Rainbow Quest

Rainbow Quest

The Folk Music Revival and American Society, 1940–1970

RONALD D. COHEN

University of Massachusetts Press

Amherst and Boston

LC 2002004333
ISBN 1-55849-346-8 (cloth); 348-4 (paper)

Designed by Jack Harrison
Set in Monotype Joanna with Runic Condensed display by Binghamton Valley Composition
Printed and bound by The Maple-Vail Book Manufacturing Group

Library of Congress Cataloging-in-Publication Data

Cohen, Ronald D., 1940–
    Rainbow quest : the folk music revival and American society, 1940–1970
/ Ronald D. Cohen.
        p. cm.
Includes bibliographical references (p.) and index.
ISBN 1-55849-346-8 (cloth : alk. paper) —
ISBN 1-55849-348-4 (paper : alk. paper)
1. Folk music—United States—History and criticism.   I. Title.
ML3551 .C58 2003
781.62'13—dc21
                                                            2002004333

British Library Cataloguing in Publication data are available.

Publication of this book was supported by a grant from the H. Earle Johnson Fund of the Society
for American Music.

To

my brother Alan,

who launched me into folk heaven in 1955

and

Pete Seeger,

who has sustained me over the last five decades

Contents

DISCARD

Preface

" 'Folk' music is experiencing one of its most robust periods since the open-ended, sometimes stigmatizing term became a popular music genre heading," *Billboard* reported on page one in July 1994. "But while young singer/songwriters seem as stylish these days as they were in the '60s, agreeing upon an acceptable definition for the genre isn't as easy anymore." Starting as the music of the peasants in the Old World, then of cowboys, lumberjacks, coal miners, southern mountain folk, and chain gangs in the United States, folk music became popularly identified with Woody Guthrie and his descendants. More recently it has taken various twists and turns: "In this respect, the growth in music represented by the term 'folk' differs from the readily identifiable folk revival of the '60s, when New York's now-extinct Greenwich Village coffeehouse scene admitted the pre-electric Bob Dylan—then a clear descendant of the itinerant troubadour tradition embodied by Guthrie—and other acoustic singer/songwriters who shared similar influences and attitudes." Today, it assumes disparate forms, "from the acoustically renewed Dylan to aggressive indie label disciples like Lach and Cindy Lee Berryhill, adult-oriented singer/songwriters like Christine Lavin and John Gorka, and major-label folk-rock groups like the Story and Indigo Girls."[1]

However defined, folk music is alive and well. Surveying the lineup at the 1993 UCLA Troubadours of Folk Festival—the Kingston Trio, Peter, Paul and Mary, Joni Mitchell, Odetta, Judy Collins, Arlo Guthrie, Richie Havens, and Ramblin' Jack Elliott—Lynn Van Matre briefly traced the history of the folk revival for the *Chicago Tribune*. In sketching folk music's family tree, she ticked off the usual litany of progenitors leading to the 1960s: the Almanac Singers, the Weavers, Pete Seeger, Lead Belly (the original spelling), Woody Guthrie, the Kingston Trio, Peter, Paul and Mary, and Bob Dylan. "Now," she wrote, "folk music's moving into the spotlight again."[2]

Any recent discussion of the folk music scene usually starts in this fashion, with a brief mention of the "folk" roots of the music, its popular upsurge in the mid-twentieth century, and its current revival. The emphasis is on personalities and locations, with not much inclination to ask why folk music became so popular for a few brief years from the late 1950s into the 1960s. Some acknowledge that the folk music revival was an important musical and cultural event, and has certainly not died away, but there is little understanding or introspection. Others see it as one small corner of the larger upsurge of rock and roll.

Though we are connected to the folk past in many ways, there seems to be little historical understanding of the convoluted, complex origins of its many musical styles. Understanding the revival can tell us much about the nature of society, culture, politics, and economics during the middle decades of the twentieth century. The gestation period of the folk music revival was long, and the music broke into wider public consciousness at a specific time for particular reasons.

Books have been written about the various musical streams that fed the folk music revival, and several anthologies, biographies, and autobiographies have put aspects of the revival under the microscope. Now it's time for a sweeping history and reinterpretation. I have attempted to get away from the time-worn dichotomy between southern "traditional" and northern "urban" folk music, as if there had been a pristine rural music untouched by external forces. With the circulation of broadsides and songsters in the nineteenth century, followed by the proliferation of songbooks in the twentieth, then the advent of phonograph records and radio, a variety of musics—hillbilly and cowboy songs, sea shanties, minstrel tunes, blues, calypso, and much more—has been not only commercially distributed but also in continual flux. The idea of pristine songs and ballads, aurally transmitted and untouched by the modern world, is hardly valid for the twentieth century, and perhaps even earlier. "Once a semi-private preserve for scholars and for the rural singers themselves," Nat Hentoff wrote in 1964, "folk music is now a pervasively commercial phenomenon." I am attempting to move away from such a simple, academic approach, by emphasizing the long-standing intersection of commercial and political forces behind the shaping and presentation of folk music, particularly from 1940 to 1970, in all sections of the country. The folk revival drew upon myriad musical syles, both topical and traditional, using acoustic instruments to capture a sound and message, but it was never simply a clash between musical purity and adulteration.[3]

My title is taken from Pete Seeger's 1960 Folkways album *The Rainbow Quest*, which includes his song "Oh Had I a Golden Thread." Written in 1958, at the official dawn of the revival, it captures his dream for a world of peace, brotherhood, and equality:

Show my brothers and my sisters
My rainbow design,
Bind up this sorry world
With hand and heart and mind,
Hand and heart and mind.

For Seeger, rainbows denoted the glimmering world of the future, the Left's continuing image of peace and harmony. Rainbows, however, also symbolized dreams of wealth, the pot of gold just over the horizon. Lyricist E. Y. "Yip" Harburg had utilized both images of the rainbow, while usually opting for the hopeful promise of the former image. In the *Wizard of Oz*, according to his biographers, it served as "a complex symbol of human aspiration. In later years, Yip sometimes called himself a 'rainbow hustler.' " In *Finian's Rainbow*, written in 1946, the pot of gold at the show's beginning, the dream of wealth in capitalist America, eventually turns to dross: "By play's end, though, the gold has lost its magic. . . . The pot of gold then turns to a chamber pot." But for Harburg and Seeger and their friends, the dream endured, despite the Depression, hot war and cold war, Red Scare, and entrenched capitalism.[4]

I am particularly interested in those influential individuals who were usually behind the musical scenes: the record company producers and executives, folk club and store owners, concert promoters, festival organizers, agents and managers, editors and writers. Virtually all white men (with the exceptions of concert promoter Mary Ann Pollar in Berkeley and café owner Lena Spencer in Saratoga Springs) and often veterans of the political and labor battles of the 1940s and 1950s, they had a commitment to changing society as well as encouraging folk music; they were also commercially savvy. Individuals such as Moe Asch, Kenny Goldstein, Irwin Silber, Harold Leventhal, Manny Greenhill, Frank Fried, and Herb Cohen represented a shrewd combination of the entrepreneurial spirit and a Left/labor commitment, probably shaped by their Jewish experience and identity. Some of them also dominated the record business: Asch (Folkways), Maynard Solomon (Vanguard), Jac Holzman (Elektra), and Orrin Keepnews (Riverside). There were, of course, many other local personalities who were key to the success of the revival—for example, Ed Pearl in Los Angeles, Ray Nordstrand in Chicago, Israel G. Young in New York, Barry Olivier in Berkeley, and Gene Shay in Philadelphia—but they had slightly more particular concerns. I have interviewed them and scores of others, to get their personal stories and insights. Indeed, Israel "Izzy" Young has emerged as a central figure. Because of Izzy's zeal as collector and chronicler, gadfly and promoter, touchstone and icon, I have depended on his writings and sensibilities to tell much of the story after 1957, when he opened the Folklore Center in Greenwich Village.

"A folk song does so many things," Theodore Bikel has written. "It tells a multitude of stories, legends, fables, and jokes. It admonishes, lulls to sleep, calls to battle, rings with hope for the prisoner, with threat for the jailer, with joy for lovers, and with bitterness for him who might have had but didn't. It heralds birth, boyhood, wedlock. It soothes the weary, the sick, and the aged, and it mourns the dead." For a brief moment, 1958–1965, it captured the dreams and allegiance, as well as time and resources, of a large segment of the population, particularly young people. How and why this happened is the central focus of *Rainbow Quest*.[5]

I remember the Weavers' hits of the early 1950s, but my love affair with folk music began about 1956, when my brother began borrowing Folkways records of Woody Guthrie and Pete Seeger; then I began to purchase my own albums, starting with the Weavers, the Almanac Singers' *Talking Union*, and others from Folkways, Stinson, Vanguard, and Elektra. My record collection grew, I occasionally labored over playing the banjo, with scant success, and I have attended many folk concerts through the ensuing decades. This book began to take shape in the early 1980s when I had the time to connect my scholarly historical interest—the postwar period (the years of my coming of age), the Red Scare, twentieth-century youth culture—and my love for the music.

As I worked on this book over the last two decades I became increasingly dependent on a number of old friends, new friends, colleagues, librarians and archivists, and assorted others, all of whom have contributed immeasurably to improving its documentation, scope, reliability, and style. Where should I start?

First and foremost, Israel G. "Izzy" Young has supported and guided me through the folk music thickets, a sincere friend and host as well as one of the key players in the unfolding drama that I have tried to portray, with all of its personalities and complexities. I have also received substantial support from the following, who have critically commented on particular chapters or in other ways rendered substantial assistance: the late Bernie Asbell, Scott Baretta, Eileen Boris, Guy Carawan, Norm Cohen, Art D'Lugoff, David Dunaway, Richard Flacks, Peter Goldsmith, the late Kenny Goldstein, Eric Gordon, the late Lou Gottlieb, Archie Green, David Hajdu, Frank Hamilton, Fred Hellerman, Ed Kahn, Dennis Mayoff, Ron Radosh, Millie Rahn, Neil Rosenberg, Dave Samuelson, Pete Seeger, Irwin Silber, Ralph Lee Smith, the late Dave Van Ronk, Stephen Wade, Elijah Wald, Dick Weissman, and Henrietta Yurchenco. Judith McCulloh continually prodded me to refine my focus and organization. I have also depended heavily on numerous scholars, the late Richard A. Reuss foremost among them, whose works have deftly guided me along the journey.

I have had extraordinary assistance from Gail Malmgreen and Ed Cray, two skillful editors, in shaping up the manuscript for publication. I would also like to thank the two anonymous readers for the University of Massachusetts Press, and particularly Joel Ray for his scrupulous copyediting. Many of my colleagues at Indiana University Northwest have been most helpful, particularly Terry Lukas, Anne Koehler and the staff of the IUN library, as well as my departmental colleagues Jim Lane, Roberta Wollons, Fred Chary, the late Rhiman Rotz, Mark Sheldon, and Paul Kern. A Spencer Foundation research grant enabled me to launch my research by visiting with Izzy Young in Stockholm, Sweden, for which I am very thankful, and ongoing support from Indiana University Northwest in the way of summer fellowships and sabbaticals was equally crucial. Paul Wright, my editor at the University of Massachusetts Press on this and the previously published autobiography of Agnes "Sis" Cunningham and Gordon Friesen, *Red Dust and Broadsides*, has once again provided just the right balance of encouragement and critical input. I will always be in his debt.

Numerous librarians and archivists have also been most helpful with their expertise and assistance, particularly Bruce Conforth when he was the Indiana University archivist for assistance in locating and using the invaluable Richard A. Reuss Papers in the university's archives; Michael Taft and his predecessors at the Southern Folklife Collection at the University of North Carolina; Jeff Place and Tony Seeger at the Smithsonian Folkways collection, part of the Smithsonian Institution's Center for Folklife and Cultural Heritage; and Joe Hickerson, head of the Archive of Folk Culture at the Library of Congress, for his unflagging assistance and unmatched expertise. Joe retired in 1998 after thirty-five years of invaluable service. Because there has been no institution separate from the Archive of Folk Culture essentially devoted to collecting and exhibiting folk music–related materials, in 1999 I joined with Art D'Lugoff, Alan Gerson, and numerous others in establishing the Folk Music Museum in Greenwich Village, which will house my growing personal collection as a start. Indeed, I would like to thank all of those who have entrusted their materials to my use and loving care, including Jacke Alper, Roy Berkeley, the late Mario "Boots" Casetta, Sis Cunningham, David DeTurk, Toni Di Francesco, Josh Dunson, Ray Flerlage, Ray Funk, Lydia Grady, Archie Green, the late Manny Greenhill, Lionel Kilberg, Barry Kornfeld, Ernie Lieberman, Ed Pearl, the late Mary Ann and Henry Pollar, Aaron Rennert, and Irwin Silber.

There are no illustrations in this volume because I am publishing separately, with the assistance of David Bonner and Kelly Blanscet, *Golden Threads: An Illustrated History of Folk Music in the United States, 1900–1970* (New York: Folk Music Museum in Greenwich Village, 2004).

Last but certainly not least, Nancy DelCastillo, my longtime companion, has continued to provide the emotional and social atmosphere that has allowed me to finish this and many other projects. Thanks!

RONALD D. COHEN

Rainbow Quest

Prologue: Summer 1953

In the summer of 1953 the folksingers Guy Carawan, Frank Hamilton, and Jack Elliott traveled throughout the South. Carawan recalled, "I wanted to go down and visit on the farm in North Carolina where my folks grew up. I also knew there was an Asheville Folk Festival and people like Roger Sprung and Harry and Jeanie West, who I met in New York, had been going down regularly to the South to the Asheville Folk Festival. I had listened to recordings of Bascom Lamar Lunsford. I had a number of reasons to go. It was all my roots down there." Carawan had met Frank Hamilton in Los Angeles a few years earlier, where they participated in the Sierra Folk Singers, part of the local progressive folk music scene. One of the singers and pickers in New York City's Washington Square Park on Sunday afternoons and a member of Bob DeCormier's Jewish Young Folksingers chorus, Carawan, who had a car, talked Hamilton, still in Los Angeles, into the southern trip. "I packed my toothbrush, underwear, and socks in my guitar case and hit the road," Hamilton remembers. "At the invitation of Pete Seeger, I arrived in Beacon, New York, to stay until I would connect with Guy."[1]

Once in New York, Hamilton joined Carawan one night to hear Brownie McGhee in a bar in Harlem, where they met Jack Elliott. The three then visited Fred Gerlach's apartment for more music, and decided to travel together. "Frank and I both [were] entranced with Jack's singing and ability and we were both still pretty young and fresh," said Carawan. "Jack had traveled some and he was also not bashful about being out and busking, singing in the street, passing the hat and raising money out in public places and so we began to discuss, 'cause Jack, when he heard we were going to the South, he said, 'Oh can I go with you? Can I go with you?' and at first we said 'No, because we don't have any money.' Anyway, at first I was resisting. I didn't know Jack all that well." But within a week the three had developed their travel plans. "Jack Elliott converted to Cowboyism," said Hamilton. "Wore a Stetson hat and was a disciple of Woody Guthrie. Carried an old Gretsch guitar with him at all times." Before leaving they visited Lee Hays, currently living with Earl and Helen Robinson and their two sons in Brooklyn. Lee talked about his early days in the South and about the Highlander Folk School in Tennessee. They also went to see Toshi Seeger, Pete's wife, while he was away. In Hamilton's words, "the three of us hit the road together in search of American folk music."[2]

Inching their way down the East Coast after a visit near Washington with Mike Seeger (unfortunately missing his musical parents, Charles and Ruth), they began busking in Norfolk, pulling in nine dollars before they were threatened with arrest. "We've been taken for everything from mountain hill-billies, Texas cowboys (Jack wears a cowboy hat), country farmers, dust bowl refugees, to hoboes and sometimes city fellers," Carawan wrote at the time. "I was getting somewhat panicky in the back of my mind about how we'd make out when our money is all gone. I feel much better now and confident that we'll not starve. Keeping gas in the car is the main problem." Guy didn't mind admitting he had been to college, but Jack thought they should pass as drifters. After a close scrape in Merry's Point, Virginia, where the sheriff and the Klan suspected them as dangerous outsiders after they had contacted local labor organizers and stayed with a black family, they visited Carawan's relatives in Mesic, North Carolina. They listened to white spirituals but were warned not to visit the black church. After quick singing stops along they way, they next arrived in Maces Springs, Virginia, to visit A. P. Carter, of the famous Carter Family trio. At the sight of A. P., with Clinch Mountain looming in the background, Hamilton remembered the words to the old song, "Way up on Clinch Mountain, a long way from home, I'm as drunk as the devil, O leave me alone!" "We stayed overnight with him in his old torn down shack full of old pictures, song sheets and books," Carawan wrote. "We found him sitting on the railroad tracks up by Clinch Mt. He talked of the past a lot that evening and the next day. We sang some and then the three of us piled into one bug-eaten bed. We left the next morning after acquiring some old song books and drove on to Asheville."[3]

Asheville was the home of Bascom Lamar Lunsford, a legendary performer and collector, and his Asheville folk festival, begun in 1928 as a tourist attraction. Carawan loved Lunsford's recordings, but "he turned out to be just the opposite of the kind of person I'd expected. He sings like an old mountain reprobate, full of glee and friendliness. He turned out to be a reactionary aristocrat however," Carawan dejectedly wrote to Noel Oliver. "The first question

he asked us was 'Are you Communists?' He claims that hundreds of Communists have been going around the country with tape recorders and collecting
songs and using them for progressive causes and that they're part of a movement against this country. Telling him we were friends of Pete and Woody and
from New York didn't help matters any. He thinks [Alan] Lomax is pink, and
on and on he went about the subversion that's taking place." Carawan was most
disturbed, having to deny his Left politics, but felt discretion was definitely
necessary. Hamilton's memory matched Guy's description: "Jack, a hippie cowboy, me, a gawky, disheveled teenager, and Guy, a squeaky clean California boy
ascended the hill to Bascom's tent that night. He was resting inside. Guy said,
'Mr. Lunsford? We're folk singers just come down from New York City to see
you.' Jack and I eyeballed each other. This booming voice roared at us in the
night from inside the darkened tent, 'YOU BOYS COMMUNISTS?' Guy was crest-
fallen. Jack and I started laughing, hysterically. Nobody answered him. Bascom
was convinced. We were there to subvert the Asheville festival and overthrow
North Carolina." The next day he warmed somewhat, but remained wary as
he denounced Pete Seeger's Left politics. Curiously, the morning mail brought
Lunsford's new Folkways Record (*Smokey Mountain Ballads*), with liner notes full
of a "glowing tribute to a great traditional singer," and he appeared content
until "he almost choked on his coffee" after noticing they were written by
Seeger. Lunsford certainly preferred to forget the painful memory that he had
introduced Seeger to the five-string banjo in 1936, when Charles Seeger had
brought his seventeen-year-old son to the Asheville festival to meet its note-
worthy director.[4]

One visit with a local family with four ragged children further tarnished
Carawan's romantic view of the South. After a night of cramped sleep in a bed
with Frank and Jack, "We ate a very repulsively dirty and fly-molested breakfast
of homemade biscuits, gravy, grits and bacon, and then made music with them
all. . . . The whole thing reminded me of Erskine Caldwell's kind of people and
happenings." The three troubadours nonetheless kept busy performing as the
Dusty Road Boys at the Canton folk festival, on the streets, and in summer
camps, finding music everywhere.[5]

Stopping briefly at the John C. Campbell Folk School in Brasstown, North
Carolina, the trio next arrived at the Highlander Folk School in Monteagle,
Tennessee, run by Myles Horton, an old friend of Lee Hays, Will Geer, Pete
Seeger, and other northern activists. Finally Carawan "felt back among some
politically akin people. It's encouraging to find a place like this in the South—
carrying on its programs and being well-liked by the community." They didn't
stay long, but Carawan would return in a few years and dedicate his life to the
school and its causes, particularly the civil rights movement. They next arrived,
broke, in Nashville, home of the Grand Old Opry, mecca for country music
fans. Attending a free show their first night, they heard Roy Acuff, Hank Snow,

Grandpa Jones, Chet Atkins, and Stringbean (David Akeman), and talked with some of them. They returned the next night: "It's a remarkable show—no dead spots, packed full of all the top hillbilly singers, instrumentalists and comedians. It's mostly commercial stuff with a few real folk (old timey) musicians on it. I'm really fed up with electric guitars." They also met Earl Scruggs. Grandpa Jones noticed Hamilton's worn banjo head and helped him replace it with one of his own.[6]

Returning to Asheville, they took a side trip to Black Mountain College where they watched the anticommunist film *Man on a Tight Rope* before their concert. Hamilton refused to take the movie seriously, but Carawan was "bothered by what to me was real filth and lies put over in a very effective manner. I was vowing to get to the truth of the matter thinking seriously about a trip to the Soviet Union to see for myself." (He would make the trip with his wife Noel four years later.) Angered by the film, he defended the progressive song movement in argument with the poet Charles Olson, head of the school and an old friend of Pete Seeger, Woody Guthrie, and Lee Hays; Olson had now soured on the idea that "culture (art) can be approached as a weapon." Returning to Asheville, they attended the folk festival, always held the first weekend of August, and Carawan wrote that Lunsford "is still suspicious and unfriendly toward us. He's a shit and how." They were particularly impressed by banjo player George Pegram.[7]

Somewhat exhausted after six weeks on the road, discouraged by their broken tape recorder, and wondering what to do next, the group wound up in New Orleans, where they looked up Billy Faier. Carawan then decided to go off by himself for a week or so and visit Noel, who was working on a Quaker project in Mexico. Originally from Woodstock, New York, Faier, an accomplished banjo player, briefly lived in California before spending a few years in New Orleans. He had met Jack Elliott earlier in New York. Faier, Elliott and Hamilton spent the time playing and listening to jazz, and Hamilton played with a Dixieland group at the Four Aces with a borrowed trombone. (Later Elliott composed "912 Green," a rambling narrative song about their visit with Faier.) After Carawan returned from Mexico, Billy, somewhat jealous of his friends' traveling experiences after listening to their stories, decided to accompany them back to New York for a visit. The trip didn't go well. "Guy Carawan's the world's worst driver," Faier later noted. "I couldn't stand it. And when we got to North Carolina, I'd had enough. I said, 'Listen. I'm getting out. I'm going to hitchhike the rest of the way back.' Also part of it was that I wanted to hitchhike through the South." Elliott decided to join him, and the two made their own way to New York.[8]

Carawan stayed briefly in New York, then returned to Los Angeles and married Noel Oliver. Hamilton also remained in the city for a time, traveled to California, and finally moved to Chicago. Jack hit the road, married in Southern

California two years later, and kept going. Billy Faier also soon moved to California, the Bay Area, where he enlivened the folk scene. All four personified the California–New York folk axis. They were young urban musicians with a strong penchant for rural, white southern music. "The kids around Washington Square had a Rousseauian view of folk singers. We were all kind of wide eyed. We were the prisoners of the big city and we romanticized the freedom and virtue of country life," Hamilton later admitted. The trip both reinforced and shattered their belief in the bucolic rural life. Lunsford's behavior was particularly appalling, despite his musical contributions. Lunsford had recently introduced a folk act at his festival "as three Jews from New York," and his apparent anti-Semitism grated on Hamilton, who was Jewish on his mother's side. Jack, his Jewish background coming to the surface, was equally mortified and nicknamed Lunsford "Bastard Lampoon Lunchfart."[9]

The trip through the South not only captured a telling moment in the lives of the folk singers, but also connected to the various traditional, commercial, and political aspects of what would become a folk revival throughout the English-speaking world.

1
Roots of the Revival

Writing in the April 1940 issue of *Etude* about Alan Lomax's *American School of the Air* radio program on CBS, Blanche Lemmon observed: "American youth are privileged this year to dip into a veritable treasure chest of Americana. . . . They are learning that this always has been a singing country and that songs of work, play, humor, lamentation, religion and love have dotted its progress throughout the years, poured forth spontaneously by its cowboys, its searchers for gold, its cotton pickers, its sailors, lumberjacks, farmers, teamsters, mountaineers, railroaders and others, each in characteristic style."[1]

Lucky students would hear these songs each Tuesday while sitting in their classrooms. In addition to Lomax himself discussing and performing folk songs, along with Lead Belly, Woody Guthrie, Burl Ives, the Golden Gate Quartet, or Aunt Molly Jackson, for example, the shows included "an orchestral work written by a noted American composer and based on one of the folk songs presented. Thus listeners hear a folk song in its original form, learn of its place in, and relation to, our national life, and then hear it again after a skilled composer has woven its themes into a modern orchestral composition." Each show featured a different theme, such as "Poor Farmers" or the "Blues." Lomax prepared a manual for every program, with an outline and supplementary materials, encouraging the students to hunt up local folk songs.

Always the teacher, Lomax combined entertainment and discovery through folk songs, connecting past and present, local pride and national patriotism, and high and low culture, and inculcating a subtle progressive, activist political consciousness. "To know these songs and to study their fascinating variety is to study the common man at close range—his conflicting moods and desires and his method of expressing or defeating them," Lemmon concluded. "It is the hope of those concerned with the Folk Music of America broadcasts that by them youth may be served, and that by means of the comprehensive outlines offered in the programs increased interest in an appreciation of our great variety of folk songs may be stimulated." More than fifty years later, after a lifetime of collecting, preserving, documenting, presenting, and shaping modern folk music sensibilities in the United States and abroad, Lomax could still marvel at the show's scope and contributions.[2]

In 1940 the study and dissemination of folk music was hardly in its infancy. In the United States and abroad, collectors and scholars had been scouring the countryside for many years, preserving and shaping the folk music legacy. Alan's father, John, an eminent folklorist, headed the prestigious folk song archives at the Library of Congress. The father's politics were considerably to the right of the son's, yet both believed in the uniting and rejuvenating powers of folk music. Their similarities and differences mirrored the complexities of the changing role of folk music in American society throughout the twentieth century. As the country emerged from the crucible of Depression and domestic strife and plunged into the horrors of international war, folk music served many as a touchstone of social, cultural, political, technological, economic, and musical change.

Folk music—non-commercial people's music—has always been around. But in the late nineteenth century scholars and collectors in England and the United States began to sharpen their understanding of what folk music entailed. In *Anglo-American Folksong Scholarship since 1898*, published in 1959, D. K. Wilgus concentrated on the formal collecting and study of ballads—essentially narrative or story songs—which scholars had assumed to be more authentic than work, religious, play-party, or folk lyric songs. "In the twentieth century folk song study had developed from an antiquarian, esthetic, and literary pastime toward a disciplined study of a segment of traditional culture," Wilgus wrote. Ballad collecting originated in England in the eighteenth century, part of an antiquarian mentality and literary style, later augmented by a nationalistic search for peasant roots and a shared past.[3]

Folksong collecting and scholarship proceeded rapidly in England in the early twentieth century, sparked by the desire by some to preserve "traditional" folk music and dance as a hedge against accelerating modernization. Disagreements among collectors and scholars did exist, however, and were rooted in contemporary political and cultural conflicts. Cecil Sharp (1859–1924) by 1914 exerted much influence through his publications and control over the English Folk Dance Society. By the 1930s folk song scholarship and promotion was almost totally divorced from any existing traditional social base because of the academic interest of Sharp and other collectors. Soon, it would also get caught up in the rise of radical politics.[4]

Meanwhile, in the United States the search for the folk proceeded apace, particularly in the South, where a rural alternative to the onrushing modernism of city and factory was thought to exist. Though Appalachia had developed a reputation in the late nineteenth century as a haven for rubes and slackers, sorely needing modernization, the discovery of rustic folk songs and folkways by the beginning of World War I helped to reshape the image. Northerners developed institutions to preserve "traditional" southern culture and promote its study, including the Hindman Settlement School, the John C. Campbell Folk School—the creation of Olive Dame Campbell, Sharp's collaborator on *English Folk Songs from the Southern Appalachians* (1917)—and the White Top Folk Festival of the 1930s. Sharp had spearheaded the romanticization of the rural folk in England, and helped to do the same while in the United States during the war, connecting Anglo-Saxon traditional ways with quaint, enduring American values and manners.[5]

Nostalgia for a seemingly lost, or at least disappearing, rural past was perhaps epitomized by the automobile king Henry Ford, who clung to older forms of music and dance as a counter to an urbanizing world he had helped create. Pupils at Dearborn High School in Michigan had square dance instruction three times a week. Benjamin Lovett, from Worcester, Massachusetts, became Ford's private dancing teacher and the caller for Henry Ford's Old Fashioned Dance Orchestra on Victor Records and other labels; Lovett led crowded dancing classes in the Ford Motor Company ballroom. Ford also brought numerous fiddlers to Dearborn, including Alanson Mellen Dunham, a snowshoe maker from Maine, who became a national celebrity.

The popular dissemination of folk music came most readily through recordings, as the songs and styles were extracted from their traditional contexts and commercially packaged. Record companies often sold the records to the communities that produced them, believing no other market existed. Corporate executives could, in fact, influence rural cultures through selecting certain performance styles or topics and neglecting others. Generally, however, the music's greatest impact fell on outsiders who were struck by the music's sound and imagery. The musicologist Charles Seeger aptly characterized the impact of the new media—radio as well as records—on both traditional and urban folk styles, which he dated from around 1940: "Almost overnight, the constant, slow, ages-old interchange of materials between city and country and between folk, popular and fine arts of music was vastly speeded up. Country singers were recorded by phonograph companies and folklorists were drawn into radio programs. City people, always on the look-out for new things and for broader cultural life, heard the records and broadcasts. . . . But in the process, the songs themselves—even the idiom in which they had been molded—began to change." Influence went in two directions, as rural performers caught on to modern sounds. "Thus the 'hill-billy' and the 'city-billy,' though using the same musical materials, crossed paths while going in exactly opposite directions."[6]

Carl Sandburg (1878–1967) was one influential outsider. Born in Galesburg, Illinois, in 1878, with little connection to traditional American folk music, particularly its black and white southern roots, Sandburg nevertheless made an early contribution to the dissemination of folk music through his publications, records, and public performances. His leftist politics and search for heroic, common themes in U.S. history led, perhaps naturally, to a love of folk music. He collected songs most of his life, and also picked up some from John Lomax, including "The Buffalo Skinners." He frequently performed during public lectures the spirituals and the hobo, cowboy, and jail songs that he had zealously collected. Sandburg's flat midwestern voice hardly captured the musical nuances of many of the songs, but his simple guitar accompaniment and unadorned style appealed to many. In 1926 the poet recorded about ten songs for the Victor Talking Machine Company, which issued two of them on one disc— "The Boll Weevil" and "Negro Spirituals."[7]

Sandburg's importance in the dissemination and popularization of the music came not through his sundry performances but rather the publication in 1927 of his *American Songbag*. A year earlier, in order to copyright those songs in the book that had been recorded, Harcourt, Brace and Company issued a preliminary edition of two hundred copies. During the stressful project Sandburg depended on the help of professionals, including composer Ruth Porter Crawford (she would marry Charles Seeger, in 1932). The published collection introduced the public to 280 native songs grouped under twenty-four headings, including "Dramas and Portraits," "Minstrel Songs," "Pioneer Memories," "Blues, Mellows, Ballets," "Railroad and Work Gangs," and "Lovely People." The book remained continuously in print, shaping public sensibilities for over seventy years.[8]

As an added bonus, Sandburg appended a list of sixteen previous publications, including John Lomax's *Cowboy Songs and Other Frontier Ballads*, Louise Pound's *American Songs and Ballads*, Cecil Sharp's *American-English Folk-Songs Collected in the Southern Appalachians*, Dorothy Scarborough's *On the Trail of Negro Folk Songs*, Charles Finger's *Frontier Ballads: Songs from Lawless Lands*, and John Jacob Nile's *Singing Soldiers*. He also steered the readers to the files of the *Journal of American Folklore* and the publications of the Texas Folk Lore Society, among other sources. Setting an influential tone and style, *The American Songbag* foreshadowed the all-encompassing songbooks of John and Alan Lomax.

As if to answer Sandburg's call for additional study and collecting, the Library of Congress established the Archive of American Folk-Song on July 1, 1928. Carl Engel, chief of the Library's Music Division, believed in the "pressing need

for the formation of a great centralized collection of American folk-songs."
Engel appointed Robert Winslow Gordon to be the collection's first director. A
student of Harvard ballad scholars George Lyman Kittredge and Francis Barton
Gummere, Gordon taught in the English department at the University of California at Berkeley from 1918 to 1924. Always a maverick, he preferred folk
song collecting among waterfront denizens and hoboes to "stuffy" academic
life, and he wrote the monthly "Old Songs That Men Have Sung" column for
Adventure magazine from 1923 to 1928, attracting a broad male audience. In late
1925 he began collecting folk songs in North Carolina. Based in Asheville, he
worked with Bascom Lamar Lunsford, who had just done some recordings for
OKeh Records. Gordon then moved to Darien, Georgia, for another few years
of collecting, before accepting the position at the Library of Congress. His
superiors rarely saw him, as he worked mostly in the field to secure materials
for the archive.[10]

John Avery Lomax (1867–1948) succeeded Gordon at the Archive of American Folk-Song in 1933 and would serve as titular head, with slight pay, for
ten years. Having grown up in Bosque County, Texas, he had begun collecting
cowboy songs early in life, but he took up the work seriously only after initiating graduate work at Harvard University in 1906. Encouraged by Kittredge,
in 1910 he published *Cowboy Songs and Other Frontier Ballads* (with revised editions
in 1916 and 1938), which broke from the traditional emphasis on British
ballads. Lomax summarized his developing views in an address to the 1913
annual meeting of the American Folklore Society. Rather than analyzing folk
songs (ballads) for their lineage and literary merit, he discussed eight types,
differentiated by occupational groups—miners, lumbermen, railroaders, cowboys—as well as the "songs of the down-and-out classes—the outcast girl, the
dope fiend, the convict, the jail-bird, and the tramp." He defined a ballad
broadly, as not just a story song with roots in the misty European past but as
a breathing representation of the living common folk.[11]

Lomax pursued materials in every nook and cranny of the country, eventually
publishing a series of influential song books: *Songs of the Cattle Trail and Cow Camp*
(1919), *American Ballads and Folk Songs* (1934, with Alan Lomax), *Negro Folk Songs
as Sung by Lead Belly* (1936, with Alan Lomax), *Our Singing Country* (1941, with
Alan Lomax), and *Folk Song: U.S.A.* (1947, with Alan Lomax). Lomax's broad
sweep almost singlehandedly redefined the meaning of folk music. During the
summer of 1932 he had traveled the length of the country with his two sons,
twenty-four-year-old John Jr. and seventeen-year-old Alan, lecturing, selling
copies of *Cowboy Songs*, and sampling the varieties of folk music heard along the
way.

Searching for song representations of the "pure folk," Lomax romanticized
the "people," particularly rural southerners, white and black, who were seemingly untouched by modernizing influences. During the summer of 1933, ac-

companied only by Alan, he began hunting for songs in remote southern lumber camps and prisons. Traveling through Texas, Louisiana, Mississippi, Tennessee, and Virginia, with a "portable" disc recorder weighing over three hundred pounds built into the back seat of their Ford, they found numerous examples of black work and religious songs. At that time they first encountered and recorded Huddie Ledbetter (Lead Belly) at Angola Penitentiary in Louisiana.[12]

Though searching for the democratic threads that linked Americans, rich and poor, northern and southern, black and white, city and country, John Lomax approached his collecting from a conservative, even romantic, position. Idealizing the "folk," he failed to question the status quo, particularly southern race relations. He found no black protest songs, underscoring his view that blacks, even convicts, accepted their natural inferiority and subservient status. "I hid my feelings" about segregation, Alan later wrote. "Nor could I discuss them with my father, who, in spite of his intense sympathy for the prisoners and a genuine concern for black welfare, believed in the overall beneficence of the Southern system. Indeed, at that time, in fact, there were very few white Southerners, and not many Americans, who held different views."[13]

John Lomax's collecting and travels continued through the 1930s. He took under his wing a former prisoner from Texas, the singer James "Iron Head" Baker, and began a second penitentiary tour in 1936 through Florida, South Carolina, and Virginia for the Library of Congress. In Arkansas he recorded Emma Dusenberry, whose large repertoire of traditional songs proved invaluable. Remaining affiliated with the folk song archive until 1942, always nominally paid, Lomax was caught up in the Depression-era rush of activities by folklorists, writers, academics, and countless others eager to document all aspects of "the folk," including their music. The proliferation of New Deal cultural programs, including the Federal Writers Project, the Federal Theater, the Resettlement Administration, and the Farm Security Administration photography project greatly facilitated this effort. Grappling with the nation's economic problems, while repairing its social and cultural dislocations, Roosevelt's New Deal sought to energize the "folk," who were perceived as the country's moral backbone.

Those searching for traditional forces and styles could have either politically conservative or radical leanings, with the elder Lomax and Bascom Lamar Lunsford representing the former. They belonged to the evolutionist wing of folklorist scholarship, those who believed that folk songs belonged to an early stage of cultural development that required respect and preservation. Both to honor and preserve, Lunsford's annual Mountain Dance and Folk Festival in Asheville, North Carolina, was organized in 1928. Here were annually displayed the talents of traditional southern performers, men and women who drew increasing attention from the North.

Although not without controversy about the meaning and value of authenticity, other festivals nourished the same purpose. Among the earliest were the American Folk Song Festival, organized by Jean Thomas, Kentucky's "Traipsin' Woman," in 1930 in Ashland, Kentucky; Annabel Morris Buchanan's White Top Folk Festival in southwest Virginia, established in 1931; and the eclectic National Folk Festival, first staged by Sarah Gertrude Knott in St. Louis in 1934 and continuing for many decades. Until its demise in 1939, White Top, featuring ballad singers and fiddle contests, attracted thousands, particularly following Eleanor Roosevelt's visit in 1933. Yet White Top had its critics, Charles Seeger for one. The musicologist, then working for the Resettlement Administration, believed the high admission charge and doubtful authenticity of some of the performers revealed that the festival was "reactionary to the core." Unlike the integrated National Folk Festival, it was also for whites only.[14]

The recurring controversy over authenticity continued through the 1930s. John Lomax sought to avoid modernization and commercialization by going into southern backwoods and penitentiaries. But while he dressed newly freed Lead Belly in prison or cotton-field garb, the singer himself preferred double-breasted suits and sprinkled his performances with vaudeville tunes and popular songs. At the same time that Lomax and other folklorists combed the hinterlands for "authentic" traditional musicians, the record companies scattered representatives throughout the South, capturing hundreds of black and white performers on disks for commercial issue. Generally snubbed by folklorists at the time, these recordings displayed a remarkable range of musical talents and styles, and were eagerly bought by rural consumers. Although Lomax did not himself promote recordings for a commercial market, he nonetheless produced the album *Smoky Mountain Ballads* for Victor Records in 1941, a landmark reissue compilation of ten recent hillbilly recordings by the Carter Family, Uncle Dave Macon, the Monroe Brothers, and other southeastern performers.

Early commercial recordings issued by Emile Berliner in the late 1890s had featured "traditional" songs, including "Dixie," "Virginia Camp Meeting," and "A Day in Country School." Record companies did not originally record rural musicians, preferring "rube" stereotypes by urban entertainers. They targeted urban audiences, somewhat divided into ethnic, racial, and regional categories. Columbia's 1913 catalog had a two-page listing of "Folk Songs and Traditional Melodies"; of the forty-eight selections only six were American in origin, and four of these were by Stephen Foster; the remainder were from Europe and the British Isles. Bentley Ball was one of the first to combine cowboy songs, drawing on Lomax's 1913 *Cowboy Songs and Other Frontier Ballads*, with a more formal parlor piano accompaniment. In 1919 he recorded thirteen sides for Columbia, including "Jesse James," "The Gallows Tree," and "The Dying Cowboy." Ball foreshadowed the recording of vernacular southern musicians targeted at a regional market.[15]

In September 1922 Fiddlin' John Carson appeared on the fledgling WSB in Atlanta. Soon other rural singers and string bands entertained their neighbors over the five-hundred-watt station. In January 1923 WBAP in Fort Worth programmed an hour and a half of square dance music with Fred Wagner's Hilo Five Hawaiian Orchestra—the first radio barn dance. Haphazardly scheduled until 1927, when it began a regular Friday night slot, the show featured various performing groups. The *National Barn Dance* aired in April 1924 on WLS in Chicago, followed by the *WSM Barn Dance* in Nashville in November 1925. (Renamed the *Grand Ole Opry* in 1927, it soon occupied a three-hour slot on Saturday nights.) Harry "Haywire Mac" McClintock launched his popular *Blue Monday Jamboree* on San Francisco's KFRC in 1925. In 1938 the former hobo and author of "The Big Rock Candy Mountain" and "Hallelujah, I'm a Bum" moved his colorful act to Los Angeles in 1938 and joined the *Happy Go Lucky* network show.

Almost simultaneously with the advent of live old-time music on the radio, record companies began to discover traditional musicians. The champion fiddlers Alexander "Eck" Robertson and Henry Gilliland traveled to New York in June 1922 and somehow convinced Victor Records to record them, separately and together. Their records sold modestly. The next year the versatile musician Henry Whitter, a Virginia textile worker, followed in their footsteps, recording for the General Phonograph Company. A major breakthrough came in mid-June 1923, when Ralph Peer recorded Fiddlin' John Carson performing "The Little Old Log Cabin in the Lane" and "The Old Hen Cackled and the Rooster's Going to Crow" for OKeh in Atlanta. Although initially not promoted or advertised, the record sold extremely well, leading to Carson's further recording in New York.[16]

The record industry experienced boom times through the 1920s. Brunswick, Gennett, Paramount, Victor, and Columbia, as well as OKeh, rushed to sign "country" or "hillbilly" acts. These recordings captured a wide range of southern white musical styles, contrasting with but also influenced by the popular tunes of the day. "Hillbilly" became the generic term used by the record companies to designate the music of the rural white South. String bands predominated, although occasionally a solo performer such as the professionally trained Vernon Dalhart succeeded. His 1924 recording of "The Wreck of the Southern Old 97," backed by "The Prisoner's Song," sold over one million copies, revealing the vast potential of the hillbilly market. The success of Jimmie Rodgers and the Carter Family, both initially recorded by Ralph Peer for Victor in August 1927, further demonstrated the breadth of the audience. Rodgers incorporated blues, jazz, and pop influences, while the Carters presented a more traditional, and religious, southern sound. Rodgers and the Carters embodied the two halves of white southern culture—secular and religious, modern and traditional, worldly and homey—that seemed increasingly at odds.

The appearance on radio and records of southern white musicians followed closely on the heels of the commercial discovery of southern black music. Black music had various wellsprings during the nineteenth century—religious and secular, domestic and commercial, even minstrelsy—which eventually came together to produce blues, jazz, and gospel, with both African and European musical roots.[17]

Developing from a mélange of southern musical styles in the early years of the century, the blues had swept the South by World War I and in the 1920s traveled up the Mississippi to Chicago and other northern cities—paralleling the spread of jazz, which musically it often overlapped. The Mississippi Delta, marked by thriving plantations and brutal segregation, proved to be one fecund source. By 1910 white collectors began to note this peculiar musical style, and soon record companies were issuing titles written and recorded by whites out of the minstrel / coon-song tradition. W. C. Handy published "St. Louis Blues" in 1914, instantly popular though owing more to jazz than rural blues. Mamie Smith's rendition of "Crazy Blues" for OKeh in 1920 captured the hearts of southern rural blacks and their urban relatives. Smith, who had been a dancer with Tutt-Whitney's Smart Set Company and a featured singer in Harlem, was a vaudeville-jazz performer rather than rural blues singer.

Soon northern record companies found a host of female blues singers, most with experience on the black theater circuit—among them Edith Wilson, Rosa Henderson, Lucille Hegamin, Ida Cox, and Viola McCoy. OKeh's ubiquitous artist and repertoire (A&R) man, Ralph Peer, created the company's 8000 Race Records series in 1921, and was soon copied by Paramount, Columbia, Vocalion, Victor, and their smaller competitors. By 1927 these companies were issuing some five hundred race records a year. While not exclusively blues— the series also included jazz bands, songsters, and string bands—the records sold well among the rural poor, tenants and sharecroppers who could scarcely afford a record player yet willingly sacrificed to hear their music. Gertrude "Ma" Rainey and Bessie Smith quickly became dominant among the female "classic" blues singers. Usually backed by jazz bands, they mixed their soaring vocals with heavy backup and show business glitz.[18]

Following on the heels of the female performers, record companies soon began to search out male acoustic guitar players with rural roots and appeal. Termed "country blues" or "rural blues," as distinct from the showbiz, jazzy style of the "classic" performers, this music had a raw, gutsy sound often heard in isolated juke joints. And yet the rural bluesmen were not beyond the reach of commercialism. Rural performers moved to nearby towns or cities, and records found their way into the most remote parts of the South, making blues an urban as well as rural musical style.

Electrical recording, becoming widespread by 1926, added significantly to tone and clarity, and new, more portable equipment allowed the companies to range father afield throughout the South, while at the same time luring performers to their studios in Chicago, New York, or Richmond, Indiana. Moreover, the growing competition of commercial radio provoked the companies into diversifying their product. By the early 1930s about two hundred solo artists had been recorded. Papa Charlie Jackson had the first rural blues hit, "Papa's Lawdy Lawdy Blues" in 1924, and the influential Texas bluesman Blind Lemon Jefferson began recording in 1926. Most significant, if not always the most popular, of the Mississippi bluesmen were Charley Patton, the Mississippi Sheiks, Peetie Wheatstraw, and somewhat later Robert Johnson, who recorded in 1936 and 1937. As well as Blind Lemon Jefferson, Texas produced Alger "Texas" Alexander, whose rough tones more than hinted of his work in the fields. The Southeast, with Atlanta as its recording center, also produced its share of performers, including Blind Blake, Blind Willie McTell, and Blind Boy Fuller. When the record companies went bust in the mid-1930s, most of these performers ceased recording, although a significant few resurfaced in the 1960s.

When the blues moved north with the black diaspora of the 1920s and after, Chicago became its mecca. Tampa Red and "Georgia Tom" Dorsey, earlier accompanist for Ma Rainey, were based in the Windy City, along with Mississippi-born William Lee Conley "Big Bill" Broonzy. By the mid-1930s jazz and blues clubs dotted the urban landscape, North and South, fostering overlapping styles of black music.

The blues had a definite influence on white country music, leading to a fascinating mélange of black and white styling. Indeed, with so much give and take, it was occasionally hard to identify the performer's race. For example, the white musicians Austin and Lee Allen's "Laughin' and Cryin' Blues" and "Chattanooga Blues" accidentally appeared in Columbia's 14000 Race series in late 1927. (They sued the company unsuccessfully for this racial affront.) The country performers Henry Whitter, Uncle Dave Macon, and Dock Boggs freely borrowed from their black neighbors.

Then Jimmie Rodgers appeared and soon reached the country music stratosphere with a series of best-sellers. Born in Mississippi in 1897, Rodgers drank deep at the blues, and he appeared in blackface with a traveling medicine show. "Blue Yodel No. 1," issued by Victor in February 1928, rocketed to instant fame, eventually selling over a million copies. He followed with scores of records, many in the blues mode, with total sales of perhaps twelve million by the time of his death in 1933. Rodgers had a legion of imitators, including Jimmie Davis, Ernest Tubb, and particularly Gene Autry.

The blues also became incorporated into the emerging western swing and proto-bluegrass styles of the latter 1930s, a melding which underscored the shared roots and close links of many black and white southern musicians. Such musical race mixing might appear surprising, considering the extent of southern segregation and the deplorable state of national race relations, but disembodied voices coming from the phonograph or radio did not necessarily carry racial markers, despite attempts by the record companies to warn their customers.

While southern musicians such as the Monroe Brothers, the Blue Sky Boys, and the Coon Creek Girls developed a sophisticated sound, further west a new musical hybrid appeared. Influenced by Jimmie Rodgers, vocalists such as Ernest Tubb and Lefty Frizzell adopted a western style of garb and performance. With Gene Autry's first movie in 1934 the mold was set for a legion of Hollywood singing cowboys—Johnny Bond, Jimmy Wakely, Tex Ritter, and Roy Rogers, initially one of the Sons of the Pioneers. Patsy Montana, an early female country star, scored with her 1935 hit "I Want to Be a Cowboy's Sweetheart." Parallel with the onset of the singing cowboy was the advent of Western Swing. After a rocky start, Bob Wills and Milton Brown formed the Light Crust Doughboys in 1932, which set the eclectic style of "country jazz." Brown soon spun off the Musical Brownies, while Wills initiated the Texas Playboys, the most influential and long lasting of the swing groups.[19]

Some rural performers, white and black, went commercial during the 1920s and the Depression, but others languished in obscurity. In the late 1930s Alan Lomax, the first paid assistant in charge of the music at the Library of Congress, traveled throughout the South recording prisoners, field hands, and levee workers. Though focused on the rural black South, Lomax also explored other regions and styles; with the help of Bascom Lamar Lunsford and the folklorist Stith Thompson, he recorded rural old-time music in Ohio and Indiana in early 1938, and on a subsequent trip to the Midwest he captured lake sailor songs from the Upper Peninsula of Michigan. In late 1938 and early 1939 he recorded black blues performers in New York with the help of John Hammond, and he also recorded Captain Dick Maitland's shanty songs. John Lomax, meanwhile, tried to keep pace with his son, making a sweeping six thousand-mile trip through the South in 1939, followed by a second shorter one in 1941, assembling one hundred disks of Mexican, black, and white songs.

If John and Alan Lomax glossed over their differing political views, Lawrence Gellert's collecting was overtly political. Having moved for reasons of health from New York to Tryon, North Carolina, Gellert became acquainted with his black neighbors and began making blues field recordings in Greenville, South Carolina, in 1924. He gained the confidence of black prisoners and sharecroppers in the Carolinas and Georgia and gathered a large number of unaccompanied hollers and group work songs that often contained strong social commentary. Indeed, the protest nature of many of the songs, so different from those recorded by the Lomaxes, brought swift criticism when Gellert went public with them. The left-wing Gellert had already written on the subject for *New Masses* before publication of twenty-four of the songs in *Negro Songs of Protest* in 1936 (the title was provided by the Communist culture critic Michael Gold). "These songs are still in the making," he explained in the Preface. "Never sung twice quite in the same way, new verses are constantly improvised, the text doggerel, nonsense, bawdy or protest, depending upon the mood of the singers or whether whites are within earshot."[20]

The folklorist Herbert Halpert, one of Gellert's defenders, toured the South in 1939, working for the Folk Arts Committee of the Works Progress Administration (WPA) as well as the Archive of American Folk-Song; upon his return to Washington he deposited 419 twelve-inch acetate discs, comprising over one thousand performances. Halpert, who also worked for the Federal Theater, argued that "folk songs that spring from new social conditions, such as the industrialization of the South makes inevitable, are songs we hail with enthusiasm because they show the true vitality of folklore in the South." For Halpert and many of his colleagues, folk music had current validity; in Kentucky, he noted, "the miner's strike songs are made up to the tunes of old ballads."[21]

The critic Paul Rosenfeld also sensed the ongoing political and cultural struggle over folk music, its appeal to both conservatives and progressives. The latter subscribed to what could be called the functionalist approach to folk music, the view that folk songs might have not only an ancient lineage but a dynamic present; they could serve practical purposes, energizing the folk to struggle against racism and oppression. Rosenfeld warned against the new southern regionalism that sought to preserve a Jim Crow South. Folk music, he argued, should not serve parochial, conservative, racist purposes, though it often did. As the 1930s unfolded, folk music abetted a broadly defined progressive politics.

The Left and Folk Music

Topical songs had existed throughout the nineteenth century, from labor and abolitionist tunes to farmers' laments and spiritual and overtly political ballads. They expressed a wide range of dreams and discontents. They appeared in thousands of songsters and broadsides, while others turned up in labor papers.[22]

In the early twentieth century the Industrial Workers of the World (IWW) used folk and popular-song melodies as well as familiar religious tunes to carry their messages and instill a cohesive spirit among members and sympathizers. The Wobblies, as they were derisively called, first published *Songs of the Workers* in 1909—better known as "The Little Red Song Book." Small enough to fit into a shirt pocket, it traveled the length of the land, spreading the songs of Joe Hill, T-Bone Slim, and Ralph Chaplin. Though their songs did not appear on records at the time, the Wobbly singers Goebel Reeves and Mac McClintock later recorded numerous sides, the former for OKeh, Gennett, Brunswick, and others from 1929 to 1938, the latter for Victor from 1927 to 1931. (The Communist party adopted Joe Hill as a cultural icon, despite the seeming clash in political philosophies—the anarchist Hill opposed any notion of centralized power, political or otherwise. The Young Workers League of America, the party's youth wing formed in the mid-1920s, included in its songbook, *The March of the Workers and Other Songs* [ca. 1925], Hill's "The Preacher and the Slave," as well as Chaplin's "The Commonwealth of Toil.")[23]

While popular (that is, commercial) music has generally avoided overt political content, particularly of a Left-leaning sort, certain musical subcultures have not shied away from complaints and controversial subjects. Blues has inherently dealt with suffering and unrest, though usually in a covert fashion and from a personal perspective. Similarly, old-time music has sometimes included protest, pro-labor, and pro-union songs, for example, the Martin Brothers's 1929 recording of "The North Carolina Textile Strike."

The composers and performers Florence Reese, Ella May Wiggins, Jim Garland, his half-sister Aunt Molly Jackson and sister Sarah Ogan Gunning, Woody Guthrie, Sis Cunningham, and John Handcox captured this mix of native radical politics and working-class trials and hardships. They often identified with such Left-led unions as the National Miners Union, the National Textile Workers, and the Southern Tenant Farmers Union (STFU), as well as the Highlander Folk School in Monteagle, Tennessee; and with Commonwealth College in Mena, Arkansas, the Southern School for Workers near Ashland, North Carolina, the socialist Brookwood Labor School in Katonah, New York, and the Red Dust Players in Oklahoma. The Kentucky Workers Alliance promoted folk-styled labor songs and published *Songs for Southern Workers* in 1937. While an organizer for the Socialist-connected STFU, Handcox penned "Raggedy, Raggedy Are We" and "There Are Mean Things Happening in This Land."

Though not steeped in Marxist rhetoric, Aunt Molly Jackson was deeply committed to labor unions. She added an authentic voice of the folk to the formation of northern urban folk music. Born in 1880, she married at fourteen; forty years later, and the wife of a coal miner in Kentucky (her second husband), Aunt Molly was a repository of local folk songs. She testified about the terrible conditions in the coal towns and sang her "Ragged Hungry Blues" in November 1931 to an investigating team composed of John Dos Passos, Samuel Ornitz, Theodore Dreiser and other concerned northern leftists. The audience of outsiders was stunned by her power and graphic descriptions, and within the month she abandoned Clay County, Kentucky, for New York.

The Communist Left quickly embraced Aunt Molly and she also caught the attention of the New York press, including the *New York Times*, the *Herald Tribune*, and even *Fortune* magazine, all captivated by her brazen, rugged charm and unvarnished expressions of rural poverty and struggle. She appeared at New York rallies, met the New York University folklorist Mary Elizabeth Barnicle, and through her Alan Lomax. The musician and writer Margaret Larkin brought Molly to Columbia Records, for which she recorded "Kentucky Miner's Wife" (aka "Ragged Hungry Blues"). For the next few years she traveled around the country, organizing and raising funds for the miners. She finally settled on the Lower East Side in New York, where she survived the Depression mostly on welfare; she was temporarily a potent symbol of rural creativity and survival.[24]

Rural protest songs, white and black, reached northern audiences through the labors of various Left-oriented collectors, publicists, and performers. The

Memphis-born, New York–based songwriter, publisher, and performer Bob Miller waxed scores of such songs (under the names Bob Ferguson, Bob Hill, and Bill Palmer), though he would become better known in radical circles for his compositions, such as "Eleven Cent Cotton, Forty Cent Meat," and for his publication of the portfolio *Songs of the Almanac Singers* (1942).[25]

Margaret Larkin (1899–1967), a poet and journalist who was born in New Mexico and raised with cowboy songs, also linked folk songs and social protest. She published *Singing Cowboy: A Book of Western Songs* in 1931, publicized the songs and struggles of Ella May Wiggins, who had been gunned down two years earlier during the Gastonia textile strike, and early on befriended Aunt Molly Jackson. Larkin performed Ella May's "The Mill Mother's Lament" and other labor songs in New York during the early 1930s.

Maurice Sugar in Detroit and Mike Quin on the West Coast were two other proletarian-tinged song writers. Sugar, an attorney, penned "The Soup Song" (1931) and "Sit Down" (1937), musical staples of the Left throughout the decade. Quin, who became a popular columnist for *People's World*, the Communist party's West Coast paper, wrote "Someday We'll Pay Our Debts" and "March, Worker and Soldier." Influenced by the IWW in the Northwest, Quin had previously published worker songs, set to popular tunes, in his column in *Western Worker*, the precursor to *People's World*. (Woody Guthrie's column in the latter, "Woody Sez," beginning in May 1939, introduced readers to a steady stream of folk-style songs.)

During the Depression a broad Left culture began to emerge, particularly in New York City, within a rejuvenated and expanding Communist party. By the mid-1930s various Left/labor musical styles and influences existed, shaped by no articulated Communist party musical line, though there seemed to be a penchant for grand labor choruses and avant-garde European influences. (Party leaders generally had little interest in folk music.) In New York the Composers Collective (1932–36), a special section of the Pierre Degeyter Club affiliated with the Communist-connected Workers Music League, attracted an impressive array of musicians including Charles Seeger, Earl Robinson, Norman Cazden, Henry Cowell, Marc Blitzstein, Elie Siegmeister, and Aaron Copland. The Collective encouraged the composition of music to stir the masses, using modern musical idioms. Heavily influenced by the music of Hanns Eisler, the revolutionary composer popular among the German working class, and the prose of Bertolt Brecht, the Collective's aesthetic hardly connected with America's masses. The Timely Recording Company, formed in 1935 by insurance salesman Leo Waldman, first issued three records that exemplified this style, featuring Eisler's "In Praise of Learning" and "Rise Up" as well as Maurice Sugar's "The Soup Song" and Degeyter's "The Internationale" (1871).[26]

Though organized socialist parties were traditionally indifferent to the political utility of music, folk or otherwise, there were notable exceptions. Music played some part in British socialist circles around the turn of the century, mostly choruses singing songs designed for moral uplift; traditional folk music also had some appeal, at least as a counter to the music hall songs favored by the working class. In the United States Charles Kerr had published *Socialist Songs with Music* in 1901, widely circulated in various editions, which was soon followed by Harvey Moyer's *Songs of Socialism for Local Branch and Campaign Work, Public Meetings, Labor, Fraternal and Religious Organizations, Social Gatherings and the Home* (1905). Both were used in the numerous socialist Sunday schools of the time. The Rand School, the socialist workers' school founded in 1906, published the *Rebel Song Book: Eighty-seven Socialist and Labor Songs for Voice and Piano* in 1935. Socialists working at the Highlander Folk School, particularly Zilphia Horton, as well as Claude Williams at Commonwealth College, utilized folk music as a labor organizing tool. And there was considerable singing at summer camps, in the garment unions, and in the Workmen's Circle, a Jewish labor fraternal order.[27]

Many folklorists, writers, academics, and enthusiastic amateurs sparked a broad interest in folklore and folk culture during the 1930s, often drawing upon nostalgic and patriotic views of the country's past. Those searching for traditional models and styles might have either conservative, liberal, or radical leanings. The folk festival organizers Jean Thomas—formerly a Hollywood scenario writer, reporter, and publicist for the speakeasy hostess Texas Guinan—and Sarah Gertrude Knott, founder of the National Folk Festival, matched Lunsford's and the elder Lomax's patriotic, conservative, traditional bent. In the North, however, folk music became generally associated with those on the liberal if not left side of the political spectrum. Such a political identification would generally carry through subsequent decades, with intriguing twists and turns. Folk music attracted a complex mix, however—hard-headed radicals and fuzzy romantics, progressives and conservatives, those strictly interested in the music and those who mixed culture and politics.

Charles Seeger loomed as a prime influence. An academic musicologist greatly moved by modernist Continental styles, he nonetheless became strongly committed to documenting and publicizing traditional music from throughout the Western hemisphere. During the Depression he wrote for the Communist party's *Daily Worker* under the name Carl Sands, and he exhibited a growing penchant for folk music. "Its current repertoire must mount into the tens of thousands of ballads, songs and dances," he wrote in 1938. "It has suffered from industrialism, commercialism, religious bigotry and the snubbing of city sophisticates. But it is still going strong, losing, as it goes, many old songs but adding many new, its technical and stylistic nature undergoing continual change through increased contact with academic and popular art." And he concluded: "Unquestionably, the musical soul of America is in its folk music, not in its academic music; and only in its popular music to the extent popular music has borrowed, stolen and manhandled folk."[28]

Early Left song books generally stuck to a formal, European classical style. The Composers Collective's first two editions of the *Workers Song Book* (1934 and 1935), generally followed this format, with songs by members Seeger, Elie Siegmeister and Lan Adomian; they argued that "the composer is the hand that writes; the audience sings and decides what shall be sung. A great audience calls forth great song." The *Red Song Book*, published by the Workers Music League in 1932, had already begun to crack this elitist view, however; along with "Red Army March" and "Oh, Tortured and Broken in Prison"—identified as "Lenin's Favorite Song"—it included among its twenty-six songs "The Preacher and the Slave," "Hold the Fort," Aunt Molly Jackson's "Poor Miner's Farewell," Ella May Wiggins's "I.L.D. Song," and "The Soup Song." Ray and Linda Auville, party members in Cleveland, continued the trend in *Songs of the American Worker* (1934). Michael Gold heaped praise on their earthy style. The socialist *Rebel Song Book* (1935) included a miscellany of musical styles, many European, but also spirituals and IWW songs, and three with music by Sis Cunningham—"The March of the Hungry Men," "The Cry of the People," and "Song of the Lower Classes"—already published in her *Six Labor Songs* at Commonwealth College in Mena, Arkansas. The Composers Collective's third songbook, *Song of the People* (1937), included many folk songs using traditional American tunes.[29]

For the second half of the decade, the Communist-led Left promoted and explored many native traditional musical and cultural styles. Charles Seeger commented: "An old woman named Aunt Mollie Jackson had come to one of the meetings of the Composers' Collective, and I learned her songs and discovered that they were folk songs simply dolled up . . . So I went up to her and I said, Mollie, You're on the right track and we're on the wrong track— [we were] professionals trying to write music for the people and not in the people's idiom." Seeger soon joined the New Deal's Resettlement Administration (retitled the Farm Security Administration in 1937), followed by a stint with the Federal Music Project of the WPA from 1937 to 1941. As the Popular Front—the Communist party's outreach effort—entered its full stride after 1935, even IWW songs—"Hold the Fort," "Commonwealth of Toil" and "The Preacher and the Slave"—entered the musical lexicon, despite the Wobblies' anarchistic bent. Earl Robinson, the choral director at Camp Unity, an adult camp in Wingdale, New York, that opened in 1936, taught a broad repertoire of American working-class songs, black and white.[30]

Left organizations made no clear differentiations among native folk, jazz, blues, ethnic, gospel, popular, and classical music in their public programs, thus leaving room for a wide variety of influences and expressions. For example, New York's Theater Arts Committee (TAC), formed in early 1937 by activist actors and writers, soon organized Cabaret TAC, located at the Princess Theater, which featured the politically sophisticated music of Earl Robinson, Marc Blitzstein and Harold Rome, sung by Tony Kraber, Beatrice Kay, June Havoc and

Michael Loring. Similar groups materialized in Los Angles and Washington, D.C. Blitzstein's prolabor musical The Cradle Will Rock opened in June 1937, soon followed by the International Ladies Garment Workers Union (ILGWU) presentation of the pop-styled Pins and Needles, with music by Rome—both instant cultural staples of the Left.

Blues and jazz also attracted Left support—particularly among younger members—with their musical allure and overtones of interracial cooperation. First, a benefit at Carnegie Hall for the Spanish Children's Milk Fund featured W. C. Handy, Fats Waller and Cab Calloway. Next, Eric Bernay of New Masses, a Communist cultural magazine, sponsored John Hammond's momentous "Spirituals to Swing" concert at Carnegie Hall on December 23, 1938. "I was not completely comfortable about Bernay's backing," Hammond later wrote. "New Masses was, of course, a Marxist publication. Eric promised he would not make political capital of our association, however, and he was true to his word. He saw the concert as a landmark event, the first major concert to be produced in New York for an integrated audience and one which would bring both profit and prestige to its sponsor." Sister Rosetta Tharpe, Sonny Terry, Sidney Bechet, Big Bill Broonzy—replacing country bluesman Robert Johnson, recently murdered—and Count Basie's band, among others, performed during the long night. A year later TAC sponsored a sequel, also produced by Hammond.[31]

Barney Josephson opened Cafe Society in Greenwich Village on New Year's Eve, 1938, also with Hammond's assistance. The first racially mixed club in New York, Cafe Society soon featured Lena Horne, Billie Holiday and Josh White. Born in South Carolina and a seasoned street blues singer before his first commercial recordings in 1932, White sang both blues and spirituals. White would also appear at Max Gordon's Village Vanguard (opened in 1935), along with Lead Belly and Richard Dyer-Bennet.[32]

Radio increasingly served as an outlet for the Left's musical ferment. Jim Garland, Aunt Molly Jackson's half-brother, had a short-lived radio folk show in New York in 1938. A coal miner and National Miners Union organizer from Harlan County, Kentucky, Garland had moved to New York in 1935. He played for various radical organizations and also assisted in Elizabeth Barnicle's English classes at New York University. (Both Barnicle and Alan Lomax recorded him for the Library of Congress.)[33]

Alan Lomax, while continuing with the Library of Congress, launched his first radio show in late 1939, part of CBS's American School of the Air. "You had the charming folk tune, simply and crudely performed by myself or one of my friends," Lomax later recalled. "Then it was to be transmute[d] by the magic of symphonic technique into big music, just as it was supposed to have happened with Bach and Haydn and the boys. This was music education." The friends included Pete Seeger, Woody Guthrie and Lead Belly, with orchestral arrangements by Aaron Copland, Charles Seeger, or Ruth Crawford Seeger. Over two years about fifty half-hour programs reached public schools throughout the country on Tuesday mornings. John Lomax praised his son's singing, but carped that Lead Belly's voice had become "weak and pitiful," lacking its natural charm, and Guthrie, the "Oklahoma Dust Bowl man," was "an absolute zero." Alan eventually agreed with his father that the formal compositions drained all validity and passion from the songs: "The experiment, which must have cost CBS a small fortune, was a colossal failure, and had failed to produce a single bar of music worthy of association with the folk tradition."[34]

For his second radio effort, Lomax introduced Back Where I Come From in August 1940, also on CBS, for fifteen minutes three evenings a week. Written by Lomax and directed by Nicholas Ray, who had worked with him on the previous show, the new show featured Guthrie, Lead Belly, Josh White, Burl Ives, and the Golden Gate Quartet, with Earl Robinson sometimes serving as an announcer. In all of his work, Lomax tried to capture "the seemingly incoherent diversity of American folk song as an expression of its democratic, inter-racial, international character, as a function of its inchoate and turbulent many-sided development."[35]

Each program centered on a theme, such as "Nonsense Songs," "Love True and Careless," "Jails," or "Work Songs of the City." Guthrie had left the show by late 1940, and Lomax wrote to Guthrie early the following February. "I really miss you a lot. . . . We don't have anybody who can come out and speak his mind with sincerity and honesty the way you can. Pete is on very regularly and his banjo playing adds a lot. Direction has improved a great deal and everyone likes the show except maybe Burl who is beginning to feel his oats these last days." In any case, CBS canceled the program in February 1941 even though Lomax considered it to be a success. "Our agent William Morris told us we were set for life. And then the great paw of America reached out and stopped it: Mister William B. Paley said that he didn't want any of that goddamn hillbilly music on his network. And that was that." Woody Guthrie wrote to Lomax from Los Angeles: "Too honest again I suppose? Maybe not purty enough. O well, this country's a getting to where it cain't hear its own voice. Someday the deal will change."[36]

Henrietta Yurchenco produced various folk programs for city-owned WNYC in 1940–41, with roughly the same performers as those Lomax featured. She believed that "through their songs life among poor whites of Appalachia, oppressed southern blacks, and dust storm victims came alive far better than all the articles in the Daily Worker of the New Masses. . . . Composers of classical music sought them out, for Americanism was in the air, and these folk singers had their finger on its musical pulse." Assisted by Yurchenco, Guthrie soon appeared on a variety of radio programs including Lead Belly's weekly series, Folk Songs of America. Guthrie regularly performed on a network show sponsored by the Model Tobacco Company, and was paid the princely sum of $200 a week.

Yurchenco staged a ten-day folk pageant on WNYC in February 1941, with the cream of the local folk establishment. Pete Seeger began appearing on WABC in New York City.[37]

Promenade, a publication of the American Square Dance Group (ASDG) since the mid-1930s, covered all the folk music radio shows in New York City as well as new record releases. Margot Mayo, a cousin of the traditional Kentucky banjo player Rufus Crisp, headed the ASDG and its newsletter for many years. The mixed bag of radio shows during the summer of 1940, continually changing, included Burl Ives, the Golden Gate Quartet, Josef Marais with South African folk songs, and international folk music. Folk music was suddenly hot, in New York and nationally, but by the next summer the pickings would be slim, with only Burl Ives and Eric Clark broadcasting regularly in New York City. The rest of country heard old-time music shows emanating from Chicago, Nashville, and elsewhere.

As an indication of the Left's increasing shift to traditional rural songs and melodies with a radical twist, in early 1937 Timely Records released six sides of labor songs including "We Shall Not Be Moved," "Hold the Fort," "Solidarity Forever," and Maurice Sugar's "Sit Down," with baritone Mordecai Bauman and Elie Siegmeister directing the Manhattan Chorus (originally styled the Daily Worker Chorus). "Daily, on picket lines, and at demonstrations, the songs serve for mass singing," Martin McCall (aka Max Margulis) wrote in the *Daily Worker*. Siegmeister, a classically trained member of the Composers Collective and early convert to folk music, formed the American Ballad Singers in 1939; the group lasted until the mid-1940s. "Listening to those authentic ballads, lullabies, dance melodies, and work songs," he wrote in 1943, "we realize that this is one of the richest, most exciting types of music on earth." And he continued: "Many folk singers today—Leadbelly, Aunt Molly Jackson, George Edwards, and Joshua White—have distinctive, individual qualities of style that mark them as outstanding artists in their field. . . . Folk song, the natural expression of our people who 'don't know anything about music,' is the deepest, most democratic layer of our American musical culture."[38]

Earl Robinson served as an important folk music conduit, exhibiting a deft combination of musical expertise and creativity and a sure grasp for idiomatic compositions that captured a native spirit. Growing up in Seattle, Robinson arrived in New York in 1934 and quickly plunged into Communist party activities including the Young Communist League and the Workers Laboratory Theater, soon known as the Theater of Action. During the summer of 1936, as musical director at Camp Unity, he composed "Joe Hill" (with words by Alfred Hayes). After a short stay at Camp Kinderland in 1937—left-wing camps played a key role in shaping and disseminating folk music for many decades—he returned to Camp Unity in 1938 while continuing to compose, with increasing success, for the Federal Theater Project. Robinson also led the IWO (International Workers Order) People's Chorus, formed in January 1938, presenting folk music to various union and Left audiences. "One of the most exciting manifestations of the growing People's Front movement is the development of a real people's culture in every artistic field," Irene Tannenbaum wrote in the *Daily Worker*. "In the vanguard of the movement to develop a true people's culture is the I.W.O. People's Chorus, which is bringing real American folk music to the masses." Robinson soon achieved national acclaim for "Ballad for Americans," written by John Latouche and performed by Paul Robeson for CBS on November 5, 1939. Even *Readers Digest* labeled it "the finest piece of American propaganda."[39]

Almanac Singers and the War Years

In 1940 the actor Will Geer organized what he later termed "the first hootenanny" (a musical program with many performers)—a "Grapes of Wrath Evening" on March 3 at the Forrest Theater in New York, where he was starring in *Tobacco Road*. The performers included Aunt Molly Jackson, Bess and Alan Lomax, Burl Ives, Woody Guthrie, the Golden Gate Quartet, Margot Mayo's square dance troupe, and the young Pete Seeger. Born to Charles and Constance in New York City on May 3, 1919, Pete dropped out of Harvard at nineteen and hit the road, sometimes traveling with Woody. The concert marked Seeger's inaugural public performance, a nervous rendition of one song.

Geer, a seasoned actor, had appeared with the New Theater League and in Mark Blitzstein's controversial *The Cradle Will Rock*; he had also traveled with Burl Ives and Tony Kraber in 1939, performing for various union and other benefits. Through his friend Ed Robbin, Geer met Woody Guthrie in Los Angeles, and they struck it off immediately; they performed in migrant labor camps around California during the summer, singing and organizing. Geer, Guthrie, and Kraber appeared in a second New York "Grapes of Wrath" concert on April 12, 1940, at the ACT Galleries, to benefit beleaguered Communist party activists in Oklahoma. In December 1941 Geer made a short film with Burl Ives and Josh White; entitled *Tall Tales*, it was the first of ten depicting the historical background of specific folk songs.[40]

Folk music was also becoming commercialized in 1940. It seemed to be "rapidly becoming a new industry," composer Roy Harris commented. "Tossed into the commercial boiling pot, it is now being processed for radio and every conceivable outlet. The more obvious melodic idioms and the word ideas are put through the work-a-day wringer by crooners, bands, small orchestral groups, radio skits, folk-feature programs, records." He predicted, "America will have many folk song vendors in the next few years. Some city boys may take a short motor trip through our land and return to write the Song of the Prairies—others will be folk song authorities after reading in a public library for a few weeks. . . . We'll have Folk Song Hot and Cold in the Pot with whiskers on it." Harris's own *Folksong Symphony* (1940) attested to his reliance on songs collected by Carl Sandburg and John Lomax. Folk music also infused the compositions of other classical composers including Aaron Copland.[41]

While continuing to provide a steady stream of entertainment for black and white rural audiences, the major record companies recognized the growing urban interest in native folk styles. Victor Records recorded Woody Guthrie in May 1940 and released in August the album *Dust Bowl Ballads*, including "Talking Dust Bowl, "Do Re Mi," and "So Long, It's Been Good to Know You." Victor also reissued the Carter Family, Uncle Dave Macon, and the Monroe Brothers—all active and quickly becoming part of an enduring country folk legacy—in John Lomax's compilation *Smoky Mountain Ballads*.

In the June 1941 *Harper's Bazaar* Chester Kallman extensively reviewed much of this recorded musical treasure trove, including Carl Sandburg, John Jacob Niles, Lead Belly, the Golden Gate Quartet, Josh White, Woody Guthrie, Paul Robeson ("Ballad for Americans"), and Earl Robinson. As for Robinson's *Songs for Americans* (Timely Records), Kallman thought the public reaction would be mixed, "One camp thinking his 'Abe Lincoln' and 'Joe Hill' genuine recreations of the American ballad spirit, while the other would probably complain that the earthiness was willful and not as artless as it pretends, and that an artist simply could not be what he wasn't—a hundred and twenty million people." The long-smoldering question of authenticity and style versus substance would continually engage folklorists, music critics, and fans throughout the century.[42]

New York City proved a stewpot for the mix of radical politics and southern music that resulted in the formation of the Almanac Singers. In late 1940 Pete Seeger met Lee Hays and his roommate Millard Lampell, who were both interested in labor songs. Hays, a music and dramatics instructor at Commonwealth College in Arkansas (1936–39), was steeped in traditional and labor songs and had been compiling a workers' songbook with choral director Waldemar Hille, whom he had met at Commonwealth. Seeger, Hays, Lampell soon moved from their cramped apartment to a cheap, grimy, but roomy industrial loft on 12th Street and 4th Avenue in Greenwich Village; their sympathetic landlord was the father-in-law of Ira Gershwin. Soon joined by others, including Peter Hawes from Massachusetts, in the communal Almanac House, the self-styled Almanacs (they assumed the name the following February) initiated Sunday afternoon musical rent parties—Mill's idea after accompanying John Hammond to one in Harlem. They began appearing at various Left meetings and labor rallies, beginning with an American Youth Congress (AYC) gathering in Washington, D.C., in February 1941.

Presenting a mixture of traditional and topical songs, generally written by Hays and Lampell, the ensemble had a refreshing sound and dynamic delivery.

Temporarily known as Pete Bowers, mostly to protect his father who was then working for the government, Seeger assumed partial leadership of the loosely knit ensemble. They were a pioneering group that paved the way for sundry offspring, starting with the Weavers, led by Seeger and Hays, a decade later. In both content and style they drew on an eclectic musical heritage including the nineteenth-century protest songs of British radicals and of the U.S. abolitionist movement. Alan Lomax provided musical counsel and connections. Almanac House attracted various Left and musical luminaries—Jim Garland, Aunt Molly Jackson, Lead Belly, Josh White, Marc Blitzstein, the Communist party organizers Mother Bloor and Elizabeth Gurley Flynn, and even the detective writer Dashiell Hammett.

Though not formally allied with the Communist party, the Almanacs—styled by *Time* as "four young men who roam around the country in a $150 Buick and fight the class war with ballads and guitars"—closely identified with the party's domestic and foreign agenda. "At a recent meeting of the League of American Writers Theodore Dreiser heard Pete Bowers and Lee Hays, the Almanac Singers, sing ballads from their endless repertoire," George Lewis opened his lengthy piece on the group in the *Daily Worker* in late March 1941, the first of numerous articles and notices. "When they had finished singing, Theodore Dreiser commented, 'If there were six more teams like you, we could save America.' " Lewis praised their antiwar songs, some included in their newly prepared song book for the American Peace Mobilization. "They are not a part of the current ballad fad," the author continued; "they feel a definite responsibility for the cultural and political standards of their work; and towards the end of creating valid material they have made thorough analytical studies of the source of a people's culture as it is found in all contemporary forms of proletarian expression." In writing contemporary topical ballads, they hoped to influence other performers.[43]

In March 1941 they recorded their first album, *Songs for John Doe*, accompanied by Josh White, for Eric Bernay's Keynote Records (a contact made by Alan Lomax). Bernay owned the Music Room on West 44th Street, a record shop described as "nothing more than a 'hole-in-the-wall.' . . . The walls are covered with shelves loaded with albums containing folk songs of all nations." *John Doe* appeared on the new "Almanacs Records" label because Bernay, former treasurer of *New Masses*, desired some anonymity; he also demanded they finance the album. Strongly antiwar and highly offensive to President Roosevelt's supporters—the Almanacs backed the Communist party's nonintervention posture following the Nazi-Soviet pact of August 1939 until the German invasion of the Soviet Union on June 22, 1941—*John Doe* appeared just as the party came under sharp attack. Its neutral stance offended many on the Left, but coincided with the views of others, including Charles Lindbergh and the right-wing group America First. John Hammond, Earl Robinson and Bernay had circulated a letter announcing the album and soliciting contributions so that it could "be distributed in the cause of peace, and in the cause of a new music which has arisen out of the people." Seeger later recalled, "Within a few weeks, the Almanacs' record was known from coast to coast in this narrow circle of leftwingers, and peaceniks of one sort or another."[44]

Someone in military intelligence heard *John Doe,* noted the songs were "highly seditious," and so reported to his superior officer. The latter concluded the records were obviously "put out by some Communist organization which had its identity under the name of the ALMANAC SINGERS," and so passed the information to the FBI in October 1941. Thus began the FBI's prolonged and fruitless attempt to document the subversive nature of the Almanacs and their recording company. Director J. Edgar Hoover finally ordered an end to the pursuit in early 1943.[45]

Soon after issuing *John Doe,* Bernay produced Paul Robeson performing the Earl Robinson–Harry Schachter antiwar "Spring Song." The Almanacs participated in a May Day peace march in New York, and later in the month they regaled twenty thousand striking Transport Workers' Union members in Madison Square Garden, introducing the song "Talking Union." Then they joined with a group of actors in a spirited revue called "Sign of the Times." Reflecting many years later on his role in the peace movement, Seeger wrote: "Should I apologize for all this? I think so. . . . At any rate, today I'll apologize for a number of things, such as thinking that Stalin was simply a 'hard driver' and not a supremely cruel misleader."[46]

The New Theater League often arranged for the Almanacs' appearances, first at antiwar and union meetings, and later at prowar rallies. It published *Eight Songs of the Almanacs* (1941) and the bouleversement *Eleven Songs to Tear Hitler Down* (1942). The Almanacs' album of labor songs, *Talking Union,* appeared on Keynote in July 1941. *Time's* mixed review reminded readers that *John Doe* had "ably hewed to the then Moscow line," but the new discs "lay off the isolationist business now that the Russians are laying it on the Germans." With the assistance of Alan Lomax and Henrietta Yurchenco, they also recorded two non-political albums of more traditional songs for Hazard Reeves's General Records, *Sea Shanteys* and *Sod Buster Ballads.* They frequently mixed topical and traditional songs in their concerts, drawing on an increasing store of materials that was greatly enhanced by Woody Guthrie, who joined the group in the summer of 1941.[47]

Germany's abrupt invasion of the Soviet Union in late June 1941 doomed the *John Doe* album, as party followers hopped on the prowar bandwagon. "Well I guess we're not going to be singing any more of them peace songs," Guthrie remarked to Seeger, who later reminisced: "He was right, of course. The day after the invasion, the *Daily Worker,* which had been preaching peace hard for the previous year, suddenly had its headline, 'All Aid to the Soviet Union.' And guess what, Winston Churchill comes out with a headline, 'All Aid to Our Gallant Soviet Allies.' "[48]

Seeking a new act, Village Vanguard owner Max Gordon contacted Nicholas Ray, a regular at the Vanguard who was then living at Almanac House. Ray recommended Lead Belly, recently returned to the city from Washington, and Josh White. "Opening night was one of those nights," Gordon recalled in his memoirs. "There was in the place a feeling that something important was going to happen. I never saw so many guitars in the place: Pete Seeger, Burl Ives, Richard Dyer-Bennet, Millard Lampell, The Almanac Singers, five strong, and Woody Guthrie—all present, with guitars slung over their shoulders." In a typically lengthy letter to Gordon, Woody praised his employment of White and Lead Belly and gave pointers on how best to present them. But Woody himself never played the club. "Every time I had an opening for him," Gordon explained, "he'd be off somewhere with his guitar, thumbing his way across the land, out into the country 'where there was more of it under corn than under concrete.' "[49]

During summer 1941 Seeger, Lampell, Guthrie, and Hays decided to tour the country. Saul Mills, of the New York CIO Council, connected them with various union locals, their target audience. Singing "Jesse James" and "Black-Eyed Susie" at a largely black housing project in Pittsburgh, they drew little response, and "Union Train" and "Union Maid" didn't fare much better, but "Jim Crow" got a good reaction. In Cleveland they sang for the National Maritime Union, whose enthusiastic, generous members tossed over $200 into the hat; they next entertained union members and strikers in Detroit, Cicero, and Milwaukee. Hays returned east after the Almanacs performed for various progressive groups and unions in San Francisco, including Harry Bridges's Longshorsemen's Union. Before leaving New York the group had recorded "Song for Bridges" and "Babe O' Mine," which were soon released by Keynote. Elated by their labor reception in the bay area, Guthrie, Lampell, and Seeger next joined a "Victory Campaign Rally" in Los Angeles, where they entertained various labor and political gatherings. Lampell returned to New York, while Seeger and Guthrie headed to Portland and Seattle. They finally arrived back in New York in late September.[50]

Seeger, Hays, Lampbell, Guthrie, and Pete Hawes soon moved into a new Almanac House, with more bedrooms but less space, on West 10th Street near 6th Avenue. They were joined by Alan Lomax's sister Bess, a recent graduate of Bryn Mawr who worked at the New York Public Library. She was full of songs and enthusiasm, but the poverty and chaos of the situation and the fact that everybody expected her to do the cooking soon forced her to find her own apartment. "She was the youngest of a large brood," Seeger remembered, "and her father somehow got wind that she was living with a bunch of radical singers. She found he was coming just in time to move out with a friend and welcome her father when he arrived from Texas to make sure his daughter was behaving herself in the big city." Then Pete Hawes moved out, temporarily replaced by his brother Butch, an artist trained at the Boston Museum School.[51]

Agnes "Sis" Cunningham and Gordon Friesen arrived from Oklahoma, fleeing political repression and poverty, and moved into Almanac House in mid-December. Gordon, a journalist and artist, and Cunningham, a performer, former teacher, and member of the agit-prop Red Dust Players, brought a healthy dose of rural radicalism to the group. Later, the blues performers Sonny Terry and Brownie McGhee occasionally stayed overnight. Alan Lomax had urged the Almanacs to invite the two seasoned musicians from North Carolina, who had only met in June 1940. "We had a wonderful afternoon, supper, and then we were making music," Seeger recalled. "We just kept on making music. It was after midnight when one of the neighbors must have been annoyed by the racket we were making, singing 'Saints Go Marching In' when good folk were supposed to be asleep. We heard a crash of a bottle against the wall."[52]

Rising friction among Hays, Guthrie, and others had forced Lee to move out of Almanac House before the arrival of Cunningham and Friesen. Despite his creativity and occasional high spirits, Hays's seeming malingering was too much for the group, which delegated Seeger to ask him to depart. Lampell, pursuing his writing career, also left to find his own apartment. Arthur Stern replaced Hays as the group's bass. The amorphous organization continually reconfigured itself, with whoever was available showing up for the sundry bookings and weekend hootenannies. "Along about noon on Sunday all the mattresses were gathered up, forced down a narrow stairway leading from the kitchen into the basement, and spread around on the concrete floor," Friesen later recalled. "Early comers (admission was 35¢) dove for these mattresses and packed themselves aboard. Later arrivals had to stand up or sit on newspapers." As for the outside concerts, sponsoring organizations were not always happy with whoever showed up for a performance; they preferred to have the "stars," despite the group's quest for the anonymity of the collective. When one program organizer, trying to arrange a concert, requested at least four Almanacs for one night at $25, she stipulated "only if Woody and the tall thin fellow who plays the banjo are among the four."[53]

In mid-December the Almanacs—in this instance, Seeger, Guthrie, Cunningham, Lampell, and Stern—auditioned for NBC radio. The network's favor marked the group's sudden popularity as the Left joined the patriotic front in the battle against fascism. Soon they were performing prowar songs for the opening show of the widely broadcast *This Is War* series, for CBS's *We The People*, *The Treasury Hour*, and assorted Office of War Information overseas broadcasts. They also had an awkward yet successful audition at the swank Rainbow Room atop Rockefeller Center, arranged by the William Morris agency. They never performed, however, because they refused to kowtow to the management's insistence that they wear hillbilly outfits. Moreover, a potential recording contract with Decca fell through because of mounting criticism in the mainstream press of their radical politics.

Amidst the intoxication of the moment, nagging economic and political problems continued. "All efforts to keep the house heated on weekdays were abandoned," Gordon Friesen recalled years later. "Frigid temperatures took over; windows frosted; pipes froze; icycles [sic] grew like stalactites in the bathroom . . . Bess Lomax broke open her hope chest and passed out all her blankets to keep Almanacs and semi-Almanacs from freezing to death . . . Only for the Sunday afternoon hootenannies was there any serious attempt made to provide heat." Eviction forced the troupe to move a few blocks away to 6th Avenue, between 9th and 10th Streets, to a third-floor loft above a dance hall. Then an attack in the liberal New York Post, headed "Peace Choir Changes Tune," reminded readers of the John Doe album and the Almanacs' Communist connections. They discussed changing their name, perhaps to "The Headline Singers," though Alan Lomax preferred something more "countrified." The peripatetic Guthrie briefly formed "Woody Guthrie's Headline Singers" with Sonny Terry, Brownie McGhee, and Lead Belly; they seem mostly to have gathered in the leader's apartment, eating, drinking, and jamming.[54]

During the late winter of 1942 a group of Almanacs, three using the surname of Bowers, toured the Midwest. In Detroit they sang at a rally in Cadillac Square for over thirty thousand auto workers, and in Chicago for the Office of Civilian Defense. Five of the group (and perhaps Guthrie) also recorded the prowar dear Mr. President album for Keynote—previously planned for Decca. Billboard's sour reviewer, labeling the group "strange and interesting," attacked "the propaganda [which] seems almost too primitive to appeal even to primitives; some of it is so casually savage that it defeats its own ends—and the practice of using lovely old folk melodies to tell these ephemeral sermons should make anyone who really loves the old songs profoundly unhappy." Only Guthrie's "Reuben James" earned praise. Meanwhile, Guthrie had been moving away from the Almanacs, involved with other projects, including writing his autobiography, Bound for Glory. Lampell had also become increasingly distracted; he was working with Earl Robinson on Lonesome Train, their cantata drawing on Lincoln's democratic legacy, for CBS. (The subsequent Decca album, recorded a week later, featured Burl Ives, narration by composer Robinson, and a cast including Seeger now a private in the army.)[55]

The Almanacs vigorously championed their win-the-war, no-strike message, but their outwardly ebullient spirit could hardly paper over mounting frictions and confusions. Who were they? What was their role in a world at war? Who would lead them—if anyone could lead so disparate a group? What songs should be sung; should the hoots continue?

In early June, Stern, Bess Lomax, Butch Hawes, and newcomer Charlie Polacheck abruptly moved to Detroit, seeking a new activist musical home. Word spread quickly, and initially the bookings rolled in, at $25–30 for a half-hour job. Between June and November they had 107 appearances, over half for unions, mostly UAW (United Auto Workers) locals, then increasingly for the International Workers Order, war relief organizations, and assorted Left parties. They also recorded locally and performed successfully for conventions of the United Rubber Workers in Akron, and for the United Cannery, Agricultural and Packinghouse Workers of America in Chicago. Their composition "UAW-CIO" proved very popular. Initially hired for the UAW convention in Chicago, they were canceled at the last minute. "We went anyway because we could not understand what had happened," Stern dejectedly reported to Seeger a few months later. "So for a week we sat and listened to the convention, sold our records at a booth in the convention hotel lobby and sang at a few convention parties." 56

Among their many frustrations, it was exceedingly difficult to obtain Almanac recordings in the Midwest. Stern believed the problem was Eric Bernay at Keynote Records, who preferred to sell the albums, particularly Talking Union and dear Mr. President, through his Music Room and its mail order business, rather than wholesale them to distant retailers or jukebox suppliers. The Almanacs also had the albatross of the discredited John Doe album. "Everywhere we go that god-damned album rears its ugly head and we are either mildly joked or heckled or kept from jobs because we were 'isolationist' before June 22nd," Stern complained to Seeger. "We should never have written such songs, and having written them and recorded them, they should now be explained once and for all and perhaps therefore to a certain extent explained away." Their current prowar repertoire apparently didn't quite fill the bill.57

Despite Pete's induction into the army in July, the New York Almanacs still managed to get sporadic bookings. Cunningham occasionally accompanied Sonny Terry and Brownie McGhee on a performing date, or Guthrie and his singing partner Cisco Houston. Party members continued to be an enthusiastic audience. Seeger had only recently joined the Communist party. "We had weekly sessions with a nice young man who tried to guide us in learning a little bit more about dialectical materialism; but none of us were really that enthusiastic about becoming great Marxist scholars," he later wrote. "We trusted the Communists to know generally the right thing that we should be pushing for, whether it was peace or war." During the war the party was thoroughly patriotic, supporting Roosevelt and the CIO's antistrike pledge; indeed, in 1944 it officially transformed itself into the Communist Political Association and backed the president's reelection. For the war's duration party affiliation hardly seemed the stigma it had been, or would shortly become once more.58

The remaining Almanacs continued performing into the fall; they appeared in It's All Yours, a musical drama set in a barroom and written by Lampell and Guthrie; it featured Earl Robinson, who also directed the music, Guthrie, Terry,

McGhee, Josh White, Lead Belly, Cunningham, Richard Dyer-Bennet, the wounded Spanish Civil War veteran Bart van der Schelling, and a square dance directed by Sophie Maslow. At the last moment Guthrie had a falling-out with Lampell and refused to appear.

Sophie Maslow staged two dance programs in New York, "Dust Bowl Ballads" and "Folksay," the first featuring the American Square Dance Group and the Lindy Hoppers, and taking inspiration from Guthrie's recent album (Maslow used his recordings during the show because his live performance, which she initially preferred, was never dependable). The 1942 *Folksay*, with Guthrie and Earl Robinson as part of the show, was inspired by Carl Sandburg's *The People, Yes* and other folk-styled texts. Folk song and dance easily mixed as a broad Left musical culture continued to hold sway, particularly in New York, drawing on rural, grassroots, democratic themes.[59]

Bess Lomax and Butch Hawes returned to New York to get married, crossing paths with Cunningham and Friesen, who ignored Hay's entreaties to stay put and moved to Detroit in December 1942. Hays had dreamed of resuscitating the Almanacs in New York, but this was now impossible. The Motor City rump group struggled on briefly, securing only a few bookings before collapsing by March. One of their last concerts was at Wayne University in mid-February, a rare college appearance. To survive, Cunningham and Friesen obtained work in war plants, then Friesen became a reporter for the *Detroit Times*. They returned to New York in May 1944.

The Almanacs had disbanded in the midst of war, but their impact and memory would filter down through the generations, indirectly through the popularity of the Weavers in the early 1950s and directly with the reissue by Folkways Records of the *Talking Union* album in expanded form in 1955. Seeger wrote in 1942, "The Almanacs will be known wherever there are good union people, but not much farther, I guess."[60]

The Almanacs' dream had been to help shape and stimulate a radical union movement, fueled by the exhilarating CIO organizing drives of the late 1930s when Communist union members had played a major role. But their security was tenuous by 1941. Some unions in Detroit and elsewhere kept their fiery rhetoric and welcomed the Almanacs' ability to stir the membership, but their numbers continually shrank. Indeed, the Almanacs never had the backing of the powerful union heads, whose agendas led in other directions. To their chagrin, the Almanacs' legacy would not be a singing, radicalized labor movement but rather a musical style alone.

The Almanacs did help to shape postwar English musical consciousness. "Bob Hinds, a merchant seaman, had brought the Almanacs 78 rpm record 'Talking Union' for me to hear in 1946," John Hasted, a musician and physicist, fondly recalled in his memoir. "I at once wanted to make music like this. But it was years before I could even [get] hold of a folk guitar, let alone find other people with similar aspirations." He finally enlisted A. L. "Bert" Lloyd, backbone of the English folk revival, and they formed the short-lived Ramblers, with help from Jean Butler (aka Rogers), "an American girl who had plenty of experience singing with five-string banjo for American Unions, and had often performed with the Almanacs." Hasted began corresponding with Seeger, then traveled to the United States in 1958, meeting with Lampell and People's Songs alumnus Jerry Silverman; Lampell took him to visit Guthrie in the hospital. Hasted helped launch *Sing*, the British counterpart to *Sing Out!* and remained active in the developing folk music scene. The British and U.S. folk revivals developed a symbiotic relationship, fueled by shared musical roots and interests, including the Almanacs' potent influence.[61]

As performers on the Left scattered to do war work at home or on the battle front, recording opportunities shrank, though many continued to give concerts. The shellac shortage and an American Federation of Musicians' strike, from August 1942 into 1944, crippled much of the commercial recording industry. Some smaller companies struggled to issue new recordings, and three adventurous entrepreneurs—the songwriter Johnny Mercer, a record store owner named Glenn Wallichs, and the songwriter and film producer Buddy De Sylva—launched Capitol Records in 1942; early on they signed Tex Ritter and Jack Guthrie, Woody's cousin. Swing and pop songs continued to dominate, but folk held its own.

A 1942 *Billboard* article reported, "Modern recorded folk music includes both old-time traditional ballads and new numbers—and these new tunes often make themselves felt on the hit parade lists." "Incidentally," the article concluded, "it is interesting to note that the war is tending to aid the folk music field. Placing greater and greater importance upon all things that are indigenously American." In late 1944 *Billboard* noted, Hillbilly disks are more popular today than ever before." Traditional and country music found a ready market in northern industrial centers such as Detroit, with large numbers of displaced black and white southerners, and in military outposts worldwide.[62]

Temporarily stationed at Fort Meade, Maryland, Seeger managed to get to New York for a few recording sessions by the Stinson/Asch company, including *Songs of the Lincoln Brigade* with Butch and Bess Hawes and newcomer Tom Glazer; the six Spanish Civil War songs, issued in 1943, reminded many of the first major victory of fascism and the Left's "good fight." Under the name Union Boys, Seeger joined Glazer, Ives, Houston, Guthrie, and White in March 1944 on *Songs for Victory: Music for Political Action*; with four Almanacs' union songs along with "Dollar Bill" and "Jim Crow," rather than blatantly prowar tunes, the album promoted a home-front victory over capitalism and racism. The Union Boys also cut the single "Solidarity Forever," backed by White's "Little Man Sitting on a Fence," for Stinson.

Moses "Moe" Asch, an electrical engineer and son of the writer Sholem Asch, had begun recording in 1939, first with "Jewish Folk Songs" by the Bagelman Sisters, then the Kol Nidre sung by Cantor Leibele Waldman, and he quickly discovered a Jewish market. After branching out to other ethnic music—Ukrainian, Italian, Greek—two years later he recorded Lead Belly doing children's songs, and joined together with Herbert Harris owner of the Stinson Trading Company, in 1943. Sometimes their label read Asch / Stinson, but usually only one or the other name appeared on the records.[63]

Asch, with his catholic approach, emerged by war's end as the major producer of folk recordings. In addition to Lead Belly, Guthrie, Ives, and other folk stalwarts, he recorded many jazz masters including Mary Lou Williams, James P. Johnson, and Coleman Hawkins. "Asch cautions against the notion that folk music comes solely from the past," Seymour Peck commented in PM in September 1944. "We today, he says, are producing folk music in war ballads, blues songs and union chants. In collaboration with the United Automobile Workers (CIO) and the Political Action Committee, Asch has produced records about the war and home-front problems, and he is now planning an album giving musical expression to the CIO's ideas on how life should be when Johnny comes marching home."[64]

For the next four decades Asch would record, preserve, and disseminate a vast store of the world's music. "Unlike most record companies," Time commented in February 1946, "which have lavished their scarce shellac on surefire songs, Asch frequently stops making an album just when it is selling well, so he can put out something else—which may or may not sell. He has put out about 40 albums in the past three years, hopes to issue another 40 this year." In a complicated legal arrangement finalized the previous December, Asch had parted company with Herbert Harris, and now he launched Disc Records with his faithful, talented associate Marian Distler, which would last until decade's end.[65]

Along with Asch, Alan Lomax kept folk music alive and before the public during the war. Working for the Office of War Information (OWI) in Washington, Lomax tirelessly labored to promote folk music, both traditional and contemporary. He formed a group of local government workers, including Jackie Gibson and Bernie Asbell, into the Priority Ramblers.

Growing up in Brooklyn, Gibson early joined the labor movement and heard test pressings of the Almanacs' Talking Union before Bernay, her distant cousin, released it. Arriving in Washington just before the war's outbreak, she became Lomax's secretary at the OWI and later met Asbell at a United Federal Workers of America (UFWA) meeting. Fresh from hanging around Almanac House, Asbell had arrived in Washington soon after Pearl Harbor and quickly obtained a job at the Government Printing Office. At Seeger's suggestion, he looked up Lomax. The Priority Ramblers performed a wide variety of music, particularly prowar and union songs including their own compositions, at union affairs in

Washington, Philadelphia, and Baltimore. Favorites of Mrs. Roosevelt, they joined her on the White House lawn, where they sang "A Dollar Ain't a Dollar Anymore" and "Looking for a Home." They also had a Saturday night radio program on WOL. Others in the shifting group, all government employees, were Tom Glazer at the Library of Congress, Helen Schnayer, Josephine Schwartz, and Edna Crumpley. Asbell had joined the army, in February 1943, by the time Rae Korson and Arthur Semming recorded the Ramblers for the Library of Congress the following September. A teenage Ronnie Gilbert, later of Weavers fame, joined her friend Gibson in the group shortly before it disbanded by early 1944. Back in New York, Gibson worked with Bess Hawes for the music division of the OWI, then handled advance publicity for the "Roosevelt Bandwagon" during the president's reelection bid; the traveling group included Guthrie, Houston, Will Geer, Mary Lou Williams, and the dancers Helen Tamiris and Daniel Nagrin.

In early 1944 Lomax assembled a lineup of folk and country luminaries for the radio show *The Martins and The Coys*—Geer, Ives, Terry, Houston, Seeger, the Coon Creek Girls, Wade Mainer, and Guthrie. Although it was recorded in the Decca studios in New York, no domestic network would air the program, so Lomax shipped it to London for broadcast on the BBC, which had bankrolled the production. Drawing on traditional stereotyping of southern mountain culture, the show, written by Elizabeth Lomax with music arranged by her husband Alan, presents two feuding families who resolve their quarreling to join the war against fascism. Another Lomax BBC radio program the same year, *The Chisholm Trail*, featured Guthrie, Terry, Houston, Ives, Hays, and two prominent hillbilly groups, J. E. Mainer and the Mountaineers and the Coon Creek Girls. The show again demonstrated the ongoing conjunction between southern rural and northern urban performers, linked by a common folk style.

During the war, Seeger and others joined the armed forces, Guthie and Houston went into the merchant marines, and Alan Lomax worked in Washington. The Almanacs had disbanded, but their dreams of a powerful labor movement, a peaceful world, and an equitable society remained just below the surface, to be resurrected at war's end. Folk music's accessible lyrics and traditional acoustic accompaniment continued to connect with the wellsprings of national identity and was poised to serve either conservative or radical purposes. Everything was in place for the coming folk music revival: the spread of southern black and white music to a northern urban audience; the evident commercial potential of folk music; the connection of folk music and Left politics, particularly for those in or near the Communist party; vibrant performers with widespread appeal and polished styles; and key promoters such as Moe Asch and Alan Lomax. Lomax, in particular, had consciously shaped the repertoires and aesthetic sensibilities of Ives, Seeger, White, and numerous others, transforming traditional music into modern styles and sounds.

2

People's Songs, Popular Folk, and the Later 1940s

"The Tin Pan Alley composer sighed. 'Competition I can stand—but who can outwrite a songwriter who's been dead before Columbus?' " The concert promoter Ted Zittel was not far off the mark. After the war, folk music exploded, particularly in New York. WNYC's Friday night programs included Josef Marais, John and Lucy Allison, Richard Dyer-Bennet, Frank Warner, and Tom Glazer, who also had his own show on WJZ Sunday nights at 8:15. In addition, WNYC offered the "Seventh Annual American Music Festival," ten days of short programs with Pete Seeger, Woody Guthrie, Lead Belly, Tony Kraber, and Oscar Brand. Tom Glazer's Ballad Box aired on ABC from 1945 to 1947, and Elaine Lambert Lewis's weekly Folk Songs of the Seven Million, starting in 1944, could be heard on WNYC for a couple of years. "That the boom in balladry is really big time stuff is indicated by some crass business details," wrote Zittel. "Burl Ives' records sell as well as those of most popular singers of the day."[1]

Oscar Brand launched Folk Song Festival Sunday evenings on WNYC soon after his discharge from the army in late 1945. "I decided to offer my songs to every radio station broadcasting in New York City," he later wrote in The Ballad Mongers. "I received a few invitations to perform and during the Christmas season I sang over WNYC, WNEW, WLIB, and WNBC." Executives at WNYC asked him to serve as coordinator of their folk shows. "At the time, Huddie Ledbetter was broadcasting for the station. Since Huddie was an old friend, my 'coordinating' consisted mainly of walking down the hall on the twenty-fifth floor of the Municipal Building and waving to him during his broadcast." Soon Brand had his own WNYC folk music show.[2]

Folk music influenced other aspects of popular culture. In early 1945 the Theatre Guild in New York offered Sing Out, Sweet Land, "A Salute to American Folk and Popular Music." The show featured musical stars Alfred Drake, Juanita Hall and Burl Ives, with music arranged and conducted by Elie Siegmeister. Siegmeister had met Aunt Molly Jackson in a New York city loft in 1934 and said her songs "set me thinking about the real roots of American music and theatre." Sing Out, Sweet Land integrated popular and folk music; a Decca album of the show appeared in 1946.[3]

After the war the country's musical landscape began to change. Country (labeled "folk" in the Billboard and Cashbox listings) began a strong challenge to Tin Pan Alley songs, with Spade Cooley, Arthur Smith, Merle Travis and Jack Guthrie (singing his cousin Woody's "Oklahoma Hills") reaching the juke boxes in 1946. Old-time music, with its rough edges, took a back seat to the smoother sounds of Ernest Tubb, Tex Ritter, the Sons of the Pioneers, and soon Hank Williams. At the same time, one of country's offshoots, bluegrass music, began to mature under the tutelage of Bill Monroe and the Blue Grass Boys. Lester Flatt and Earl Scruggs joined Monroe in 1945, recording for Columbia, and they soon perfected the modern bluegrass sound. Big band swing, dominant from the mid-1930s, fell on hard times.

Believing that folk music, broadly understood, could retain its niche market, Moe Asch launched a new venture, Disc Records, soon after the war ended. Continuing his eclectic approach, he started with American's Favorite Songs with Bess and Butch Hawes, Pete Seeger and Tom Glazer, Lead Belly's Negro Folk Songs, and Frank Warner's Hudson Valley Songs. Asch soon followed with Hebrew and Palestinian Folk Tunes by the Palestinian String Quartet, Calypso songs by Lord Invader, and Josh White's Women Blues. Though short-lived (1946–49) Disc established itself as a significant presence on the folk scene, foreshadowing Asch's monumental Folkways label.[4]

A discharged Pete Seeger's thoughts turned to reconnecting folk music and Left politics. He had broadened his musical tastes during the war. Working with the Armed Forces Radio Service on Saipan Island in the Central Pacific, he helped out "three times a week on a 'hillbilly' program," he wrote home in his periodic "Report From the Marianas" on June 9, 1945. "Here our hillbilly program has evolved considerably from a doleful collection of sentimental southern songs, to a much more varied program now. In our 15 minutes we'll have a couple of fiddle tunes, a southern number, a popular song, maybe a spanish song, or ragtime, and a steel guitar Hawaiian number, and maybe an old banjo song by me. Nothing pleases everybody, but everybody likes something—which is best, considering our varied soldier audience."[5]

Music and politics consumed Seeger's life as he contemplated the mechanics of reaching a mass audience; he had already written to Moe Asch, "After seeing how poorly Victor plugged Woody's album, and Decca other folkmusic albums, I am thoroughly of the opinion that for a person like myself, it is far better to record for a small company—unless there seems to be a better chance of getting on juke boxes." And he wrote to friends on August 12: "Well, the war is over— and now the fighting will begin. That is, we will all start fighting to get home. Business will start fighting each other to see who can grab the first millions spent for civilian goods." He prepared to plunge into the postwar political battles, armed with his banjo and organizational skills.[6]

Seeger had met Mario "Boots" Casetta on Saipan just before war's end. Familiar with the Almanacs' recordings, Casetta one day recognized Seeger's voice over the camp loudspeaker. He introduced himself and they began discussing what could be done musically "to advance a cause, a cause of freedom of every man, for everybody." Along with USO singer Betty Sanders and fellow GI Felix Landau, they discussed a possible postwar organization to carry on the work of the Almanacs. Casetta returned to Los Angeles upon his discharge in the fall of 1945. In Philadelphia, meanwhile, Lee Hays had similar thoughts of a progressive, politically active musical organization. Back in New York and excited over the prospect of a singing Left / labor movement, Seeger put into motion a new association, national in scope and considerably more comprehensive than the Almanacs.[7]

It was a moment of left-wing optimism. "1945 was like walking on air with impossibly long dream-like strides," CIO *News* editor Len DeCaux recalled. "Fascism was vanquished. Ahead lay peace and good will." And conflict with management. "By the winter of 1945–46, industrial disputes had brought two million workers to strike at one time in January, and involved five million before 1946 was over. The biggest industries were hit—auto, steel, coal, electrical, packinghouse, oil, railroad, maritime." The country appeared ripe for radical change. The Communist party's membership reached upwards of seventy thousand, and the Sunday edition of the *Daily Worker* had about the same circulation. Wartime party leader Earl Browder's moderate views no longer seemed appropriate. In July 1945 the Communist party of old reappeared at Moscow's behest, replacing the expedient Communist Political Association; the militant William Z. Foster became party chairman, with day-to-day affairs managed by general secretary Eugene Dennis.[8]

Seeger had assistance from Norman Studer in exploring the connections between folk culture folklorists, musicians, and activist politics. Studer, a student of John Dewey, began teaching at the Little Red School House in New York in 1932, and founded Camp Hilltop in Plainfield, New Jersey, six years later; in 1940 it moved to Phoenicia, New York, and became Camp Woodland. The progressive, integrated children's camp promoted the study of folk music of the Catskills, with Seeger often a guest. Along with other children's and adult camps around and near New York City—Wo-Chi-Ca, Kinderland, Unity, Followers of the Trail—Woodland played a crucial role in instilling a love of rural and urban folk music in countless children.[9]

In March 1945 Studer organized the conference "Folklore in a Democracy" at Elizabeth Irwin High School in Greenwich Village. With papers by Benjamin Botkin and Charles Seeger, music by Woody Guthrie, Sonny Terry, Alan Lomax and the Jefferson Chorus led by Horace Grenell, the conference directed its attention to whether folklore could help "in building a truly democratic culture for the people's peace that must follow this people's war." Studer followed up the next year with "Folklore in the Metropolis," including the folklorists Botkin and Herbert Halpert.[10]

During these heady times a singing Left—promoting labor unions, racial and economic justice, and a cooperative world—appeared crucial to Seeger and his friends. Margot Mayo's American Square Dance Group (ASDG) sponsored a "home-from-war" party in late 1945, with Lead Belly, Seeger, Richard Dyer-Bennet, John Jacob Niles (a political conservative), and Guthrie, and this gathering provided the opportunity for Seeger to discuss his ideas with Oscar Brand, whose mimeograph machine, he thought, would certainly be useful. In the waning hours of the year Seeger and Lee Hays convened a meeting of more than two dozen of their musical friends in Seeger's basement apartment in Greenwich Village. "The main thing is to get the songs ready," Hays wrote to Earl Robinson. "We have been content during the war years to take the crumbs which have fallen from the master's table—i.e. the feeble offerings of the Hollywood and Broadway and Madison Avenue Boys."[11]

The organizational meeting "was more of a singing party," Guthrie later wrote, "a hand shaking get together, a joke telling, tale swapping session, and then in the middle of all the singing and laughing, we all found a vacant inch somewhere on the floor and sat down to listen more than to talk." Bernie Asbell, out of the army and back in New York, recalled that "most of the energy came from Pete." The group made plans for a newsletter and an organization to promote a singing radical movement, to be named People's Songs, Inc. As Seeger soon wrote, "While at this stage of the game there is a preponderance of folk material, we aim eventually to have People's Songs cover every kind of musical expression which can be of use to people's organizations: folk, jazz, popular, or serious cantatas for union choruses."[12]

"Maybe I'm beating the gun," Mike Gold enthusiastically proclaimed in the *Daily Worker* on January 2, 1946. "But I will report the little fact that a group of former Almanac Singers, plus others concerned with labor music, started to organize something again the day before New Year. Songs, songs of, by and for the people! . . . The spirit has not died—it has only been unemployed." The first issue of *People's Songs* reflected his optimism: "The people are on the march and must have songs to sing. Now, in 1946, the truth must reassert itself in many singing voices . . . it is clear that there must be an organization to make and send songs of labor and the American people through the land."[13]

People's Songs significantly expanded the boundaries of what the Almanac Singers had begun. A somewhat separate entity, People's Artists, under the direction of Bob Howard, served as a booking agency for the musicians and other performers. Originally centered in New York, People's Songs branches quickly sprouted in Los Angeles, Chicago, and on college campuses. Though not officially connected to the Communist party—indeed party leaders hardly considered the importance of musical (or any) culture—People's Songs had a link with the organization through certain key figures such as Irwin Silber. This affinity provided People's Songs with a dependable audience and formal recognition (not to mention increasing public suspicion and official hostility).

The organization hit the ground running, sponsoring concerts in New York with Guthrie, Hays, Lead Belly, Seeger, Betty Sanders, Sonny Terry and Brownie McGhee, Tom Glazer, and Alan Lomax. Asbell, who had some newspaper experience, became the bulletin's editor with the second issue, and his wife Millie took over as office manager. He remained on the masthead until August, then was temporarily replaced by Butch Hawes. A prolific song writer and active performer, Asbell moved to Chicago in early 1947 where he took over the People's Songs office there. Seeger and Hays guided the national organization.

Additional support came from a handful of younger New York activists affiliated with American Youth for Democracy, successor to the Young Communist League, who had formed the American Folksay Group in 1943. Their biweekly "Dance-a-Rounds" included a break for singing the Left folk repertoire; they also produced occasional "folk plays," particularly Irwin Silber's *Circle Left* and *Tomorrow Is Good Morning*. Many alumni became People's Songs stalwarts. (American Folksay faded away in 1948.)

"The first People's Songs Hootenanny was thrown in the Ohta home [Pete's in-laws], and Eighty people came," wrote Guthrie.

> The second Hoot was up in Brother's apartment on Thompson Street, and Hundred and Twelve came. The third was in the Newspaper Guild Hall on East 40th Street, and Three Hundred sang for a half a day. . . . Our next session was in the Little Red School House on Charlton Street, and the seats flooded over with faces and faces, wild hands, clapping, yells and cheers for Leadbelly, Blind Sonny Terry, Brownie McGhee, that came to help out Pete Seeger, me, Lee Hays, Betty Sanders, Tom Glazer, Alan Lomax, the CIO chorus, and to hear Bernie Asbel[l] sing his newest one, 'My Hands.' Seventy Five people in the balcony had to stand up. Everybody else stood up because they couldn't set still. I saw these Peoples Songs raise up storms of stiff winds and wild howls of cheer from the people in their seats, and saw also, that almost every chronic headache was eased and made quieter. I mean your headaches about writing, singing, copyrights, fees, pay finances and money.

Discounting for Guthrie's usual literary license, he does not seem to exaggerate by much the heady musical and political atmosphere.[14]

People's Songsters were particularly eager to appear at labor union rallies and strikes, entertaining and joining forces with the working class. At a Westinghouse strikers' rally in Pittsburgh in March 1946, Guthrie, Seeger, and Hays—characterized in the local press as a "hillbilly trio"—regaled the assembled five thousand who "whooped through the refrains, and . . . laughed over the 'Westinghouse Blues.'" Louise Levitas captured the mood in PM, the progressive daily: "The reason why union songs are in the majority is that People's Songs' first response has been from union leaders, who have a special need for such tunes."[15]

People's Songs threw itself into the fall 1946 elections, connecting with the CIO-PAC—the union's political wing in a struggle to keep progressive, prolabor representatives in Washington. Waldemar Hille sent a form letter to various songwriters in August, informing them of an emergency meeting to select new material for the CIO-PAC radio spots. Of the eight jingles requested, "three are to be on the subject of inflation, three on housing, and two on security (65¢ wage, union preservation, social security, etc.). . . . These jingles are to be angled in such a way that they can be used as a plug for any good candidate." The September release of the album Songs for Political Action, custom-pressed by People's Songs for CIO-PAC, featured Seeger, Glazer, Hally Wood Faulk, and Hays singing "A Dollar Ain't a Dollar Anymore," "No, No, No Discrimination," and other civil rights, pro-union ditties.[16]

Frequent large hootenannies in New York generated considerable local as well as national attention and enthusiasm. A "Union Hoot," including Big Bill Broonzy, and a "Freedom Hoot," with Josh White and calypso singer Lord Invader, captured People's Songs's central commitment to organized labor and civil rights. A positive article in The Afro-American newspaper praised the new organization as assuring "that Americans of all races, creeds and colors might have new songs, songs that would tell of their battles against discrimination, against a rising cost of living, of the acute housing shortage, of reactionary legislators in the Senate and Congress." Though a review in Time magazine sarcastically commented that "singers tried to best each other at songs whose tunes were simple, and whose lyrics were black and white (or sometimes red) versions of current events," Alan Lomax had the last word in the article: "We're going to put more into our songs than June moon croon spoon swoon, and sing [Mississippi Senator Theodore] Bilbo out of Congress." A hoot at the Hotel Diplomat in late October, "Free World Singing," with Seeger, Hays, Bess Lomax Hawes, and Earl Robinson, included some refreshing songs Seeger had recently heard in California, such as the "Fertilizer Song," "A Newspaperman Meets Such Interesting People," and "Talking Atom," the last two by the newspaperman Vern Partlow. "The issue of the Atomic Bomb is put squarely," said the Daily Worker. "Peace in the world, or the world in pieces."[17]

Waldemar Hille became music editor of People's Songs in mid-1946 and assumed the editorship in November 1947. Briefly a concert pianist, and more recently director of music at Elmhurst College, Hille had collected songs from the legendary Emma Dusenberry, a blind singer living in Mena, Arkansas who was a repository of hundreds of songs and ballads. Hille, Seeger, and their colleagues solicited and organized a library of thousands of songs, which People's Songs disseminated through various songbooks, broadsides, sheet music, and phonograph records; over three hundred eventually appeared in the bulletin. A flattering article in the *New York Times* remarked, "People's Songs keeps a musical stethoscope on the heartbeat of the nation, translating current events into notes and lyrics."[18]

Based on democratic ideas, People Songs promoted sharing and equality, but certain performers quickly garnered special attention in the press. Burl Ives, for one, was already a celebrity. A popular singer and actor under contract to 20th Century Fox, he was initially listed as a People's Songs sponsor. Josh White, a regular at People's Songs hoots, often shared the spotlight with Ives. Born in Greenville, South Carolina, in 1914, by the early 1930s he had become an influential East Coast bluesman, recording extensively both blues and sacred songs for Paramount, ARC, and other labels. Moving to New York during the height of the Depression, he turned somewhat to social protest songs as his career took off. White joined the Almanacs on *Talking Union* (1941) and Tom Glazer on *Songs of Citizen C.I.O.* (1944), accompanied the Union Boys on *Songs for Victory: Music for Political Action* (1944), and appeared alone on the torrid *Southern Exposure: An Album of Jim Crow Blues* (1941). By 1947 he was pulling down $750 a week at Cafe Society Uptown while continuing his political odyssey.

People's Artists increased its outreach, artfully promoting its growing lineup of performers. "People's Artists, Inc., is set up to supply talent for any affair, be it a house-party, a membership meeting, a summer-camp show or a Madison Square Garden rally, at a moment's notice," Bob Howard proudly announced. One 1946 notice listed six People's Songsters and the writer Dorothy Parker making appearances on the summer borscht belt circuit, a clear sign of New York popularity.[19]

The organization's membership neared two thousand by mid-year. "Right now the boys and girls of People's Songs, Inc. are getting ready for the November elections," reported the *Daily Worker* in May 1946, "and for the big maritime strike. They're determined to help organize America against fascism, finishing up the job that wasn't done in the war itself." Margot Mayo, writing for *Promenade*, was skeptical, fearing that "folk music is becoming big business." Behind the growing careers of Ives, Seeger, and Richard Dyer-Bennet, who was set to open at the Blue Angel, lurked "the 'big time' commercial promoter, to whom art is very little more than a commodity. What almost all night clubs want of art is already clear—sex and laughs. Radio and film, the great levelers, transmute these into slapstick and romance."[20]

Seeger and the other did dream of reaching a mass audience. A report to the national board meeting in late October, probably written by Seeger, complained that recent hootenannies had not been very successful, financially or otherwise, because of their sloppy organization. In the future "we must provide professional, rehearsed shows, since that is what the audience expects. We can no longer attract our audiences without big name performers, an attractive or unusual show idea or something of the sort." Though a grassroots organization, People's Songs nevertheless had to remain solvent. To this end John Hammond and composer Alec Wilder were now elected to the national board. The tension between authenticity and popular outreach would never be resolved.[21]

While Seeger sought more organizational structure, others reveled in informality. People's Songster George Margolin began singing in Greenwich Village's Washington Square Park on warm Sunday afternoons, generating a small crowd. "We Rolled The Union On with gusto," he wrote in the bulletin in early 1947; "gave Bilbo his Lesson in History; Cracked Corn with Jimmy (an outstanding favorite); Worked On The Railroad; Wept On Top Of Old Smokey (another favorite), and mourned over Aunt Rhodie's Old Gray Goose." Inadvertently, Margolin had launched the weekly summer fountain gatherings, soon to be a vibrant focus of local folk life. [22]

As People's Songs picked up steam, the conservative opposition took note. The House Un-American Activities Committee (HUAC), mostly fighting fascism during the war, returned to Red hunting before the guns had cooled. After 1946 it became a permanent congressional standing committee, closely allied to J. Edgar Hoover's FBI. The CIO-PAC publicity director Alan Reitman launched a campaign to put pressure on radio station to run union spot announcements, with Seeger and Glazer doing the music, and Broadcasting, a radio industry newsletter, characterized both singers as former "members of the Young Communist League, and of the Almanac Singers." The piece credited HUAC investigators for the information. The New York Sun's anticommunist columnist George Sokolsky, somewhat out of date, warned readers "to be vigilant when they see or hear a song issued by the People's Songs, Inc. or by the Almanac Singers, a related outfit, that here is propaganda designed to destroy the American form of government by every means usable, including songs." Frederick Woltman followed in the World-Telegram, using the same information to alert the public that "the lyrical Leftists have been furnishing their propaganda-with-music to Communist and Red-front affairs until CIO-PAC recently decided to give them a national audience."[23]

People's Songs tried to slough off the mounting censure. A report to the national board in October 1946 argued that "because of their obvious red-herring technique content, these articles do not particularly harm People's Songs." Guthrie attacked not only the Red-baiting, but also the attractive lure of fame and fortune for the performers, echoing Mayo's strictures. "Yes, we are going to have lots of fun watching the poets and the artists and the players, dancers, and the singers come up from the ranks of the workers and drift over onto the side of the owners, one by one, ten by ten, and then some more," he wrote to Moe Asch in July. "I am keeping my eyes open and my ears, and my mouth just to see what twists and turns, what shapes and forms, the works of Josh White, Burl Ives, Richard Dyer Bennett [sic], and others will take. I have already watched and seen several dozens walk up the money plank and turn to an oily pile of rope."[24]

By late 1946 the postwar spirit of optimism was definitely waning; the year had been a political and economic roller coaster of hope and despair. As cooperation among the victorious allies began to crumble in Europe, in early March, Winston Churchill gave his "iron curtain" speech at Westminster College in Fulton, Missouri warning of the Communist takeover of Eastern Europe. Henry Wallace resigned as Secretary of Commerce in September over President Harry Truman's increasing suspicion of the Soviet Union.

New Deal programs, hardly healthy when the war began, came under mounting attack from the rejuvenated Republicans and the southern Democrats. Truman had struggled to maintain the Office of Price Administration (OPA) in June, to control prices and rents, but Congress cut its powers and prices immediately shot up 25 percent. The GOP's crushing victory in the fall elections gave Republicans a lock on Congress and left Truman an embattled president. Labor and its allies were soon sent reeling by the passage, over Truman's veto, of the Taft-Hartley Act, a bill that outlawed the closed shop, required union leaders to swear they were not Communists, and permitted right-to-work laws. It was the stake in the heart of an already flagging militant unionism.

But People's Songs was undeterred. The album *Roll the Union On* appeared in December 1946 on the Asch label, featuring Seeger, Hays, Hally Wood, and Butch and Bass Hawes. In his press release on the album, Asch optimistically averred that "only folk artists of authentic standing will build the Asch list. . . . The present democratic ferment has created a broader acceptance than ever before for such music growing out of the everyday life and basic traditions of the American people." Records had always been part of the organization's agenda, and the first issue of *People's Songs* had promoted a number of albums, including various Asch releases. Irwin Silber, the executive secretary starting in June 1947, and Brownie McGhee released two records on their fleeting Encore label (subtitled "People's Songs"). The first featured Seeger singing "Newspaperman" and "Talking Atom," and the second McGhee doing "Black, Brown & White Blues" and "High Price Blues."[25]

Though much of the organization's activity centered in New York, branches sprang up in several other cities, particularly on the West Coast (hootenannies had begun in Los Angeles in November 1945). The following June, Earl Robinson reported in the bulletin the opening of a local People's Songs branch office. Boots Casetta, Seeger's buddy on Saipan, had returned to Los Angeles and quickly become involved with a dynamic group of composers and performers, particularly Lewis Allan (born Abel Meeropol), Vern Partlow, Bill Wolff, Morry Goodson, Sonny Vale, Bill Oliver, and Ray Glaser. Casetta soon became director of People's Songs of California.[26]

A particularly stimulating program in October, "I Hear American Singing," featured Goodson and Vale doing their popular parodies, the calypso singer Sir Lancelot, Oliver, Seeger, Earl Robinson, and even the cowboy performer Tex Ritter. Talented writers, always in abundance in the movie capital, supplied a steady stream of clever, timely songs, which often appeared in the Daily People's World, the feisty West Coast equivalent of the Daily Worker. Returning from a national tour and reporting to the national board in late October, Seeger said that "whereas in a limited sense we have reached a level of saturation here in New York (in the progressive movement), we have hardly scratched the surface in the rest of the country, especially in Los Angeles."[27]

Los Angeles People's Songsters appeared on picket lines and joined a motorcade to the state capitol to lobby for better housing. Founding member Harry Hay proved a key figure, "the theoretician of People's Songs," according to Earl Robinson; he was also a leader in organizing the Mattachine Society, the pioneering gay rights organization. Hay held monthly meetings at his home, sometimes with Seeger or Malvina Reynolds, before launching his class on the history of popular music at the People's Educational Center, a worker's education project, early in 1948. Bill Wolff and Robinson worked with Hay on another series, "Folk Music and People's Songs Today." Wolff had been education director for the International Ladies Garment Workers Union (ILGWU) in Chicago, then relocated to Los Angeles in the early 1940s where he headed the People's Educational Center and became a radio writer.[28]

Before his move to New York in mid-1948, Boots Casetta kept People's Songs visible in the Daily People's World; in addition to publishing the "People's song of the week," he had a frequent column. The songs were generally written by Casetta and other local songwriters, though some were traditional. The L.A. organization limped through 1948, heavily in debt (partly to the Daily People's World for ads), then survived the demise of the national organization in 1949, renaming itself People's-Art Songs and forming the core of a vibrant, progressive local folk music community into the 1950s.[29]

In 1947 Casetta initiated Charter Records, an outlet for People's Songs performers and composers, locally and nationally. The first recording was of the calypso singer Sir Lancelot performing "Walk in Peace" and "Atomic Energy." Casetta believed that "not only will he do good stuff from a political/social standpoint, but maybe commercially we can make something with this guy." Soon the cabaret-style performers Goodson and Vale, Seeger, the Berries (a female vocal group), the emerging Weavers, and others recorded folk and topical songs. Goodson and Vale's jaunty "Unity Rhumba" apparently sold well. But with spotty national distribution, the company was hardly a commercial success.[30]

In January 1947, Casetta traveled with Goodson and Vale and the Berries to stage two hootenannies in the Bay Area. "It was an organizing trip," he reported in the national bulletin, "and now San Francisco is set to roll—not as a San Francisco People's Songs alone, but as the northern half of People's Songs of California." The core of activists included Jerry Walter and Lou Gottlieb. The latter was attending UCLA on the GI Bill studying classical music when he heard John Jacob Niles and Bascom Lamar Lunsford perform on campus, followed by Seeger and Josh White at a People's Songs fund-raiser in mid-1946. Gottlieb moved to the Bay Area in the summer of 1948 for graduate work at Berkeley.[31]

The California Labor School in San Francisco, loosely affiliated with People's Songs, served as the center of the Bay Area's Left culture. Opened in 1942, the school early attracted both AFL and CIO union activists. Two years later a labor chorus, made up of "more than 40 longshoremen, street car conductors, waitresses, office workers, welders and working men and women ad infinitum," formed under the direction of Leo Christiansen. (Appearing on the U.S. attorney general's 1947 list of "subversive organizations," the Labor School soon lost its tax exemption and was ordered to pay back taxes. It finally closed in 1957, after years of struggle, though it staged folk concerts as late as 1955.) People's Songsters Walter and Gottlieb, later the core of the Gateway Singers, affiliated with the school. Singing and acting during his childhood in Chicago, Walter had a short-lived nightclub career, then moved to San Francisco and quickly developed "an interest in folk singing as a genuine manifestation of true people's music." Led by Walter, Gottlieb, and Barbara Spillman Cahn at decade's end, the small Bay Area radical folk scene served as a vital spawning ground for the developing folk revival.[32]

People's Songs also burgeoned in Chicago and Detroit. Seeger and Hays journeyed to the Windy City in September 1946, appearing before the CIO-PAC labor school to spark a local chapter. Win Stracke, Studs Terkel, Jack Conroy, and Raeburn Flerlage formed the core group. Flerlage, a record reviewer and music journalist, assumed the role of Midwest executive director. He also contributed a record column to the national bulletin, while organizing local hootenannies and house parties for Lead Belly, Guthrie, Josh White, and Big Bill Broonzy. The local chapter raised funds through ticket sales and by raffling records sent by Moe Asch.

Flerlage eagerly touted Seeger, who seemed to pass through the city regularly, commenting in his *Chicago Star* column, "the 'Musicians Musician' in the folksong business is not the highly-touted Burl Ives, but an underpublicized banjo wizard named Pete Seeger." Flerlage also interviewed Ives, whom he quotes saying: "If they try to push me around when I get back to Hollywood, I'll walk off the set. . . . American folk songs have dignity, and people have to recognize that folk singers have dignity, too. If I let them make a clown out of me I wouldn't be doing folk music any good, and I wouldn't be helping People's Songs or anybody else." Despite the brave talk, as his movie career took off

Ives parted company from his erstwhile colleagues. Some of his activist recordings with the Union Boys appeared following the war, but Ives had already turned to more politically palatable songs.[33]

Detroit's People's Songs chapter had been stimulated by Seeger's and Asbell's appearances; Seeger performed with Glazer, Charlotte Anthony, and Al Moss at two AYD hootenannies. "The hit of the night was Barbara Kahn [Cahn], of Detroit," Mike Scott wrote in the national bulletin in October 1946, "who sings with a sweet and mellow voice." A trade union alumna, Barbara Spillman married German immigrant Rolf Cahn following the war, and they temporarily sparked the local folk scene. Cahn had served in the Office of Strategic Services (OSS) during the war, then returned to Detroit as a labor organizer. Cahn later remembered, "We considered ourselves isolated. . . . We were very serious, very young Communists. We sang very heavy, not quite charming, political songs. Our heroes were Woody Guthrie, Pete Seeger, Huddie Ledbetter." (The local People's Songs had already folded following the debacle of the Henry Wallace presidential campaign when Barbara and Rolf Cahn moved briefly to Los Angeles in 1949, then to the Bay Area.)[34]

In early 1947 People's Songs, still centered in New York City and attempting to become more professional, began to develop a new type of leadership. Hays, lacking the requisite executive skills, resigned in late 1946 as executive secretary, replaced briefly by Felix Landau, then by Silber in April 1947. Leonard Jacobson, a professional promoter, headed People's Artists; Wally Hille assumed control of the bulletin, though Seeger remained as nominal editor until the November issue. The list of sponsors on the masthead now included many prominent show business names—Leonard Bernstein, Marc Blitzstein, Aaron Copland, Oscar Hammerstein II, E. Y. Harburg, Judy Holiday, Lena Horne, David Kapp, Elia Kazan, Gene Kelly, Dorothy Parker, Paul Robeson, and Josh White. An emergency meeting of the national board in early April discussed the current financial plight and made various plans, particularly for a national convention to be held in Chicago in September. All board members were encouraged to organize fund-raising concerts and each was asked to loan $100 to the national office.

Meanwhile, the independent Alan Lomax maintained his frenetic pace in promoting both folk music and radical politics. He was featured in a November 1945 *Time* article, entitled "Miserable but Exciting Songs," about the Library of Congress five-album reissue of his collected southern ballads, blues, and sacred songs. "By last week the Library of Congress had employed four clerks to handle 30,000 inquiries about his records," the article noted. As editor of Decca Records' American Folk Music Series and organizer of the midnight concerts at Town Hall sponsored by People's Songs, Lomax shaped and broadened musical tastes and styles.[35]

Newsweek praised Lomax's projected series for Decca, and also two reissue albums on the Brunswick label, *Listen to Our Story—A Panorama of American Ballads and Mountain Frolic*: "The two old-time albums are the real McCoy, for here, on disks, is a permanent record of the music pioneer America grew up with." They included 1920s and 1930s recordings by the traditional performers Bradley Kincaid, Uncle Dave Macon and His Fruit Jar Drinkers, Bascom Lamar Lunsford, and Buell Kazee. Lomax wrote in the introductory essay to Decca's American Folk Music Series, "Our songbag is bulging with tunes from Europe and Africa, and with hundreds of ballads and ditties that have grown up in the developing democracy of the western world. . . . In our back files are hundreds of records of country singers—from the Southern mountains, from the Spanish Southwest, from Negro communities and from the Louisiana Cajun country." A Sing-Along Book accompanied each album, "enabling the listener to take the songs from the phonograph and work them out for himself with his own piano or guitar accompaniment."[36]

The first Decca album, Carl Sandburg's *Cowboy Songs and Negro Spirituals*, had the poet singing "I Ride an Old Paint," "Jesse James," "Go Down, Moses," and eight other traditional tunes. Folk music was not just entertainment for Lomax but a way to revitalize contemporary life, connecting past to present, professional to amateur performers, the hinterlands to the nation's commercial centers. The back page of the accompanying booklet listed an eclectic variety of Decca's "folk albums": Bing Crosby's *Cowboy Songs*, Burl Ives, Josh White, Marais and Miranda's *Songs of the South African Veld*, Louis Chartier's *French Folk Songs for Children*, Dorothy Lamour's favorite Hawaiian songs, and Michael Coleman's *Irish Jigs and Reels*.

Lomax's biweekly show *The Midnight Special at Town Hall* illustrated his wide-ranging musical, cultural, and political interests. "Blues at Midnight," first in the series on November 9, 1946, headlined Big Bill Broonzy, Sidney Bechet, the boogie-woogie piano player Pete Johnson, Sonny Terry, Brownie McGhee and McGhee's brother "Stick" with his "Gold Tub" band. Lomax "intends to bring America to New York," PM reported. "Fortunately for Mr. Lomax, he does not mean to move America into the city physically, tree by tree or mountain by mountain. He will do it culturally, folk song by folk song, folk singer by folk singer." The composer Virgil Thomson praised the blues musicians, whose "renderings were as authentic as the musical material." Heavily narrated and orchestrated by Lomax, the series included "Strings at Midnight" with Carlos Montoya and Seeger and "Calypso at Midnight" with Gerald Clark, the Duke of Iron, Lord Invader, and Macbeth the Great. The concerts stretched into the next spring, including "Spirituals at Midnight," "Honky Tonk Blues at Midnight," "Ballads at Midnight," and "Mountain Frolic at Midnight."[37]

Lomax expressed his musical aesthetic through the mass media. "Nineteen forty-six will be remembered, among other things, as the year that American folk songs came to town," he announced in *Vogue*. "There is likely to be a ballad singer in Scene 1 of any new Broadway show, nowadays . . . In Town Hall, at the Irving Plaza, in Times Hall and Madison Square Garden, in fact all around the town—Lead Belly, Woody Guthrie, Josh White, Peter Seeger, Tom Glazer, Susan Reed and many more, step up to the microphone and entertain war-weary New Yorkers with songs as old as Scotch heather and political ditties as new as last week's headlines." While "there may be an element of escapism in this trend," Lomax said in the *New York Times Magazine*, "the causes . . . lie deeper in our national life: first, in our longing for artistic forms that reflect our democratic and equalitarian political beliefs; and, second, in our hankering after art that mirrors the unique life of this western continent." Lomax even tried, unsuccessfully, to host a "Hootenanny" radio show on CBS, but it was vetoed by the network bigwigs.[38]

The *Christian Science Monitor*, in an editorial on People's Songs' first Boston hootenanny in March 1947, favorably commented, "the signs of a newly receptive public have been unmistakable, especially the salable showing of folk musicians on records and their popularity in such places as New York supper clubs." Downplaying the organization's politics, the editorial speculated that Seeger and his colleagues could "certainly do much to circulate the still all-too-neglected folk heritage of poetry and song." Seeger, for one, had already appeared at the trendy Village Vanguard; the *New Yorker*, in December 1946, described him, rather archly, as "an enormous young ex-G.I. who looks like a telescope . . . He sings Smoky Mountain ballads in the matter-of-fact monotone that best sets off their violent and bloody lyrics, and at the same time he stamps heavily on the floor with his left foot and bounces like a jumping bean, somehow or other making you feel that you must square-dance or die." The article glossed over his political songs. When Seeger reappeared at the Vanguard the following March, *Billboard* seemed to prefer him over the well-established Richard Dyer-Bennet.[39]

Other performers also captured media attention. Susan Reed, an attractive teenager originally from South Carolina, was featured in *Life* magazine in late 1945: "Three times a night Cafe Society Uptown's choosy customers sit enraptured while Susie sings old Irish, English, Scottish and Appalachian ballads and accompanies herself on the zither or the Irish Harp." The media cast Reed as a welcome ingenue, naive but intriguing. As her singing and acting career advanced during the next few years she attracted considerable publicity, and appeared frequently on NBC network shows. She also performed at Bascom Lamar Lunsford's Mountain Dance and Folk Festival in Asheville in 1948, keeping a foothold in her southern past.[40]

But although she was indeed born in South Carolina, her parents were midwesterners who had been part of the Chicago literary renaissance before World War I and lived only briefly in Columbia, South Carolina, before they returned to the North and Greenwich Village. There Susan grew up, with periods in

Hollywood when her father worked in film. She had absorbed some southern music, and later spent time collecting more, but her experiences were primarily urban—studying at the Little Red Schoolhouse in the Village and later with some of New York's professional music instructors. Her mother worked with the Stagedoor Canteen in New York during the war, and Susan began performing at military hospitals around the area while in high school. She met Barney Josephson through John Hammond's wife, Jemy, and agreed to work at Cafe Society. She opened at war's end, launching a career that even took her to Hollywood for one movie, *Glamour Girl*. Reed performed into the 1950s, though she felt she was greylisted (a subtler form of blacklisting). Though somewhat unusual in its professionalism and swiftness, her success mirrored that of a few other folk performers who captured the public's fancy.

For example, in the *Daily Worker* in late 1946 David Platt praised Josef Marais, a South African native who had met his partner Miranda, from Holland, when both worked for the Office of War Information (OWI) in New York. They soon had a radio program on WOR and a Decca album of South African songs, the first of many. "Tin Pan Alley has a formidable opponent in the small but compact group of folk singers who have come up during the past decade," Platt began. "Notable among the troubadours from abroad who have contributed much to the trend away from commercial swing and other degraded forms of popular music is the team of Josef Marais and Miranda." Representing the growing appeal of international music, one aspect of the Left's search for peace and brotherhood, they quickly became a fixture of the folk music scene.[41]

John Jacob Niles remained ever popular on the concert stage. A native of Louisville, Kentucky, with deep musical roots nurtured by his parents, he became a versatile performer, influential songwriter, and avid folk song collector, publishing *Songs of the Hill Folk* (1936), *Ballads, Carols and Tragic Legends from the Southern Appalachian Mountains* (1937), and finally the *Ballad Book of John Jacob Niles* (1960). Since the early 1920s he had given concerts at universities throughout the country and in Europe. His landmark midnight concert at Town Hall in 1946 featured his standards: "Black Is the Color of My True Love's Hair," "The Seven Joys of Mary," and "I Wonder as I Wander." Some of his compositions quickly entered the urban folk song repertoire.

Richard Dyer-Bennet also maintained a visible presence on the folk scene. Born in England and a graduate of the University of California at Berkeley, after studying folk music in Sweden he arrived in New York in 1941. The next year he sang at the Village Vanguard, and at war's and he signed with concert impresario Sol Hurok. "With Sol Hurok's contract in my pocket, I packed my lute, sold my furniture on Charles Street, and with my wife and two daughters moved to Aspen, Colorado. And for years, with Aspen as my base of operations, Hurok sent me concertizing all over the land, as far north as Alaska." When funds ran short he returned to the Village Vanguard or Max Gordon's uptown

Blue Angel. His annual recital at Town Hall, begun in 1944, always attracted a crowd, part of the healthy market for his steady stream of recordings. "He and Leadbelly were there [Village Vanguard] for a while at the same time," Elaine Lambert Lewis recalled in late 1946, "and occasionally sang together. I'll never forget a version of the 'Midnight Special' with Leadbelly leading, and in lieu of a chain gang, Dick and his Swedish lute supplying the chorus." "Almost every New York City singer of folksongs," wrote Lewis, "did a turn at the Vanguard." Owner Max Gordon "likes folksongs to sound like something. They used to be sung by people who were a little too precious, and listeners were bored. Now they have flesh and blood on them."[42]

The publication of John Lomax's autobiographical *Adventures of a Ballad Hunter* in early 1947 also sparked some media attention. In the *New York Times Book Review*, Horace Reynolds recalled Lomax's collecting experiences, when he "met the common people: old gnarled women in floorless Arkansas cabins whose eyes brightened as they sang of knights in golden armor caprioling on caparisoned horses; Negro convicts like Iron Head and Clear Rock, the former he got out of the pen to be his traveling companion and act as the china egg in the song basket." Lomax senior, who died in 1948, had collected many bittersweet memories while preserving vital slices of the South's musical legacy. Reynolds wrote often about the country's rural musical bequest in the *Christian Science Monitor* praising the Library of Congress's recent field recording releases, which "bring the life of cabin, field, levee, river, smack into our living rooms."[43]

Folk song books proliferated, as the music's popularity visibly mounted. The folk singer Tom Scott's *Sing of America* appeared in mid-1947, shortly followed by Ruth Crawford Seeger's *American Folk Songs For Children* and Margaret Boni's soon-to-be-ubiquitous *Fireside Book of Folk Songs*. "There is no doubt that America in the last decade has begun to sing again," Courtlandt Canby wrote in his review of the latter in the *Saturday Review of Literature*. "Young people with a guitar singing together the cowboy ballads, or the songs of the Spanish Civil War, the *aficionados* of the ballad-singer cult, the more staid discovers of English folk songs, the blues devotees, the college and school glee clubs with their arrangements of songs from many lands—all have helped pull us out of the nineteenth-century slough of sentimentality and cheapness." People's Songs secured a commercial press, Boni and Gaer, to publish *The People's Song Book*, edited by Waldemar Hille, which sold well. The Capitol album *Jo Stafford Sings American Folk Songs*, released in 1948, epitomized the ultracommercial lure of folk music. Though Stafford had learned the songs from her mother while growing up in Tennessee, she argued "that the orchestra lures some listeners who'd flee in terror at a guitar or zither."[44]

While folk music enjoyed growing popularity through 1947, the cold war, foreign and domestic, escalated. The Truman Doctrine and the Marshall Plan, both designed to bolster European economies and combat Communism; the

Federal Employee Loyalty Program; FBI snooping; the House Un-American Activities Committee (HUAC) investigations of alleged Red subversion in Washington and Hollywood—all denoted heightened official (and popular) fear and suspicion of Soviet schemes. The president tried to beat back Congress's more extreme measures to chip away at New Deal programs with a futile veto of the Taft-Hartley Act, and by supporting civil rights measures and a progressive housing bill.

CIO president Philip Murray and his allies initially opposed many Taft-Hartley Act provisions, including the anti-Communist clause, then cracked and initiated an internal purge of eleven Left-led unions, making up about 20 percent of the CIO's total membership. The FBI, lurking in the shadows, compiled its growing files on Seeger and People's Songs, while Frederick Woltman continued to warn readers of the *New York World-Telegram* about "the Communists' musical troupe that sells the class struggle to the masses the easy way" through the folk shows on WNYC. After complaints to the station, Herman Neuman, the musical supervisor, assured the *World-Telegram* that WNYC would control the political propaganda.[45]

People's Songs held its first national festival/convention, "Sing Out, America," at Hull House in Chicago in mid-October 1947, with the FBI ever present. Various workshops and a concert at Orchestra Hall, attended by over two thousand, kept the forty-five delegates busy and entertained as they tried to hammer out a more formal organizational structure. Forum leaders from around the country included Vale and Goodson, Betty Sanders, Lomax, Stracke, and Guthrie. Seeger, Asbell, and Robinson performed for a square dance called by Silber. "Running through all the debate, disagreement, fun, etc., however, was a serious note of purpose," Silber later wrote. "This was no businessman's convention, but a gathering of people who are afraid for their country and its democratic heritage—and who are determined to chart a path for people's music in the gigantic struggles looming up ahead."[46]

Over the winter, concerts and hootenannies continued in New York and elsewhere. In a publicity pamphlet issued at the time, titled *Hootenanny*, People's Songs featured its "stars"—Seeger, Robinson, White, and Guthrie—and focused on its work in colleges. "The presence of People's Songs Workshops at Harvard University, the University of Chicago, and Brooklyn College in New York attest to the immediate popularity which the concerts enjoyed, and to the wide interest which they stimulated," the pamphlet stated. "It has been found that a large percentage of the general membership of People's Songs are students. These are the young, alert Americans who realize the double import of folk songs and singing—the historical and cultural importance as well as their importance as a common bond among all the peoples of our country and of our world." Many who were later active in the folk revival got their first exposure to the music at these events.[47]

The political ground continued to shift as People's Songs entered the organization's decisive year in 1948. "We're scared—and every day's paper makes us a little bit more scared," declared the bulletin's editors. After calling upon the readers to encourage their congressmen to abolish the HUAC, they begged for "some brand new songs; let's rewrite some old ones; let's hit it from every angle with slams at the un-Americans and their activities, new exposés of red-baiting and anything else we can think of." The songs and the political will were surely vital, but the organization could not continue without financial support, always a nagging problem. The national chairman wrote to the members in January, "You understand . . . how tragic it would be if we could not continue to do this job. The lack of a few dollars for rent, telephone, printing, may mean just that. . . . The repeal the Taft-Hartley Law, to fight high prices, to campaign for a Third Party—these add up to a huge organizing job."[48]

The publication of The People's Song Book predictably got a warm welcome from the Daily Worker reviewer, who optimistically connected past and present: "The years of the Thirties, with their fighting people's movements, were also years when such songs as are in The People's Song Book came naturally from the throats of men and women on picket lines, in mass rallies, at home and in social gatherings. Such times are with us again." Seeger encouraged the organization's performers to hustle the book, "our greatest single concrete achievement in the last two years." He shared some of his selling tactics, like plugging it from the stage, or better yet distributing copies to the audience to sing from, then asking to pay or return the book. Best of all, performers could keep 20¢ for each copy sold.[49]

Wallace Campaign and Demise of People's Songs

Roosevelt's vice president, then briefly Truman's secretary of commerce, Henry Wallace had become a magnet for disgruntled liberals and leftists throughout the country. He articulated their support for civil rights and recognition of continuing poverty, their dread of escalating world tensions, and their fears of mounting domestic anticommunism, all under the shadow of the atomic mushroom cloud. Through 1947 progressive forces including Communist party and CIO leaders discussed organizing a third party; in December Wallace announced his presidential candidacy on the fledgling Progressive party ticket. People's Songs early threw itself into the campaign.

The new party attracted many show-business notables, in New York and Hollywood. A "Show-Time for Wallace" review at Cafe Society Downtown in in April featured songs and sketches by E. Y. Harburg, Jerome Robbins, Marc Blitzstein, Harold Rome, Jay Gorney, and John Henry Faulk. During the party's nominating convention in Philadelphia in July 1948, Glen Taylor, a cowboy musician and U.S. senator from Idaho, became Wallace's running mate. Seeger traveled extensively with Wallace, as did Paul Robeson. Harry Belafonte, just beginning his musical career, performed at youth meetings. Alan Lomax enlisted as the party's musical director, juggling this commitment with his weekly Mutual Broadcasting Network show *Your Ballad Man*. Boots Casetta moved to New York in August to staff the People's Songs music desk, as it officially became part of the campaign. Silber continued to manage the organization's daily activities. In October, five hundred members of the National Council of the Arts, Sciences and Professions signed a statement supporting Wallace, among them Aaron Copland, Morton Gould, Burl Ives, Marc Blitzstein, Earl Robinson, and Artie Shaw.[50]

"It's all a little incredible—yet, here am I at party headquarters on Mr. Wallace's staff in charge of music," Casetta exuberantly informed Bill Oliver in Los Angeles. "This has been a tremendous stride forward for People's Songs. The fact that People's Songs literally 'made' the convention was immediately recognized by the party and, with the leadership of Alan Lomax, they set up a Music Desk to handle that vital phase of the new party's campaign and sent for me. I feel pretty goddam humble." Casetta and Lomax issued the campaign's two lamented paper records—"Great Day" and "The Same Merry-Go-Round" with Michael Loring, and Loring singing "I've Got a Ballot" backed by Paul Robeson doing "Battle Hymn of '48." Each sold for 25¢ through the bulletin, the *Daily Worker*, and at rallies. "The Same Merry-Go-Round" became the party's unofficial theme song. People's Songs issued two editions of the twelve-page *Songs for Wallace*, as well as numerous song sheets and other songbooks. During the campaign "an ideal program always opened with a song," Casetta told Oliver. "There were always songsheets on the seats. . . . And we would encourage the Progressive party headquarters for that town in advance to try to find songwriters, poets, or whatever who could write something that would be for the local situation too." He concluded, "In fact, there is hardly a facet of campaign and public relations activities here that doesn't coordinate and make use of music—and music to each member of the Wallace movement means PEOPLE'S SONGS."[51]

The Wallace campaign, while intertwined with the Communist party, maintained an air of independence, but People's Songs explicitly retained its ties to the Left. Lee Hays, Laura Duncan, and Ernie Lieberman appeared on stage at the party's twenty-ninth anniversary celebration at Madison Square Garden in late September, with songs protesting the recent indictment of eleven party leaders for violation of the Smith Act and supporting the candidacy of Simon Gerson for New York City Council.

People's Songs temporarily benefited from the infusion of Wallace campaign funds, which accounted for 50 percent of all its musical bookings during 1948. But audience enthusiasm didn't translate into electoral muscle, and Wallace drew only about one million votes in the fall election. He lost badly because of a combination of labor union hostility, Truman's unexpected strength as he moved to attract Wallace voters, and the mounting conservative tide. Oddly, *People's Songs* scarcely mentioned the campaign, except in a eulogy on the cover of the November issue: "The votes have been counted and the machine politicians have put away the flags and bunting for another four years. But the issues which made 1948 a crucial year will not wait four years."[52]

Indeed, seeming to take the defeat in stride, Seeger, Silber, and their friends rededicated themselves to the development of a singing Left. The organization appeared healthy, with Casetta now editor of the bulletin and four other employees in addition to Silber. Harvey Matt (aka Matusow), was hired to run the People's Songs Music Center, where he would sell records and books; "Harvey can invariably be seen at labor and progressive meetings representing PS, 'getting the music to the people,' " commented the bulletin. He had joined the Communist party in 1947.[53]

During the December 1948 national board meeting, attended by the New York inner circle—Casetta, Bob Claiborne, Herbert Haufrecht, Hille, Lomax, Betty Sanders, and Silber—Seeger listed the organization's shortcomings: "The continued lack of activity in the labor movement, the still tremendous limitations of audience and participation imposed by monopoly control of the main channels of communication, and the neglect of the whole question of affiliations to and from People's Songs." Seeger always worried about outreach and organizational matters, while the mounting debt clearly loomed as the thorniest dilemma. In January, Silber summed up People's Songs election activities for the members: 12,000 copies of *Songs for Wallace*, 300,000 wordsheets, 25,000 campaign records, and various musical tours for Wallace and Vito Marcantonio, who was successfully reelected to Congress from East Harlem. There were fourteen branches, with another six waiting in the wings. Yet the debt totaled over $5,000, most owed to staff members. The January 1949 bulletin nonetheless mentioned plans for expanded coverage in future issues and a two-week summer workshop, along with an obituary for Moe Asch's Disc Company, notice of Seeger's self-published *Five-String Banjo Manual*, and announcement of the upcoming third anniversary issue.[54]

After protracted, convoluted bankruptcy proceedings, Moe Asch had finally folded Disc Records. Folkways Records emerged from the ashes on May 1, 1949, under the nominal ownership of Marian Distler. Asch miraculously continued to issue records, but People's Songs had less luck. The delayed "February" bulletin, the last to appear, carried a short message from the national board's March 11 meeting: "The national office has been forced to close its doors for lack of funds." The New York office was abruptly abandoned and plans made to pay all outstanding debts. A few days earlier, on March 7, Lomax had staged the lavish and well-attended "New York, A Musical Tapestry" in Carnegie Hall. With a script by Norman Corwin, the elaborate show featured the jazz musician Artie Shaw playing classical music, Art Hodes, Brownie

McGhee and a jazz ensemble, Betty Sanders, Pee Wee Russell, Yma Sumac and her Inca Trio, Harry Belafonte, the Weavers (Pete Seeger, Lee Hays, Ronnie Gilbert, and Fred Hellerman), and two Palestinian dancers. Intended to be the organization's financial salvation, it surprisingly lost money. Ironically, less than a week before the national board called it quits, Sidney Finkelstein, in the *Worker Magazine*, hailed the organization's many accomplishments representing "that part of the American musical genius which is neglected and ignored by Hollywood, Broadway, the concert hall, and most of the music schools." Praising "People's Song's, which now is a lusty baby of three, and has a bright future," Finkelstein inadvertantly penned their obituary.[55]

Barnard Rubin, the culture columnist for the *Daily Worker*, lamented the organization's passing but believed the flame should be kept burning: "Obviously, the work begun by People's Songs will continue, for, more than ever, America needs the singers, musicians, and composers who have said that they know which side they are on. We suggest that people's songsters in every city get together immediately to discuss the singing and song writing activities in their own communities." The *Daily Worker* had never particularly favored folk music, giving more coverage to classical music and jazz, yet it was obvious that the demise of People's Songs would leave a deep cultural hole, at a particularly perilous time for the Left.[56]

The Popularization of Folk Music

The closing of People's Songs, while deeply discouraging to its members, signaled neither the demise of Left folk activities nor a flagging of a national interest in folk music, broadly defined. In a review of hillbilly and western records in the *Saturday Review of Literature* in early 1948, Roger Butterfield praised recent releases by Bradley Kincaid, Charlie Monroe, Fred Kirby's Carolina Boys, Bob Atcher, and Eddy Arnold, while scorning Dale Evans and the Pine Ridge Boys. For Butterfield, the more artless the better: "I really don't know what folk music is, unless it is any kind of music that catches the fun and sadness and adventurousness and ultimate hopes of a whole lot of people, in a form that is not too contrived or sophisticated or smooth."[57]

Gilbert Chase, the educational recording specialist for RCA Victor, celebrated the vibrant, creative nature of folk music: "If the folk singer is a bearer of tradition, he is also, in his own way, a renovator and even a creator, for he refashions and remolds and remakes his traditional material to suit his fancy or his needs." He appreciated the Library of Congress reissues of field recordings from around the world, as well as Alan Lomax's current American Folk Music Series for Decca and Moe Asch's various musicians, ranging from Seeger and Guthrie to Texas Gladden, the Two Gospel Keys, and Lonnie Johnson. Similarly, a long article in the *New York Times* in April 1949 praised the Folklore Section of the Library of Congress's ongoing record releases: "Here is material that should warm the heart of anyone who cares about this country's vast treasury of folklore. . . . The very lack of professionalism and polish gives the disks a special charm."[58]

Charles Seeger popularized and elevated the study of folk music with a lengthy record review in the *Journal of American Folklore* in April 1948, the first in an academic journal. He covered Lomax's newly released *Listen to Our Story* and *Mountain Frolic*, as well as the Almanac Singers' *Sod Buster Ballads* and *Deep Sea Chanteys and Whaling Ballads*, now reissued by Commodore Records. In tracking the commercial trend from "authentic folk idiom . . . to the comparatively authentic fine-art or concert idiom" epitomized by John Jacob Niles and Burl Ives, he noted that "it does not require the fatherly solicitude of this reviewer to distinguish in Peter Seeger's singing and banjo-picking a progress every bit as great as that of Niles or Ives, but in the opposite direction." As for Lomax, his contributions loomed large, though Seeger thought he overplayed his "sentimentalization of 'The Folk' and of the social and cultural role he believes it is playing." In a similar vein, in a dual review of John and Alan Lomax's *Folk Song: U.S.A.* and People's Songs' *The People's Song Book*, Horace Reynolds hailed both volumes for adding to the public storehouse of folk music. Regarding the latter, he reminded readers of the *Saturday Review of Literature* that American folk music has long included propaganda songs, starting with the abolitionists, then the IWW early in the century, and the Okies during the 1930s.[59]

Bascom Lamar Lunsford, long a hillbilly celebrity, easily captured media attention while searching for the authentic folk and their songs and dances. A lengthy profile appeared in the *Saturday Evening Post* in mid-1948: "He has warred ceaselessly, but with no noticeable success, against the whooping, cowbell-ringing, type of music played on electric guitars by synthetic hillbillies wearing cowboy hats. This sort of thing offends him sorely, for he considers it a loutish caricature of something which in its pure form is beautiful and fine."[60]

Lunsford welcomed Zilphia Horton and a musical group from the Highlander Folk School to his Asheville folk festival. But he cautioned, "I would prefer that your group would not be costumed, especially do I ask that they do not come in caricature. A mighty good rule to follow is to have uniformity as to style but a variety of color, that is taking the group as a whole." Lunsford did not let Highlander's radical reputation influence his musical tastes. Zilphia and Miles Horton, the school's directors, generally preferred a more Left-and-labor-oriented crowd, however. They naturally connected with People's Songs. Founded in 1932 and one of over two hundred labor schools in the early decades of the century, Highlander trained labor organizers, using folk music and dance as teaching and socializing tools. Zilphia Horton had published a songbook, *Labor Songs*, in 1939. She collected songs for a CIO songbook following the war, and was even approached by Seeger about cooperating on the planned People's Songs music book. Her friend Jessie Lloyd O'Connor, grand-daughter of Henry Demarest Lloyd and a crusading journalist herself, invited Horton to the People's Songs convention in Chicago in October 1947: "That's the kind of convention I do not creep like [a] snail unwillingly to—sounds like the most fun of the century!"[61]

Folk music reached into sundry nooks and crannies of society and popular culture, including the nation's college campuses. In 1940, Alice Gates, of the Women's Physical Education Department at Swarthmore College, near Phila-delphia, organized a regular square dance event that developed at war's end into the first annual college folk festival; Richard Dyer-Bennet anchored the inaugural program. (Fearing increasing hordes of outsiders who seemed to overrun the tiny campus, the college administration canceled the 1956 festival, but soon relented when faced with student pressure.) Other colleges lagged far behind; Oberlin College's folk festival, for example, only began in 1957.[62]

The folk outpouring reached such proportions that in November 1948 Ben Gray Lumpkin, teaching folk songs and ballads at the University of Colorado, issued his second mimeographed "*Folksongs on Records*" only a few months after the first issue. He divided the hundreds of recordings into seven categories, starting with Anglo-American songs and ballads, and including black spirituals and secular songs, foreign music, and folk-dance recordings. He preferred his stylings as unvarnished as possible: "For example, heavily orchestrated versions like Jo Stafford's 'Barbara Allen' seem out of keeping with the folk manner; but Richard Dyer-Bennett's [sic] and Susan Reed's versions of the same ballad, though different from one another, and through slightly polished for concert purposes, are sung in a manner close to the folk style." While top-heavy with records by Dyer-Bennet, Ives, Guthrie, Lead Belly, Seeger, and other familiar names, the list also included a wide range of folk, hillbilly, and western per-formers, gospel groups, and Library of Congress releases; it included, for ex-ample, *Greek Liturgical and Folk Songs* by the Byzantine Singers (Disc), Olga Coelho, *Latin American Folk Songs* (Victor), Los Rancheros, *Mexican Cowboy Songs* (Decca), and recordings by Marais and Miranda. Lumpkin ended with a substantial sampling of folk song books.[63]

People Artists and the Weavers

People's Artists continued to book concerts through early 1949. Its acts included folk and popular singers, comedians (Jack Gilford, Irwin Corey and Sam Lev-inson), dance bands, dancers, instrumentalists, and novelty acts. The previous September a new group—Lee Hays, Pete Seeger, Fred Hellerman and Ronnie Gilbert—resembling but more organized than the Almanac Singers, had begun to jell; they publicly emerged at the People's Songs Thanksgiving hoot. Hays characterized the group's range of songs as "juicy, lusty, serene, mellow and down-right holerin'." Initially called the No-Name Quartet, they also performed at the packed 1948 Christmas Eve hoot at Irving Plaza.[64]

Former People's Songsters, and the Left in general, found the times confusing and frightening as Cold War hysteria mounted. During 1949 the Soviet Union detonated its first atomic bomb, the Communist party came to power in China, Alger Hiss's perjury trial began, the CIO purged eleven Left-led unions, and the trial of the Communist party's leadership continued at the Foley Square court-house in New York City. Curiously, as the dark clouds of anticommunism swelled, at Elsa Maxwell's rustic "American Party" in May at the newly reno-vated Park Sheraton Hotel, Seeger joined an odd assemblage, including Ives, Stanley Melba and his Orchestra, and the "Golden Girls" in the hotel's pool ("Sea Nymph bathing suits in Lurex fabric by Jordan')." Both Margot Mayo's American Square Dance Group and Eddie Smith's "North Carolina Ramblers," "representing the hog and hominy belt," appeared for the square dance and hoedown segment of the evening, staged by Lomax. Seeger, "vocalist, and the slickest five string banjo picker in the country," was backed on guitar by Fred Hellerman.[65]

At a large meeting on July 8, a committee more or less reorganized People's Songs as People's Artists, Inc., to be headed by Paul Robeson and Betty Sanders; the steering committee included Seeger, Silber and Bob Wolfe. They argued: "The commercialized standards of Hollywood, radio and Tin Pan Alley have subverted the musical life of our country. The concert halls reach, at best, only a very small portion of the American people, and then at prices usually beyond the reach of working people." The answer was to promote "a music rooted in the democratic past of America and which is an integral part of the struggles shaping our country today." National in scope, yet centered in New York, combining music (jazz as well as folk) and radical politics, People's Artists would carry on where People's Songs had so abruptly left off. On August 26 the group staged its first production, an eclectic, integrated "Hootenanny Mid-summer," coordinated by Casetta, including Seeger and his eighty-strong Good Neighbor Chorus, a jazz band, Irish pipes, Guthrie, and Hope Foye at the air-cooled Penthouse at 13 Astor Place.[66]

The following day People's Artists planned an outdoor concert, featuring Robeson and Seeger, to be held in Peekskill, just up the Hudson River from New York City. Proceeds were slated for the Harlem chapter of the Civil Rights Congress (1946–56), the civil rights wing of the Communist party. Robeson was a tower of strength to the singing Left through the 1940s and 1950s. Beginning in the 1930s, he had combined a stellar international singing and acting career with an activist political agenda, particularly combating fascism and racism. Silber said, "Paul symbolized so much for us: the new motion stirring in the black community, which was to shortly mature into the mass civil rights movement; the Left and communist movements' potential for developing a mass social base; the persecution of those trying years and the spirit of resistance which a few of us tried to keep alive. Most particularly, he was, for us, the quintessential role model of the committed artist."[67]

An armed and angry mob, shouting "dirty commie" and "dirty kike," forcibly prevented the first Peekskill concert from even starting. Despite threatened violence from local patriots and authorities, party stalwarts organized a second concert on September 4, with Seeger, pianists Ray Lev and Leonid Hambro and Robeson; guards, many of them war veterans and union members, prevented an attack during the enthusiastic concert. But when the energized twenty thousand tried to leave in their cars and buses, local police forced them down a narrow road lined with a shouting, rock-throwing mob. Many concertgoers were injured, some seriously. People's Artists immediately shot off telegrams to local, state, and national politicians, demanding punishment for all involved. They got no satisfaction. Lee Hays pondered Peekskill's insanity: "What is there in the music of Chopin, Bartok, Mendelssohn, and in the people's songs of Paul Robeson and Pete Seeger and Hope Foye to inspire this savagery, this hatred? Who but beasts are menaced by a culture which brings people together in peace and understanding?"[68]

The Peekskill riot had been a shattering experience, an ugly example of the anticommunist hysteria sweeping the country. But it did not slow Seeger and his colleagues. In late September a hootenanny with his new group and Brownie McGhee featured a film strip on the Peekskill riot. In October, Seeger issued an"Interim Newsletter" for People's Artists, because "we all have an immediate need to keep in closer touch." Seeger always believed in written communications, linking together the scattered adherents of the musical Left throughout the country. "Before People's Artists was barely out of swaddling clothes it was almost overwhelmed by being in the center of a crisis involving fascist violence, and subsequent investigations, lawyers, suits, etc.," he began. Nonetheless, progressive songsters continued to sing and organize, and he reported on the activities of Bernie Asbell in Chicago, Bess and Butch Hawes in Boston, Jennie Wells Vincent in New Mexico, Earl Robinson in Los Angeles, Wally Hille in St. Louis, and those in New York.[69]

Burl Ives, Josh White, Tom Glazer and Oscar Brand had begun drifting away from People's Artists by late 1949, for political and/or artistic reasons. Still, the organization could easily put together an eclectic lineup of first-rate performers, including Seeger's new quartet, soon named the Weavers, which quickly became one of People's Artists' most popular attractions and the indelible prototype for a host of folk groups soon to follow. Their name came from a militant nineteenth-century German play by Gerhart Hauptmann, which Hellerman was reading in his European drama course at Brooklyn College. In mid-June, quickly broadening their repertoire, they appeared at a rally for the new China: "For at this meeting, this quartet . . . will introduce for the first time to an American audience some of the new songs and chants which the Chinese Liberation Armies have carried along with them all the way to Shanghai and beyond." They would offer such revolutionary hits as "The Song of Hoes." "The Weavers are frankly not 100 percent certain that they'll be singing these and other Chinese songs exactly as the victorious Liberation Armies and the toiling peasants are singing them," a *Daily Worker* article cautioned.[70]

On Christmas Eve 1949 a "Peace on Earth" hoot featured Christmas carols as well as songs of peace and brotherhood, with Seeger, Hays, Gilbert, Hellerman, Betty Sanders and Joe Jaffe; Silber called the square dance. That same week the Weavers began appearing at the Village Vanguard, an experiment that soon proved dramatically successful. They were initially paid $200 a week plus free hamburgers (after Gordon discovered a hungry Pete using a half a pound of meat, he revised the contract to stipulate $250 a week, but no food). They remained at the Vanguard for six months, attracting rave reviews and a record contract with Decca; seemingly overnight they had found economic security and struck a musical nerve throughout the country.

Folk music had become big business by decade's end. *Newsweek* commented in mid-1946, " 'The corn is as high as an elephant's eye—and so are the profits.' A hard-bitten Tin Pan Alley character shook his head in amazement, for he was talking about hillbilly songs—the current wonder of the music world." Once generally confined to the southern market, this music now dominated in the North as well, with "Riders in the Sky"—successful versions by Vaughn Monroe (number one for three months), Peggy Lee, Bing Crosby and Burl Ives—setting the pace. (Ives also had hits with "Blue Tail Fly" and "Lavender Blue.") White soldiers from the North had discovered the music in southern training camps during the war, then brought it home; at the same time, white and black southerners had moved north, bringing their musical styles and tastes. In *Newsweek's* shorthand version of the story, country music had already gone commercial in the 1930s, starting with Gene Autry, later followed by Hank Williams, Roy Acuff and particularly Eddy Arnold.[71]

Quite apart from its political and commercial incarnations, folk music continued to be played throughout the country, at house parties, socials, festivals, and local gatherings. The collecting, preserving, and distributing of this noncommercial music was still centralized at the Library of Congress whose Folklore Section was headed by Duncan Emrich (1945–56), assisted by Rae Korson. The advent of magnetic tape-recording machines in 1949 allowed for a more flexible recording program, along with higher quality. "The pioneering phase of the field collecting and the establishment of Archives has come to a close," Emrich reported in June 1950. "The future emphasis should be directed to coordinated efforts, to elimination of duplication, and to strong encouragement for scholars and others to use—in fairly exhaustive studies—the materials already gathered." He continued the influential recording series begun by John Lomax, with ten new albums appearing in 1948.[72]

Lead Belly died in Bellevue Hospital on December 6, 1949, and following services in Harlem his friends Brownie McGhee, Pete Seeger, Josh White, Ronnie Gilbert and Fred Hellerman performed for the small crowd. "The story of Leadbelly is the tale of a man's redemption by music," one article noted. "When word of his death became public yesterday, Alan Lomax, collector of American folk music and onetime sponsor, disclosed that he and Josh White and other students and singers of American ballads are planning a Leadbelly memorial concert in New York next month." As one vibrant member (and symbol) of the folk community passed into legend, his temporary resurrection loomed near, in the form of the Weavers' hit recordings. "There are few in a position to know . . . who would dispute that Lead Belly was America's greatest and most creative folk singer," Earl Robinson remarked about his old friend in early 1950.[73]

The five years since the war's end had seen a marked growth in folk music. Rural vernacular music had found a home in northern cities, shaped and nurtured by many including those with a Left folk agenda. Not that People's Songs and its allies dominated the scene completely, for there were many concert performers, such as John Jacob Niles, and others on the local level, who kept the music alive for various social, cultural, and aesthetic reasons. While the political dimension of People's Songs directly motivated Pete Seeger and the leadership group, people became involved for a variety of other purposes. "It was a way to get bookings for square dances or perform or lead singing," Joe Jaffe later remembered. "It was a way to show off what you'd learned, show off your stuff." Love for the music loomed large for all—the thrill of mastering an alluring instrument and developing a repertoire of songs, old and new. Folk music styles struck a sympathetic chord among those in the cities, for it was a natural sound that contrasted with their urban surroundings. For Jewish youth, most with immigrant parents, folk songs and instruments connected them to American history and culture, legitimizing their search for belonging, and at the same time serving as an outlet for their alienation from the political status quo.[74]

"My first conscious recollection of folk music as folk music was during the Henry Wallace campaign of 1948," recalled Mike Fleischer, prime organizer of the first University of Chicago folk festival in 1961. "My mother dragged me somewhat reluctantly to a concert at the UE hall on Madison and Ashland. And the three guys that were singing, there was a fella named Seeger, and there was a fella named Houston, and there was a fella named Guthrie. So that was my first real exposure, my first conscious memory of real folk music. Music of the people, not crap you got off the radio. These three men singing and playing for a pretty much left-wing audience." Fleischer soon gravitated to the more traditional sound of southern black and white folk music, but his first exposure to Seeger, Guthrie and Houston was not unusual. They and their colleagues served as the entryway for many into the world of folk music.[75]

At the century's midpoint, urban folk music retained many of its earlier personalities and characteristics as the broader milieu was shifting. Since the war the music had included both a Left orientation and commercial aspirations and overtones, in an awkward relationship that bothered some, was hailed by others, and caused confusion for many. The escalating Red Scare would serve to create a growing chasm between the two—radical politics and market forces—as the Weavers woefully discovered. For its promoters on the postwar Left, folk music had remained only one element of a much broader progressive culture, including dance, jazz and classical music, literature, and theater. But this, too, was about to change, as folk spun off substantially on its own, developing a new audience among young people.[76]

3

The Weavers and the Red Scare, 1950–1954

Soon after the start of their spectacular six months at the Village Vanguard, the Weavers participated in the Lead Belly memorial concert at Town Hall on January 28, 1950. Organized by Alan Lomax, the evening attracted the cream of the folk, blues, and jazz worlds. "Woody Guthrie sang duets with Tom Paley right after Hot Lips Page and Sidney Bechet blew some wild riffs into the rafters," Oscar Brand vividly recalled in *The Ballad Mongers*.

> Pete Seeger led The Good Neighbor Chorus in a program of folk songs, and W. C. Handy followed with a few of his original blues. Jean Ritchie quietly strummed her Kentucky dulcimer with a goose quill and then left the stage to Count Basie and his real gone piano. Tom Glazer sang some old ballads, the Lord Invader jangled some calypso tunes on a West Indian cuatro, The Weavers sang "Irene," Reverend Gary Davis raked the audience with his crude gutter gospels, and Bill Dillard's band jazzed from one side of the stage to another. There was genial Frank Warner singing a few songs from his special, private collection—songs like "He's Got the Whole World in His Hands" and "Tom Dooley." Finally, Leadbelly's close friends, Sonny Terry and Brownie McGhee, joined Sticks [sic] McGhee in some sophisticated blues.

Brand argued that "American music today is almost a direct reflection of the kind of amalgam which Town Hall provided that night—blues, ballads, calypso, and jazz mingled in what is now popular song."[1]

Jazz and blues scholar Frederic Ramsey penned a loving but blunt portrait of Lead Belly for the *Saturday Review* in late January: "Leadbelly's voice was not beautiful. It was rough and grainy, and some of its raw tones came up as if scraped out of his throat. It rang out with intensity because he often shouted with violence. It had a nasal twang. The excitement he engendered came from his understanding of each melody he sang and from a strong, precise sense of rhythm." He had been heard on radio in New York, and recorded extensively for a variety of record companies and the Library of Congress, but most of his early recordings, unfortunately, resided in company vaults (particularly at Columbia and RCA Victor). "It would be cultural mayhem of the first degree if Columbia Records, Inc., were to lose track of those [American Record Company] masters," Ramsey concluded. Only Moe Asch's Folkways had plans for more releases—vol. 3 of *Leadbelly's Legacy* would soon appear. Assuming that Lead Belly's music would live on through his own performances, Ramsey had little inkling that a very different fate awaited at least some of his songs. Indeed, the Weavers had ended their first night at the Village Vanguard with Lead Belly's "Goodnight, Irene," soon to be a runaway hit for Decca.[2]

The Weavers' burgeoning political as well as commercial career continued into the spring. They appeared with Paul Robeson and Howard Fast in late March to raise money for a lawsuit by the Peekskill victims against the Westchester County police, and joined Gypsy Rose Lee, Judy Holiday, and others in a packed show to help fund the People's Drama Theater. After a rather shaky start at the Village Vanguard, the group began gathering larger crowds and public notices. As commercial success beckoned, they obtained a manager and a record contract. Harold Leventhal, a song plugger for Irving Berlin before the war, first heard the group at the Vanguard and loved both their music and their politics. "I knew nothing about managing," he later confessed, "but I was a good organization man. . . . Of course, the Weavers did want someone who saw politically eye to eye with them, and that was me." He was joined by the considerably more cautious Pete Kameron, who knew the record business and had contacts with radio disk jockeys and other artists. The Weavers soon began to limit engagements; a notice in the *Daily Worker* in May noted they would "make a rare concert appearance" with McGhee and Terry, part of a Sunday evening folk series at the Panel Room.[3]

Kameron took over the quartet's day-to-day management, including arranging concerts and the lucrative song publishing. In April, bandleader Gordon Jenkins, working for Decca Records, heard the Weavers at the Village Vanguard and, decidedly smitten, discussed a recording contract. Decca head Dave Kapp walked out after taking one look, but Jenkins persisted. After all, the company had developed a strong lineup of folk (and country) performers, including Burl Ives, Marais and Miranda, and Josh White. And Alan Lomax had produced Decca's impressive American Folk Music Series. Kameron next approached Mitch Miller, who was interested in bringing them to Columbia Records. Using this leverage Kameron persuaded Kapp to sign the group. The Weavers first recorded

"Tzena, Tzena," backed by "Goodnight, Irene," on May 4, a day after Seeger's thirty-first birthday. Years later Gordon Jenkins wrote to Lee Hays: "I still have your first Decca audition tape, which I often play, whilst sipping a touch of vodka, and gazing back into a little cellar saloon [the Vanguard] where music, talent and truth had such a wonderful blending. It was a wonderful privilege to hear you all, and thank God for tape."[4]

"Tzena, Tzena" shot up the pop charts in midsummer, peaking at number two. Mitch Miller rushed out his own version for Columbia, which reached number three. Covers by Vic Damone (Mercury) and Ralph Flanagan (RCA) also made the charts. "Goodnight, Irene" promptly followed suit, skyrocketing to number one; it remained popular for twenty-five weeks. As usual in the music industry, a hit resulted from some combination of audience enthusiasm and commercial hype. In this case, the music publisher Howard S. Richmond mailed promotional copies of "Goodnight, Irene" to fifteen hundred disk jockeys, many of them personal acquaintances cultivated when he was a press agent for Dinah Shore and Frank Sinatra. The song got considerable airplay, and during the first month Richmond sold 250,000 copies of the sheet music, in addition to the half-million records. A parody soon appeared, "Please Say Goodnight to the Guy, Irene (So I Can Get Some Sleep)."

Pursuing popular recognition, the Weavers seemingly compromised both their artistic and political integrity. First, they temporarily abandoned their overt Left politics, at least in their songs. "Tzena, Tzena" and "Goodnight, Irene," followed by "The Roving Kind," "So Long (It's Been Good to Know Yuh)," "On Top of Old Smoky," "Kisses Sweeter Than Wine," "Wimoweh," and "Midnight Special" had no obvious political content. Perhaps performing songs by Lead Belly, a black ex-convict, and the outspoken Woody Guthrie made a political statement, but this could easily be lost on their vast, expanding audience. Guthrie, present during the group's recording of "So Long," instantly penned new verses upon hearing a Decca executive complain that references to dust storms were outdated. "It wasn't as good as the original version," Seeger later complained, "but it was good enough for the Weavers to take it to the top of the Hit *Parade*."[5]

Time blessed the group with a glowing article in mid-August. The piece focused on "the murderous old Minstrel Lead Belly" and his singing of "Irene," "his coal-black face gleaming fiercely and his horny hands scratching his twelve-string guitar. . . . Last week the old minstrel's old song, prettied up and cut in half, was in fifth place on the hit parade. A quartet called the Weavers, recording (for Decca) with Gordon Jenkins' band, had used it as a filler to back *Tzena, Tzena*. Helped along by Jo Stafford, Frankie Sinatra, *et al.*, the filler had just about caught up with third-place *Tzena*." *Time* pointed out, with obvious relish, that all the new recordings left out Lead Belly's closing verse, "An' ef Irene turns her back on me—I'm gonna take morphine an' die."[6]

There were also problems with the Weavers' musical rectitude. Their experience and inclination stressed a simple acoustic accompaniment, led by Seeger's banjo and Hellerman's guitar, and straightforward arrangements. Nothing fancy, no horns or strings, and certainly no orchestrated backup. But they soon found themselves in Decca's studios at the mercy of the conductor and arranger Gordon Jenkins. In short order they were backed by Leroy Homes's Orchestra, Jenkins's Orchestra, Terry Gilkyson with Vic Schoen's Orchestra, Leo Diamond and His Orchestra, and eventually Larry Clinton and His Orchestra. The slick, upbeat music captured the general public but must have grated on the ears of the Weavers' regular audience. In their live performances the Weavers stuck with their usual format, and their concerts also included a wider variety of songs, including some with political content, such as Spanish Civil War tunes.

The Weavers temporarily occupied an awkward musical niche, bringing a sweetened, compromised folk music to a national audience. They created a professional, polished prototype of subsequent trios and quartets. "Jenkins never asked us to change a note of anything we sang," remembered Hays. "He surrounded us with fiddles and French horns and trumpets and things, but when people sang 'Goodnight Irene' they didn't sing the fiddles, they sang the words." Besides, Hays proudly boasted, "Songs like ours getting on the Hit Parade broke down the barriers between country and pop. And the charts began to get into big trouble because we were crossing the borderline and knocking them off on both sides of the fence."[7]

In the first long article on the Weavers in late September, Time pontificated, "Professional folk singing in the U.S. is mostly the province of a few long-haired purists who rarely get a hearing outside the clubs and recital halls where their small but fervent public gathers. Last week a group of four high-spirited folksters known as the Weavers had succeeded in shouting, twanging and crooning folk singing out of its cloistered corner into the commercial big time." In sketching the backgrounds of the four, Time wrote, "Sponsored by Red-tinged People's Songs, they got enthusiastic but unremunerative backing from fellow travelers who have long claimed folk songs as their particular province. Mostly, however, they kept up their singing 'for the hell of it.'" Now headliners at Manhattan's Blue Angel nightclub and Broadway's Strand Theater, they were pulling in over $2,000 a week.[8]

The music publisher Howie Richmond worked tirelessly to plug "Goodnight, Irene." Soon, as James Dugan reported, "Lead Belly's mighty runaway was spreading into all fields of commercial music—folk, country and western, and 'race,' the trade name for Negro blues and jazz. Such artists as Lost John Miller, Quarantine Brown, Hardrock Gunter, Bull Moose Jackson, Grandpa Jones, and Ivory Joe Hunter took 'Irene' down into the swamps and the sagebrush." Hits were born, but also made, with considerable sweat. "There are 2,563 radio stations, ninety-nine television stations and roughly 400,000 juke boxes in the

United States," Gilbert Millstein explained in the *New York Times Magazine*. "In one recent month 'Goodnight, Irene,' was heard about 100,000 times over radio and TV, according to Broadcast Music, Inc. [BMI]." *Billboard* calculated the song could be heard fourteen hundred times a minute on jukeboxes. "Some people in the trade believe that no other song ever sold so fast." Pete Kameron insisted the Weavers shun leftist functions as they toured the country's poshest night-clubs. Seeger had doubts about commercialization, but he could hardly disagree with success: "I thought to myself, we were just as successful in 1941 when we sang 'Union Maid' for 10,000 striking transport workers," he later wrote. "But those months of early 1950 were an interesting experience. And at that time millions of teenagers first heard the words 'folk song.' "[9]

In early 1951 the Weavers' version of Guthrie's "So Long (It's Been Good to Know Yuh)" climbed the charts, finally reaching number four. Guthrie was elated by the recognition, though worried about the song's copyright. "I ran down via rollerwheels of all kinds and caught Pete Kameron over in the Decca Building helping the Weavers & Gordy Jenkins to record my very own 'So Long', and a backside for it by the name of 'Lonesome Traveler," he told Moe Asch at Folkways. "All well done by a twenty piece choral chorus and a thirty piece orchestra of Jenkins's. I shot the copyright certificate over to Pete Kameron and he eyed it up and down like it was good news from somewhere." Guthrie seemed unfazed by the elaborate musical setting, perhaps even flattered, though he added, "I still claim that you folks at Folkways are putting out the stuff and the real life kind of stuff that is ten to one the best kind of stuff getting put down and spun around on records." Asch assured him "that we had copy-righted the SO LONG song before PETE KAMERON, the WEAVERS, DECCA, could as you put it 'swipe' it from you."[10]

Guthrie was surely aware that Howie Richmond copyrighted many of the Weavers' songs, originally in the public domain but now slightly revised, under the name "Paul Campbell" to satisfy Decca and also reap the profits. Guthrie received a $10,000 advance for "So Long"; moreover, Richmond gave him a tape recorder and began paying him $20 a week to record scores of his songs. He eventually gave Richmond fifty hours' worth of music, including the pre-viously unheard "This Land Is Your Land." Kameron had become Guthrie's business manager, while he also worked for Richmond. Guthrie, meanwhile, increasingly demonstrated signs of his crippling Huntington's disease, though his friends still assumed he was deranged by drink.

Battles over copyright infringements have always plagued the music industry, and the Weavers' hit "Tzena, Tzena" was a good example. Joe Jaffe has recalled that he or Ernie Lieberman, both New York performers, first heard the song from a friend, who had learned it as a camp counselor in about 1949. They began singing it at People's Artists hoots, where Pete picked up on it. He contacted Joe at his Bronx apartment, and copied the lyrics and music over the

phone. The Weavers soon began performing it. Before they recorded it, however, Howie Richmond researched the song and found it in a book of Israeli
folk songs, arranged by Julius Grossman, an American school teacher. Richmond had someone (using the fictional name Spencer Ross) doctor the melody,
had Gordon Jenkins construct English lyrics, took out a copyright, and issued
the sheet music. When the song hit he received a rude surprise. Mills Music
quickly published its own version, with words by Mitchell Parish and the music
attributed to Grossman and Issacher Miron (aka Michrovsky), an Israeli who
claimed he had composed the song's third part. Mills then sued Richmond's
firm, TRO, and won a judgment concerning the music. Since TRO still controlled Jenkins's popular English lyrics, this created a legal dilemma essentially
preventing anyone from duplicating the Weavers' version.[11]

Music and Politics

The Weavers had no monopoly on "folk songs" during the summer of 1950.
Versions of "Goodnight, Irene" were recorded by Frank Sinatra (on Columbia—
175,000 sold), Dennis Day (Victor—147,000), the Alexander Brothers (Mercury), Jo Stafford (Capitol—68,000), and Red Foley (Decca—95,000). Sinatra's
rendering became his most popular record for a few years. Folk, pop, and
country began to merge. Patti Page's "The Tennessee Waltz," first released in
1948 as a hillbilly song, had limited play until its resurrection by Page in late
1950. Her pop rendition quickly sold almost five million records and sparked
a country music upsurge. In particular, the success of Hank Williams's songs
and recordings demonstrated country's growing national appeal.

Overall record sales during 1950 reached $189 million, a 10-percent jump
since 1949 (though far below the $224 million of 1947), and the total climbed
to $277 million in the mid-1950s. Six companies dominated the market: Co-
lumbia, RCA, Decca, Capitol, MGM, and Mercury. Numerous smaller labels
supplied the niche markets—rhythm and blues, country, gospel, jazz, and ethnic. Most companies still issued 78-rpm records, but they could not compete
with the new 45-rpm records among younger buyers, and the adult market for
LPs. Radio, and increasingly television, challenged the phonograph for consumers' entertainment time and dollars, but they also served as additional musical
outlets.[12]

Though show business tried to keep aloof from politics, it was unsuccessful.
Senator Joseph McCarthy had given his first headline-grabbing anticommunist
speech in January 1950 in Wheeling, West Virginia. During the summer North
Korea invaded South Korea, Julius and Ethel Rosenberg were arrested and
charged with atomic espionage, and the publishers of Counterattack issued Red
Channels: The Report of Communist Influence in Radio and Television, a listing of 151 "Reds"
in show business, including Pete Seeger, Oscar Brand, Richard Dyer-Bennet,

Tom Glazer, Burl Ives, Tony Kraber, Millard Lampell, Alan Lomax, Earl Robinson and Josh White. *Counterattack*, a smear sheet founded by three FBI alumni and launched in May 1947 by American Business Consultants, specialized in scurrilous attacks based on information from the Left press, FBI leaks, and hearsay.

"Fred Hellerman recalled, We were about to get a TV summer replacement show for Van Camps Beans, and we were all buddy-buddy with them and chummy-chummy and they were sending us all cases of their goddam Van Camp Beans!" But the show was suddenly canceled as a result of a piece in *Counterattack* on June 9, 1950: "This folk-singing quarter . . . well known in Communist circles. The folk songs they sang for 'Broadway Open House' [NBC-TV] are not the 'folk songs' they sing for the subversive groups they frequently entertain. On such occasions they usually sing fighting songs of the Lincoln Brigade (which fought for Stalin in the Spanish Civil War) and other Communist song favorites."[13]

Distraught over the impact of the story, Pete Kameron visited the editor. *Counterattack* reported:

> His problem: the folk-singing quartet had been scheduled for another program sponsored by a nationally known product. The COUNTERATTACK story had led to its cancellation . . . and promised to hurt him and The Weavers financially. He explained that he didn't know anything about Communism, or much about the Weavers' past. Since some facts had been brought to his attention, he had spoken to the "boys" about the problem and felt that they were just gullible and well-meaning. He said that he would try to persuade them to cease their pro-Communist activity as individuals and, as their manager, would refuse engagements for any Communist front groups.

The newsletter's editor assured Kameron "that COUNTERATTACK was eager to cooperate and help people break with the Communist Party and its fronts." The Weavers would continue to have commercial success, but from the very beginning the Red-baiting would take its toll.[14]

While the Weavers' career remained on course for another year or so, others were not so lucky. Anticommunist hysteria intensified. The assault on the Left came from corporations and labor unions, churches and veterans' groups, national and local governments—the political mainstream abetted by the radical Right. The Communist party, riddled with internal problems, sank under the weight of the attack. Party membership, perhaps twenty thousand in 1950, declined by half by the end of the decade. The party's eleven top leaders were convicted of conspiring to overthrow the government during the Foley Square trial, a verdict upheld by the Supreme Court in June 1951. The anticommunist crusade rippled throughout the country, snaring many for civil rights organizing in the South, labor union activities, suspect teaching in the nation's schools and colleges, and every sort of political or personal transgression. Congressional committees, led by the House Un-American Activities Committee (HUAC) and the Senate Internal Security Subcommittee (SISS) of the Judiciary Committee, supported by state and local clones, worked overtime rooting out Reds. FBI head J. Edgar Hoover, continuing his decades-long crusade against scandal or "subversion," instigated and supported Red squads in countless city and state police departments.[15]

Show business personalities became an early and continuing target for the Red hunters, furnishing publicity and glamour to the crusade. Film personalities were a particularly attractive and vulnerable quarry, but other aspects of the industry—music, theater, television and radio—felt the onslaught. In September 1950 *Billboard* alerted its readers, "In the past week, two incidents [the firing of Jean Muir from the "Aldrich Family" TV show and the political troubles of Josh White] occurred which have clearly demonstrated the effectiveness of *Counterattack*, anti-Communist newsletter, on the destines of showbiz personalities who have become involved in the Commie issue." The weekly regularly documented the mounting hysteria, scattered attempts to fight back, and the weakening spine of the show business establishment.[16]

Jerry Wexler, a music writer for *Billboard* and close friend of Howie Richmond, vividly recalled his editor asking him in 1951 "to get a dossier on a folk group called the Weavers. The dark days of Joe McCarthy and blacklisting were upon us, and I wasn't about to do that kind of dirty work. I refused." He soon jumped ship for Atlantic Records and went on to have a stellar production career. Folk music's spreading Red taint influenced the trade press to substitute "country" for "folk" in labeling rural-sounding commercial music.[17]

Despite the mounting paranoia, People's Artists struggled to establish its identity and keep progressive folk music alive, at least in New York City. In May 1950 the first issue of *Sing Out!*, the organization's successor to *People's Songs*, reached a few hundred subscribers. Among the group of postwar activists in People's Artists, Irwin Silber soon emerged as the central figure. Born in 1925, he had been a camper and counselor at Camp Wo-Chi-Ca (Workers Children's Camp), president of the American Student Union (ASU) chapter in his high school, and member of the Young Communist League (YCL) and American Youth for Democracy (AYD), then the Communist party upon turning eighteen. He attended Brooklyn College during the war, and became executive director of People's Songs.

An excellent organizer with strong political and artistic opinions, Silber recognized that his forceful, even abrasive, personality was both a weakness and a strength. In a lengthy critique of one People's Artists' hootenanny in January 1950, he confessed, "I've got a feeling somewhere that there's a certain kind of resentment towards me. . . . But if that exists, some people are not going to be able to take advantage of my experience and know-how in Hoot productions. This much is safe to say without being immodest: I know more about Hoot publicity, advertising and mechanics than anyone else in the organization."[18]

The unprepossessing *Sing Out!* comprised sixteen pages in a small format. Each monthly issue included current and historical songs from the United States and other countries, articles, letters, record reviews, and occasional editorial commentary. Robert Wolfe served as the first editor, followed by Wally Hille and Ernie Lieberman, until Silber officially took over in October 1951. He remained fixed at the helm until 1967. Paul Robeson, Howard Fast, Walter Lowenfels, Alan Lomax, Earl Robinson, Mike Gold and Pete Seeger graced the masthead as contributors. The editors took a broad view of "People's Music," believing that "no form—folk song, concert song, dance, symphony, jazz—is alien to it. By one thing above all else we will judge it: 'How well does it serve the common cause of humanity.' " About five hundred national subscribers had signed up by the end of the first year.[19]

A vibrant left-wing folk scene continued to develop in California. The First Annual People's Choral Festival in Los Angeles in 1950 spotlighted six Left choruses: the Fraternal Songsters of the Jewish People's Fraternal Order; the Luvenia Nash Singers; Earl Robinson's Southern California Labor School Chorus; the Jewish People's Chorus; the California Labor School Chorus; and the Mexican American Singers. Alumni of People's Songs remained the heart of Left musical culture in Los Angeles: Bill Oliver, Bill Wolff, Vern Partlow, Lewis Allan (aka Abel Meeropol), Malvina Reynolds, Will and Herta Geer and Dave Arkin. Some of these formed as the Sierra Folk Singers and produced hoots at the Gateway Theater. Ernie Lieberman moved from New York to Los Angeles in early 1952, followed by Wally Hille later that year. Lieberman picked up odd jobs, continued his singing, composed for musical shows, and taught folk classes. Core members of the group—Arkin, Rich Dehr, Oliver, Partlow, Ray Glaser, Hille and seven others—gathered to form the Songmakers Workshop on June 2, 1953. (By 1960 the group had split into various workshops for performers, teachers and songwriters, with the goal of creating and promoting "songs of our time.") Though the Red Scare escalated—Oliver and Partlow were blacklisted as journalists—the Left folk scene nonetheless served as a springboard for many who were soon to be prominent in the burgeoning folk revival, including Guy Carawan, Frank Hamilton, Odetta, Jo Mapes and Frank Miller.[20]

Bill Oliver had arrived in Hollywood in the early 1920s and soon became a drama critic for the Hearst-owned *Herald*. With the Depression he moved to the Left and joined the Newspaper Guild. He also began playing the piano, then guitar, wrote songs and became a mainstay of People's Songs in Los Angeles. When HUAC called him to testify in 1952 he lost both his job at the (now named) *Herald-Express* and his newspaper friends. His daughter Noel painfully recalled that "when he got called up he had me type up a letter in multiples and send it to all these people that he thought were his friends, telling them what had happened and that he had gotten a post office box, and that they were going to need some legal help, and if anybody wanted to send anything they could send it there. Nothing ever came to that box."[21]

Born in Santa Monica, Guy Carawan grew up in Los Angeles. He graduated from Occidental College in 1949 with a degree in mathematics, and along the way developed an interest in jazz, playing the clarinet and ukelele. In the late 1940s he began moving into folk music, as part of People's Songs and the Sierra Folk Singers, and he switched to the guitar. During a Weavers visit to Will Geer's house in Topanga Canyon he first heard Seeger on the banjo and was immediately taken with its sound and allure. His two years at UCLA, 1950–52, led him to study sociology as well as folklore with Wayland Hand, a ballad and folklore scholar, who cautioned Guy against involvement in People's Songs. Marais and Miranda, Guy's neighbors, seconded Hand's preference for performance over politics.

Frank Hamilton shared Carawan's interest in jazz and folk music. Born in New York City, Hamilton moved to Los Angeles when a year old in 1935. A musical virtuoso, he began playing guitar and trombone at a young age. He learned folk songs from Carl Sandburg's *American Songbag* along with the records of Burl Ives, Josh White, Lead Belly and the Weavers. At his first hootenanny at Bart and Edna van der Schelling's house he heard Cisco Houston. "Something inside clicked. I wanted to do that," he remembered. "The same evening I met Guy Carawan. . . . I was charmed by the evening. There was a duo, Rich Dehr and Frank Miller, who later became one of the first popular folk music groups" (the Easy Riders with Terry Gilkyson).[22]

Hamilton's musical interests and circle of friends grew quickly in Los Angeles. He recalled a night in 1951:

> One night, when I sang at a concert put on by the Sierra Folk Singers, a large rugged looking older man approached me and complimented me on my rendition of the bawdy ballad, "Sam Hall." I was singing it with the verve of a seventeen year old. He invited me to a party at his home in Santa Monica to meet some of his friends. That was the first time I ever met Will Geer, the famous actor. At the party that night were the Weavers, and my idol Cisco Houston.

In 1951 the Geers moved from Santa Monica to Topanga Canyon, which quickly became one of the local folk music centers. Will was struggling to survive the Hollywood blacklist. He had been listed in *Red Channels*, and his thriving movie career came to a screeching halt after he refused to cooperate with HUAC during his appearance in April. (Woody Guthrie arrived in the fall of 1952 to take up residence on the property, and somewhat later he purchased eight acres nearby; but he returned to New York in early 1954, with his new wife, Anneke, as he became increasingly impaired by Huntington's chorea.)[23]

Bess and Butch Hawes had moved from New York to Boston in 1946, and a year later to Cambridge; Butch prospered as a book illustrator, while Bess was busy with three children born in quick succession. At first barely performing, Bess taught guitar and other stringed instruments to mothers at a cooperative nursery school in Cambridge. Because of Butch's serious health problems, they relocated to Los Angeles in 1952. Bess would soon revive her unique group-teaching technique and become a vital catalyst in the local folk revival.

Frank Hamilton journeyed briefly to San Francisco in 1952 and attended "one of the most enthusiastic concerts of folk music that I have ever seen presented with Jo Mapes, Rolf Cahn and an innovative five string banjo player and performer, Frank Robinson." Mapes, born in Chicago, moved to Los Angeles with her mother during the war. Her first day at Thomas Starr King Junior High she met another newcomer, Odetta Felious, and they quickly became friends. With dreams of becoming a famous singer or actress, Jo roamed around Hollywood picking up odd jobs and occasionally singing. In 1957 she moved to San Francisco and quickly became involved with Rolf Cahn and other members of the budding folk scene, including Stan Wilson, Billy Faier and Ella Jenkins. Other remnants of the People's Songs group, such as Lou Gottlieb and Jerry Walter, also remained musically active.[24]

The Weavers Succumb

The Weavers' career managed to continue on track into 1951. Pete Kameron ordered the group not to perform at political events, including the funeral of the Communist stalwart Mother Bloor, or even commercially record "The Hammer Song." "We kept on with personal appearances, but it got to be more and more of a drag," Seeger recalled. "Our then manager would not let me sing for the hootenannies and workers' groups." The group felt increasingly trapped, with political brickbats flying from all sides. In *Sing Out!* Irwin Silber complained that they "would have sounded far better in the more vital and vibrant Hootenanny setting than they did in their formal attire on the Town Hall stage." Their success, he continued, "signifies a new concern on the part of the entertainment industry monopolies with providing mass outlets for genuine expressions of people's culture. Doubtless, many people's singers will have more of an opportunity to make a living at their craft as a result of the sudden commercial popularity of the 'folk idiom'. But the achievements here can only be of a limited nature and it would be completely near-sighted to have any illusions on this score." If anything, he was overly optimistic.[25]

Wally Hille astutely sketched their situation. "I don't see them as having done so much that they did not foresee," he remarked to former People's Songster Bob Black in March 1951. "A commercial venture is just that. They went out to make a living thereby—to try to have some influence on the type of songs prevalent on the market . . . without delusions of any complete turnabout. . . . Another thing, the Weavers never were a successful 'out and out' progressive team. They only got good as a commercial outfit, and then decided to keep making a living." He believed Seeger had "many bitter twangs of conscience," and Hellerman a feeling of "glee." Hays was "finally feeling the thrill of large success for the first time—after many years of frustrating achievement in the back yard," and Gilbert projected "a somewhat naive idealism—perhaps filed off somewhat by now." Hille observed, "The Weavers haven't hit a crisis yet," and he wondered "what will they do when this comes . . . as I expect it will some day."[26]

Hays wrote to Earl Robinson:

> Poor Pete is in anguish, so unwilling to accept the demands of this new day. I am myself fearful of what is to come but at least I have broken with the restrictive notion that we can go on forever in the same old way and with the same old methods and techniques. . . . I am so wrapped up in the problem of what to say to this big new audience of ours that I am not in the least ashamed that the old audience is gone, or that we did so little to keep it alive. Wherever we go, you know, local progressives report at the stage door on the first night. But the lineup is nowhere nearly as long as it used to be. We are in for some hard days.[27]

Throughout 1951, People's Artists and its allies struggled to survive. Needing a recording outlet, Irwin Silber and Ernie Lieberman, representing the organization, had established Hootenanny Records in late 1949, issuing the Weavers' "The Hammer Song" and "Banks of Marble." The poet Walter Lowenfels, a close friend of Hays, greeted the new company in the *Daily Worker*: "Let the voice of America, singing for peace and brotherhood, be known, rather than the 'Voice of America' broadcasts." Over the next few years Hootenanny would issue eight 78s, selling for 89¢, and one LP album. Silber later said, "At the time the Weavers still felt, OK they were gonna sort of lead two lives. . . . They still felt committed to what we were about. And they knew that Decca was not going to be interested" in Hootenanny's circulating these two sides. The album, *Hootenanny Tonight*, appearing in 1954 and later reissued by Folkways, was the first recording of a live hootenanny. In contrast to the 1930s and 1940s, when small progressive labels were fairly prolific, Hootenanny Records was practically alone in circulating "dangerous" songs. Folkways, however, would soon help fill this niche, reissuing albums by Guthrie and Lead Belly, and the Almanacs' *Talking Union*. Decca also recorded Guthrie and Cisco Houston, now that the Weavers had hit; but the Guthrie sides never appeared.[28]

Through the political turmoil, *Sing Out!* remained staunch. In the first anniversary issue, a month late in July 1951, the editorial aggressively noted: "The events of the past year—the struggle for peace and liberation of colonial peoples, the Korean War, the fight against Jim Crow with the martyrdom of the Martinsville Seven and Willie McGee, and then the freedom of four of the Trenton Six, the McCarran Act and the persecution of the leaders of the Communist Party—all these have shown the sharpening struggle between the peaceful peoples of the world and the imperialists who would divide them and use them against each other."[29]

The folk Left represented by *Sing Out!* always had some difficulty accepting the Weavers' popularity and modern styling. Fred Moore's generally positive review of their Decca album, *Folk Songs of America and Other Lands*, complained that the presentation of "Easy Rider Blues" "sounds pretty stiff," which could be expected "from any all-white group, which attempts to present some aspect of Negro music." For their enormous national audience, however, the sound appeared just right. *Newsweek* touted the group's popular and financial success in August 1951: "Just a year and a half ago, The Weavers burst upon the New York scene in a tiny Greenwich Village night club called the Village Vanguard. Since then, they have toured the country and their salaries have zoomed from $200 to $4,000 a week." They kept releasing hits. "So Long (It's Been Good to Know Yuh)" reached number four in early 1951; "On Top of Old Smoky" almost made number one and remained popular for twenty-three weeks into late 1951; "Midnight Special" went to number thirty in September 1952 (two months before Decca dropped the group). As late as January 1954, after their official demise, "Sylvie" managed to break into the top thirty for two weeks.[30]

The FBI escalated its surveillance of the Weavers, and the pressure from right-wingers resulted in their replacement on the Dave Garroway television show. Next, the Ohio State Fair canceled their appearance for the summer of 1951. Frederick Woltman followed with a red-baiting article in the *World-Telegram*. Senator Pat McCarran's Senate Internal Security Subcommittee mounted an investigation. Though the Weavers had initially appeared at the country's fancier nightspots—the Shamrock Hotel in Houston and the Palmer House in Chicago—by early 1952, they found themselves reduced to the cramped Duffy's Stardust Room on the outskirts of Cleveland.

On February 6 and 7, 1952, Harvey Matusow testified before HUAC about the Weavers' Communist links. A few weeks later Matusow repeated his charges at more length before the Ohio Un-American Activities Commission. The group's popularity, he said, "was used to attract many young people to the movement because they respected the Weavers and thought they were good singers and entertainers. The bobbysoxers go for that. Once the young people were at the affair, the Communist Party organizer took over. He had a good chance to recruit many of the young people." When Matusow was asked, "you are not testifying, or want to give the impression that there is anything subversive or un-American about folk singing or square dancing," he readily agreed. The publicity following his testimony, combined with continued FBI dirty tricks and the ongoing anticommunist assault, doomed the Weavers, who straggled along for about a year, entertaining at such venues as a dinner club in Kansas City and the Rotary Club of Pasadena. "Very quickly our work came down to nothing, there was no work to be had," Ronnie Gilbert recollected. "We stuck together as long as we possibly could, and then it was pointless." They disbanded following their annual concert at Town Hall in December 1952.[31]

The Red Scare's Widening Net

"There's a revolution brewing in the music business," Allen Churchill reported in the New York Times. "Already it has gone so far as to drive Tin Pan Alley's prolific composers out of Brill Building cubicles and send them, hand-painted neckties flapping in haste, to music libraries, where they startle attendants by demanding, 'Where do I find folk songs? You know, stuff in the public domain.'"[32]

But folk music's commercial glory was tortured. Burl Ives, for one, weathered the enveloping political miasma but emerged agitated and tarnished. Though he had not been involved in Left causes for a few years, Red Channels listed him anyway. In September 1950 administrators at the University of Washington challenged his appearance on campus. "I believe you were informed at the time of your appearance here a year ago," one notified him, "that the University had received some protests relating to the Communist movement in America, and, in effect, challenging your loyalty. Now, similar objections again have been made, quite emphatically and by a friend of the University who occupies a position of considerable influence in the community." Of course, the university "steadfastly maintained that academic freedom, which means the intellectual freedom of its personnel, must not be infringed," but since the "Communist Party does not allow its members this kind of freedom," the university "will not allow members of that Party the use of University classrooms and platforms." Ives quickly issued a public statement denying membership in the party, yet he defended his appearances "at benefits for organizations later declared subversive. . . . I was there for the purpose of that particular benefit, usually to feed, clothe or help someone."[33]

His denials and dodgings did not initially suffice. His acting and singing career still appeared shaky and vulnerable. So, on May 20, 1952, Ives voluntarily appeared before the Senate Internal Security Subcommittee. He confessed that in the 1930s he "did not believe in the Communist philosophy," but said that in New York his "first audience as a singer was various unions and so-called progressive organizations." After a number of preliminary questions about his appearances and affiliations, he demonstrated his patriotism and salvaged his career by naming names. He identified four people, including concert performer Richard Dyer-Bennet and Ives's former publicity agent Allen Meltzer. "I am very sorry that I have to bring up names in this manner, because I would like to be able to not mention other names, but I can't [avoid it]," he said. In conclusion, trying to ensure his salvation, Ives admitted he had "made some mistakes, and I want to thank this committee for the very fair and democratic way in which you have heard my story. I believe that in no Communist country would such a hearing be possible at all."[34]

The expected blast came from Irwin Silber at Sing Out!: "The well-known folksinger, who once joined in singing 'Solidarity Forever,' has a different tune today. It might be called 'Ballad For Stoolpigeons' or the 'Strange Case Of The Wayfaring Stranger.' . . . The future of Burl Ives should be interesting. We've never seen anyone sing while crawling on his belly before." Five years later, in a review of Ives's book of sea songs, Pete Seeger uncharacteristically raked over his old colleague's political sins: "Burl Ives went to Washington, D.C. a few years ago, to the House Un-American Committee, and fingered, like any common stool-pigeon, some of his radical associates of the early 1940's. He did this not because he wanted to but because he felt it was the only way to preserve his lucrative contracts; and that makes his action all the more despicable."[35]

Silber's wrath was certainly fanned by his own political difficulties. He and Betty Sanders had already been subpoenaed by HUAC. The committee canceled the summons a week before their scheduled appearance, however, prompting the editor to argue that "we must use the partial victory [of not being called] already achieved as the springboard for further mass action in defense of all people being harassed by the witch-hunters." (He finally appeared in 1958 and refused to discuss his politics.)[36]

Josh White, also listed in *Red Channels*, was another popular performer who bent, but did not break, under the pressure. A piece in the black monthly *Our World*, in early 1949, praised White's belief in race pride and human rights, well demonstrated by his acting in the film *The Walking Hills*: "Josh waited a long time for this kind of thing and turned down several offers because he didn't think the role did the race any good. He's also seen to it that Josh, Jr., is not typed as the buck-eyed, hair-on-end 'pickaninny' too often given Negro kids in films." As for his songs, "whether it's Hard Times Blues, One Meat Ball or The House I Live In, when Josh sings it, it has a real meaning, for both he and his music put a lot into each other." In June of the next year, however, while in London on one of his frequent concert tours, he heard the news that he was marked as a Red and returned immediately to meet with the people at *Counterattack* and *Red Channels* and two FBI agents. In order to avoid a subpoena, White volunteered to appear before HUAC, but although under extreme pressure, he blunted any attack on Paul Robeson. The popular performer and civil rights leader had recently faulted President Truman for plunging the country into the Korean War, urging blacks to fight against racism at home, not in foreign adventures. The State Department immediately moved to void Robeson's passport. White had secretly discussed his necessary testimony with his old friend, who advised him to try to clear himself, but name no names.[37]

White appeared on September 1, and testified: "I have never knowingly belonged to or supported any organization designed to overthrow the Government of the United States. But I did on many occasions appear at benefits and rallies which I was led to believe were for worthwhile causes. I did not even suspect that some of them were Communist inspired." He proudly admitted, "Often I sang the powerful song, 'Strange Fruit,' which is an indictment of the horror of lynching. But I always followed it with what I call the answer to 'Strange Fruit'—'The House I Live In' or 'What Is America to Me,' which expressed the other side of the story—my profound love for our America. Why shouldn't a Negro artist—and for that matter any decent person—raise his voice against lynching?" He sang the two songs, both written by Lewis Allan, with the music for the latter composed by Earl Robinson, then left the stand.[38]

Counterattack's editors gloated that they had brought White before HUAC, where "he told how he had been duped into supporting Communist fronts, and dealt an effective propaganda counterblow against the CP and its deception agencies." But White was not done with his obeisance, as far as it went. The December 1950 issue of *Negro Digest* featured "I Was a Sucker for the Communists," a reprise of his HUAC testimony, in which he reaffirm his patriotism as well as his commitment to "singing of the hope, joys and grievance of ordinary folk. I shall stand shoulder to shoulder with those who are pushed around and humiliated and discriminated against, no matter what their race or creed may be." White had done as much as he could, or would. "Erasing my name out of *Red Channels*, well, it never happened," he later stated. "Yet I would do the same thing again. People said I went to Washington and called names, even though I didn't. I'm singing and will sing songs that are good for America. . . . I don't believe in Uncle Tom."[39]

White and Ives had publicly struggled to salvage their careers, and both had succeeded, more or less; White continued his nightclub appearances, discovering a particularly receptive audience in England and western Europe. Others, such as Tom Glazer, had political problems as well. Glazer appeared frequently on radio as well as in concerts, and his children's records sold thousands of copies. When a patriotic ballad by Vaughan Monroe, with lyrics by Glazer, reached the top ten on the Hit Parade, Silber penned an assault on those who "try to get so small and insignificant that the red-baiters will not see them. . . . Josh White didn't get small enough for them until he publicly repudiated every decent thing he had ever stood for. Tom Glazer has a sweet smell about him these days because he is busy writing paeans to [General Douglas] MacArthur."[40]

Glazer had performed with the Priority Ramblers, appeared on numerous labor and protest albums during the mid-1940s, and toured for People's Songs, but his politics were far from unambiguous. He had also sung for Democrats backing Eisenhower as their candidate in 1948, performed for an Americans for Democratic Action (ADA) rally, and appeared at a testimonial dinner for the Socialist party leader and vocal anticommunist Norman Thomas in 1950. Yet *Red Channels* listed him, after an attack in the New York *Journal-American* in March 1949; the short *Red Channels* piece mentioned his connection with People's Songs, but little else.

In a letter to the *Journal-American*, the singer countered the charge that he was a Red sympathizer and threatened a law suit if there was no public retraction. "Folk singer Tom Glazer says he is anti-communist,"*Counterattack* proclaimed the following April. "Glazer declared: 'I am unalterably opposed to Communist tyranny or any other kind of tyranny or dictatorship, wherever it exists in any country, organization, industry or union.' *Glazer admitted the accuracy of all facts* cited after his name in 'RED CHANNELS.' " The *Counterattack* piece added to his frustrations. In anguished letters to family, friends, and potential allies, Glazer expressed his anger at being attacked from both the left and right. Merle Miller, in *The Judges and the Judged*, his 1952 study of Red Scare casualties, noted that despite the declaration in *Counterattack*, "the number of Mr. Glazer's radio and television appearances, which dropped sharply after the publication of *Red Channels*, has not increased much." But his career as a songwriter and children's entertainer eventually revived.[41]

Oscar Brand found himself similarly caught in the political crossfire, a painful experience that long rankled. Irwin Silber complained in late 1951, "Folk-Singer Oscar Brand joined the ranks of the 'ex's' [ex-progressives] last month when, in a public statement at Cooper Union in New York, he indulged in some wild red-baiting in an attempt to atone for past digressions from the path of 200% Americanism. As a result, the attempts to remove Oscar's WNYC 'Folk Song Festival' from the New York air-waves seem to have subsided." Brand had presumably criticized the Communists for their "pernicious influence upon the American folk-music field." Occasionally quizzed by the FBI, listed in *Red Channels*, and informally interviewed by a staff member of HUAC, he never publicly testified. Brand has forcefully argued that he had no firsthand knowledge of party meetings or membership, "so they never called me." Nonetheless, he felt shunned by the Left and stigmatized by the establishment. He later deplored the situation that "many incipient folk singers had to try to live down the taint of their subscriptions to the *People's Songs Bulletin*," and concluded, "Blacklisting is a despicable act."[42]

While the performers and activists reacted variously to the political pressure—cooperating, dodging, or with defiance—the climate worsened. Even Harry Belafonte, on the periphery of People's Songs and People's Artists—he had appeared at various concerts in a minor role—and with growing popularity, found himself mentioned in *Counterattack* in late 1951: "He has been billed as entertainer for several functions of the Committee for the Negro in the Arts, the party's Negro cultural front, since the start of the Korean war." That same month Belafonte opened at the Village Vanguard to rave reviews. Although the Red taint lingered, it hardly seemed to matter, as his career skyrocketed.[43]

Others had less luck. In early 1953 *Counterattack* named Robert DeCormier (director of the Jewish Young Folk Singers), Laura Duncan, Martha Schlamme, and Leon Bibb as "stars in the circle of top entertainers for Communist fronts" and active in People's Artists, "the party's entertainment booking agency." Earl

Robinson, Robert Claiborne, and Paul Robeson were harassed and blacklisted, along with Pete Seeger. HUAC eventually summoned many, and a few cooperated. Seeger appeared in mid-August 1955, along with Tony Kraber and Lee Hays. The latter agreed to discuss general issues, but took the Fifth Amendment when questioned about specific political matters concerning himself or others. When asked what songs he had written, Hays proudly mentioned "one which, according to the *New York Post* has been quite useful here lately [during] ceremonies for former Air Force Secretary Talbott on August 12—I see that the Air Force Band played a Weavers song, So Long It's Been Good to Know You." In the *New York Times*'s terse summary, the "burly, sandy-haired folk singer" invoked the Fifth when questioned about People's Songs and the Communist party, but readily admitted his membership in the mainstream American Federation of Musicians and the American Guild of Variety Artists.[44]

Tony Kraber, who was listed in *Red Channels*, named by Elia Kazan and Clifford Odets in their congressional testimony, and blacklisted since 1951, proudly stated: "I am well known as an American folk singer. Some 20 or 25 years ago I was perhaps one of only a half-dozen folk singers known to the Library of Congress, people like Carl Sandburg, who was a good friend of mine, and who has taught me many songs, and whom I have taught songs, even, and other great folk singers of that sort, and I claim my small share in the renaissance of American folk music, which is nearly lost at this time." He continued, "the reason I am here, I am sure, is the fact that I have been called a guitar player." The committee chairman, Francis Walter, shot back, "We are not interested in whether you are a guitar player or a piccolo player." Talkative but uncooperative, Kraber took the First Amendment. Curiously, when he volunteered to sing some of his songs, Walter responded, "I agree your songs are splendid, and I bought most of them, and I enjoy them very much," but he only wanted to know if Kraber had performed for the Communist party. The singer and actor again took the First and also the Fifth. Seeger followed Kraber and cited the First for his defense. "Never have the specious charges of un-Americanism [against Hays, Kraber, and Seeger] been more ridiculous," announced Silber. In 1955 Fred Hellerman also used the Fifth Amendment.[45]

In this political climate, songs could appear as subversive as individuals and organizations. HUAC was particularly exercised over "Wasn't That a Time" (Seeger unsuccessfully offered to sing the troublesome song during his testimony). Vern Partlow's "Old Man Atom" especially rankled. Originally written in 1945, when Partlow had interviewed nuclear scientists as a reporter for the *Daily News*, and published in *People's Songs* as "Talking Atomic Blues" in January 1947, it oddly caught on with the general public. For a few years following the atomic bombing of Japan scientists and the public alike pondered, questioned, and feared the new ultimate weapon, but by 1950 a dulled acquiescence had generally settled over the country. Atomic imagery quickly seeped into popular culture. Even the Communist party occasionally made light of the weapon. At the end of 1947 the Brooklyn Communist party invited "You Atoms and You Eves" to a "New Year's Atom and Eve Ball."[46]

"It is . . . or was . . . a hit," *Counterattack* informed its readers in September 1950, in a capsule summary of recent events surrounding "Old Man Atom." "*Protests were made that it aped the Communist line.* It was banned on some radio stations. Columbia and RCA-Victor withdrew their recordings." The anticommunist syndicated columnist Victor Riesel hopped on the bandwagon: "So you haven't had the 'Atom Talking Blues' sung to you? And you haven't had one of the 'people's singers' croon the ballad in your ear—giving out with lines like 'we hold these truths to be self-evident: all men may be cremated equal?' Then you're not living, pal."[47]

Sam Hinton first recorded the song for ABC Eagle in early 1950, a small label in Southern California, which sold the master to Columbia Records; the release had some success until the mounting criticism led to its withdrawal. The Sons of the Pioneers, hardly Stalinist stooges, had their popular RCA-Victor version pulled from the stores and airwaves by the fall. Partlow later recalled:

> The rave reviews in *Billboard, Variety, Cash Box* and other music industry trade publications on the "Atom" recordings ceased. Decca Record's part-owner Bing Crosby stopped rehearsing his own surefire version; the Decca artists and repertoire man, who had auditioned me for an earthy follow-up album of OMA and other originals, titled "The Singing Newspaperman," told my publisher the attack on the song was crazy, but the company's stockholders, under the circumstances, could do without a "controversy." Moon and June still paid off and always would, it was decided.

Six different versions hit the stores and just as swiftly vanished. *Cash Box* listed Bob Hill's (aka Fred Hellerman) Jubilee recording as its "Sleeper of the Week" in mid-July. "Tune itself is essentially a folk item," ran the notice, "but as offered here, it should and will go in any type of location. Sock punch of the song is its lyrics which weave a timely message hard to match."[48]

Life initially opposed censorship, in July linking the problems of "Old Man Atom" with the recent firing of Jean Muir from "The Aldrich Family" TV show. Flashing its anticommunist credentials and admitting that the song "is not in line with the latest military views of the atom bomb's effectiveness," the magazine nonetheless argued that "that's no reason why any private group of censors should be allowed to keep the rest of the U.S. people from buying or refusing to buy a recording of 'Old Man Atom' as they choose." A few months later, in a piece entitled "The 1950 Silly Season Looks Unusually Silly," the *Saturday Evening Post* noted: "A recording company withdraws platters of a song called 'Old Man Atom,' apparently on the theory that people have become so hysterical that they are demanding a cheery attitude toward destruction." The *New York Times* also weighed in on the side of sanity after Columbia and RCA withdrew their recordings. Despite such mainstream support, the disks disappeared. "Peace in the world, or the world in pieces," the song's close, became too disturbing a refrain in the midst of the Korean War and with the reality of the Soviet bomb. Partlow swiftly followed his tune onto the blacklist.[49]

About the Left cultural events of his youth in Washington, D.C., Carl Bernstein recalls "There were songs about owning those banks of marble and sharing those vaults of silver, but allegiance to a foreign power? Taking violent action against the government of the United States? Spying? Treason? Pete Seeger sang sometimes, and Cisco Houston. Listen to those songs. I remember speeches also, not the words exactly, but the feel, a lot of talk, no doubt, about making this country a better place, decent, more humane." The adult journalist deemed it folly to think of his parents' folk music as subversive. But at the time it was no joke.[50]

The war in Korea ground on, and the Red Scare escalated. Sing Out! backed the practically moribund Progressive party and its presidential candidate, Vincent Hallinan, in 1952, but with little enthusiasm. The election of Dwight Eisenhower and running mate Richard Nixon hardly signaled any relief (rather, perhaps, increased harassment and intimidation) though the new president had promised to end the fighting in Korea. Moreover, some on the Left, with their own folk legacy, attacked the Communist party. In 1952, Joe Glazer, education director of the United Rubber Workers, and Bill Friedland, an organizer for the Michigan CIO, issued the album Ballads for Sectarians, foreshadowing the satirical Bosses' Songbook: Songs to Stifle the Flames of Discontent (1958). Both the album and songbook lampooned the party's ties to Moscow and its rigid policies.[51]

Still the hootenannies and musical shows continued in New York, providing a diversion and spark of light for those weathering the Red Scare. Oddly, the Saturday Review of Literature chose this time to celebrate the "Golden Age of Hootenany [sic]," writing in late 1951: "Back in the days of Federal Works projects, folk singing was a wholesome, inexpensive way for people to entertain themselves and each other. One group of citizens even decided to emulate the old minstrels, traveling about, echoing the workers' plaints, but eventually camped out for long runs in small Greenwich Village night spots. For Pete Seeger, Burl Ives, Cisco Houston, Tom Glazer, Woody Guthrie, and others of this hard core the struggle is over—they have arrived." Hardly. Perhaps the Weavers' fortunes had blinded the writer to the current state of affairs. Success had always been fleeting, and all of those named had (or would have) various political problems.[52]

In September 1951 the United Electrical, Radio & Machine Workers (UE), one of the radical unions expelled by the CIO in 1949, sponsored a "Freedom Festival," featuring the People's Artists Quartet (Laura Duncan, Ernie Lieberman, Betty Sanders, and Osborne Smith), along with Earl Robinson, the Duke of Iron, and a jazz ensemble. Irwin Silber and Mike Stratton wrote the script.

Master of Ceremonies Howard Da Silva, a blacklisted Hollywood actor, gave a running commentary, for example introducing Bernie Asbell's "Song of My Hands" with: "Did you ever stop to think that a song could be written about plain, everyday things—like the price of food, like putting the kids to bed, or like a pair of hands?" There were also skits about the Red Scare and fighting back together: "It's gonna be a tough walk—they have the money, they have the newspapers, radio, TV, movies, they have everything, almost. Almost. All we have is 150 million working people—miners, seamen, farmers, steel, auto, rubber—and electrical. That's all we got—and that's all we're gonna need. That's the power of UE. That's the power of freedom." This format generally became standard for People's Artists programs—a variety of performers and narration from a prepared script, connecting the music to an uplifting, instructional political message.[53]

During the summer of 1953 *Sing Out!*, heavily in debt, missed three monthly issues. Then it reported in October: "On June 19, 1953—in the face of an avalanche of world protest—the government of the United States murdered Ethel and Julius Rosenberg." Despite this crushing news, and continuing political and economic struggles, People's Artists managed to publish *Lift Every Voice!: The Second People's Song Book*, edited by Silber with an introduction by Paul Robeson. Silber also happily greeted the release of John Greenway's *American Folk Songs of Protest*, "a valuable contribution to the growing body of literature which helps us to know our fighting past and provides the base for the full flowering of a people's music." The Korean War ended in July, four months after the death of Stalin, both events possibly causing some cracks in the Cold War's veneer. A year later the Senate stripped Joe McCarthy of his political power, further easing internal tensions.[54]

Attending to the Music

Folk music scholarship provided a growing body of songs and their contexts for performers. While academic work flourished, typified by the publication of Malcolm Laws's *Native American Balladry* and Tristram Coffin's *The British Traditional Ballad in North America*, more popular compilations reached a broader public audience. The *New York Times* welcomed the completion of Vance Randolph's four-volume collection, *Ozark Folksongs*. Comparing Randolph to the indefatigable John Lomax, John Gould Fletcher, a poet born in Arkansas, marveled that he had found such treasures in Arkansas and Missouri, where "according to legend, shoeless natives chase razorback hogs, or spend their time drinking moonshine whisky under the trees." The songs illustrated the traditional and religious nature of Ozark life. Just when the Weavers were shaping a northern urban audience and sensibility for folk music, Fletcher (and Randolph) reminded New Yorkers of the music's roots.[55]

The jazz scholar Charles Edward Smith made a similar point in his July 1950 article "Folk Music, the Roots of Jazz," a survey of recent field recordings collected by Harold Courlander and titled "Negro Folk Music of Alabama." Reminding readers of the ongoing importance of John and Alan Lomax in documenting rural black music, Smith stressed the diversity of the music, its African roots and rural setting, and its connection to contemporary popular music. "Courlander's Alabama researches acquaint us with a spring of folk influence still feeding, if remotely, the gushing flow of jazz—and perhaps, vice versa." This was a living music. Alan Lomax underscored the point in his just-published *Mister Jelly Roll*, based on extensive interviews with the influential jazz musician Jelly Roll Morton and his friends.[56]

Through his book and record reviews in the *Christian Science Monitor* and *New York Times*, Horace Reynolds kept the public informed of the latest folk music scholarship. He covered album releases of field recordings of Anglo-American songs and ballads by the Library of Congress. This was the real stuff, "sung not by trained singers but by the people who have preserved them, by the workers—cowboys, sailors, mountainers [sic], sod-busters, steel-drivers, roustabouts, okies, and their women folk—[and] they reflect the timbre and tempo, the common sights and sounds of American life." His review of William Doerflinger's *Shantymen and Shantyboys: Songs of the Sailor and Lumberman* stressed the unpolished nature of the 150 songs collected from Yankee and Canadian sailors and woodsmen.[57]

Through 1952 popular coverage of folk music included both its traditional and popular sides, usually linked and yet somewhat estranged. Recordings of "primitive folk music" continued to generate interest and surprise, and the major collectors received praise in an overview article in the *New York Times*. Moreover, wrote the *Times*, "thanks to a host of performers, including Burl Ives, Gene Autry, the Golden Gate Quartet, Los Panchos, Eddie [sic] Arnold, and a variety of square dance bands, one can hear folk music as it merges with our own popular music." The early recordings of old-time and black music occupied a particularly complex niche within the genre. Folkways Records' unique packaging of selections from Harry Smith's extensive collection of rare 78s into the three-album, six-disk *Anthology of American Folk Music* proved particularly influential. This eclectic sampling of late 1920s and early 1930s recordings, with extensive, heavily illustrated notes, introduced a large new audience to the Carter Family, Clarence Ashley, Buell Kazee, Furry Lewis, Mississippi John Hurt, and Blind Lemon Jefferson—many of whom still survived, often in rural obscurity. One *New York Times* article noted the compilation's importance "in what it reveals about American popular music before it became so standardized by coast-to-coast radio programs, nationally distributed talking pictures, and phonograph releases that blanket the country." Smith's collection would have a prolonged musical impact.[58]

The ballad singers Josef Marais and Miranda continued to be popular, and some of Marais's songs were recorded by such singers as Jo Stafford and Doris Day. "The vogue of hillbilly and 'country' tunes may have something to do with Marais' new popularity with the jukebox trade," a *Time* article noted, referring to his music as "South African Country." In mid-1953 the music historian Sigmund Spaeth attempted to capture the scope of the current folk revival in *Theatre Arts* magazine. He preferred the authentic songs, such as "On Top of Old Smoky," and was an admirer of Burl Ives. "It took the Columbia [Records] people a long time to discover the commercial value of this fat man's singing," he quipped, but "Burl Ives must today be considered the high priest of real American folk music interpretation." Spaeth also relished the evident authenticity of Bob Atcher, Susan Reed, and Harry Belafonte, while sarcastically critiquing the "purveyors of pseudo folk music," such as country performers Jimmie Rodgers (long dead), Hank Snow, and Eddy Arnold. "It all adds up to the fact that America is now fully cognizant of its heritage of folk music," Spaeth summed up, "the indigenous realities as well as the adaptations and imitations. It can well be left to the whirling discs to decide upon the permanent survival of the fittest."[59]

Oscar Brand tackled the thorny question of "authentic" folk music in an article in the *Saturday Review of Literature*, covering new record releases by John Jacob Niles and the Canadian performer Alan Mills. For Brand, no slouch at shaping and rewriting older songs, what counted was "the artistic merits of the song and the performance." Many singers composed new folk songs, such as Niles's "Black Is the Color of My True Love's Hair" and "Venezuela," or rewrote others formerly in the public domain. Despite Niles's "weird, hoarse falsetto," Brand welcomed him, Mills, and other contemporary performers because "as they sing the new songs and refashion the old they support the practice of balladry as a living, breathing art," rather than clinging to "frozen folk songs."[60]

From his perch as head of the Folklore Section at the Library of Congress, Duncan Emrich replied that older folksongs were hardly "frozen," but always in flux, while "an excellent entertainer such as Burl Ives blankets America with his version of a 'Lolly Toodum' or 'Blue Tail Fly,' in effect 'standardizing' the songs so that 'incorrectness' are pointed out to other singers, both on the folk and popular levels." Emrich faulted Brand for neither differentiating between "folksingers" and the "singer of folk songs" nor recognizing that a song had to circulate among the folk before it could legitimately be called a folk song. This debate over authenticity and creativity, long brewing, within a few years would reach a fevered pitch.[61]

Pete Seeger had thought long and hard about how to define a folksinger and folk music. He explained himself in early 1953 to Ray Lawless, who was compiling a folk music handbook:

> I am honored by your interest, but must emphatically disclaim the title "authentic American folksinger." First, while I am a singer of folk songs, I am not a folksinger in the musicological or anthropological sense of the term: a member of a folk

community who performs for his neighbors and friends. Rather, as a student unusually fortunate in hearing many kinds of music, and fortunate also in other
aspects of education, I picked on this particular branch of our culture as the one
in which I was most deeply interested in participating.

Further, the term "authentic" is so debated as to be almost meaningless without
elaborate definition. I am authentically Pete Seeger when I sing, but my singing
betrays many influences of sophistication foreign to the folksingers from whom I
have learned. I will say this: that I believe strongly in the value of maintaining an
idiom, a tradition, in its strength and homogeneity (others would say "purity"
but this term, too, is misused).

Seeger more or less held to this view over the musical evolution of several
decades. But others had difficulties in making such distinctions. Cisco Houston
boasted that he was "referred to many times as one of America's most authentic
folk artists," yet readily admitted he had recorded with Gordin Jenkins and
other orchestra leaders for Decca: "I did record material with folk flavor, several
of which were my own compositions based on old folk songs."[62]

Mid-Decade

As *Sing Out!* limped into its fourth year, editor Silber continued to rail against
"this atmosphere of fear and suspicion, [when] all free cultural expression is
stifled. Honest expression of the people can reach out only through a few
harassed channels." With a strong spirit but a weak bank account, following
another four- or five-month publishing hiatus the magazine emerged as a substantial thirty-two-page quarterly in late 1954, a format that survived for many
years. Pete Seeger announced his permanent return in his new "Johnny Appleseed" column, dedicated to "the thousands of boys and girls who today are
using their guitars and their songs to plant the seeds of a better tomorrow in
the homes across our land. . . . For if the radio, the press, and all the large
channels of mass communication are closed to their songs of freedom, friendship and peace, they must go from house to house, from school and camp to
church and clambake"—a fitting description of Pete's own peripatetic activities
as the blacklist shut him out of commercial establishments. He joined Sonny
Terry, Leon Bibb, Jack Gilford and others for a National Lawyers Guild concert
in New York in early 1953; a year later he appeared with a similar group at
the "Lift Every Voice" concert against discrimination at the Manhattan Center,
sponsored by the Bronx County American Labor Party.[63]

The advent of ten-inch and twelve-inch LPs seemed to promise added scope
for reaching a growing market, particularly among college youth, and as commercial and political folk music struggled to survive, a few visionaries began
in limited ways to shape and promote the music. Jac Holzman initiated Elektra
Records in 1950 while a student at St. John's College in Annapolis, Maryland.

Growing up in New York City with an early interest in electronics and recorded sound, in college he discovered Lead Belly and Guthrie as well as old blues records. He first recorded a fellow student, Glenn Yarbrough, and after dropping out of St. John's he moved to Greenwich Village and began hanging around Peter Carbone's Village String Shop, along with other folk addicts. Concerned with quality as well as documentation, and aware of the dearth of competition (except for Folkways), he launched his small recording enterprise and the Record Loft on West 10th Street, a shop specializing in folk and Baroque records. The Record Loft's mail order catalog listed a range of recordings from Folkways, Mercury, and Decca, as well as Elektra. Within a year he had issued ten-inch albums by Jean Ritchie and Frank Warner, followed by Shep Ginandes's *British Traditional Ballads in America, Voices of Haiti, Turkish and Spanish Folksongs, Mexican Folksongs,* and others by Hally Wood, Cynthia Gooding, Sonny Terry, and Oscar Brand. Tom Paley's *Folk Songs from the Southern Appalachian Mountains* proved highly influential, a rare early recording in the old-time style by a northern urban performer. Jean Ritchie, born in Viper, Kentucky, and steeped in local songs, recorded her mountain dulcimer music for Holzman and spent a year in the British Isles, performing and collecting songs.[64]

The first Elektra album to make a profit appeared in 1953, but the company did not break even until 1956; Holzman kept costs to a minimum, usually recording people in their homes and apartments. He managed the Record Loft until 1954, when he began to devote all of his time to the label, issuing eleven albums that year and the first sampler album. Holzman initially marketed the records through national distributors, then established his own sales network. Each early album contained a pamphlet with song lyrics to help the listeners sing along. "Now the booklet also had one other major advantage," he later said. "I would put an outlandish price on the book, never intending to sell it. But in calculating the Federal Excise Tax I could deduct that from the price of the album and calculate my Federal Excise Tax on the lower base. But that was secondary. I found that although I was inclined artistically to do it because I really felt it was the most complete package, I found a way of making it work financially as well." Moe Asch had included booklets in his Disc and Folkways albums, but Holzman insists he did not borrow the idea from his friendly rival. Besides, unlike Folkways, he also added extensive notes to the back of the album covers, an art soon perfected by Kenneth Goldstein on the hundreds of folk albums he produced.[65]

As Elektra struggled to stay alive and supply the small folk market, Folkways continued with a steady stream of albums, oblivious to market concerns. "Folkways has been the outstanding manufacturer of folk-music recordings in the long-playing era," the *New York Times* announced in early 1954. The recent release of *Leadbelly's Last Sessions,* ninety-four selections on four records, established a high standard that was "sure to be historic." Frederic Ramsey explained to

High Fidelity Magazine's readers how he had managed to capture so much of Lead Belly's vast repertoire in late 1948, thanks to the recent invention of recording tape. With the success two years later of the Weavers' "Irene," "there was a flurry of interest among all the companies who had neglected Leadbelly. Several wanted to bring out part, or some of the material that Leadbelly had recorded on tape, but not one of the major companies cared to preserve the sequence which is so vital a part of the feeling of these recordings." Only Moe Asch, scorning profits, finally had the inclination. In addition to his recording, Jac Holzman inaugurated the "Folk Lore / Folk Song" department in the *Record Changer*, essentially a jazz magazine edited by Bill Grauer and Orrin Keepnews of Riverside Records, with a survey of Folkways's *Leadbelly's Legacy* series and previous recordings for Asch, Disc, Columbia, and Musicraft.[66]

By mid-decade, folk music was still searching for a larger audience and greater recognition. Charismatic performers, an increasing youth market, eclectic styles and themes, the waning Red Scare—all combined to boost folk music's commercial potential and cultural influence. Concluding his survey of the story of American folk song, published in 1955, Russell Ames optimistically argued that there "has recently been a considerable revival of good folk singing in the cities among lovers of the arts, students, young trade unionists, and others, providing new artists and new audiences for the singing of old and new songs. . . . Perhaps 'folk' song will not long be an accurate name for the roving, changing, people's songs of the atomic age. But if we listen for what is honest, truthful, and human in the songs being made today, we need not worry much about the name we attach to them."[67]

4

Stirrings of the Revival, 1955–1957

In late 1954 the classical composer Roy Harris, who had arranged "Folksong Symphony 1940," drawing on a range of native folk sources and classical models, gave *House and Garden*'s mostly suburban, female readers a short course in folk music. He tried to differentiate between real folk songs, hillbilly jingles, and Broadway hit tunes; the latter deserved praise, he said, and might even be considered urban folk songs, but he dismissed the Grand Ole Opry, "some of the poorest music that ever entered human ears and yet it seems to give pleasure to many people." Preferring the "genuine folk song," he lamented that "today the air waves are flooded with commercial versions of old folk tunes set to June-moon-swoon rhymes, sung by confection-like voices accompanied by slick bands." Harris approached folk music with an elevated musical aesthetic, combined with cultural nativism, even patriotism. He made no mention of folk music's past left-wing connections, urban or otherwise. Harris's version of folk music, suitable for his proper *House and Garden* audience, hardly foresaw its upsurge of popularity just over the horizon. The few years before the Kingston Trio's leap into musical stardom in 1958 witnessed considerable ferment in folk circles.[1]

Stirrings of a popular folk revival at mid-decade could be readily discerned, particularly in California. Stan Wilson, for one, demonstrated folk music's infectious possibilities. Born in Oakland, California, in 1922, he moved to Berkeley as a child. Soon after the war—having survived kamikaze attacks on his merchant marine ship—he began playing a folk guitar, heavily influenced by the blues of Josh White, though he also picked up ballads and folk songs from Richard Dyer-Bennet and other concert performers. He started professionally at the Black Hawk in San Francisco, a popular jazz nightclub, and soon moved to the new hungry i in the North Beach neighborhood.

Enrico Banducci had opened the hungry i (the "i" standing for "id") at 149 Columbus Street in 1949 as a hangout for actors and other artists, with informal shows on Sundays. Starting with Wilson in 1952, however, the eighty-two-seat venue began nightly entertainment. (Banducci also co-owned the Purple Onion across the street, which initially attracted the hungry i's overflow crowd after opening in 1953.) In 1954 Banducci moved into larger quarters around the corner at 599 Jackson Street, and the hungry i, now with a regular liquor license and seating over four hundred, became the city's favorite nightspot for folk music and topical comics. Wilson continued to attract large crowds for a few years, often sharing the bill with the comic Mort Sahl. The first of his numerous albums appeared in 1953 on local Cavalier Records, with a smattering of folk, blues and calypso tunes.

Wilson spearheaded the folk revival in San Francisco, which quickly attracted a range of styles and talents. Odetta Felious first traveled to San Francisco with a stage production of "Finian's Rainbow." There she reconnected with her school friend Jo Mapes. They mostly hung around the Vesuvios bar and began playing folk music with Wilson and Nan Fowler. After a brief return to Los Angeles, where she improved her guitar playing, Odetta came back for a longer stay and Jo talked Banducci into letting her perform at the hungry i. She temporarily filled in on Wilson's night off, and after she moved to the tiny Tin Angel she became an immediate hit. She had a brief stint at the glamorous Blue Angel in New York, then returned to the Tin Angel for another year, through 1953 and into 1954, when she recorded her first album with Larry Mohr for Fantasy.

In 1953 Barbara Dane (an adopted surname after her divorce from Rolf Cahn), who briefly had her own folk music show on San Francisco television in 1950, Folksville USA, formed the Gateway Singers with Lou Gottlieb, Jimmy Wood and Jerry Walter, friends from the California Labor School. They were a clone of the Weavers, with Gottlieb trying to copy exactly their musical arrangements. The quartet performed for labor unions, house parties, anywhere they could find an audience. Gottlieb was the perfectionist leader, while Dane opted for a looser style. One day Gottlieb and Walter, both Communist party members, met with Dane to tell her that the party had ordered them to replace her because Cahn had earlier been expelled. Though she was now divorced from Cahn, she was nonetheless forced out. Searching for a black woman to replace Barbara, they first auditioned Odetta, then hired Elmerlee Thomas, on Dane's suggestion. Now integrated, and ready for the expected commercial success, they wheedled Banducci into letting them perform at the hungry i on

Monday nights, not long after his move to larger quarters. Combining Left politics and strong commercial aspirations, the Gateway Singers symbolized the increasingly contrary impulses of the revival.

The quartet's humor, musical skills and creative spirit attracted growing crowds, and they quickly found themselves performing six and then seven nights a week, through 1955 and 1956. They sprinkled their sets with sprightly songs by Malvina Reynolds, the Los Angeles People's Songster who had moved to Berkeley in the early 1950s. Travis Edmondson soon took Jimmy Wood's place on guitar, and during their second year at the hungry i, Decca Records (previously the Weavers' recording company and for this reason Lou's choice over Capitol) released their debut album, *Puttin' on the Style*, with added musical accompaniment by a small jazz combo. Although Decca had dropped the Weavers a few years earlier, the company retained its interest in folk music, releasing albums by Burl Ives and Sam Hinton. In a glowing review of the Gateway Singers, the *San Francisco Chronicle* music critic Ralph Gleason reminded local readers that the group "have been playing at the hungry i for so long that older settlers have begun to confuse their beginnings with the Gold Rush or the coming of the first windjammer." The local favorites "have been given an impressive accolade—their song 'Puttin' on the Style' is going to be made into a beer commercial with the Gateways singing it. Aside from selling a million records, this is the ultimate in recognition in the world of popular music."[2]

Gottlieb left the Gateway Singers in the summer of 1957 to return to his graduate studies in Berkeley and was replaced by Ernie Lieberman (now Ernie Shelton for political reasons). "They are certainly as good as and probably better than ever before," Jim Walls wrote in the *Chronicle* in March 1958. Combining Left politics, Weavers-like musical style, clever semitraditional and topical lyrics, and careful attention to timing and harmony, the Gateway Singers managed to shape and focus urban folk music at mid-decade.[3]

What about Rock and Roll?

"Our music, like our other national products, had been frozen by the War," Jeff Greenfield remembered. "By midcentury, the tastes of young Americans were in kind the same as their parents in the 1930s. *Billboard*, the music industry's paper of record, had polled America's kids in 1951: they liked the Mills Brothers, the Ink Spots, the Ames Brothers, Bing Crosby and Perry Como, Stan Kenton and Ray Anthony and Les Brown. Television was pulling people away from their phonographs and radios, and the record business was losing 10 percent of its business every year. Music did not seem to matter." Then rock and roll—the sound from "the hidden other world of the country: in the heart of black America"—hit big. Black groups began selling in white markets, while the record companies increasingly issued white cover versions since musical arrangements had no copyright protection. Technological and commercial changes—particularly the unbreakable vinyl 45-rpm record, the flood of transistor radios from Japan, the sudden appearance of many small, independent record companies, and the increase in local AM radio stations—facilitated the spread of pop music.[4]

Although the bulk of the baby boom generation would not reach adolescence until the 1960s, a sizable youth market existed in the mid-1950s, shaping the expanding consumer culture. Distinctive teen magazines such as Dig and Teen began appearing in 1955. Elvis Presley released his first single for Sun Records in 1954, and the next year moved to RCA Victor, marking the commercial acceptance and explosion of rock and roll. The barriers between black and white music, long maintained by marketing strategies and audience segmentation, were collapsing.[5]

A backlash against the escalating youth culture quickly developed; the assault was both aesthetic and moral, with racial overtones. In mid-1950s America the nuclear family was seen as the bedrock of democracy and capitalism, freedom and prosperity, security and stability, in contrast to Communist tyranny and collectivism. Yet youth—the heart of the family and hope of the future—were seemingly running wild. There was considerable alarm. "The accusation [was] that rock and roll was obscene," Jeff Greenfield recalls, "a menace to the morals of the young. Part of the reason for this sense was the source of the music: niggertown, the other side of the world, where men went to buy forbidden pleasures. Part of the feeling was in the sound of the music: raw, frenetic, basic. Part of it was the fact that, on occasion, rhythm and blues music was pretty strong stuff." Reaction mounted on diverse fronts. First songs came under fire, then live rock shows, with the deejay and promoter Alan Freed heading the list of degenerates.[6]

While rock and roll appealed mostly to adolescents, their parents and older siblings became increasingly attracted to folk music. Generally not danceable, folk music represented a political and/or aesthetic sensibility, a search for understanding amid the commercial clatter of electric guitars, raucous lyrics and gyrating performers; it linked past to present and commented on current social, cultural and political matters. The protagonist Sonny in Dan Wakefield's novel Going All the Way (set in Indianapolis in the mid-1950s), accompanying his friend Gunner to a party, heard "a record of a guy singing and playing the guitar, but it wasn't hillbilly music exactly. It sounded to Sonny more like old English folk songs but it was about America. Something about This land is your land, and it's my land. . . . The words seemed a little communistic." Noticing scattered about the apartment "those little egghead weeklies that were printed on rough paper and didn't have any pictures on the covers just names of articles," he feared that "maybe the whole place was a secret communist cell; with the magazines and the folk music and everything."[7]

In Marge Piercy's novel Braided Lives, the college student Jill was relieved to hear folk music at a party, the "only music actually sung and played in our peer group. Pop music is crooners soggily serenading our parents. White rock music belongs to the high-school crowd none of us were in with. Black music I knew only because I lived in a partly Black neighborhood. We think folk music is real, gritty, authentic. We like songs about old labor struggles." Folk music held the promise of solace and intrigue, romance and adventure, history and maturity, anything but establishment politics, suburban life and teenage hijinks.[8]

Calypso

"Folk songs are the articulated expression of the experiences of a people (a nation)," Burl Ives argued in Variety in early 1955. "These songs are a shared heritage, and when the people of a country can sing of these things together, it can only strengthen their national bonds." This seemed the central core of folk music's importance, illustrated in the repertoires of Ives, Josh White, John Jacob Niles and Richard Dyer-Bennet. The common wisdom dictated that folk music had native roots, connecting to a real or mythical rural past. One strand of mid-1950s folk music, however, violated these parameters, and its chief exponent established a new performance style that transcended traditional expectations.[9]

Born in New York in 1927, Harry Belafonte spent part of his childhood in his mother's native Jamaica, then returned to finish school and serve in the navy during World War II. After various odd jobs and short stints as an actor and singer, he studied and collected folk songs, and opened at the Village Vanguard in late 1951. While listening to Belafonte in an audition singing "Take This Hammer," Vanguard owner Max Gordon thought, "Harry's no Leadbelly, no prisoner swinging a hammer on a chain gang down in Georgia." Next, doing a calypso number, "left arm uplifted, right hand on navel, Belafonte moved his hips as if he were dancing with some imaginary broad. I hate a phony Caribbean accent," Gordon recalled. "I've had the real thing at the Vanguard—Calypso singers from Trinidad: the Lion, Atilla the Hun, King Radio, Macbeth the Great. What the hell am I going to do with a phony Caribbean accent?" Yet upon hearing "The Banana Boat Song"—though annoyed that Harry did not play the guitar but was accompanied by a piano—Gordon hired him. Following a successful run of fourteen weeks, Belafonte moved to the Blue Angel for four months. He promptly signed a record contract with RCA Victor, which finally released "Mark Twain" and Other Folk Favorites in 1954. The previous year he had followed Josh White into the posh Black Orchid in Chicago, and proved he could equal the master's drawing power. His initial acting foray in Hollywood resulted in the lackluster, little-seen Bright Road (1953);

although a starring role in *Carmen Jones* (1954) proved more rewarding, his film career faltered. Hollywood, hardly in the vanguard of the civil rights movement, had few roles for strong black men, preferring the muted image of Sidney Poitier, Belafonte's closest friend.[10]

A reporter for *Down Beat* explained that Belafonte was not a traditional folk singer: "Belafonte is a native New Yorker, the possessor of a not-large but extremely flexible voice and a flair for theatre . . . a guy who collaborates with others to revamp different folk tunes." Still, he was usually termed a folksinger. "Mr. Belafonte is a self-made folk singer," Howard Taubman explained in his review of the Broadway production of John Murray Anderson's *Almanac*. "When he sings 'Mark Twain,' he makes you feel the weight of the Mississippi riverman's labor as well as the struggle of the human personality to dominate it. When he does something simple, moving and familiar like 'Shenandoah' he gives it the true dignity of a great folk song." Not exactly authentic, yet Belafonte gave the songs the feel of authenticity. He toured the country in "Three for Tonight," co-starring with the dancers Marge and Gower Champion, and the CBS television version of the show on June 23, 1955, brought him before a national audience. Belafonte's popularity was based on various factors, including his sexual allure, not usually considered an aspect of folk's attraction. Following a wildly enthusiastic reception at New York's Lewisohn Stadium, he was warned, "Get scarce, kid, the guards can't hold back that mob of girls much longer." *Ebony* gushed with racial pride, remarking that Belafonte "began playing chi-chi night clubs where Negroes had never performed before" and that "he fights hate with song, tries through the media of music and drama to show that the Negro is a 'proud, creative human being who wants recognition on his merit alone.' "[11]

Belafonte adapted various musical genres, particularly calypso, first developed among former slaves and other Creoles in Port of Spain, Trinidad, as part of Carnivals in the late nineteenth century. A particular style developed before World War II, which told stories, conveyed news, and was led by chantwells, or singers, such as Atilla the Hun, the Roaring Lion, and Lord Invader. Some calypso stars had begun performing and recording in New York during the 1930s. In 1944 the Andrews Sisters had a surprise runaway hit with "Rum and Coca-Cola," written by Lord Invader and brought back from Trinidad by comedian Morey Amsterdam. By the early 1950s the Duke of Iron and Sir Lancelot had gained a wide following, particularly in New York, Miami and California, and they heavily influenced such eclectic singers as Stan Wilson and Belafonte.[12]

In 1956 RCA Victor released Belafonte's *Calypso*, an album recorded some months earlier and based on his television show "Holiday in Trinidad"; it included "Day-O" (aka "The Banana Boat Song"), "Jamaica Farewell," "Man Smart," and eight others from the singer's well-developed West Indian repertoire. Irving Burgie, better known as Lord Burgess, had written most of the songs, drawing on various folk sources. The album topped the charts for a year and a half. It was not his first album success—"Mark Twain" had reached number three in early 1956, and Belafonte became number one for six weeks during the spring—but Calypso remained number one for eight months and sold over a million and a half copies. Then An Evening with Belafonte almost made the top in April 1957. Even more impressive, his single of "Day-O" hit number five in early 1957 and stayed in the top one hundred for twenty weeks. Belafonte's albums continued to make the charts into the mid-1960s.[13]

While Belafonte soon became the King of Calypso, his recording of "Day-O" joined a crowded field, and was not even the first big seller. That honor went to the Tarriers, whose version of the "Banana Boat Song" on the tiny Glory label appeared on the charts in late December 1956, hitting number six, a few weeks before Belafonte's. Sarah Vaughn, the Fontaine Sisters, and Steve Lawrence also had somewhat successful covers, and satirist Stan Freberg managed to reach number forty-three with his humorous version in midyear.

The interracial Tarriers, composed of Alan Arkin, Erik Darling, and Bob Carey, had a simultaneous hit backing Vince Martin on "Cindy, Oh, Cindy" (written by Burt D'Lugoff and Bob Nemiroff, husband of playwright Lorraine Hansberry), also with a calypso beat and released by Glory. Alan Arkin, son of the People's Songster Dave Arkin, had grown up in Los Angeles, and studied acting, his first love, at Bennington College; Bob Carey, the black member of the group, had a law degree but preferred music. Raised in upstate New York, Erik Darling grew up listening to jazz and the popular folk performers. Developing his skills on the guitar and banjo, by the early 1950s he started hanging around Washington Square in Greenwich Village on Sunday afternoons, picking and singing with regulars Roger Sprung, Tom Paley, Billy Faier, and Tom Gerasi. In 1954 he toured with the show "Musical America," and also recorded with Sprung and Carey as the Folksay Trio for Stinson Records. Strongly influenced by the Weavers, Darling envisioned a similar group and eventually formed the Tarriers.

Belafonte made some effort to dampen the calypso fad and to reinforce his career. "The present hysterical type of fervor for any melodies that even remotely resemble Calypso will wear out and drive it to premature obscurity," he wrote to the New York Mirror in May 1957. "I wish to be accepted strictly on my merits as an artist who sings songs of all the world, rather than be representative of any specific area—and certainly not as a symbol of a contrived craze." A flattering story in Life concluded: "A moody, quick-tempered man of 30, he steers his course between high principle and crass fame." A Look article emphasized his recent interracial marriage to the dancer Julie Robinson and his featured role opposite Joan Fontaine in the movie Island in the Sun. Indeed, racial issues always marked his public life; the Saturday Evening Post remarked that "he was acclaimed by white audiences long before he faced an all-Negro audience," although he "considers himself a representative of his people." Belafonte's ability to cross racial lines, even in the South as the civil rights movement heated up, persisted as a hallmark of his career.[14]

A few other calypso-style tunes became hits during the first half of 1957, including Belafonte's "Jamaica Farewell" (number seventeen) and "Mama Look-A Bubu" (number thirteen) and Rosemary Clooney's "Mangos" (number twenty-five). Exotic music obviously appealed to a middle-class society awash in bland entertainments and distractions. Terry Gilkyson's "Marianne" reached number five, and the Hilltoppers' cover managed a respectable eight. Cheesy magazines, one-hit wonders, quickly hit the newsstands, such as *Calypso Stars*, *Calypso Song Craze*, *Calypso Songs*, *Calypso: The Belafonte Story*, and *Calypso Album*, filled with stories about performers—Tarriers, Lord Flea, Lord Invader, the Talbot Brothers, Johnny Barracuda, Lady Calypso, and the like—and with selected songs. *Tommy Sands vs. Belafonte and Elvis* and *16: Elvis vs. Belafonte* deftly explored the contrived "Big Battle of 1957—Rock 'n' Roll vs. Calypso." A few movies joined the crowded field, such as *Calypso Heat Wave*, *Bop Girl Goes Calypso*, and *Calypso Joe*. But just as quickly as it had mushroomed, the calypso craze faded, as Belafonte had warned. The Tarriers continued to perform widely, even appearing on the *Ed Sullivan Show*, though they had no further hits.[15]

Skiffle

In mid-1956 an English skiffle performer named Lonnie Donegan made a splash on the U.S. charts with "Rock Island Line," borrowed from Lead Belly, which was number ten by June. Donegan's "Lost John" also skipped through the U.S. charts for a week in June. A passing commercial fad in the United States, skiffle persisted a bit longer in England, peaking in 1957, and it served as a springboard for many budding rock and roll bands (the Quarrymen, for example, a skiffle group with John Lennon and Paul McCartney, would become the Beatles). The left-wing *Sing* advertised "Studio Skiffle Night" at the Princess Louise club, with worksongs, ballads, blues, and union songs; the "Forty-Four" Skiffle & Folksong Club featured the John Hasted Skiffle and Folksong Group, with Hasted, *Sing*'s music editor, playing twelve-string guitar and banjo. Hasted readily admitted that "some skiffle groups make a dreadful noise; that many of the folksongs are badly interpreted; that some skiffle is indistinguishable from Rock 'n' roll." Drawing on American folk songs, black and white, skiffle groups added jazz stylings with drums, perhaps even a clarinet.[16]

Not particularly traditional folk, skiffle seemed to bubble up from below, a healthy sign of musical democracy in an age of crass commercialism. Hasted wrote in *Sing*, "Unlike the older skiffle groups, the new ones make no distinction between a rock 'n' roll number and a folk song, and I think this is only to be expected and is not a bad thing anyway." But he also complained that "the real music is being strangled in a welter of skiffle clothes, skiffle outfits (with specially designed washboards) and skiffle toilet rolls. Old music is being recomposed and the people who first made it (Leadbelly, Uncle Dave Macon, [Ken] Colyer) quietly forgotten. But the music behind the ballyhoo will survive."[17]

Perhaps skiffle's prime defender, Hasted tried to explain the music to Sing Out!'s readers in early 1957, in his piece "Don't Scoff at Skiffle": "For years, people had been battling to get youngsters to sing, and not just listen and jive to the pops. And now, there are Skiffle groups everywhere . . . The fact is, Skiffle is very easy to perform, much easier than instrumental Jazz." The enthusiastic Hasted stressed skiffle's democratic nature and lack of overt commercialism, which he assumed would lead to its continued popularity. But skiffle promptly waned. "Rock and Roll took over most of skiffle, and left the rest of us to merge into the new Folksong Movement," Hasted wrote in his autobiography. Somewhat of a passing fancy, popular as another exotic import, skiffle had slight impact in the United States. Its audience scarcely recognized its American roots, and it generated no domestic spawning of skiffle bands or styles. Soon enough, however, the music would double back over the Atlantic in a new form of rock and roll, a cross-pollination with significant musical, cultural, and economic consequences.[18]

Sing Out!

Settling into its new identity as a quarterly in early 1955, Sing Out! struggled against the popular musical tide, Editor Irwin Silber toned down the magazine's overt politics, but concerns about class and race still dominated his decisions, for he "always believed that political and topical songs were a fundamental part of our folksong heritage." In the fifth anniversary issue he boasted of the four hundred songs that had been published: "If our songs and articles have helped the American people in any way in their search for peace, in their defense of our democratic liberties, in enriching their lives with the best of our American song tradition, then we think that we have served our country—and our people—well." Seeger agreed and, as usual, remained outwardly optimistic. He announced in 1956, "The American folksong revival [is] in full force, with 500,000 guitars sold last year, and millions more having fun singing folk songs together."[19]

Essentially shut out by the commercial blacklist since the Weavers' demise, Seeger continually toured the country, appearing at summer camps, colleges, public schools, and private homes while turning out a steady stream of albums for Folkways Records. Silber's enthusiastic review of the Folkways reissue of Talking Union, with liner notes by the blacklisted historian Philip Foner, reminded readers of Seeger's earlier work with the Almanac Singers. Silber also praised the addition of seven new selections by Pete and the Song Swappers (a New York group including newcomers Tom Gerasi, Erik Darling, and Mary Travers).

In the same issue the editor attacked the House Un-American Activities Committee for calling Tony Kraber, Lee Hays, and Seeger to testify: "Never have
the specious charges of un-Americanism been more ridiculous."[20]

"Folk songs are making the Tin Pan Alley cash registers ring again," Silber
announced in early 1956. "Since the fabulous popularity of 'Sixteen Tons,' the
pop publishers are scouring the hills and libraries once again in search of American folk songs which can be turned into coin of the realm. Among the latest
releases making their 'hit parade' bid are Rock Island Line, John Henry, and
This Land Is Your Land." While normally leery of the profit motive and cau-
tioning that "commercial publishers and arrangers frequently distort both music
and words of these songs," Silber believed "this development of interest in folk
song must be heartily welcomed. Our American music can only be made health-
ier by it."[21]

In 1955 the Weavers reunited for a Christmas concert at Carnegie Hall. Since
their breakup, Ronnie Gilbert had moved to Los Angeles with her husband to
raise their infant daughter; Fred Hellerman had been studying musical theory
and harmony with Milt Okun and Bob DeCormier, and functioning as a music
producer-arranger-publisher; Lee Hays was writing ads and stories for *Ellery
Queen's Mystery Magazine*, while living with the blacklisted composer Earl Robinson
and his family in Brooklyn Heights. Harold Leventhal, the Weavers manager,
decided the time was politically and artistically ripe for a reunion concert—
and they could certainly use the money. Leventhal wanted to help his friends
and also challenge the blacklist. "During that whole period that it went on so
intensely with the Weavers, the Weavers were the only group, or single or
whatever, in the music business, that was hit by the blacklist," he recalled.
"Unlike the movies, there was nobody else. No bands were knocked out, no
singers, but the Weavers. Nobody in the music business came out in their
defense. Nobody."[22]

Turned down by his first choice, Town Hall, Leventhal rented the plush
Carnegie Hall, without giving the stuffy management many details; apparently
they had not heard of the Weavers. An instant sellout, the concert attracted a
combination of musical and political fans. "The air was charged as at few
concerts," music critic Robert Shelton wrote in 1960. "The fans had returned
in multitudes, and the group's electrical rapport with its admirers was fully
reestablished." Fortunately, Leventhal had the concert recorded. After a number
of refusals, Maynard Solomon, co-owner of Vanguard Records with his brother
Seymour, agreed to release the album, one of their first featuring folk music.
Fred Hellerman edited the tapes, emphasizing the concert's dynamism and
dropping its quieter moments. *The Weavers at Carnegie Hall* appeared in 1957 and
set the aesthetic standard for the folk revival. On the front cover of the album
was a photo of the group, in formal attire, and the back included a quote from
the *New York Times*: "They enchanted a capacity and wildly partisan audience.

And small wonder; they do their kind of repertoire to perfection with plenty of spirit and enthusiasm."[23]

Maynard and Seymour Solomon, borrowing $10,000 from their father, had launched Vanguard Records in 1950 as an elegant classical label which took full advantage of the length and fidelity of the new twelve-inch 33-rmp records. Seymour, a graduate of Julliard, was a classical music reviewer and radio commentator, and he and Maynard were sticklers for the finest sound quality. They also had left-wing inclinations. Before the Weavers' album they had already issued a few ten-inch recordings of folk music, including *Russian Folk Songs*, and at least two by bluesman Brother John Sellers. Vanguard would quickly develop into a premier folk label.[24]

Silber ardently welcomed the Weavers' triumphant return in *Sing Out!*'s fifth anniversary issue: "The reunion of The Weavers after a three-year absence shows just how much the American people have suffered from the cold war." Certainly, he suggested, "the political as well as the musical significance of the concert was implicitly understood." Silber had to swallow his pride and apologize for his earlier lack of enthusiasm, admitting it was now "possible to see how many of us (and this writer not the least) seriously underestimated both the artistic achievement and overall cultural impact of The Weavers during the period from 1949 to 1952 when their songs were on the lips of tens of millions of Americans." Perhaps success did not always imply a political sellout. "The isolation (all too often self-imposed) of the cultural left from the mainstream of American cultural expression was the cause of many such errors of judgement." In *Sing Out!*'s next issue, he wondered if Decca would consider issuing the concert's album: "Now that Tin Pan Alley has rediscovered American folk song, who will 'rediscover' American's finest folk song group? There's a lot of money in it for someone—and there's a lot of good music in it for all of us." Silber no longer connected Mammon with the devil, yet as his prophesy came true he would continually have second thoughts. The reunion concert would become the touchstone for the revival: attendance would be a badge of honor and the memory a prized possession.[25]

The Weavers commenced to tour—generally only on weekends—and they continued to record for Vanguard. They quickly gathered an enthusiastic following, including friends across the political spectrum. Reviewing a May 1956 Chicago concert, Seymour Raven reported in the rabidly conservative *Tribune*, "There is plain theatrical intent in their style of singing. Within this frame of reference there is no noticeable violence to 'authenticity.' " And he concluded: "There apparently is a large revival of folk song interest at the moment. The phenomenon is cyclical. Some earlier manifestations were accompanied not only by guitars, banjos, and the like, but grinding axes. This time it may be different."[26]

Popular interest in folk music seemed to be on the rise. Yet *Sing Out!* and its parent People's Artists continued to wallow in debt, and so the principals folded the latter in late 1956, a casualty of political malaise and newer folk interests. Besides, People's Artists had pretty much ceased to function as a booking agency. "As you can imagine," Pete wrote to the few surviving members on November 2, "this was not easy to decide. However, we came to the conclusion that the important function originally served by People's Artists since its inception in 1949 could best be carried forward in new ways." He argued that because of People's Songs and People's Artists, "there are today, many groups and individuals carrying forward the job of promoting and popularizing folk music."[27]

Counterattack, on the wane as the Red Scare wound down, found cause to rejoice in *Sing Out!*s troubles. After noting the passing of the Jefferson School and the recent demise of People's Artists, it observed: "On the cultural front, Communist dismantling crews were also hard at work. . . . A well-identified name is gotten rid of and the folk singers magazine can move forward without the embarrassment of a Red tag. A little re-tooling will be necessary; the Fall issue of Sing Out was cancelled, but a big, new Winter number was promised." Silber, Seeger, and Jerry Silverman assumed People's Artists's remaining assets, and on February 28, 1957, formed Sing Out Incorporated. Silber was hardly able to support a family, for neither he nor the rest of *Sing Out!*'s skeleton staff were paid a salary. (The magazine now had only about fifteen hundred subscribers.) He worked briefly for the *Daily Worker*, and as a promotional writer at Avon Books. A year later, Moe Asch became a silent partner when he invested enough to put the floundering magazine on its financial feet, just in time to reap the harvest of the coming folk boom. Silber was also hired by Asch to design advertising materials and Folkways album booklets, the job lasting until 1964; he worked after hours to edit *Sing Out!*[28]

Along with much of the old Left, Silber experienced considerable soul-searching as he tried to survive economically, politically, and intellectually. In early 1957 he candidly admitted to the folklorist Archie Green, a political maverick with a deep-rooted anticommunist bent, "I have come to realize that I developed a number of glaring blind-spots in my political outlook (particularly concerning the Soviet Union and communism abroad) and that I also lost a certain amount of ability to think independently. This led to the kind of one-sidedness and sectarian, arbitrary judgements which you have referred to on occasion." At year's end, he pointed out to Green that *Sing Out!* had taken a sharp turn when it switched to a quarterly, reflecting a "modest, sounder political outlook," and the editorial page had been dropped, "thus removing from ourselves the temptation to issue the same kind of left-wing dogma for which we had achieved an unenviable reputation." Now, he said, "we have decided that only the most unusual and incredible circumstances should cause us to move out of the realm of musical concern—and that our comments on the rest of the world should be made only as a result of singing in the news." Not that the magazine would completely ignore political concerns. For example, the winter 1957 issue praised the Montgomery, Alabama, bus boycott, while stressing its use of civil rights songs.[29]

New York City

With its rich history of political and cultural activism, New York City proved a lush environment for the developing revival. Lou Gordon moved to Greenwich Village in 1953, where he already knew Jean Ritchie and Paddy Clancy. Paddy and Tom Clancy, Irish brothers who had arrived in the late 1940s, had rented the Cherry Lane Theater for their Sean O'Casey play "The Plow and the Stars," but were not making ends meet. Paddy convinced Gordon and Jean Ritchie's husband, George Pickow, to help pay the rent through staging midnight folk shows on the weekends following the play. Known as "Swapping Song Fair," the first show, on March 5, 1954, included Oscar Brand, Ritchie, Robin Roberts, Phil Raiguel, and Bernard Krainis trading songs from England, Ireland, Scotland, and the United States. Over the next few years the list of performers included Josh White, Richard Dyer-Bennet, Jo Mapes, Tom Paley, Frank Warner, Bob Gibson, Jack Elliott, Ed McCurdy, Guy Carawan, and the two Clancy brothers, soon joined from Ireland by their brother Liam and Tommy Makem.

Gordon calculated that it would not be difficult to fill a one-hundred-seat theater in the Village. The successful shows prompted a move the next year to the larger Circle-in-the Square, where Gordon worked with Harold Leventhal and also, briefly, Art D'Lugoff. Although a veteran of the Abraham Lincoln Brigade during the Spanish Civil War and a long-time labor organizer, Gordon tried not to inject politics into the shows. Despite these efforts, Cynthia Gooding, one of his first performers, objected to Guy Carawan's appearance on political grounds. "Perhaps you feel you should not judge these people," she wrote to Gordon in April 1954, "but a man who sings political songs for People's Artists—even though he says he doesn't like to—is either foolish or an opportunist, or really believes what he's singing. . . . I think you have done yourself and the Swapping Song Fair a great disservice, lowered the standards of what is, after all, an art, not a humanitarian endeavor and permitted what could have been a wholly admirable series to become far less than that." The loss of Gooding, with her expansive international repertoire, was troublesome, but did not doom the popular concerts.[30]

Swapping Song Fair's high point was a production of " 'Bound for Glory': A Musical Tribute to Woody Guthrie" in March 1956 at Pythian Hall, with over a thousand crowding the auditorium. Seeger, Earl Robinson, Lee Hays, Ed McCurdy, Robin Roberts, Reverend Gary Davis, the twin sisters Ellen and Irene Kossoy, and Jim Gavin supplied the music; Marge Mazia, Woody's former wife, and her dance group performed. Robinson and Hays did the narration from a script by Millard Lampell, crafted around a medley of Guthrie's songs. An ailing Guthrie appeared in the balcony, grey and wizened though still in his forties, and proudly raised his shaky fist when given the spotlight. The evening was a vivid symbol of the legacy of the Almanac Singers, People's Songs, and People's Artists—a potent brew of protest politics and vernacular folk styles.

The concert was originally Seeger's idea to raise some money for Guthrie, then languishing in the Brooklyn State Hospital. But the take exceeded expectations, and drew the attention of the IRS. So Leventhal, Seeger, and Gordon established the Woody Guthrie Children's Trust Fund to benefit the family. Guthrie soon checked himself out of the hospital, but he could barely function, Huntington's chorea increasingly limiting his motor skills, and he quickly wound up in Greystone Park Hospital in New Jersey, where he would remain for the next five years. Later in 1956 Folkways Records issued an album of his songs, Bound for Glory, interspersed with Will Geer reading from Guthrie's writings; the script from the show along with the songs was published as California to the New York Island.[31]

Guthrie became the spiritual and musical godfather of the budding revival, which came to life every Sunday afternoon from spring to fall in Washington Square in Greenwich Village, adjoining New York University. By the early 1950s these gatherings had become a standard feature of local social and musical life, despite occasional complaints from the neighborhood. The journalist and writer Dan Wakefield remembered the Square in his memoir, New York in the Fifties. He was reminiscing with a friend while sitting near the fountain, "where we used to go on Sundays to hear the folksingers and mingle with the crowd, which always included people we knew. It was a community scene, like people in a small town gathering for a concert, but instead of a brass band we had guitar players, and we sang along with them, telling Michael to row the boat ashore or proclaiming this land is your land, this land is my land."[32]

George Sprung, brother of the banjo player Roger, was originally a devotee of jazz and blues in the 1930s and drifted to folk music in 1946, though not for political reasons. He soon began going to Washington Square on Sunday afternoons; he also joined Pete Seeger's Good Neighbor Chorus and briefly worked for Stinson Records in the 1950s. Sprung held the park department's monthly permit for the Sunday folk gatherings for a few years until 1952, when Lionel Kilberg took over the responsibility. Initially a jazz musician, Kilberg couldn't play his clarinet in the Square, since the permit specified only stringed instruments. He modified a washtub bass and dubbed it the Brownie bass (named after his dog). Whoever carried the permit had to be present, since park officials did check to see if it was displayed, and so Kilberg became a weekly fixture and performer. In the mid-1950s he formed the Shanty Boys with Roger Sprung and Mike Cohen, one of the first northern bluegrass groups that appeared frequently in the Square and at concerts. Initially the permit allowed playing for only two hours, but Kilberg managed to have it expanded to four. For a few years during the winter months the Washington Square regulars moved indoors to the nearby Labor Temple, with a smaller turnout.

When Jo Mapes moved to New York from California in the mid-1950s, she dropped by the Square and found bluegrass groups, blues players, and protest songs. "It was a warm day in early spring and the fountain wasn't yet filled with water," she recalls, "just beer cans and bottles, and junk food wrappers. Assorted Village types spread out on the inner steps [of the fountain], dirty jeans rolled up, denim shirts opened to show bony pallor. Blood shot eyes squinted through dark glasses." Theodore Bikel began frequenting the Square soon after his arrival from England in late 1954. He wrote in his autobiography,

> One of the most important places at the time was Washington Square, preferably around the fountain in the center of the Square. Where else could young—or not so young—singers test their mettle in a public place? Sure, there were political rallies and sometimes a picket line or two. But those were few and they were, moreover, theme-oriented and did not lend themselves to languid folk ballads or rural country dances. Washington Square was an ideal location for folk music because there was a built-in audience of students. . . . No one played in the Square for any reason except the satisfaction of playing and the honing of musical skills in front of an audience.[33]

Occasionally friends would bring Guthrie to the Square, not to play but just to enjoy the scene and get away from his hospital room. With Guthrie too incapacitated to perform, Jack Elliott eagerly took his place. Born Elliott Adnopoz in Brooklyn, "Ramblin' Jack" had taken on the persona of Guthrie, his close friend since 1951, touring the United States and England in his stead. A *Cosmopolitan* article, with photos by George Pickow, recounted, "He often sings at impromptu socials held Sunday afternoons around the Square's fountain, where the entertainment may include anything from acrobatics to authentic Indian dances." After recording three songs for the early Elektra album *Bad Men, Heroes and Pirates*, recorded in Jac Holzman's bedroom on 10th Street in the Village, Elliott moved to England in 1955 and quickly cut an album arranged by Alan Lomax, *Woody Guthrie's Blues*. (He often performed with Derroll Adams, originally from Oregon, on his European travels.) Except for half a year in California in 1958, Elliott stayed in Europe until 1961, and he had trouble adjusting when he returned because the musical landscape in the United States had shifted considerably. (Curiously, while visiting Guthrie in the hospital the day after his reappearance, he met Bob Dylan, newly arrived in the Village, who had collected Elliot's Topic records and closely copied his style.) Elliott continued to tour and record for Prestige Records, remaining a vibrant musical presence, yet without the fame that would come to so many of his performing colleagues by the early 1960s.[34]

After performing in Washington Square, some would drift over to Allan Block's sandal shop, the hangout for the old-time string crowd. Arriving in New York from the University of Wisconsin in 1940, Block shipped out to India as a volunteer ambulance driver, then returned to the city and worked for People's Songs. He soon opened the sandal shop, which became a Village fixture for many years. At one point he led singing at Gabe Katz's studio on East 10th Street, attracting a fair crowd including Billy Faier and occasionally Tom Paley. A regular group soon frequented the shop. They kept alive a string-band tradition just making its northern impact. John Sebastian, later of the Loving Spoonful, lived in the Village as a teenager and hung around the shop on Sunday evenings playing his harmonica.

Tiny Robinson's apartment on the Lower East Side served as another magnet, particularly for older black musicians. Tiny, a seamstress and the niece of Lead Belly, lived downstairs from Martha, Lead Belly's widow, and welcomed their old and new friends including Reverend Gary Davis, Sonny Terry, Brownie McGhee, and John Lee Hooker. Theo Bikel's apartment was another meeting ground for the city's musicians, including the Clancy Brothers, Cynthia Gooding, and Dov Seltzer and his wife Geula Gill of the popular Israeli trio Oranim Zabar.[35]

A counterculture was developing by the mid-1950s, particularly in the Village, centered on modern jazz, abstract art, and the Beat writers. Between the Beat and folk worlds there was some surprising overlap. For example, John Cohen, David Amram, the Clancy Brothers, Mary Travers, Harry Smith, and Izzy Young bridged the two groups. New York's avant-garde political and musical cultures rubbed shoulders, yet generally retained their distinct audiences, styles, politics, and contexts. "The Beatniks hated folk music," according to Dave Van Ronk, who lived in the Village.

> The real Beats liked cool jazz, bebop, and hard drugs, and the folkniks would sit around on the floor and sing songs of the oppressed masses. When a folk singer would take the stage between two Beat poets, all the fingerpoppin' mamas and daddies would do everything but hold their noses. And when the Beat poet would get up and begin to rant, all the folk fans in the house would do likewise. But in the eye of the media, folk music and Beatniks were one and the same. So a lot of people came to the Village to see the Beatniks and they ended up seeing folk music.[36]

Concerts abounded in the mid-1950s, yet there were no strictly folk venues. Nightclubs like the Village Vanguard still booked the more expensive acts, but there was no equivalent to San Francisco's hungry i. Art D'Lugoff had begun staging folk concerts at the Circle-in-the Square Theatre in November 1955, and after a year switched to the Actor's Playhouse, a prelude to launching the Village Gate in 1958, where he opened with Pete Seeger, followed by Earl Robinson. "I was one of the first folk impresarios in the U.S.," said D'Lugoff.

"I personally liked the music, and I thought it would be good commercially. I first heard it at political rallies, and hootenannies at people's houses. I felt the public was looking for some alternative to the bland music of the time. Jazz had become cool—there was no dancing with it, the melody had gone out of it." Despite these feelings, he loved and would feature jazz at the Gate, along with comedians, who were generally cheaper than the big-name folk performers at the time.[37]

If folk music was not welcomed in the clubs and coffeehouses, it found a more congenial atmosphere among a smattering of New York recording companies. By 1955 or so, Folkways, Stinson, Elektra, and an assortment of offbeat labels had established themselves in the small folk market, though they were hardly a challenge to RCA Victor's and Decca's long-standing domination of the commercial marketplace. The Clancy Brothers, particularly Paddy, with help from Diane Hamilton (a member of the wealthy Guggenheim family and active in the Country Dance Society), initiated Tradition Records in 1956 as an outlet for themselves and their friends, including Paul Clayton and Jean Ritchie. Riverside Records also recorded folk music. Bill Grauer and Orrin Keepnews started it as a jazz label in 1953, reissuing Fats Waller, Ma Rainey, and Louis Armstrong, and recording Thelonious Monk and Dixieland bands. Keepnews believed "that there was obviously a substantial element of what can fairly be described as folk music in traditional jazz and in the linkage between jazz and blues, and so there was a kinship." Moreover, he said, "these are both kinds of records that appeal to a small specialized highly dedicated audience. It's not the same, there's not that much audience overlap, but it's the same kind of audience." Though Keepnews had a chance to issue Pete Seeger albums, he was advised by the popular radio announcer Ben Grauer, his partner's cousin, that it would be commercial suicide, and so refused.[38]

Kenneth Goldstein sparked Riverside's move into folk recordings. Born in Brooklyn in 1927, Goldstein entered City College of New York after an army stint and following graduation worked for Fairfield Publications doing market research and at the Newspaper Guild, all the while plunging into folklore and folk music. He developed an encyclopedic musical knowledge along with an elaborate record collection. Beginning in 1951 with Bob Harris's Stinson Records, Goldstein produced and edited reissues, including extensive notes, of Guthrie, Seeger, Ives, and Dyer-Bennet. He next produced Patrick Galvin, A. L. Lloyd, and Ewan MacColl performing Irish and English folk material, using his transatlantic connection with the British Workers Music Association. In 1955 Goldstein began developing Riverside's Folklore Series, starting with Ed McCurdy and soon including Paul Clayton, Oscar Brand, Bob Gibson, Jean Ritchie, and his established stable of British performers. He eventually produced over a hundred albums.

Goldstein quit Fairchild in 1956 and produced records full-time (about one a week), as well as selling and publishing folklore books. He had already been working for Holzman at Elektra and the Solomons at Vanguard, as well as Folkways and Tradition, and in the early 1960s would produce albums for Prestige. Before becoming a professor of folklore Goldstein was instrumental in shaping the folk aesthetic through the 1950s into the early 1960s, producing well over five hundred albums, all with detailed, scholarly notes. He provided the growing consumer market with a wide range of performers and styles— traditional and commercial, urban and rural, young and old, from North America and the British Isles. It was a remarkable and lasting achievement. Though not a collector of country disks, he early recorded Harry and Jeanie West for Stinson, which he believed to be "the first commercially issued record of . . . hillbilly stuff in the revival movement. . . . I really wasn't into it. But I thought I liked it and I thought that the people in the folksong movement and the revival would like hillbilly singers as well." He later recorded Bascom Lamar Lunsford and George Pegram at the Asheville folk festival.[39]

Goldstein also produced four volumes of The English and Scottish Popular Ballads (The Child Ballads) and one volume of Great British Ballads Not Included in the Child Collection, all sung by Ewan MacColl and A. L. Lloyd. "A major effort in the recording of balladry, Kenneth Goldstein's five-volume series for Riverside is indeed noble in purpose," William Jansen wrote in the Saturday Review. Quite esoteric, the series captured Goldstein's penchant for musical tradition and scholarship, his two great loves. "I really liked the revival," he told the folklorist Neil Rosenberg. "I always liked singers of folksongs as well as traditional singers." He felt an ethical responsibility to the record companies and the performers: "I saw the issue of the pragmatics and the business promotion of performers as being related to the end of furthering folk music and I was really gungho on promoting folk music." Combining his left-wing politics, scholarly bent, and musical sensibilities, Goldstein became one of the key figures behind the scenes.[40]

Folk record companies issued albums of international songs, ballads, bawdy songs, and songs about topical subjects. These fads hardly lasted beyond the 1950s, but for a few years they supplied an expanding college and adult market with lively, informative, and often humorous entertainment. The main focus was on ballads and songs from the British Isles—Goldstein's speciality—but a wide range of international folk songs, sung by Theo Bikel, Cynthia Gooding, Oranim Zabar, Marais and Miranda, and others appealed to those searching for international harmony and understanding, or to those just curious about the wider world and its music. Gooding early recorded Turkish and Spanish Folksongs for Elektra, closely followed by Mexican Folksongs, and Martha Schlamme issued German Folk Songs on Folkways. Albums of Israeli folksongs by Hillel and Aviva, Bikel, and Oranim Zabar sold well.

Ed McCurdy, a Canadian, was a key performer of the period who recorded prolifically after moving to New York in 1954. He was often accompanied by Erik Darling, one of a handful of accomplished session banjo players in New York, and by Alan Arkin on recorder. McCurdy turned out a series of albums with such titles as *Barroom Ballads, Blood, Booze 'N' Bones, Sin Songs, Pro and Con*, and he hit on a winning formula with the first *When Dalliance Was in Flower and Maidens Lost Their Heads* album for Elektra. Holzman and McCurdy dreamed up the idea in 1956 for an album of double-entendre Elizabethan songs, decorous yet titillating, with suitable covers showing some cleavage. After they shipped the record "all hell broke loose," Holzman recalls. "By that I mean that a couple of distributors felt they were a little on the bawdy side and didn't quite know whether they wanted to sell it or not. But it became a palpable hit on college campuses. And we sold a lot of them." The album's glossy cover featured "some nubile Playmates of the Month and some horny dallying dudes," among them Holzman and his partner Leonard Ripley in jerkin and tights. They issued three more albums before the well ran dry, and sold over a hundred thousand copies. A year earlier Goldstein had produced Will Holt's *Pills to Purge Melancholy*, based on Thomas D'Urfey's salty collection of "love" songs, *Wit and Mirth: Or Pills to Purge Melancholy*, published in 1719–20. Goldstein capitalized on similar sources a few years later for McCurdy's *Lyrica Erotica*.[41]

Drawing on a more contemporary legacy, Oscar Brand began a steady stream of *Bawdy Songs* albums in 1955, about ten in all, on the Audio Fidelity label. A walking musical encyclopedia, Brand had accumulated numerous bawdy songs but was unable to perform them on his radio show or in most concerts. "I remember a lot. And what I didn't remember I made up" he once explained. "Songs like 'The Four Prominent Bastards' I made into a song. 'The Bastard King of England' had been sung with different melodies. 'Blinded by Turds' was originally 'Blinded By Shit.' . . . I mean my contribution to American folklore consists of thousands of songs, rewritten or new." Whatever their source, the songs included in the first *Bawdy Songs and Backroom Ballads* album and its numerous successors made them popular in college dorms and teen bedrooms, offering a strong contrast to current pop songs, even controversial rock and roll lyrics, though Brand regretfully expurgated most of them. "What I did to the poor 'Bastard King of England' is unbelievable, because that I wrecked," he later conceded. "The chorus was, 'he was dirty and lousy and full of fleas and his terrible tool hung down to his knees, God bless the bastard king of England.' . . . So I wrote, 'he was dirty and lousy and full of fleas and he had his women by twos and threes.' . . . And unfortunately that's the version most people know."[42]

Brand also recorded popular song albums for Riverside, including *American Drinking Songs* and *G.I. American Army Songs*. Holzman wanted to issue a bawdy songs album on Elektra, but Brand felt obligated to Audio Fidelity. "My songs are fist songs," he explained, in contrast to Ed McCurdy's *Dalliance* albums; "his songs are wrist songs, they're slaps on the wrist. And my songs are a good punch in the nose. I say my songs, they're the songs of the people whom I knew. Hard driving people, farmers, truck drivers." A few years later Elektra issued Brand's album of U.S. Air Force songs, which sold well, then albums for the Marines, Army, Navy, skiers, boaters, and golfers, to name just a few. "Oscar could find these songs, or he and I, or he would write them or I'd sit down and write them," according to Holzman. "And we'd go out and record them and we'd sell enough of these things. We knocked them out in two days. I mean everybody knew the melody and Freddy Hellerman would wince but he'd take the money and he'd go into the studio and we'd do them." Perhaps not of the highest artistic quality, the albums kept Elektra in business into the early 1960s.[43]

Brand churned out his records while continuing his radio show and maintaining a wide-ranging performing career. He had little radio competition until George Lorrie (aka Levine) initiated "Folklore with Lorrie" on WBAI in 1957, one hour on Monday nights, with both records and live performers. Brand was the most prolific, but Paul Clayton, from New Bedford, Massachusetts, and steeped in folksong and folklore, also recorded a steady stream of albums, starting in 1954, for Tradition, Elektra, Folkways, Stinson, and Riverside. He mostly recorded traditional songs and ballads, including Bloody Ballads, Wanted for Murder, and Timber-r-r! Clayton joined the growing list of generally youthful performers who appealed to the expanding urban market.

Chicago and Points West

New York garnered the most media attention and remained the mecca for aspiring folkies, but colleges such as Oberlin provided willing, eager audiences. Joe Hickerson arrived at Oberlin from New Haven, Connecticut, in 1953; mainly a pop music fan, he was also familiar with the Weavers and other prominent folk performers. Grey Gables Co-Op, an eating club that attracted the campus folksinging crowd, became his hangout. He inherited from Steve Taller a folk record distribution service, selling Folkways, Elektra, and Stinson records on the campus, and he took over Taller's campus folk radio show. Seeger had appeared at Oberlin in February 1954, his first Midwestern small college performance following the blacklist; he would return each year, his audience swelling from about two hundred the first year to one thousand in 1957.

Hickerson's trips to New York included hanging around Washington Square on Sundays and hearing as much folk music as possible. He joined the Folksmiths at Oberlin, eight students who formed a singing group in late 1956; the next summer they traveled around the children's camps of New York and New England and also recorded for Folkways. Hickerson entered graduate school in folklore at Indiana University, where he formed the Settlers with fellow graduate students Bruce Buckley and Ellen Stekert. Bob Black—a mandolin player, alumnus of N.Y. Folksay and People's Songs and neighbor of Woody Guthrie in Coney Island—had begun graduate school at Indiana in 1954, and there he met Buckley and played on his local folklore television show. He also sold Folkways on campus. Eventually Hickerson worked out an arrangement to take over Black's business ordering from Folkways.

In the late 1950s folk activities mushroomed on campuses, attracting not just the politically active but also those who preferred a respite from rock and roll and pop music in general. Ronald Radosh, who had attended Elizabeth Irwin High School in Greenwich Village with Mary Travers, arrived at the University of Wisconsin and roomed for a while with Marshall Brickman and Eric Weissberg. He organized his friend Pete Seeger's first Wisconsin campus concert, sponsored by the Labor Youth League. Roz Baxandall remembers "these bearded men, many of them accomplished folksingers, several from New York City's Music and Art High School (Marshall Brickman, now of Woody Allen fame, Eric Weisberg [sic], who cut a few Weaverlike hit records, and Ronald Radosh, now a Cold Warrior, who played a mean banjo), and Bob Dylan, undiscovered at the time, who came down from Chicago and played with a harmonica around his neck, had hootenanies outside on the patio by the lake."[44]

After a slow start, the new Folk Arts Society organized an exchange with Moe Hirsch and Bob March at the University of Chicago, then brought Seeger back and sponsored a series of sings. Despite problems with the cautious university administration, there was a successful hoot featuring Guy Carawan, Brickman, and Weissberg. Radosh reported on the scene in *Caravan* in late 1958: "From the situation where nobody at the school either sang or wanted to hear folk artists, we now have appearances at the University by Pete Seeger, Odetta and Theo Bikel, all in one year."[45]

Growing up on the Lower East Side, Eric Weissberg had attended Camp Woodland with Radosh and gone to children's parties at Seeger's Greenwich Village apartment, hearing Guthrie and Lead Belly. A fan of bluegrass, he early picked up the banjo, and at Wisconsin in 1957 he hooked up with Brickman and Radosh. The three banjo players became active in the left-wing folk music club and played often on campus. Weissberg left after one year, along with fellow student John Herald, and returned to New York and the Julliard School of Music.

Albert Grossman and Les Brown's Gate of Horn in Chicago became the midwestern magnet for folk music. A Chicago native, Grossman had attended the new Roosevelt University, graduating in 1947 with a Bachelor of Science in commerce and going to work for the Chicago Housing Authority. In the mid-1950s Grossman reconnected with Brown, a college friend and fellow folk enthusiast. Brown realized Grossman was a bit unscrupulous, eager to make a buck, yet their mutual interest in folk music drew them together. Brown had started as a reporter for *Variety*, then moved to *Down Beat* in 1955–56, and he was open to a change when Grossman approached him with the idea of launching a club. They had just attended an exhilarating folk concert by Fleming Brown and Big Bill Broonzy, and so agreed to feature folk music. Brown recalls, "A certain kind of person went to those concerts that we didn't see at nightclubs and jazz clubs and other places like that. We thought that was a niche." Vaguely aware of the hungry i in San Francisco, they had no specific model in mind. Grossman suggested they call the club the Shingled Banjo, but Brown won out with the Gate of Horn, a reference from Virgil and T. S. Eliot. They rented the basement of the Rice Hotel, a Northside fleabag that had survived the great Chicago fire.[46]

Using their connections in Chicago, San Francisco, and New York, they opened in July 1956 with Robin Roberts, soon followed by Bob Gibson, who appeared for eleven straight months; then Big Bill Broonzy and Odetta. The next year they featured Theo Bikel, Jo Mapes, Peggy Seeger, Glenn Yarbrough, Shelly Berman, Frank Hamilton, and Martha Schlamme, with Gibson the club regular. Odetta had been singing around California, then got the call from Grossman and performed in October with Gibson, staying four months. "When I pulled up in a taxi cab in front of the Gate of Horn to do a sound check or whatever, there was standing Big Bill and Josh White, who had just finished there. And Josh White and Big Bill came just to make sure that their baby sister was going to be all right." She remembers Grossman as "a distant person, a friendly person, a brilliant mind, and impeccable taste"; he subsequently became her manager. Grossman had already convinced Bikel to appear, then introduced him to Odetta during a layover of Bikel's railroad sleeper car: "We sang for each other in my compartment—not an audition, exactly, but a mutual feeling out. We decided then and there that the two of us would share the bill at the Gate a few weeks later." And so a stable of performers was developed that would pack the house night after night.[47]

Les Brown quit his job at *Down Beat* and began managing the club despite sundry problems that increasingly grated on him. He protested Grossman's policy of paying Broonzy only $100 rather than the regular scale of $125 a night. "I said 'now why are you doing that?' And he answered, 'Because the black musicians have a different union scale, lower scale. . . . It's their fault, not ours.' " Brown also feared that the mob, ubiquitous in the entertainment industry, would intervene, and sure enough one day a man named Wally introduced himself as their consultant, for $100 a week, which he always collected. The mob had a jukebox delivered, but they refused to use it, explaining that folk clubs didn't need a jukebox; Wally finally had it removed. Wally also informed them that the "big hats want to come in and see the place. . . . So we arranged for them to come in on a slow night . . . [so] these Mafia types wouldn't scare the hell out of the college type clientele." They tipped well but "thought that we had something kind of weird here, strange." Then they asked Grossman and Brown to help them manage some troubled jazz clubs on Clark Street. They agreed to think about it, but Brown reminded Grossman, "We decided a long time ago when Wally came in here the first day, that that's as far as we're gonna go with these guys, you don't want to get mixed up with these guys."[48]

Brown began to have second thoughts about the folk music business. Besides mob interference, he also discovered drug and other problems with the staff and performers, particularly Bob Gibson, and after two years he decided to return to *Variety*. He agreed to sell his half of the club to Allan Ribback, who finally made a deal with Grossman. Brown left feeling cheated and betrayed— Grossman insisted on paying him less than the sum previously agreed on—and permanently ended their relationship.

The Gate of Horn dominated Chicago's folk landscape into the 1960s. The city had no central location for folk singers to congregate, no Greenwich Village or Washington Square, just scattered venues and local groupings, with little direct connection to the vibrant Southside blues scene. Radio station WFMT-FM became an important catalyst. Soon after its founding in 1953 the announcer Mike Nichols began a one-hour folk show on Saturday nights. For a brief period he featured live music, particularly the Willow Singers—Fleming Brown and his wife Jean, Betty Wills, and Bernie Asbell. The singer Gerry Breen met the bagpiper George Armstrong on the show, and they soon married and began an influential career together. After Nichols left, Norm Pellegrini and Ray Nordstrand replaced him, alternating weeks. They expanded the show, now named *The Midnight Special*, to two hours in 1956, and the station issued a monthly program guide including a local music calendar. Pellegrini and Nordstrand collected a large variety of folk and comedy records, supplying listeners with an increasing range of performers and styles as well as notices about local shows, events, and personalities.

Studs Terkel also had a show on WFMT, *Almanac*. A local media personality, actor, and alumnus of People's Songs, Terkel had long promoted folk music, in 1948 helping to initiate the touring show "I Come for to Sing," which appeared mostly on college campuses. First sponsored by the Renaissance Society at the University of Chicago, the show featured Win Stracke, Larry Long, and Big Bill Broonzy, with Terkel as narrator. A professional singer and actor and host of a popular Chicago children's television program, Stracke had also been active in People's Songs. Originally from Mississippi and Arkansas, Broonzy moved to Chicago in the early 1920s and recorded successfully into the 1930s, becoming a noted folk-bluesman. "I Come for to Sing" became established as the Monday night folk entertainment at the Blue Note, a jazz club, for over a year beginning in July 1952.

On his *Almanac* radio show, Terkel hosted a variety of visiting musicians, including Pete and Peggy Seeger, Marais and Miranda, Burl Ives, Mahalia Jackson, and Odetta. Listeners "have a rare opportunity to learn about folk music from many different points of view," Gerry Armstrong wrote in *Sing Out!* "It enables them to form a broader and more intelligent approach to their enjoyment of folk music by hearing the personal views and learning the backgrounds of the outstanding artists in the field." Through Terkel's *Almanac* and *The Midnight Special*, WFMT played a prominent role in shaping local musical tastes; reportedly, after Terkel played selections from the *Weavers at Carnegie Hall* on *The Midnight Special*, one record store sold over four hundred of the albums in one week.[49]

A separate music scene developed in Hyde Park around the University of Chicago. Moe Hirsch had grown up in New York, attended Camp Wo-Chi-Ca with Ernie Lieberman as his counselor, hung around the hootenannies in the later 1940s, and learned music from Tom Paley and Harry and Jeanie West. After traveling to Los Angeles in the summer of 1952, where he met Will Geer and Frank Hamilton, he entered the graduate mathematics program at the University of Chicago in the fall. Hirsch immediately fell in with the university folk crowd—Pete Stone, Pete Stein, Carl Gottesman, and Bob March—and they formed the campus Folklore Society in 1953, staging square dances and concerts. They brought Peggy Seeger, Odetta, Bob Gibson and Sonny Terry and Brownie McGhee to campus in 1958, when Hirsch graduated.[50]

The lack of a local Chicago folk record label prevented performers from having a convenient outlet. Terkel's relationship with Moe Asch proved of some value, for he would record his friends at WFMT and send the tapes to Folkways. First came *Radio Programme Number 4, Studs Terkel's Weekly Almanac on Folk Music Blues on WFMT with Big Bill Broonzy and Pete Seeger*, issued in 1956. Terkel pushed Asch to issue other Broonzy albums, but he held out for an advance of $250, a tough sell to the penurious Folkways owner. After midnight on May 7, 1957, Terkel gathered Broonzy, Sonny Terry, and Brownie McGhee in the studio to trade songs and stories. "There is a great deal of banter and overlapping of voices, at times," he explained to Asch when sending the tape. "Didn't edit it—because I think this supplies a great deal of its charm. I know there are some cuts to be made—repetition [sic], etc. But in the main, I'd suggest leaving in most of byplay—Bill was feeling good as were the others . . . The humor is kind of Negro freewheeling variety—that I have never heard on a record. Don't cut it." The engaging album appeared in 1959 as *WFMT-Chicago-Presents the Blues with Studs Terkel Interviewing Big Bill Broonzy, Sonny Terry, Brownie McGhee*.[51]

Terkel's letter also mentioned a recent benefit for Broonzy in November 1957 (the singer would die the following year). A full house of fifteen hundred heard Odetta, Seeger, Stracke, Gibson, Frank Hamilton, the blues performers Sunnyland Slim and J. B Lenoir, and the gospel star Mahalia Jackson. The sixty-four-year-old center of attention, recovering from an operation, sat silent; said Terkel; "his big frame was shrunk in his double-breasted suit, his hair was graying and not a note passed the lips that had helped bring his people's music out of the South to the rest of the world." The evening clearly demonstrated the close links between the urban folk revivalists and traditional blues, with gospel somewhat bridging the two—a stimulating mixture of vernacular music.[52]

In late 1957 the several threads of the Chicago folk scene came together with the founding of the Old Town School of Folk Music. Dawn Greening, her husband Nate, and their two children lived in Oak Park, near Chicago, and frequented the Gate of Horn, where they met Gibson. They often invited the club's performers to their house for dinner and sometimes to stay the night. (Grossman had only a small, cheerless apartment for performers near the club.) Her first night at the Gate, Odetta met Dawn, "this friendly, outgoing person. . . . I just didn't believe it. Go over to her house with her four kids and other strays, me being one, coming in it was like a community center." They became lifelong friends. Sometimes people would perform at the Greenings', but Dawn wasn't pushy. Eventually Nate purchased a Vega banjo and took a few lessons from Gibson. Soon Frank Hamilton began giving lessons in their house two days a week. Stracke, who had met the Greenings during the Henry Wallace campaign, was impressed with Hamilton's ability to teach various instruments at different levels, a technique he had developed from Bess Hawes's group classes in Los Angeles; Stracke also appreciated the group singalongs after refreshments. He envisioned a formal folk school, with a homey touch. "One night, about three weeks into those classes, as I was driving Frank home I put the idea to him," said Stracke. "I suggested that we could organize a school around him and his teaching techniques—a school in which he would use the same dining room approach, but for larger classes."[53]

The Old Town School of Folk Music opened on December 1, 1957, at 333 West North Avenue, with several hundred people greeted by Hamilton, Broonzy, and the bagpiper George Armstrong. By the second year, with a few additional teachers (and Gertrude Soltker managing the finances), the school held classes two nights a week and Saturday afternoons; Dawn prepared the refreshments and generally oversaw things. It quickly became a vibrant part of the local folk scene, not only through the classes but also concerts. The Weavers and Mahalia Jackson, accompanied by Broonzy in one of his last appearances, held a successful fundraiser to help purchase a sound system. Believing the Old Town School could be a musical United Nations, Hamilton and the other teachers ventured into the ethnic communities—Greek, Polish, Serbian, Croatian, black—meeting and bringing back local musicians to teach and perform.

Hamilton remained with the school until 1962, a vital presence and leader while others took over much of the teaching. He had strong feelings about Grossman, after working for him at the Gate: "He could be ruthless, tough and charming in the same breath. He had a sense of what would sell. He saw the rise of folk singing in the popular music field and set a strategy to reap the benefits of it." Frank felt more comfortable at the not-for-profit Old Town School, away from the rough and tumble of the market place, but he continued performing at the Gate as the house musician, his versatility invaluable as a variety of performers filled the stage.[54]

Los Angeles

Folkways and other labels had some outlets in the Midwest, but outside of Denver there was little organized folk activity between Chicago and the West Coast. Odetta, Hamilton, and Jo Mapes left Los Angeles, but other alumni of People's Songs formed a strong local folk community. Bess Hawes began teaching guitar class in the adult education program at UCLA that soon stretched to six a week. Bess also taught guitar for two weeks in the summer at the Idyllwild Arts Foundation School of Music and the Arts near Palm Springs; started by Bea and Max Krone in the summer of 1950, the Idyllwild school was an adjunct of the University of Southern California School of Music. Sam Hinton, a performer steeped in traditional music, became a yearly presence at Idyllwild, joining Bonnie Dobson and Marais and Miranda in 1956. Hinton met Moe Asch at Idyllwild, beginning his relationship with Folkways. Hinton did not call himself an authentic folk singer; he wryly claimed membership in the "Urban Literate Southern California Sub-Group of the Early Atomic Period." Insisting "I cannot sing authentic folk music, no matter what I do," he could nevertheless preserve its "emotional content. My desire is to arouse in the audience emotions similar to those felt by the 'original' folk audience." Hinton became a stalwart of the folk revival in the state.[55]

Folk music flourished in scattered patches throughout the sprawling Los Angeles area, but with no central focus, no folk club or magnet neighborhood such as Greenwich Village. "By 1957, I was spending more and more time in California working in movies and television." Bikel recalls. "I bemoaned the fact that Los Angeles had no places where folksingers could hang out and sing or play when they felt like it." He discussed the problem with Herb Cohen, and they soon opened the first folk coffeehouse, the Unicorn on Sunset Boulevard. Born in Brooklyn in 1932 into a left-wing family, Cohen had early attended People's Songs concerts, then joined the merchant marine in 1949, shipping out of L.A. as an organizer for the Marine Cooks and Stewards Union. Somewhat involved in the early 1950s folk scene that was centered around the Geers' place in Topanga Canyon, Cohen began organizing concerts in 1952 with Jimmy Gavin, Hamilton, Odetta, and Marcia Berman. He later arranged concerts for the re-formed Weavers, Pete Seeger, and Martha Schlamme in L.A. and also a few in the Bay area. From his contact with the owners of San Francisco's Purple Onion, in 1956 he was hired to manage their floundering club in L.A., and he brought in his friends Gavin, Bikel, and Berman. But the owners had little interest in folk music, so he jumped at the chance to open the Unicorn with Bikel, a small place seating less than one hundred. "On hooks on the wall there were a couple of guitars and a banjo. Anyone who had a mind to picked one up and played . . . The cops could not understand the success of the place. They kept coming in, first the uniformed cops and then the plainclothes men, to see what underhanded hippie-type business we were conducting that attracted such crowds." Bud Dashiel met Travis Edmondson there and they soon launched their successful duo, Bud and Travis. The place attracted an eclectic crowd, with "beards and sandals . . . sitting next to tuxedos and evening gowns." Within a year a dozen coffeehouses had opened through-out the area.[56]

Six months after opening Bikel and Cohen spotted another location on Cosmo Alley behind the Ivar Theater in Hollywood, where they opened a folk night-club named after the street; it seated about 150, and served beer and wine. "Here I performed regularly," Bikel writes, "to keep the customers coming, but we had a wonderful array of artists, not only folk performers but comedians as well. Lenny Bruce would come regularly to try out new material, and Maya Angelou read her poetry." Cohen helped book folk acts into the proliferating coffeehouses and clubs throughout the country, establishing connections for traveling musicians. The Unicorn and Cosmo Alley remained open for about three years, until Cohen's departure in 1959.[57]

Cohen and Bikel paved the way for other folk spots as well, particularly the Ash Grove, opened by Ed Pearl in 1958. Starting at UCLA in 1954, Pearl joined the campus Folk Dance Club and fought to bring Pete Seeger to campus despite the blacklist. He became active in the university's Folk Song Club, with Guy Carawan as its advisor, and organized the weekly Friday hootenannies and other activities. Developing a particular attraction to southern vernacular music, Pearl listened to Spade Cooley, Merle Travis, and Joe Maphis, as well as Harry Smith's *Anthology of American Folk Music.*

The local folk community also spawned Terry Gilkyson and the Easy Riders, a clone of the Weavers. They had a national success with the calypso-style "Marianne" in early 1957 for Columbia, which reached number five and re-mained on the pop charts for four months. (The Hilltoppers' simultaneous version on Dot almost matched their success.) Frank Miller, a building con-tractor, and Rich Dehr, a painter, had met in 1950 and soon formed the Easy Riders. Miller had been in Greenwich Village before the war and hung around Almanac House, and both he and Dehr became active in People's Songs activities in Los Angeles and the Topanga Canyon folk scene at Will Geer's. Gilkyson, a professional musician, had written "The Cry of the Wild Goose" and recorded with the Weavers on their hit "On Top of Old Smokey." Around 1952 the three met at radio station KGIL in the San Fernando Valley and soon teamed up.

Miller and Dehr had a vast musical repertoire, some learned from their friend Bess Hawes, and the trio became adept at writing songs, including "Memories Are Made of This." (Dean Martin's version, with their backup, reached number one in early 1956.) They also wrote "Mr. Tap Toe," "Everybody Loves Saturday Night," "Fast Freight," "Greenfields," and "South Coast," all hits for others over the years. The Easy Riders disbanded in early 1959, having sparked a growing popular interest in folk music on the eve of the Kingston Trio's breakthrough.

New York

"Israel Goodman Young was born in Manhattan on March 26, 1928. He lived on the top floor of 110 Ludlow Street, surrounded by the largest Jewish community in America. He never used his full name until late in High School or early in College. He loved his name. He loved to play with his name." So begins Israel G. "Izzy" Young's *Autobiography. The Bronx. 1928–1938*, a quirky little paperback with photos by David Gahr. The family soon moved to the Bronx, where Izzy lived until 1948. He attended the High School of Science, then Brooklyn College until 1950, leaving without a diploma. Of greater importance, he began attending Margot Mayo's American Square Dance Group in 1945, combining folk music and dance, his two lifelong passions. He remained an integral part of the group while working at his family's bakery into the 1950s. Curiously, he was generally oblivious to the left-wing aspects of the folk revival, including the Folksay square dance group and People's Songs. During the summers in the early 1950s he worked as a waiter in the Catskills, along with performers John Cohen and Tom Paley, whom he had known in Greenwich Village; Izzy led the square dancing. In the mid-1950s he met Kenneth Goldstein, who not only produced scores of folk albums but also collected and sold folklore books. Already a bibliophile, Izzy was taken under Goldstein's wing, and in March 1955 he issued his first folklore catalog, fifteen pages of common and rare publications, new and used. The books were stored in his parents' basement in Brooklyn.[58]

By early 1957, when Izzy published his second book catalog, he chafed at the commercial nature of popular folk music, represented by such performers as the Tarriers and Harry Belafonte. Attending the New York Folklore Society annual meeting, he felt part of the academic milieu, yet he remained an outsider. At age 29, Izzy felt ready to launch a folk enterprise, sensing the growing market for books and records. Ben Botkin, in the *New York Folklore Quarterly*, noted that "Israel G. Young, a young bookseller with ideas (and possibly idioms) . . . has a feeling that there are going to be 'some changes [and not just square dance changes] made' and that new forces and movements are about to burgeon in the American folklore field." In 1965 Young told folklorist Richard Reuss,

"Then in [February] 1957 I heard of this store being vacant on MacDougal Street and I bought it and I hadn't the slightest idea what was going to happen when I opened it. I had about $50 in the bank, and I had a batch of books I put up on the shelves and a few records and I started doing business from the first minute." He cashed in a $1,000 insurance policy to cover the lease.[59]

Sing Out! happily greeted Izzy's opening, which finally answered the question, "Wouldn't it be wonderful if there were one place which sold everything available in the folk song field?" During the Folklore Center's first week he sold about $300 worth of books to Burl Ives and perhaps another $400 to Harry Belafonte. Izzy was particularly thrilled about stocking cheap ten-inch LPs from Stinson and Elektra, then being phased out, which would allow him to "see who is on my side in Folk Music"; he purchased the records for fifty cents and sold them for one dollar. He worried that "folksingers just do not buy books and they will be a problem—and if they expect discounts etc." On the positive side, he wrote in his journal that "I hope to interest the general public more in folklore—cater to specialists and libraries so I can sell rare books etc. and start distributing books & publishing books so I can make a living. I have the future." He had a hunch, based on his years of reading, dancing, and hanging around the local folk establishment, that a market existed.[60]

The ebullient folklorist and entrepreneur could scarcely imagine just how important his tiny Folklore Center at 110 MacDougal Street would shortly become, as the Greenwich Village scene rapidly evolved. He soon heard from Grossman at the Gate of Horn that Peggy Seeger would be coming to New York and wanted a concert. Izzy organized one in June at the Actor's Playhouse on Sheridan Square, which launched him in the promotional business. Over the next fifteen years he produced a steady stream of concerts, big and small, at first at the Actor's Playhouse, local Provincetown Playhouse, or in the cramped Folklore Center itself. Following Peggy Seeger he featured John Cohen, Robin Roberts, and Logan English, then Tom Paley and Paul Clayton, Dick Weissman, and the Ivy Leaguers, a British skiffle group composed of five members from the crew of a British ship. In her review of the concert, Lee Shaw halfheartedly praised the seamen, but saved her enthusiasm for Jo Mapes, Weissman, and particularly Cohen and Paley, who filled in during breaks, and who, "against the protests of the audience . . . finally quit for the evening. It had been quite a show." Izzy's one principle: share the gate equally with the performers.[61]

Locally and nationally the Folklore Center became a locus for folk music, supplying books, records, new and used instruments, and all sorts of information, and offering folk performers and fans a convenient gathering place. Hardly a businessman, Izzy's chaotic practices could be maddening to his customers. "Because I am caught up by the people that come into the store," he explained to Archie Green, "I neglect my mail completely. I have five hundred dollars of orders to mail out on my shelves and I am powerless to do anything about it." He admitted, "I keep no records either [and] it is a wonder I am still in business." These headaches haunted Izzy, his friends, and customers during the store's fifteen-year existence.[62]

Another who hitched her star to folk music was Lee Hoffman, who edited the relatively short-lived *Caravan*. Having moved from Georgia to New York in 1957, she met Dave Van Ronk through the Libertarian League, and he took her to Washington Square, followed by sessions at Rick Allmen's apartment (Allmen later owned Café Bizarre). A member of the Fantasy Amateur Press Association, Hoffman edited two issues (May and Summer 1957) of their fanzine *Choog* devoted to folk music, which were printed on her mimeograph machine. Following a loose definition of folk music—"the Child ballads, Horace Sprott's field calls, Woody Guthrie's dustbowl ballads, Paul Clayton's whaling songs, Oscar Brand's bawdy songs, the IWW's songs of protest, etc."—she filled the first issue mostly with song lyrics and a chatty piece on three Oscar Brand performances. In the second issue she remarked, rather critically, "Folk music is turning into Big Business nowadays, with specialized recording companies springing up like toadstools, and everytime you turn around, you run into another Authority on the subject (including the self-appointed amateurs like me)."[63]

Soon Hoffman plunged into a more ambitious project, a monthly folk fanzine aimed at the local scene. (Jon Pankake has described a fanzine as a magazine printed on a mimeograph machine. "For a few pennies you could write your profound thoughts on as many sheets as you wanted to pay for, ditto up copies, and send them into the world." The fanzine was cheap and represented the editor's opinions, a personal publication with no pretense or hint of professionalism.) She gave the first issue of *Caravan* away, then with the second traded copies with Izzy for records. "I couldn't pick, I couldn't sing, I wanted to participate in what was going on," Hoffman later explained. "What I did was publish amateur magazines." She gathered a stable of writers and others including Van Ronk and the photographer Aaron Rennert, who had been hanging around Washington Square since 1955. With two friends Rennert formed Photo-Sound Associates and began documenting the local folk scene and supplying *Caravan* with a steady stream of photos. Run on a shoestring, *Caravan* depended mainly on contributions and support from Jac Holzman of Elektra and Paddy Clancy of Tradition.[64]

In *Caravan*'s first issue, August 1957, the editor (now known as Lee Shaw) explained that the monthly would be reader-dependent and reader-oriented, and that it would pull no punches. Indeed, the first article, by Dave Van Ronk (writing as "Blind Rafferty"), chastised Elektra Records: "The aim of the A and R . . . men seems to be to avoid frightening or offending anyone. Whether or not this is literally true, I am amazed at Elektra's ability to turn out one innocuous little album after another—genteel, sophisticated, and utterly false." John

Brunner followed with his report from England, a regular column, marking Lee's awareness of the transatlantic links in folk music. Brunner explained the skiffle music fad, then going strong, and mentioned that Ewan MacColl and A. L. Lloyd continued to perform in a traditional style; he also noted various Americans passing through London, including Guy Carawan, Jack Elliott, Derroll Adams, and Peggy Seeger. Hoffman concluded the first issue with a summary of local happenings, which were slim during the summer except at the Folklore Center, where "quite often there's something really interesting going on, what with people like Tom Paley drifting in to sing a bit to the bystanders. Sometimes it really swings."[65]

Despite various difficulties, Caravan generally appeared on time and grew modestly. Each issue had letters taking various sides in the persistent authenticity-versus-commercialism debate. In October the editor praised a midnight concert by Tom Paley and Paul Clayton, sponsored by the Folklore Center, and in the December issue Dick Weissman drew a loving portrait of Brownie McGhee. Caravan and the Folklore Center quickly formed a symbiotic relationship.

By late 1957 a folk music national infrastructure seemed in place, with important beachheads in major urban centers. Folk clubs and coffeehouses existed in Chicago, L.A., Philadelphia, and San Francisco, and folk radio shows in New York, Chicago, and San Francisco. Folk had lost much of its former left-wing political gloss, but Seeger, Silber, and Sing Out! maintained a semblance of overt radical politics, as did pockets of musical activists throughout the country. The major names of the past—Burl Ives, Josh White, Richard Dyer-Bennet—still performed, joined by a growing host of young and not-so-young performers. The prominent folk record labels—led by Folkways—included Elektra, Riverside, and Tradition, and a few of the majors such as Decca remained interested. Folk music had broken through into the larger public consciousness during the decade—first with the Weavers, and again with the Tarriers and Harry Belafonte—so the potential existed, particularly as the college and youth market began to grow. But except for Sing Out! and Caravan there was yet scant folk journalism.

Pete Seeger persevered as the Johnny Appleseed of the revival. He left the Weavers in 1957, replaced by Eric Darling, and pursued a solo career, mostly touring the nation's schools and colleges, while continuing to appear at political events. Darling, who quit the Tarriers when he decided he needed the Weavers' stature and talent, energized the quartet. Hays, Gilbert, and Hellerman had questioned their future without Seeger but they quickly adjusted to Darling's virtuoso style, eclectic tastes, and youthful energy. Through their sporadic travel schedule and stream of Vanguard recordings their popularity and influence persisted.

In the spring 1955 issue of Sociologus, Arlene Kaplan analyzed her interviews

with former members of the East Bay Folk Music Association, originally organized at San Francisco State College in 1950. After studying the individuals and
the songs they sang, she concluded: "Folksingers in the mass society are participants in a deviant group. They have interests which are deviations from the
accepted goals and standards of the society and which are tolerated rather than
approved. In the long run, however, these interests may come to be accepted
in the larger society as a legitimate variation or novelty. Folksingers can return
to the larger society with their newly legitimated interests." Her prediction
would be exemplified by the startling success of the Kingston Trio.[66]

5

The Kingston Trio and the Emerging Revival, 1958–1959

"The folksingers are coming back into their own," *Variety* trumpeted in February 1958. "With many jazz concerts finding it tough sledding around the country this past fall and winter season, the folksong packages are picking up lots of concert coin." The article listed Marais and Miranda, Josh White, Cynthia Gooding, Susan Reed, Oscar Brand, Bob Gibson, Richard Dyer-Bennet, Pete Seeger, and Theodore Bikel as "racking up hefty grosses in their concert stands" at New York's Carnegie Hall and Town Hall and Chicago's Orchestra Hall. "Bikel also hit an SRO [standing room only] stride in college dates at Indiana, Oklahoma, Antioch, Oberlin, Berkeley, and Palo Alto." Bikel's tour was arranged by Albert Grossman, who understood folk music's commercial appeal.[1]

The proper definition of folk music—involving judgments about who or what to include or exclude—continued to plague folklorists as the decade wound down. For instance, in 1958 Sven Eric Molin, in the *Journal of American Folklore*, took D. K. Wilgus and other folklorists to task for their too academic definition, particularly their criticism of Burl Ives. Certainly, wrote Molin, Ives had altered "any song just as he pleases, in the manner of eighteenth century ballad collectors. But this manner, one must note, is also the manner of actual one hundred percent authentic folksingers who . . . feel none of the compunctions about total fidelity to source that bother the collectors and reviewers."[2]

Called upon to defend his denial in *Western Folklore* that he was an authentic folk singer, Sam Hinton tried to clarify his position and preference for traditional performers:

One of the first things I do with each of my classes in folk music is to compare selected performances of both types: Burl Ives' "Divil and the Farmer's Wife" vs. Horton Barker's L.C. recording of the same song; Dyer-Bennett's [sic] "Barbara Allen" vs. that of Rebecca Tarwater; my own commercial recording of "Long John" vs. the L.C. field recording of "Long John" sung by a chain gang. The techniques are different, but both kinds show artistry, and, after a critical, unprejudiced listening, most listeners find the commercial recordings comparatively pallid and lifeless.

Perhaps so, but "most listeners" had no exposure to "real" folksingers, and they increasingly nurtured the urban, commercial folk revival. Hinton believed "that the distance between folk society and literate society is ever decreasing, and Teresa Brewer will yet shake hands with Mrs. Texas Gladden. But until that happens—until my own culture, and Teresa Brewer's, develops a folk tradition of its own—if I want to learn something about real folk music, I'll stick with Mrs. Gladden." But most listeners preferred Brewer's easily digestible melodious style.[3]

Berkeley

While the academics debated the pros and cons of Burl Ives and Teresa Brewer as proper folkies, the revival continued to broaden, often boosted by local organizers. Barry Olivier served as an important spark and conduit in Berkeley. Born in San Francisco, Barry heard the Library of Congress field recordings in the mid-1940s, as well as Burl Ives's commercial disks. "I've always felt that Burl Ives really was the most important single catalyst in the whole folk music movement," he later said. "As important as Pete [Seeger] is . . . I think Ives was just a giant figure." After his family moved across the bay to Berkeley, Olivier began attending local concerts with Carl Sandburg, Sam Hinton, Guy Carawan, Barbara Dane, Marais and Miranda, Odetta, and Pete Seeger. He began playing guitar in high school, and in 1952 he launched a folk spot on KPFA, the local avant-garde FM station, fifteen minutes once a week, expanded to the one-hour weekly Midnight Special in 1956. Somewhat modeled on its Chicago namesake, the show featured a variety of live folk personalities such as Andrew Rowan Summers, Jean Ritchie, Theodore Bikel, Billy Faier, and Bob Gibson. Those performing locally but unable to appear at the station—Paul Robeson, Pete Seeger, Cisco Houston and Odetta—were taped for the show. Olivier also accompanied the folklorist Archie Green to tape Aunt Molly Jackson, then living in Sacramento, in January 1958.[4]

Before leaving the Midnight Special show in late 1958, Olivier launched Friday night folk sessions at the Northgate restaurant in mid-1957. "The response so far has been somewhat astounding," Al Fischer reported in the Daily Californian, "with crowds averaging between 300 and 500 people each week." Morton

Cathro followed with an article in the *Oakland Tribune*: "Has your appetite for music been curbed by calypso, jaded by jazz or reined by rock 'n' roll? If so, tuck your guitar under your arm and drop by Cooper's North Gate in Berkeley one of these Friday nights for a refreshing evening of just plain old folk songs." Olivier also circulated *Folk Song Arts*, a free weekly newsletter full of information about local events.[5]

The Blind Lemon, a local night spot opened in the mid-1950s, also began featuring folk performers on Tuesdays and Thursdays. "Opening night was a concert of K. C. Douglas, Larry Moore, Odetta, and me," the owner, Rolf Cahn, remembered. "It was a sellout. It was the hub of the folk music community."[6]

In 1956 and 1957 Olivier had staged concerts on the campus featuring local musicians. "Barry has promoted the most successful concerts in the Bay area," Billy Faier reported in *Caravan*. "He is the best concert promoter I have ever known because he has a real love for the field." Olivier, no longer a student, next convinced the University's Committee for Drama, Lecturers and Music to fund a full-blown summer folk festival in late June 1958. Emphasizing the occasion's educational contributions, he told the committee that "I believe this would be the finest folk music festival ever assembled outside the actual states where much of our folk music originated."[7]

Olivier invited to his "Weekend of Folk Music" familiar names whose local drawing power had already been tested: Marais and Miranda, Jean Ritchie, Sam Hinton, Frank Warner, Margarita and Clark Allen (who specialized in Spanish and Gypsy songs and dances), Andrew Rowan Summers, and Billy Faier. There would be four main concerts, four workshops, and assorted other events, combining entertainment with the proper academic touch. "The greatest event in folk music ever to take place in the Bay area will take place in Berkeley at the University of California late this month," Olivier modestly announced in *Folk Song Arts* on June 6. While hardly original—Swarthmore College had hosted a festival since 1945, and Oberlin followed suit in 1957—campus folk festivals were still a rarity.[8]

Billy Faier enthusiastically informed *Caravan*'s mainly New York readers, "This weekend of folk music was the most exciting musical event of my life." "It is difficult to explain about the Fraternal spirit that I felt among the singers and the audiences," he concluded. "It is due, I believe, mainly to a complete lack of any competitive spirit between the various artists," unlike "the feeling of competition that I had always found (and contributed to) among singers of my own immediate generation." The festival was also a financial success, earning Olivier $500 after expenses.[9]

Over the next year folk musicians, including Jean Ritchie, Cisco Houston, and Sandy Paton, continued to visit the Berkeley campus. "The 1958 'Weekend of Folk Music' Festival at U.C. was one of the most important events in the history of folk music, and certainly last year's most outstanding contribution to the art of folk song throughout the world," Olivier wrote, in order to obtain support from the campus for a second weekend in 1959. Expanded to five days of concerts and workshops, the 1959 Second Annual Folk Music Festival, again in late June, included Alan Lomax, Jimmy Driftwood, Jesse Fuller, Sam Hinton, Pete Seeger, and the local singer Merritt Herring. The format was now set for yearly festivals until their demise in 1970. Olivier wrote, "We were concerned about a *product* of the folk music process—the finished, traditional, pure, real, good, old folk songs. With popularizers all about—the Kingston Trio and its school—we had almost a religious fervor about laying out what we considered to be real folk music, so it would be fully appreciated and so that people wouldn't waste their time and energy with the watered-down, 'impure' stuff."[10]

The six-days 1960 Berkeley festival included old and new names, black and white styles, foreign and native music—Ewan MacColl, Peggy Seeger, Sam Hinton, the cowboy singer Dick "Slim" Critchlow, Sandy Paton, the New Lost City Ramblers, John Lomax Jr., and the blues performer Sam "Lightnin' " Hopkins. The music critic Alfred Frankenstein, in the *San Francisco Chronicle*, wrote, "But this folk music festival still brings us far too few folk artists and draws a bit too heavily on that intermediary borderland where Seegers take mainly from Lomaxes and the Lomaxes mainly from God." He noted the presence of two Seegers, Peggy and her brother Mike, and one Lomax. About Mike's New Lost City Ramblers he said, "If they really were a hillbilly string band, they would be intolerable for more than a few minutes, but because they are actually eggheads exercising a genius for mimicry, their performance takes on about 87 different nuances of satire all at once and rises to monumental stature in the process."[11]

Billy Faier was another who shaped the local community's evolving folk aesthetic, performing in the first festival, presenting a weekly program on KPFA, teaching guitar and banjo, and giving concerts throughout the Bay Area. Born in Brooklyn in 1930, after high school he visited Washington Square for the Sunday folk singing, where he picked up the banjo. In 1951, fearing the military draft, he took off for Oregon, only to learn he was classified 4F. From Oregon the rambling Faier moved to San Francisco and connected with Barbara Dane, Rolf Cahn, and Stan Wilson, then wound up in New Orleans for a couple of years. In 1953, he welcomed Frank Hamilton, Jack Elliott, and Guy Carawan to his house during their southern swing, and returned with them to New York. After a few years in Southern California he drifted back to Berkeley in 1957 and met Barry Olivier. Faier initiated *The Story of American Folk Music* on KPFA that November. Seemingly omnipresent on the folk scene, he reappeared in New York in late 1958.[12]

Once back in New York he became one of the few local banjo virtuosos, appearing frequently in recording sessions for Oscar Brand, Ed McCurdy, and Logan English; he also made *The Art of the Five-String Banjo* for Riverside. He told

Ray Lawless, who was compiling information for his *Folksingers and Folksongs in America*, "As a professional, I feel I have a great responsibility to my audience (being billed as a folk singer), to transmit to them as honest an account of folk music as I can. I avoid 'tricks' calculated to get attention."[13]

Michael Rossman has recalled Berkeley's heady folk music climate during the later 1950s. Raised in a left-wing family, while briefly a student he had joined the University of Chicago Folklore Society and reveled in the weekly folk sings. Returning to Berkeley in 1956, he joined the local folk scene. "It beckoned me at the Blind Lemon, comforted my studious midnights from KPFA, offered itself more vigorously in new coffeehouses' rotations," he wrote. Rossman connected with the nascent activist political scene on campus, yet he never strayed far from the folk culture: "Every so often we partied in a friendly basement on Regent Street, maybe sixty people, passing the gallon jugs of rough red wine and singing the songs of politics—the union songs, Wobbly songs, revolutionary songs, miners' and slaves' and Spanish Civil War songs, that extended the political core of the folk music canon."[14]

Olivier and Faier had close contacts with local performers, yet they also welcomed nationally known singers, fostering a healthy mix of professionals and amateurs. Mary Ann Pollar, on the other hand, specialized in the big names. Born in Texas, she had moved to Chicago to live with her grandparents, then relocated to the Bay Area in 1950. In the mid-1950s she and her husband Henry allowed Rolf Cahn to use their house in Oakland for his weekly guitar classes, and they participated in staging yearly folk concerts at the Berkeley Little Theater. Pollar had earlier met Odetta, and when, in late 1958, Odetta's manager Albert Grossman contacted Pollar about producing a show in Berkeley she jumped at the chance, thereby inaugurating her "Mary Ann Pollar Presents" concerts and business. She next featured Theo Bikel, also represented by Grossman. Using flyers, strikingly designed posters, and a growing mailing list, she reached out to a community obviously eager for folk music, producing concerts by Billy Faier, Sonny Terry, Brownie McGhee, and Barbara Dane. In many ways, Pollar fit the style of promoters in other cities—thorough and aggressive—but otherwise she differed significantly. The rest were white, male, and mostly Jewish; she was female and black, though she shared their generally Left politics. With scant connection to community performers, Pollar featured mostly national names, using her ties to folk managers and national music networks.

The Kingston Trio

In September 1958 a new trio appeared at the Berkeley Little Theater, attracting a middling crowd. The Kingston Trio—Bob Shane, Dave Guard, and Nick Reynolds—had formed the year before and recorded their eponomyous album for Capitol in February 1958; it was released on June 1, following the single "Scarlet Ribbons" by a few weeks. They appeared at the hungry i through June, where they recorded what would become their second album, released the next January. In September, receiving air play in some markets, they were as yet little known.

Both Guard and Shane, born in 1934, had grown up in Hawaii and moved to California to attend college. Guard graduated from Stanford University and Shane attended the nearby Menlo Park School of Business. Nick Reynolds, born a year earlier in San Diego, first met Shane in Menlo Park, then Guard. The latter and Reynolds, joined by various others, formed the Calypsonians in 1956, later variously known as the Dave Guard Quartet, The Kingstons, and the Kingston Quartet. They performed at San Francisco's Purple Onion in early 1957, where Shane joined them on May 1. Now the Kingston Trio, they became the headline act in July. Guard first heard Pete Seeger in a Weavers concert in San Francisco in 1957 and immediately took to the banjo, learning from Seeger's *How to Play the 5-String Banjo* and from Billy Faier. Urged by their manager, Frank Werber, the trio cut a demonstration record, which made the rounds of Los Angeles recording studios, including Dot, Capitol, and Liberty. They signed with Capitol and hit the road for some seasoning, playing before tough crowds at the Holiday Hotel in Reno, Nevada, and similar establishments with their new bass player, David "Buck" Wheat. Their first Capitol album, *The Kingston Trio*, produced by Voyle Gilmore, appeared in early summer.

The trio borrowed from various sources and models for their first album's songs: "Fast Freight" (Easy Riders), "Saro Jane" (Gateway Singers), "Sloop John B" (Weavers), "Hard, Ain't It Hard" (Woody Guthrie), and "Bay of Mexico" (Pete Seeger). Lou Gottlieb of the Gateway Singers recalls his role in shaping one song:

> I had a wife and children, no money . . . so I started working as a stand-up comic and got a job at the Purple Onion. There were three guys there who used to hang around the hungry i all the time. In fact, they'd even be in the dressing room half the time. But they were cute. Dave Guard, Bob Shane, and Nick Reynolds. And they were the opening act at the Purple Onion. . . . Well, sir, these kids really had something different. There was a magic about that act that was hard to explain. . . . When they made their first record, which was probably in February of '58, they needed a tune. I had a couple of old charts from the Gateway Singers that I quickly rescored for three voices. They did a song that I stole from Uncle Dave Macon called "Rock about My Sarah Jane" and put it on their first album. And they let me publish it. The royalties ultimately came out to thirty grand.

Gottlieb was impressed by the trio's style and verve and not offended by their slick, popular approach. After all, the Gateway Singers, the Easy Riders, the Tarriers, and indeed even the Weavers (old and new), the trio's prototypes, could hardly claim rustic authenticity, and each sought commercial success. The Kingston Trio just became more popular, and quickly so.[15]

Public recognition first came from a remote corner of the country. Paul Coburn, host of *Coburn's Caravan* on KLUB in Salt Lake City, played the cut "Tom Dooley" from the album on June 19. The deluge of positive calls surprised him, and local record stores immediately sold out of the album. "Don't mean to brag," the DJ informed the trio in early August, "but hooper [rating] shows I have the most popular show in this market and I'll always take the best care of your future releases." Word spread east and west, encouraging Capitol to release the single in early August. It began to appear on the charts in late September, and before Christmas "Tom Dooley" hit number one; it remained popular into February 1959.[16]

The public erroneously connected "Tom Dooley" with Thomas A. Dooley, the Navy doctor recently in the news for his missionary and medical roles in Vietnam and Laos following the French defeat in 1954; he had published part of his story, *Deliver Us from Evil*, in 1956, helping fan the flames of Catholic anticommunism. Thus accidentally the trio reaped the fruits of anticommunism while they drew inspiration and songs from the Weavers and Gateway Singers. When Dooley was in St. Louis in early December 1959 to receive a gift of $18,000 from the local Jaycees, the hometown hero eagerly sought out the trio after their performance at the local Chase Club. Guard, Reynolds, and Shane returned with Dooley to the Sheraton-Jefferson Hotel, where they played into the early morning hours for the doctor and Laotian Prince Souphan, in town to honor Dooley. Dooley, in turn, introduced the trio to his mission's catchy theme song, "I Was a Cooley for Dooley." The next year the trio played several benefits for the doctor's work in Southeast Asia.[17]

Unlike most other hit tunes recorded by various artists and labels eager to take advantage of the moment, neither "Tom Dooley" nor the trio's other successes had any rivals doing cover versions. Their unique style must have dissuaded the competition. Whatever the reason, they briefly had the popular/folk market pretty much to themselves. Television appearances with Milton Berle, Perry Como, Dinah Shore, and Patti Page assured their popularity.

"Hanged Man in Hit Tune," *Life* headlined in mid-December 1958. The article, with scant substance, featured the song rather than the trio: "Out of the jukeboxes in almost every bar and candy store came the same three-part harmony plea of an old folk song imploring a gay blade headed for the gallows to hang his head in shame before the hangman fitted it through a noose." Moved to action by hearing of Dooley's sad plight, a bar owner in Galesburg, Illinois, collected money for a small commemorative tombstone and wreath, now adorning his establishment. But the original Tom Dula's life had little romance and less pathos. The sensational murder trial in 1867 took place in Wilkes County, North Carolina, where Dula, not quite twenty years old and a Civil War veteran, along with his former lover Ann Melton, was accused of the murder of Laura Foster, Ann's cousin. Dula alone assumed the guilt. Perhaps he blamed Laura for giving him a venereal disease, or perhaps he had gotten her pregnant.[18]

Dula's hanging a year later generated numerous ballads. The blind hillbilly fiddler G. B. Grayson, a descendant of the man who had supposedly arrested Dula, with his partner Henry Whitter recorded a version for Victor in the 1920s. Frank Proffitt, of Pick Britches Valley, Tennessee, had his rendition collected by Frank Warner in 1938. Warner himself played the song for decades, and eventually recorded it on the 1952 Elektra album *Frank Warner Sings American Folksongs and Ballads*; a few years earlier Alan Lomax had printed it in *Folk Song U.S.A.*, attributing Warner. Bob Carey, Erik Darling, and Roger Sprung, known as the Folksay Trio, also recorded the song in mid-decade for Kenneth Goldstein at Stinson Records. Dave Guard claimed the Kingston Trio first heard it performed by a folk-singing psychologist auditioning at the Purple Onion, then he copied the words from Dick and Beth Best's *New Song Fest*, first published privately in 1948 and commercially in 1955, which listed no copyright. A lawsuit between Ludlow Music, representing Lomax and Warner, and Capitol, which had noted the song as "Traditional—arranged by Dave Guard," finally resulted in their splitting the royalties after 1962. Frank Proffitt received nothing. In 1959 Columbia Pictures released *The Legend of Tom Dooley*, loosely based on the song, with the Kingston Trio on the soundtrack.[19]

Following hard on the heels of their monster success, the Kingston Trio produced a second album and string of hit singles: "Tijuana Jail" reached number twelve in April 1959, "M.T.A." number fifteen in July, and "A Worried Man" number twenty in late summer. After *The Kingston Trio's* number one ranking in late 1958 (for only one week, though it remained a bestseller for 114 weeks), *From the Hungry i* reached number two early the next year, then *The Kingston Trio at Large* remained number one for fifteen weeks and *Here We Go Again* was the top seller for eight weeks. In 1960, *Sold Out* and *String Along* also climbed to the pinnacle of the charts. During their first four years they had a dozen bestselling albums, the first six certified gold (over 500,000 sold). In its zeal to reap quick rewards before the craze died, Capitol forced the group to release three albums per year, which quickly depleted their stock of songs and their fervor. "I liked just about all our first four albums," Guard later said. "The first three for sure. I'd say the quality of our work went up, but the enthusiasm for the songs didn't. On the first three albums in particular, we were very interested in all the tunes, those were songs we really liked. Later on we were just looking for tunes that would keep up the quality of the group, that sounded like Kingston Trio songs."[20]

On the Roy Rogers and Dale Evans television show in early 1959 the trio shared billing with Johnny Cash, Jimmy Dean, the Everly Brothers, and Roy Acuff. Publicity centered as much on the trio's physical image and domestic lifestyle as on their folksy, upbeat musical appeal. "It is hard to recall an instance when as wholesome a group of entertainers as the Kingston Trio has won as swift and widespread a popularity as they have." *Redbook Magazine* began its puff piece in mid-1959. Telling the soon-to-be-familiar story of their college backgrounds and sudden rise to stardom, the article stressed that they "score sensationally without catering to any of the current 'sure-fire' vogues." Certifying their pop status, *Life* featured a cover photo and two-page spread. "The brightest new sounds heard through all the racket of rock 'n' roll come from the voices and the instruments of three college grad cutups," the article intoned. Accompanied by a photo captioned "Dutiful wives tend[ing] to their tired husbands in club dressing room between song sessions," the *Life* story said without irony that "with success, domesticity came to the softsell folk singers." Shane married an heiress from Atlanta, Guard the daughter of the treasurer of a chain of department stores, and Reynolds a comedienne also due to inherit a fortune.[21]

They had the perfect combination of charm, wealth, security, and modesty. "Rockless, roll-less and rich," *Time* proclaimed the next year. Only recently Guard had been a "prebeatnik who was heading nowhere," Reynolds a tennis bum, and Shane a Waikiki Beach surfer and drinker. But with their triumph at the Purple Onion "they acquired purpose," then wives, which "stabilized them further." Despite their instant success, and being crowned with the honor of appearing at both the Newport Jazz and folk festivals in 1959, they "still divide up the household chores as they did in the days when they used to sleep three in a bed in fleabag hotels." What saints: professionals yet with youthful zest; a refreshing alternative to the scruffy, rebellious, lewd rock and roll singers, according to the mass media.[22]

Thrilled by their style and songs, teenage fans consumed their records and packed the auditoriums. "Now don't get me wrong, we're typical teens and like rock 'n' roll, but you have interested us in a new type of music," two Southern California fans wrote in early 1960. "And as my mother says 'the Kingston Trio records teach you something about people that you wouldn't ever have a chance to meet' (such as zombies). . . . Thanks ever so much for introducing a new world of music to us." Years later the traditional performer Arthel "Doc" Watson, from Deep Gap, North Carolina, said, "I'll tell you who pointed all our noses in the right direction, even the traditional performers. They got us interested in trying to put the good stuff out there—the Kingston Trio. They got me interested in it!"[23]

The Kingston Trio emerged as moral gatekeepers at an optimal time. Rock and roll's upsurge during the mid-1950s had shaken adult society's aesthetic and moral foundations, leading to escalating recriminations, censorship, and soul searching. Could middle-class culture survive? Were young people out of control? The baby boom generation was just reaching its teens, and the youth market was growing. More important, teenage consumer spending, fueled by the general prosperity, increased, and producers and advertisers paid close attention. "The American teenagers have emerged as a big-time consumer in the U.S. economy," Life reported in 1959. "Counting only what is spent to satisfy their special teenage demands, the youngsters and their parents will shell out about $10 billion this year, a billion more than the total sales of GM." Hardly a monolithic group, teenagers nevertheless appeared to be a cohesive subculture, set apart by their somewhat rebellious dependence. The decade's emphasis on family values, continually stressed in school, church, and the mass media, ran up against a more complex reality. Fear of juvenile delinquency changed into anxieties about youthful exuberance and independence in general.[24]

Throughout the decade contrary and unsettling social, cultural, and intellectual tendencies had surfaced, troubling in their implications. Life in suburbia, shaped by increased consumer spending and images of televised life, fostered conformity, but brought new strains and conflicts. These were confusing times, with the Bomb hanging over everyone's head. Social critic Paul Goodman, in Growing Up Absurd, described "groups of boys and young men disaffected from the dominant society. The young men are Angry and Beat. The boys are Juvenile Delinquents. These groups are not small, and they will grow larger."[25]

Within a few years the baby boom generation would create a massive market for youth-oriented goods and music, but the record companies realized that adults still made up the bulk of their audience. Teens preferred single records and radio programs featuring rock and roll, an expanding segment of consumer culture. In arguing against the tyranny of the Hit Parade, in 1958 Pete Seeger noted that classical LPs made up 25 percent of the record market, other LPs 40 percent (popular, jazz, folk, etc.), children records and country and western singles 8 percent, with pop singles appealing to only the remaining 27 percent of purchasers. But the latter controlled the Hit Parade. The Kingston Trio's appeal illustrates the complications of the musical marketplace. They attracted an adult audience that had enthusiastically responded to the Weavers early in the decade and other folk favorites a few years later, such as Harry Belafonte and the Tarriers. But the Kingston Trio's reach was broader, thanks to pop radio programs, proliferating 45-rpm records, and college venues.[26]

Reaction and Debate

As a wide range of folk recordings continued to pour forth, the New York Times music critic Robert Shelton kept up a steady drumbeat for the music, and would soon be positioned to make (or perhaps break) careers. In an early column in January 1958 he covered a range of albums, from the trained baritone Milt Okun to Samuel Charters's Folkways reissue of the religious street singer Blind Willie Johnson, who had recorded for Columbia in the late 1920s and died in 1949. Shelton appreciated both Okun's "musical refinement" and Johnson's "simple, primitive directness and 'authenticity' of expression." He also threw in praise for new releases by Robin Roberts, Pete Seeger, Burl Ives, Carl Sandburg, and Josh White. Later in the year he lauded Erik Darling, Peggy Seeger, Guy Carawan, Carolyn Hester, and other singers.[27]

Shelton pondered how to develop his lofty position at the country's premier daily. "The assignment has worked out well, and I feel that I am getting more and more in control of what I am doing with each article," he confided to Archie Green in early 1959. Still there were problems, for "I am not writing for the small sect of devoted folkniks who know what it is all about, but for the general record-buyer, who expects only polished, slick performances. How to straddle the big area between a Belafonte and a Buell Kazee without having a dozen sets of critical criteria is, as you can imagine, not easy." Shelton subscribed to music magazines, joined the American Folklore Society, met many performers, and cultivated a fruitful friendship with Alan Lomax. Through the 1960s he would promote and mediate, but he often found himself caught in the crossfires of heated debates.[28]

Always the tug between traditional styles and commercialism went on. In early 1958 the British scholar A. L. Lloyd found that "the picture of U.S. folk song is confused, for it seems that most country performers are ambitious to modify their traditional style with a view to being 'discovered' by the agents of recording companies or radio stations. Thus, a once rich, varied and free tradition becomes progressively more uniform, more regularised, distorted to fit the moulds established by the professional minstrel and, beyond him, the popular entertainer." Nonetheless, he concluded, American folk music, an amalgam of black and white influences, "with a range of musical types that is almost unique in breadth," had much to offer.[29]

The Kingston Trio's instant popularity generated little immediate public reaction from the folk music establishment. Sing Out!'s editor Irwin Silber had long been the gatekeeper, but now he remained silent. Ron Radosh, fresh from radical politics and folksinging at the University of Wisconsin, fired the first salvo in the quarterly magazine. He went after the "groups who are supposedly building upon the folk tradition and enriching American music [and] are actually commercial 'pop' singers using guitars and banjos, letting themselves snugly fit into the Tin Pan Alley notch, ruining the music which they could have decently portrayed." As for the current Weavers (Erik Darling having replaced Seeger), they "had to resort to ruining good songs"; the music of the Tarriers "was of the most mediocre sort"; the Gateway Singers larded their act with "the dullest type of night club humor," followed by lackluster song arranging, "destroying what was good in the music and adapting it to the stereotyped beat and style of a decadent musical culture." He saved his sharpest barbs for the "atrocious" Kingston Trio, whose album "brings good folk music to the level of the worst of Tin Pan Alley music, and is even worse because it is advertising itself as folk music." Radosh concluded with a call to arms: "It is about time that fans of folk song and those who hope to spread it, sing it, or perform it in the folk tradition stop patronizing prostitutes of the art who gain their status as folk artists because they use guitars and banjos." *Sing Out!*'s few hundred readers might have agreed, but the Trio's millions of fans kept the record bins empty and the cash registers ringing.[30]

Sing Out!'s following issue contained three essays to further the debate. The topical songwriter Malvina Reynolds argued against the dead hand of the past, for "every generation has to discover music for itself." She proclaimed that "the stuff that is coming over the air is the folk music of our time. Some of it is awful, and some of it is not awful at all." Alan Lomax, returned from England in 1958 and once again in the thick of the debate, attacked the "city-billies or folkniks" for mastering the musical style without absorbing the music's emotional content. In reply, John Cohen, a member of the old-time revivalist New Lost City Ramblers, cautioned Lomax to take the "city folksingers" seriously: "The emotional content of folk songs is a different thing to different people— and it is hard to say that there is a single, correct way to emotional content." Lomax should stop preaching and listen, for "if folk music is valid and has force, the attitude of the folk singer towards his music will be communicated to and felt by those who hear it."[31]

Cohen and the New Lost City Ramblers had little thought of commercial success as they struggled to master the performance techniques of the southern string-bands recorded in the 1920s and 1930s. Indeed, the controversy over authenticity was actually a three-way struggle among the unadulterated commercial performers (such as the Kingston Trio) and their defenders, those who preferred only traditional performers (Lomax and most folklorists), and the city revivalists, whose love for the music translated into their own performance style as they strove to duplicate or reconstruct the older sounds. The battle would continue for decades, often a tempest in a teapot but vital to those involved. Lomax had no truck with most popularizers. He accepted younger performers only if they adhered to prescribed aesthetic and stylistic standards:

> Thus when a good jazzman, symphonist, or gypsy snatches up a folk song and plays with it, the results may be interesting or, occasionally, important, but important as jazz, symphony or gypsy music, not as folk song . . . But when a so-called folk-singer, with no respect for or knowledge of the style or the original emotional content of the song, acquires the shell of the song merely and leaves its subtle vocal and interior behind, there is a definite expressive loss.[32]

Greenwich Village

Through 1958 Izzy Young promoted the Folklore Center, which served as a local (even national) magnet for performers and fans alike. In his column in the *New York Folklore Quarterly* the folklorist B. A. Botkin reminded readers that Young had predicted that "new forces and movements are about to burgeon in the American folklore field." As for Botkin, briefly reviewing some of the recent folk music controversies, "If the burgeoning resembles the dandelions on the spring lawns, then we should be thankful that there are not more weeds and that the greensward is still there, that spring is in the air, and that the sound of banjoes and guitars heard in the land is a pleasant relief from the power-mowers." No doubt Izzy could not have agreed more. While the Folklore Center limped along financially—Izzy preferred to talk and organize rather than make a profit—the proprietor began reaching out to publicize the music. *Caravan* repeatedly mentioned the Folklore Center as the place to purchase folk supplies or concert tickets, meet people, or obtain information.[33]

From April to October, on warm Sunday afternoons, Washington Square, just around the corner from the Folklore Center, captured the essence of the burgeoning revival—amateur, enthusiastic, eclectic. "Musicians, many with guitars, some with banjos, a few with mandolins and one or two with bass viols, share the fountain with Greenwich Villagers, tourists, cats and dogs and a clicking corps of photographers," Michael James happily reported in the *New York Times*. The Square attracted young people from throughout the city. " 'The Village used to be a refuge from Iowa,' one Villager noted, 'but now it's a refuge from Brooklyn and the Bronx.' " The young folksingers who filled the park during the early afternoon, singing, picking, and listening, would be slowly replaced, first by "the beatniks with beards and tattered jeans, their girls with long untidy hair. To these beatniks, Mr. Rinaldo [foreman of the park], the police and even the ballad singers are 'square' and 'ain't nowhere nohow.' "[34]

Barry Kornfeld, sketching in *Caravan* the history of the singing in the Square, stressed the tensions and clashes with the police, often over types of instruments—currently bongos were banned. He ended the piece pessimistically: "It is interesting to note that what remains of the political and social climate is somewhat cynico-nihlistic, as opposed to the former prevailing optimism. . . . Further, few, if any of today's folksingers link themselves with the Washington Square tradition." Despite such carping, crowds gathered each week, generating enthusiasm and publicity, though frictions with the neighborhood and city authorities would continue.[35]

One activist group of performers and fans, allied with Lee Shaw and *Caravan*, coalesced as the Folksingers Guild. Organized by Dave Van Ronk, Roy Berkeley, and their Village friends in 1957, the loose group first rented the Young Socialist League's hall. "I was very scrupulous," remembered Berkeley. "I had asked the YSL to let us use their hall. But I didn't want to turn the Folksingers' Guild into a front for the YSL. I didn't want to do to the Folksingers' Guild and to our music what I felt the Communist Party had been doing to other organizations and to their music." Over the next two years they had enough money to rent Adelphi Hall for their monthly concerts, then other neighboring locations, often at midnight when the space was available.[36]

Affiliated with various noncommunist left-wing organizations, the Guild, led by Van Ronk, rebelled against performing for free (or whatever they could get by passing the hat) at the few coffeehouses springing up in the Village, such as Rick Allmen's Café Bizarre. "They tried to instill in the rest of the folksingers that the coffee houses were exploiting them, using them to draw people without paying them," Aaron Rennert recalls. "And this thing just seemed to snowball into what was originally supposed to be a folksingers' union." The organization raised just enough from one concert to put on the next. Rennert, along with Joel Katz and Ray Sullivan, formed Photo-Sound Associates, and struck an arrangement with the group to obtain exclusive control over photographing and recording the concerts. Besides the ubiquitous Van Ronk and Berkeley, performers included Roger Abrahams, Luke Faust, Gina Glaser, Dick Weissman, Happy Traum, John Cohen, Tom Paley, and toward the end in 1959 Frank Hamilton, Tony Saletan, Cynthia Gooding, Billy Faier and the Greenbriar Boys. Van Ronk remembers: "We would never do solo concerts. There were always about three or four people on the bill. Somebody would be up there for about fifteen or twenty minutes and we'd yank them off just before everybody left and then hit them with the next screecher."[37]

Unlike Chicago, San Francisco, and Los Angeles, New York lacked a full-fledged folk club. Art D'Lugoff filled that vacuum by opening the Village Gate in early 1958, "featuring beer, barbeque and folk songs." A graduate of New York University in 1949, he had sampled various jobs—newspaper work, labor organizing for the United Electrical Workers, waiter, freelance writer—until entering the concert promotion business in the mid-1950s. His left-wing politics easily meshed with his love of jazz and folk. After promoting numerous concerts at the Circle-in-the-Square, Town Hall, and Carnegie Hall (including a jazz series with Louis Armstrong in 1956) and managing a few performers such as the Tarriers, he decided to create his own large (450-seat) concert hall/cabaret. Before opening he had traveled around the country, picking up tips from the operations of the Gate of Horn, the hungry i, and Cosmo Alley, his closest models. Some pressure from local gangsters and crooked cops caused D'Lugoff a few uneasy moments, but he refused the payoffs and they backed off. A born optimist, he also believed in the commercial potential of folk music.[38]

"When he opened the Village Gate in 1958, d'Lugoff [sic] wanted to feature folk music," Dan Wakefield later remembered, "but he couldn't afford it." He told Wakefield, "The Weavers I couldn't buy, or the Kingston Trio, and I couldn't afford Joan Baez, so I turned to jazz." The Village Gate became a major jazz (and comedy) venue, but continued with a steady stream of folk performers, particularly Pete Seeger, one of D'Lugoff's favorites, and various Israeli singers. The Village Gate and Izzy Young's nearby Folklore Center, on MacDougal between 3d and Bleeker, served as the bookends of the Village folk scene. Young shared D'Lugoff's penchant for folk, but he also loved jazz. Indeed, starting in late 1958 he briefly copublished the short-lived *Jazz Review*, edited by Nat Hentoff and Martin Williams.[39]

Barry Kornfeld sketched a graphic portrait of the Folklore Center in *Caravan's* midsummer 1958 issue:

> Inside is a long, narrow shop lined with ceiling-high shelving. On the right wall are books and periodicals dealing with all phases of folk music, lore, and dance, plus jazz, some Elizabethan music, and whatever else may have struck Mr Young's fancy. On the left wall, front, is a display of concert announcements, local notices, and business cards of guitar and banjo teachers. A row of posters just below the ceiling gives a chronological history of Folklore Center sponsored concerts. The left rear wall is piled high with folk and jazz records.

Izzy's shop not only served as the focal point of local folk activities but also attracted national attention. Always eager to reach out, assist, and inform, Izzy had been developing national connections through his book business for a few years. The president of the folksong society at Baldwin-Wallace College in Berea, Ohio, wrote in late 1958 asking for advice. Despite "the general lathargy [sic] on campus as well as an opposition to anything new," the club had sponsored two successful concerts, the first by Pete Seeger and Sonny Terry, followed by Guy Carawan. He now wondered, what next? Club members had seen neither *Sing Out!* nor *Caravan* and were "hungry for any information, advice, or help which you can give us."[40]

In early 1959 Young made a deal with Irwin Silber to write a regular column for *Sing Out!* titled "Frets and Frails," which would be free from censorship or constraints. The column, first appearing in the spring 1959 issue, would quickly become a much read and discussed feature, essentially a gossip column of the folk world. With no introduction or fanfare, Izzy began with a notice of Alan Lomax's return to the United States (he also feted him at the Folklore Center). *Newsweek* had already recognized Lomax's accomplishments and reappearance "after seven years of tireless folk-song collecting across Europe. . . . In possibly a thousand villages he had become a familiar figure, swinging along lopsided with the weight of his tape recorder, laughing, scowling, cajoling, and bullying local singers to record in bars, on threshing floors, and even in sulphur mines." Seeger told *Sing Out!* readers that Lomax had planted the seed, and folk music "flourishes now like any happy weed, quite out of control of any person or party, right or left, purist or hybridist, romanticist or scientist."[41]

Upon his return, Lomax quickly made his presence felt in early April with "Folksong '59," a musical extravaganza at Carnegie Hall. Performers ran the gamut from the Arkansas singer Jimmy Driftwood to the gospel Selah Jubilee Singers and Drexel Singers, the blues performers Muddy Waters and Memphis Slim, the Stony Mountain Boys playing bluegrass, Pete and Mike Seeger, the Cadillacs (a rock and roll group), and Lomax himself doing prison work songs. "The time has come for Americans not to be ashamed of what we go for, musically, from primitive ballads to rock 'n' roll songs," Lomax declared, defending his eclectic approach and acceptance of change. John Wilson, in the *New York Times*, praised him for producing "an array of artists who gave a fascinating display of the source material that the juke boxes have diluted and distorted," and favorably compared the event to John Hammond's "Spirituals to Swing" concert twenty years earlier. Others expressed more skepticism. Aaron Rennert, in *Gardyloo*, generally admired the performers but criticized the sound system, obvious lack of rehearsals, and jumbled program. Lomax made little attempt to explain the various styles, seemed "discourteous to both the performers and his audience," and some booed and hissed him, or even left the hall, when "he told them to lay down their prejudices and listen to rock 'n' roll." Izzy Young recalled a few years later that Lomax "put on what is probably the turning point in American folk music. . . . At that concert the point he was trying to make was that Negro and white music were mixing, and rock and roll was that thing."[42]

Perhaps the show's main contribution came in opening Carnegie Hall to bluegrass, still a little-recognized style in the North. Pete Seeger had added a section on Earl Scruggs in his banjo instruction book as early as 1954, and Mike Seeger produced *American Banjo Scruggs Style* for Folkways in 1957 including the New York–based Eric Weissberg, followed two years later by *Mountain Music Bluegrass Style*. Roger Sprung had introduced bluegrass banjo to Washington Square, and in 1957 he formed the bluegrass-style Shanty Boys with Mike Cohen (John's brother) and Lionel Kilberg. Still, Roger Lass had to apologize in *Caravan* for seeming to have overlooked the music; giving a short description and history, he concluded with a plug for the Shanty Boys. Mike Seeger, Eric Weissberg, and Roger Sprung were now regulars in Washington Square, along with Marshall Brickman, Ralph Rinzler and the Greenbriar Boys (Bob Yellin, Paul Prestopino, and John Herald). In July 1959 the Stanley Brothers and Earl Scruggs, playing with Hylo Brown and the Timberliners, appeared at the first Newport Folk Festival, marking bluegrass's official recognition as an element of the revival.

Lomax, fittingly, anointed the music in the October 1959 *Esquire*, in his influential "Bluegrass Background: Folk Music with Overdrive." He pronounced: "Out of the torrent of folk music that is the backbone of the record business today, the freshest sound comes from the so-called Bluegrass band—a sort of mountain Dixieland combo in which the five-string banjo, American's only indigenous folk instrument, carries the lead like a hot clarinet. . . . The result is folk music in overdrive with a silvery, rippling, pinging sound." According to Lomax, Bill Monroe had recruited Earl Scruggs and Lester Flatt in 1945, launching a new music that drew on the rich, vibrant legacy of old-time music. Short and to the point, the article stamped bluegrass with a patriotic pedigree and with Lomax's valuable seal of approval.[43]

Izzy Young covered a wide swath of folk news in Sing Out!, ranging from Odetta, Theo Bikel and the New Lost City Ramblers to the Idyllwild summer folk workshop. He particularly delighted in giving travel itineraries. The blues performers Champion Jack Dupree, Lightnin' Hopkins, Muddy Waters, Lizzie Miles and Howlin' Wolf were appearing in England—"American Blues are being recognized in England and Europe while they are not encouraged enough here," said Izzy—and he applauded the State Department for sponsoring a tour of India by Brownie McGhee, Sonny Terry, Marilyn Child, and Cisco Houston, as well as Tony Saletan's two-year trip to the Far East.[44]

Not satisfied with the quarterly appearance of "Frets and Frails," in late 1959 Izzy launched an expansive monthly publication, Folk Music Guide, USA. He expected "to list every folk music event in America—concerts, festivals, club dates and college programs of folksingers, etc." Mentioning bits and pieces of news about peripatetic folksingers home and abroad—which were too late for his last "Frets and Frails" and too early for the next Sing Out!—he also included listings of concerts, book and record reviews, ads, and a few essays. Ambitious in scope, it was too much even for the energetic Izzy, and it folded after four issues.[45]

Izzy fought to be the conscience as well as the town crier of the revival. He predicted in mid-1959: "There will be so much money to be made in Folk Music in the next two to three years that politics and personal differences will be forgotten in the desperate attempts to copyright every folksong that was ever written." Certainly, he had "nothing against Tin Pan Alley as they are in the business to make money." Yet he felt "bad about all the new music that will parade as Folk Music just the way a lot of new music was called Calypso a few years ago." In predicting increasing commercialization of folk music, he also advised prospective store owners on how to make money: "Don't be married. Have faith in your genius. Put on concerts which only 60 people will attend to attest to your integrity. Lend money to any itinerant folk singers. Let them sleep in back of your store and feed them. Once your ego is established start your own magazine. Brag if you can pay the bills."[46]

Always a maverick, bighearted though with no activist political background, Izzy worked with anyone in order to promote the music he loved. Silber charged that Izzy had been approached by both Archie Green and Billy Faier to drop his Sing Out! column "because that meant that he was lending himself to the unsavory political reputation of our magazine." He queried Green, "Do you feel that we must prove our anti-Communism to your satisfaction before you will believe it legitimate for someone to write for us?" As for Izzy, he had no thoughts of surrendering his quarterly podium and gossip column.[47]

Izzy constantly tried to stir the pot, tugging folk music back to its traditional rural roots while commercial pressures strongly pulled in the other direction. He certainly had difficulty accepting the arguments of Jac Holzman, now prospering as head of Elektra after years of struggling to survive. "I have been suggesting a wider television exposure of folk music to interest the general public," Holzman wrote to Izzy in October 1959, and "perhaps the most important factor is the accent on personalities such as the Kingston Trio which have the ability to capture the interest of a large number of people who have never been conscious of folk music before. In this respect, the Kingston Trio has put us on the map."[48]

Commercial (as well as academic) aspirations also appeared in *Caravan*. Despite her modest goals, the readership grew, and so editor Lee Shaw switched from mimeo to photo-offset for the August/September 1958 issue, a large, slick bimonthly with a press run of two thousand (up from two hundred a year earlier). By year's end, Roger Abrahams was serving as record review editor and Kenneth Goldstein as book review editor. The February/March issue announced a new editor, Billy Faier, recently returned from California, with no mention of Shaw. *Caravan* now revealed a more academic thrust with a piece on the American Folklore Society (AFS) by MacEdward Leach; Archie Green's critical analysis of the limited discography in Malcolm Laws's *American Balladry from British Broadsides: A Guide for Students and Collectors of Traditional Song* (American Folklore Society, 1957); and Faier's report of the annual AFS meeting (with some chatty news about the Village crowd). Scratching for new subscriptions and fresh copy, Faier struggled along: "I have been abismally [sic] busy with this frigging mag and trying to make a living etc.," he wrote to Archie Green.[49]

A marvelous performer with a strong following, Faier tried "to do a more balanced scholarly thing" than *Sing Out!* "I was trying to bridge the two worlds—the scholar's and the urban folk singer's. And I did to a great extent." Not everyone appreciated the new approach. "The changeover from a gossipy fanzine to a responsible, informative publication has lost us many readers, as was expected," he said. "On the other hand, many others have subscribed specifically because of the change." Since he hoped to make a profit, this was a serious situation. Simultaneously, he worked for WBAI, where he had a folk show, *Midnight Special*, live music on Saturday nights.[50]

Aside from the change of editors, *Caravan*'s staff remained about the same, with Faier also writing his share of articles, including a glowing review of *The Bosses' Song book*, a parody of the old *People's Song Book*. First issued in 1957 in a small run of five hundred, the expanded version, still published by Dick Ellington, took a biting look at the old Left as well as at capitalism from a socialist/anarchist perspective. The songs, some written by Roy Berkeley, others by Dave Van Ronk, gained instant notoriety. "BOSSES' SONGBOOK is aimed exclusively at people who are (a) radicals, (b) folksong enthusiasts, and (c) people who don't mind seeing their little tin gods kicked around. Turns out there are a surprising number of people who fit all three categories," Ellington bragged to Archie Green. Fred Hoeptner contributed a fascinating two-part piece,

"Folk and Hillbilly Music," to *Caravan* in mid-1959, one of the first serious treatments geared to an audience beyond the slight group of dedicated hillbilly record collectors. He made a strong case for the ongoing relevance of old-time string-band music: "The early hillbilly performers obtained their style and material from the previous non-commercial folk song and style and developed on it; todays [sic] 'folk' performer, usually the urban folk singer, is obtaining his style and material increasingly from hillbilly styles and developing on them, especially the instrumental style."[51]

Constantly broke, Faier kept up with his monthly schedule for a few issues, then ran into additional misfortune later in 1959. Issue no. 20, dated June/July 1960, was the last to appear, but *Caravan* had made its mark, locally and nationally. Combining gossip and scholarship, news and complaint, celebration and nitpicking, both versions of the magazine had introduced countless musicians and fans to the rapidly changing folk scene, focusing on tradition and style and disdaining commercial glitz (the Kingston Trio barely rated a mention). Moreover, both Shaw and Faier acknowledged that the Village folk scene was not unique, and they continued to publicize national folk happenings, particularly in Chicago and on the West Coast, as well as in England. Yet Shaw had never taken *Caravan* very seriously—"What I was doing was a fanzine," she said. "It was a hobby thing. We were local gossip, whatever people wanted to put in print."[52]

Shaw was not quite done with folk music and magazine publishing, however. "Although I've been somewhat aware of the 'hillbilly' field for sometime, I've only recently 'discovered' it myself," she informed Archie Green in early 1959. "With the release of the New Lost City Ramblers record and several other things, including my acquisition of the Folkways [Harry Smith] anthology, I find a whole vast genre of music before me." Combining her newfound musical interest and desire to continue publishing, she launched the mimeographed *Gardyloo*—titled after the traditional city cry before emptying the slop jar out the window—in April 1959, again with mostly New York news. Now she could go back to "the way things were done with the early *Caravan*, strictly for fun. Not have to worry about advertisers, printers, and all that kind of stuff. Just messing around." Publication would be sporadic; it would last for seven issues, eventually running out of gas in 1960. Only a hundred or so copies circulated locally. She started with a gentle portrait of Erik Darling, followed by Izzy Young's defense of city folksingers, in which he explained that he meant nothing critical in coining the word "folknik." Shaw praised the artistry and enthusiasm of an eclectic concert hosted by Oscar Brand, with the Shanty Boys, Hally Wood, Andrew Roman Summers, Cynthia Gooding, Pete Seeger, Frank Warner, Lord Invader and the Tarriers.[53]

Above all, *Gardyloo* served to publicize the New Lost City Ramblers. Fellow students John Cohen and Tom Paley had played together at the first hoot at

Yale University in 1952, and later in the Village. A seasoned banjo player and alumnus of People's Songs, Paley had quickly developed a legendary reputation; his ten-inch Elketra album, *Folk Songs from the Southern Appalachians* (1953), proved most influential on urban folksingers. He remembers meeting Peggy Seeger at Yale along with her younger brother, Mike. The son of Charles and Ruth, and half-brother of Pete, Mike Seeger had been weaned on folk music and soon became a versatile performer. Cohen, Paley and Seeger assiduously listened to old hillbilly recordings, including the Alan Lomax reissues *Listen to Our Story* and *Mountain Frolic* and the earlier John Lomax compilation *Smokey Mountain Ballads*.

Cohen, Seeger and Paley began playing together in mid-1958, first on a radio program in Washington, followed by a concert at the recital hall of Carnegie Hall, organized by Izzy Young. Folkways released their first album, *The New Lost City Ramblers*, in early 1959 to solid local reviews; it was soon followed by a second and third. "Our repertoire was largely drawn from old hillbilly records of the 1920s and '30s," Cohen notes, "and although many people thought that we sounded exactly like the old records, we didn't. We introduced the name 'old-time music' on our second album, *Old Time Music for Children*. We stood in opposition to the commercialization of folk music." Other skilled bluegrass and string bands began to emerge on the local scene, but the Ramblers would be most successful in planting the seeds of an old-time revival throughout the country. Their appearance at the first Newport Folk Festival in 1959 marked their indubitable coming of age.[54]

The folk revival proceeded on two parallel, slightly divided, tracks. Local performers, promoters, scholars, and fans struggled over authenticity, style, and performance, relishing yet trying to make sense of the vibrant folk scene. Simultaneously, the forces of commerce and publicity recognized the new sounds. Grace Jan Waldman fueled the national publicity with her May 1959 description, "Life among the Guitars," in *Mademoiselle*. Beginning with the requisite description of Washington Square on Sunday afternoons—"modern minstrels, bards and troubadours revive the ancient art of story-singing, their guitars substitute for ancestral lyres and Irish harps"—Waldman's colorful guided tour stretched to Chicago's Old Town School and Gate of Horn and to the Unicorn in Los Angeles. She mentioned concerts at college campuses scattered around the country, academic folklore departments, the Library of Congress, and Big Bill Broonzy's impact on Iowa State University, where he worked as a janitor before his death in 1958. She concluded: "It is hard to tell whether there is truth in the traditionalist's lament that the increasing popularity of folk music will result in its distortion. It does seem certain, however, that this art will not easily be returned to the custodianship of the archives set now that folk music has been discovered by thousands of people." Thoughtful and wide-ranging (with no mention of the Kingston Trio), Waldman's piece endeavored to achieve a sense of balance.[55]

"The folkniks are on the move as never before," reported *Billboard* the following month. "The emergence of folk music and artists as big business is highlighted by more folk records in release, more periodicals on folk music in publication, more frantic activity on the doubtful front of copyrighting the largely public domain material of the folk field, and more folk music concerts, particularly on the outdoor front, than at any time in recent memory." The piece covered the Newport Folk Festival, Richard Dyer-Bennet and Brother John Sellers at the outdoor Ravinia Festival in Chicago, and other concerts and festivals. T. E. Rafferty (a pseudonym) added a sour note in *Knave* (men's magazines increasingly covered folk music), questioning the authenticity of those "drooling 'Tom Dooley,' wailing 'Wimoweh,' and limning out 'Hey Lilly Liley Oh.' " After furnishing a brief, sarcastic overview of the revival, the author ended with a warning: "It shows every sign of being a big, healthy fad for quite a while. But it's fake, not folk." He recommended the New Lost City Ramblers, Pete Seeger, and Oscar Brand.[56]

Billboard's reporters took a somewhat different tack, focusing more on popular country performers such as Johnny Horton, Stonewall Jackson, and Carl Smith who drew on traditional rural styles. Horton's "The Battle of New Orleans" reached number one on the charts in May 1959, where it remained for over two months; Jackson's "Waterloo" reached number four and stayed popular for four months; Smith's "Ten Thousand Drums" broke into the top one hundred for two months, peaking at number 43. Whether labeled folk or country, such music proved that "only authentic, American-based material appears to last in the pop world. . . . Jazz, r.&b.[,] country and folk are all basic American forms which last."[57]

The Newport Folk Festival

George Wein and Albert Grossman struggled to merge the various strands of the burgeoning folk revival in the first Newport Folk Festival, July 11–12, 1959. The wide range of performers included: Odetta, Leon Bibb, Jean Ritchie, Jimmy Driftwood, Pat Clancy and Tommy Makem, Pete Seeger, Frank Warner, Martha Schlamme, Brownie McGhee and Sonny Terry, Memphis Slim, Barbara Dane, Earl Scruggs, the Stanley Brothers, the New Lost City Ramblers, Reverend Gary Davis with Barry Kornfeld, Billy Faier, Frank Hamilton, John Jacob Niles, Professor Alex Bradford, Oscar Brand, the Kossoy Sisters, Cynthia Gooding, Ed McCurdy, Bob Gibson, and the Kingston Trio. Pretty much something for everyone—citybilly and hillbilly, traditional and popular, gospel, white and black blues, bluegrass, traditional and revivalist. Studs Terkel traveled from Chicago to share master of ceremonies duties with Seeger and Brand.

Long a summer watering hole for the rich, and more recently a tourist attraction, Newport, Rhode Island, had much to offer, yet was off the beaten path and difficult to get to. Seeking to enliven the local cultural scene, residents Elaine and Louis Lorrillard first decided in the early 1950s to organize a concert by the New York Philharmonic, which flopped. They next hit upon the idea of a nonprofit jazz festival in July 1954 and hired George Wein, recommended by John Hammond, as the organizer. An accomplished jazz pianist, Wein owned two jazz clubs, Storyville and Mahogany Hall, in Boston, as well as a record label. The jazz festival clicked, but in subsequent years it increasingly drew a beer-swilling college crowd, annoying many of the locals. Rock and roll had crept in during the 1958 festival, and Wein planned on adding folk artists the next year—an afternoon with Seeger, the Kingston Trio, and Odetta. As plans ripened, Wein decided a separate folk festival was in order, officially sponsored by the nonprofit Newport Jazz Foundation.

Wein hired Albert Grossman to produce the first festival. Still living in Chicago, Grossman traveled back and forth, organizing and arranging, shaping an eclectic event considerably more expansive than the Berkeley folk festival. Advance ticket sales indicated a small crowd, and publicity had been minimal. Yet twelve thousand attended the three concerts, a workshop on instrumental techniques, and a seminar. The festival was a popular if not yet a financial success.

Robert Shelton's coverage in the New York Times celebrated "perhaps the most ambitious attempt ever made at delineating a cross-section of the nation's folk music." He praised Grossman for his ample reach and all of the performers, particularly Odetta, though he cautioned that a few—Jean Ritchie, John Jacob Niles, and Reverend Gary Davis—seemed out of place performing in a baseball park. Somewhat more expansive in a follow-up piece in the Nation. Shelton again wondered, "How do you transplant the 'root' singers and put them on side by side with the large-voiced, polished and earnest professionals?" This conundrum would plague future festivals. Shelton's generally positive comments, however, belied his private complaints. "I rather consciously held back on negative criticism at Newport in both my Times piece and Nation piece," he revealed to Archie Green. "I may be wrong, but I think a new venture like this needs public support now. There'll be time enough to tear into [it] after it is old enough to stand on its own feet. . . . It seems to me that when they get an advisory panel that a good many of the fights about the Kingston Trio vs. ethnic singers can take place there and the festival will ultimately move in a more representative direction."[58]

Writing in the Christian Science Monitor, Robert Gustafson praised most of the performers, particularly Frank Warner, while criticizing the "slick and distorted" offerings of the Kingston Trio. He thought the Sunday morning seminar, with the folklorist Willis James, Alan Lomax, Moses Asch, and the critic Stanley Edgar Hyman, added the proper critical, scholarly touch. Frederic Ramsey, in the Saturday Review, dwelled more on the rain and fog, but predicted that the festival "will be followed by the other folk concerts and tours of folk artists throughout the country." He recalled the old days "when a folk performer like Lead Belly had to be towed from one college to the next to entertain small campus audiences. That which no one performer could achieve by himself—an arena for his voice—has been established by many."[59]

The Greenwich Village pundits weighed in with detailed scrutiny. "When Pete Seeger, singing *Darlin' Cory*, stepped into the swirling mist—colored by the lights blue and red and amber—to open the first concert of the Newport Folk Festival, it was as though by some magic we were witnessing the birth of our folk music revival," Mark Morris reported in *Gardyloo*. "The concert that followed, the most dazzling I've seen, brilliantly bore out this theme." He stressed the crowd frenzy over the Kingston Trio on Sunday night, though "what connection these frenetic tinselly showmen have with a folk festival eludes me." When Earl Scruggs, playing with Hylo Brown and the Timbeliners, followed the Trio onstage for the finale, it took Oscar Brand fifteen minutes to control the unruly crowd, and he had to promise the Trio's reappearance. Morris concluded, "If their presence will assure the audience which enables the festival to present the other performers on the program, I shall grit my teeth and welcome them." *Sing Out!* editor Silber hailed the festival as "the most ambitious folk song fest since Joshua's army sang down the walls of Jericho," but noted that Alan Lomax had "dismissed the event as 'a publicity stunt.'"[60]

Izzy Young hailed the festival in *Caravan*: "Where Alan Lomax failed in FOLKSONG '69 at Carnegie Hall a few months ago, Albert Grossman succeeded at Newport without making cerebrations of what the singers should sing. Grossman did not demand that the show revolve around his idea of what folk music should be." Izzy flattered the refreshing newcomer Joan Baez, but griped about the Kingston Trio: "Only one person was heard booing (this writer) when the Kingston Trio returned to another great ovation." In the following issue Izzy complained that his article had been largely rewritten: "No two of my sentences were left in order and the rest you rewrote so that my sense, style, thought and integrity were violated grossly." Perhaps he had been more critical in the first version; after all, editor Faier had a stake in the festival, having written the introduction to the festival's official program.[61]

Few mentioned Joan Baez's brief appearance, the festival's most important legacy to the revival. Joan had begun to perform while at Palo Alto High School in the late 1950s, influenced by Belafonte, Seeger, and Odetta. She moved with her family to the Boston area in 1958 when her physicist father began teaching at MIT. She recalled listening to the Kingston Trio driving across country; they remained her secret favorites. Joan briefly attended Boston University and promptly joined the Harvard Square folk scene, singing at Club Mount Auburn 47, better known as Club 47, where she built her repertoire.

Preceded by the Cafe Yana in Boston and Tulla's Coffee Grinder in Cambridge,

Club 47 was opened by Joyce Kalina and Paula Kelley in January 1958. Originally featuring jazz, which caused legal problems because it did not have a cabaret license, the club reorganized as a nonprofit educational institution after a few months, offering memberships to the patrons. Folk performers appeared two nights a week, and Baez became the club's first regular "professional." She even cut a local album with Bill Wood and Ted Alevizos, *Folksingers 'round Harvard Square.* Rather at loose ends, in July 1959 she accepted Grossman's offer to perform at the Gate of Horn, two weeks for $200 a week. Here she shared the stage with Bob Gibson and met Odetta. Gibson invited her to appear as his guest at the upcoming Newport festival, and she found herself driving east with Odetta.

Joan's memories of Newport are burnished with feelings of excitement and dread, recalling "tents full of folksingers, banjo pickers, fiddle players and gospel groups, and streets full of hitchhikers. The kids who flocked to the festival were trim and had short hair." On Sunday night, in the midst of his act, Gibson gave her a short introduction.

> In that moment there was only the speeding of my heart; all movement was a silent film, and all sound was surface noise. . . . Bob was giving me a bright and cheery smile, and his cocky look which meant that life was only one big joke anyway, so not to worry. We sang, "Virgin Mary Had One Son." He played the twelve-string, and with eighteen strings and two voices we sounded pretty impressive. I had a solo part next, and my voice came out just fine. We made it to the end and there was tumultuous applause. So we sang our "other" song, an upbeat number (thanks to Bob) called "Jordan River." The two songs were religious, and I looked and sounded like purity itself in long tresses, no makeup, and Bible sandals.

She left the stage and plunged into much commotion. The next day she joined Gibson at a local private concert, earning $100, a fortune that sealed her fate. Word of her triumph at Newport quickly spread, and when she returned to Club 47 for her regular Tuesday night stint students lined the block trying to get in. The smitten Grossman strenuously tried to enlist her as a client, promising a Columbia Records contract. She preferred, however, to sign with Maynard Solomon at Vanguard, a small but glossy label and home of the Weavers, and she soon took on the low-key, politically receptive Manny Greenhill as her manager.[62]

Raised in New York and early exposed to labor songs and left-wing theater, Greenhill moved to Boston in 1950 and within a few years began to organize children's concerts, some with folksinger Tony Saletan. Art D'Lugoff's New York midnight concerts seemed an intriguing idea, and he presently developed relationships with D'Lugoff, Moe Asch, and the folk establishment of New York. An organizer of the Folksong Society of Boston, Greenhill helped stage concerts at the YMCA, charging a modest 99¢. Pete Seeger appeared at MIT in 1956, to a packed house of over one thousand. Willing to confront the American Legion and other obstructive groups, the amenable and politically committed Greenhill agreed to serve as Seeger's New England agent, an arrangement that continued through the 1960s.

Not much impressed with the Kingston Trio, Greenhill preferred "a more rootsy sound," yet recognized the quickening commercial folk scene and hung around Club 47, where he first heard Baez. By late 1959 he billed himself as "New England's most active folk impresario and agent," with his Folklore Productions concerts at Jordan Hall featuring Alan Lomax, Sonny Terry and Brownie McGhee, Josh White, Merle Travis, Sister Rosetta Tharpe and Alex Bradford, and Oranim Zabar; his ten to twelve concerts a year would stretch into the 1970s. Also in late 1959 he and George Wein opened the Ballad Room, a folk night club, beginning with Bud and Travis, joined by Rolf Cahn. Greenhill connected with a growing list of regional folk entrepreneurs—D'Lugoff in New York, Frank Fried and Grossman in Chicago, Paul Endicott in the Midwest, Ed Pearl in Los Angeles, and Mary Ann Pollar in Northern California.[63]

Chicago

Bernie Krause grew up in Detroit during the 1940s surrounded by classical music, which was gradually replaced by jazz, pop, blues, and folk by the early 1950s as he learned to play the guitar. Present with his parents at the Weavers's 1955 Christmas concert at Carnegie Hall, he later recalled, "When the Weavers began to sing, the atmosphere was palpable. . . . The crowd was on its feet most of the time. Even standing on my seat, I rarely caught a glimpse of the group that night." After joining the Folklore Society at the University of Michigan, he found himself typed a folksinger. Folk music at the university combined performance and activist politics, as the members quarreled about authenticity, generally disparaging the Kingston Trio and their ilk. In the spring of 1959 Krause's friends in the Folklore Society, Al Young and Bill McAdoo, helped launch *Folkways*, grandiosely subtitled *A Magazine of International Folklore*.[64]

In May 1959 Krause heard a Bob Gibson concert in Detroit, and after the show he demonstrated to the master that he could precisely imitate his guitar style. Highly impressed, Gibson invited Krause to sit in as his backup guitar player during his regular stint at the Gate of Horn in Chicago the following month, for five dollars. Elated at the prospect, Krause packed his clothes in his guitar case and hopped a freight as far as South Bend, where he was thrown off and had to hitchhike the rest of the way. Arriving broke in the Windy City, Krause embarked on a remarkable daylong odyssey. He first visited Grossman's office to meet Gibson. When he asked the secretary for Al, she directed him down the hall. "I walked into a room where, to my youthful amazement, Al was in bed with a woman," Krause recalled. "He brought his hand up from under the sheet for me to shake. Wet and sticky, his handshake was memorial. . . . I left—feeling a bit sick—and sat on the floor in the waiting room." Gibson arrived and suggested they walk over to the Gate for a sound check. On the way Gibson pointed to an old man on the sidewalk just ahead, whom they followed into a record store. "Approaching him, Gibson said, . . . 'Bernie, this is Carl Sandburg.' Catching my breath, I struggled to say something intelligent but was silent from shock." The poet invited them to his apartment, where they sipped iced tea, singing and talking for an hour or so. They finally arrived at the club, where Krause spotted "a fragile-looking young woman with long, black hair, bare feet, and marvelous, enigmatic eyes." Joan Baez. "I fell in love with her in a nanosecond. . . . I sat down next to her at the table, and we began playing guitar together, exchanging tunes, and singing to one another." After the sound check he called his grandfather in Chicago, inviting him to the club that night, but he declined. That evening the packed audience gave Baez mild applause, waiting eagerly for Gibson and his unknown accompanist. "Walking up on the stage with Gibson and playing the opening tune was one of the most emotionally charged moments of my life. In my mind, I was finally a pro," Krause recalled.

> Toward the end of the first song, I caught a glimpse of three figures elbowing people aside as they forced their way toward the stage. I couldn't see very clearly because of the spotlight glare and the haze. But I did notice that two of them didn't stop shoving until they reached the lip of the stage. As we launched into the opening bars of the second tune, these two goons jumped up on the stage and shoved their way past the mics and cables to where I was standing. One grabbed my guitar and the other gripped my arm; they lifted me off the platform, through the room, up the stairs, and out the door—my feet barely touching the ground during the whole transaction. I thought they were cops and felt utterly helpless. . . . Dragging me outside, one of these jerks pushed me up against the wall and pinned my arms. The other stood in the background, gripping my guitar by the sound hole. It was only then that I saw my grandfather standing in the shadows. He gave a nod. The fellow holding my guitar smashed it to pieces on a fire hydrant. Then my grandfather bounded over to me in a rage, and with one goon still restraining me, he slapped me hard across the head and screamed, "No grandson of mine is going to play these dives with whores and prostitutes!"

The two "thugs" hustled him into a limo and deposited him at Midway Airport, where a waiting plane whisked him back to Detroit. "I was so embarrassed and furious that I never spoke with my grandfather again." Twenty-five years later Krause regaled Gibson with the evening's events, and he responded, "So, that's what happened?" Within a few years Krause would be a member of the Weavers.[65]

Chicago's dynamic folk scene offered much to musicians and fans. Gibson anchored the stream of talent at the Gate of Horn, including the Gateway Singers, Josh White, Odetta, Brother John Sellers, Theo Bikel, Barbara Dane, Bud and Travis, and Stan Wilson. The plush Orchestra Hall featured concerts by many of the same performers, as well as Pete Seeger, Oscar Brand, and Jean Ritchie. Studs Terkel continued his "I Come for to Sing" shows, area universities hosted concerts, and Grossman sponsored various programs. Toward the end of 1959 Bud and Travis appeared with Lenny Bruce at Mister Kelly's nightclub, and the Kingston Trio performed at Navy Pier.

Frank Fried, a laid-off steelworker, began working for Grossman in early 1958. Initially selling tickets for White and Bikel shows, after a year he struck out on his own. A social and labor activist, Fried had grudging admiration for Grossman, who "had no moral code or a political outlook that gave him a sense of morality so he was essentially an amoral person. He led a very consistent life, which is more than most people can say, and he stayed the course." Fried soon formed Triangle Productions, staging concerts at Orchestra Hall or wherever possible, gauging performers by their level of intensity and shunning the overly slick. Soon a folk manager and record producer, he later produced mammoth pop, folk, and rock concerts.[66]

The Old Town School continued with a four-day-a-week schedule, with guitar and banjo classes taught by Frank Hamilton, Win Stracke, Ted Johnson, and John Tangerman. Hamilton, a vital presence, sought to feed off but also counteract the growing popularity of the Kingston Trio and such popular acts: "It was our job to patiently reeducate the students. If it wasn't 'Tom Dooley' it would have been some other tune or music. As it was, we made sure that the students knew that 'Tom Dooley' had been collected from Frank Warner and originated from the singing of Frank Proffitt, the fretless banjo maker." The school grew over the years, producing a steady stream of amateur and soon-to-be professional musicians.[67]

Alan Ribback, born in the late 1920s, grew up in Chicago, and attended Northwestern University and graduate school at Indiana University. Early exposed to the prominent folk names, he joined the folk music club at IU, began performing locally, and helped organize a concert for Seeger at the Bloomington veterans' hall when the university refused the use of campus space. Returning to Chicago in 1957 he discovered the newly opened Gate of Horn. Ribback asked Grossman for advice and soon found himself managing the club, then became a copartner. The partnership had its problems. Grossman "more or less did what he wanted to do and he didn't share the work very well and we didn't agree sometimes," Ribback remembered, and the limited seating meant tight finances. Grossman, beginning to understand that folk music could be lucrative, moved more into concert production, including the Newport Folk Festival. The club relocated from its cellar on Dearborn Street to larger, plusher quarters on State Street. Ribback soon bought Grossman's half, and the latter moved to New York in 1960, launching a spectacular management career.

Paul Endicott, based in Garden City, Michigan, near Detroit, combined Left politics and extensive musical connections. In the mid-1950s he began booking concerts for Seeger and the Weavers in the Midwest, West, and Canada. He continually badgered Moe Asch for records, as promos or to be sold at the concerts, and kept up a steady correspondence, full of plans and suggestions. In October 1958 he informed Moe, "I am expanding the publicity end of things and will have one and two column mats set up for Pete, all photos will be captioned at the bottom with my name and address plus a blurb, new brochures are being printed, a list of records available for sale is going out." Guy Carawan had met Endicott in Detroit before Carawan's trip to Moscow and China. Endicott scheduled an extensive tour for him soon after his return, where he could perform and also show his travel photos. At a time when many performers were taking the topical sting out of the music, Carawan continued in the tradition of the Almanac Singers and People's Songs. By early 1959 Endicott also represented Sonny Terry and Brownie McGhee; later in the year he arranged Peggy Seeger and Ewan MacColl's concerts in Canada.[68]

Carawan's travels were interrupted by legal problems at the Highlander Folk School, where he had settled to revive their music program. The school was already under intense community pressure because of its deep involvement in civil rights organizing and interracial activities, and its alleged communist connections. On July 31, 1959, the last night of a community leadership workshop, county and state police raided the school. After Carawan and a few others were arrested, the raiding party terrorized the group for over an hour and ransacked the buildings. To steel themselves, the students sang "We Shall Overcome" during the ordeal. Carawan was soon arraigned on minor charges, and subsequently indicted by a grand jury, but charges were dropped the following year. "I spent a night in the Grundy County jail as a result of the hoax raid and am out on bail now," he informed Izzy Young on August 24. "Now they are trying to padlock the place." Brushing aside such troubles, he supplied more information on his recent trip to the South Carolina Sea Islands, excited that "the surrounding area of the Cumberlands here is full of Fiddlers, ballad singers, white and Negro church singing and more. We're planning a Cumberland Mt. Folk Festival next summer (a truly integrated one for all kinds of old & new Negro and white music which will be open to every one to attend)."[69]

Despite his work for Highlander, which paid little, Carawan kept a hectic tour schedule to the West Coast during the spring, then through the West, Midwest, and Canada in the fall and winter, while he continued to record for Folkways. Endicott informed Moe Asch of Carawan's travels, financial troubles, and other matters. For instance, he advised in late August: "Rev. King's church in Montgomery is under continuous surveillance and in view of the fact that the raid on Highlander made the front pages in Alabama, the Church people do not think that it would be wise for Guy to appear in Montgomery at this particular time. Therefore, the projected LP has been postponed until some time in the future." Perhaps the least commercial folk performer, Carawan toured the colleges, clubs, and progressive organizations in order to continue his work with civil rights and music preservation, in Tennessee and on the Sea Islands. Songwriter Ernie Marrs, visiting Highlander late in the year, sensed some friction between Carawan and Asch. He assured Asch, "Like me, he's trying his level best to learn all he can from these folks here—and to help in any way that he possibly can. They have sensed this, taken him as one of themselves, as nearly as possible, it seems." Carawan would become a key figure in stimulating and documenting the unfolding southern civil rights movement.[70]

Los Angeles

Billy Faier surveyed the Los Angeles scene in the April/May 1959 issue of *Caravan*. He began with a brief discussion of Herb Cohen's opening of the Unicorn, a coffee house featuring folk music but also "the headquarters of the Beat Generation." It catered to "tourists, 'beat' types (whom the tourists come to see), and the following of whatever folk singer happens to be singing"—perhaps Logan English, Dick Rosmini, Jimmy Gavin, or Faier himself. Cohen's other establishment, Cosmo Alley, with Barbara Dane, Theo Bikel, or Leon Bibb appearing, was more expensive and upbeat, frequented by "the Hollywood night club set." The Club Renaissance on Sunset Boulevard, owned by Ben Shapiro, also had folk performers on Thursday nights, such as Ramblin' Jack Elliott. The Unicorn's noisy crowd often frustrated the acoustic performers. Ed Pearl's Ash Grove seemed "the only place in Los Angeles where folk singers could present their material without any commercial coating." Faier also noted the opening of Gerald McCabe's guitar shop in Santa Monica, which became a magnet for performers and fans.[71]

Pearl, a guitar player and teacher who was heavily committed to Left politics, had been involved in local folk activities, particularly at UCLA, during the mid-1950s. He organized a flamenco show in late 1957, sponsored by his new creation, the L.A. Folk Music Society, and he followed with a concert by Logan English and Marcia Berman hosted by Ralph and Marcy McGlaze on Pico Place (known locally as Goat's Gulch) in Santa Monica. (The couple were close friends of Bess Hawes, Pearl's guitar teacher and a potent influence on him; Berman lived nearby, and the street had become a folk hangout.) Pearl was struck by the success of the Kingston Trio, not his favorite group but a sign of folk music's commercial potential, and by the crowds that turned out for his own concerts. Thinking a folk club was now feasible, he obtained financial backing and opened the Ash Grove in July 1958. Brownie McGhee, Carawan, and Pearl's flamenco guitar teacher, Jeronimo Villarino, performed on opening night. Charging $1.25 admission, he soon booked Barbara Dane, Leon Bibb, and Bud and Travis, creating the area's liveliest folk venue.

Pearl promptly connected with folk promoters and performers throughout the country. He traveled to the first Newport Folk Festival, where he met Grossman, Greenhill, Lomax, Baez, and the New Lost City Ramblers, who were soon to have a major impact on the Ash Grove. "Things have been terribly hectic here as I am forming a record company and a concert promotion company, and what with Barbara Dane and then Odetta here at the Ash Grove and my secretary ill I didn't get it out," he informed Izzy Young in late 1959, with news for the *Folk Music Guide USA*. Pearl did not initiate a record label (others recorded many of his performers), but he did launch Edwin M. Pearl Enterprises, promoting concerts throughout the state.[72]

Ed Kahn had grown up in Indianapolis and become involved in the folk scene while a student at Oberlin College in the mid-1950s, meeting Pete Seeger, Gibson, Carawan, Peggy Seeger, and Frank Hamilton. He recorded the traditional banjo player Pete Steele, who lived in Ohio, and produced an album for Folkways. After visiting the Asheville folk festival during the summer of 1957, he transferred to UCLA and began to study folklore with Wayland Hand, while selling Folkways records to Bess Hawes's students. A city product, he became attracted to southern white vernacular music, particularly as commercially recorded since the 1920s. Following graduation Kahn entered UCLA's doctoral program in anthropology and continued his study of traditional music. Starting in December 1958, McCabe's guitar shop furnished him with space to sell a complete line of folk records and a few books, with a branch at the Ash Grove; he remained at McCabe's for ten years. "I am now in a position to promote more folk music than I have ever been in in the past," he informed Moe Asch in mid-1959, "but I request your conscious cooperation so that I can do the best job." In addition to his business with McCabe, he sold records out of a coffeehouse in Hermosa Beach "which seems to attract a middle aged crowd which spends" and had begun concert promotions, starting with Pete Seeger.[73]

By the end of 1959 folk fans in Los Angeles had a rich but still limited choice of venues. The entrepreneur Herb Cohen, soon to depart the scene, later described a local (as well as national) two-tier folk circuit, the coffeehouses and the nightclubs. Performers might progress from a "basket house" in New York or Chicago, where they collected donations, to a "class A coffee house where they charged a few dollars admission. And from there you could be hired as an opening act, if you got great reviews," at a nightclub. A national folk circuit had been casually formed in recent years, with Southern California as one terminus. "A lot of the commercialism in the music and a lot of the sound in the music originated on the West Coast," Cohen has argued. "New York was much more a purist operation in terms of people performing. . . . I think it originated here with the Kingston Trio, Stan Wilson, Limeliters, that whole thing." "There was just no political emphasis out here," he concluded. "And so when I'm talking about a California sound, I attribute it to the essence of trying to become commercial." Remnants of the old Left, the People's Songs crowd, along with Ed Pearl and other local organizers, fought this trend, with some success. Nonetheless, Hollywood asserted its potent influence, promoting a commercial style that had grabbed the public's attention with the Kingston Trio and would continue to craft a popular folk sound. (Cohen himself would later be a potent force in pop music.)[74]

"I first see America through the window of an airplane. I expect it to be big," Mariam Makeba recalled in her autobiography. "This is the next to last day of November 1959. . . . The plane lands at Idlewild. Mr. Belafonte has a car there to meet me. I am to go directly to his offices on West Fifty-sixth Street. From the ground, Manhattan is just as impressive. But there is no time for sightseeing. In two days I have to be in California to do the *Steve Allen Show*. And they tell me I am to open at the Village Vanguard here in New York in five days." A rising musical star in apartheid South Africa, Makeba had only recently fled to Europe and now was on the folk fast track in the United States. On her opening night at the Village Vanguard, she spotted the Belafontes, Sidney Poitier, Duke Ellington, Diahann Carroll, Nina Simone, and Miles Davis in the crowd. Makeba quickly signed with RCA and began touring the country.[75]

About the same time, a record collector in Greensboro, North Carolina, wrote to Moe Asch at Folkways. "This age has been called the Atomic Age but in the world of entertainment it is actually the age of mediocrity both on television, radio, and records," he said. "There have popped up literally thousands of so-called singers who are creations of imaginative publicity men. I think you would do a service by issuing more records by artists of the caliber of Cisco Houston and also increase your distribution of recordings so that record stores in southern areas, like Greensboro, would carry your records." Soon to be the site of integration sit-ins, a new militant phase of the civil rights movement, Greensboro with its segregation would certainly have looked familiar to Makeba. But even here a folk audience existed, one quite removed from the glitz of the Village Vanguard and *Steve Allen Show*.[76]

Folk music's growing audience never dealt with the issue of its definition and scope. "Folk music comes from the people, but it is kept alive today by Pete Seeger, Woody Guthrie, Josh White, Burl Ives, The Weavers, Lead Belly, The Golden Gate Quartet and other individuals and small groups," Erik Darling wrote in late 1959. "True, folk music is intended for the people, but it only occasionally filters through to the masses of America." Still, he saw signs that folk music "is just becoming a young healthy tree; whether it will be an oak or a willow, only time will tell." Darling struggled to maintain a sense of authenticity and professionalism, while appealing to a growing commercial market; after all, he had crafted the Tarriers's first hit, "The Banana Boat Song."[77]

Simultaneously, a more traditional sound and interest continued to be promoted. Robert Gustafson apprised *Christian Science Monitor* readers of the work of the Pinewoods summer camp on Cape Cod, sponsored by the long-established Country Dance Society of America, a week of playing and studying folk song and dance. Teachers included Frank Warner, Billy Faier, and Dick Best, with May Gadd, previously associated with Cecil Sharp, as director. They used song-books produced by the Cooperative Recreation Service of Delaware, Ohio, which issued a steady stream of widely distributed musical publications. The camp remained one surviving outpost of traditional music and culture. "The prevailing feeling among folklorists at the camp was that some sort of folk tradition will probably survive, but it may well be that of an urban culture," the author concluded. "Because of the inroads of civilization the ancient ballads and songs which could formerly be found in the back hills and valleys soon may be no more."[78]

A few scholars continued to scour the South, hunting up and recording traditional performers. Following in the Lomaxes' deep footprints, Harry Oster, who taught literature at Louisiana State University, recorded bluesman Robert Pete Williams and others at Angola prison, as well as local Cajun singers. Samuel Charters also kept his recording machine busy. D. K. Wilgus's 1959 publication *Anglo-American Folksong Scholarship since 1898* eloquently detailed the lives and battles of folk music collectors on both sides of the Atlantic. Moreover, the Archive of Folk Song at the Library of Congress extended its collecting and preserving of the country's treasury of vernacular music, under the guidance of Rae Korson.[79]

The final years of the decade witnessed a flowering of folk music throughout the country. Record companies, clubs, coffeehouses, magazines, reviewers, managers, promoters, radio programs, festivals, and performers all fueled the revival. Various personalities created a national web, connecting urban centers, particularly New York, Boston and Cambridge, Chicago, Los Angeles, and the Bay Area. "The music was acoustic and fresh, simple rhythms and gentle voices," Ellen Sander recalled a few years later, "a relief from the vinyl love masquerading as radio rock and roll. Audiences would clap and stomp along and participate in the music they were experiencing. When it was over, audi-ence and performers would applaud each other with an ovation that was as lusty as it was genuine."[80]

6
Into the Heart of the Revival, 1960–1962

In *Home Fires*, Donald Katz's sensitive, panoramic study of the Gordon family of Harbor Isle, Long Island, the author writes of Lorraine, who was fifteen in 1962: "It was not the first time in recent months that Lorraine had invited 'new friends from the Village' to camp out on the playroom floor. Most of the young folkies Lorraine met at clubs or in Washington Square Park were urban kids, and they seemed to relish the chance to visit a typical suburban home, almost as anthropologists looked forward to a dig." Lorraine rigorously copied Joan Baez's looks and guitar style and took every occasion to hang around the Village, frequenting the Gaslight or the Fat Black Pussy Cat. One evening at Gerdes Folk City she sat "next to a skinny kid wearing a striped cap like a railroad engineer's. The kid had on a blue salt-of-the-earth shirt, and he looked much too young to be hunkering over his glass of wine legally. He was sucking deeply on a cigarette less than an inch long." Bob Dylan, "the skinny kid," had only recently arrived in the city. With her friends Maris and Susan, Lorraine visited Washington Square on Sundays, rejecting the Kingston Trio and Peter, Paul and Mary for more authentic performers. "Lorraine loved the Weavers and Pete Seeger. She understood that their songs were connected to the romance of ancient political dreams that lived on, even in places like Harbor Isle."[1]

In the early 1960s folk music strongly grabbed the attention of the youth market. Jay Milner, in a *New York Herald Tribune* piece called "The Folk Music Craze," wrote, "The teenagers provide the momentum for most of the fads these days, and, as they did with rock and roll, teenagers are singing and playing folk music as well as listening to it." *Mad* magazine, bellwether of adolescent culture, included in its January 1960 issue a parody of "record albums of authentic folk songs" such as "Authentic Old Syndicate Songs," "Ballads of a New England Accountant," and "Madison Avenue Work Songs." During the spring of 1960 the Kingston Trio's *Here We Go Again* topped the list of best-selling albums (followed closely by *The Sound of Music*). "The tenure of folk music's appeal to the mass audience cannot be estimated with accuracy, of course," Milner concluded. "Record companies, music publishers and professional performers who depend on the trends are continually trying out new material they hope will catch the public fancy."[2]

As folk music became increasingly commercial and lucrative, Alan Lomax tried to remind people about its roots. In "Getting to Know Folk Music," an article he coauthored with Carroll Calkins for *House Beautiful*, he gave a nod to Belafonte, the Kingston Trio, the Tarriers, Eddy Arnold, and Frankie Laine; but he pointed out that "under the smooth bland surface of the popularized folk songs lies a bubbling stew of work songs, country blues, field hollers, hobo songs, prairie songs, spirituals, hoedowns, prison songs, and a few unknown ingredients." The article concluded: "This music belongs only to us, because only in America are there so many different cultures mixed together. The songs are the oral history of our country." About the same time, in mid-1960, Lomax recounted his youthful forays with his father and his later experiences collecting in Europe for the readers of *HiFi/Stereo Review*, and he recalled teaching traditional songs to Burl Ives, Josh White, and Pete Seeger. Now, he said, all the world's folk treasures needed preserving, for "we of the jets, the wireless and the atom-blast are on the verge of sweeping completely off the globe what unspoiled folklore is left," which is in "danger of being replaced by a comfortable, sterile and sleep-inducing system of cultural super-highways." Lomax's lifelong musical crusade had expanded considerably, and he would continue to shape and mold a vibrant folk aesthetic. But he seemed to be fighting a rear-guard action, as commercial forces poised to assume expanding control of the folk revival.[3]

The Expanding Folk Scene

On May 20, 1960, Michael Rossman reported to his friend Kathy Greensleaves about the recent protest against the House Un-American Activities Committee hearings at the San Francisco City Hall. "That night," following the demonstration, "in Berkeley we had a small party, attended mostly by the 'hard-core, experienced agitators' as we had been described," he wrote. "And it was a victory party: we sang 'We shall not be moved' as I have never heard it sung, as a saga of the three days, event by event, and we sang it for a full half-hour of intensity and enthusiasm, stopping only when the guitarists could play no longer. . . . Meanwhile, elsewhere in the City, picketing of Woolworth's and Kress's was continuing in force as it has for several months. And a peace parade, the Little Summit March, was marching toward Union Square and a meeting of 3,000 people." Civil rights, peace, and government repression were issues that inflamed Rossman and a growing number of students and citizens of the Bay Area. He envisioned a new political movement: "I see the rise of a new Left in this country, a Left of a nature that has not been seen within this century."[4]

College enrollments had increased from 2.5 million in the late 1950s to over 3.7 million in 1962, and with the baby born generation coming of age it climbed precipitously thereafter. Demographic shifts resulted in social and cultural upheavals. Jack Newfield, a student at Hunter College, summarized the scene: "By the end of the 1950's there were not only the subcultures of Beats, but the irreverent satire of Lenny Bruce and Mort Sahl, the stirrings of SANE, Martin Luther King's local protests against segregation, and the slow growth of dissident publications like I. F. *Stone's Weekly, The Village Voice,* and *The Realist.*" On February 1, 1960, in Greensboro, North Carolina, four black students launched a sit-in at the local Woolworth's, protesting segregation. Facing intimidation and violence with quiet fortitude, they sparked a rash of sit-ins in fifty-four cities throughout nine southern states. Two months later Ella Baker, associated with Martin Luther King's Southern Christian Leadership Conference (SCLC), called a meeting that attracted about 120 students representing fifty colleges and the Student Nonviolent Coordinating Committee (SNCC) was born. SNCC became the spearhead of the southern civil rights movement, although joined by the older Congress of Racial Equality (CORE), the newer SCLC, and even the mainstream National Association for the Advancement of Colored People (NAACP).[5]

In the fall of 1960 much of the country was absorbed with the tense battle between Richard Nixon and John F. Kennedy for the White House. Todd Gitlin, a second-year Harvard student, joined Tocsin, the campus peace group, and became involved in regional anti-nuke protests. He also connected with the student Committee for a SANE Nuclear Policy (SANE). Meanwhile Robert "Al" Haber at the University of Michigan had transformed the insignificant Student League for Industrial Democracy (SLID) into Students for a Democratic Society (SDS), recruiting a core group of active members (including Tom Hayden) who supported civil rights, peace, and other progressive causes. Student activists such as Haber, Gitlin, and Rossman shared a disillusionment with both mainstream politics and old Left preoccupations, but Gitlin credited the Communist party with one abiding, vibrant legacy: "From the Forties through the early Sixties, the music of the Weavers, Woody Guthrie, and others was an embattled minority's way of conjuring an ideal folk. . . . The political generation of the Fifties was missing, but folk was the living prayer of a defunct movement, the consolation and penumbra of its children, gingerly holding the place of a Left in American culture."[6]

Folk music could be heard at campus rallies and also on television. CBS-TV daringly attempted an unusual one-hour *Folk Sound USA* show, sponsored by Revlon, in June 1960. The eclectic lineup featured Cisco Houston, Joan Baez, John Jacob Niles, John Lee Hooker, Earl Scruggs and Lester Flatt, Frank Warner, and Peter Yarrow. Harriett Van Horn complained in her *Variety* review that the show's work songs, blues, and western ballads were "the kind of folk music I associate with far-out Bohemian types. I mean the kind who wear leather thong sandals and entertain you after dinner (a casserole of garlic bulbs and goat hearts, stewed in bad wine) with their scratchy old recordings of blues songs by Leadbelly and Blind Willie Johnson." Her review mixed praise with some skepticism.[7]

In midsummer 1960 *Newsweek* and *Time* spotlighted folk music's increasing visibility. "The new aficionados will haggle over the merits of Earl Scruggs' three-fingered banjo-picking technique as rabidly as jazzmen debate the far-out trumpet playing of Miles Davis," noted *Newsweek*. Odetta, Pete Seeger, and Theo Bikel now attracted large crowds, and "the bulk of their supporters come from colleges and large urban centers." *Time* addressed what it called the "Folk Frenzy": "The U.S. is smack in the middle of a folk-music boom, and already the TV pitchmen have begun to take advantage of it. Pseudo folk groups such as the Kingston Trio . . . are riding high on the pop charts, and enthusiasm for all folk singers—real or synthetic—has grown so rapidly that there are now 50 or so professional practitioners making a handsome living where there were perhaps a half dozen five years ago." The article singled out seven for particular praise, Odetta, Bikel, the New Lost City Ramblers, the Brothers Four, the Weavers, Baez, and Seeger: "An ardent left-winger, he once sang many industrial songs, now is better known for Appalachian mountain songs (*Pretty Polly*) and Negro classics."[8]

Both articles mentioned the Newport Folk Festival. *Newsweek* favorably reviewed the three-volume Vanguard Records album of the 1959 festival, recently released, and noted the upcoming second festival, which *Time*, a few weeks later, alluded to as a prime example of the do-it-yourself allure of the music: "At Newport last week, many spectators brought along banjos and guitars with their sleeping bags and sat around campfires on the beaches strumming far into the night. (In the last three years, U.S. banjo sales have increased by 500%.)" Newport had become the folk mecca, at least for a few days each year.[9]

The second festival, again organized by Albert Grossman, brought together a broad range of performers and the eastern folk establishment—Harold Leventhal, Manny Greenhill, and Irwin Silber—and the oversized program included a section promoting *Sing Out!* The three dozen acts spanned the folk spectrum: Oscar Brand, the Clancy Brothers and Tommy Makem, Pete Seeger, Odetta, Jesse Fuller, the Brothers Four, the Weavers, Peggy Seeger, Bud and Travis, Robert Pete Williams, Ewan MacColl, and John Lee Hooker. The three days, expanded from two the previous year, featured evening concerts, a Sunday afternoon hootenanny—where "youngsters in dungarees and Bermuda shorts eagerly waited their turns to sing old ballads, blues songs or topical ditties that ranged from the U-2 [spy plane] to psychoanalysis"—and a morning seminar with a five-member panel debating "authenticity versus ersatz folkmusic." Overall attendance, hovering around ten thousand, seemed disappointing, though the Vanguard, Elektra, and Folkways recordings would carry the sounds far beyond the milling crowds.[10]

The popular headliners captured the bulk of the publicity, and the debate raged over folk music's growing commercialism. "The twenty or so minutes of ethnic music presented at the Festival more than held its own against the fifteen hours of commercial music heard," Izzy Young remarked in Sing Out! Toshi Seeger, Alan Lomax, and Moe Asch had already begun to voice their concerns about the festival's slickness. But they would have to wait three years before implementing their ideas, for riots at the jazz festival led the Newport community to temporarily cancel all festivals. Though the jazz festival would return the next year, George Wein hesitated before initiating another folk festival.[11]

Izzy began envisioning a new folk festival, a small affair featuring traditional musicians—"to be as ethnic as possible and not to give a damn about the managers—or the Weavers and Brothers Four etc. though they have their perfect right to exist as they see fit." He suggested such traditional performers as Frank Warner, Hobart Smith, George Pegram, Lonnie Johnson, and Roscoe Holcomb, though he would also include some city performers, perhaps Paul Clayton, Ellen Stekert, and Dick Weissman. "My head is swimming with ideas," he told Pete Seeger, "and I've got to keep one ear open for the good things I'm interested in and one ear closed to the managerial group and the touters and a lot of my friends." Seeger responded immediately: "This kind of thing has got to be done if we don't want the commercial people to simply take over and ruin the whole situation. I will be glad to perform on it for free if you want me to, or serve in any other capacity you feel necessary." Such ideas—less commercialism and more emphasis on traditional performers and grassroots involvement—would resurface with Newport's revival in 1963.[12]

Robert Shelton at the New York Times had chronicled the Newport Folk Festival and would continue through the decade to champion folk music's various facets and personalities. In a December 1960 piece he roamed around New York City as tour guide, huckster, and skeptic:

The army of folk musicians on night maneuvers wears many uniforms and uses varied tactics. A 20-year-old beauty, soignée in gold lamé, Beverly Wright, yodels folk airs at Trude Heller's Versailles and proudly tells a visitor that she is "booked to sing folk in Vegas"; a bearded Yemenite in the Cafe Sahbra plays on a Miriam drum an Israeli medley laced with fragments from the "Rhapsody in Blue"; an actor in vest and button-down collar, Jimmy Gavin at the Phase 2, lampoons "Mary

Had a Little Lamb," and a Southern-born singer, Len Chandler, confidingly tells a group at the Cafe Wha? that he has thrown over his classical study to rediscover his people's music.

Shelton pointed out the attractions of Gerdes Folk City, the Cock 'n' Bull, the Blue Angel, the Gaslight Cafe, Café Bizarre, and the Village Gate, mostly grouped in Greenwich Village. Among the performers, he preferred Dick Rosmini, Billy Faier, Dave Van Ronk, Carolyn Hester, and Varda Karni. "Folk music," said Shelton, "is leaving the imprint of its big country boots on the night life of New York in unparalleled fashion, from the grimiest Greenwich Village espresso joint to the crooked-finger elegance of the Waldorf Astoria."[13]

Izzy

The Village's established reputation as America's bohemian heartland lingered into the 1960s, although Beat culture had already begun to fade. Jazz remained the music of choice for Beats, yet "a few . . . invariably among the youngest, are not so much interested in jazz as in the folk music of the 'ethnic' set," Ned Polsky concluded in his 1961 *Dissent* article "The Village Beat Scene." He described the folk crowd as "historically minded, middle-class youths, mostly Jewish, who are trying to disown their parents' culture not by becoming beat but rather by proving that ancient proverb, 'New York ain't America.' "[14]

To most outsiders, however, Beats (or Beatniks, the derisive media term) and folkies overlapped. Joan Baez, characterizing herself as a "Harvard Square," remembered that during her infrequent visits to New York, she "wandered around with black eye-makeup on, did all the appropriate things." For Ellen Sander, "The beats had been brained into existentialism, but the folkniks were full of piss and vinegar and ready to make a lot of noise about change. Greenwich Village was alive and radiating young talent and enthusiasm, fucked-over kids of the Fifties, in from wherever, disgusted with what they left behind, open to whatever was waiting for them, with a burning desire to express themselves with music of their own making, with a lifestyle of their own contrivance." Richie Havens, newly arrived from Brooklyn, said, "There was so much talent and energy in the Village of the early 1960s that we instinctively knew that big changes in our American culture were brewing all around us. The air was electric and it was going to be like that for most of the decade."[15]

But the Big Apple still trailed San Francisco, Chicago, and Los Angeles in furnishing folk venues. Izzy Young was prepared to correct the situation. In early January 1960, "a dapper, well-dressed advertising man, Tom Prendergast, walked into my store and convinced me to take a look at a dilapidated bar on West Fourth Street near Broadway where we might open up a folk music club," Izzy recalled. "Why not? We walked over to the bar and met Mike Porco, who was serving the entire clientele of two or three regular customers. We quickly came to an agreement and made the following disastrous (for us) deal with

Mike: We would pay all the publicity; we would pay all the singers; and we would keep the gate. He would sell drinks and food. He couldn't lose. We couldn't win." The Fifth Peg (name suggested by Erik Darling) opened with Ed McCurdy and Brother John Sellers on January 8, followed by the Clancy Brothers and Billy Faier, the Tarriers, Brownie McGhee and Sonny Terry, and Dick Weissman. Harold Leventhal, Bob Shelton, and Art D'Lugoff dropped by to check out the talent. "It is my latest attempt to become a self-made foundation," Izzy quipped in Sing Out![16]

By March the crowds began to dwindle. "Theo Bikel showed up to do a set. There were only three people left but he sang for two hours—a house record!" Porco forced Izzy and Prendergast out in late April, bringing in Charlie Rothschild as his manager and Logan English as the emcee. The renamed Gerdes Folk City opened in June with Carolyn Hester. Izzy posted a notice in the Village Voice in mid-May: "Everything I do turns out to be successful artistically only. Now the FIFTH PEG is added to the list; but I'll be back on the active folk scene soon and so will my marvelous partner Tom Prendergast." Bitter about the experience, he continued producing concerts at the Folklore Center and other spots. "I understand the place will be called 'Folk City,' " he wrote in his diary; "the palace guard Logan English, Bob Shelton, Molly Scott are all in on it and I feel quite bad about it. Except that their taste is execrable and no proudness accrues to anyone singing for them." Some performers, including Dave Van Ronk, at first staged a boycott to support Izzy, but they soon capitulated. Folk City became the premier folk spot in the Village.[17]

In May Izzy wrote in his diary about Lomax, Shelton, and others who drifted into the Folklore Center during the spring. Lomax "thinks the Kingston Trio is great and he still believes in rock 'n' roll as an important force," but Lomax suggested that "if I wanted to hear folk music, I should live in a mountain town of Haiti for a month. Then I would see how weak city music is." Izzy didn't trust Shelton, who "secretly tries to shape it [folk music] to a very weak view. . . . He is already preparing himself for the equivalent of a record-jacket-writing career of fluff posing under serious journalism." (Indeed, Shelton used aliases when writing record jacket blurbs.) When the Reverend Gary Davis came into the Folklore Center, borrowed a banjo, and began picking and frailing, "stupid on-lookers walked in, didn't understand what they were observing, and walked out. But a lot of people stayed around to hear him." On May 15 "Lomax walked into the store sporting a Stevenson button. . . . He met some friends and they discussed Mort Sahl vs. Lenny Bruce."[18]

Archie Green, newly installed as the librarian of the Institute of Labor and Industrial Relations at the University of Illinois after years as a carpenter and shipwright in San Francisco, wrote to congratulate Izzy on his popular but short-lived Folk Music Guide USA. "It is a breath of fresh air in this closed square community." Coming from San Francisco, a musical hotbed, Green welcomed news of the outside world, complaining that "the U.I. campus seems hardly affected by the folksong revival. . . . The University seems to attract a few big concert names such as Dyer-Bennet, Seeger, Odetta, and Bikel, but apparently no one here has invited Frank Warner, Jean Ritchie, Jess Fuller, or any of the less well known youngsters who play it straight. My complaint, really is that folksong here always seems to be theatrical." Ellen Stekert, in the Indiana University graduate folklore program, could report happier tidings from nearby Bloomington in mid-February: "Jean Ritchie is coming out here this Saturday—20th—to give a concert on campus! Hooray—we have scored our first step toward not being 'stuffed shirt' folklorists!"[19]

Barbara Dane, acquainting Izzy with her busy performing schedule, including the Ash Grove in Los Angeles, the Ballad Room in Boston, the Gate of Horn in Chicago, and the first Newport Folk Festival, wanted some notice in the Guide, which "fulfills an important function and . . . besides being a handy guide to who is where, the articles and reviews are very interesting." Like many others, Dane used Izzy as both a bulletin board and a sounding board. Dick Weissman, performing at the Exodus in Denver, remarked on the "Ivy-Leagueish" crowd that preferred the Tarriers to Sonny Terry and Brownie McGhee. "The main problem in a town like this, as I see it, is education. My music, or even Brownie & Sonny's stuff sounds peculiar to these people. They end up being most enthusiastic about the loud and fast pieces. I think this is because of the trio and quartet boom." He was impressed by a young local singer, Judy Collins, who had the makings of a "very commercial sound." Yet she had been musically sheltered—"Brownie was quite literally the first blues guitarist she had ever seen, and Eric Weissberg the first banjo player."[20]

Irwin Silber and Moe Asch launched another element of the revival in 1960 with Oak Publications, beginning with Woody Guthrie's Ballads of Sacco and Vanzetti, Songs of Joe Hill, and Harold Courlander's collection Negro Songs of Alabama. Producing songbooks, instrument instruction books, and much more (eventually over a hundred titles), Oak served as a vital aid and stimulus, particularly for budding musicians. The co-owners finally sold their lucrative company to Music Sales, Inc., in 1967. Along with Sing Out! and the prolific Folkways Records, Oak managed to encourage the do-it-yourself impulse of folk music, which was always part of Silber's and Asch's agendas.

Little Sandy Review Emerges

As Izzy and his friends struggled with the tug, even friction, between commercial and traditional music, two undergraduates at the Minneapolis campus of the University of Minnesota quietly initiated the Little Sandy Review, a little magazine that would shake up the folk world. Silber gave the magazine a buoyant send-off: "Two young, ardent and extremely articulate folkniks in Minneapolis have managed to kick up more of a fuss in folksong circles over the past few months than almost anyone has done since Jesse Cavanaugh and Arnold Stanton began (copy)writing folksongs." With pointed, sarcastic, and sometimes outlandish record reviews, Paul Nelson and Jon Pankake laced the Little Sandy Review with their sharp wit and idiosyncratic tastes. Said Silber, "Pankake, Nelson and their magazine are not just phrase-mongers creating havoc with their rapier-like thrusts. They are serious and determined about their ideas."[21]

Nelson and Pankake launched their ambitious, small-format monthly in March 1960, announcing: "We are two people who love folk music very much and want to do all we can to help the good in it grow and the bad in it perish. After reading this issue, it should be very apparent to anyone who we think is good and who we think is bad and why. If you disagree, fine. More power to you." They planned to review numerous new recordings, starting off with three dozen albums. They reserved their praise for the more traditional performers, while the records of the Kingston Trio, the Limeliters, and the Brothers Four, as well as Sing the Folk Hits with Jack Narz, were thoroughly panned. By the third issue the editors listed upcoming albums and included other assorted folk news, along with letters to the editors. "People remember the bad reviews that we gave to records we didn't like, records we raked over the coals," Pankake later explained. "Oddly enough, no one seems to remember that we were just as fanatic and excessive on the other side, on records that we praised."[22]

Though seemingly isolated in central Minnesota, the editors connected directly with New York and the proliferating commercial folk establishment east and west. They personally delivered a shipment of the first issue to Izzy Young at the Folklore Center. "This is a thing to get free records, right?" Izzy quizzed Pankake. "Wrong, it wasn't," he later said. "We never got a free review copy of a record—we didn't want free records. . . . We did not want to be beholden to record companies." Thirty years later Pankake recalled that initially they made at least one important exception. In an early letter to Moe Asch at Folkways Records, Paul Nelson enclosed the first issue and pointed out the printed notice of five Folkways records. "To show our appreciation for your work (which is practically the only good, honest folk music produced today), we will donate to you free each month, a full-page ad." In exchange Nelson wondered "if you would send us covers on all your new folk releases well in advance, and also send us two complimentary copies of each new American and English folk release or any record concerning an American or English folksinger." In response, Asch didn't "think it is fair to you people to give us free ads. We would rather pay as your other advertisers do. Separately we are sending you some records at no charge and we will send you regularly, covers on new releases."[23]

Whatever the final arrangement with Asch, the magazine continued to review dozens of Folkways issues and run the ads. But they cherished their financial and intellectual independence. "To use a current word, we were marginalized,"

Pankake later boasted. "And we loved being marginalized. We liked the distance from the center that gave us the freedom inherent in the fanzine medium to say anything we wanted. We weren't responsible to anyone for anything, and we had fun with that freedom from responsibility. We found it exhilarating to be twenty years old and in love with writing and to fall in love with folk music, and just have a blast putting those two loves together." They relished praising older white and black traditional performers, increasingly heard on LP reissues of 78-rpm records or newer field recordings. Issue no. 5 was dedicated to Woody Guthrie.[24]

The letters column served as a sounding board for various thoughts on the magazine and the current folk recording scene. "I think your magazine is in a rut, and should do something about it," Vanguard's Maynard Solomon advised the youngsters in the sixth issue. "Free-wheeling iconoclasm is OK, so is shooting from the hip whenever you spot a folk outlaw, but it gets terribly dull after a while. LSR is becoming a glib magazine, whose opinions are readily predictable, produced according to formula." Certainly bothered by their mostly negative reviews of Vanguard releases, he nevertheless concluded, "Have fun." In a lengthy response, the editors summed up their philosophy, "that folk music should and CAN only be performed by people in the folk tradition or by people who have taken the trouble to learn it." Emboldened by their surprising critical stature, they concluded with a poke in Solomon's commercial eye: "We're pretty sick and tired of your brand of 'snob-appeal folkum,' Mr. Solomon. We're afraid that it and the Kingston Trio–type folkum are going to displace real folk music—people love the idea of 'easy-listening' folk music and you at Vanguard are certainly doing your share to give it to them. Let us hope they choke on it, Mr. Solomon."[25]

Pankake and Nelson ended their first year on a high note: "The year 1960 was, among other things, the Year of the Folk Boom. Folk LP's and singles sold across record counters like hotcakes; the Kingston Trio was on everybody's Top Ten list; guitar and banjo sales soared; coffee houses sprang up like weeds in college areas; everyone had Odetta's new LP; and Jean Ritchie and John Lee Hooker even got on television. Strange things were happening. For the first time in history, American folk music became Big Business." Mixed among the swarm of commercial releases were some real gems, from a variety of record companies. The editors listed their top ten releases, starting with Alan Lomax's Southern Folk Heritage Series for Atlantic Records; the remainder included white and black rural compilations, ending with the Reverend Gary Davis. *Belafonte Returns to Carnegie Hall* topped their list of "Ten Lousiest Records of 1960," closely crowded by Bob Gibson's *Ski Songs* and *The Limeliters*. The *Little Sandy* never reached more than two hundred subscribers, with another one hundred copies distributed through bookstores, yet it managed to make its mark during its four-year run. Billy Faier, in the June/July 1960 issue of *Caravan* (its last issue), exclaimed: "Little did we know that this innocently titled, mimeographed magazine would turn out to be a crusader marching into our midst from the wilds of the mid-west. For the editors of LSR have something to say and say it they do, leaving little to the imagination as to their feelings about the current folk-music-on-record scene."[26]

Just as the *Little Sandy Review* and its defenders geared up to attack the commercial monster, *Rogue*, a men's magazine featuring nonfiction, fiction, and pin-ups, devoted much of the October 1960 issue to the emerging folk scene. With a cover shot of the Kingston Trio, followed by full-page photos of Pete Seeger and Alan Lomax, among others, the section began with Cynthia Gooding describing folk music's democratic ethos: "Blues, ballads, and folk songs all accept and express the fact that life is hard, that a man's deeds for good or ill are his own, not society's, that a man may stand or fall on his own actions, pay the price or take the reward for the things he has done." Shelton, in his usual cheerleading role, conducted a brief guided tour of the revival, sprinkled with the familiar names, old and new. The Kingston Trio rated their own profile, furnished by Bruce Cook, a chatty piece with reprise of their brief career: "The Trio was the one-in-a-million of such groups that had managed to promote a college gig into a smash professional success. But you're not collegiate forever and three slim, carefree campus types enthusiastically having a ball with a folk song is a picture that's bound to age. . . . At the moment, of course, there appears to be few hazards for the Kingston Trio beyond hitting a higher tax bracket." Cook glossed over their connection to traditional folk music.[27]

If *Rogue's* male readers picked up some additional information but perhaps little comprehension of the folk revival, *Mademoiselle's* female clientele gained a narrower yet deeper understanding after reading Susan Montgomery's "The Folk Furor." Struck by the youthful enthusiasm at the last Newport Folk Festival, Montgomery wrote that "this generation of college students is not exactly beat, but it is composed of young people who are desperately hungry for a small, safe taste of an unslick, underground world. Folk music, like a beard and sandals, has come to represent a slight loosening of the inhibitions, a tentative step in the direction of the open road, the knapsack, the hostel." First purchasing records, "starting out, perhaps, with one of the popularizers, Harry Belafonte, or a group like the Kingston Trio, and moving slowly toward the ruggedly authentic," the students, Montgomery wrote, quickly begin to visit the coffee-houses and folk clubs, and finally pick up an instrument. She pointed out that student singers and collectors had carried their music throughout the country and even overseas. "If the folk movement qualified, in some respects, as a religious movement—it is one led by seekers, value hunters and extremists who are willing to go all the way for something they believe in—it must be admitted that along with the high priests and faithful disciples it also harbors its share of hangers-on."[28]

Montgomery's piece earnestly tried to capture folk music's current lure and ambience, yet for some it stopped short of full comprehension. A few months later in the *New Republic* the folklorist Gene Bluestein attacked the article for slighting young people's rebellious nature, particularly in the developing civil rights movement. "That spirituals, work songs, and other protest songs should figure prominently in the expression of students in the South is not surprising," he explained. "What is significant is that the main stream of the song traditions that interest college students in general derive from similar materials." Bluestein sketched folk music's radical legacy, which continued to attract "students who are filled with the stubborn idealism that permeates the songs of Negro slaves, miners, hoboes, and blues singers. If the Kennedy administration is serious in its proposal to recruit them into a corps which will work to push into new frontiers, they will respond en masse and bring their guitars with them." Blue-stein linked folk music, protest, and the emerging youth rebellion north and south. *Mademoiselle*'s Nancy Lynch responded in the *New Republic*, attacking Blue-stein's "irresponsible inaccuracies and puerile snideness." Lynch challenged Bluestein for linking folk music too closely with campus protest, since "students' interest in folk music preceded the picket lines by at least three or four years; and their current passion, in the folk field, is for Bluegrass and country music." The exchange produced more heat than light, but did capture some dimensions of the debates over folk music's aesthetic versus political roots and dimensions, the values and motivations of the young, and authenticity versus commercialism.[29]

University of Chicago Folk Festival

In his April/May 1961 *Sing Out!* column, Izzy Young wrote, "Imagine having tea with Elizabeth Cotten, Roscoe Holcomb, Frank Pro[f]fitt, Dick Chase, Horton Barker, along with dozens of your favorite City Singers. And being able to swap anecdotes and experiences in an informal way. And then be able to hear these performers in the best series of concerts that any Folk Festival in America has yet presented. That's what happened at the First University of Chicago Folk Festival last February. When Horton Barker, only heard on Library of Congress Records, sang his traditional ballads I felt I had heard my first American Traditional Singer." Izzy enthusiastically congratulated festival organizer Mike Fleischer "for a fine and honest job which should point the way for other interested groups, schools and promoters around the country."[30]

The midwinter University of Chicago Folk Festival established a high standard, featuring only traditional performers without commercial glitz. Chicago native Fleischer remembers his mother dragging him to a concert during the Henry Wallace presidential campaign in 1948; there he first heard Pete Seeger, Woody Guthrie, and Cisco Houston. Big Bill Broonzy and others entertained at

Circle Pines summer camp in Michigan, the Midwest equivalent of Camp Woodlands, with folk music and folk dancing stimulating Fleischer and many other young people. As a deejay in the Navy during the mid-fifties, he played the records of Bill Monroe, the Stanley Brothers, the Blue Sky Boys, and Hank Williams. He arrived at the University of Chicago in 1958, joined the Folklore Society, and soon became president; he attended the concerts and wingdings with fellow members Paul Butterfield, Mike Bloomfield, and Elvin Bishop, future stellar performers. He frequented the Gate of Horn, Seeger concerts at Orchestra Hall, and traveled to the first two Newport Folk Festivals.

Shying away from the Kingston Trio and similar groups, Fleischer hustled to put on a campus concert for the New Lost City Ramblers. "In the spring of 1960, against the counsel of Harold Leventhal (Pete Seeger's manager, who was trying to advise us), we accepted three jobs in the Midwest, without any guarantee that we would be paid," John Cohen recalls. "Traveling as three men in a Volkswagen beetle with suitcases and seven instruments (two guitars, two banjos, fiddle, mandolin and Autoharp), we played at Oberlin College, in Ann Arbor, and at the University of Chicago. The Chicago concert was put together on three days' notice." With little time for publicity, the Folklore Society, charging a dollar, easily managed to fill the auditorium's three-hundred seats for two shows. (University of Chicago students also packed the Gate of Horn for the Ramblers's first club date in the city.) Following the concert the trio began discussing a larger affair, with more traditional performers such as Roscoe Holcomb or Elizabeth Cotten.[31]

In planning for the festival, Fleischer and his fellow students reached out locally to those more experienced in such matters, such as Fleming Brown and George and Gerry Armstrong, teachers at the Old Town School, who had valuable contacts and advice. The Folklore Society picked the long February weekend during the semester break in order to attract students from around the Midwest, who arrived in substantial numbers despite a snowstorm. Josh Dunson, active in the Folklore Society, and with a New York old Left and Village folk background, recalled a battle with the dean of students over staging the festival, partly because of some of the students' radical politics. Fleischer, however, denies there were any political frictions.

In addition to the performers mentioned in Izzy Young's column, the festival featured Frank Warner, the blues artists "Wee" Willie Dixon and Memphis Slim, the blind street singer Arvella Gray, Alan Mills, the National Barn Dance star Bob Atcher, Sandy Paton, and the New Lost City Ramblers—thirty-four in all. Studs Terkel and Archie Green shared emcee duties. There were also workshops, hoots, and academic presentations, including Alan Ribback on "Urban Folk Music." The Little Sandy Review began its laudatory assessment: "Ewan MacColl remarked after the most recent Newport Festival that he had seen every imaginable kind of singer there 'except a folk singer.' He was, of course, pointing out the basic weakness of 99% of the 'folk' festivals—most of them merely turn into a potpourri of city singers, college amateurs, pop music groups, and night club professionals; and there are no 'folk' in sight. . . . Happily, this was NOT the case at Chicago." The blind singer Horton Barker particularly captivated the audience as well as the editors—"ballad singing that could rival anything in the world for sheer magnificence."[32]

While unable to attend, Pete Seeger, responding to a postcard from Izzy, urged him to explain in his *Sing Out!* column "why this folk festival was so much more important than any of the so-called 'festivals,' such as Newport. If you wrote it up in strong enough language and well enough to persuade people you might even start to sound the death knell of the phony festivals and see more festivals like this take place." Robert Shelton also graced the festival with his imprimatur: "In a period when the popularization of folk music has led to many specious species of dilution and hybridization, the bulk of the music at the festival was as pure and refreshing as a swig of spring water. The key words were tap-roots, tradition, authenticity, and non-commercial." While clearly an artistic success, the expansive weekend nonetheless lost money. To make up for the shortfall, Fleischer contacted Manny Greenhill, who arranged for Joan Baez to perform in a benefit concert on campus the following fall. The popular singer invited Horton Barker, who just happened to be in the audience, to join her for two songs, bridging the musical generations.[33]

The triumphant Chicago festival brought increasing attention to the city's already rich folk life. Six month's earlier the staid *Chicago Tribune* had given a lengthy, somewhat arch overview of such activities called "Are You a Folknik in a Hootenanny?" A caravan of three hundred "folkniks" were traveling to Newport for the folk festival, "which is quite a *coup* considering that some still call folk music a national menace that is fast pushing classical and jazz albums out of the home. It has already replaced rock 'n' roll." The article boasted, with some exaggeration, that local folk impresario Albert Grossman had created the festival, and lauded the accomplishments of the Old Town School of Folk Music. "Folk music doesn't cure dandruff, epilepsy, or hydrogen bomb jitters but it is said to fill a basic need in this age of anxiety." And despite the lingering notion "that a folksinger has to look like a retired Apache dancer," most "of them do wear shoes."[34]

While the *Tribune* tried to dress folk music in proper garb, making it palatable to its respectable readers, Archie Green worked to demonstrate its traditional working-class, grassroots legacy. Excited by the success of the festival, he returned to the University of Illinois ready for action. "It was good to talk to you in Chicago," he informed Izzy in mid-March. "The fans here at Illinois enjoyed the Chicago bash. So they came back and organized a Campus Folksong Club. We put on a nice weekend with the New Lost City Ramblers." With support from Green, its adviser, the club staged concerts, lectures, and hoot-

enannies. "Folksing planners favored 'pure' representation of traditional mate-
rial but exercised no censorship over those who burlesqued or sanitized folksong," he later recalled. "One night, a fraternity duo coupled a saccarine [sic]
'Johnny, I Hardly Knew You' with a Chad Mitchell–flavored 'Lizzie Borden.'
Club partisans felt that they had been dragged to the precipice of vulgarity, but
they tempered outrage in the knowledge that 'obnoxious' Fijis (Phi Gamma
Delta members) courageously offered then-current majority views of folksong.
Although our club grew to more than five hundred members, sober leaders
know that they formed but a tiny enclave within a huge campus geared to elite
and popular culture."[35]

The club's mimeographed newsletter, Autoharp, lasted for thirty-three issues,
until 1968. Originally conceived as a folk bulletin board, Autoharp became more
of a forum for discussions of traditional music. Green launched the dialogue
by explaining the campus setting for folksong: "To wrench a ballad or blues
out of its culture context for concert presentation is, by definition, an act of
violence. Yet college audiences cannot invade, en masse, Appalachian mountain
hamlets, or Nova Scotian fishing villages to hear 'pure' folksong. If traditional
folksong is to be heard on campus, other than via record and tape, it must be
heard by importing true folk singers, or by imparting to collegiate singers of
folksongs some respect for traditional material and styles." These would remain
his guidelines for campus concerts, with the appearance of Sonny Terry and
Brownie McGhee, the bluegrass group Red Cravens and the Bray Brothers,
Jimmy Driftwood, the blues singer Curtis Jones, and Josh White, among others,
during the first year. One student convert returned brimming with enthusiasm
from a concert at the University of Wisconsin by Clarence "Tom" Ashley, along
with Clint Howard, Doc Watson, and Fred Price. "His humor is raw and healthy,
and the audience, for all its collegiate sophistication, ate up all the jokes that
Ashley could dispense." Ashley had recently come from a month at the Ash
Grove in Los Angeles, "not usually a haven for farmers, but Ashley made a hit
there as he did in Madison and as he did at the University of Chicago Folk
Festival." Rural music and its authentic interpreters was quickly conquering the
clubs and campuses throughout the North.[36]

The second annual University of Chicago Folk Festival in 1962 continued to
feature traditional performers—Ashley, Big Joe Williams, the New Lost City
Ramblers, Reverend Gary Davis, Jean and Edna Ritchie, Ramblin' Jack Elliott,
the Bluegrass Gentlemen, Speckled Red, and the Staple Singers, with scholars
D. K. Wilgus and Sam Eskin. The Little Sandy Review's glowing review particularly
lauded Ashley and Doc Watson, as well as the Reverend Gary Davis, though all
performers came in for much praise. "Another Chicago Folk Festival was over,"
Paul Nelson and Jon Pankake said. "We can hardly wait until the next one. It'll
probably be bigger and better than ever."[37]

Clubs and performers proliferated in the Windy City, offering something for virtually any folk fan. Frank Fried, with Triangle Productions, increasingly produced large concerts, cornering the growing commercial market. Through late 1961, for example, he showcased the Limeliters, Miriam Makeba with Chad Mitchell, Josh White, Pete Seeger, the Clancy Brothers, and Carlos Montoya at Orchestra Hall. A year later Fried added Peter, Paul and Mary to his lineup in November at Orchestra Hall; and paired Lester Flatt and Earl Scruggs with Ramblin' Jack Elliott at the Old Town School. His success as the premier folk entrepreneur in the Midwest, gained through astute advertising and the sale of season tickets, landed him the job as consultant and independent producer for Mercury Records, which established a separate folk department.

Traditional Music

Ralph Rinzler played a vital role in the resurrection of old-time performers. Raised in New Jersey, son of a doctor with roots in Russia and Austria, Rinzler was steeped in a vast range of folk music and folk arts, domestic and foreign, from a young age. He early took to the piano, later switching to the banjo and then mandolin. While at Swarthmore College in the mid-1950s he became heavily involved with the yearly folk festival, and during holidays and summers he began hanging around Greenwich Village, learning from Woody Guthrie; through Mike Seeger he also discovered that traditional southern performers were alive and well. He joined the Greenbriar Boys in 1959, and with John Herald and Bob Yellin helped introduced bluegrass to enthusiastic northern audiences.

A skilled performer, Rinzler preferred to act the interlocutor, discovering and introducing traditional musicians such as Clarence Ashley. Born in 1895, Ashley had been active through the 1920s and 1930s with the Blue Ridge Mountain Entertainers and the Carolina Tar Heels, occasionally recording, and he continued to perform over the decades. Rinzler had heard Ashley on the Folkways *Anthology of American Folk Music*, but assumed him long dead. Appearing with the Greenbriar Boys at the Union Grove Fiddlers Convention in North Carolina during Easter weekend in 1960, Rinzler was stunned to come across Ashley. Four months later, Rinzler and the hillbilly collector Eugene Earle traveled to east Tennessee to record Ashley, where they also met Doc Watson, who generally played rockabilly on his electric guitar. Rinzler convinced Watson to switch to a traditional acoustic guitar, and recorded him along with Ashley and his family; *Old Time Music at Clarence Ashley's* soon appeared on Folkways Records. The Friends of Old Time Music invited Ashley, Gaither Carlton, Fred Price, Clint Howard, and Watson to perform at P.S. 41 in Greenwich Village on March 25, 1961, their inaugural concert in the North and the formal launching of Doc Watson's phenomenal career.[38]

The Friends of Old Time Music (FOTM), a seminal group committed to preservation and presentation, was the creation of John Cohen, Ralph Rinzler, and Izzy Young. In his *Sing Out!* column in late 1960 Izzy announced that Cohen "is apace with ideas for a non-profit organization to further Old Timey Music that will bring singers from the mountains to the Big City." In addition to his role in the New Lost City Ramblers, Cohen spent much time collecting and recording traditional music in the South and photographing the musicians. In the summer 1960 *Sing Out!* he explained his work in Kentucky. "If the city wants and needs folk music in its soul, then its exchange with country musicians must be a two-way affair. If we feel a desire towards their outlook on music, we must be willing to understand their way of life and to respect them as people who have something to offer in their way." Cohen, Rinzler, and Young officially launched the nonprofit FOTM in December 1960. Their first New York concert in February 1961 featured Roscoe Holcomb, from Daisy, Kentucky, along with Jean Ritchie, the Greenbriar Boys, and the New Lost City Ramblers. *Sing Out!* warned, "In many cases the performance may seem foreign or unpolished. However much this may be so, it is our intention to bring people whom we feel have something to offer in artistry if not in slickness of presentation." The second concert, with Ashley and Watson, was soon followed by programs featuring traditional performers Bill Monroe, Bessie Jones, Gus Cannon, and Furry Lewis. In late 1962 FOTM presented a concert in Carnegie Hall with Ashley, Watson, and Pete Seeger, coproduced with Harold Leventhal.[39]

Rinzler introduced Ashley and Watson at the University of Chicago Folk Festival in February 1962, followed by their appearance at the Ash Grove in Los Angeles in March and April. Ed Pearl had presented a mix of popular and rural performers, but the success of the New Lost City Ramblers, Ashley, Watson, and Lightnin' Hopkins, and the influence of Alan Lomax, pushed him toward the traditional performers; he decided he could "take the more meaningful music—or what I felt was the real stuff—and have it slowly replace the more sophisticated stuff." He welcomed Ashley and Watson with no hint of how important their presence would become. When Ashley got laryngitis Rinzler urged Watson to take center stage, and he quickly became a star. Rinzler had not only provided Doc with a braille slate and pocket watch, but also had encouraged him to drop his electric guitar and Eddy Arnold imitation and concentrate on a traditional repertoire. Indeed, Rinzler structured the group's program, creating a mix of ballads, love songs, story songs, and instrumentals. "I was mediating between my sense of how Pete did a show or the Greenbriar Boys, or Joan [Baez] or anyone would do one," Rinzler said. "And how these guys who were used to getting up and doing vaudeville, black faced and slapstick, Tom [Ashley] actually was still doing black face with cork, burned cork in Round City, Tennessee, at the time. Now I couldn't let him get up and tell nigger jokes on the stage, but he would have if I, someone didn't tell him. Nor could they get up and do a show of five parlor songs, 'Silver Haired Daddy,' this is folk songs, folks."[40]

While Pearl provided an ongoing formal venue for folk music in Los Angeles, many performers and activists worked in more casual settings. Hootenannies continued at the McGlaze home on Pico Place, with their friends Bess Hawes, Marcia Berman, Ed Cray, and others. Idyllwild featured Moe Asch, Charles Seeger, Sam Hinton and Brownie McGhee and Sonny Terry. During the summer of 1962 a local group of folk fans organized the first Topanga Banjo and Fiddle Contest, with Bess Hawes as emcee, establishing a long-running annual fixture on the local folk scene. John Cohen told Izzy Young. "There was a banjo-fiddle contest in Topanga canyon (first time that has ever been tried in any city that I know of, outside the south), and on twenty dollars worth of mimeographed publicity, and a dollar & 24¢ admission, there were over 500 people there and about 30 contestants." (Actually there was a long lineage of fiddle contests throughout the North.) "The level of music was very high, and everyone seemed to have the right idea. There was but one Kingston Trio type, and one Pete Seeger type. The rest were all old time and bluegrass type musicians. . . . We must have such a contest in NY this year!" Cohen noted a lively interest in FOTM concerts in Los Angeles, and he concluded, "I unnerstan that the lads from Lil Sanity Review are going to be drafted soon in an attempt to make the world safe for bad folkmusic to go unmolested."[41]

While traditional music took firm root in Los Angeles, Barry Olivier expanded the Berkeley Folk Festival now in its fourth year. He thanked the *San Francisco Chronicle*'s Alfred Frankenstein for his coverage and prompted him to attend the workshops in addition to the formal concerts: "They are perhaps the most important facet of the Festival and one which I think you have felt was lacking." The festival's university setting heightened Olivier's emphasis on the workshops' teaching, rather than purely entertaining, aspects; topics ranged from "What Are Folk Songs?" and "Out of Touch with Tradition" to "How to Collect Folk Songs." Performers included many familiar names—Marais and Miranda, Sam Hinton, Frank Warner and Jean Ritchie, along with a newcomer, the Texas bluesman Mance Lipscomb.[42]

Lipscomb had only recently been "discovered" by Chris Strachwitz, one of the enthusiastic collectors scouring the South for "lost" blues and old-time performers. Following the publication of Sam Charters's *The Country Blues* in 1959 and with the continuing impact of Harry Smith's *Anthology of American Folk Music*, northern collectors began hunting up and recording rural bluesmen, many of whom had last recorded thirty years earlier. The British scholar Paul Oliver and Larry Cohn in New York spearheaded a growing number of serious collectors and record producers. Strachwitz had emigrated from Germany as a teenager in 1947, moved to the Bay Area in 1953, connected with Charters, and became hooked on Lightnin' Hopkins's recordings. He traveled through Texas in 1959 and met Hopkins in Houston through Hopkins's agent, Mac McCormack; the next year Strachwitz returned to the state with collector Bob Pinson and recorded Black Ace, Melvin "L'il Son" Jackson and Lipscomb, who worked on a plantation in Navasota. Lipscomb's album was released on the Arhoolie label, launching the national careers of both producer and artist. The ever alert editors of the *Little Sandy Review* happily noted that "when Sam Charters wrote his book, *The Country Blues*, in 1959, it was generally conceded that the era of genuine traditional blues recording was over. Such has not turned out to be the case— the well that looked very dry in 1959 is a veritable geyser in 1961." They welcomed the three Arhoolie releases of Black Ace, Jackson and the sampler *Blues 'n' Trouble*.[43]

In *Down Beat*, Pete Welding began to explore the mounting interest in folk-blues: "It's almost as if the death of the superb blues artist Big Bill Broonzy in the early summer of 1958 had spurred every collector, musicologist, folklorist, and owner of a tape recorder to invade the rural South in an effort to preserve as much of the rough; natural; vigorous, and it was feared, perishable music of the Southern Negro—especially the secular blues—as possible before all the older practitioners had died." Lightnin' Hopkins, Mance Lipscomb, Snooks Eaglin, Robert Pete Williams, Jesse Fuller and Furry Lewis were some of the musical treasures recently unearthed, and certainly more remained hidden in the southern countryside. Others had already migrated north and were playing weekends on Maxwell Street in Chicago for crowds of locals and tourists. Though heartened by the reawakening, Welding feared that most of the rural musicians would not profit much from their newfound celebrity status, lacking steady work on the folk music circuit.[44]

Traditional performers had more than financial difficulties. Lipscomb's experiences in Berkeley highlighted the gulf between the rural (black) South and urban (white) North, particularly in a college town. "Course, I didn't make no money until I got to Berkeley," Lipscomb later recalled. "And I didn't want to go out there. California was a place I had never been to." But the university's offer of five hundred dollars proved most persuasive. He arrived in Berkeley very disoriented and struggling to make sense of the odd surroundings. Once on stage he "never looked up. Played about three numbers. I was trembling and nervous." His musical success, however, and quick friendships with Jean Ritchie and Sam Hinton, who served as his unofficial hosts, soon calmed him. After over a dozen years of traveling, visiting dozens of universities as well as many festivals, he had mostly adjusted to his new life as he crossed the vast racial and cultural divide.[45]

There were other awkward moments as cultures clashed throughout the 1960s. "I recall in 1965 when J. E. Mainer brought his band from North Carolina to Minneapolis to perform at the Guthrie Theater as part of a folk music festival we had been asked to book," says Jon Pankake. The band wanted to perform one of their usual minstrel routines, "Sambo Sues Eliza for Divorce," but had forgotten their blackface makeup, and J. E. asked Pankake to locate some. "There was, of course, a budding folklorist within me that wanted to see this performance of purely racist entertainment before it passed into history forever, but unlike the *Little Sandy Review*, this concert series had an obligation to the community. I found myself in the absurd position of trying to convince J. E. Mainer that there was no black greasepaint or burnt cork within miles of Minneapolis, and that the show would have to go on without the skit. I felt like a character in a Samuel Beckett play."[46]

Despite the potential for awkward or uncomfortable cultural moments, the 1962 Berkeley festival continued to move into a more traditional format, with Roscoe Holcomb from Kentucky, Bessie Jones from the Georgia Sea Islands, Scotland's Jean Redpath, the New Lost City Ramblers, Jean Ritchie, and Charles Seeger—and none of the current crop of popular performers. But all were not satisfied. One critic asked Olivier if he hadn't noticed "the tremendous number of guitars and banjoes being carried around from workshop to workshop and to the concerts? Many, many kids came here to sing and learn, not just to sit and listen." The *New York Times*'s Robert Shelton returned from his western trip with general praise for the festival, with its wonderful setting and organization; he lamented the slow pacing of the concerts, boring presentations of Slim Critchlow and Andrew Rowan Summers, as well as lack of local ethnic music, Chinese, Mexican, or Indian. (Shelton also noted the upsurge of folk clubs up and down the West Coast, with five in Seattle, a dozen in San Francisco, and eighteen in the Los Angeles area.) Despite some sour notes, Olivier immediately began preparations for the first winter folk festival, during early December, to feature the Greenbriar Boys, Bessie Jones and the Georgia Sea Island Singers, Sam Hinton, Jean Ritchie, and Charles Seeger (then teaching at UCLA), with the usual mix of concerts and discussions.[47]

New York

As the revival gained momentum, a *Look* survey assessed changing teenage musical tastes: "In the tough, realistic sixties, teen-agers will not accept 'mush.' They may move toward authentic country music, blues or folk music. Or they may start going to symphonies. But one thing is sure. The whole field of popular music as we once knew it is gone forever." In the eyes of the mainstream press, however, folk music had no overtones of rebellion—generational, political, or otherwise. The popular Limeliters, led by the erstwhile radical Lou Gottlieb and playing before nightclub audiences at night and college students during the day, seemed the epitome of respectability. Their "music—which is alternately light and serious, old and new—is as pleasant as an international blend of good coffees," intoned a *Time* reporter. For Herbert Kamm, in the *New York World-Telegram and Sun*, "An ancient mode of song with fresh new trappings has risen above the racket of rock 'n' roll to restore a measure of sanity to the beleaguered world of popular music. . . . By vocal and instrumental manipulation, its practioners have captured the college campus and the concert hall, the candlelit bistro and the floodlighted stadium, the beatnik beer joint and the posh supper club, the avant-garde and the square." Considered safe, the Lime-liters, the Chad Mitchell Trio, and the Brothers Four had joined the pop pantheon with the Kingston Trio.[48]

The general public had little awareness of urban folk music's radical political past and struggle for survival during the years of the Red Scare, yet for some participants the battles scars remained fresh. Pete Seeger still felt the conservative political lash. He had appeared before HUAC in August 1955, refusing to co-operate, was cited for contempt of Congress, and finally convicted in March 1961. The previous August Seeger had distributed an informational letter to his friends, anticipating growing legal expenses. "Despite such a gloomy picture, we feel far from despondent," he assured them, with his usual aplomb. "I am able to travel and sing to larger numbers than ever before, and whenever we have a chance to talk to people about the whole 1st Amendment situation, we get encouraging support from Americans of widely differing backgrounds." College student Richard Reuss, an avid and acerbic Seeger watcher, noted during a concert at Carnegie Hall in mid-December, 1960: "The audience seemed to enjoy posing as a liberal leftist audience—anytime Seeger mentioned anything that could possibly coincide with a position taken by varying degrees of liberals, the audience cheered or clapped (some of them). I think it unlikely that very many actually made a big cause for these positions outside the theater in regular life, but rather just enjoyed cheering on any cause because of Pete's reputation as a liberal, and just for the plain heck of it." Harold Leventhal and a group of friends hurriedly organized a defense committee, raising funds for legal fees.[49]

Seeger remained out of prison pending his court appeal, while monetary and moral support poured forth from around the world. The flyer for a benefit concert in England, featuring sister Peggy, Ewan MacColl, and A. L. Lloyd, condemned his conviction as "a hangover from a witch hunt we had thought was long dead." (A few months later while touring with Peggy Seeger, MacColl, considered an "undesirable alien," would be refused entry into the United States from Canada.) Support groups also organized in Canada and Australia. In Los Angeles, a "For the Love of Pete and Freedom" benefit featured Sam Hinton, Bill Oliver, and other friends. Although still blacklisted by commercial television, Seeger signed a record contract with John Hammond at Columbia Records, the onset of a prosperous musical marriage. At year's end, the Seeger family toured Great Britain for five weeks, and the crowds were large and boisterous. Seeger's legal victory came a year later, on May 18, 1962, when the U.S. Court of Appeals overturned the conviction. The Weavers, with Eric Darling rather than Seeger on the banjo, also faced a continuing blacklist. Refusing to take a loyalty oath, they were barred from The Jack Parr Show on NBC in January 1962. In a sharp retort, "They charged that blacklisting had contributed to the wasteland that is television." The issue of blacklisting would arise again in 1963 in connection with the *Hootenanny* television show.[50]

On April 9, 1961, shortly after Pete's conviction, a "riot" broke out in Washington Square. While apparently unrelated, the two incidents marked the potentially fractious nature of folk music, just as its commercial appeal mushroomed. The new commissioner of parks, Newbold Morris, bending under community pressure regarding racial mixing, unwelcome noise, and sandaled youth, refused to grant the monthly permit. Izzy Young, who had recently replaced Lionel Kilberg as the individual responsible for obtaining the permit, explained in *Sing Out!*: "A protest was staged in the Park by some 300 folk singers and their friends, and 3,000 onlookers brought by the publicity of the press and radio. By some incredible bungling the Police Inspector in charge called the riot squad as the demonstration was ending and caused a 'riot.' " Challenging the police, Izzy and Art D'Lugoff had led a group of fifty, fronted by an American flag mounted on a banjo, into the park, resulting in the subsequent attack by the police and arrest of ten. According to the cautious *New York Times*, "At the height of the battle, hundreds of young people, many of the boys with beards or banjos and many of the girls with long hair or guitars, fought with fifty policemen in clashes across the square. Hundreds more, including some baffled tourists, watched."[51]

The Washington Square "riot" resulted in a few bruised heads and egos, much heated rhetoric, and for some symbolized the heights of absurdity. *Time* magazine characterized Morris as "a blueblooded liberal Republican," whose concern for the park's grass seemed somewhat misplaced: "There is some grass in the square, pushing its way up through a mulch of ice-cream wrappers, but there is none within a beer can's throw of the folk singers' fountain." "It looked like a bloodless victory for law, order and organized dullness," but by week's end the parks commissioner appeared to be caving in to public pressure, and "chances seemed good that Sunday afternoons would again be filled with seditious G-sevenths."[52]

When Pete Seeger appeared at the nearby Village Gate in late April, facing friends and Columbia Records executives, he sang the newly minted "Ballad of Washington Square." During a Weavers concert at Carnegie Hall in early May, at one point some of the group left the stage and Lee Hays quipped, "They're going to stick pins in their Newbold Morris Doll." Police continued to barricade the park on Sundays, faced by large demonstrations. After four weeks protesters marched back into the park, with guitars held aloft covered in black crepe, and proceeded to sing unaccompanied, which was legal. Mayor Robert Wagner's support for the singers eased the pressure, with weekly permits again being issued by late May, though state Supreme Court justice William Hecht had rejected the New York Civil Liberties Union's brief backing the performers. Total victory finally came in July, with a favorable ruling by the state appellate court.

Izzy Young, who was legal complainant and official spokesperson for the pro-testers, wrote, "Washington Square is again a peaceful place to hear folkmusic on Sunday afternoons." Dan Drasin's short film *Sunday* would soon present the "riot" to a wider audience. "Don't miss it," Izzy said. "You'll see all your friends in it." Long-time Village denizen Oscar Brand said, "Perhaps the lesson of Washington Square may help bring folk music to the public parks of other cities and towns, and coffee houses to the Main Streets of the world."[53]

Broadside Magazine

The mass media was continually filled with stories about popular folk singers. Herbert Kamm's series in the *New York World-Telegram and Sun*, in late August 1961, focused on the Limeliters, the Brothers Four, the Chad Mitchell Trio, and the Kingston Trio. While the masses of young people welcomed the torrent of commercialized folk music, some bucked the current. Following a show at Ohio Wesleyan University, the folklorist Richard Reuss wrote: "The worst elements of commercial folk music or rather the bastardization of folk music manifest themselves quite obviously in the Brothers Four's concert." Yet, despite their obvious shallowness and lack of musical talent, the "audience response was great and the chapel was packed (1500 app.) but the more discerning listeners tended to be critical (from a folk standpoint)."[54]

The jazz and folk critic Nat Hentoff seconded Reuss's qualms about the slick performers, but also included in his attack Harry Belafonte and even Odetta, reserving his praise for the more traditional repertoire of Baez and the New Lost City Ramblers. Echoing the *Little Sandy Review*, he also leveled a blast at the growing number of topical performers. The Freedom Singers, in their recent album *We Shall Overcome*, had demonstrated that "it's certainly possible to adapt folk material to current action," but Hentoff generally condemned the "trans-mogrification of folk song into hoarse self-righteousness. . . . Basically, the schools and students that support 'causes' support folk music. Find a campus that breeds Freedom Riders, anti-Birch demonstrators, and anti-bomb societies, and you'll find a folk group."[55]

People's Songs had long since folded, and *Sing Out!* hardly recognized current topical songwriters, so the field seemed promising for a folk magazine that would fill the political gap. "Pete Seeger and I have been discussing, cross continent, a project that we'd like to put before the readers of SING OUT for advice, comment and discussion," Malvina Reynolds wrote to the magazine in late 1960. "I am proposing the publication of a song book or journal of topical songs, to be called BROADSIDE. This would begin to round up, and make avail-able all over the country, the songs that are arising out of the peace, labor, civil rights movements in different areas." Seeger eagerly seconded the idea, his commitment reinforced by his firsthand experience with the flourishing English political song movement in late 1961. He soon announced in *Sing Out!*, "Whereas here in America our new songs either are strictly fly-by-night satirical, or sentimental, or flat—footedly earnest, there the best songs like those of Woody Guthrie, seemed to capture glints of humor in the middle of tragedy." But neither Reynolds nor Seeger had the time or inclination to edit such a new publication.[56]

Following their involvement with the Almanac Singers and People's Songs, Sis Cunningham and Gordon Friesen had barely managed to persevere and raise their two daughters, Aggie and Jane, through the 1950s; Friesen had been blacklisted as a reporter since the late 1940s, while Cunningham's poor health and sporadic employment meant a fitful survival. Yet with radical and musical commitments intact, they eagerly welcomed the chance to publish a topical song magazine. Soliciting advice and money from a few score friends, they launched *Broadside* in their public housing apartment, using a mimeograph machine left over from the American Labor Party. Over the years financial help came from Pete and Toshi Seeger, but it was never enough. Cunningham and Friesen lived on a shoestring "that stretched over the entire expanse of *Broadside's* existence" into the late 1980s.[57]

Issue no. 1, subtitled "A Handful of Songs about Our Times," appeared in February 1962; the run was three hundred copies and the price 35¢. Izzy took fifty copies for the Folklore Center. "BROADSIDE's aim is not so much to select and decide as to circulate as many songs as possible and get them out as quickly as possible," the editors proclaimed on the front page. "BROADSIDE may never publish a song that could be called a 'folk song.' But let us remember that many of our best folk songs were topical songs at their inception." The brief issue contained five songs, including "Come Clean Blues" by Malvina Reynolds (about strikers at the Colgate-Palmolive plant in Berkeley), "Carlino" by Gil Turner (referring to a New York politician who supported building bomb shelters), and newcomer Bob Dylan's "Talkin' John Birch Society Blues."[58]

A key figure during *Broadside's* early years, the performer and songwriter Gil Turner served as emcee at Gerdes Folk City, where he met many of the songsters. He was also a member of the New World Singers, who had sung in Mississippi in August 1961 for the civil rights movement. Since Cunningham and Friesen seldom ventured out to the folk clubs, Turner would bring the young performers to the monthly meetings at their apartment—Dylan, Phil Ochs, Tom Paxton, Len Chandler, Peter LaFarge, and many more—where they would sing into the Revere tape recorder supplied by Seeger. Cunningham then transcribed the songs and she, Friesen, Turner, and whoever else was present would decide which songs to publish. Songwriters began sending their taped songs, and *Broadside* quickly emerged as the premier national platform for topical songs—and the Friesens' apartment a beehive of activity. "It was non-commercial in the extreme," Josh Dunson wrote, "and owed its life to the enthusiasm of Seeger, the toil and the inventiveness of the Friesens, and the songs corralled by both Seeger and Gil Turner. It operated on the faith that throughout the United States there were song writers desperately needing a place to air their musical thoughts and the ideals of the student movement." *Broadside* also published reprints of news articles and editorial that gave background and substance to the songs and running commentary on current events.[59]

Broadside's third issue contained Dylan's "I Will Not Go Down under the Ground," an antiwar song, and the sixth issue headlined "Blowin' in the Wind." Dylan had already established his local reputation, but *Broadside* decidedly facilitated his national reach. Born Robert Zimmerman, and raised in Hibbing, Minnesota, after a brief fling at college life in Minneapolis, Bob Dylan arrived in Greenwich Village in February 1961 and made the rounds of the MacDougal Street folk hangouts—the Commons, the Gaslight, the Café Wha?, and Izzy's Folklore Center. Dylan's waiflike appearance and outlandish stories quickly captivated the locals. Modeling himself on Ramblin' Jack Elliott, and with the help of Dave Van Ronk, Dylan's folk persona swiftly formed. He was quick to visit the hospitalized Woody Guthrie, his musical and cultural idol. Dylan appeared on stage at Gerdes Folk City for two weeks beginning April 11, on the bill with the Mississippi bluesman John Lee Hooker, and he became a regular at local hoots and as a backup harmonica and guitar player.

"After listening to Jack Elliott for two nights last week I now think that he will not 'make' it," Izzy Young recorded in his sporadic diary in mid-October. "Grossman thinks that Bob Dylan has a much better chance of making it. He thinks Peter, Paul and Mary will be one of the top commercial groups. . . . I just made an arrangement with Bob Dylan to do a concert early in November— Al Grossman spurred me to do it." And he continued a bit later: "I am very excited by Bob Dylan. I am producing the concert so I can hear him entire. Purely from the way he talks he seems to have greatness in him—an ability to stand on his own." Izzy produced Dylan's first concert at the small Carnegie Chapter Hall on November 4, 1961; it attracted only fifty-three people, hardly a success. But Dylan had already been spotted by Robert Shelton of the *Times*, who would heavily promote his career. "A bright new face in folk music is appearing at Gerdes Folk City," Shelton had written on September 29. "Although only 20 years old, Bob Dylan is one of the most distinctive stylists to play in a Manhattan cabaret in months." Folk music had long ago gone bigtime, but Dylan would add a new dimension, in the process changing the nature of popular music. He hired Albert Grossman as his manager and signed a record contract with John Hammond of Columbia Records, where he recorded his first album in November (though not released until the following March, to lukewarm reviews; less than five thousand were sold in the first few months).[60]

"Bob Dylan blew into New York just a year ago," Izzy announced in early

1962 in *Sing Out!* "He came from the Midwest where he sang sentimental cowboy songs, jazz songs and top forty Hit Parade stuff at Carnivals and wherever he was. He hardly knew the word 'folkmusic' until he began to appear in Village coffee houses where the patrons especially liked his own songs such as 'California Brown Eyed Baby.' He hasn't changed at all in the past year—he dresses and talks the same, only now he is recording for Columbia Records." Izzy had a hard time separating fact from fiction in Dylan's life as he kept up his drumbeat of publicity. "He has a true poetic touch that smacks of the best folk tradition in many of his songs," he continued in the next *Sing Out!* Bouncing between the Friesens' apartment, Folk City, and clubs up and down the East Coast, Dylan quickly made his impact. One night Gil Turner heard Dylan sing the hastily written "Blowin' in the Wind" and immediately performed it himself at Gerdes. "He sang the song, sometimes straining to read the words off the paper," David Blue later recalled. "When he was through, the entire audience stood on its feet and cheered. Bob was leaning against the bar near the back smiling and laughing." It soon appeared in *Broadside* and became a prime anthem for the youth revolt. *Sing Out!*'s readers had their first full accounting of Dylan in the October/November 1962 issue, a most flattering portrait by Turner. Three songs, "Blowin' in the Wind," "Letter to Woody," and "Ballad of Donald White," accompanied the article.[61]

The editors of the *Little Sandy Review*, showing pride in their friend, lavishly praised Dylan's first album, *Bob Dylan*, after summarizing his rather prosaic background in Minneapolis "before he hoisted himself up by his bootstraps to singlehandedly conquer the folksong big time." They prized both his captivating style, based on Guthrie and Jack Elliott, and his songwriting talents. "All in all, this LP is a magnificent debut," they concluded, "and, we sincerely hope that Dylan will steer clear of the Protesty people, continue to write songs near the traditional manner, and continue to develop his mastery of his difficult, delicate, highly-personal style." Pankake and Nelson tried to separate the traditional from the topical Dylan. But they stuck to their guns, panning his second album, *The Freewheelin' Bob Dylan*, in a review titled "Flat Tire": "As a songwriter, he has become melodramatic and maudlin, lacking all Guthriesque economy; his melodies bear more relation now to popular music than folk music." The editors also leveled a lengthy blast at *Broadside*. They devoted the bulk of issue no. 25 to their attack on the "sappy and idiotic simple-mindedness found in the majority of the songs printed in the East Coast BROADSIDE and in parts of SING OUT!" They preferred the two new *Broadsides* that had sprouted in Boston and Los Angeles, neither much concerned with political songs. The controversy over "traditional" versus topical songs would remain at the center of the revival through the decade.[62]

Broadside attracted many new singer-songwriters. Via Ohio State University, Phil Ochs arrived in the Village in mid-1962 and participated in his first Folk

City hootenanny in July, doing more country than folk, but he soon moved into protest music. Gil Turner brought him around to the *Broadside* meetings and he became a regular. When the editors called for a song about James Meredith's troubles at the University of Mississippi, Ochs responded in November with "Ballad of Oxford, Mississippi." Ochs, Dylan, and their colleagues developed an intense and sometimes competitive fellowship. Josh Dunson described one stimulating taping session at the Friesens' in *Broadside* no. 20, with Turner, Dylan, Seeger, Ochs and Happy Traum. Dylan sang "Masters of War" followed by "Playboys and Playgirls Ain't Gonna Run My World," then Ochs did one about striking miners in Hazard, Kentucky. "We were all out of breath without breathing hard," Dunson concluded, "that feeling you get when a lot of good things happen all at once. Pete expressed it, leaning back in his chair, saying slowly in dreamy tones: 'You know, in the past five months I haven't heard as many good songs and as much good music as I heard here tonight.'"[63]

Moe Asch, who early on gave *Broadside* financial support, suggested issuing an album of songs by the regulars under a new Broadside Records label. Ochs, Turner, Matt McGinn, Seeger, Peter LaFarge, Mark Spoelstra, Happy Traum, and Dylan (aka "Blind Boy Grunt" because of his Columbia Records contract) gathered at the Cue Recording studio to cut the sides for *Broadside Ballads*, which appeared in late 1963. Five of the fifteen songs were Dylan compositions, starting with the New World Singers' performance of "Blowin' in the Wind."[64]

The Civil Rights Movement

Folk music soon fueled the civil rights movement. The Kennedy administration's lukewarm support for civil rights hardly put a crimp in the movement's progress, though it probably heightened the threat of violence. The Student Non-violent Coordinating Committee (SNCC), formed in 1960 and led by Bob Moses, had targeted Mississippi for their voter registration project during the summer of 1961. Older organizations, including Martin Luther King's Southern Christian Leadership Conference (SCLC) and the Congress of Racial Equality (CORE), remained active in other places. Freedom songs had aided the Montgomery bus boycott in 1955–56 and would continue through the 1960s to encourage solidarity in the midst of extreme opposition and hardships. With new words set to familiar gospel and popular tunes, the songs were easily learned and shared. Miriam Makeba, a protégé of Harry Belafonte, quickly found herself on the front lines. First in a trip with Belafonte to Atlanta, then on tour with the Chad Mitchell Trio (formed in Seattle in 1958), she confronted Jim Crow in various southern cities through 1960. The next year she traveled widely with Belafonte, who held frequent press conferences. She has written in *Makeba: My Story*: "All the newspapermen and the radio and TV people give me a valuable chance to speak up about the crimes that are being committed against my people at home." Comparisons through stories and music between South African apartheid and Jim Crow seemed natural and logical. Meanwhile, the Nashville student sit-in movement heightened the use of music to forge solidarity and a defiant spirit, as the outside world soon learned through the promotion of the Folkways album The Nashville Sit-in Story, released in 1960 and as fresh as the headlines.[65]

The music's vitality also infused the North. "Happy election day!" Joe Hickerson greeted Marian Distler at Folkways Records on November 8, 1960. "Here we are, listening to the Nashville Sit-in Story, Bill McAdoo, and the Investigator [a satire on Joe McCarthy], hammering posters together and mimeographing leaflets to distribute and display on our march this afternoon in the great liberal stronghold of the KKK and American Legion, etc., i.e. here in Bloomington. Part of the nationwide demonstrations for universal suffrage in the South."[66]

Civil rights workers, mostly black, garnered support from a small coterie of southern whites, particularly those connected with the Highlander Folk School. Originally organized to foster the labor movement, Highlander had switched in the early 1950s to spurring and facilitating the civil rights movement. Guy Carawan, hired in 1959, had become a valuable asset in championing the use of music in the movement. Black and white students left an organizing conference in April 1960 singing "We Shall Not Be Moved," "Keep Your Eyes on the Prize," and "We Shall Overcome." "Somewhere in the South today there is a tall, good-looking, clear-eyed young man with a banjo—and a mission," Irwin Silber said of Carawan in Sing Out! in the summer of 1960. "At this moment, he may be standing on a platform at a prayer meeting in a Negro church, head thrown back, leading an audience in an old hymn of hope and determination, singing along with a new generation in the Negro South." "We Shall Overcome" quickly became the anthem of the civil rights movement. For a week, in late August, Highlander hosted a "Sing for Freedom" workshop, with a few dozen civil rights workers from throughout the South. Joining them from the North were performers Gil Turner, Pete Seeger, Hedy West, Wally Hille, and Ethel Raim.[67]

"Freedom singing in the current movement is not something that spontaneously developed," Carawan later explained. "There were some definite cultural resistances to it." Black college students had generally rejected their rural musical backgrounds and preferred formal hymns at their meetings "or Rotarian type songs like 'The More We Get Together, The Happier We'll Be'. At colleges like Fisk in Nashville, many of the students initially reacted with embarrassment to new freedom songs that were sung with hand clapping and in a rural free-swinging style." But the ever-confident Carawan "found that my presence at mass meetings and workshops, introducing new songs in place of the usual dull and inappropriate ones, added a lot of spirit and enthusiasm. I could tell that it was more than the novelty of seeing a white, foot-stomping banjo-picker at an all-Negro meeting. The songs really provided a meaningful outlet for people's feelings." Highlander had become a prime training ground for civil rights leaders by late 1959, when Carawan met Martin Luther King and others at the annual Southern Christian Leadership Conference meeting in Columbia, South Carolina, and by the next spring he was teaching "We Shall Overcome" and other songs to numerous sit-in students. At the founding conference of the Student Nonviolent Coordinating Committee (SNCC) he led the singing for the two hundred present. One of the few whites traveling around the South, through 1960 and into 1961 Carawan successfully spread the civil rights message and spirit through music, though he began to spend more time documenting the movement rather than leading the singing.[68]

"The Civil Rights Movement was gaining strength at that time and songs from the sit-ins and the jails were coming North," Tom Paxton recalls, "songs with the immediacy and snap of a police dog or a fire hose. . . . They had choruses that could raise the courage of those who sang them—a courage that was far from rhetorical when sung in the face of the Bull Connors, the Cecil Prices and the Klansmen." In the Army and stationed outside New York City, Paxton frequented the Village folk clubs and one Saturday joined Len Chandler on a desegregation picket line outside a Woolworth's. The next week he composed his first topical song, "Mister Woolworth," on an Army typewriter, and after his discharge he became a fixture on the Village folk scene.[69]

In early February 1961, a benefit concert for Highlander at Carnegie Hall featured Carawan, Seeger, Memphis Slim and Willie Dixon, as well as two southern groups, the female Montgomery Gospel Trio and the male Nashville Quartet, fresh from the civil rights trenches. Before they departed, Moe Asch got them into his Folkways studio and soon issued We Shall Overcome: Songs of the "Freedom Riders" and the "Sit-ins." After the release of The Sit-in Story: The Story of Lunch-Room Sit-ins, however, Folkways's joint venture with SNCC temporarily soured, when the frugal Asch refused to donate one thousand records to the organization to assist with fundraising. SNCC turned to Vanguard, which helped distribute Freedom in the Air: A Documentary on Albany, Georgia 1961–2, produced by Carawan and Alan Lomax. But the Folkways-SNCC rift soon healed, and the sympathetic Asch released Birmingham, Alabama, 1963, The Story of Greenwood, Mississippi, and two compilations from the Selma, Alabama, movement. In 1962 CORE issued Sit-in Songs: Songs of the Freedom Riders on the Dauntless Records label. Drawing on his field recordings during 1963 and 1964, Alan Ribback (aka Moses Moon) would produce Movement Soul on the ESP label (reissued by Folkways). Guy and Candie Carawan published two volumes of civil rights songs, We Shall Overcome: Songs of the Southern Freedom Movement (Oak, 1963) and Freedom Is a Constant Struggle: Songs of the Freedom Movement (Oak, 1968).[70]

From Nashville and Highlander freedom songs spread throughout the South and North, and they reverberated among the CORE-inspired Freedom Riders in mid-1961. "In most instances field secretaries were good songleaders. By the end of the Freedom Rides, the songs of the Sit-ins, bus and jail experiences were considered essential for organizing," Bernice Johnson Reagon has explained. "No mass meeting could be successfully carried out without songs led by strong songleaders. In the early stages this responsibility fell on the field workers, gradually being shifted to local songleaders as they were identified." A member of the Albany movement during early 1962 and then the Freedom Singers, Reagon later explored the "Songs of the Civil Rights Movement" in her 1975 doctoral dissertation.[71]

Folk music and civil rights seemed a natural fit. In March 1962 Pete Seeger, Bess Hawes, and Sam Hinton raised money for UCLA's freedom riders during a concert in Santa Monica organized by Ed Pearl. A benefit for SNCC at the City College of New York featured Dylan, Ramblin' Jack Elliott, John Cohen, Ralph Rinzler, Dave Van Ronk, and the Tarriers. Robert Shelton's lengthy August 20 article, "Songs Become a Weapon in Rights Battle," drove home the connection between music and civil rights. Back from a hectic ten days in the South, Shelton wrote, "Negro folk music, which has been singing of a promised land since the days of slavery, has become a vital force in the attempt to fulfill that promise in the South today." Quoting from King and other activists, Shelton surveyed the racial hot spots, focusing on Albany, and the songs that energized the civil rights workers. Though echoes were found in the North, in the music of Bob Dylan and the recent release of Peter, Paul and Mary's rendition of "The Hammer Song," it was "in the churches of the South that the script of the drama of desegregation is being written. The essential musical background to that drama is adding new voices and new songs every day."[72]

At the end of 1962 Shelton had reprised his article in *Sing Out!*, and added some political barbs and impressions: "The Negroes of the South know what they are singing about and what they want out of life. Because they know, their music rings with more meaning and conviction. Because their music is not just a 'kick,' a hobby, a form of exhibitionism, or a 'gig,' it is a different sort of folk music than one encounters among the pampered, groping, earnestly searching young people one meets in the Greenwich Villages of the North." Shelton's comparison of urban, white folkie angst with black organizing passion, however, came just as the student and labor movements began sparking campus and community civil rights protests throughout the North.[73]

Seeger, paying his own expenses, had traveled to Albany, Georgia, and performed before a packed church crowd, with mixed reactions (mostly indifference) until he closed with the moving "We Shall Overcome." The trip resulted in his renewed commitment to civil rights, and he now salted each concert with a selection from his proliferating freedom songs repertoire. He had already met Albany activist Bernice Johnson. After her expulsion from Albany State College for civil rights work she entered Spelman College in Atlanta, and to earn money during the summer of 1962 she worked as a waitress in Saratoga Springs, New York, where she met Lena Spencer, owner of Caffé Lena, a folk club opened in 1960. Lena introduced her around, which resulted in Gil Turner inviting her to join Sing Out!'s late September Hootenanny at Carnegie Hall. Shelton's review of the packed program praised Johnson, whom he called "a teenage Odetta." After briefly making the rounds of the Village folk clubs, she flirted with a solo career, but Seeger urged her to help form a SNCC quartet; SNCC field secretary Cordell Reagon received similar encouragement from Executive Director James Foreman. The rapidly organized Freedom Singers (Bernice Johnson, Charles Neblett, Cordell Reagon, and Rutha Harris), managed by Toshi Seeger, began touring the country by year's end. Their first fund-raising event, "The Gospel Sing for Freedom" in Chicago's McCormick Place, proved a financial debacle, but things soon picked up, particularly in their concerts with Seeger. They traveled for about a year, raising money for SNCC; their appearance at the 1963 Newport Folk Festival proved the highlight of their musical career. (A second, all-male group briefly replaced them in 1964, recording one album for Mercury Records.) Through the fall and into the winter of 1963 civil rights songs filled Broadside's and Sing Out!'s pages, as the movement heated up, continually propelled by the outpouring of music.[74]

The civil rights movement served as a focal point for activist folk singers, but the languishing peace movement also attracted attention. Seeger and Turner joined three hundred marchers on 5th Avenue in late January 1962, singing "You Can Dig Your Grave in Your Own Back Yard" and other topical numbers. "The beards and 'leotards' of Greenwich Village moved down Fifth Ave. yesterday chanting peace slogans and singing folk songs in a 'General Strike for Peace,' " the Herald Tribune announced. Marching the two-and-a-half miles from the Hotel Plaza at 59th Street to Washington Square, the marchers joined in on "a number of folk songs with peace themes, including many contemporary ones about the H-bomb, but kept coming back to a favorite, 'I Ain't Gonna Study War No More.' " Many of the new songs came from Broadside.[75]

Popular Folk

Time described the folk scene in early 1962: "Guitar atwangle, eyes aimed into a far corner, the voice pitched in a keening wail, the singer holds the rapt attention of the shaggy boys, girls and dogs scattered around his Greenwich Village pad. In a campus dormitory in Ohio, in a café along San Francisco's North Beach, in a living room in upper-class Grosse Pointe, Mich., other singers with guitars chant tales of tragic love. In fact, all over the U.S., people of all descriptions—young and middle-aged, students, doctors, lawyers, farmers, cops—are plucking guitars and moaning folk songs, happily discovering that they can amuse both themselves and their friends." Six months later the magazine devoted a few columns to the emerging "folk-girls": "It is not absolutely essential to have hair hanging to the waist—but it helps. Other aids: no lipstick, flat shoes, a guitar. So equipped, almost any enterprising girl can begin a career as a folk singer." Lavishing praise on Baez, the article also mentioned newcomers Bonnie Dobson, Judy Collins, and Carolyn Hester. *Newsweek*, not to be upstaged, focused on Gerdes Folk City and Dylan, a "raffish type who has a colorful way with words" and who "looks and acts like a square's version of a folk singer." The mainstream press insisted on confusing the folk crowd with the caricature of a beatnik.[76]

At the end of 1962 *Time* put Joan Baez on its cover. With folk clubs springing up, it seemed time to survey the national landscape, but author John McPhee larded the sketch with snide remarks, in the usual *Timespeak*: "On campuses where guitars and banjos were once symptoms of hopeless maladjustment, country twanging has acquired new status." Turning from the masses to the professional musicians, he divided the latter into three camps—the Popularizers (Kingston Trio, Limeliters), the "Semipures, the Adapters, the Interpreters" (Baez, Guthrie, Seeger, Dylan), and the smallest group, "Pures, the Authentics, the Real Articles" (Jean Ritchie, Frank Proffitt). Focusing on commercial success, the article buried the performers in an avalanche of clichés, while generally ignoring the music's allure. McPhee ended on an upbeat, patriotic remark: "At its best, it [folk music] unpretentiously calls up a sense of history. . . . And, unpontifically, it dusts off the sturdier and simpler values of American life." Though mentioning that folk "singing has always been been closely allied with social protest and liberal politics," McPhee made no reference to the civil rights movement. The glossy *Song Hits Magazine* said that "country [that is, folk] music is basic, and the simple folk twang brings satisfaction to students everywhere. There's corn on the campus, folks, and it looks like it's there to stay."[77]

New performers mined the clubs, campuses, and record companies, searching for folk gold, and some discovered the mother lode. After a hesitant start, Judy Collins launched her career at the Exodus, a new folk club in Denver, from 1959 into early 1960, followed by six weeks at the Gate of Horn in Chicago. Moving east with her husband and young son that fall, she quickly took to the Village and opened at Folk City over the winter. She also reconnected with Albert Grossman, who suggested putting her in a trio with Jo Mapes and another female singer, an idea she rejected. As her solo career accelerated she was approached by Jac Holzman, who had been searching for Elektra's counter to Baez. "Jac was ambitious, smart, and very good at what he did. He had great taste, and he wanted me on his label. After the shock wore off, I was flattered," she recalled. Holzman remembers, "What I saw in Judy was a captivating voice, a good story sense, but still unsure of herself and lacking authority." Collins recorded primarily traditional folk songs, backed by Fred Hellerman and Erik Darling. The album, *A Maid of Constant Sorrow*, appeared in late 1961. By 1963 she was singing more topical numbers, by Dylan, Seeger, and Shel Silverstein.[78]

A strong rivalry developed among the "Folk Queens"—Collins, Baez, Carolyn Hester, Buffy Sainte Marie, and a few others. "About 1962, Joan appeared on the cover of *Time*, and it was one of the most important moments for women in folk music," according to Hester, who had come to New York from Texas in 1955. "They had a whole article about her and I was one of the little blurbs. I felt like my life was either changed or over. I wasn't sure." After knocking about for a few years, Hester recorded an obscure album for Coral Records, and in the early 1960s she got involved with the Village crowd, particularly the Clancy brothers. Their label, Tradition Records, produced *Carolyn Hester* in 1961, which led to her signing with Columbia Records later that year. According to John Hammond, "I wanted to continue signing folk singers. I passed on Joan Baez, whom I had heard at the Newport Folk Festival, because she was asking a great deal of money while still a relatively unknown artist. Vanguard signed her instead. I decided to look further. Carolyn Hester, a Texas girl with a good voice, was in town, so I went to one of her rehearsals and heard a kind of folk music I knew nothing about." Columbia's *Carolyn Hester*, with Dylan accompanying on harmonica on three tracks, was released in June 1962 to rave reviews. Meanwhile, Robert Shelton had introduced her to the musician and writer Richard Fariña and they married and moved to Boston.[79]

Through 1962 topical and popular folk music somewhat overlapped with Dylan and particularly with Peter, Paul and Mary, a group put together by Albert Grossman. Coming off his success with the first two Newport Folk Festivals, Grossman worked with George Wein while developing his contacts in New York, and they formed Production and Management Associates (PAMA). Mary Travers had long been a part of the Village scene, Noel Stuckey was developing a reputation as a standup comic at local clubs, and Peter Yarrow had been slowly building his performance skills, appearing at the Gate of Horn, Ash Grove, and similar establishments on the national folk circuit. "Peter had been advised by his friend and manager Albert Grossman to form a group for a year. Albert thought he'd get a little more work that way," Mary recalled. "They were looking at the wall of Izzy Young's Folklore Center where there were pictures of everybody in folk music and there was a picture of me, and Peter said, 'Who's that?' And Albert said, 'That's Mary Travers. She'd be good if you could get her to work.' So he called me." Travers suggested including Stuckey, whose name soon became Paul, forming the more euphonious Peter, Paul and Mary. Yarrow remembers that Grossman initially ordered Travers not to speak, thereby maintaining her mystique, since she "was the sex object for the college male. She was 'the' woman in America when Peter, Paul and Mary were the Number 1 recording artists in the country. To be with Mary was like being with Brigitte Bardot, she was so desirable."[80]

Grossman had previously considered other configurations, possibly Bob Gibson with Carolyn Hester and Ray Boguslav, or Mary, Peter, and Logan English or Dave Van Ronk. "Albert Grossman was standing right next to me and asked me what I thought after they finished" an early show at Folk City, recalled Eric Weissberg. "I didn't really like what they were doing. . . . He may have asked what I thought, but he didn't really care, because he said to me, 'Well, they're going to be huge.' And he was right." They were both right, for the group definitely needed a musical tuneup, if not overhaul, which Grossman understood. He turned to Milt Okun, who had been kicking around as an arranger and musician for about a decade, working with Harry Belafonte for a few years, then the Chad Mitchell Trio, a Kingston Trio clone. As their arranger, he fed the apolitical group topical songs, and in May 1962 "John Birch Society" reached ninety-nine on the pop charts.[81]

Okun found the new group highly problematic. Mary would admit they "were untrained singers who didn't write music. I had a tendency to sometimes go flat, Peter had a tendency to sometimes go sharp, the guitars would go out." Okun tried to palm them off on other arrangers without luck, so he stuck with the job, at first suggesting that Mary wear different clothes and both Peter and Paul shave their beards. But Grossman had an image of an offbeat group, to counter the Kingston Trio's buttoned down image, and stuck with his formula. Unlike his work with the Chad Mitchell Trio, Okun only did the arranging of songs chosen by the group, which slowly jelled (he would remain with them until 1970). As their club career began to take off, Grossman searched for a record company, and finally hit upon Warner Bros. Records, founded in 1958 in Los Angeles and still struggling in early 1962. Grossman had first contacted Jerry Wexler at Atlantic Records, who eagerly arranged a recording session. "At the last minute," Wexler recalled, "with musicians standing by, Albert called to say Mary had laryngitis, and the session was scrubbed. In fact, Grossman had been mugged by Artie Mogul[l], who offered him more money and whisked them down the street to Warner." Mogull, a publisher at M. Witmark & Sons, served as Warner's East Coast representative and had agreed to attend a Peter, Paul and Mary concert; he didn't make it, but he told company president Mike Maitland that they were great and should be signed. Maitland arrived in New York soon after, caught the show at the Blue Angel, and was appalled; they sounded rough and looked like beatniks, but were obviously popular. The next day he visited a company executive, who called Mogull and asked him why he had said nothing about beards. Since Mogull had never seen them he wasn't sure if this was a trick, so he hung up, called a friend to check on this unlikely story, then called back and assured Maitland this was Grossman's shrewd gimmick to make them stand out in a crowded field. The group signed the Warner's contract on January 29, 1962, receiving a hefty $30,000 advance and the freedom to record in New York rather than in Los Angeles, and to design their own albums.[82]

Peter, Paul and Mary appeared in March, with "Lemon Tree," Seeger and Hays's "If I Had a Hammer," and Seeger's "Where Have All the Flowers Gone" (also a current single by the Kingston Trio). The single of "Lemon Tree" and "Early in the Morning" hit the charts in late April, and the album stayed at number 1 for seven weeks in the fall; it was certified gold in December and would eventually sell over two million copies, staying high on the charts for an amazing 185 weeks. With records selling like hotcakes, PPM also developed a stage charisma, with Peter as the leader, Paul the comic, and Mary the silent, mysterious beauty with marvelous energy. In July Warners issued "If I Had a Hammer" as a single. Originally named "The Hammer Song," it climbed to number 10 by mid-October 1962. It won 1962 Grammys for Best Performance by a Vocal Group and Best Folk Recording, and Peter, Paul and Mary barely lost to Robert Goulet as Best New Artist. (*Moving*), their second album, released the first week of 1963, shot into the top ten; the single "Puff (The Magic Dragon)" peaked at number 2 in May. Soon Grossman paired the trio with Dylan's songs.

Boston and Cambridge

In the Boston/Cambridge area, Club 47 and Manny Greenhill were the twin poles of the local scene, bolstered by *The Broadside*, which cultivated local as well as national material and performers, with an emphasis on traditional styles. Baez remained the musical focal point until she moved to California in late 1960. Club 47 generally monopolized the cream of the local talent, such as the Charles River Valley Boys, Eric Von Schmidt, Mitch Greenhill, Dayle Stanley, Tom Rush, Bill Keith, Jackie Washington, and Jim Rooney, along with outsiders Rolf Cahn, the New Lost City Ramblers, Doc Watson, and Bonnie Dobson. Club 47 developed a loyal following, nurtured by the in-group "membership" atmosphere as well as its stimulating music, film series, experimental theater, and art gallery. But other venues also welcomed the music. In one week toward the end of 1962, local folkies had a choice of Miriam Makeba at John Hancock Hall, Sleepy John Estes at Harvard, Jesse Fuller at a local YMCA, the Limeliters at Symphony Hall, Peter, Paul and Mary along with the Clancy Brothers at Doneely Memorial Theatre, or the Moonshiners at Jordan Hall.

Initially designed as a bulletin board, full of announcements of local folk activities and ads, the ambitious biweekly *The Broadside*, launched by David Wilson on March 9, 1962, had no desire to compete with its politically slanted namesake in New York. An Air Force vet returning to Boston in 1960, Wilson became program director of the local Folksong Society, promoted by Manny Greenhill, and began running hoots at the Café Yana and the Unicorn. He also had a folk radio show, "Raising a Ruckus." "I kept discovering folk music concerts that had come and gone in the Boston area that I didn't know anything about. I thought that there should be some way to know about them," he later said. "I decided that a newsletter would be the answer, so I cranked out the first one on a hectograph," about nine hundred copies. Although the magazine generally avoided overt politics, it lauded Seeger's appearance in August for the senatorial peace candidate and Harvard historian H. Stuart Hughes, where he sang "Stand Up and Sing Out for Hughes," to the tune of "Roll On Columbia, Roll On."[83]

The *Broadside*'s ambivalence about political matters surfaced in its treatment of the police assault on Jackie Washington, a Club 47 regular. On December 3, 1962, two Boston policemen stopped him, roughed him up, fracturing his nose in the process, then charged him with assault and battery against a police officer. Found guilty and fined $10, he appealed the case. The *Broadside* applauded the pressure on the police by local supporters, and especially Washington's fortitude and humor while telling his story at Club 47 of his night in jail: "The most important factor in this whole case we feel after hearing Jackie's story both from the fact sheet and Jackie's own words is that here is a young man of excellent reputation throughout the Boston Community as a folk singer, as a youth worker, and last but not least, as a person who has the courage to stand up for his rights in this so called 'cradle of liberty' and use his case as a precedent to show the citizens of Boston the police brutality which does exist." But nowhere did the magazine mention that Jackie was black and the officers white, or even hint at possible racial overtones to the affair. The next month, however, the magazine published a notice about a panel discussion on civil rights and the Boston police, including Washington as a special guest, and also announced a local tour by the Freedom Singers coming in March 1963.[84]

The *Broadside* not only shied away from overt politics, it avoided almost any form of controversy. Eric Von Schmidt and Jim Rooney would later take David Wilson to task: "Very rarely was anyone except the most commercial hack criticized. . . . Everyone was worth going to see. Every club had a good lineup. It was as if there were no musical standards by which folk music could be judged." But they grudgingly recognized the magazine's informational value. Though Wilson felt shunned by the folks at Club 47 (who were perhaps jealous of plugs for the competition) and sensed lukewarm support in Boston, he maintained a regular biweekly schedule for most of the decade. He was one of a handful of folk magazine pioneers; within a short time similar publications sprouted throughout the country.[85]

Baez, with strong backing by Manny Greenhill, had early committed herself to the civil rights movement. Thrilled by her commercial recognition, capped by the *Time* cover, the activist Greenhill yet might have withdrawn as her manager "if we didn't mesh in this political level, because all these exciting things were happening. And I felt I was making a contribution to all these things just by booking her." Her commitment to integration and civil rights mounted through 1961 and 1962, but her southern tours drew no blacks, through a combination of segregation and lack of local recognition. In 1963, she performed at black Miles College in Birmingham and stayed at the integrated Gadston Motel, where she met the Reverend Martin Luther King, in town for massive demonstrations. "I sang and talked, and no one seemed bored," she wrote. "Perhaps it was partly because of the electricity we could feel emanating from the center of town, miles away, where the kids were at that very moment being arrested and filling paddy wagons, singing and praying, scared to their bones but bolstered by each other's presence and by the knowledge that they were doing right in the eyes of God."[86]

Through various personal connections, a bond developed between Cambridge and Berkeley, both avant-garde university communities. Rolf Cahn, by way of Detroit and Berkeley, settled in Cambridge in 1959 and quickly became established as the community's guitar teacher, whether folk, blues, or flamenco. His students included Jim Kweskin, Debbie Green, Jackie Washington, and Manny Greenhill's son Mitch. Cahn began working with Eric Von Schmidt, a graphic artist and blues guitarist, and they recorded for Folkways. The Cambridge-Berkeley nexus was later nurtured by Baez as well.

There were also strong ties between Cambridge and the Village folk crowd. During a flying visit to Greenwich Village, Bill Keith and Jim Rooney rushed to Izzy's Folklore Center, a cornucopia of books, records, magazines. "Soon he was grilling us about what was going on up in Cambridge," Rooney recalled. "He'd been getting reports from people like Barry Kornfield [sic] and Bob Dylan. As a matter of fact, did we known Dylan? No, we didn't. He said, 'Come back. He's back here.' With that we went into the back room, and there was Dylan sitting at a cluttered desk, banging away on a typewriter." They also met John Herald of the Greenbriar Boys, joined Roger Sprung in Washington Square on Sunday afternoon, picking for almost five hours, and played a hoot at the Bitter End, hosted by Theo Bikel.[87]

With no central control, the Revival accelerated into the early sixties, propelled by grassroots patronage, fueled by gathering commercial forces and mounting political activism, and enlivened by a proliferating number of talented (and not so talented) musicians and songwriters. Toward the end of 1962 Allan Sherman's satirical album *My Son the Folk Singer* began making the rounds, becoming the nation's top seller in mid-November for two weeks, and remained among the top forty albums for half a year. Folk music seemed to know no bounds.

7

The Revival's Peak, 1963–1964

In early March 1963 *Billboard* announced that " 'Hootenanny,' the first regularly scheduled network TV program devoted to folk music, will make its debut on ABC, Saturday, April 6, Jack Linkletter will host the weekly series. The Limeliters, the Clancy Brothers, Theodore Bikel, the Chad Mitchell Trio, Miriam Makeba and other performers who have become famous in the exploding popularity of folk music, will be making appearances on 'Hootenanny.' The series will originate at various college campuses before audiences of students."[1]

Izzy Young also noted what was to come on television in his midwinter *Sing Out!* column. He announced both the appearance of a bluegrass group, the Garret Mountain Boys, including David Grisman, on an upcoming ABC-TV show, and the videotaping by Bitter End owner Fred Weintraub of a concert at Syracuse University, featuring Jo Mapes, the Limeliters, and the Clara Ward Singers, for a television series to start in the spring. Bob Gibson, with Ed McCurdy as host, had initiated a series of Tuesday night hoots at the Bitter End in the Village the previous year, and ABC subsequently bought the club's concept. Theo Bikel also taped his WBAI radio show at the Bitter End. Weintraub's "enthusiasm for his work is immense," remarked Joan Barthel in the *New York Times*, "perhaps because he reached The Bitter End last year by way of Scarsdale and Madison Avenue."[2]

A half-hour show on Saturday nights, *Hootenanny* was produced by Richard Lewine and hosted by Jack Linkletter, son of the television personality Art. The burgeoning college campuses seemed the logical home for a televised folk show

194

and ITA's *The Scene* noted that "the role of the nation's colleges, universities, civic organizations and other such basically non–show business institutions in shaping entertainment patterns is rapidly developing in the eyes of the talent industry." A major talent management concern representing numerous folk performers—Peter, Paul and Mary, the Limeliters, the Journeymen, the Brothers Four, Odetta—ITA recognized the college appeal. (CBS was considering a similar show, to be titled *Folk Festival*, with Oscar Brand as the emcee and the Tarriers as the regular quartet in an informal setting. The program planned to present the Limeliters, the Kingston Trio, Peter, Paul and Mary, Joan Baez, Pete Seeger, and the Weavers. But it arrived stillborn.[3]

Hootenanny, representing the maximum commercial potential for folk music, can perhaps serve as the slippery touchstone of the revival. Featuring an array of performers who were mostly on the slick side and packaged in the standard mass media manner (no rough edges), the show allowed numerous musicians to reach an audience previously unimagined. Once hooked, many in the audience went out to purchase the records, and some may even have discovered the music's rural roots and traditional performers. But the program also generated other passions. ABC's decision to continue the blacklist of Pete Seeger and the Weavers not only excluded them from the show but also galvanized a performers' boycott and media debate. (The Weavers had a rare appearance on Theo Bikel's noncommercial *Directions '61* show on ABC, singing "Wasn't That a Time," but they were canceled from NBC's *Tonight Show* in January 1962 for refusing to sign a loyalty oath.) The thaw in the Cold War had only been partial.

Hearing of the blacklisting of Seeger, *The Broadside* in Boston waved the caution flag two months before the first show. Editor Dave Wilson, usually shunning politics, was shocked "that a major network sees fit to record him on their major record label, but not to televise him." The next month New York's *Broadside* wrote, "A major network has a weekly T.V. show to be called 'Hootenanny' all ready to go—big money sponsors, performers, etc., all lined up. Even before the airing of the 1st show, however, the project has been crippled—and probably doomed—by the application of the BLACKLIST." Joan Baez had refused to appear if Pete Seeger was not invited. "So Joan won the biggest Emmy of the year hands down without even stepping before the T.V. camera." Lewine desperately wanted Baez for the pilot show, taped at the University of Rochester, and her manager Manny Greenhill suggested she hover nearby in case they dropped the blacklist. But when the producers remained adamant, she packed up and continued on her current tour. The network proceeded to tape a number of shows before the April unveiling, including Judy Collins, the Clancy Brothers, Theo Bikel, and the Journeymen at Brown University. Some initial dealing with Harold Leventhal, the manager of Seeger, the Weavers, the Tarriers, Bikel, and soon Collins generated fleeting hope among many that the network would yet back down.[4]

After checking the story, Nat Hentoff wrote in the *Village Voice* that the Weavers were also banned, and that the interracial Tarriers had passed muster only after a threatened disclosure of network racial discrimination. He applauded Baez's stand and wondered "whether some of the other performers who have agreed to be on 'Hootenanny'—and they include a number of resplendent liberals—know about the Seeger blacklisting." Hentoff supported a boycott. He also discussed the recent refusal of CBS to permit Seeger or the Weavers to appear on a show with President Kennedy, sponsored by the Anti-Defamation League of the B'nai B'rith (Odetta, Josh White, the Clancy Brothers, and Judy Collins, seemingly unaware of the situation, joined the president). *Newsweek*, on the other hand, covered the taping at Brown University and enthusiastically previewed the series. If the mass circulation magazine gave no clue the show had political problems, *Variety*'s readers were alerted on March 20 in a lengthy piece summarizing the situation. Many performers would stick with Seeger but *Variety* said that "ambivalence is suspected by some observers . . . since the network exposure, a big promotion for performers and the medium generally, and the loot involved are strong lures."[5]

An initial boycott meeting took place at the Village Gate on March 17, organized by Judy Collins and Carolyn Hester. Izzy suspected "that money will talk at this meeting and few will dare to lose money for principle," but he wouldn't miss the action and took detailed notes. The packed crowd included Collins, Tom Paxton, Bob Dylan, Dick Weissman, Tommy Clancy, Jac Holzman, Dave Van Ronk, Erik Darling, Ralph Rinzler and Harold Leventhal, some of whom had already taped a show or two. Even Izzy fretted, "It would be a terrible thing to cut folk music off TV when it took so long to get on," yet he backed the boycott.[6]

Meetings of the protesters continued into April, and their position hardened, though there were disagreements and much confusion about how to proceed. Some dwelled on specific tactics, others stood on higher principles. Alan Lomax, always more interested in republican ideas than organizing details, argued on March 25, "It is because we're folksingers, attached to democratic traditions, that we are taking such a strong position. We are specially sensitive to the invasion of the rights for Americans to express private viewpoints as an artist." The next day Izzy wrote, "Lomax was absolutely necessary for the meeting. He brought it the poetry of America—folk traditions—its simple ideals, fair ideas for individuals, and a great spirit. It fired us all." Soon the Folksingers Committee to End the Blacklist emerged, with Tom Paxton, John Herald, Logan English, and Billy Faier taking some responsibility; the group began collecting signatures and formalizing the protest. Producer Lewine claimed full responsibility but denied any political motivation, and he hid behind the rationale that Seeger and the Weavers could not hold a vast audience. When Nat Hentoff asked Izzy about Bikel's role, Izzy responded that "he had hurt us so far and that we did not expect help from him. He has a reputation for talking liberal and acting in just the opposite manner." Izzy's suspicions seemed warranted. As quoted in *Billboard*, after taping two *Hootenanny* shows Bikel called any blacklist "sick and evil," but also took "an oblique swipe at methods of protest employed by others, [and] said that artists like the Weavers can get on TV if all involved act as sane, responsible people and not engage in ineffectual public protests or boycotts by folk singers." (Bikel does not mention the boycott or even the show in his autobiography, *Theo*, though he discusses the Weavers' other television problems and his own media career at the time.[7]

ABC launched *Hootenanny* on time and the boycott proceeded. Jack Gould, in the *New York Times*, praised the opening show with Bob Gibson, the Limeliters, Bud and Travis, and Bonnie Dobson at the University of Michigan—"a thoroughly pleasant and enterprising departure from the staid programing norm"—but questioned the Seeger ban. Barry Kittleson, in *Billboard*, had a more jaded view of a show that "is in desperate need of a suitable format"; "they've whipped up a monster that is reminiscent of the amateur days of early television," with announcer Linkletter lurking "in the background only to come on like a reporter at a wrestling match." But the show caught on, and the network agreed to expand it to one hour in the fall, the prime 7:30–8:30 P.M. slot, preceding the powerful Saturday night lineup of Lawrence Welk and Jerry Lewis.[8]

If the viewers embraced the show, the controversy simmered among countless performers and political sympathizers. *Broadside* devoted four pages to the imbroglio in the April issue. "In Franco Spain the laws provide that even musical notes (but first the lyrics) in songs have to be approved by the censors," Gordon Friesen noted. "Here we do not have as yet a 'Handbook on Un-American Musical Notation.' But we do have people who would no doubt like to get one out and put it into use." In the end, many of the big names refused to appear—Dylan, Baez, Peter, Paul and Mary—while others trimmed their sails, flattered by the attention and publicity. "It was quite amazing to us (the New Lost City Ramblers) that we were even considered for this show, and we went through a great deal of soul searching to arrive at our decision" to appear, John Cohen has explained. "Central to our argument was to balance our repugnance at the blacklist industry with the opportunity to bring traditional music, played in a traditional style, to the widest possible audience." That Seeger's brother Mike was a member of the Ramblers complicated the situation. Tom Paxton, Peter LaFarge, and Dave Van Ronk organized a protest campaign during July's Newport Folk Festival, collecting two thousand signed postcards complaining of Seeger's and the Weavers' blacklisting.[9]

Even Izzy Young, an ardent leader and supporter of the boycott, relaxed his vigil by year's end, as the group he managed, the Even Dozen Jug Band, secured a spot on the show taped at Fordham University. Eager for the exposure, he

still grumbled about the taping session: "No one respects the show and everyone sang the song ['Hootenanny Hoot'] making fun of it—and that's where
the brainwashing comes in. While lampooning the song they all do a good
job—their sarcastic enthusiasm parodying quartets etc. comes over as great fun.
The first step in degradation." He learned that the producers would not let the
singer Will Holt include a variety of songs, such as "House of the Rising Sun"
and Dylan's "A Hard Rain's A-Gonna Fall," but finally relented on "Lemon
Tree." "No song with content can get through the show," Izzy concluded. In
any case, he was there, part of his temporary immersion in the commercial
side of the music, and he made a few pennies from each of the Even Dozen
Jug Band's records that sold.[10]

Pete Seeger's attitude toward the show was predictably complex. Devoting
one of his *Sing Out!* columns to the affray, he welcomed a show that could "be
a breath of fresh air on TV. But with the producers of the show knowing little
about folk music besides what they learn from the pages of *Billboard* and *Variety*,"
they could not accomplish much, and besides they would never feature the real
folksingers, such as Doc Watson, Horton Barker, or Bessie Jones. And what did
he recommend? Perhaps start another television show, or at least have people
write to ABC and the sponsors critiquing forthcoming shows. When performers
asked his opinion about the boycott, he refused to take a stand. "In the summer,
Harold Leventhal called a meeting with Pete Seeger, Theo, and me to discuss
the situation at ABC," Judy Collins has written. "I was surprised at Pete's response. He said that *Hootenanny* would help to make folk music popular, which
was something he had fought for all his life, and urged Theo and me to accept
invitations to go on the show again." So, with mixed feelings—after all, she
had launched the protest group—Collins did two more shows, but she found
the "artistic direction to be slick and commercial. The production staff changed
lyrics and insisted on cuts in material that made no sense. After those performances, I told ABC I would not do the show again." She later regretted her
appearances.[11]

Leventhal shared Collins's confusion. After much faltering and lame excuses,
and somewhat tired of the protesting, ABC finally offered Seeger a spot if he
would sign a loyalty oath. He curtly rejected the offer, writing to ABC: "I just
finished a seven-year court battle to prove the principle that such oaths are
unconstitutional, and I was acquitted and vindicated." Perhaps there was some
solace in the fact that his half-hour television show, *Two Links in a Chain*, appeared
on Canada's CBC-TV. *Hootenanny* survived without him, introducing its weekly
audience of eleven million to a packaged, sanitized version of folk music, with
some spark and variety yet limited to "safe" sounds and performers.[12]

By the end of 1963 *Hootenanny* had become one of ABC's most popular shows.
Colleges vied to be the lucky host, and the network had to pay damages when
eager students at four of the shows trampled over locked gym doors to get

good seats. Paul Gardner wrote in the *New York Times*, "In the collegian's blue book, football games are routine; fraternity parties are passé and homecoming weekends have never been able to stimulate interest. But the appearance of a television unit for a 'Hootenanny' sequence almost makes four years of academic isolation worthwhile." With no mention of any performers, he focused on the students' excitement. "The object is not to impair the school's curriculum or lure students from class," Gardner said, "but to inject a spontaneous campus atmosphere into a program that might otherwise emerge as a straight variety show."[13]

Jo Mapes had bittersweet memories of the show. Her initial qualms about breaking the boycott were undercut by Seeger's argument that folk music needed such national exposure, so she proceeded to appear and enjoyed the experience, renewing old acquaintances and meeting new stars such as Johnny Cash. "We presented a wholesome, spanking clean, all American show, our songs being screened for possible subversive messages and other unwelcomed elements," she recalls. "I was not allowed to sing Woody Guthrie's 'Little Sack of Sugar,' as it was considered 'sexually suggestive.' . . . Yet we sang 'Wimoweh,' " about racial oppression in South Africa. She and Cass Elliott, soon of the Mamas and the Papas, referred to the host as Jack "Lackluster."[14]

While the weekly *Hootenanny* grabbed the spotlight, other television shows also featured folk performers, sometimes offering a more political message. Bob Dylan, just beginning his climb, in one leap reached the pinnacle with an invitation to appear on the popular *Ed Sullivan Show* in mid-May 1963. There was only one catch. The CBS-TV censor refused to allow him to sing the abrasive "Talkin' John Birch Society Blues," though Sullivan had already given his approval. Dylan refused to appear if he could not sing the song, and so he canceled. Various columnists raked CBS over the coals for such censorship, pointing out that Dylan was already under contract to Columbia Records. Dylan tried to get the Federal Communications Commission to intervene, with no luck. In any case, he performed on a rival network with the Brothers Four, Carolyn Hester, Barbara Dane, and the Staple Singers.

Despite the hype—including a package of "Hootenanny ABC-TV Paper Dolls"—ABC dropped *Hootenanny* for its fall 1964 lineup. "The program changes mean that folk music no longer will have a regular weekly showcase on network television," one article concluded. "The moves probably grew out of a failure to obtain full sponsorship for *Hootenanny* and also to compete early Saturdays with CBS and NBC, where both will have shows designed to attract children." Irwin Silber cheered the news: "And so, as Jack Linkletter sinks slowly into the undulating waves which gently wash the shores of Seahawken U., we bid fond farewell to ABC-TV *Hootenanny*, Madison Avenue's Answer to Folk Music."[15]

The Folk Craze

For about two years the words "folk music" and "hootenanny" had a magic, commercial ring. The country seemed to go folk crazy. "Hootenanny" became attached not only to a show and countless records, but also sweat shirts, pinball machines, shoes, paper dolls, even vacations and Ford dealerships; the New Jersey's Palisades Amusement Park had a Miss Hootenanny contest. "Beach Hoot a Splashing Success," trumpeted *Billboard*; over seven thousand college students during their week's spring break at Daytona Beach, heard thirty-six college folk groups compete for a Mercury Records contract. "Trucks filled with folksingers drove up and down the beach stirring up interest and local clothing and record stores tied in with window displays featuring Mercury albums." Some fifty radio stations had hootenanny shows. Indeed, WCPO in Cincinnati switched to an all-folk format in August, a "Summer Hootenanny." At least a hundred albums (and some songbooks) sported "hootenanny" as part of their title.[16]

Eighteen-year-old Maggie Puner explained to her fellow teens in *Seventeen*:

> Folk music is living music, an expression of human emotions—despair, joy, hope. It has no ulterior motives, just a few basic hopes: to preserve the heritage of every country throughout the world in song; to express firsthand the thoughts of the people, be they about the outlaw Jesse James or the atom bomb; to become a part of the mind and heart of everyone willing to let it. Folk music is here to stay. But don't just take my word for it—go out and hear for yourself, then decide.

She recommended Seeger, Baez, Peter, Paul and Mary, the Weavers, Josh White and Odetta. Joyce Maynard recalled that Seeger "always made me feel generous-spirited" when as a pre-adolescent she joined in during one of his energizing concerts. "We applauded ourselves at the end, and stood up, wishing there was something more we could do than give a standing ovation." As for Baez, "She was the champion of nonconformity and so—like thousands of others—we joined the masses of her fans."[17]

Maynard had no awareness of, or interest in, the vital and barely concealed commercial forces at play. The Kingston Trio earned between $8,000 and $12,000 for each concert, and another $300,000 per year from their records, much of which they invested. "The investments are designed to give the singers income and something to do when the Kingston Trio is no longer a box-office hit," their manager, Frank Werber, explained to *Business Week*. Unlike Maggie Puner they realized that the fad would soon run its course.[18]

There was no dearth of guides to the burgeoning folk scene. Art D'Lugoff, proprietor of the Village Gate, took *Cavalier*'s male readers on a sprightly tour of Greenwich Village night life: "This year and next year, and long after, more great entertainment will come out of Greenwich Village than from anywhere else in the nation for the simple reason that more good and great talent has a chance to begin in the Village." With the loosening of cabaret licensing requirements, practically anyone could open a place and feature music. The Village Gate, Manny Roth's Café Wha?, the Gaslight, the Bitter End, Folk City, Trude Heller's Versailles, and others were part of a national network that provided venues for the escalating scores of folk performers—Caffé Lena (Saratoga Springs, New York), the Gate of Horn (Chicago), Second Fret (Philadelphia), Shadows (Washington, D.C.), Purple Onion (San Francisco), La Cave (Cleveland), Ash Grove and Troubador (Los Angeles). Some of the most popular performers headlined the posh night clubs, such as the Coconut Grove (Los Angeles) or Copacabana (New York). On the other end of the commercial scale, coffeehouses were springing up everywhere, offering the singers atmosphere and an audience though scant financial security.[19]

Folk attracted a wide range of performers and fans. Dion DiMucci, lead singer of Dion and the Belmonts, a white doo-wop group with a string of hits in the late 1950s, soon switched to acoustic music. He left the Belmonts in 1960 to record his own chart-toppers and, visiting with the legendary record producer John Hammond at Columbia Records, Dion heard Aretha Franklin, Lightnin' Hopkins, the Reverend Gary Davis, and Bob Dylan in the studio. He also discovered the Greenwich Village folk clubs. "It was another big surprise—all the while I'd been belting the Bronx blues, a scene had been mushrooming under my nose, with music that was a lot closer to the simple storytelling I'd learned from Hank Williams than most of the Broadway melodies that I'd been forced to croon." Hanging around Washington Square with the folk performer John Sebastian and the comedian Richard Pryor, Dion also listened to Mississippi John Hurt and Sonny Terry and Brownie McGhee. "The music, especially the old stuff I'd started collecting, was opening me up to all sorts of new ideas, but, to be honest, half the stuff I was hearing from the folk elite left me a little cold. I always got the feeling that guys like Tom Paxton and Phil Ochs—two singer/songwriters touted as the best back then—were really just reporters, putting the news to music." Picking and choosing among the folk styles, he was caught by the thrill of "expressing yourself, not trying to please people who'd never know the real you anyway." But by 1964 he had become a junkie, and music took a backseat in his life; he did, however, include some Dylan and Guthrie songs on one Columbia album.[20]

Ethan Crosby and his younger brother David were members of the Les Baxter Balladeers, one of the countless pop folk groups making the rounds of the Los Angeles clubs and Las Vegas casinos. "It was a hot little group and we got hired by Jack Linkletter to go out on tour," Ethan recalled. "We were the Jack Linkletter Folk Caravan, with Joe and Eddie and their guitar player; the Big Three, which was Cass Elliott. . . . We did thirty one-nighters on a lousy bus; it was a grim trip. . . . It was a crazy tour." But it was a typical experience for the performers and promoters who hopped on the wobbly folk bandwagon.[21]

The folk craze caught the eyes of countless journalists. "When a college student wanted to let off steam, there were always such tension relievers as panty snatching, bed pushing and elbow bending at hand, part of the charm of which lay in calculated naughtiness," Meryle Secrest suggested in the *Washington Post*. "But these well-tested pursuits have lately been passed over in favor of a fad the very innocuousness of which gives pause." College students, male and female, were listening, picking, and singing throughout the country. "You are going to find folk music wherever you find a group of people who are concerned," one student explained. "The kind of people who join student Peace Union [sic] and CORE or go on Freedom Rides are the kind of people who will like folk signing." At the crosstown *Washington Daily News*, James O'Neill judged "this modern 'folk music' to be a step forward from the cacaphonic depths of rock and roll, but still a long way from a true form of art."[22]

The folklorist Roger Abrahams, only recently a mainstay of the Village folk scene, helped organize the popular Thursday night folk sings in the University of Texas student union after his arrival as a member of the English department in 1960. Activist politics played little role in bringing students to the Texas hootenannies, but the audiences identified as outsiders, alienated from the dominant fraternity and sorority crowds. The university's overwhelmingly conservative students still preferred the twist, but a growing group of rebels drifted to folk music, as it increasingly connected to the civil rights movement. Many of the performers, including Janis Joplin, lived together in the Ghetto, a run-down apartment complex, and they also hung around Threadgill's Bar on the edge of town, absorbing live traditional country and bluegrass. In January 1963 Joplin took off for San Francisco and freedom; soon after that the 11th Door opened as Austin's first commercial folk club, featuring Doc Watson and Mance Lipscomb.[23]

Ensconced on college campuses and in various bohemian neighborhoods, folk music was also becoming part of mainstream popular music. The Rooftop Singers' "Walk Right In" reached the musical stratosphere in January 1963 and remained on the charts for three months. Izzy Young applauded their seeking out the song's originator, Gus Cannon of the Memphis-based Jug Stompers, who received $500 outright plus 25 percent of the royalties. "This is just about unheard of. And beautiful." Only recently working as a gardener, the elderly Cannon joined other older bluesmen on the folk circuit. Led by Erik Darling, the Rooftop Singers also had a hit with "Tom Cat" a few months later. During the year other folk records became top sellers. Peter, Paul and Mary, the Kingston Trio, the New Christy Minstrels, and the Chad Mitchell Trio crowded into the pop charts along with Jan and Dean, Little Stevie Wonder, the Beach Boys, and the Singing Nun. Tom Glazer and the Children's Chorus briefly reached number fourteen in midsummer with "On Top of Spaghetti." Trini Lopez followed Peter, Paul and Mary's hit of late 1962, "If I Had a Hammer," with his own version which made it to number three about a year later.[24]

Controversy swirled around the music, as usual, while its popularity grew. Nat Hentoff regaled *Playboy*'s readers with a lengthy overview of the scene. "The expanding folk carrousel [sic] [is not] limited to the folkum style of the Kingston Trio or the earnest pamphleteering of Pete Seeger. It is, in fact, the growing diversity in the current folk farrago that makes this phenomenon so absorbing and increasingly difficult to compartmentalize." He preferred Dylan, Baez, and the New Lost City Ramblers, and he questioned much of the pious radicalism of young folkies, but he ended on an upbeat note: "Whether the ancient gold will indeed be transmuted into something nobler is seriously open to question, but the weight of current evidence is shifting to the side of those performers and listeners who are convinced that even though the folk—in the traditional sense—are dying, folk music can continue to live boisterously and change more unpredictably than ever before."[25]

While the pundits of the popular press dissected the various musicians and styles, a group of mostly scholars gathered in March 1963 during the winter meeting of the New York Folklore Society to share their views and feelings. "At the Symposium Saturday I felt alone again—with 12 apostles on the dais," Izzy wrote in his notebook. "Lomax said we all make our money from folk music— therefore we're not honest. But that was only a cloak to cover his copyright operations. . . . All decried mass media. Only I spouted enthusiasm. And I'm out of step. I have kept a little light shining but there is no need for it now." As the proceedings were published in the *New York Folklore Quarterly*, the lively exchange among Izzy, Lomax, Oscar Brand, Irwin Silber, the folklorist Ben Botkin, and Ralph Rinzler became public. They played their respective parts. Izzy praised the role of city musicians who drew on tradition as well as writing their own topical songs. The group discussed the role of commercial forces in promoting folk or any other kind of music, for good or ill, and the tension between urban and rural styles, as well as their cross-fertilization.[26]

Izzy, the Samuel Pepys of the Revival, was growing increasingly alarmed at the musical compromises many preferred to make. His longtime friend Dick Weissman, one of the most versatile and sensitive banjo players in the Village, had become a member of the popular Journeymen, led by John Phillips. Izzy said that Dick "does only junk, and writing it, too. . . . Two years ago he said he was in the business to make enough money to retire and do good work. No more of that." Weissman had his own doubts, but he could hardly pass up the applause and money. The Journeymen's moderately successful albums for Capitol and their crowded performing schedule temporarily served to blunt his concerns about quality and style. "On one level it was sheer pop fluff," he has explained, "but I took pride in playing as well as I could and in learning a bit about group singing from John Phillips, who was an excellent though untrained vocal arranger." After three and a half years the group folded; Phillips went on to organize the Mamas and the Papas, and Weissman became a successful performer and studio musician.[27]

Mike Gross in *Variety* captured the contrary winds of the revival: "The song accents now are more on entertainment values than on ethnic sources. Show biz's influence on the folksters, and vice versa, has disturbed the purists who are pointing to commercialism as the corruptor of an art form. But the big demand for the folk performers in virtually all areas of show biz (records, concerts, college dates, tv, pix) is stimulating a new folk form that can appeal to a mass audience. Whether the new form is folk or not doesn't militate against the impact this new material is having on the music business."[28]

The Civil Rights Movement

From the abolitionist movement of the mid-nineteenth century, topical songs had long been connected with civil rights organizing, and a direct line continued into the mid-1960s. Indeed, "We Shall Overcome" resonated nationally and internationally, connecting with worldwide liberation movements for five decades. By 1963 the civil rights movement could claim substantial achievements, yet it seemed mired in partial victories and it faced increasing local white resistance, even violence. Freedom songs stimulated and cemented the resistance to discrimination and segregation. *Broadside* published a string of freedom songs and informed its readers of the latest news. In May 1963, for example, editors Cunningham and Friesen led off with the song "Bull Connor's Jail" and news of the arrest of Guy and Candie Carawan in Birmingham (they had been detained as they tried to enter the New Pilgrim Baptist Church). "The racial crisis in the South has become a theme of major importance for folk singers of the North," Robert Shelton proclaimed. "New songs on this theme are not only weapons in the civil-rights arsenal, but are also developing into valuable commodities in the music industry." Peter, Paul and Mary's version of Dylan's "Blowin' in the Wind" began to shoot up the charts in early July, reaching number two in August. Phil Ochs, Len Chandler, and Tom Paxton were also writing topical songs that caught the media's attention.[29]

Various performers filtered into the South, including Pete Seeger, who reported: "I was three days in Greenwood, Mississippi, this past July lending some small support to the Negro voter registration drive down there. Sang in a small Baptist church, at a large NAACP meeting in Jackson, and out in an open field. The last was a songfest also attended by Theodore Bikel, Bob Dylan, and several hundred of the most enthusiastic Freedom fighters and singers one could imagine. All ages." Bikel had become a prominent supporter of SNCC. A seasoned civil rights worker already arrested during a demonstration in Birmingham, he was the first northern performer after Seeger to venture south. *Time* matter-of-factly covered the Greenwood voter registration rally and presence of the three singers: "All over the U.S., folk singers are doing what folk singers are classically supposed to do—singing about current crises. . . . Instead of keening over the poor old cowpoke who died in the streets of Laredo or chronicling the life cycle of the blue-tailed fly (the sort of thing that fired the great postwar revival of folk song), they are singing with hot-eyed fervor about police dogs and racial murder."[30]

The March on Washington propelled folk singers into the national spotlight. Joan Baez joined Dylan, Odetta, Josh White, and Peter, Paul and Mary in a morning pre-march concert. "I was in Washington in 1963 when King gave his most famous speech: 'I have a dream,' " Baez recalled in her autobiography. "It was a mighty day, which has been described many times. . . . In the blistering sun, facing the original rainbow coalition, I led 350,000 people in 'We Shall Overcome,' and I was near my beloved Dr. King." Dylan, the Freedom Singers, Peter, Paul and Mary, the opera star Marian Anderson, and Mahalia Jackson sang during the later formal program.[31]

"On the march the air was filled with the sounds of the jail-ins, Sit-ins, and street marches of Southern campaigns," said Bernice Johnson Reagon. "These songs were led mostly by local leaders who had come from their areas to be present in Washington. . . . Once at the Monument, the music of the Movement was represented only by the Freedom Singers; there was no recognition given to local songleaders. This group was invited to the March as an afterthought through the grace of Harry Belafonte who chartered a plane from Los Angeles to the capital for the occasion." Robert Sherman, in the *Saturday Review*, welcomed the lineup of folk singers, but reminded his readers, "It is, of course, on the Southern battlefields of the war against discrimination, that these freedom songs have served, and are serving with the greatest effectiveness. Acting in a sense as common denominators of the Negro people, they weld individuals—with individual doubts and terrors and weaknesses—into a dynamic and inexorable striking force."[32]

Many white southerners were so nervous that they construed anything culturally challenging as promoting civil rights. John Phillips, part of a "Hootenanny Tour" with Glenn Yarbrough and Jo Mapes, recalled "The 'Hoot Tour' was never conceived as a political event, but in the south during the end of 1963, if you were white, on a bus and played a guitar and sang for a living, it didn't matter—you *were* political. Suddenly we found ourselves in the thick of the civil rights movement." At the University of Alabama Phillips mentioned the name of Josh White and was greeted with shouts of "Nig-GER, Nig-GER." At another stop they were welcomed with Louisville Slugger bats, roughed up and sent on their way. When they refused to play in Jackson, Mississippi, because of a local ordinance barring blacks from the city auditorium, "the city's rednecks went crazy, smashing hotel windows, baiting us with chants of 'Nigger lovers,' and surrounding the hotel." They performed instead at the nearby black Tougaloo College. "The young students, with tears in their eyes, walked up to the stage and asked us to sing freedom songs." The whole troupe ended the show holding hands and singing "We Shall Overcome."[33]

Guy Carawan continued to be a vibrant force. In early May 1964 he organized a "Sing for Freedom" workshop at the Gammon Theological Seminary in Atlanta, three days of music and organizing sessions. Southern activists— Fannie Lou Hamer, Bernice Johnson Reagon, Bertha Gober, Doc Reese, and Andrew Young—joined with northern songwriters—Phil Ochs, Len Chandler, and Tom Paxton—to offer a series of closed workshops and open songfests. Highlander Folk School had attempted a preliminary music workshop four years earlier and now, in a headier political climate, the revamped Highlander Center joined with SCLC and SNCC to spur new songwriting. Theo Bikel attended, representing the Newport Folk Foundation.

Josh Dunson issued reports to *Broadside* and *Sing Out!* about the exuberant music and the sharp exchanges between older performers, such as the Sea Island Singers, defending their slave song legacy and those who preferred fresh songs of freedom. "Many of the people who had come to Atlanta ashamed of their own vibrant tradition went away with a deepening sense of pride in it," he concluded in *Broadside*. "A number left somewhat troubled, not convinced, but thinking. All had many new songs to take home." He ended on a more upbeat note in *Sing Out!*: "As the singers returned to their homes in Savannah, Albany, Americus, Aikins, Wagner and Hattisburg [sic], Mississippi, they carried new songs and new ideas. They took with them a growing sense of the effect the Freedom Movement had on the Northern songwriters, and, more important, a deepening pride in the heritage and tradition that had been hidden from them because of its militancy, depth and power." This was Len Chandler's first real trip into the South (aside from a brief Army stint), and he came away with new friends and commitments. Indeed, Cordell Reagon immediately dragged him off to Nashville, where he was "arrested about four or five times in about a week, and that was real important because the songs that you make up and you sing in jail and all those things really had an incredible impact on me."[34]

Julius Lester joined the *Broadside* stable of writers discussing freedom songs. Like Chandler, he was born in the Midwest, but he moved to Nashville in his teens, graduated from Fisk University in 1960, and soon headed for New York; he also worked at the Highlander Folk School, singing at mass meetings and voter registration workshops. In his article, "Freedom Songs in the South," Lester connected new and old freedom songs, both necessary to bolster resistance and foster community: "Not only do the songs help to keep the people 'marching up to freedom land'; they serve to crumble the class barriers within the Negro community." A few weeks later he published "Freedom Songs in the North," where he argued that all passion seemed drained from the songs when pulled from the South. He contended that "the city-singer has a *responsibility* to Leadbelly and to the southern freedom fighters in whose songs live the blood and body of every Negro who has wept and laughed, suffered and exulted at life in America. It can be nothing more than a travesty when the city-singer forgets them. . . . Being Negro is not a necessary prerequisite for singing freedom songs. Being willing to understand the Negro and his history is."[35]

In 1964 Lester had been fully committed to race cooperation as the route to black freedom. By the end of the 1960s, however, he had passed through the furnace of race rebellion and emerged a black power advocate. In *Search for the New Land*, published in 1969, he dropped any hope for race empathy. He recalled the earlier time with much bitterness:

> What did they know of these songs we would sing in church and in the field, songs the old folks sang when they were ironing or just settin' on the porch in the evening as the sun went down and the frogs came out? Nobody had ever hated them. And who was this Joan Baez talking about all her trials would soon be over. The bitch was white, wasn't she? Plus, she was good-looking and was making money. The only kind of trials she could have had was deciding whether she should fly first-class or tourist. . . . Blacks have always served as a path which whites have used to try and get out of the concentration camps of their souls.[36]

The Mississippi Freedom Summer project came hard on the heels of Congress's quarrelsome passage of the Civil Rights Act of 1964. *Sing Out!* reported, "A number of professional folksingers will participate in Project Mississippi this summer, traveling throughout the state giving performances at freedom schools and community centers, and attempting to instill an interest in the music of Mississippi among its people." Seeger, Ochs, Peter LaFarge, Lester, and Collins committed themselves to a few sweaty, frightening days in the Delta; they also took donated banjos and guitars to share among the local young people. Organized by the Council of Federated Organizations, an umbrella group of various civil rights organizers, the larger project combined voter registration, freedom schools, and other activities in the heart of the segregated South. White and black activists worked side by side, sharing the dangers and personal triumphs.[37]

Bob Cohen, a member of the New World Singers, directed the Summer Caravan of Music. Part of the Greenwich Village scene and strongly committed to SNCC, Cohen had visited Mississippi the previous summer to perform freedom songs. Working with Harold Leventhal, and sponsored by the New York Council of Performing Artists, he recruited a flashy lineup of over twenty performers who would play throughout the state for a week or so during the summer. Barbara Dane, another volunteer, remarked, "It seemed an important surprise that people like Phil Ochs, July Collins, Jean and Jim, the Eastgate Singers and others of us would come all the way from New York or California on our own money just because we cared enough about what was happening there."[38]

For some the experience was less philanthropic, more personal. Julius Lester later said, "I've been traveling through the country that birthed Robert Johnson, Muddy Waters, Charlie Patton, Eli Green, Son House and Fred McDowell. . . . Officially I came to Mississippi to sing in Freedom Schools, at mass meetings and to hold workshops on black music. Unofficially, though, I came to learn and to be born again. I came to see my family's beginning in this country." For others, fear mixed with a strong personal commitment. Carolyn Hester concluded that "the only place we were really safe was in the black part of town." The experience was a mixture of anxiety and exhilaration for most, including Ochs, who dreaded violence even when performing in New York. But they left their mark. *Newsweek* reported: "Back in New York last week, Judy Collins got a letter. It was from Barbara McClinton in Clarksdale. She wrote: 'Well, "It Isn't Nice" has become very popular here. Some kids from Cleveland [Mississippi] wanted it so I sent it to them. That song is going to be here forever and ever. I'll never forget you.' " As for Collins, who was terrified during much of her stay, "I returned from Mississippi with more experience but fewer illusions."[39]

Pete Seeger conducted his own tour of Mississippi in early August. He performed in Hattiesburg on August 2 and in Meridian the next day. While on stage in Meridian he was informed that the bodies of civil rights workers Andrew Goodman, James Chaney, and Michael Schwerner had been found buried in an earthen dam. He began to sing, "O healing river, Send down your water," then ended with "We Shall Overcome" as the audience stood in shock.[40]

Countless folk singers would continue their involvement in furthering racial harmony and black advancement through the rest of the decade, but they generally limited their activities to the territory north of the Mason-Dixon Line. The civil rights struggle took on new twists and turns, especially with the rise of the Black Power movement, and fresh issues, particularly the antiwar struggle, began to absorb the energies of most activists.

Newport and Other Folk Festivals

The cult of the personality, often dictated by commercial forces, was nothing new in the folk world, but it took a particular twist during the revived Newport Folk Festival. The planned 1961 festival had been canceled because of the city's temporary ban following riots at the 1960 jazz festival and without the leadership of George Wein (who returned the following year) financial problems plagued the 1961 jazz fest. Joined by his wife Joyce, Wein soon began to consider reviving the folk festival in 1963, and following discussions with Pete and Toshi Seeger and Theo Bikel, plans began to unfold. "Our rationale for putting the festival back on the map was that we owed a debt to the grass roots of the folk field, a debt that needed to be acknowledged and repaid," Bikel later wrote. "Occasionally we might give credit along the lines of 'I learned this from a blind blues singer in Mississippi,' but we owed that singer more than just a mention from the stage." Moreover, the expanding folk scene called for a high-profile national festival.[41]

The Seegers had earlier decided to dim the spotlight on the stars and include newer as well as more traditional performers. *Sing Out!* announced the rationale for the new format in early 1963:

> George Wein, who also runs the Newport Jazz Festivals, responded to criticism of the '59 and '60 festivals ("too many city professionals; not enough folks") and has asked a committee of performers to take responsibility for choosing the program. . . . First decision: all performers to get union minimum, no more no less, plus travel and hotel expenses. Aim is to combine on the same program some well-known names with unknown but exciting and genuine folk performers.

The seven-member planning board for the nonprofit Newport Folk Foundation was initially composed of performers: Bikel, Jean Ritchie, Clarence Cooper, Erik Darling, Bill Clifton, and Peter Yarrow, in addition to Seeger. Wein would serve as the nonvoting chairman of the board and the festival's producer. Any profits were to be earmarked for promoting traditional music. The three-day festival would include three evening concerts and a dozen or so afternoon workshops, plus informal hootenannies and assorted other activities. In order to promote a sense of equality, all performers would receive $50 a day in addition to meals, lodging, and transportation.[42]

Toshi Seeger took prime responsibility for the performers' needs and comfort, and with an exciting lineup of old and new faces, the late July festival garnered rave reviews. The performers included: Peter, Paul and Mary, Dylan, Seeger, Baez, Collins, Bikel; bluegrass bands (Bill Monroe, Jim and Jesse); traditional performers (Doc Watson, Clarence Ashley, Bessie Jones and the Georgia Sea Island Singers, John Lee Hooker, Mississippi John Hurt); topical performers (Freedom Singers); and assorted urban singers (Dave Van Ronk, Jackie Washington). Workshops focused on instruments (fiddle, banjo, guitar) and musical styles (blues, ballads, international, topical). The festival program described all the performers and included a poem/song by Dylan and a variety of short essays. With attendance nearly forty-thousand, Robert Shelton reported in the *New York Times*: "A listener reels away from this resort city as from a buffet of rich food. There was a cross section of the top level of professionals, and a legion of lesser-known performers." Leroy Aarons, in the *Washington Post*, appreciated the underemphasis on commercial singers, the strong lineup of traditional southern performers, and the warm greeting for Dylan, representing the new breed of singer-songwriters. *Newsweek* described the colorful but sober young people, guitars at the ready. Mississippi John Hurt, Baez, and Dylan seemed to stand out. At the closing concert, during Baez's third encore, "she shared the triumph, leading Dylan out, and together they sang his 'With God on Our Side.' " A fitting climax to a festival movingly launched the first night with Dylan, Peter, Paul and Mary, Seeger, Bikel, Baez, and the Freedom Singers joined together in "Blowin' in the Wind" and "We Shall Overcome."[43]

Old met young at the topical song workshop, bridging thirty years of rebellious creativity. Dylan, the Freedom Singers, LaFarge, Paxton, and Ochs performed their newest compositions. Josh Dunson reported that when LaFarge finished "Ira Hayes," "Alan Lomax, deeply stirred, came up to congratulate him, and one of the Indian performers lifted off Peter's cowboy hat and replaced it with his own head-dress of many feathers." "Traditional music's influence on topical music was exemplified at the very beginning of the workshop when Aunt Molly Jackson's brother, Jim Garland, led things off with his now classic composition, 'I Don't Want Your Millions, Mister," Dunson wrote. Izzy Young preferred the informal afternoon settings, where "the audience could get close to the performers, meet and talk with them, even though three or four things were happening at one time, and you had to go to various parts of the park in double-time to attempt to keep up." The slick *Song Hits Magazine* gave its pop music blessing: "The success of the Newport Folk Festival proves that there is a demand for America's folk music heritage in its many forms."[44]

If Newport regained its place as the premier showplace for folk talent, it joined an increasingly crowded field of folk festivals. *Sing Out!* folded in a review of Newport as part of a broader overview of summer festivals: "Where once there was ample cause for cries of 'commercialism' (and the First Annual Chicago Folk Festival was the only island in a sea of folkum) this no longer seems the case. Even the most dedicated purist would be hard-pressed to to find fault with such city talent as Bob Dylan, the New Lost City Ramblers, Hedy West . . . when they team up with traditional performers of the quality of Roscoe Holcomb, Frank Proffitt, Horton Barker." Aside from Newport, the piece mentioned Jimmy Driftwood's Arkansas Folk Festival, Brandeis University's inaugural festival in May, the Monterey Folk Festival, the 26th Annual National Folk Festival in Kentucky, and others in Asheville, Berkeley, Ontario, Pasadena, and at Grossinger's Hotel in the Catskills. The First American Folk Festival in Asheville naturally included local celebrity Bascom Lamar Lunsford on its board of advisors, along with Alan Lomax and Carl Sandburg; its eclectic lineup included Doc Watson, Bill Monroe, Judy Collins, John Jacob Niles, the New Lost City Ramblers, and Frank Warner, along with Lunsford's old nemesis, Pete Seeger.[45]

While Newport mingled popular and traditional performers, glitz and the plain style, politics and religion, the earlier midwinter University of Chicago Folk Festival adhered to its original format. John Cohen and Ralph Rinzler stressed the 1963 festival's "respect for the folk traditions as well as an interest in present day developments based on these traditions." The audience was warmed by the performing of Bessie Jones from the Georgia Sea Islands, Virginian Hobart Smith, and the Mississippi bluesman Fred McDowell, joined by

Sunnyland Slim, Jimmy Driftwood, and Bill Monroe (his first urban/college festival appearance). Archie Green and Sam Charters added the proper academic touch. Three months later the first UCLA Folk Festival kicked off with a similar format, mixing old and new interpretations of rural sounds with academic presentations, to great acclaim. Organized by Ed Pearl and the UCLA folklorist D. K. Wilgus, the three days featured Clarence Ashley, the Dillards, Roscoe Holcomb, Bill Monroe, the New Lost City Ramblers, Hedy West, and Pete Seeger. Participant Rita Weill believed "the inter-play between artists as well as audience and performers, gave the entire weekend a family feeling . . . On the strength of traditional music alone, the Festival attracted a segment of the city population which was oriented only to The Weavers a scant five years ago."[46]

The festival "was just an astounding success," Pearl recalled. "And for a little while there, traditional music was considered very sellable and commercial." The UCLA festival not only promoted a traditional sound, but also encouraged the audience, ten thousand strong, to participate. Bess Hawes (one of the planners) unfavorably compared Newport with UCLA: "I had the sad feeling [at Newport] when I saw so ma[n]y people wistfully fingering their instruments, that they had been invited to bring them to the party, and nobody had asked them to play."[47]

Pearl followed up by helping produce the first Monterey Folk Festival in May 1963. Headliners included the Weavers, Dylan, Peter, Paul and Mary, Bill Monroe, Doc Watson, and Mance Lipscomb. Attendance was disappointing and the festival lost money. Ralph Gleason added his sour note in the *San Francisco Chronicle*: "After a weekend at the Monterey Folk Festival, I confess that I owe an apology to the ABC television people and the 'Hootenanny' show," he began. "I thought they were making folk music dull. I was wrong. Folk music IS dull." Nothing seemed to please him. "It's the cult of the primitive, the sublimation of big city anxieties in ersatz rural dress, behavior, accent and songs. A substitute for reality. University students from Boston, New York and the West Coast, trying to imitate Dogpatch America with the fervor of Harvard lads playing New Orleans jazz." Perhaps the professionalism of Peter, Paul and Mary gave them some cachet; as for Dylan, "I find he tends to bore me and sound oppressively mournful." Gleason preferred rhythm and blues. (Monterey served as the reunion of Dylan and Baez. Living in nearby Carmel, Baez had met Dylan the year before at Gerdes Folk City, but remained unimpressed until Manny Greenhill shared Dylan's more recent recordings; his startling lyrics and delivery now induced her to sit in the audience, launching an intense personal and musical relationship.)[48]

In late June the Berkeley festival, a crowded weekend of concerts, panels, workshops, and films, set a high musical standard. Pete Seeger headlined, along with J. E. Mainer's Mountaineers, Tony Kraber, Jean Ritchie, and Mance Lipscomb. Organizer Barry Olivier adhered to his policy of featuring traditional performers, yet realized it was increasingly necessary to include some topical songs. "It wasn't until 1963 that we loosened up and began a middle phase of exploration, breaking out of the narrow defining role . . . There were song-writers starting to come to life," he later recalled. Olivier welcomed Seeger introducing Dylan's "Hard Rain's A-Gonna Fall," Paxton's "Ramblin' Boy," and his own "Bells of Rhymney," and he was equally proud of the impressive panel, with Charles Seeger, D. K. Wilgus, and the Berkeley ballad scholar Bertrand Bronson discussing "The Folk Music Revival in the United States." Future fes-tivals would more directly connect to contemporary musical styles and topics.[49]

On the opposite coast the Philadelphia Folk Festival, embodying the devel-oping down-home festival style, closed the summer season. Theo Bikel joined Elizabeth Cotten, Mississippi John Hurt, Dave Van Ronk, Hobart Smith, and the Jim Kweskin Jug Band. Josh Dunson noted in *Broadside*, "With all the satchel-carrying managers and agents crawling in, and around folk music these days, it was a real pleasure to run into a folk festival that is definitely not dominated by them."[50]

Folk in the Media

Through late 1963 and into 1964 the folk craze reached high tide. "Hooten-annies are the thing this year," *Billboard* trumpeted in August 1963. "There hasn't been anything like it since rock and roll exploded on the music scene a decade ago, for the interest it has stirred up on radio, TV, concert, one-nighter and festival level." Coffeehouses were prime training grounds for the gathering hordes of guitar and banjo pickers. Packaged traveling hootenanny shows cov-ered the country. Even protest songs could make a buck; *Billboard* noted: "The folk craze that is engulfing the country, as witness the many hootenannies, has given vent to a couple of 'hollers' as well with an upsurgence of protest songs going pop. This new breed of popular song offers 'meat' in place of 'beat,' and roots its growing appeal in human compassion rather than the long-popular form of self-pity." About seventeen thousand folk fans almost overflowed the Hollywood Bowl, cheering Peter, Paul and Mary, Odetta, and Bud and Travis. "Just how big a force is the folk movement?" *Billboard* asked in October. "From all indications it is very big and at the moment shows little signs of a let-up in the pace." Most record labels had at least one folk performer or group and numerous hootenanny albums. Pete Seeger imparted his wisdom to *Seventeen*'s teenage readers: "We've got a big world to learn how to tie together. We've all got a lot to learn. And don't let your studies interfere with your education." The Bally company produced a short-lived Hootenanny pinball machine, to be played while munching a Hootenanny candy bar, while the Fuller Brush com-pany captured a special market niche with a Hootenanny bath powder mitt, appropriately decorated with young performers playing guitars.[51]

The new year would produce an even more frenzied folk marketplace, just before the bubble burst. *Billboard Music on Campus* saluted the four and a half million college students who constituted a formidable music market: "And while the collegians didn't discover folk music, they were certainly responsible for its wide public acceptance. Many of today's top folk groups got their start as undergraduates and most of the top current folk names first hit it big on the campus." In February 1964, eleven thousand Ohio State University students crowded into the basketball arena for "The Big Hoot," featuring Josh White, the New Christy Minstrels, and the Journeymen. For the 1963–64 school year, Johnny Mathis and Connie Francis topped *Billboard's* college poll for most popular male and female vocalists; the Beatles captured first place as top vocal group (with the Kingston Trio trailing in fourth place, and Peter, Paul and Mary in ninth); Harry Belafonte ranked first among male folk singers, just ahead of Pete Seeger, Josh White, and Bob Dylan; while Joan Baez placed first over Odetta, Miriam Makeba, and Judy Collins. Peter, Paul and Mary ranked number one among the folk groups, followed by the Kingston Trio, the Chad Mitchell Trio, and the Limeliters. "Tradesters agree," said *Billboard*, "that the continual influx of new names is what's keeping the folk field alive and vibrant."[52]

The mass media struggled to categorize the performers and their audiences, trying to get a grip on a mass phenomenon that was obviously beyond simple assessment. Students supplied "a rousing enthusiasm for the old favorites, as well as for some of the newer adaptations," and always "the mood is cheer," said the *Christian Science Monitor*. In a mostly pictorial spread, the *Saturday Evening Post* typed the phenomenon "a strange one. It consists of a rediscovery by city youth of what is essentially a country idiom, an urban folk revival that feeds upon songs of love, hate, birth, death and work that were born in the fields and on the prairies." *Life* focused on the increasingly newsworthy Dylan, "The Angry Young Folk Singer": "His biting protests against poverty, injustice, segregation and war are revitalizing a folk movement which was bogging down in dying cowboys and blue-tail flies. . . . Unlike the new crop of well-scrubbed collegiate folk groups, Dylan scorns clothes, baths and razors." The *New Yorker's* Whitney Balliett disdained popular folk music, "so bland and cherubic and homogeneous. Its performers exude health and bonhomie." He preferred another side of the revival, the trend "instigated by John and Alan Lomax and dedicated to the ferreting out of blues singers who went underground twenty or thirty years ago," currently represented by Roosevelt Sykes, Lightnin' Hopkins, Mississippi John Hurt, and Reverend Gary Davis.[53]

It was not Alan Lomax but Tom Hoskins who in 1963 unearthed Mississippi John Hurt, known only from his 1920s recordings, in Avalon, Mississippi, a remarkable feat that startled the folk world. John Fahey and Ed Denson, two California blues fans, tracked Booker White to Memphis. Then Dick Watterman found himself crammed into a Volkswagen with Phil Spiro, Nick Perls, and the bluesman Reverend Robert Wilkins, driving the back roads of Mississippi in June 1964 searching for Son House. They discovered that House was living in Rochester, New York, and on June 21 they called him and were soon happily on their way north. Two days later they met House, and on the same day John Fahey, Bill Barth, and Henry Vestine located the bluesman Skip James in Tunica, Mississippi, which Waterman and his friends had just left. These and other older southern bluesmen quickly found themselves on the folk circuit.

Into the flourishing folk market stepped a few short-lived national magazines, attempting to capture the music's slick yet complex image. Editor Irwin Silber of *Sing Out!* wrote, "Already, the lure of the fast-buck has attracted the gimmick slickers and fly-by-night promoters who are moving in for the quick kill. With the halo of folk music protecting their efforts, the jackals are making their bid to take over—bending, twisting, distorting the living body of genuine creative expression to the hokum-folkum which can only turn out to be the same dish of muddy soup which we rejected in the first place." But for now *Sing Out!* would ride the high tide.[54]

Robert Shelton had been considering starting a popular folk magazine for a couple of years. "There is a crying need for a magazine that would be on the news-stands, on every campus, on every coffeehouse cashier's counter," he confided to Archie Green in July 1962. "I have no axe to grind against *Sing Out!* or *Caravan* or *Autoharp* or the three *Broadsides*. There is room for many publications, but there seems to be a real need for one good, slick, professional, adult national magazine." He requested Green's confidentiality, as he didn't want the word out before he was ready to leave the *New York Times*. It took more than a year before *Hootenanny* appeared, with Shelton as editor (and still music reviewer for the *Times*).[55]

The first issue of *Hootenanny* appeared in December 1963; it was a substantial magazine with features, songs, cartoons, and much information on the popular folk scene. "There will be stimulating debate in these pages about ends and means in folk music, about integrity and expediency, about elevating taste or pandering to it," Shelton explained. "We define folk music broadly. It is antique balladry of unknown authorship. It is also topical broadsides written yesterday by the guy next door. Folk music in America is truly international. It is blues, bluegrass, cowboy yodels, flamenco, doinas, work songs, come-all-ye's, love laments, breakdowns." Irwin Silber sneered that *Hootenanny* "seems to be on the general level of Modern Screen (which it greatly resembles)," but he welcomed Dylan's projected column. Though the magazine was planned as a bimonthly, the second issue didn't appear until March 1964. Highly annoyed with the shallow inaugural number, Shelton felt more in control with the second, and he assured Green, "We're planning on being in business for a long time to come. . . . I'm not turning from editor to drum-beater, but I am quite pleased with the book and I want to see it solidly established now with the collegiate folk fans." Green obliged by ordering fifty copies for the University of Illinois Folksong Club, which he had profiled in the second issue. In addition to Green's piece, there was Shelton's article on Baez and Dylan, another on the New Christy Minstrels, Theo Bikel discussing freedom songs, Richard Fariña on traveling in England, a profile of Enrico Banducci and the hungry i, and record reviews. Shelton revealed Judy Collins's rocky relationship with the Hootenanny television show. "She made it clear that her action was not linked to the dispute over the blacklisting of Pete Seeger, although she had participated in early meetings of the committee to oppose that blacklist." Rather, she objected to the show's lack of artistic sensibility.[56]

By Hootenanny's third issue Shelton had assembled an impressive stable of writers—Kenneth Goldstein, Ralph Rinzler, Nat Hentoff, and John Greenway. The latter's discussion of Woody Guthrie focused on his degenerative disease, Huntington's chorea, and his songwriting abilities, while taking a swipe at his postwar output: "His hate became factitious as he wrote to the order of a small group of leftists who had captured him and countless others." (Starting on the Left, Greenway had shifted to the Right since the late 1950s.) A mixture of scholarly discussion and folk kitsch, Hootenanny struggled to find its identity and market. The fourth and last issue, dated November 1964, reverted to cheaper paper and less academic analysis. Shelton's lead article scrutinized "The Kingston Trio vs. Beatlemania." Highly skeptical of the Beatles, though hardly a fan of the Trio (he did recognize their seminal influence), he wrote that "both groups are products of the assembly-line, new products thinking that dominates American popular music." Still, the "Kingston Trio started something very constructive in American music. If The Beatles end it, we'll all be the losers."[57]

Shelton's dream soured even before the folk wave crested. "Hootenanny, ah, Hootenanny," he moaned to Archie Green, late in the year. "This god-damn magazine has been nothing but trouble and battles since I started. I think it is going under, although the publisher says he'll try to make it a quarterly. It's been selling about 40 to 50 thousand, which is not enough for him to make his quick profit, so he pulls the cheap-paper bit, and the 'hypnotism' ads." Shelton became music editor of Cavalier, a Playboy imitator; he envisioned reaching a larger college crowd through record reviews and perhaps a folk music yearbook.[58]

Shelton's Hootenanny lasted longer than its ragtag competitors, which were eager to cash in on the obvious folk bonanza. The eclectic, bimonthly Folk Music, seemingly a rival to Hootenanny though not as slick, lasted for two issues in mid-1964. Publisher-editor Joe Wysong and his coeditor Herb Dexter rounded up a mix of performers and scholars—Judy Collins, John Hammond, Billy Faier, Jo Mapes—to discuss aspects of folk music and review records. Wysong had some money and a fondness for folk music, while Dexter, with writing experience, preferred avant-garde jazz. With meager capital and little outreach, they quickly folded. The sole 1964 issue of *Hootenanny Songs and Stars*, as its name implied, printed a medley of songs, profiles of pop performers, plugs for ABC's *Hootenanny* and MGM's folk musical *Hootenanny Hoot*, along with an illustrated guide to the "Hootenanny Hoot" dance. (Featuring Johnny Cash, Judy Henske, Sheb Wooley, the Gateway Trio, and the Brothers Four, *Hootenanny Hoot* shamelessly exploited the folk trend. The exhibitor's campaign book suggested that theaters promote hootenannies in their lobbies, organize a family barbecue and hootenanny in a local park, or stage "Hootenanny Hoot" dance contests.)

ABC-TV Hootenanny Show Magazine was launched in January 1964 with a bang, only to fold in midyear after just three issues. With no formal connection to the television show, the magazine initially focused on the program's stars, yet supplied intriguing, even challenging information and perspectives, with a touch of humor from Jean Shepherd. In the first issue Theo Bikel wrote, "The word 'hootenanny' belongs to the people; Pete Seeger, Woody Guthrie and Lee Hays, among others, have given it its present meaning . . . But they didn't do it for profit or glory. Nor are they offered any—is it not ironic that, in the case of Pete, the very reverse seems to be happening? And why should he, like Moses, show the Children of Israel the Promised Land and yet not be allowed to enter?" Will Holt followed with a discussion of "Weill, Brecht, and Protest Songs." The second issue opened with a glowing editorial on Earl Robinson and Millard Lampell's "The Lonesome Train," then profiled Flatt and Scruggs, Judy Henske, the Bitter End in Greenwich Village, and the Boston/Cambridge folk scene. The magazine's editor, Linda Solomon, gave a rosy review of Seeger's records. With something of a folk background, as well as stints as an ad writer for the *Howdy Doody* television show and a contributor to *Cosmopolitan* and *Escapade,* Solomon had lofty expectations. Unlike its competitors, *ABC-TV Hootenanny* generally avoided the standard folk performers and academics for its contributors, often substituting freelance writers. What turned out to be the last issue focused on session musicians, Southside Chicago blues, Ella May Wiggins, and Phil Ochs—hardly popular folk topics and a far cry from the style of the fading television program.[59]

Along with the short-lived attempts to establish national magazines there was a flowering of local folk newsletters, some fleeting, others more enduring. Community and campus folk clubs had been publishing newsletters for some years, but the mid-decade upsurge of enthusiasm sparked a new crop. Faith Petric launched the San Francisco Folk Music Club's *The Folknik* in October 1964, full of notices, news, and perspectives. Chicago's *The Folk Scene* offered a similar, although leaner, menu of information, photos, and interviews, with increasing coverage of Greenwich Village before its collapse after six issues. *Good News,* published by the Los Angeles Folk music Society, was launched in April 1962 to supply news of local folk happenings. "No longer will we have to wait for the latest copy of eastern-published folk music 'fanzines' to learn of events and personalities in the field on the West Coast," the editors boldly proclaimed. It barely survived a year, however. The slack was temporarily taken up by both a local *Broadside* (soon the more emphatic *Broadside!*), launched in March 1962 by Ed Pearl with a few friends and lasting until mid-1963, and the more secure *Songmakers Almanac*, heavily connected to People's Songs alumni. The latter, also begun in 1962, struggled on through the decade, presenting listings of concerts, bits of local news, and the like.[60]

The singer Country Joe McDonald inaugurated the mimeographed *Et Tu* in Los Angeles in August 1964 as a forum to publish his own and friends' songs; he announced his desire to "clarify some of the controversial issues of our time and bring into the light some of the little known facts concerning social and political movements of our times." McDonald soon moved to Berkeley, and he briefly continued *Et Tu* before changing the name to *Rag Baby* in September 1965. Others sprang up in 1965, including *The Broadside* of New Britain, Connecticut, a thin publication with songs and a few record reviews in its six or so issues; *Folkin' Around* in Cambridge, Massachusetts, soon changed to *Sounds*, a substantial, ambitious monthly that lasted into early 1966; and the sole issue of New York's *The Pointer* in May, sporting "New York's only complete calendar of folk music." *Stray Notes* from the Atlanta Folk Music Society, a thin, large-format affair, was temporarily impressive and lasted through the year. There were many others, most of them passing monuments to musical zeal and economic myopia.[61]

One idiosyncratic publication definitely marked folk's commercial aura. "The *Folk Music Yearbook of Artists 1964* is a must for anyone concerned with the still rapidly growing national interest in 'folk music,' " Izzy Young announced early in the year. "The *Yearbook* is an amazing compendium of bits of information and photographs of hundreds of individuals who are folksingers, who purport to be folksingers, or who were folksingers. . . . I can't wait to see next year's expanded edition." With well over one hundred pages of photos, mini-biographies, lists of performers, music executives, talent agencies, albums, and books, short articles, and ads, Jandel Productions' publication was a grab bag of miscellaneous information. But its utility was soon questioned. Irwin Silber concluded that this "is one of the oddest products of the folk song boom I've ever come across. It contains more information and less knowledge about folk music than can possibly be described in a few paragraphs." But because of its fascinating details, he recommended it to those involved in the music business. The 1965 edition never appeared.[62]

Whatever the fortunes of other publications, *Sing Out!* reaped the harvest of the revival. After thirteen years, with a circulation of fifteen thousand per issue and growing steadily, Silber announced in early 1964 that the magazine would immediately expand from five to six issues a year. "There are still lots of good songs that need singing—and lots of good ones that need writing as well. There are still tales to tell and battles to wage in the process of rediscovering, appreciating and expanding our folk traditions."[63]

The Summer of 1964

The folk frenzy crested during 1964's hot summer, sending mixed messages. "A consolidation of fan loyalties, focused on a hard core of time-tested talents, appears to be in the making in the folk music field," *Music Business* told its readers in July. "As folksters across the land turn their eyes toward the annual Folk clambake in Newport . . . , most key observers feel that hard truths must be faced." A few acts—Peter, Paul and Mary, the Kingston Trio, Baez, Seeger—dominated the marketplace, to some extent squeezing out lesser performers. The recent breakup of the Journeymen, the Tarriers, and the Highwaymen marked "an over-populated folk group field."[64]

Topical songs, dominated by Dylan's hard-hitting paeans to civil and personal rights (artfully interpreted by Baez and Peter, Paul and Mary), captured a large segment of both the college and the adult markets. Protest was in the air. Gordon Friesen surveyed the field for *Sing Out!*'s readers in late 1963, focusing on Dylan, Ochs, Spoelstra, Chandler, Paxton, and LaFarge. "They all share basic similarities," he observed. "They are unafraid of 'controversial' ideas and are determined that what they say shall be heard." A year later Betty Rollin summed up the new music in *Vogue*: "It is hard to know exactly what effects the new songs are having upon the young people. . . . It seems, at least, a slice of the younger generation has moved into a post-beat era. It seems, at last, it is no longer square to care." (Rollin used the crowd at Club 47 in Cambridge to make her point, though the club was hardly known for promoting political activism.)[65]

In 1965, Josh Dunson, a frequent contributor to Cunningham and Friesen's *Broadside*, outlined the topical song movement in *Freedom in the Air: Song Movements of the Sixties*, a brave and insightful attempt to capture the moment. From a left-wing family and steeped in the lore of political and movement songs, he had begun circulating a sketch of the proposed book during the previous summer. "Before the people who slaved to bring the new singers forward are completely forgotten, and middle age sets in for the topical song writers, I think it is important and have convinced International Publishers to include a short book on topical and freedom songs," he informed Pete Seeger. He sent a prospectus to Seeger, Guy Carawan, Sis Cunningham and Gordon Friesen, and Julius Lester.[66]

In his book Dunson wrote of the civil rights movement: "The freedom songs owe much to the initial spurt provided by the Nashville Quartet, Guy Carawan and the Freedom Singers, but the influence of the pioneers has been eclipsed. Every marcher has become a freedom singer, and it is they, rather than the outstanding individuals, important as they were, who have made the movement rock with songs." If the common folk had become the bedrock of the southern freedom song movement, individual songwriters remained at the heart of the northern rage for topical songs. Dylan, Ochs, and Pat Sky represented an upsurge in songwriting, but their approach differed from that of their southern contemporaries: "The movement in the South sings 'we,' and in the rest of the country hundreds of individuals sing about problems as they relate to themselves . . . Both want to sing to the greatest number of people, who will, hopefully, listen and learn. In doing this they face a most difficult common problem, the conflict of interest with profit-oriented mass media." Essentially optimistic, Dunson yet deftly sketched looming conflicts—authenticity versus commercialism, self versus community—that would plague the folk revival and activist society more generally.[67]

Many performers were torn between some sort of political/artistic/personal commitment and beckoning commercial success. Mark Spoelstra, an up-and-coming topical songwriter, fulfilled his contract by cutting two albums for Folkways before moving to Elektra in late 1963. He begged the notoriously stingy Asch not to complain to Elektra but to realize "I'm the one that wants to reach a wider audience. I'm the one that wants to feel more secure when I get through my alternative service. . . . I hope you react to this like the Moe Asch I respect and admire; and not the ol' tyrant I've heard about." Spoelstra moved to California and worked with a semimigrant black community in West Fresno in lieu of his military service.[68]

Newport 1964

Robert Shelton prefaced his coverage of the July 1964 Newport folk festival with a review of Vanguard's recently issued six records covering the previous year's performers. "The happy admixture of entertainment with education is extracted from the work of some 75 performers in three days and nights of music-making," he reported of the eclectic albums. The 1964 festival was more of the same—evening concerts, broadsides, blues, and old-time and bluegrass—dished up in larger doses, now four days and three nights with over two hundred performers in the several concerts and seventeen workshops. Fittingly, Alan Lomax introduced the opening roots session, with Seamus Ennis, Bessie Jones and the Georgia Sea Island Singers, Jean Ritchie, Jimmy Driftwood, and a Cajun band. The next day's workshops included vernacular performing, topical songs (Ochs, Paxton, and Dylan), and a freedom song session with Guy Carawan and the Freedom Singers. Fifteen thousand crowded Freebody Park for an evening concert featuring Hawaiian songs, "Yank" Rachell, Fred and Annie May McDowell, Elizabeth Cotten, the Moving Star Hall Singers, the Greenbriar Boys, as well as the Chad Mitchell Trio and Phil Ochs.[69]

Total attendance topped 70,000, almost twice that of the previous year. While the stars made their appearance—Bikel, Collins, Dylan, Peter, Paul and Mary—Shelton emphasized that "the musicians were real folksingers, humble amateur or semiprofessional musicians dealing in traditional vocal and instrumental styles . . . Prison-born work songs or blues were not merely interpreted this weekend, but were also brought here by singers who had been in the jails of Louisiana and Texas. Many of the performers had waged their personal war on poverty long before it became national policy." Shelton was referring to Doc Reese, Sarah Gunning, the Staple Singers, Jesse Fuller, Robert Pete Williams, Mississippi John Hurt, Skip James, perhaps even Johnny Cash. Foundation member Bikel lauded the festival's democratic approach, with every performer receiving the same compensation. More important, many "thousands who came because their curiosity was piqued left with some respect for musical traditions and with melodies swirling inside their heads that their parents had long forgotten."[70]

In retrospect Bob Shelton realized that Newport had three remarkable ingredients: "The historic moments at Newport '64 tended to pass people by. Only when Dylan later appeared with rock backing, and, still later, went to Nashville, did all the pieces fit together. It was all brought back home at Newport '64, when Dylan went beyond topical songs, [Johnny] Cash sang of country troubles, and Muddy Waters brought on his band to show that music, if it is alive, is always in motion." Cash was trying to recoup his career, and Waters expressed the sensibilities of Chicago's urban electric blues scene. But neither Cash nor Waters garnered much notice at the time. Cash would later acknowledge being indebted to the folk revival: "I took note of Bob Dylan as soon as the Bob Dylan album came out in early '62 and listened almost constantly to *The Freewheelin' Bob Dylan* in '63. I had a portable record player I'd take along on the road, and I'd put on *Freewheelin'* backstage, then go out and do my show, then listen again as soon as I came off." He fondly recalled sharing a precious moment in a hotel room at Newport with his wife June Carter Cash, Dylan, and Baez, "so happy to meet each other that we were jumping on the bed like kids."[71]

Seemingly all sparkle and enthusiasm, the festival had its disquieting reverberations. Newport residents complained of excessive noise after midnight, unruly politics, and bothersome concertgoers, as the rainy weather forced many of the overflow crowd to scramble for nightly shelter in their cars or city parks. The city barred the next year's festival from Freebody Park, but a deal was struck and George Wein leased thirty-five acres of vacant land in the city's northern section, where he built a music shell.

Brickbats also flew from various other directions. Dylan's three appearances caused much unease. At the Friday afternoon topical song workshop he introduced "It Ain't Me, Babe" and "Tambourine Man," hardly political songs, and he repeated "It Ain't Me, Babe" with Baez that night. The audience began to grumble. Opening with "All I Really Want to Do" on Sunday night, he shakily proceeded with "To Ramona," "Tambourine Man," and "Chimes of Freedom," calling on Baez to conclude with "With God on Our Side." The seemingly stoned Dylan hardly connected with the audience. Shelton, his staunchest patron, scribbled in his notebook, "Has the American Yevtushenko turned into the American Edgar Guest?"—more a comment on his lyrics than his behavior. "As I headed toward the press tent, I conveyed the general disappointment to Charlie Rothschild [Al Grossman's associate], who was suggesting that I had just seen a great Dylan performance." The next month's release of *Another Side of Bob Dylan*—with "Motorpyscho Nightmare," "My Back Pages," and "Spanish Harlem Incident"—marked his turn away from overtly political songs toward dark introspection.[72]

Despite the obvious commercial and artistic triumph of Newport, questions about folk music lingered. In September's *Sing Out!* Irwin Silber welcomed the mounting general enthusiasm yet feared that "the fundamentally healthy and human content of the folk tradition was lost in the caverns of Tin Pan Alley." Paul Nelson, recently named *Sing Out!*'s managing editor while he continued as the *Little Sandy Review*'s coeditor, questioned Newport's contribution to the revival. He preferred the traditional performers and the "new talent," with little mention of the big names, yet concluded: "One piece of candy is good, or even three or four, but a whole boxcar full at a single sitting proved more than anyone could handle; such 'extremism' in quality, far from heightening one's critical appreciation as one would think, instead proved too rich a dish, and many simply wandered in a dazed state, 'accepting' (if, indeed that is the word) everything, but comprehending nothing."[73]

Nelson saved his rhetorical scorn for the *Little Sandy*'s more discerning readers. For them he sketched the "two hundred nameless, faceless teddy bears who sang a song or two, were amazed by the many thousands in the audience, and watched their music float uncaptured out into the acres of air above Freebody Park. Whether they played well or badly, the reaction was the same: none." Mockery followed insult, with the audience singled out for special contempt: teenage folkies following "the teachings of [their] Great Saints of Modern Times, the trinity of [their] socio-religious convictions, Pete Seeger, Bob Dylan and the Virgin Mary, Mary H. Magdalene, Joan Baez." Nelson attacked all the "sham" aspects of the revival, such as Judy Collins ("an IBM Baez") and most of the topical song writers, particularly Phil Ochs and Len Chandler. To Dylan, Nelson gave a mixed review, but chastised the audience for demanding only two encores as Dylan "chose to show off his more personal, introspective songs rather than shoot the obvious fish in the barrel. . . . Dylan was taking his first faltering steps in a long time in a productive direction for himself as artist, and not himself as hero."[74]

In *Broadside,* the *Little Sandy's* sparring partner, Josh Dunson praised Newport's topical songs, particularly Ochs's "I Ain't Marching Anymore," Tom Paxton's "Daily News Song," and Dylan's "Tambourine Man," while reserving special compliments for the Cuban Rodriguez Brothers, particularly their "Soy Negro" ("I am a black man"). He worried that at the topical workshop "there was no direct confrontation with the most disturbing and meaningful events of this 'long hot summer' " in Mississippi. He also carped privately to Theo Bikel about what he saw as Newport's pretense of equality: "A great area of friction and bitterness arose out of the accommodations. This was NOT purely a racial matter but pointed to a great differentiation between the well to do commercial artist and the traditional singer." He found Sleepy John Estes, Yank Rachell, and Hammie Nixon crammed into "a shabby room," and noted other examples of racial insensitivity by Newport's organizers and concert emcees. As for festivals, he preferred the smaller, more focused one near Philadelphia, where Ochs, Paxton, and Bernice Reagon connected with pressing contemporary issues.[75]

Others entered the fray over Dylan's change of musical direction, their touch-stone for the essence of the revival. Dylan's friend (and Baez's brother-in-law) Richard Fariña captured the allure of Dylan (and Baez) for *Mademoiselle's* mature female audience: "To the young men and women who listen, the message is as meaningful as if it were uttered in the intimacy of their own secluded thought." Fariña did not mention topical songs specifically, only Dylan's artic-ulation of youthful bewilderment and anguish. Shelton expressed his disap-pointment with Dylan in a glowing review of a Baez-Dylan concert at Forest Hills tennis stadium soon after Newport. He felt that Baez could interpret Dylan better then the composer could himself, though their duet "With God on Our Side" shined. Dylan "disappointed at least one listener with the lack of control of his stage manner, his raucously grating singing and the somewhat declining level of his new compositions."[76]

In an "Open Letter to Dylan," Irwin Silber wrote, "I saw at Newport how you had somehow lost contact with people." Noting the trappings of fame, the traveling entourage, he added, the "new songs seem to be all inner-directed now, inner-probing, self-conscious—maybe even a little maudlin or a little cruel on occasion." Whatever happened to the Dylan who "never wasted our precious time?" Paul Wolfe followed up in *Broadside,* once home to Dylan's songs, remarking "the emergence of Phil Ochs as the most important voice in the movement, simultaneous with the renunciation of topical music by its major prophet, Bob Dylan. It was the latter event that proved most surprising" at Newport. He matched the two, Ochs and Dylan: "meaning vs. innocuousness, sincerity vs. utter disregard for the tastes of the audience, idealistic principle vs. self-conscious egotism."[77]

Many, including Ochs himself, strongly defended Dylan and their letters piled up at *Sing Out!* and *Broadside.* Ochs argued that his friend's writing "is as brilliant as ever and is clearly improving all the time. . . . How can anyone be so pretentious as to set guidelines for an artist to follow?" The mainstream press concurred. Reviewing *Another Side of Bob Dylan*, Ralph Gleason wrote in the *San Francisco Chronicle* that at first "the album did not reach me, but as I played it over a few times it made a deeper and deeper impression until now I feel it may have some of his best and most important work on it." He hailed Dylan as "the voice of the New Generation." In a lengthy *New Yorker* profile, Nat Hentoff described Dylan's background and the rather chaotic recording session for *Another Side*. In a response to Hentoff's comment "that there were hardly any songs of social protest in the collection," Tom Wilson, Columbia Record's recording producer, had replied: "Basically, he's in the tradition of all lasting folk music. I mean, he's not a singer of protest so much as he is a singer of concern about people. He doesn't have to be talking about Medgar Evers all the time to be effective." Hentoff appeared to concur, and his tribute concluded with Dylan inviting him for a ride on his motorcycle, then he "hunched his shoulders and walked off quickly." Dylan's baffling, beguiling personality remained intact.[78]

Even Shelton soon came around. Reviewing Dylan's fall concert at Philharmonic Hall, he appreciated the older songs ("Times They Are A-Changin'," "Talkin' John Birch Society Blues") as much as the recent compositions ("Gates of Eden," "It's All Right, Ma") and ended on a high note: "Dylan seems to have returned his enormous musical and literary gifts to a forward course," and he was still "the brilliant singing poet laureate of young America." Izzy Young, also in the Philharmonic audience, had mixed feelings about his friend's artistic turn: "His old songs are his best—his new songs are murky, introverted and too occupied with death and the fighting of it. But this is just a phase and he should not let himself be trapped into a corner by left wing friends, purist idolaters, and a hoodwinked public."[79]

In late 1964 *Life* wrote of Pete Seeger: "He's been called America's tuning fork and he looks it. He also looks rather like a nervous garage mechanic—until he unslings his guitar or banjo, leaps to the stage in rumpled chinos to croon and holler his songs—('some bitter and mad, some joky, some pure sunlight and love') and gets his audience—any audience in the world—to sing and holler along with him." The brief article, mostly photos, mentioned his earlier HUAC problems but nothing recent. Moreover, his recording of Malvina Reynolds's "Little Boxes," released by Columbia as a single, had briefly broken into the pop charts, reaching number seventy the previous February.[80]

As the revival reached its peak in 1964, Seeger and his family oddly disappeared from the frantic scene; they set out on a heavily planned world tour, to include thirty countries. Harold Leventhal staged a "Bon Voyage Concert" at Carnegie Hall on June 8, 1963, though they didn't leave until August 18th. "Will be singing in schools and colleges, concert halls, villages, radio and (whee!) TV," Seeger announced in the program notes. "No government agency is sponsoring this tour. It is Free Enterprise pure and simple." Sis Cunningham was left in charge of his correspondence, and he showered her and Friesen (and others) with messages and suggestions throughout the trip. They first headed west, stopping in Japan to visit his wife's father's birthplace, then through Southeast Asia and India, Africa, and eastern and western Europe, before returning in early June 1964. Leventhal kept the media apprised of their progress, and Seeger's reports appeared in *Sing Out!* Upon his return he materialized at Newport, then rushed off to Mississippi.[81]

Politics

In late May 1964, Joan Baez joined a gathering of celebrities at Madison Square Garden—Gregory Peck, Woody Allen, the Swingle Singers, the New Christy Minstrels, the New York City Ballet—for the New York Democratic party's salute to President Lyndon Johnson, soon up for election. She dedicated "The Times They Are A-Changin' " to the President, and closed with "Blowin' in the Wind." But Baez soon turned away from mainstream politics. "I have never been involved in the campaign of any major political candidate, preferring to work entirely outside of the party structure," she averred in her autobiography. "I did not vote in 1964 and would not go to the polls until it was time to vote against Nixon in 1972." If Baez shunned partisan politics, she had no reservations regarding political causes. "The organizers of the Free Speech movement at Berkeley got hold of me, and I went up to sing and speak. Ira [Sandperl] and I raised the subject of nonviolence, and developed a small following. But when I was asked back again and again to take part in their marches and rallies it was not so much because of an overwhelming interest in nonviolence but rather because I drew huge crowds."[82]

Controversy broke out on the Berkeley campus on October 1 when the university administration decided to ban off-campus political activities from the Sather Gate area, the campus's main entrance. With the arrest of former graduate student Jack Weinberg, who had just returned from southern organizing along with Mario Savio and other student activists, the Free Speech Movement got its quick start. Well into the second day of Weinberg's spell in the police car, surrounded by thousands of student protesters, he was released, but this was only the start of a tumultuous fall semester. Baez was already scheduled to perform in Berkeley on October 2, but she temporarily remained politically uninvolved. She returned on November 20, however, to sing at a noon rally at Sproul Hall, the campus administration building, and again on December 2 to join the sit-in at Sproul. Later she wrote:

> I was there when they went into the hall. Up in front of thousands of kids and press from all over the country and the world. I told them to go into that building

with "as much love as they could muster," and then I sang to them. Some of the
more "radical" kids didn't like me talking about "love" at such a serious revolutionary movement. Inside, the halls and rooms were filled with students holding
seminars on everything and a seminar on civil disobedience led by Ira and me.
. . . We left the building [about 2:30 A.M.], planning to return in the morning,
and as we were pulling out of the parking lot, the police moved in. . . . Berkeley
marked the beginning of a new level of activism and risk taking in the universities
of the United States of America.[83]

Music infused the Free Speech Movement, as Michael Rossman vividly recalls.
With Baez leading the throngs in "The Times They Are A-Changin' " and "We
Shall Overcome," he followed her into Sproul Hall, where "the spirit of song
flickered throughout our communal life. All afternoon and evening, rotations
of guitarists occupied the resonant stairwells. . . . Periodically, the spirit would
flicker over each section of human pavement in the corridors, as it broke into
song for a quarter-hour before resuming the endless collective debate until
night drew on, when we hushed to save what rest we could until the dawn
arrests, when we sang again." The locally distributed Free Speech Songbook included
folk song rewrites, as well as parodies of Christmas carols, the latter quickly
released on thirteen thousand copies of the 45-rpm record Joy to U.C. Ralph
Gleason echoed Rossman's fervor, saying the "Cal students who marched 7000
strong Friday in a quiet, orderly, responsible demonstration to University Hall
are not only making literature, they are making folk music. . . . Friday night,
after the Harry Belafonte show, student parties all over Berkeley were entertained by college songs, Beatles records, and the new folk music of the FSM
movement." He applauded the students for drawing on pop and show tunes,
as well as the Beatles and folk songs, for their parodies—the true folk process. Irwin
Silber highlighted the students' clever redoing of "I Don't Want Your Millions,
Mister":

We don't want mass education,
From IBM machines so blind.
But just to be treated as human beings,
Our cause is freedom of the mind.[84]

Baez had appeared at the Berkeley Folk Festival the previous June, joining
the New Lost City Ramblers, Mississippi John Hurt, Doc Watson, and Almeda
Riddle in a tribute to traditional songs. Indeed, there was scant mention of
topical songs to mar the enthusiasm of the thirty thousand attendees. Lawrence
Linderman concluded his rather sarcastic overview of the festival in Cavalier:
"The Berkeley Folk Festival is the most important event of its kind in America
and is also the best run (I had seen only one campus cop in the five days)."
When the story finally appeared in the November issue, Berkeley was hardly

so quiescent. Next year's festival would have a slightly more contemporary tinge, though major musical changes would not come until 1966.[85]

The Big Picture as 1964 Ends

"There is, of course, nothing puzzling about the rise of folk music in recent years," the music critic Gene Lees carped in *HiFi/Stereo Review*. "The taste of the American public had been consistently depressed for more than a decade by concerted actions of the broadcasting and recording industries, whose entente is based on the fact that both have a sole and simple motivation, namely greed. With a decade of rock-and-roll behind us, the appearance of another type of music based on twanging guitars and amateurish singing constituted only a shift of emphasis." The revival had produced no musical geniuses, he said, certainly not Dylan; besides, their "protests mewl and whine, and one sometimes gets the impression that they are secretly glad of the conditions they protest. Otherwise, what justifications for their existence could they find?" Arnold Shaw, a music publishing executive and black music scholar, indirectly countered Lees with a lengthy, upbeat review of the folk scene in *Harper's Magazine*. "Whether one sings, listens, ponders or just beats time," he concluded, "the folk frenzy is a matter for rejoicing, reflecting as it does an affirmative change in the temper of the college generation, a still-to-be-assessed turn from cool spectatorism to active involvement." Shaw's muted praise of folk music that connected with student activism did not frighten the conservative *Reader's Digest*, which republished the article in its usual condensed format. Robert Shelton more directly challenged Lees, countering that "[the] word genius scarcely seems excessive for even such turbulent, erratic, unpredictable literary-musical giants as Guthrie and Dylan."[86]

A conservative backlash against folk music lurked in the shadows, however, mimicking an attack dating back almost three decades. Though Barry Goldwater had been trounced at the polls by Lyndon Johnson in early November, a Republican groundswell, centered in the Midwest and West, was definitely building. A few even tried to promote a conservative folk music revival. The California Young Republicans briefly opened a "Rally Right" folksinging club in Newport Beach, raising funds for Goldwater's campaign. "Entertainment will be 'clean-cut, novel, high class and, of course, right-wing,' and will feature the 'Goldwaters' and local talent during the three-week trial period," an article explained, "Hoots are OUT, rallies are IN." The "Goldwaters," a southern quartet, issued one album, *The Goldwaters Sing Folk Songs to Bug the Liberals*, with such songs as "Barry's Moving In," "Down in Havana," and "Row Our Own Boat." But it was obvious that the Left had long ago captured popular folk music. "Along with the hand-clapping, the guitar strumming, the banjo-picking, the shouting and the howling, comes a very subtle, but highly effective, presentation of standard Communist-Party propaganda," Jere Real asserted in the right-wing *American Opinion*. He had plenty of evidence, what with raking up Seeger's political past and documenting the political sins of Baez and Dylan. Real's voice might have seemed faint at the time, but he was a forecast of the dawning conservative age. Moreover, in a bit of déjà vu, Ewan MacColl again had his visa cancel in October, and though it was soon restored, his U.S. tour with Peggy Seeger had to be postponed.[87]

Despite the demise of the *Hootenanny* television show and the glitzy folk magazines, the year ended with folk music definitely in the commercial saddle. Commercialism and activist politics, particularly the civil rights movement, had continued uncomfortably in tandem, while traditional performers and styles, white and black, had made a showy comeback. Exactly who and what constituted folk music remained muddy. Nonetheless, college students nationwide, along with many of their parents, lavishly spent their money and time on guitars, records, literature, radio and television shows, and concerts. Folk music spoke to them, invigorating civil rights demonstrators in the South, students at Berkeley, fans at the numerous folk festivals in Newport, Chicago, Los Angeles, and Philadelphia, club- and concertgoers in Greenwich Village, Detroit, and on virtually every campus in the country. Both the big names and the newcomers garnered attention, with a few financially well compensated. Folk music had definitely come of age, in all of its many-colored glory, just when the Beatles' invasion and Dylan's sudden turn toward introspection launched a new wave of rock and roll passion. But perhaps its commercial time had come and gone.

In what were billed as their fifteenth-anniversary concerts, the seven Weavers reunited at Carnegie Hall on May 2 and 3, 1963, regaling the audiences with much of their repertoire. Pete Seeger, Lee Hays, Ronnie Gilbert, Fred Hellerman, Erik Darling, Frank Hamilton (who had replaced Darling in 1962), and Bernie Krause (about to fill in for Hamilton) crowded the stage. "Folk singing in the U.S. didn't really begin with the Weavers, of course, it just seems that way sometimes," said *Newsweek*. "The new folkniks revere the Weavers."[88]

The reconstituted group limped along through 1963. Hellerman kept busy as a record producer and recording musician and Gilbert had plunged into acting. Then it was over. "A fabulous chapter in the history of folksinging came to a close this past December when The Weavers presented their final concert (ever) at Chicago's Orchestra Hall," Silber announced in *Sing Out!* "The Weavers had been hurt in recent years by the changing tastes of the new folksong audience, the emergence of a swarm of groups patterned after the original, the rapid turn-over in banjo-pickers, and the political blacklisting which had kept them off of television. But for 15 years, The Weavers were among the best of their kind. We hate to see them go. An era has come to an end and folk music in America won't seem quite the same again." The year 1964 witnessed the birth of dozens of Weavers's clones after the demise of the prototype. Was this progress or a symbol of bigger troubles ahead, as Silber envisioned?[89]

Ellen Sander would sum up the current feeling. "By the time most of the folksingers had records out, the material took on a more permanent aspect—and it happened simultaneously on campuses, in cities, and small towns, wherever kids were aware, listening, feeling, and laying their hands on guitars. In trains and bus stations, in barracks and parks, people would get together and make music."[90]

8

Folk's Transformation, 1965–1966

"The youth of 1965, the college students who stood on the steps of Sproul Hall to hear Joan Baez tell them to have love in their hearts, have lived with The Bomb all of their lives," Ralph Gleason explained in *Ramparts*, the radical monthly popular on the campuses. "They are the true fallout from the blast that changed the world, the real Bomb Babies." He praised Dylan, Baez, and their folk colleagues, for the "times, indeed, are a-changin' and these young artists are among the reasons why and they have served notice on their elders to get out of the way." Connecting folk music and rebellion seemed natural as the year unfolded. Lenore Hershey told *McCall's* readers, "Rock 'n' roll has animal spirit, a get-up-and-move compulsion. Folk is the idiom of the individual, seeking, rebelling. Tuned into the current college generation, it seems destined to spread even farther."[1]

Underground papers such as the *Berkeley Barb* and *East Village Other* supplied the political, cultural, and consumer needs of the mounting youth rebellion. Students challenged campus rules throughout the North, while their southern black counterparts, led by SNCC, continued civil rights demonstrations, and the antiwar movement fostered a mounting level of confrontation. Young people increasingly preferred the energizing rhythms and lyrics of rock and roll to the more mellow sounds of folk music, though the two became briefly fused into the hybrid labeled folk rock.[2]

In late 1962, students at Indiana University in Bloomington had launched the campus Folk Song Club, which organized concerts, lectures, instructional workshops, films, and other activities. Yet it "all seems to have fallen apart . . . after about 1965. Things suddenly started to go downhill," Neil Rosenberg recalled. What with the rise of student activism, marked by the Students for a Democratic Society and the growing antiwar movement, combined with the British invasion and folk rock, folk definitely lost its musical luster. "All of a sudden rock 'n' roll was acceptable to intellectuals and college students. And that was another kind of a drain in another direction—artistic, that is. Some of the best performers who had been involved in the club's activities suddenly got electric guitars and formed bands, and they were off in another direction." As the club's last faculty advisor, Rosenberg watched the students get stoned and the club disintegrate in 1967.[3]

In early 1965, however, folk music's gloss had scarcely faded, and few could anticipate its sharp commercial decline. Jack Newfield, in the *Village Voice*, celebrated folk music as "one of the battlegrounds where the hegemony of the established canons and values is being challenged by a creative cadre of insurgents" led by Phil Ochs. For John Denver, however, newly emerging as a performer, the glory days were quickly waning. "When the Christy Minstrels broke up, I knew that was it," he later recalled about the opening months of 1965, shortly after the group's founder, Randy Sparks, had sold his interest for $2,500,000. "I knew that was it; the folk music movement of the Sixties had passed into the history books." As his own career would prove, though, Denver's obituary was slightly premature.[4]

Music and Civil Rights

Broadside continued to publish dozens of new compositions about the freedom movement. Pete Seeger picked up a few on the Selma-to-Montgomery march in late March, where the demonstrators "were creating one great song after another, right before our eyes." While Seeger stressed the creative, energizing role of the local demonstrators, Bernice Reagon, formerly of the Freedom Singers, lamented that once the march arrived at the state capitol outsiders again took center stage. "The music and speeches stood out as different from the music of the March just completed and the earlier Selma campaign," she wrote in her study of freedom songs. "The Selma Freedom Choir did not sing. Music was provided for the marchers by professional entertainers like Harry Belafonte, Joan Baez and Peter, Paul and Mary." Media-attractive outsiders, making a brief appearance but hogging the spotlight, began to rankle many of those on the civil rights firing line. Other frictions between sojourners, generally white, and local activists, mostly black, led into the black power movement the next year. Reagon concluded, "Musically, this trend was reflected by the decline in the use of songs and singing as an integral part of the continuing struggle."[5]

During the summer's Southern Community Organization and Political Education (SCOPE) training sessions for northern volunteers, Margaret Long noted in the *Progressive*, "the singing, black and white together, seemed predominantly and wildly rock and roll, pounding with thunderbolts of hand-clapping. . . . Rock and roll, observed the Reverend Andrew Young of SCOPE, has done more than perhaps any other Negro expression to span the culture gulf between young blacks and whites."[6]

Drawing on his musical preservation work on John's Island, South Carolina, and following a festival on the island the previous Christmas, Guy Carawan, along with Willie Peacock and Willie McGhee, helped organize a musical workshop in May in Edwards, Mississippi. Including the Moving Star Hall Singers, the Georgia Sea Island Singers, Doc Reese, the fife player Ed Young, and Alan Lomax and Ralph Rinzler, the sessions introduced local organizers to traditional and contemporary folk music. Many of the young black activists found the older songs strange, smacking of slavery and oppression, and Lomax's remarks offensive. "Some of the young people seemed a bit brash" to the older performers, Carawan recalled, "and their outspoken behavior raised concerns about their safety in the repressive South." A few months later, former Mississippi SNCC workers Sam Block, McGhee, and Peacock carried out the first Northern District Mississippi Folk Festival in Mileston; African and local music and dance were showcased, with no outsiders. Peacock had originally envisioned four separate, similar events in Mississippi and Alabama.[7]

In October almost two dozen activists—including Carawan, Peacock, Reagon, Lomax, Rinzler, and Julius Lester from the Newport Festival board, and Charles Sherrod and Miles Horton—gathered in Knoxville, Tennessee, as guests of the Highlander Center to discuss the possibilities of a broader southern cultural movement. While Reagon served as prime organizer and leader, Lomax worked hard to shape the discussions, and he authored the final report. The group drew up a blueprint for future cultural undertakings. They visualized "a cultural revival in the South at the community or grassroots level; that we will deal first with Negro culture and music, since this seems to be in greatest immediate danger of being lost to posterity, and to have the greatest immediate advantage, that of enriching the newly aware and modern Negro with a sense of identity in his own and American culture." Festivals were planned for John's Island, Charleston, and southwest Mississippi. Lomax stressed the value of church music, particularly the spiritual tradition of the Holiness or Sanctified Church; his hand can also be seen in the emphasis on the value of collecting songs from prisoners, railroad workers, and levee workers. "We intend to encourage the Negro community to come alive in its own spirit and on its own terms," Lomax argued in the final report.[8]

In a draft report of the conference Lomax wrote that songs "are a record of the trials that the Negro people have undergone in slavery and in the forced isolation of the social ghetto. Every one of them is in one sense a song of protest and an affirmation of the Negro's unswerving drive toward freedom, justice, and self-realization." Lomax still believed in the transforming power—political, social, and spiritual—of cultural preservation and rejuvenation. In covering the conference, The Southern Patriot, organ of the Southern Conference Educational Fund, an integrated group of southern civil rights activists, stressed as well the importance to whites of being exposed to black music.[9]

In December, Block, Peacock, and McGhee staged their second festival, in Greenwood, Mississippi. Julius Lester, reporting to the Newport Festival board, noted that religious singing dominated the festivities, though two local blues-men touched off a strong reaction among the older, pious members of the audience. Hurried planning, poor publicity, and dreadful weather kept the crowd to a minimum. The highlight for Lester was an African fashion show and display of African and African American paintings, sculpture, and pottery. He encouraged the Newport Foundation to fund future cultural events in Mississippi and other southern states.

Northern support for civil rights continued through the year. In July a two-day Freedom Folk Festival in Cambridge, Massachusetts, raised $1,500 for the Congress of Racial Equality (CORE). On very short notice forty performers donated their time, including Tom Paxton, Peter LaFarge, Eric Andersen, Ronnie Gilbert, and Tom Lehrer. Hurried planning definitely hurt attendance, but the optimistic promoters anticipated a second festival the next year. Popular music was also connecting with civil rights and black cultural awakening. Nina Simone recorded "Mississippi Goddam" (first published in Broadside) in 1965, and Sam Cooke's militant "A Change Is Gonna Come," posthumously released, reached the pop charts early in the year. Black-owned or -influenced companies—Mo-town, Stax-Volt, Fame, Atlantic—turned out a stream of fresh, exhilarating soul recordings. Racial politics and identity had become big business, as the civil rights movement began to fragment and urban violence escalated.[10]

Into 1966 an interracial group of musicians gathered by Bernice Reagon (Len Chandler, Hedy West, Mable Hillary, the Reverend Pearly Brown, Barbara Dane, and occasionally Pete Seeger) toured the South for a month, playing eighteen cities, to raise funds for the Southern Students Organizing Committee and SNCC educational projects. Local performers also joined in. Barbara Dane wrote "We went mostly for the chance to use ourselves and our songs to tell about the people we come from, and to show how the music has always intertwined—to show that no kind of wall could have separated 'black' music from 'white' music." Such ongoing commitments attracted little outside attention, however, as civil rights organizing was replaced by more violent headlines.[11]

Black culture and the civil rights movement remained vital to the revival, but other pressing issues began to take center stage. Irwin Silber, who had delib-erately downplayed Sing Out!'s radical politics since the late 1950s, now began to incorporate a political agenda. He inaugurated a new column, "Fan the

Flames" (the name taken from the IWW's songbook), designed to rattle readers' complacency. Coming off his recent critique of Dylan, he argued that the "identification of folk music and social conscience annoys some modern-day hippies who seem to think that commitment is square and political awareness naive." In the next issue he attacked the Vietnam buildup, and particularly two folk singers (Stephen Addiss and Bill Crofut) who were currently touring in South Vietnam, sponsored by the State Department; "their folk songs of love and brotherhood are being echoed by the bombs dropped by our planes on North Vietnam."[12]

Sing Out!'s overall politics were partially shaped by managing editor Paul Nelson's musical aesthetics (and lack of Left connections). In addition to increased international coverage, Sing Out!'s definition of folk music broadened. For instance, Tony Glover's coverage of rhythm and blues recognized Chicago electric blues. In the same issue Izzy added, "There is a mad rush on to record and document every new white blues singer or songwriter—but where is the equivalent for the new Negro blues singer or songwriter? They appear elsewhere and on other labels like Excello, Chess, Vee Jay, and King. In fact, they don't need us and they reach a far larger market. We should reach out to them and not wait for them to come to us."[13]

On April 17, 1965, the peace movement mounted a massive march on Washington organized by the SDS. Twenty thousand gathered at the Washington Monument to hear a parade of speakers and performers; then they descended on the Capitol. Phil Ochs introduced "Love Me I'm a Liberal," but not all were laughing at his sarcastic jabs. Ochs's searing lyrics skewered friends and foes alike. Joan Baez used a different approach, saying she would refuse to pay the 60 percent of her taxes that she calculated went into military spending; her protest lasted for ten years, becoming as much a part of her image as her long hair and lovely voice.

Newport

At the beginning of 1965, in a stab at greater independence, Izzy moved the Folklore Center from MacDougal Street, the heart of action in the Village, just west to a larger space on Sixth Avenue, one flight up. He was free from selling instruments, which were now handled by his partner Marc Silber at the adjacent Fretted Instruments, and he also dropped records for the time being, concentrating on books and magazines. "Moving to a new location . . . is my new way of meeting the world," he announced in Sing Out![14]

Dick Reuss, a folklore graduate student at Indiana University and contributor to Broadside, accepted a grant to organize the People's Songs collection, housed in Sing Out!'s office. This job presented him with the perfect opportunity to query the staff, particularly Paul Nelson, and note office comings and goings.

Simultaneously, he was tape-recording dozens of hours of interviews with Izzy, and also visiting the *Broadside* scene at Cunningham and Friesen's apartment. He kept voluminous notes, which he compiled into the "Folk Scene Diary Summer 1965." Reuss scrutinized the inner workings of *Sing Out!* and the adjoining Folkways Records office. Nelson, *Sing Out!*'s managing editor for two years, was having increasing problems with Silber, and seems to have felt rather isolated. Reuss learned that Silber had offered Nelson's position to Julius Lester, who gracefully declined. Nelson officially informed Silber in late July that he would be leaving in early October, to be replaced by Ed Badeaux, a musician and journalist from Texas who had briefly worked for *Sing Out!* in the late 1950s.[15]

Reuss initially had little inkling of *Sing Out!*'s internal tensions and convoluted politics, which had been building through the year. Pete Seeger, officially an associate editor, had expressed his thoughts to Silber in early January, sketching his blueprint for the future. Since the magazine could not do everything, it should concentrate on the possible: "What do we aim at? It seems to me the key is in those two words: peace and freedom. Well, let's add another one: and music. These words, like every other good word, are in danger of being prostituted by demagogues." He particularly objected to the sappy copy in a Kay guitar ad—"you strumming a happy tune on your KAY guitar"—and threatened, "there's going to be some desks overturned in the SING OUT! office if this ad goes in one more month." So, he continued, "if we think of SING OUT! as representing a ground swell of mass resistance to the whole mass media of fokum I think we have the key to future growth," which would come not only through sensitive ads but also better copy, broader coverage—Vietnam, the World Youth Festival in Algeria—and in general more of a political thrust. In his response, Silber agreed with some of his points, but took a more expansive view of the magazine, which should be "applying the real, honest values implicit in popular music (a much better term, I think, than folk music) to contemporary life and problems." Believing that "we do have something of a public trust," Silber preferred to be increasingly inclusive, despite his recent swing to a more radical political stance. Conflicts between political integrity and commercial success were to mount in the coming months.[16]

As sort of a prelude to the Newport Folk Festival, the theatrical manager Manheim Fox, figuring to cash in on the folk boom, staged a mammoth folk festival at Carnegie Hall spread over a week in mid-June 1965—eleven events and sixty performers. The opening concert featured Mississippi John Hurt, Son House, Muddy Waters, and Chuck Berry, followed through the week by Phil Ochs, Johnny Cash, and Billy Edd Wheeler, with Archie Green, Hamilton Camp, and Sam Charters serving as articulate narrators for the thematic concerts. The festival met with general approval, though Carnegie Hall hardly matched the greenery and freedom of an outdoor site. Silber gave a mixed review, praising Muddy Waters, Otis Spann, the Blue Sky Boys, Dock Boggs, and Phil Ochs, the only topical singer on the bill, while panning others. He preferred the "low-key music-making" of the June Berkeley festival to New York's "show business extravagance." Fred McDowell, Jean Redpath, and the Hackberry Ramblers were musically refreshing, he said, while the three panel discussions, including "The Beatle Mystique vs. the Folk Mystique," added a provocative academic touch.[17]

"Very quiet and busy today," Reuss noted for July 19. "Paul, Irwin and Deanna [Oak Publications' secretary] are going to Newport at the end of the week, and one can sense that the hub of folk affairs is shifting in that direction for the moment." Predicting a monster turnout, the Kiwanis Club of Newport, running the food stands, had ordered 23,000 hot dogs, over eight thousand pizzas, and 1,100 gallons of coffee for the hungry throngs—which would number over 75,000 for the four days. There would be 175 performers in six concerts and twenty-six workshops. The English singer-songwriter Donovan (the British "Dylan"), Baez, Son House, and old-time fiddler Eck Robertson played on opening night.[18]

In his *Times* report, Robert Shelton focused on the Friday blues stage, where "Alan Lomax, the folklorist, was an articulate, illuminating, fluent, but sometimes maddeningly pedantic host-narrator. Likening the blues to the Italian stornella, the Spanish copla and the Mexican corrida, Mr. Lomax described the Afro-American blues and its variations as 'our most powerful, pervasive popular musical form.'" Five former Texas prisoners, a quartet from the Mississippi Delta, Mance Lipscomb, the Bill Monroe Band, and Willie Dixon demonstrated blues variations. "Finally, after the narrator's challenge for them to prove themselves capable of playing the blues, came the Paul Butterfield Blues Band. . . . They proved themselves an exciting present-day link in the long chain of the blues."[19]

The Chicago harmonica player Paul Butterfield had brought together Elvin Bishop and Michael Bloomfield into the dynamic Butterfield Blues Band in 1963. Gaining a well-deserved local reputation, the racially mixed group soon attracted the attention of Paul Rothchild, a producer for Elektra Records, who rushed to Chicago and signed them as the label's first electric group. Jac Holzman arranged for them to join a blues workshop at Newport. According to Rothchild, who would play his own controversial role in the weekend's proceedings, Lomax introduced the group: "Today you've heard some of the greatest blues musicians in the world playing their simple music on simple instruments. Let's find out if these guys can play at all." Lomax left the stage and was immediately confronted by Grossman, who had already decided to manage the group: "What kind of a fuckin' introduction was that?" After a few more harsh words, "there were these two giants, both physically and in the business, wrestling around in the dust!" For Rothchild, this "was the exact moment of transition between the old roots music which we loved and cherished, and the next evolution of that music." Yet this was only the prelude to further bedlam.[20]

Because of their success at the blues workshop, coupled with pressure from

Rothchild and Grossman, the festival directors agreed to allow the Butterfield band to perform while the audience was filing in for the Sunday evening concert. At the sound of their electric instruments, a dispute broke out backstage among Seeger, Grossman, Holzman, Peter Yarrow, George Wein, Bikel, and Harold Leventhal; Yarrow and Grossman lined up against Seeger, Wein, and Lomax, who felt the music inappropriate, too revolutionary, and too screeching. Very agitated, Seeger threatened to cut the power lines until talked out of it by Bikel. Rothchild said, "It was like somebody reminded him about his revolution, and he was witnessing another revolution and . . . he was the right wing all of a sudden."[21]

After Seeger opened the concert, Ronnie Gilbert and Theo Bikel sang two of Phil Ochs's topical songs (while the angry author, excluded from the program, sat fuming in the audience). After the flamboyant, crowd-pleasing Cousin Emmy, Bob Dylan finally appeared in an orange shirt and black leather outfit, trailed by a pick-up band with whom he had secretly been rehearsing—Butterfield band members Mike Bloomfield, Sam Lay, and Jerome Arnold, along with Al Kooper and Barry Goldberg—and carrying an electric guitar. They opened with "Maggie's Farm," followed by "Rolling Stone" and "It Takes a Train to Cry," then, shaken by the crowd's raucous behavior, Dylan hurriedly left the stage. While some had appeared shocked and shouted their disapproval—"Bring back Cousin Emmy," "Play folk music," "Sell out!"—others clearly enjoyed Dylan and his new group. Part of the problem was the inadequate sound system, loud, unbalanced, and obscuring the words. Rothchild, who had already recorded the Butterfield Blues Band, was running the sound mixing board, and quickly found himself caught in another fracas. Rothchild: "We were just getting the music up there to where it was exciting and here comes Pete again" (as well as Peter Yarrow); "here we are two diminutive guys, Pete Seeger towering over us by a foot, easily, just screaming and threatening." Grossman and Holzman joined the struggle over the sound level, and finally "Peter Yarrow said, Pete get away from here or I'll fucking kill ya. And Pete turned on his heel and left. . . . So that was the pivotal moment."[22]

Yarrow, back as emcee, prodded and begged Dylan to return to the stage with his acoustic guitar. After some delay, he ended the set with "It's All Over Now, Baby Blue" and "Mr. Tambourine Man," to wild applause. Peter, Paul and Mary, Ronnie Gilbert, Oscar Brand, Josh White, and Theo Bikel came next, then Mel Lyman of the Kweskin Jug Band had the last song, lulling the crowd with "Rock of Ages" on his harmonica. "At the party afterwards, everyone was still talking about the concert," Maria Muldaur recalled. "The Chambers Brothers started to play. Dylan was off sitting in a corner buried, and [Richard] Fariña told me to go over and ask Dylan to dance because Fariña was always into starting some rhythm going and starting to boogie and dance and stuff. So I went over to him and said, 'Do you want to dance?' and he looked up at me and said, 'I would, but my hands are on fire.' "[23]

Bikel, who seems to have played a crucial role in defusing Seeger's anger, has little to say about the festival in his autobiography. "For the moment we were all upset about what seemed an intrusion by rock-and-roll into what we considered to be our pristine world of folk," he writes. "We had used amplification for only one purpose: to make sure that the performers would be heard. . . . This was different; this music did not exist apart from the amplification. I remember saying to Pete that I was sure this kind of music had a place somewhere, but that the place was not here." Still, upon reflection, he understood that Dylan's "retreat into self-absorption was a kind of salvation for him. The music blared outward, but the texts had turned inward."[24]

Dylan's unveiling of what would quickly be called "folk rock" at Newport was a continuation of his move to electric instrumental work paired with imaginative, introspective, sometimes nightmarish lyrics. No newcomer to electric guitar, a staple of his high school rock and roll days, Dylan easily returned to his musical roots, marked by the release of the semi-electric *Bringing It All Back Home* in March 1965, featuring "Mr. Tambourine Man," "Gates of Eden," and "It's All Over Now, Baby Blue." The album would soon reach number six on the charts, and the single "Like A Rolling Stone" shot up to number two by September.

Various groups, including the Animals, had begun to pioneer folk rock, a melding of folk-style lyrics, electric guitars, and a rock-and-roll beat, before Dylan's tumultuous Newport showing. In Los Angeles, a new group called the Byrds included David Crosby, a regular at the Troubadour and former member of Les Baxter's Balladeers; Gene Clark, fresh off a tour with the New Christy Minstrels; Jim McGuinn, a product of Chicago's Old Town School of Folk Music and guitarist with the Chad Mitchell Trio (he had been booed playing Beatles songs in Greenwich Village); and Chris Hillman, a bluegrass mandolinist. Accomplished musicians, they signed with Columbia and turned Dylan's "Mr. Tambourine Man," released in April 1965, into a number one hit single by early summer. At year's end their upbeat version of "Turn, Turn, Turn," a biblical passage set to music by Pete Seeger, reached similar heights. Their album, *Mr. Tambourine Man*, climbed to number six in midsummer.[25]

The day following Newport, as people straggled into the *Sing Out!* office, Dick Reuss, who could not attend, asked what had happened. Deanna had "a wonderful weekend," and remarked that "Dylan got booed off the stage for his rock 'n' roll stuff. . . . Deanna said his rock and roll stuff was good but it didn't remotely approach folk music and she went to Newport to hear folk music." Paul Nelson had just the opposite reaction, "talking about the Dylan fiasco which made a very great impression on him, and he kept saying how dramatic it was and how it overshadowed everything else. . . . Dylan was absolutely the greatest, Paul said." Reuss also heard about the fight between Lomax and Grossman over the former's insulting introduction of the Butterfield Blues Band during the blues workshop. Deanna reported that Shelton had tried to describe the fight in his coverage, but the passage was removed through a *Times* editorial decision.[26]

"Generally, the festival reflected the growing breadth of taste among the folk-music audience," wrote Shelton. He preferred the workshops to the rather helter-skelter evening concerts, and he praised the abilities of Dick and Mimi Fariña, Mark Spoelstra, Gordon Lightfoot, and the Kweskin Jug Band. He did not mention Dylan. Yet Dylan's performance would dominate all memories and future discussions, marking the festival as a watershed, both real and symbolic.[27]

Sing Out!'s Silber wrote, "The era of Folk-Music-as-Show-Business reached what may prove to be its ultimate peak in the mammoth four-day 1965 edition of the Newport Folk Festival." Dazzled by the array of traditional performers, he preferred them to the commercial types, while touting the Chambers Brothers' charged mix of gospel and rhythm and blues. Silber also liked Len Chandler, Mark Spoelstra, the Kweskin Jug Band, and Richard and Mimi Fariña, while panning Ian and Sylvia, Peter, Paul and Mary, Baez, Odetta, and Josh White. Dylan's windup elicited little comment.[28]

Paul Nelson, in his swan song as managing editor, compared this year's Newport to last year's, which "seemed determined to fuse elephantiasis to social pretentiousness, to the detriment of both Man and beast." He applauded the paramount roles of roots performers Cousin Emmy, the McGee Brothers, and Lightnin' Hopkins, as well as newcomers Jim Kweskin, John Koerner, and the Fariñas. He loved the new Dylan, "an angry, passionate poet who demands his art to be all, who demands not to be owned, not to be restricted or predicted, but only, like Picasso, to be left alone from petty criticisms to do his business, wherever that may take him." Nelson believed the audience had unfortunately chosen Seeger over Dylan. "It was a sad parting of the ways for many, myself included. I choose Dylan. I choose art." And with that swipe at *Sing Out!*'s founder Nelson was no longer managing editor, though still a contributor; soon he would become an influential rock journalist. In a letter to Jon Pankake, Nelson praised the new Dylan, "whereas before I wouldn't have given much of a damn what happened to him at Newport. But, by God, he was so great in those three numbers! . . . I'll bet my critical judgment I'm right (and particularly so because Irwin hated it) and I'll stand behind Dylan and his new songs. He's made it back to Hero with me."[29]

Broadside began its brief thoughts on Newport with the disgruntled Ochs, who complained of the rude police, renaming it the "Newport Fuzz Festival." He had been refused a pass and had to sneak backstage. Ed Freeman, in the Boston *Broadside*, repeated the Dylan story, and was cheered to discover that the audience all knew the difference between rock and roll and folk and preferred the latter. He enjoyed the performers but found the four days too long and confusing, the quieter performers having to compete with the likes of the boisterous, crowd-pleasing Chambers Brothers. A week after the festival, Robert Shelton praised the Newport Folk Foundation for raising a large sum that would go to supporting traditional music and musicians. He quoted George Wein claiming the festival board was still united, though others "saw growing rips in the canvas that covers the three-ring circus of American folk music"; and he finally revealed without mentioning names, that a "folklorist and a personal manager scuffled on the ground over a fine point of courtesy in the folklorist's introductions." Arthur Kretchmer, in the *Village Voice*, labeled Newport "schismatic and disjointed. The festival committee tried to force-feed a May Day atmosphere complete with militant Socialist restrictiveness to a generation that doesn't trust anybody who wants to run a machine—there ain't no poetry in the bureaucracy, baby." Newport seemed a chameleon, changing colors for each reviewer.[30]

A few months later, in a lengthy article in *Cavalier*, Shelton compared and contrasted the New York and Newport festivals, finding "they both reflected, backstage at least, the growing tentacles of show-businessmanship." Perhaps considering that *Cavalier* had helped promote the New York show, he bestowed general praise on its artistic reach. As for Newport, after some criticism of Dylan and Baez, he lamented "that no young performer is stepping out to assume the role of leadership which Pete Seeger has long wanted to relinquish." Only Peter Yarrow showed promise, if he could free himself from Grossman's grasp. Longing for the good old days of folk brotherhood and idealism, Shelton feared that competition and commercialism had finally taken over, but he promised that "*Cavalier* will do what it can to keep the folk movement in general and its best festivals on the track of honesty, representativeness, and wholesomeness in music."[31]

Mary Travers had a more personal, and highly negative, take on Newport. She confided to Archie Green that she much preferred 1964, when the "brotherhood and goodness of man was everywhere," but this year "an air of tension and agitation . . . ran through the city singers." Of course, "the country singers were, as always, friendly and open; and without any of the sophisticated hostile nuance that the city singers displayed throughout." After taking an initial swipe at Baez, and wondering about the Grossman-Lomax spat, she thought the finale "had all the component madnesses of our present culture." She "felt that I never wanted to be forced to play a part in such a fiasco again."[32]

After having issued multiple-record albums from the 1963 and 1964 Newport festivals, Vanguard released only one LP from 1965, a skimpy overview including the Butterfield Blues Band, Chambers Brothers, Son House, and the Lilly Brothers with Tex Logan, but no Dylan. Seeing a dwindling folk market, and perhaps having difficulty including performers signed to other companies, Vanguard then gave up on the festival.

Following Newport, Dylan was soon back in the studio, continuing to record cuts for the all-electric *Highway 61 Revisited*, released in September, along with the single "Positively 4th Street," which reached number seven on the pop charts by November. The Lovin' Spoonful, a mellow folk rock group led by John Sebastian, delivered "Do You Believe In Magic?," which reached number nine in a couple of months. The Butterfield Blues Band followed up their Newport triumph by appearing at Club 47 in Cambridge, breaking the club's acoustic tradition. Jim Rooney then booked Muddy Waters and his band, which opened the urban blues floodgates. Albert Grossman and Elektra's Jac Holzman, excited by the mounting enthusiasm, staged a combined Butterfield Blues Band press party and recording session at Café Au Go Go in late August. Wrangling an invitation, Izzy found himself quite impressed by their musical skills: "There is a certain reserve to them that is infectious so that your moving feet are not out of order. The crowd whistles and the electricity squeals back . . . I'm really glad I'm here tonight."[33]

But in late August Dylan received another harsh shock at Forest Hills in Queens, a tennis stadium seating fifteen thousand. "Facing a rude and immature audience, Bob Dylan gave a program Saturday night . . . in which he was a model of patient composure. . . . Most of the audience's attitudes were concerned with Mr. Dylan's excursions into 'folk rock,' a fusion of rock 'n' roll with folk-based songwriting," Shelton explained in the *Times*. The generally young audience first started booing Murray (the K) Kaufman, a popular disk jockey, whose introductory remarks lauded the singer's conversion to rock and roll. Dylan's opening acoustic set was well received, but when he returned with an electric band—Robbie Robertson, Al Kooper, Harvey Brooks, and Levon Helm—the audience exploded in shouts of "we want the old Dylan." Dick Reuss wrote that during the closing number, "Like a Rolling Stone," "a whole mob of kids run out from the stands, and play catch as catch can with the fat, out of shape cops, who are total losers—the whole concert now takes on a visual approximation of Dylan's mad imagery in his songs." Shelton predicted: "By the time they get to know his excellent new folk rock songs, such as 'Tombstone Blues,' maybe the noisy young boors who ruined an artistically strong concert may have grown up a bit." Indeed, the booing would quickly subside, replaced by cheering and swelling excitement. Dylan's September concert in the Hollywood Bowl generated wild enthusiasm, and it was the same in Dallas and the rest of his thirty-six stops during the fall. But his subsequent swing through England raised many hackles when he plugged in during the second half of his shows.[34]

As folk rock was experiencing its birth pangs, there was much talk about the Newport festival's future. The board of directors discussed the festival's size, the role of the "big" names, the number of workshops, the balance between traditional and contemporary performers, and the absurd number of singers crowding the stage during the finale. Seeger accepted the continuing role of rhythm and blues, but only if there was some "connection in form and content to what we in general call the traditions of folk music." Such a caveat was, of course, the core of the dilemma, given the increasingly fluid definition of folk music. Ralph Rinzler preferred to stress the festival's role as an educational tool, with traditional performers and artists demonstrating their skills, the format he would fully develop with the Smithsonian Institution's Festival of American Folklife.[35]

The new manager of Club 47, Jim Rooney, had a list of telling suggestions for the festival's directors. Pointing out that the audience easily preferred the traditional performers, he suggested limiting the role of the older popularizers such as Bikel and Brand. As for Dylan, despite the obvious sound problems, Rooney argued that his disturbing songs and presentation were invaluable and should be encouraged. "Even as it was, it was head and shoulders above the easy mouthing of conventional liberalisms such as the Phil Ochs song about freedom (done identically by Theo Bikel and Ronnie Gilbert)," he asserted. "Maybe he didn't put it in the best way. Maybe he was rude. But he shook us. And that is why we have poets and artists." Dylan underscored the increasingly evident generational split, which had to be addressed.[36]

While these debates raged through the hot summer, Dick Reuss toiled away in the *Sing Out!* office, remarking on the swirl of events and odd personalities. Nelson's imminent departure from the masthead was only one indication of editorial controversies, though the circulation continued to soar. Silber and Moe Asch believed it was time to enlarge the format to 8 1/2 × 11 inches in order to be visible on newsstands and drugstore racks, which might expand circulation from 25,000 to 100,000. Izzy had doubts about the proposed format, but he figured that "*Sing Out!* is ready to go for all the marbles. . . . There is a lot of money at stake for Moe Asch and Irwin Silber. I do not think Irwin can do it."[37]

Izzy spelled out his concerns to Seeger. He greatly enjoyed writing for *Sing Out!*, but became nervous when "my employers seem to becoming real capitalists. And *Sing Out!* seemed to become softer. And Irwin started those foolish editorials to fan flames." "*Sing Out!* has no roots outside of NYC and that must be worked on," he continued. "Regular ways to accumulate information must be developed." By year's end the magazine's future would be further clouded as Irwin combined the perhaps incompatible aims of commercial outreach and escalating political involvement. And *Sing Out!* seemed to have growing competition, particularly from Larry McCombs, an editor in Cambridge who had launched *Folkin' Around* (soon changed to *Sounds*) earlier in the year, an ambitious national listing of concerts, records, and news, combined with various creative columns and even a few songs.[38]

The boisterous summer thankfully faded with another mellow gathering at the Philadelphia Folk Festival, a refreshing alternative to the fireworks of Newport. The cowboy singer Glenn Ohrlin, Mississippi John Hurt, Bikel, the Greenbriar Boys, Ochs, the Butterfield Blues Band, Judy Collins, and Skip James kept the audience musically engrossed. On the last day, Dick Reuss joined a group taking shelter from a sudden rain storm. "Some girl with an autoharp started singing some of the old favorites of the folkniks of seven or eight years ago, things like 'Down in the Valley,' 'Brown Eyes,' and 'Strangest Dream,' and even though I first said 'Oh no, not one of these refugees from a Jewish summer camp again,' it turned out to be pretty good." The Boston Broadside's Robert Lurtsema similarly appreciated Philadelphia's lack of commercialism, the "well-rounded, well-balanced presentation of the best available performers," and especially the freedom and hospitality. Sing Out!'s reviewers, Silber and performer Michael Cooney, summed up the general consensus: "Good fun. Good music. Good people. These days, that's worth writing about."[39]

Politics, Commerce, and Folk Rock

Political activism and musical creativity joined occasionally in the fall of 1965. Barry McGuire, recently of the New Christy Minstrels, recorded "Eve of Destruction," a doomsday prophecy by teenager P. F. Sloan (inspired by Dylan) which hit the charts in late August and quickly climbed to number one, selling six million copies despite a widespread broadcasting ban because of its "radical" message. Paul Simon and Art Garfunkel followed with "Sounds of Silence," which became a gold record. "With a dozen more songs of protest snapping close behind, it ["Eve of Destruction"] heralds a radical change for rock 'n' roll," Time pronounced in mid-September. "Suddenly the shaggy ones are high on a soapbox. Tackling everything from the Peace Corps to the P.T.A., foreign policy to domestic morality, they are sniping away in the name of 'folk rock'— big-beat music with big-message lyrics." Sonny and Cher also hopped on the folk rock bandwagon with "We Gotta Get Out of This Place." Newsweek noted, "Billboard's latest tabulation of best sellers crowds six folk-rock disks into its top ten. . . . The folky rollers protest—against being put down, being hung up, being drafted, Vietnam, Selma, the FBI, the Bomb." Disturbing yes, but still big business. "The future of folk rock is anyone's guess," Nora Ephron predicted in the New York Post, "and most anyone who is asked guesses that it is unlikely that the messages will remain so hard-sell."[40]

Dylan always took center stage in the popular press, but the mounting crowd of performers loosely grouped under the folk rock rubric garnered serious attention as well. Folk rock partly connected the generally mellow Southern California music scene with the hard-bitten New York folk and recording establishment. The music publisher Lou Adler had encouraged the young P. F. Sloan, who had previously penned pop ditties for Connie Stevens, to write trendy political songs. "Adler is well into the protest biz, although until recently he was riding the surf trend," the British musician Ian Whitcomb commented. "Dunhill, his record label, is by all accounts a 'protest factory.' Meanwhile, the rest of Hollywood hasn't been slack." As a telling aside, Whitcomb added: "While all this pop business had been going on, there had been a civil war in a suburb of Los Angeles called Watts. Between August 11 and 16, rioters in this ghetto set fire to their neighborhood, looted shops and businesses, and fought the police and soldiers. There were thirty fatalities. But I didn't know where Watts was and none of my friends ever went there, nor did I associate its black residents with the ebony heroes who sang R&B."[41]

The shift of both musicians and much of the recording industry to the West Coast gathered steam by mid-decade. "The heavies evacuated the Village and split for California," Ellen Sander remembered. "Folk had become too commercial to be comfortable, tourists jamming every coffeehouse were degenerating the scene, cover charges and minimums every place we used to hang out for free were a drag, the stars of the folk world were off the streets and on the road or in secluded, exclusive enclaves. The Spoonful played in the Night Owl to hundreds of teenyboppers in from the boroughs."[42]

Southern California's protest songs were quite abstract, unlike the caustic output of Len Chandler, Phil Ochs, and others in New York who had thrown themselves into the civil rights and antiwar movements. Whitcomb quoted a radio station program director near San Francisco discussing "Eve of Destruction": "A lot of the lyrics I can't make out, but what I can is goddamn *treason*! Can you believe a guy who knocks our Draft, our senators, our church, our H-bombs—and all on a pop record? . . . It may knock the U.S.A., but I don't knock success. I grab it by the balls and hang on tight. That 'Eve' disc is Dylan made commercial. . . . It's a new kind of *loot* music under the title of *protest*, remember that!" (Randy Sparks, founder of the New Christy Minstrels, allegedly labeled "Eve of Destruction" "communist fodder," and was composing a rejoinder, "Song of Hope.")[43]

"What is happening is that we are into a Combination thing, an Era of Amalgamation, the latest manifestation of which seems to be Folk & Rock & Protest," Boston *Broadside*'s Freeman explained to his readers. "The idea is to take two dissimilar forms of music, stick 'em together, and ZONK! instant fame & fortune." What next? Perhaps a combination of Bossanova and "Rock-Folk," "otherwise known as BAR-F." Phil Ochs worried that with most of the protest music, "the quality has been terrible and the philosophy has been juvenile. Dylan has made such an impact with his style that these guys who are writing songs are writing like tenth-rate Dylan." Dave Wilson reported from Boston "that the Pro-Dylanites rant a bit longer than the Anti's. One possible reason could be that this city seems to be a spawning ground for a number of groups picking up on the 'folk-rock' thing."[44]

Paul Williams, a student at Swarthmore College, early touted folk rock in his articles in *Folkin' Around*, which relocated from Cambridge to Chicago during the summer. In October the magazine became *Sounds*, the subtitle changed from

"National Folk News and Schedules" to "National News & Schedules: folk, country, blues, rock, jazz, pop, comedy." Editor McCombs favorably reviewed a sparsely attended folk concert on August 20 at the roomy Arie Crown Theater, which could not compete with the thousands packed into White Sox ball park for a Beatles show—both organized by Frank Fried of Triangle Productions. The former included Tom Rush, the Georgia Sea Island Singers, Koerner, Ray & Glover, Ochs, and the Jim Kweskin Jug Band. "The boundaries around and within folk music have become very blurred, if not totally meaningless," McCombs noted, "and I think it's great . . . People are really listening to all kinds of music, not only in the folk clubs but on the Top 40 shows. As a firm believer in the benefits of a reasonable amount of chaos and anarchy, I applaud the trend." The ambitious *Sounds* barely survived into the new year, but the gutsy young Williams was already launching his own mimeographed newsletter, *Crawdaddy*, initially a five-page review of rock-and-roll records. Williams's publication pioneered rock reviewing well over a year before Jann Wenner launched *Rolling Stone* in San Francisco in late 1967.[45]

Josh Dunson, clearly on the side of protest music, ventured to capture the essence of folk rock in a January 1966 *Sing Out!* piece, "Folk Rock: Thunder without Rain." Having championed in the previous issue Chicago's urban blues scene, he wrote, "I would argue that there is more protest and guts in one minute of good 'race music' than in two hours of folk rock. What should be meaningful to folk song enthusiasts is not that Dylan broke the top forty or that folk rock is big in pop music but that 'race music' has made its own bridge to the 'folk world' with the gospel and rock of the Chambers Brothers and the Chicago blues of the Butterfield Blues Band."[46]

The Peace Movement

Antiwar actions had been building all year: the Vietnam Day Committee attempts to block troop trains in Berkeley, the Congress of Unrepresented People demonstrations in Washington, and coordinated national parades and teach-ins. Though Joan Baez joined a peace march in London in the spring, along with Donovan, Carolyn Hester, Tom Paxton, and Theo Bikel, the folk community remained largely mute. "Len [Chandler] is also one of the most outspoken of performers," the Boston *Broadside* commented. "At Newport this year, he made a statement from the stage which seemed to be what many people had been waiting for all through the festival. While changing a string that had broken during his first song, he said, 'I would just like to go on record as disagreeing with our policy in Viet Nam.' The remark was greeted with both cheers and boos. But the point was made that he made the statement every other performer who might have been expected to speak, had skirted."[47]

"On [our] way to Newport Barbara [Dane] and I had the idea of a Sing In for peace," Irwin Silber explained to an organizing committee in late August, including Harold Leventhal, Jac Holzman, Paul Krassner, and Izzy Young. "We had a date on Sept. 24 for a *Sing Out!* annual concert but felt it was just one more concert. Received favorable response so we paid no attention to difficulties and we plunged right ahead. Some 40–50 people have already agreed to participate. . . . The war has escalated since. What we propose seems to have dramatic value [and] influence on others." Worried about adequate press coverage, the group discussed two concerts at Carnegie Hall as well as other activities. They formed an executive committee of Leventhal, Holzman, Silber, and Art D'Lugoff, with Barbara Dane as coordinator, who wound up doing the bulk of the organizing work. "Enthusiasm has been channeled into Negro movement," Leventhal worried. "Crisis has tapered off. It's hard to raise money. PP&M will sing for freedom and not for peace (Irwin—PP&M said that if they sang in peace concerts it would hurt their effectiveness in the civil rights movement)." (Martin Luther King would not publicly oppose the war until early 1967.) Leventhal continued, "Most managers of rock 'n' roll don't know about war in Vietnam." Leventhal, Holzman, Moe Asch, and a few others loaned over $12,000 for expenses (and all were repaid).[48]

Five thousand or more filled Carnegie Hall for two "Sing-In for Peace" concerts, one starting at 8 P.M. and the other following at midnight, with a total of sixty performers. "The audience was a mixed group," the *Christian Science Monitor* reported. "This reporter talked to a number of them and at least half of those interviewed said they were at the performance strictly for the entertainment. Some were even strongly against the peace movement." When the second concert ended at 4 A.M. the crowd marched three miles to D'Lugoff's Village Gate, where the singing continued. Baez (who counseled draft resistance), Bikel, Bernice Reagon, Fannie Lou Hamer and the Mississippi Freedom Singers, Seeger, and Mimi and Richard Fariña regaled the buoyant crowd. Many made a strong connection between civil rights and peace, with Fannie Lou Hamer asserting, to loud applause, "Until we straighten out the mess in this country, we should stop messing around in other places." Silber rejoiced that for "the first time, almost, since the Hootenannies of the 1950's, the essence of the creative union between folksong and social value had been recaptured. It may very well have been a milestone that will have untold reverberations in the years to come."[49]

Bothered by Dylan's glaring absence from the concert, Izzy penned one of his most creative essays, "Bob Dylantaunt," in the inaugural issue of the *East Village Other*. Reflecting on Dylan's lingering image as a protest singer, Izzy recalled his previous political lapses, for instance when Dylan originally "allowed Columbia Records to delete the 'John Birch Society Talking Blues' from his second album. This was after he swore that Columbia would have its way 'over his dead body.' (I was hoodwinked at the time into arranging an abortive protest march against the entire matter which I cancelled by dumping signs and literature into the trash basket when Dylan and management pulled a no-show on our line of six brave marchers.)" Izzy voiced displeasure at Dylan's abandonment of political protest. "Where he has obscured his words he has intensified his voice. His voice now tells the true story of Bob Dylan. He screams from the bottomless pit and it is truly heart-rending. But it is like sharing something dirty. It is no longer in the open arena of life's possibilities and we mourn for it."[50]

Part of the concert's proceeds were used for a large ad in the *New York Times*, signed by scores of performers and activists calling for an end to the war. Moe Asch's name was missing, however. He had already objected to the use of his name in promotional materials for the "Sing-In" and now argued that giving money to the *Times* or *Washington Post* for ads was a waste: "I am sure that the coffers of these bullwacks of the government policy do not need to be lined with the money collected for a peace movement." Asch recommended giving the money to King's SCLC or for an ambulance or blood for the Vietcong. Barbara Dane responded that the committee preferred to pursue their particular goal, to influence the country's war policy in Vietnam through newspaper ads. Despite Asch's (lucrative) professional relationship with Silber, he preferred to stay away from overt political commitments. Besides, his recent deal with MGM Records, setting up Verve/Folkways to recycle older Folkways albums as well as issue new records, denoted his intensifying plunge into the commercial marketplace (while surrendering considerable control over his beloved company). He also completed a deal with Scholastic to market and distribute the noncommercial titles in the catalogue, mostly to schools and libraries. Both Verve/Folkways and Folkways-Scholastic collapsed after a few years.[51]

Meanwhile Silber was occupied with censorship issues. In early November, two FBI agents paid a visit to Campbell's Music Co. in Washington, D.C., and confiscated three Oak song books, including the Carawans' *We Shall Overcome*. Suspecting that some of the songs promoted civil rights and other subversive ideas the store had requested the visit. Rushing to Oak's defense, the Discount Record and Book Shop ran an ad in the *Washington Post*: "The fact that an otherwise reputable store would call a Federal Agency to tell them what they should stock—in other words, to act as 'thought police'—is expected in the Soviet Union, not in America. How was Oak Publications undermining our country—by using the wrong kind of chords in their folk music books?" The incident quickly turned into farce. Ralph Gleason prophesied, "The next thing you know the FBI will be picking up on The Byrd's hit, 'Turn, Turn, Turn' and, like the record buying public, they'll be singing verses from Ecclesiastes with that most subversive line of all subversive lines, 'a time for peace, I swear it's not too late.' "[52]

The FBI imbroglio was without consequence, but Silber created other difficulties in the November issue of *Sing Out!* In his "Fan the Flames" column, the

editor included a few quotes, some highly salacious, from the recently published Born to Win, a collection of Woody Guthrie's writings edited by Robert
Shelton. The reaction was swift, with a few advertisers registering their disgust.
"Do we want our next generation to grow up with the feeling that this sort of
language is associated with the guitar?" the incensed president of the Harmony
Company complained to Silber. "If you were the parent of teen-agers, would
you permit them to take up the guitar, if you felt that the background of folk
music contained this kind of language reflected in the article?" And from the
Vega Instrument Company: "This is great stuff for a stag party, but certainly
degrading to your publication, and, in my opinion, to its advertisers." They
threatened to take some action, but the issue died down. In reply, Silber drafted
an editorial defending Sing Out!'s independent nature and value to the folk community. Meanwhile he wrote to Michael Asch, Moe's son: "If you could read
some of the obscene letters that have come into this office protesting this par-
agraph of Woody's (a piece of writing that I find to be Woody in his best
Whitmanesque style and viewpoint) you would indeed fear for the future of
America." Sing Out!'s role, said Silber, was "not only to document the music
and the expression, but to discuss the ideas let loose and to be a force in its
own way on its generation."[53]

1965 Ends in a Whimper

In his paean to folk music, Ballads, Blues, and the Big Beat, published in 1966,
Donald Myrus devoted a short section to Izzy Young.

> To get a feeling for the magnetic attraction of 321 Sixth Avenue, consider the scene
> at 11 A.M., November 23, 1965. In the kitchen of Izzy's tiny, three-room apart-
> ment, two flights above the center, Big Joe Williams was in the midst of preparing
> a second batch of southern fried chicken, rice, and espresso coffee for Izzy, himself,
> and any fans or musicians who happened in. The extemporaneous breakfast de-
> veloped because Big Joe had just arrived from Chicago—where he had been per-
> forming his blues at the Yellow Unicorn—to take part in a four-day blues session
> conducted at the Cafe Au Go Go on Bleecker Street.[54]

At home with the blues, as well as mainstream folk, hillbilly, even folk rock,
the proprietor of the Folklore Center was about to earn $200 hosting the four-
day Thanksgiving affair, sponsored by Verve/Folkways, partly as a fundraiser
for the financially troubled club. In addition to Big Joe, lineup included Son
House, Eric Andersen, Bukka White, and Skip James. Izzy loved the traditional
bluesmen, "who went through so much [but] could come up with such positive, definite music of great power and beauty. It was dazzling to see a single
guitar fill the room with ideas right after a six member electrified group would
appear on the stage with nascent forms of fascism." He could make little sense

out of the white performers, at one point mistakenly introducing Eric Anderson as John Hammond Jr. "because there was no difference to them." "The Beatles are about the only great people of the white musicians around today," he wrote in a letter to Seeger.[55]

Often disgruntled, Izzy pushed ahead, promoting, commenting, instigating—whatever he felt was called for to keep the scene alive. Hearing a rumor that Asch had had a parting of the ways with Silber and was pulling out of *Sing Out!*, Izzy queried Seeger in December concerning the actual ownership of the magazine (still a mystery to him). Next, following a meeting of the advisory board, he wrote Silber, praising him as editor, saying *Sing Out!* "can start a new life now and make an important contribution to the contemporary world." Izzy wanted to write more stories, perhaps about Motown Records, and he requested $50 to travel to Detroit and Chicago to cover the scene. He concluded the letter, "I do not give up the right to privately and publicly conspire against you." He held poetry readings at the center and was planning a large exhibit of Greenwich Village memorabilia. "I don't have cash but I do owe less than I ever did so I don't feel people breathing down my neck as I used to," he reported to a friend. "The new store is doing less business than the old, but it is building up slowly. I am more human here."[56]

Cavalier, having positioned itself as the voice of the revival, published its folk popularity poll in November. Peter, Paul and Mary reigned as most popular group, edging out Ian and Sylvia, with Baez and Dylan topping the lists of male and female performers; Dylan also won for best single ("Subterranean Homesick Blues") and best album (*Bringing It All Back Home*). *Life*, adding its own imprimatur, dated folk rock from "when Bob Dylan, a prolific folk singer with a Cause, in fact a number of Causes relating to the harsh ways of the world, tacked the rampaging rock 'n' roll tempo to one of his sermons of lament." Seemingly antiestablishment, folk rockers were not against making money, both *Life* and a lengthy profile of Dylan in the *New York Herald Tribune* explained. "Dylan, and his managers, get royalties on everything that is sold, of course," the paper commented. "He gets a performer's fee on each of his own discs, and he gets a composer's fee on everything else. It is estimated that he will earn $1.5 million in the next 18 months from composer's royalties alone. . . . Pretty good for a guy whose first job in New York got him only $2 for an evening's work in a coffee house in Greenwich Village."[57]

On the other hand, the pundit Russell Baker thought one "of the more alarming social phenomena of the past year has been the commercial success of the misnamed 'protest song,' a pop religious musical form aimed chiefly at the youth market." He could not understand anyone being troubled by the rather shallow songs, particularly "Eve of Destruction." "When the young start swinging to laments about not getting no satisfaction and society's mindless pursuit of color TV and democracy's sellout by the school board, they have moved into premature adulthood. This is unhealthy. . . . The modern world is impossible enough as it is without having to cope with millions of kids who are convinced that destruction can be averted if the Chinese will switch to love and dad will turn off the color TV."[58]

1966 and More of the Same

As folk rock merged into full-blown rock, more traditional folk, including blues, bluegrass, hillbilly, ethnic, and other forms of vernacular musical expression continued to attract audiences. Sing Out! entered the new year poised for expansion. "Today SING OUT!, once the hip-pocket companion of a few hundred guitar-pickers, has become a national magazine of influence with more than 25,000 regular readers," Irwin Silber boasted in the January issue, the last in the old format. The new, expanded version, he said, "will enable us to give you more songs, more articles, more news about folk music activities—and better coverage of the field." Starting with great optimism, and certainly more visibility, the experiment would be most controversial and last two years. Sing Out! continued to have some dissenters. John Cohen reported to Archie Green, "After several years of hassles with Irwin Silber about some of his editorial positions, and some deep concern on my part about the resignation of Paul Nelson from Sing Out, I had something of a showdown with Moe & Irwin." He desired a column on traditional music, by himself, Green, or perhaps Ed Kahn, with no interference from Silber. "Some schnook at Sing Out complained that Sing Out should cut out all political aspects, because folk songs aren't connected with politics. In my mind, I could see another dreary explanation from Irwin, but would much rather see a stimulating statement from you based on your scholarly wrestling with both tradition and contemporary problems." The column never appeared.[59]

The colorful, large-format Sing Out! debuted with the February/March fifteenth anniversary issue, including a miniature LP containing eleven songs, ranging from Phil Ochs to Frank Proffitt to the Old Harp Singers. Seeger challenged the readers to get involved, writing letters, songs, even articles. "For many years we have been a cozy little group all to ourselves, congratulating ourselves on our exclusiveness," he candidly admitted. "Now we are daring the dangers of the marketplace. We are daring to grow ten times as big as we ever were." Concerns about too much commercialism dominated much of the issue, including a lengthy section titled "Folk Songs & the Top 40," with over two dozen critical comments by a range of professional voices. Just how far things had gone toward market economics was illustrated in a full-page ad for Hagstrom Go-Go electric guitars, "the Free Ridin' Beat of Folk-Rock." Still, the issue included articles on Jesse Fuller, Frank Proffitt, John's Island, South Carolina, and "Folk Songs of Faith."[60]

The new year witnessed a rapid escalation of the Vietnam war. Stokely Carmichael became chairman of SNCC and launched black power, driving whites out of influential roles and splitting the civil rights movement. A few months later Huey Newton and Bobby Seale formed the Black Panther party in Oakland, and soon resorted to using guns to protect the local citizens from the police. *Time* named "youth" (those under twenty-five) as their "Man of the Year," for "that generation looms larger than all the exponential promises of science or technology: it will soon be the majority in charge. . . . For better or for worse, the world today is committed to accelerating change: radical, wrenching, erosive of both traditions and old values." Still, Barry Sadler's prowar single "Ballad of the Green Berets" was one of the year's top sellers (as was his album *Ballads of the Green Berets*).[61]

Folk music had slid off the magazine covers and front pages, but folk rock continued to generate enthusiasm. Robert Shelton found himself a convert; he wrote in the *New York Times*: "But from this corner the new music can generally earn praise as a healthy movement. No one says that every folk and topical performer need add a beat, long hair and outlandish clothes to his act." In passing Shelton took a swipe at *Sing Out!* for continuing to pan folk rock. Silber shot back that folk rock was bland and derivative, a muted version of the music of Chuck Berry, Willie Dixon, Muddy Waters, and Sonny Boy Williamson. "Its superficial electronic frenzy cannot cover up its fundamental noninvolvement with life."[62]

In response, Shelton scolded the "conservative wing of the folk Establishment" that was "becoming aware of its loss of influence on and communication with a new generation of folk listeners. These listeners are playing truant from the authoritarian folk school and finding equal mental-musical-emotional excitement in the post-Beatles resurgence of rhythm-and-blues, white, Negro and integrated." Paul Nelson took Shelton's side and lambasted Silber: "Where other men dream of gods and devils, Mr. Silber's nightmares are always in capital letters. Cash Registers, Success Syndromes, Machine, and Systems haunt him and keep his mind from contemplating Mankind and its Problems. . . . Such cheap and calculating emotional tabloidism would make even the most primitive of the muckrackers [sic] blush."[63]

Izzy Young entered the fray with an impassioned letter to the *Times* denouncing Shelton, who "will not treat of something unless it has the word 'folk' in front of it. That is a technique to win favor with the powers that be in NYC so that Mr. Shelton can continue to write liner notes, program notes (un[d]er such interesting names as Stacey Williams and Dan Auerbach). It is a method of not dealing with Negro music. Now that they call it 'folk rock' the Negro is easily separated from rock and roll and Mr. Shelton can write paeans to all the white imitators and ignore every Negro group." He sent copies of the correspondence to Reuss, Seeger, and numerous others, receiving various reactions, including Grossman's counsel to be less emotional. Shelton immediately called and threatened to sue. "Said he could lose his job," according to Izzy's notes. "Said that he told me pseudonym as a confidence. Did not bring up second name I uncovered—Dan Auerbach. Said I was inaccurate, obviously hysterical."[64]

Nervous over the threatened suit, Izzy solicited support and advice. When he mentioned to Moe Asch that he "felt bad that Shelton was the victim he [Moe] said that it was bad to think that way. . . . Moe said that it was terrible to have a man [Shelton] bastardizing a field and making of it a ground for himself and no one else." Further emboldened, Izzy sent copies of his correspondence to various papers. Shelton distributed his own nasty letter ("NOT FOR PUBLICATION"), deciding not to sue but rather pledging $100 "to start a fund to ensure a rest for Mr. Young from the burdensome responsibilities of running the Folklore Center and to get him the psychiatric care he apparently needs. One does not need to be a trained diagnostician to discern in Mr. Young's letter symptoms of hysteria, paranoia and megalomania." The lengthy letter proceeded to detail Shelton's position, his many positive reviews of black musicians, his criticisms of prominent white performers, and his standing as a professional journalist. "Now, since he finds my criticism of a low-level, unprincipled, dishonest and personally biased nature, Mr. Young, the George Bernard Shaw of the puberty set, attempts a rejoinder to my piece in praise of some, but not all, folk-rock." As for Izzy's indication "that my work for The Times displays a 'slovenly cravenness' and suggests an investigation. I am fully prepared to face such an investigation if the bleatings of an over-emotional shop-keeper can undo eight years of dedicated service to this field."[65]

Shelton finally got to the heart of the issue: "Mr. Young and the editors of Sing Out! magazine do not seem to be aware of the crisis in leadership that exists in folk music. Now, tastes are fragmented, and the searing voices of jealousy, frustration, sour grapes, petty rivalry, are replacing the harmonious voices. . . . The anti-folk-rock voices have lost their sense of reason. They are howling in the night, and howling is not persuasive." While lamenting the shattered folk establishment, Shelton did little to heal the wounds, which would continue to fester. As the revival shriveled commercially, the stakes seemed to escalate. Shelton had tried to capture the field with the ill-fated Hootenanny magazine, then turned to Cavalier, with somewhat better results, but not what he had hoped; there was no real national competition for Sing Out!, which rankled. Shelton would continue to rehash the great debate, getting the final word in his 1986 biography of Dylan: "I had accused Sing Out! of disturbing narrow-mindedness and opposition to an avant-garde. . . . Silber riposted testily, and my editors offered fees to Nat Hentoff and Paul Nelson . . . to enter the debate. . . . Silber was on the run."[66]

Izzy Young's concerns went beyond his quarrel with Shelton. He continued to lament the takeover by crass commercialism. Everyone was making a buck, except the lowly folk singers. "I assure you that these people [the club owners, such as Art D'Lugoff of the Village Gate] are as much friends with rock and roll, the new youth, as they were with folkmusic," he wrote to The Broadside. "And as for you folk singers in Boston that want to come to Greenwich Village to be exploited and allowed to practice in front of hippies and bearcats come prepared. You won't get a job without electricity. The 'New Youth' has to have a thousand dollars worth of equipment today to be exploited." He missed the good old days, when a semblance of equality reigned in the Village, when an acoustic guitar sufficed to hold an audience, and when the clubs and coffee-houses were accessible to all.[67]

Paul Krassner moderated the next round, a discussion among Silber, Shelton, Murray the K, and Tom Paxton at the Village Vanguard. Cavalier cosponsored the meeting and published the proceedings. The panelists discussed the importance of song lyrics compared to the music, and the role of protest songs. Shelton, branding Silber "the Walter Lippman of the folkniks," criticized him for denouncing the mass media, mass culture, and the Hit Parade. "I have no interest in putting down anybody who is trying to make a genuine expression— a genuine protest," Silber countered, with the emphasis on "genuine." Something of a tempest in a teapot, the discussion underscored the notion that popular music could be taken seriously. But even Shelton championed message music, if it reached the masses.[68]

The three-day Boston Winterfest (aka Boston Folk Festival) in March typified the current nature of the revival. Headliners included Doc Watson, the New Lost City Ramblers, the Stanley Brothers, Son House, the Chambers Brothers, the Muddy Waters Blues Band, Tom Paxton, Phil Ochs, Roscoe Holcomb, and Richard and Mimi Fariña. But concertgoers were in for a surprise treat. Ralph Earle reported in the Boston Broadside that on Saturday night to "the cadence of muffled boohs, in marched STAFF SERGEANT BARRY SADLER!!! (and chorus). They kindled patriotic fervor first with 'Bamiba,' a mournful lament about a G.I. who was 'in the Pleiku Jail' because he had been 'caught on the Ho Chi Trail.' . . . Next, we heard a pseudo-calypso ballad with Vietnamese lyrics and a dramatic recitative, then an uproarious ditty about the modern-day 'gold-bricker' or 'Garret trooper,' I think he was called. By now, what else could cap the surge of emotions swelling in our breasts but 'The Ballad of the Green Berets'?" The appalled Earle could only conclude that Sadler's last minute appearance "seemed to be an attempt to represent the hawks versus the doves (Tom Paxton and Phil Ochs?). It's too bad there weren't a few more owls among those making the decisions."[69]

The West Coast

The Bay Area music scene was undergoing a seismic shift, led by the combination of LSD and rock music. Emerging from 1950s rock and roll and early 1960s folk, then scorched by the Beatles-led English invasion, musicians were abandoning folk rock. Neither mellow nor openly political, bands such as the Grateful Dead, the Jefferson Airplane, and Big Brother and the Holding Company readily connected with the tremors of youthful rebellion. Large rock concerts at the Fillmore and Avalon ballrooms attracted swelling crowds of stoned, painted, feather-bedecked young people.[70]

Troubled by the rather low attendance and financial problems of the 1965 Berkeley Folk Festival, organizer Barry Olivier vowed to modernize the lineup by adding rock. "I knew a lot of people who were starting to do it," he recalled, including Jorma Kaukonen and Paul Kantner, members of the Jefferson Airplane. "I went over to talk to those guys and had a big talk with them one afternoon and wanted to get them in the festival, and they went for it." Though the band had already signed a record contract with RCA for an astounding $20,000 advance, "they'd all looked at the festival and Pete Seeger and stuff like that as like Mecca." Barry also snagged another new electric group, Country Joe and the Fish. They appeared alongside Pete and Charles Seeger, Phil Ochs, Sam Hinton, Malvina Reynolds, Los Halcones de Salitrillos from Mexico City, the Greenbriar Boys, Robert Pete Williams, Rabbi Shlomo Carlebach, and Bess Lomax Hawes. Panels and workshops covered string-band music, topical songs, traditional fiddle styles, and contemporary rock. A "Dance Happening" featured the Jefferson Airplane and the Greenbriar Boys.[71]

The Airplane had already appeared on campus in April with the Butterfield Blues Band at the Berkeley Blues Festival. That same month the generally mainstream fifth annual San Francisco State College folk festival featured Mark Spoelstra, Guy Carawan, Doc Watson, Richard and Mimi Fariña, and Malvina Reynolds. Since every festival now needed an electric band, the New York–based Blues Project band also appeared. Faith Petric, editor of the local *folknik* newsletter, extolled the entire festival, but was taken off guard by the clamorous Blues Project. "If they speak a musical idiom foreign to me, that is my problem and loss," she frankly admitted.[72]

The Berkeley festival reviews were mostly positive. "The Berkeley Folk Festival's adventuresome experiment in bringing a modern, electronic band to its audience was a success," Ralph Gleason announced. "The Jefferson Airplane's appearance was greeted enthusiastically." Gleason also applauded the "idea of bringing in representatives of cultures other than the dominant American one." Bill Haigwood in the *Berkeley Daily Gazette* noted the "clusters of strumming, beating, whistling hippies, folkies and interested bystanders [who] arranged themselves across the steps, buildings and lawns of" the university. Olivier "showed he wasn't behind the musical times bringing to the concert rock and roll as well as electronic amplification in the form of the Jefferson Airplane, for the first time." A couple of weeks later, Gleason clarified the significance of the new music: "One of the aspects of contemporary music which links it to folk music in my opinion is the increasing tendency to write songs about personal experiences and as an expression of a personal outlook on life, just as the blues singers did for years. In any case, the leap of the Berkeley Folk Festival into the modern electronic world (the first folk festival to do so, I believe) was not only historic but successful."[73]

Joe McDonald had moved to Berkeley in May 1965 "to join the beatniks and play guitar and be a folk singer," but he discovered "hippies, of course, and the beginning of the psychedelic scene." Having already published *Et Tu* in Los Angeles, he started the expansive *Rag Baby* in September, coedited by Ed Denson and Mike Beardslee, covering the local folk scene. Focused on traditional music, with a long piece on the bluesman Fred McDowell, the first issue also included McDonald's "I-Feel-Like-I'm-Fixin'-to-Die Rag," performed at an antiwar rally in October and soon to become well-known and controversial. McDonald met Barry Melton at the Berkeley Folk Festival, and they soon got together with Arhoolie Records owner Chris Strachwitz to record the rag and three other antiwar songs for an EP, issued as *Rag Baby*'s fourth number, the first of three recorded magazines. They first sounded like a jug band, with McDonald on acoustic guitar, but soon they switched to electric. Thus was born Country Joe and the Fish. With complicated views of radical protest, stemming from his parents' Left politics, McDonald represented more cultural than traditional political dissent, if a distinction can be made.[74]

Others followed the trajectory from folk to rock, often acknowledging and incorporating their roots. Janis Joplin was a renegade from the Austin folk scene, for example, while Jerry Garcia, a proficient banjo and guitar player, was steeped in folk, gospel, bluegrass, and hillbilly music. Garcia "catapult[ed] a band that started out as folkies into new, danceable rhythms." Beginning as the Warlocks, they became the Grateful Dead in late 1965. "Their approach . . . is different from most other groups in that they are navigating these genres in search of a hybrid of folk and rock that is not, however, folk-rock," Rock Scully, the band's manager, later explained. "Jerry's genius at this point is in finding a way to incorporate his past into the new configuration of the band by applying a psychedelic rock momentum to jug-band music and country blues."[75]

While acid rock ruled the roost in the Bay Area, to the south a somewhat different scene began unfolding. Ed Pearl remembers that " '65 really was a watershed of where music was going in ten different directions, and society was being questioned in ten different directions. And at the Ash Grove it was very interesting because it was almost split down the middle, honest to God, between people who became very hippy and people who became very politi-

cal." The club continued to book the more traditional and mainstream performers through 1966: Mark Spoelstra, the Kentucky Colonels, Bill Monroe,
Sonny Terry and Brownie McGhee, Skip James, and Sir Lancelot, the legendary
calypso singer. Pearl also initiated the Free University of California, with a
variety of "academic" classes supplementing the club's school of traditional
music. Nearby, on the Sunset Strip, Love, the Byrds, the Lovin' Spoonful, Marvin
Gaye, the quasi-acid-rock Kaleidoscope, and the developing Buffalo Springfield
held sway. Steve Stills and Richie Furay had recently been part of the Village
folk scene, then moved to Los Angeles and, together with the Canadian folkies
Neil Young and Bruce Palmer, formed Buffalo Springfield. The local scene, quite
alienated from its northern counterpart, was becoming frenetic. The changing
lineup at Doug Weston's Troubadour captured the gyrating situation. Having
begun as a mainstream folk club in the late 1950s and become the home of
performers such as David Crosby, Gene Clark, Linda Ronstadt, and Jackson
Browne by the mid-sixties, it was soon on its way as the center of L.A. rock.[76]

The Mamas and the Papas, recently arrived in Los Angeles from New York,
dominated the charts by May 1966, a surprise and delight to John Phillips,
who had made the smooth transition from folk, as had Denny Doherty, formerly of the Halifax Three, and Cass Elliot, recently with the Big Three and the
Mugwumps (Michelle Phillips was too young to have had a folk past). When
they first appeared at the Hollywood Bowl, opening for Sonny and Cher, the
crowd went wild. "Our music was far from political or antiwar," John has
remarked, "but America's freaks and 'heads' in their faded, ragged jeans, sandals, beads, long hair, and hippie headbands had embraced us and discovered
Cass as the ultimate Earth Mother for rock's new counterculture."[77]

Running parallel with rock and drugs in Southern California was the ongoing
cultivation of a traditional folk style. Taj Mahal, a member of the Rising Sons
with Ry Cooder, had won one of the categories at the Fifth Annual Topanga
Banjo and Fiddle Contest in 1965, along with Dick Greene of the Greenbriar
Boys and Scotty Stoneman of the Stoneman family and lately of the Kentucky
Colonels. It was hardly an amateur event, but judge Frank Hamilton nonetheless
saw it as "an oasis of good taste in musicianship in a field filled with hyper-
technicans and tyros." Hamilton returned the next year, joined by Sam Hinton,
with Bess Hawes as emcee. The Song-Makers continued to hold concerts
throughout the area and encourage song writing.[78]

The UCLA Folk Festival continued to attract crowds in 1965, cultivating
respect for traditional music, with the Blue Sky Boys, Moving Star Hall Singers,
Jimmy Driftwood, and Glenn Ohrlin. Revenues fell $2,000 short of costs, how-
ever, and the deficit was contributed by the Newport Foundation. Festival director D. K. Wilgus defended the festival's format, for "the best way to understand traditional art is through the traditional performers themselves"; but
pressure mounted from the students to invite Dylan or another exponent of the

new, popular sound. "We must first consider that the UCLA Folk Festival, unlike festivals at Berkeley and the University of Chicago, is produced by the University and cannot therefore simply represent student tastes, enthusiasm, or crusades," he explained to a campus administrator in the fall. "In one way or another the 'folk-rock' show would override, if not destroy, the traditional aspects of the festival." Besides, Dylan, the Byrds, the Rolling Stones, or Sonny and Cher were filling the Hollywood Bowl. "One function of the festival is to present performances not easily available elsewhere."[79]

Wilgus considered combining the 1966 festival with a student-instigated "Sound of the Sixties" show, then decided to pull out altogether. "The history of the UCLA Folk Festival has been a struggle to present traditional performers in an atmosphere consonant with the value of their art and their dignity as human beings," he explained. "I cannot return to the conditions under which traditional art and artists are given at best the crumbs of the feast, and at worst are humiliated and degraded by cult adulation and crass commercialism." He insisted that when the students presented "Sounds of the Sixties" "that the terms *folksong, folk music, folksinger* not be used to characterize the non-folk performers and performances in this program." Though abandoning the festival, Wilgus and his folklore colleagues—Ed Kahn, Gene Earle, Archie Green, Norm Cohen, and Ken Griffis—continued to oversee the John Edwards Memorial Foundation and its newsletter, vital links to the world of traditional music preservation and scholarship. Over the next few years a special series of monographs, a record reissue project, a reprint series, and the hefty *JEMF Quarterly* were launched. Wilgus also edited the ground-breaking "Hillbilly Issue" of the *Journal of American Folklore* in 1965, setting a high standard for this new scholarship.[80]

Newport

If the UCLA festival fell victim to the shifting winds of popular tastes, in Newport it was business as usual in July, albeit without the fireworks of the previous two years. Directors Oscar Brand, Judy Collins, Julius Lester, Alan Lomax, Ralph Rinzler, Mike Seeger, and Peter Yarrow produced a hefty booklet and lineup of two hundred musicians. About 65,000 souls sat through four days of concert, contests, and workshops; a record-setting eighteen thousand attended one concert, with another six thousand turned away. No longer top-heavy with the "stars," Newport filled the stages with a variety of roots musicians. The bluesmen Son House, Howlin' Wolf, Skip James, and Bukka White, the gospel groups the Dixie Hummingbirds and the Swan Silvertones, the topical songsters Rosalie Sorrels and Buffy Sainte-Marie, and the bluegrass musicians Flatt and Scruggs along with Jim and Jesse McReynolds joined Bob Gibson, Eric Andersen, Joseph Spence, and the first (and almost only) black Grand Ole Opry star, Deford Bailey. Judy Collins, Phil Ochs, Carolyn Hester, Pete Seeger, the Lovin' Spoonful, and Tom Paxton were also slated.

With folk music relegated to the back pages of the daily press, if noticed at all, there was little coverage of the festival. "Although some board members of the musician-run festival were pleased that the event was getting smaller, the winds of discontent were blowing strongly over the dusty Festival Field," Robert Shelton wrote in his *Times* piece. There were few electric groups, among them the Lovin' Spoonful, "a bizarre op-art rock quartet that scored a spiritual triumph for modernity in folk music." A late-night incident at the Student Non-Violent Coordinating Committee (SNCC) booth disturbed many, when a group of uniformed guards attacked and ejected a dozen members of the organization. Shelton concluded: "The ambitious and diffuse festival had many high points and frequent plateaus, but the low points were prevalent. Clearly, what is needed was a stronger hand at the tiller—in philosophy, production and staging." The lack of musical fireworks seemed to dim his enthusiasm.[81]

In a lengthy piece in the September *Sing Out!* the folklorist Bruce Jackson covered the festival's history since 1962, focusing on the functioning of the Foundation (along with an accounting of finances for 1963–65), and ladling out advice to the directors about future concerts and workshops. "The idea is to bring together the best and most representative of each school, not to say which school or form is best, to bring them together and offer them all a receptive home," he suggested. He followed up in the next issue with an overview of the 1966 festival. He preferred the Sunday evening finale, with Seeger singing his antiwar song "Bring Them Home," which "made Friday and Saturday nights seem even more grotesque than they were." On Saturday night the performers were rushed and the script by Alan Lomax, read by Tom Clancy, Jackson denounced as "international dreck"; "1966 substituted bad taste and lack of consideration for the chaos of 1965 and 1964." Still, he concluded that some performers saved the weekend, particularly Fannie Lou Hamer, "ending it all with a feeling that was both honest and appropriate." Irwin Silber also took a swipe at the heavy-handed staging, and recapped the assault on SNCC: "Half a dozen SNCC leaders, including 'black power' advocate Stokely Carmichael, came to Newport for a weekend of fun and were treated to some 'blue power' games by out-of-town special cops who got all up tight with the new black man who takes crap from no one."[82]

Broadside added more of a political slant in reviewing the dismal weekend: "How can there be a time of rejoicing anywhere in this land while the forces of fascism, fattening on the escalating Viet Nam war and the resistance to Negro rights at home, grow more menacing by the day. The mood at Newport only reflected the dark clouds gathering over every American."[83]

Sing Out!

The dispute between Irwin Silber, Robert Shelton, and Izzy Young, partly a struggle over aesthetics, also reflected a broader social and political confusion.

Despite his appetite for commercial success, Silber's nagging radical conscience had propelled him to create a new, more belligerent Sing Out! "Where does the proper area for a folk music magazine begin—and where does it end?" the editor queried in the November issue. "Some readers think we overstep our bounds when we report on the happenings of the Beatles, Bob Dylan, Chuck Berry and other artists in that generally murky area known as rock-and-roll or folk-rock. Others think that topical-political songs have no place in a folk music magazine." Whatever the case, he now announced the breaking of a new barrier—an article that had no direct connection to folk music however defined. Julius Lester, one of the magazine's associate editors, published "The Angry Children of Malcolm X," an impassioned analysis of recent transformations in the southern freedom movement. "We believe that Julius Lester's article which reflects the new mood of this movement is one of the most provocative and revealing pieces we have ever read," Silber explained. "It will tell you more about the music of the black man in America today than a desk drawer full of learned analyses of the sound of the blues, jazz, R&B, rock, or whatever." In the same issue Silber published his own "La Huelga! Songs of the Delano Grape Strike."[84]

"The world was moving fast in 1966," Lester wrote a few years later. "In Afroamerica there was no time for flowers. Flowers were for cemeteries and cemeteries were where you went any time a white cop decided that was where you should be. The civil rights movement had pushed white youth into their initial confrontations with the society. Black Power and the urban rebellions pushed them further. Where whites were concerned about defining their lives, blacks were, too. So they went to war." In the 1966 piece he declared that the black man will live "within the framework of his own blackness and his blackness links him with the Indians of Peru, the miner in Bolivia, the African and the freedom fighters of Vietnam. What they fight for is what the American black man fights for—the right to govern his own life."[85]

In early October, Silber announced that Moe Asch has sold his 45 percent (of the total of one hundred shares) of Sing Out! stock to the editor, who in turn proposed selling the shares to members of the editorial advisory board, creating a cooperative. Silber would retain his current forty-five shares, Seeger had ten shares, and Ethel Raim and Ed Badeaux desired ten each, leaving twenty-five to be divided among the rest. With power no longer concentrated in the Silber-Asch partnership, the reality for the last decade, there would certainly be a greater semblance of corporate democracy; Silber would also have a chance to pull out, if necessary. It would take a few months before an arrangement was worked out, dividing power and responsibilities—without, however, solving the escalating complications and frictions, or the money problems.

The Year Finally Ends

Robert Shelton struggled to capture the year's achievements, without reaching much of a conclusion. "Folk music was no longer booming, it had become a standard part of the popular-music diet of America as well as overseas," though with shrinking crowds. But how to define folk music, now undergoing much experimentation? "The Byrds, The Velvet Underground, The Fugs, The Mothers of Invention were breaking out of all bounds and heading toward a totally new avant-garde sound. Some described it as electronic pop music, others saw it as acid-Buddhist music, and others, including this commentator, ran out of catch-phrases for such complex new musics. What was clearly emerging in this furthest-out manifestation of the folk scene was an almost tenuous link to any past tradition. Soon, this music would, at its present pace, be out of the folk fold completely." He repeated his critique of Newport while praising the New York Folk Festival, then couldn't avoid taking a swipe at his former friends: "Irwin Silber and Izzy Young have turned *Sing Out!* magazine into a vehicle for kicking the inert body of the defunct New York Folk Festival. The entire sour-apple tone of *Sing Out!* has been increasingly irking the more thoughtful people in the field." He lamented the shocking death in a motorcycle accident of Richard Fariña on April 30, the day his book *Been Down So Long It Looks Like Up to Me* was published.[86]

Shelton's concluding peroration was a call to arms, a further challenge to Silber and his crowd: "We are with those who are still saying yes to the longevity of folk music in its infinite variety, whether political or not, whether modern or traditional. . . . Those who will affirm, not destroy, the value of any popular art that has become emblematic of a generation are those for whom *Cavalier* will speak and to whom we will continue to speak." The publication of *The Face of Folk Music* two years later, featuring Shelton's text along with Dave Gahr's lush photographs, would underscore his eclectic approach and, he hoped, set his mark on the revival.[87]

Izzy Young prided himself on keeping up with musical and cultural trends, despite Shelton's labeling him as one of the mossbacks. Because he now merged the Folklore Center with Marc Silber's Fretted Instruments, Paul Williams arranged to move *Crawdaddy's* editorial office into Silber's former adjoining space. "He's a real burrower and hard worker," Izzy privately commented about Williams. "I welcome the opportunity to be next to what is happening in the music industry." And he publicly boasted, "I will be apprised of new cultural change weeks before the newstand [sic] readers and that's heartening. CD is to be the magazine of rock and roll." *Crawdaddy* was already making its mark; for example, several of its writers were ejected from the Café Au Go Go because of Jon Landau's negative review of the Blues Project, the club's house band. Landau, a college sophomore, represented the new brand of rock journalists,

decades younger but certainly of interest to Izzy. Running a blues evening at
the Café Au Go Go in early September, with Eric Andersen, Tom Rush, and
Dave Blue, Izzy thought the music paled in comparison to that of black performers. During the concert Artie Gorson, a prominent manager, remarked to
Izzy that "White Blues" was "the music of the Sixties." When Izzy suggested
that the drummer for the Muddy Waters Blues Band was much better than the
white drummer then playing, "he replied, 'if a Negro is good then the white
audience will listen to him' . . . It took me an hour to figure out the horror of
his last statement," Izzy later wrote in his notebook. "The white audience is
the judge of all things in America. And he thought he was being 'liberal' in
saying it."[88]

Izzy was not shy about giving advice to any and all, including Maynard
Solomon, august owner of Vanguard Records—"Recordings for the Connois-
seur." (Country Joe McDonald later suggested to Solomon that this phrase didn't
seem quite appropriate for a Country Joe and the Fish rock album.) "I said that
I felt bad to see him record a group he didn't know personally such as "LOVE"
on the Elektra label," Izzy recorded in his diary. "He said 'I think you're confusing someone else's work with our own, Izzy.' 'No, no, you have a group
like them.' 'Not Ian & Sylvia.' 'No.' 'Oh, you must mean THE VAGRANTS.' 'That's
it,' I said. 'You've never met them, you'll never have them in your house,
you'll never want to have anything to do with them and that's why I feel bad
about the new trend, for one thing." Then Izzy admitted he was listening to
the Beach Boys, and Solomon countered, "They're professional. They're not
folk singers, they don't believe in what they're doing. Izzy, please.' And he
spoke correctly and I said that I would not allow myself to be stampeded into
touting them as Shelton does and others." Definitions now had hardly any
meaning; purity had flown out the window; commercialism prevailed. Sam
Charters, a producer for Vanguard, informed Izzy he was going to San Francisco, " 'It's all there, Izzy, now,' and I got the sinking notion that to make
money in any field you have to be there the minute it happens, nip it financially,
crush it with mass promotion and onto the next important source of civilization."[89]

Elektra and Vanguard, fierce competitors, had just about cornered the folk
market. In 1963, Elektra had even launched a classical and ethnic label, None-
such, countering Vanguard's baroque recordings. Meanwhile Jac Holzman and
Maynard Solomon remained close friends. "I very quickly moved more toward
rock and roll, signing the Paul Butterfield Band," Holzman recalled. "And that
led to frequent trips to California, where Vanguard was not functioning. And
I found Love and the Doors, and . . . the competitive advantage swung my way,
in my direction at that point. I mean Vanguard was never able to keep up. We
had the horsepower at that point, and I must say we used it." Holzman established an L.A. office in 1962, well positioned across from the Troubadour and

poised to almost rival the major labels; three years he later announced Elektra was branching out into "r&b, country, pop and blues . . . not so much prompted by a desire to cover all musical categories as specialized markets, but as a recognition that musical categories now have little meaning." But the scene finally soured. "If I have an overriding, contrasting memory of dealing within the folk music world and dealing with the rock and roll world, the former was civilized people who truly care about the music," he later said. "The role of the record company was understood. We were midwives to the artistic endeavor. . . . We were not financing and distribution organizations only. And I left the record business when that's what the business became." He sold Elektra to Warner Bros. in 1970, after he had made his West Coast presence felt with the first Doors album, released in early 1967.[90]

Confusion seemed pervasive, and the scramble for success, if not security, escalated. "There was an awful lot of money kicking around in 1965," Dave Van Ronk later recalled. "My God, it was the Big Rock Candy Mountain. There was incredible prosperity for all of us. . . . We had five or six real fat years. Some people bought houses in the country, some people built recording studios, some people acquired expensive drug habits. And all of it was taken for granted. . . . By 1969 the cold snap had set in." Van Ronk remained in Greenwich Village. "I think there was more talent around the Village after Dylan," the anarchist believed, "but there was more hokey shit around, too. Money always attracts talented people; money also attracts greed."[91]

Such a confusing situation called for some sort of response, but who knew what it should be, other than reaching out to grab the brass ring as it flew past? Jim Rooney of Club 47 in Cambridge recalled, "By sometime in the fall of 1966 I started to become aware of what was going on in San Francisco and New York. "My friends Charlie Roth[s]child and Peter Edminston had opened up a place in New York on St. Mark's Place called the Balloon Farm. It was the first psychedelic dance hall in New York." Rothschild, formerly associated with Albert Grossman, also moved into management. As Izzy reported in Sing Out!, "The people who run folkmusic are just beginning to latch onto other scenes. The latest example is Charlie Roth[s]child, who now manages Andy Warhol's pop art groups, The Velvet Underground & The Plastic Inevitables, along with the Fugs." Rothschild had aspirations of opening another club in Boston, but a corporate lawyer from Kansas, Ray Riepen, opened the Boston Tea Party in 1967, the area's first hippie hangout. He checked with Rooney at Club 47, however, to learn about running a night spot. Folk clubs still had some utility.[92]

"With the advent of folk-rock, which blends urban 'folk' and pop idioms, we have the epitome of subjectivization of the urban folk movement," wrote Ellen Stekert. "Today 'folksong' to most young urban people is almost completely equated to personal protest song and with pop professional entertainment. Folksong to the scholar is a matter of oral tradition, change, and generally non-professional transmission. We are in a humpty-dumpty age of ambivalent and misapplied words and although it is not our province to dictate usage, at the very least we can clarify what is happening." A cry for serious scholarly appreciation and understanding of the revival, Stekert's essay also made distinctions between authentic and derivative, serious and shallow, homespun and slickly commercial folk music.[93]

As 1966 faded into 1967, the revival, having clearly peaked and now on the slide, demonstrated the fragile, continuing interaction between commercial thrust and political commitment. But who could tell the difference? Rock had captured, with a vengeance, the imagination and pocketbooks of the young and it continued to incorporate various folk performers and styles, influenced by Dylan's personal lyrics and the Rolling Stones' blues-inflected instrumental techniques. "The Beatles shut us down," Ian Tyson (of Ian and Sylvia) recalled, with some exaggeration. "It was over. OVER. We didn't know how to play with electric instruments. . . . All us folkies were just standing there with egg on our faces. The only one who had the guts to challenge the rock 'n' roll guys on their own terms was Dylan. He just jumped in."[94]

For the last two years Newport had served to punctuate the folk scene, actually and symbolically, yet the action in this summer resort was part of the waves of change sweeping over the country. There were slight local variations, in Los Angeles, Berkeley, Cambridge, Chicago, and elsewhere. But the patterns were clear. As rock swept the commercial scene, roots performers, black and white, continued to surprise and please audiences throughout the country, countering the electronic sounds. Mostly old, they would be fading from the scene within the next few years, though followed by much younger musicians eager to learn their traditional styles and repertoire. The urban bluesmen proved most popular among younger audiences, either in themselves or in the guise of their acolytes, mostly white, carrying on the tradition with some success. This lively folk scene would continue through the remainder of the decade, mixing commercial sounds with musical commitments, as the country plunged into cultural chaos and heightened political activism, fueled by the war in Vietnam.

9
The 1960s End
(But Not Folk Music)

"Long talk with Pete Siegel yesterday," Izzy Young recorded in his notebook in early January 1967. "How work at Elektra has changed in the year and a half that he's there—now when he auditions tapes he doesn't listen for good or bad, only if the sound could make a hit, of the blowing your mind category. Jac Holzman feels that he will have his first top ten single hit with THE DOORS and they'll know if its [sic] so in a week or so—otherwise back to the drawing board again." Holzman's Elektra had pioneered modern folk recordings in the early 1950s, but now electric music, the louder the better, seemed the commercial way to go, though the label retained a strong folk lineup. The Doors, their first album, did strike it rich, reaching number two on the charts by midyear.[1]

Izzy viewed the passing music parade with a combination of detachment, aesthetic criticism, political scrutiny, and occasional mental blocks. "I did not write my regular column for the last issue of Sing Out! because I did not want to be stampeded by everything new—as if, for example, I had to treat of the Beach Boys as folk music because they write songs of today. I admitted to myself that I couldn't do an honest column so I didn't write it with the attendant loss in business for I hid out from Sing Out! and I didn't buy any Oak Publications for the same reason. So, if that happens again and I can not write I shall say so openly quickly so I don't have to disappear." Surprisingly, he would soon be one of Sing Out!'s owners, with heightened obligations.[2]

"Though the bloom has long since left the rose, what is loosely termed 'folk music' is still a potent force on college campuses, and for the handful of artists who came to dominate their field, business is better than ever," wrote Kristin White in Billboard Music On Campus. "Meanwhile, younger artists who a couple of years ago might have essayed the coffeehouse route are instead organizing rock groups and storming the bastions of pop music, as groups like the Blues Project, the Youngbloods, the Jefferson Airplane, and the Mothers of Invention have done. Thus the new blood which might otherwise replenish the lower ranks of folk music is flowing in other directions." Some movement stalwarts and older vernacular musicians still performed, although John Hurt had died in early November 1966, the long-suffering and silent Woody Guthrie just about a year later, and other old-timers continued to fade from the scene.[3]

For the remainder of the decade folk music would survive, scarred and battered, incorporating as well as influencing the broader music scene. All the while, the folk establishment in New York and throughout the country struggled to accommodate itself to changing conditions, with continuing frictions, particularly at Sing Out! Commercial and political forces were still closely intertwined, while academic scholarship attempted to understand the history and meaning of folk music, however construed—Child ballads, bluegrass, blues, old-timey/hillbilly, sea shanties, Cajun, gospel, Mexican, folk rock, cowboy, Native American, and so on. The country, meanwhile, plunged further into internal chaos and external warfare. Political, cultural, economic, generational, racial, and other conflicts escalated, creating confusion, fear, and widespread official retaliation.

Sing Out!

Sing Out!'s internal squabbling during 1966 was a prelude to a major eruption the following year. In early 1967 Silber gave a faint hint of a new structure; six months later readers received more details. "A new chapter in the 17-year history of Sing Out! begins with this issue," the editor announced in late summer. "We are now the joint property of the working editors and editorial advisory board members whose efforts go into the making of this magazine." Formal transfer of ownership on May 31 listed thirteen owners, including Silber, Pete Seeger, Paul Nelson, Barbara Dane, and Izzy Young. Harold Leventhal, Manny Greenhill, Judy Collins, and Lee Hays loaned money.[4]

In July, Silber, temporarily remaining as editor, proposed a number of changes, starting with dropping the subtitle, "The Folk Song Magazine," which he thought too narrow. Something more inclusive seemed appropriate, as the U.S. government had "become the fountainhead for the exploitation of people throughout the world, and the destroyer of their lives when they attempt to throw off our domination. . . . I believe that the time is coming when every American will have to choose his side. I believe that some of us who work in the arts and in the fields of communication have the opportunity at this moment in history to help Americans choose the side of opposition to this government, first of all, and ultimately to this system." Those who knew Silber's radical background were not surprised by his thoughts, but he had generally refrained since the late 1950s from using the magazine as a soapbox. "We must be concerned primarily . . . with the CONTENT AND SOCIAL PURPOSE of music, and most especially of song." The politically charged music he espoused included not only what could be labeled folk music, but also "the 'New Music' of the alienated and disenchanted youth of today." Old music, new music, foreign or domestic, whatever represented political struggles and elevated consciousness, should be included.[5]

The editorial board reacted mostly negatively, some calling for Silber's resignation; he seemed not only too pessimistic, but his editorial work had become sloppy. Michael Asch, Paul Nelson, and John Cohen, for instance, grumbled to Pete that "although Irwin, currently, pays lip service to the notion that many new areas of musical expression should be explored by Sing Out, he has unfortunately shown little ability to discern these elements in the past." Ed Badeaux, still managing editor and caught in the crossfire, refused to join what he perceived as a lynch mob. Who could replace Silber, he wondered, particularly in such a charged and emotional climate? He thought an editorial cooperative, as some suggested, would be "the kiss of death to Sing Out." There was much backbiting. "We spoke of Pete Seeger a lot," Izzy confided in his notebook, about a conversation with Julius Lester in mid-August, "and why he doesn't fight harder and his 17–18 year relationship with Irwin Silber and how lately Irwin has been setting us, as individuals, against Pete but not doing the dirty work himself. I said that I did Irwin's dirty work with Shelton . . . I'll continue my dirty work but others will have to do their own from now on."[6]

An editorial meeting in early September allowed for an exchange of views. "I feel very old," Pete confessed, "and [feel] like resigning from the whole shebang, partly for any kind of sectarianism has always wearied me. I and Lee Hays started a magazine—saw clearly that ruling powers were providing music for American people through NYC and Hollywood—keeping them from music that would lead to a better future. To bring out traditional and new [music] to wake up [the] American public . . . Because we saw [the] enemy so clearly we didn't argue so much. We knew we were small and weak." But things had drastically changed. We are "no longer small and weak, so we say let's concentrate on [the] guy beside me—not the big enemy. I can tell you that the ruling powers of America are just as restrictive as in 1946 about letting real traditional music be disseminated [sic] to make people proud of their heritage, from wherever. Nor are they interested in new music that can threaten our security."[7]

Seeger's high-toned plea for harmony in the face of government and corporate animosity did not immediately sweep the field, as the other board members continued their carping and calls for editorial changes. Julius Lester concluded that Sing Out! was now irrelevant, not keeping up with the musical and political times. "Only thing unpredictable in Sing Out is Izzy's column," he charged. The meeting ended with a surprising agreement that editorial policies and responsibilities would now be controlled by an editorial executive board, including Silber, Ed Badeaux, Ethel Raim, Paul Nelson, and Julius Lester. "Naturally, a change of this kind has great emotional overtones for me personally," Silber informed the magazine's readers. "I've sailed this ship through a lot of different weather . . . I've been midwife (and mother and father, too) to more than 100 different Sing Out! babies in the course of these 17 years. But the past belongs to the past. The times cry out for something new. New ideas, new people, new ways of looking at the world."[8]

For a while Silber remained part of the awkward cooperative arrangement, continuing to make organizational suggestions in order to publish on time and pay off the various loans. But in early April 1968 he finally confessed to his colleagues "I'm afraid the time has come for us to part company. As you must all undoubtedly realize by now, I am not very happy working with the Editorial Executive Board. . . . This has now become too much of a drain on my insides, so I simply have to discontinue a situation which is both frustrating and unhappy for me." He wanted to contribute an article from time to time, and he remained on the editorial advisory board as he moved on to work for the Guardian and other radical publications. The collective editorial arrangement soon collapsed, and within a few months Happy Traum surfaced as managing editor, with Raim as music editor; Traum finished out the troubled decade at the magazine's helm. Growing up in the Bronx into the 1950s, Traum heard his first Seeger concert around 1953 and soon began hanging around Greenwich Village, quickly emerging as an adept performer. A member of the New World Singers from 1962 to 1964, he early gravitated to Sing Out! In his own terms he became the "fall guy." With muted politics, Traum hoped to broaden the magazine's appeal and the definition of folk music, while digging out of the financial hole. One step was to shrink the format, starting with the June/July issue, somewhere between the original handy size and the short-lived magazine-rack jumbo layout.[9]

"It looks pretty grim for Sing Out!" Izzy confided to his notebook in May. With slumping advertising revenue and a growing debt, the magazine limped along. In late 1967 Silber and Asch had sold Oak Publications to Music Sales, Inc., collecting a tidy sum; the new company, in turn, hired Silber for five years to maintain continuity and supervise new titles for Oak. Silber was extracting himself from the folk business, but not too hurriedly. While Traum disagreed with Silber's politics, he remained part of Oak's stable of authors.[10]

"Once we were the challengers of this system and its values," Silber explained to Seeger in late 1968, laying out the reasons for his recent metamorphosis. "Once we represented an alternate culture that was both democratic and liberating. Once we were in the artistic vanguard, charting new paths in a jungle of tradition-bound mediocrity. . . . This is no longer true." And so he had to depart for fresh political and artistic territories. Fully committed to the peace movement, he and Barbara Dane soon published *The Vietnam Songbook*: "This book, then, is designed as an act of solidarity, a testament of friendship, between men and women of the United States of America who oppose and work against the criminal policies of their government and their comrades of Vietnam—both north and south." Openly challenging the establishment's war policies and including songs by Phil Ochs, Tom Paxton, Nina Simone, and active-duty GIs, even six songs from North Vietnam, *The Vietnam Songbook* eventually sold fifteen thousand copies.[11]

Through 1967 *Sing Out!* dished out a mix of political articles, contemporary songs—for example, the controversial "Society's Child," on interracial themes, by the precocious 16-year-old Janis Ian—historical pieces, record reviews, and current news. But the attempt to fatten newsstand sales produced rather dismal results, with an escalating debt, exacerbated when the new editors missed some publishing deadlines. Gordon Friesen lamented in *Broadside*: "We understand that these hopes went glimmering as the year proceeded, not so much because of what *Sing Out!* did or did not do, but simply because the expansion unfortunately coincided with a sharp drop-off interest in folk music per se." Paul Nelson, only recently the champion of vernacular performance, now favorably reviewed the Rolling Stones, the Lovin' Spoonful, Buffalo Springfield, the Kinks, and the Jefferson Airplane, pushing his colleagues to recognize an expanded definition of folk music. After hearing the latter at the Café Au Go Go, Nelson wrote, "the Airplane radiates all those things the folkies say an electric group can't: warmth, love, a natural excitement, taste, unity, art."[12]

Silber unleashed a barrage of criticisms designed to rouse debate: "The symbol of America before the world today is the napalm bomb—and all the music that America has to offer the world—folk music, jazz, rock and roll, country and western, Broadway shows etc.—is being listened to in every corner of the earth as background to that exploding bomb." The rot began at home, he said, for the "mass arts in America today are more corrupt than ever. . . . There is no other country in the world where the cult of nothingness has been raised to such a high philosophic and esthetic principle." In the next issue, revealing *Sing Out!*'s internal differences, Nelson defended youth—"a tribal entity that cares, an international oneness to whom national boundaries are all but meaningless"—against Silber's diatribes. Ed Badeaux generally supported Silber, wondering what would happen to real folk music with the commercial takeover of "groups, electronically turned on LOUD to obscure the individual music, employing colored lights and film images to obscure the visual image. It is amplified. It is stoned. It is completely removed from life. . . . And it is a truly accurate reflection of the America of this moment. For we live in a faceless, corporate, materialistic society spoon-fed electronic pap to crush whatever might remain of our individuality."[13]

If to many Silber represented the magazine's far Left, he had stiff competition from Julius Lester. Returning from a month's trip to North Vietnam as part of a team investigating bomb damage for the War Crimes Tribunal and the Bertrand Russell Foundation, he swiftly became more militant. Two years later he admitted, "I felt completely free for the first time in my life. . . . [T]heir gentleness was mine, their mud was mine, and their enemy was mine." Back home the cultural revolution among young whites obviously solved no problems, he argued, and served no larger causes. They "tried to be Negro and some went South to be bludgeoned, jailed and murdered because they wanted to save themselves." At least, though, they had become involved, compared with the hippies who "have no outrage and they gave flowers to policemen, and carry balloons . . . White youth dropped out into non-involvement. . . . A red balloon and a peacock feather are no answer for napalm." Black power, on the other hand, had substituted guns and bricks for picket signs and leaflets in an "arena of life or death and blacks didn't care which." When a white friend reacted with surprise to the racial violence in Newark, Lester thought: "He didn't understand. One day he will, when it is his life staring Death in the eyes each morning, but then it won't matter if he understands. It will be too late for the explanations and the understanding. . . . Maybe, though, maybe he will learn to fight back and truly come alive. Maybe." This was heady stuff for Sing Out!'s readers.[14]

Izzy invited Lester to discuss his trip to North Vietnam at the Folklore Center on June 8. Soon after that Lester wrote a long angry letter to Broadside, requesting that his name be removed as a contributing editor:

> I stay angry most of the time now, because it's against everything human for people to have to live with rats and roaches and not have enough to eat and to worry about being evicted and getting evicted and not being able to eat if they don't have money. And then I think about North Vietnam and Cuba and what I felt when I visited them this year and they made sense. . . . It's so easy to be human, you know. So damned easy, and this country works 24 hours a day at being inhuman. . . . I don't sing much now, because nothing short of destroying this country will satisfy me. . . . I look forward to the day when I will place a person in my rifle sight, squeeze the trigger, hear the explosion and watch that person fall. And after the shooting has stopped I will continue that act of love that began when I started to hate by helping others to build a country that will exist for its people and not vice-versa.

Dick Reuss thought the letter very moving, and lamented "the days of greater hope and optimism of five years ago when it looked like black and white would be able to make a good start on solving race and poverty problems together in voluntary association."[15]

Lester struggled to balance his fierce, creative independence with the need to cooperate in the revolutionary struggle, whether racial, political, or artistic. Trying to make sense out of their mutual arrangement for running *Sing Out!*, he explained to Silber, "it's a very difficult thing to have to listen to criticism and sometimes bow to the decision of the group. i'm writing for the guardian now and any article that goes in has been read and criticized by the committee before. and it's been good for me to learn that opposition to my ideas does not mean opposition to me, but it's one of those things that every revolutionary must learn, as possibly your experience in the party indicated." Lester said he hoped that the collective would be able to continue to work together.[16]

Years later, Lester was still sorting out the whirl of events in the late 1960s, with music at the core: "The Movement, then, was not only Martin Luther King, Jr., writing a letter from Birmingham jail, but Pete Seeger singing 'We Shall Overcome' at Carnegie Hall, and Jefferson Airplane singing 'White Rabbit' in Golden Gate Park. It was flowers placed in the rifle barrels of soldiers at the Pentagon antiwar demonstration in the fall of 1967, and it was burning draft cards . . . Ultimately, it was too much, a time too big to grasp, or to understand, or even to know what it was you were experiencing."[17]

While the Left was confused, the Right continued its onslaught on folk music, sometimes with serious repercussions. Pete Seeger still had problems appearing on network television. He had taped a series of shows for educational television, *Rainbow Quest*, with numerous popular and traditional performers, which now reached broader circulation, but he was not able to break through into prime time until *The Smothers Brothers Comedy Hour* on CBS, hosted by Tom and Dick Smothers, a folk-comedy duo. Appearing on September 10, Pete performed "Wimoweh" but not his current antiwar, anti-Johnson song, "Waist Deep in the Big Muddy" (both a single and the title of a recent album for Columbia, on which he was rather unsuccessfully backed by the Blues Project—one of his rare attempts to go electric). During the show's taping he had sung the song, with the support of Tom and Dick, but CBS "said they reserved [the] right to cut it as it was their network show. Curious to see what happens Sunday . . . if the song is not cut out," Pete told the *Sing Out!* board. His worst fears were realized when the network omitted the song. Seemingly trying to avoid controversy, CBS provoked a hornet's nest of criticism; they relented a few months later, and for his return engagement in February 1968, Dick and Tom's vast audience heard Pete's "Big Muddy" a month before President Lyndon Johnson announced he would not seek reelection.[18]

Reaction from the corporate establishment was hardly surprising, even in 1967, and neither was an attack from the far Right. "I've been expecting some of these far-out right-fielders to make the looneysville scene ever since old Barry Goldwater got busted in 1964," Silber quipped in *Sing Out!* "But now they've gone past the end of the line and I don't think the trolley's coming back." What aroused his sarcastic wrath was the appearance of David Noebel's *Rhythm, Riots, and Revolution,* published by Christian Crusade Publications in Tulsa, Oklahoma, in 1966. A religious colleague of Billy James Hargis, the notorious anti-Semite and racist, and author of *Communism, Hypnotism, and the Beatles,* Noebel followed in the footsteps of W. S. McBirnie's right-wing *Songs of Subversion,* with considerably more documentation. Indeed, his research is impressive, and he included a fascinating appendix with relevant documents and a helpful list of "subversive" songs and where they were published. "This study is concerned with both the cultural and the psychophysiological, i.e. Communist use of music capable of producing a generation of neurotic and emotionally unstable youth," Noebel wrote. "The study is, in parts, 'unbelievable,' but then so is $E=MC^2$, and since knowledge is the irreducible requirement for intelligent action, the following material is offered with the sincere prayer that those concerned will take the proper action to assure a free Republic based on Christian precepts and Constitutional concepts."[19]

So the Communist takeover would not come from Moscow's tanks and missiles, but rather Pete Seeger's banjo and Phil Ochs's guitar. In a graduate history paper at the University of Tulsa, Noebel analyzed and scrutinized *Broadside* magazine, a potent Communist weapon (surprising news to Cunningham and Friesen, who struggled to publish each monthly issue). Silber had fun lampooning Noebel's book: "Actually, Noebel is a kind of clerical 007—like if Bond didn't booze or ball the chicks and turned out to really be Norman Vincent Peale or Bishop Sheen or Ronald Reagan." But the rise of the new Right was no laughing matter, as George Wallace's surprising showing in the 1968 presidential primaries would indicate, along with various other signs of a potent conservative backlash. *Counterattack,* having survived twenty years, used an alias, "Carol Ascher," to subscribe for one year to *Sing Out!* in 1967 in order to keep its files updated.[20]

Al Capp added an odd note of conservative sarcasm, introducing in his widely syndicated cartoon the character "Joanie Phoanie," a hippy folksinger pulling down $10,000 per concert. Joan Baez objected not to the caricature but to Capp's simplistic politics: "Either out of ignorance or malice, he has made being against war and for peace equal to being for communism, the Viet Cong and narcotics. It is this kind of social distortion, this kind of untruth which has always been a partner to violence." But ridicule came with the territory, as political polarization gripped the country. Two decades later Baez found humor in her being characterized as "a slovenly, two-faced, showbiz slut, a thinly disguised Commie, who traveled around in a limousine" singing "Lay Those Weapons Down, McNamara," "Throw Another Draft Card on the Fire," and "Let's Conga with the Viet Cong." "I got huffy, and huff turned to rage," she recalled. "I never sued Al Capp. I asked for a retraction but did not get one. Al Capp publicly denied to all who asked that Joan Baez was Joanie Phoanie."[21]

Perhaps more troubling than Seeger's problems, Capp's satire, or the other assaults from the Right was the crumbling of folk music's activist consensus, for example concerning the civil rights movement. Julius Lester's move toward black power signified one response to heightened racial and political tensions. Theo Bikel bolted in the opposite direction. "Actor and folksinger Theodore Bikel resigned from the Student Non-Violent Coordinating Committee (SNCC) yesterday and branded as 'obscene' the group's charges that the Israeli army had committed atrocities against the Arabs," *Louisville Courier-Journal* reported in August. Born in Austria, Bikel had fled with his family to Palestine in 1938, relocated to London in 1946, then moved permanently to the United States in 1954, but he always maintained strong emotional and religious ties to Israel. Proud of his strong support for civil rights, particularly in Mississippi, he was repelled by SNCC's rejection of white support. "Much to my dismay, SNCC underwent a change after the first few years," he recalled in his autobiography, "when Stokely Carmichael took over the reins of the organization. . . . Most of the white Northern allies the movement had were Jewish liberals. It became evident after a while that this wing of the civil rights movement was espousing the theory of the Third World being pitted against the rest."[22]

In Bikel's eyes, Carmichael and SNCC had made three very bad decisions. Besides turning their backs on whites and defending Palestinians against Israel, even using anti-Semitic caricatures, they provoked domestic racial violence, abandoning the legacy of nonviolent resistance. "Finally, in 1967, SNCC engaged in openly violent actions in the ghettos, which most often hurt innocent blacks, and continued to commit excesses much against the advice of Dr. King and most other responsible leaders," he wrote. Bikel circulated a lengthy open letter to the press, detailing his grievances and declaring his independence: "You may want to spit in my face for being 'Whitey.' But do not look to me for silence while you insult the memory of my people so recently martyred; you have no right to tamper with their graves." He welcomed support from Martin Luther King and Bayard Rustin, and fended off expected jabs from Carmichael and SNCC and from Julius Lester, "a onetime ally of mine in organizing the folk field. His broadside was particularly saddening to me, as I had known him to be a scholarly and intellectual person." Lester was not alone in questioning Bikel's letter, which was discussed at a *Sing Out!* board meeting, with additional criticisms from Silber.[23]

Newport and Other Festivals

Barry Olivier remained at the helm of the Berkeley Folk Festival, now ending its first decade. "1967 approached and we consciously decided to emphasize electric rock music," he wrote. "We arranged to have six electric bands from six different cities." Stretching through a long weekend and ending on July 4, the festival highlighted Doc Watson, Jimmy Tarlton, Janis Ian, Reverend Gary

Davis, and Richie Havens in addition to the rock bands—the Steve Miller Blues Band, Country Joe and the Fish, Kaleidoscope, and Crome Syrcus. Intellectual stimulation came from Archie Green, Ralph Gleason, and the pop record producer Phil Spector. Olivier tried to create a contemporary cultural event, inviting hippies and black activists, and scheduling more dances and free events. Perhaps Red Crayola from Houston stretched the concept beyond the breaking point; they played "deafeningly loud music with no discernible structure (at the Greek Theatre, one of their 'instruments' was a block of ice suspended from a rope, which dripped upon another surface and caused electric impulses to be transmitted to the audience)." "Their screeching, eerie music had something of the supernatural to it," Olivier recounted, and a local television station, broadcasting live, "missed about 12 minutes of the Red Crayola's 15 minute set, because the television people thought they were still just setting up for their music!"[24]

"The Berkeley Folk Music Festival has gone pop," Julia Bidou reported in the folknik upon hearing of the lineup. "Although we know this is a trend somehow it is a bit of a shock to have it happen at home. . . . A vast section of [the] folk music audience in the Bay Area has been ignored." More traditional sounds continued to find a home throughout California, but confronted increasingly stiff competition.[25]

John Phillips, of the Mamas and the Papas, was approached to participate in a rock festival on the fairgrounds in Monterey, slightly down the coast from San Francisco. He organized a board of directors with Paul Simon, Art Garfunkel, John Lennon, Paul McCartney, and other heavyweights, and soon had a stellar lineup playing for free because this was a charitable event. "To the suspicious Bay Area rockers, L.A. was Star City—slick, moneyed, plastic, and elitist," Phillips recalls. "Haight-Ashbury was becoming the universal hippie mecca for both the drug and rock cultures. Musicians saw themselves as organic post-capitalist advocates of 'power to the people.' " The festival drew thousands and presented a wide array of talent: Simon and Garfunkel, the Animals, Lou Rawls, Janis Joplin with Big Brother and the Holding Company, Quicksilver Messenger Service, the Paul Butterfield Blues Band, Country Joe and the Fish, Otis Redding, the Jefferson Airplane, Laura Nyro, the Byrds, Hugh Masekela, Jimi Hendrix, the Grateful Dead, and the Who. "For that one brief, glorious time, Monterey showed how peace and harmony could thrive and triumph amid social and cultural gaps, political upheaval, great rock, and weird drugs," Phillips concluded.[26]

Members of the folk community also expressed their enthusiasm. Ellen Sander in Sing Out! pronounced it "a monumental event in every aspect." She reviewed the scene more than the performers, surprised there were no arrests though a "measurable excited energy level prevailed." As for the music, "Rock was presented, proudly, as an art form, a serious but gleeful development of unquestionable talent rather than a fast buck, teenybop curiosity." Sing Out!'s readers could have no doubt that the magazine had accepted electric music.[27]

At the essentially acoustic folk festival in Newport, the usual eclectic array of performers crowded the main stage and various workshops for five days, and there was little pandering to the growing hordes of rock fans. Jimmy Driftwood, Jean Ritchie, and Theo Bikel appeared, as did El Teatro Campesino, the Glinka Russian Dancers, the Chang Ming Quang Group, Bill Monroe, Merle Travis, Muddy Waters, and Sarah and Maybelle Carter, performing jointly for the first time in many decades. The trio of Joan Baez, Mimi Fariña, and Judy Collins left few dry eyes in the audience. Thematic evening concerts included one on New York music and folklore. Arlo Guthrie unveiled "Alice's Restaurant" to loud acclaim.

Ralph Earle, reviewing the festival in Boston's *Broadside*, was pleasantly surprised by the tasteful, intimate, educational workshops and well-paced evening concerts. Expressing his preference for the traditional performers, he reluctantly admitted the "most impressive performance on Saturday and Sunday night was given by Joan Baez."[28]

Irwin Silber charged George Wein with adding Baez at the last minute in order to jazz up ticket sales. Welcoming the numerous roots musicians, the appearance of El Teatro Campesino, representing California's striking farm workers, and New York's street-action Bread and Puppet theater, he complained that no one confronted the reality of burning black ghettos, with Newark going up in flames the day before the first concert. Julius Lester had previously resigned from the festival's board, and no one was left to represent his views. The problem, Silber said, was a combination of poor planning and the unfortunate locale of the festival in a "wealthy and relatively inaccessible Rhode Island resort city," so "nothing that happens there will really seem important"; he suggested moving the festival closer to the streets of Boston or New York.[29]

Increasingly frustrated with Silber's running of *Sing Out!*, Pete Seeger hit the roof over his Newport diatribe. "I feel that if you are trying to kill SING OUT Magazine before you are no longer its editor, you're doing a good job," he wrote in November. "For 15 years I've defended you against all kinds of attacks, saying that even if I disagreed with you I appreciated your self-sacrifice in keeping the magazine going, and saying at other times, that I agreed with you, but didn't think much of the way you expressed yourself." He had a litany of complaints. Seemingly "too self-righteous," Silber attacked the commercial stars, while "it was you as editor of SING OUT, who continually boosted personalities, when SING OUT should have been writing about working people and songs and their uses and their meanings." Concerning Newport, he said, "I've tried to persuade you to downgrade these commercial festivals, and all you do for issue, after issue, after issue, is to boost them up." And he concluded, "I am only sorry that I have been so uncriticizing of you as editor of SING OUT. I am afraid that even if you leave immediately its too late to save the magazine." Yet *Sing Out!* struggled along, with Silber involved a bit longer, as did Newport for two more years.[30]

Other festivals triggered much less controversy. Philadelphia, for one, continued on its merry way. Boston *Broadside* praised its every aspect, from the casual atmosphere to the impressive lineup—Son House, Arthur "Big Boy" Crudup, Jesse Fuller, Doc and Merle Watson, the Rooftop Singers, the Beers Family, Bill Monroe and the Bluegrass Boys, Eric Andersen, Pete Seeger. Bob Lurtsema's short piece in *Sing Out!* echoed these sentiments.

Izzy

Izzy Young proudly offered a smorgasbord of performers in his Sixth Avenue store. "Monday continues to be folk night at the Folklore Center with Cynthia Gooding scheduled for Oct. 2, John Hammond on the 9th, and Des & Juliet Rainey on the 16th," Kathy Kaplan added to her "New York News & Notes" column in Boston's *Broadside*, in September 1967. "If at all possible, patronize these events. It's very possible that the FLC is our last hope for decent music in NYC." In addition to his ongoing *Sing Out!* column, "Frets and Frails," Izzy launched a newsletter in 1967, with notices of concerts, additional gossip, and his random thoughts, published haphazardly but steadily into the next decade.[31]

"We're on to a new concert series," he announced in February. "I'm doing this now that folkmusic is dead, to bring back the feeling of the old days of 1957 when we put on concerts by Peggy Seeger, Billy Faier, Tom Paley. . . . I had no idea of 'first' concerts at the time. It was all part of a communal life of sorts. Now I'll be presenting some concerts just so I can hear what a West Coast singer sounds like in person." He started out with Spider John Koerner, Tim Buckley, and Jack Elliott, followed by a melange of whichever performers struck his fancy. He also launched poetry readings on Sunday nights. As for the store, he assured clients in a hand-written ad in *Sing Out!* "that we shall have two salespeople working full time, seven days a week." Despite the magazine's mounting problems, and the country's escalating ills, he seemed to be rejuvenated. "I'm in love with folkmusic again. The Monday night concerts are a huge success. Tim Buckley is the first new young singer to make me flip for a long time."[32]

"You know, I've put on 100 poetry and folk song events at the Folklore Center in the last year, forgetting about the nine years before that, without a cent of subsidy," Izzy told the readers of the *Village Voice*. "I don't want $180,000 to continue but I think my powerful friends in the Village (I'll name them next week, if necessary) should get me a thousand dollars a year so I can continue exactly as I have in the past and be able to pay the artist a bit more than I have and to keep up my V[illage]V[oice] advertising. Not a cent for me or my intelligence." He learned that Paul Clayton had electrocuted himself on April 6; he was not the first suicide and would not be the last, but all sudden deaths of friends were shocking. "So Paul Clayton who recorded more LPs than anyone on more labels, who knew more of poetry, who knew more of drugs, who knew more of all sex, couldn't take it any more," Izzy recorded in his notebook. "I used to kid him on the failure of his attempts to cash in on the folkmusic craze with watered down lyrics based on traditional material. . . . I felt again as I did with the suicides of Peter LaFarge and Woody Wachtell that our twenty year old idea of folkmusic had to be changed not to conform to present day standards, but to survive."[33]

"I came back from my first trip to the West Coast three weeks ago and I'm still happy about the experience," Izzy reported in August. He had visited the Ash Grove, Fillmore, Avalon, Haight-Ashbury, the Berkeley Folk Festival, and the Sweets Mill Folk Music Camp. At a scenic mountain retreat in Northern California, Virgil and Edith Byxbe had launched Sweets Mill in the 1950s as a children's camp; sometime later, influenced by the Idylwild music camp, they switched to summer folk sessions, and finally to a folk music camp in the mid-sixties. "For me the most important experience at Sweets Mill was a talk Israel Young gave on what he calls 'The Death of Folk Music,' " Ellen Faust recounted in *the folknik*. "His basic statement is that folk music is dying. He seems to feel that the psychedelic rock scene is where it's at and that is the new 'folk' music. His attitude toward the festival at Sweets Mill was contemptuous. . . . In his talk he mentioned the death of Paul Clayton, who recently committed suicide. This to him was an indication that those who cling to the past structure of folk performance would be plowed under if they didn't get out." Faust thought the flamboyant proprietor of the Folklore Center much too pessimistic.[34]

In late 1967, students in Margaret Mead's methods class at Columbia University chose Izzy as the subject for a project. They filmed discussions and photographed the store. Michael Asch, son of Moe Asch and one of Mead's students, had organized the venture. Looking back over his experiences during an interview by Asch, Izzy suspected "that guy who opened the store 10 years ago was a great guy because he wasn't afraid. He just did what he had to do. . . . And sometimes I [now] resent the fact that I don't have all kinds of money and all kinds of equipment to put on things but somehow I'm putting on more things than the 'Y' and the Guggenheim together in terms of poetry alone."[35]

The next month Izzy joined the students to hear and see their report, with Mead's running critique. "I am glad that the students swarmed around the store for their term's work," he recorded in his notebook. "It forced me to think more closely of what it is I stand for. . . . In terms of folkmusic I represent perhaps the last person whose work is public that is holding on to his original beliefs and keeps them in practice." Shortly thereafter, Billy Faier wrote of Izzy for the *Woodstock* (N.Y.) *Week*, echoing Izzy's self-image: "But the most colorful, anarchistic and romantic organization to be involved in folk music, and nothing but folk music, for the past ten years, always resisting the encroachment of slick pop sounds, good or bad, always in the vanguard of proselytizing for the authentic sound is the one and only Israel Goodman Young."[36]

1967 Ends

Woody Guthrie died at the age of fifty-five on October 3, 1967. His long hospital incarceration had prevented all but his family and closest friends from having much contact for over a decade. A week after his passing Marjorie, Arlo, Nora, and Joady Guthrie threw his ashes into the ocean off Coney Island, Woody's favorite spot. Ralph Gleason quickly took the measure of the bard's impact. "Just a short few days before Woody died, Pete Seeger had appeared at the Berkeley Community Theater in a poignant concert filled with reminiscences of Woody and old labor union songs, which left me with an uneasy feeling that it was all irrelevant now, symbols of another era. . . . If there was one thing that Woody Guthrie contributed to American popular music above all else, I think it was the idea that anything you really felt strongly about could be a song. . . . The topical song, the protest song, the individual statement, all became big business and mass media material in the past dozen years, while Woody Guthrie died inch by inch in a hospital bed. It's ironic, to say the least."[37]

If his heart had stopped, his voice still rang out loud and clear. Elektra released a three-record set of Alan Lomax's 1940 Library of Congress interviews with Guthrie, and there were numerous Folkways records in circulation, enough to satisfy most appetites. Harold Leventhal organized two glittering concerts, the first at Carnegie Hall on January 20, 1968, followed by a second, with a somewhat different lineup, at the Hollywood Bowl in Los Angeles two years later. At Carnegie Hall, Judy Collins, a bearded Dylan in his first public appearance since a motorcycle accident in August 1966, Richie Havens, Jack Elliott, Odetta, Tom Paxton, Arlo Guthrie, and Seeger headlined the evening. Millard Lampell prepared the script, based on Guthrie's writings, which was read by Robert Ryan and Will Geer. Ellen Willis, in the pop music magazine *Cheetah*, wrote, "Sure it was sentimental. Sentimentality was one reason we deserted to pop. But pop has its own softnesses, and between that Indian Norman Vincent Peale snowing the Beatles and Pete Seeger glorifying just plain folks, I'll take the latter." Clive Davis, head of Columbia Records, noted shrewdly, "A great musical figure, Woody Guthrie, was being honored, but all attention was riveted to the return of the young, mysterious poet who had haunted so many minds"—Dylan.[38]

The Guthrie tribute presented the unified face of the folk establishment, but behind the scenes there was much grumbling. Bob Shelton, the revival's cheerleader in the mass media, privately had become quiet alienated. He wrote to Archie Green in mid-1967: "I am going to be seriously looking at Europe this summer as a possible future home. Maybe the same problems exist there, but I am so deeply disappointed with the present pulse, texture and malperspectives of American society that I must think of somewhere carving out a more congenial environment for myself and my wife." In late 1968 he moved to England. Phil Ochs, increasingly embittered yet the strongest voice following in Guthrie's footsteps, found himself in the audience rather than on the Carnegie stage. He left during the finale, "This Land Is Your Land," and afterward complained to Leventhal about his exclusion, to little effect. Izzy smelled conspiracy, while Sis Cunningham and Gordon Friesen in Broadside hinted that "Woody himself might have walked out on the whole proceedings, in the sense that the ESTABLISHMENT, which he had resisted with all his strength while he was able, took him over when he was dead and couldn't do a thing about it." Still, they appreciated that many young people, there to see Dylan, were exposed to Woody's songs. Izzy promised a long critique in his newsletter, but never wrote it. Ochs soon moved to Los Angeles.[39]

As folk music struggled to survive in the chaotic musical marketplace, its definition remained elusive. David DeTurk and Al Poulin tried a broad approach in the first anthology of essays on the revival, The American Folk Scene, which included thirty-two selections, most previously published. They stressed the music's social context rather than musical characteristics. "It is the relevance of folk music to the great social upheavals that literally define the limits of our existence today that captivates the imagination," they explained. "Folk music and song are no longer 'other-directed' by tradition, but have become 'inner-directed' extensions of the search for a palatable and viable future." Responding to the book's call to understanding the music's social impact and manifestations, the folklorist Joe Hickerson, working at the Library of Congress's Archive of Folk Song since 1963, preferred its meatier, less topical selections. Relying on the academic distinction between "folk music"—with distant, oral, community roots—and "folksong-revival music"—with contemporary origins—he called for a more scholarly approach to the subject. Still, he wrote, "It will probably be a long time before people, other than folklore students and knowledgeable performers, will be able to converse with each other about folk music and know exactly what they are talking about."[40]

Antiwar songs, hardly new among folk performers, continued to capture public attention. Tom Phillips's overview for the New York Times cautioned that the outpouring lacked "a song that could serve as a theme for the movement, a rallying call of the kind that's been common in movements with wide support on the American left." He listed Seeger's "Waist Deep in the Big Muddy," Baez's "Saigon Bride," Malvina Reynolds's "Napalm," the Fugs's "War Song," Arlo's "Alice's Restaurant," all more bellicose than Ochs's earlier "Talking Vietnam." Because the movement desired "an end to what they consider a national disgrace . . . the songs are sometimes satiric, sometimes sorrowful and sometimes indignant, but the tone is always negative." *Broadside* maintained a drumbeat of antiwar songs, marked by Ochs's "The War Is Over," appearing in early 1968.[41]

1968: Anno Mirabilia

"Traditional folk singers—including the modern figure of Bob Dylan—have usually been purveyors of a musical heritage, chroniclers of their time, pro- testers against injustice," said *Time* in early 1968. "But today's troubadours are turning away from protest. Their gaze is shifting from the world around them to the realms within." The piece mentioned Janis Ian, Arlo Guthrie, Tim Hardin, Richie Havens, and Leonard Cohen. "It has been said of the late Woody Guthrie, one of the great folk singers of an earlier generation and the father of Arlo Guthrie, that he was the root, that younger singers after him were the branches; and that the flowers were yet to come. In a sense, today's new singers are the flowers." Perhaps that was because they seemed so safe.[42]

Dylan, though out of action for over a year, continued to hold center stage. Albert Grossman had been renegotiating his contract with Columbia Records, even proposing a switch to MGM, but Columbia came through and Dylan returned to the studio. Grossman still served as his manager, though their re- lationship had noticeably cooled. The acoustic *John Wesley Harding* appeared in January 1968 and went gold by April. "The new LP has a unity that has not characterized any previous album by the 26-year-old folk poet," Shelton pro- nounced in the *New York Times*. "Nearly all the dozen songs are linked into a pageant about life's outsiders: gunmen, renegades, immigrants, tenants, saints, hobos, drifter convicts, lovers and losers." The album ended with a touch of country, presaging *Nashville Skyline* eighteen months later.[43]

Dylan's songs and persona appeared to retreat from the hustle and bustle of an increasingly chaotic world, yet his lyrics still resonated with the country's growing number of activists. "More and more the conviction grows that Bob Dylan is an important American poet," Ralph Gleason wrote. But this was not poetry to lull the masses or encourage navel gazing. On the contrary, "On Telegraph Avenue [in Berkeley], as well as Greenwich Village and other gath- ering places of the young these days, lines from Dylan songs are excerpted and put on cardboard signs and tacked on the tables where the fund raising con- tainers and the petitions and the buttons are on display." Tellingly, the cover of *The Times They Are A-Changin'*, not *John Wesley Harding*, accompanied Gleason's article in the *San Francisco Examiner and Chronicle*.[44]

Student and community activism mounted as the war ground on. "Joan Baez spent 45 days [actually only thirty] at the Santa Rita prison farm in California, alongside her mother and sister and many friends, for trying to stop an induc- tion center at work in Oakland," Izzy noted in *Sing Out!* in early 1968. "Ed Sanders, Marc Silber, Mika Seeger, and myself were among hundreds arrested in NYC, although we never got anywhere near the Whitehall Street induction center."[45]

Thousands flocked to Chicago for the Democratic party's national convention in late August 1968. At the end of one lengthy day, after the majority of delegates had voted to support President Johnson's war policies, several hundred others, many from New York, huddled on the floor of the International Amphitheater singing "We Shall Overcome" in protest. The orchestra countered with "California, Here We Come" and "Happy Days Are Here Again," while the demonstrators concluded with "The Battle Hymn of the Republic." "Shortly after 5:15 P.M., the singing and chanting began to subside and the marchers began to disperse," the *New York Times* reported. "The New York delegates began looking for their caucus, which had been scheduled, to poll the delegation on how it would cast its votes for the Presidential candidates." While the convention dutifully nominated Hubert Humphrey, Chicago's finest, on orders from Mayor Richard Daley and the police chief, continued to beat the protesters and anyone else within easy reach throughout the downtown parks and streets.[46]

Just a month before, folk fans had flocked to Newport for the ritual annual gathering of the clan. Robert Shelton celebrated a stimulating, eclectic show which attracted a record-breaking crowd of seventy thousand and featured B. B. King, Janis Joplin with Big Brother and the Holding Company, Doc Watson, Roy Acuff, Tim Buckley, Taj Mahal, and the Young Tradition. Shelton discerned various current trends in the revival: "Commercial country and Western music is gaining acceptance as a folk music form," and folk rock continued to hold sway. "Topical and protest songs are still gushing out in profusion," and the old heroes, particularly Woody Guthrie, "are still in the pantheon."[47]

Others were far less charitable. Richard Goldstein, in the *Village Voice*, believed the high point was the frustrated anticipation of Dylan's appearance, followed by "Jerry Rubin's latest near-bust (for handing a Yippie newspaper to a nun)." Ellen Willis thought Newport lacked the feel of a festival: "Instead of camaraderie, there was tension; instead of participation, consumership. All weekend, the management was busy trying to manipulate a sullen audience and a bunch of equally hostile, if more reticent, performers." The bulk of the audience "had apparently come not as true believers but as businesslike consumers, determined to get their money's worth." The rock critic Jon Landau chimed in with similar, somewhat nostalgic, sentiments. "With interest in traditional forms of folk music apparently at a low ebb," he lamented in *Rolling Stone*, "the Festival was torn between the presentation of big names who brought out the crowds, and traditional artists who, for the most part, generated little attention or enthusiasm."[48]

Izzy Young, another firsthand witness, recorded his thoughts. Attending the party after the Friday night concert, he noticed that "it was disgustingly filled with folksingers and their agents and managers many of whom I hadn't realized

were ever interested in folk music anymore. Business was going on as usual.
. . . Buell Kazee was standing all alone with a plate of food in his hands, no
one coming over to him, or anything, and I saw him, neatly dressed." Izzy's
disappointment would be reinforced in the coming months.[49]

While the Newport crowd seemed little interested in protest politics or the
traditional performers, both attracted the attention of the conservative press.
National Review columnist Anthony Dolan took a few swipes at "the flower children. The ones whose army surplus look and long hair the town people obviously resented." He appreciated old-time banjo player Kazee, a conservative
who felt out of place, and he wrote that the audience "were far more interested
in discovering beauty and feeling groovy than in revolutionizing the world."[50]

Irwin Silber also tolled the death knell of the protest song movement, part
of his increasing disenchantment with the folk revival. The older performers—
Dylan, Phil Ochs, Tom Paxton, Len Chandler—had mellowed or disappeared,
and the newcomers showed little political promise. "Today, the topical song
revolution is a memory—not quite nostalgia yet, but an echo from another
time which serves to remind us of intervening battles waged and miles traveled." He found some hope in particular contemporary artists—the Beatles,
Jefferson Airplane, Aretha Franklin, James Brown—that expressed generational
and racial angst while remaining part of the commercial matrix: "Current rock
would seem to be the music most suitable for the disaster which is today's
America."[51]

Across the continent, the Berkeley Folk Festival had been staged, with considerably greater apprehension and tension, in early July. "As it turned out,"
organizer Barry Olivier later wrote, "the Festival had been a calming influence
on the political activities of revolutionaries on Telegraph Avenue—at least in
the short run." Months and years of protests culminated in nighttime clashes
between angry demonstrators and city police on Telegraph Avenue just off the
campus, resulting in numerous arrests and the enforcement of a curfew. The
militants vowed to block the street for a political rally on July 4, the planned
opening of the folk festival. Dreading more violence, the city council wisely
lifted the curfew and agreed to the street closing for a rock festival. Both the
folk festival and the rock festival proved successful. Dr. Humbead's New Tranquility String Band, Jesse Fuller, and Howlin' Wolf joined Joan Baez for the
final Sunday afternoon concert; rock music was provided by Quicksilver Messenger Service at the evening dance.[52]

Musical Possibilities

"Yep, the Friends of Old Time Music is getting up steam," Izzy announced in
his *Newsletter* in early 1968. Starting with Libba Cotten, then the blues singers
Yank Rachell and Shirley Griffith, the FOTM concerts would be coordinated

with the Philadelphia Folk Song Society and the Folklore Society of Greater Washington. "Now that folk music is dead, and I wish I wouldn't be quoted so often on it, we have it all to ourselves and we're going to help set up an underground circuit that doesn't have to depend on mass media and mass fast fads for existence," he proclaimed. Indeed, despite the lukewarm reception for noncommercial performers at Newport and elsewhere, the concert series, a mix of urban and rural performers, foreign and domestic, connected with an expanding nationwide audience for traditional sounds.[53]

During the dead of winter the University of Chicago Folk Festival continued rolling along, with only roots performers such as Bukka White (rural blues), the Osborne Brothers (bluegrass), Johnny Shines (urban blues), and Clark Kessinger and Kilby Snow (old-timey). "At the conclusion of last year's festival, several of us held the dim view that since most everything else is going rock, we might just turn around and find that there was no more festival," John Cohen wrote. "This year we all left believing that the festival and its music will continue as an institution of America's non-conforming traditions." Banjo and fiddle contests sprouted up throughout the country. The Topanga festival, on the outskirts of Los Angeles, continued in July 1968 with Frank Hamilton, Sam Hinton, and Earl Robinson among the judges.[54]

Also in July, Ralph Rinzler presided over the free inaugural Smithsonian Folklife Festival in the nation's capital. Over half a million visitors explored the dozens of crafts exhibits, food booths, displays of folk arts, and performance stages. "With all this talk about food, money and crafts, don't get the idea that music was left out in the cold," Jonathan Eberhart assured *Sing Out!*'s readers. Indeed, Rinzler had managed to gather a dazzling array of vernacular performers—the Preservation Hall Jazz Band, Skip James, Muddy Waters, Lightnin' Hopkins, Ralph Stanley, Grandpa Jones, Doc Watson, and the Georgia Sea Island Singers, among others. Josh Dunson especially appreciated "the Saturday night concert where all the performers watched the stage from the side and jumped and applauded with the rest of the audience, so when they were on stage the nervousness was almost gone." This was a far cry from the commercial circus of Newport. The expansive, well-attended festival continued through the remainder of the century, vibrant testimony of the country's living folk heritage.[55]

Izzy wrote, "Things are happening so quickly in America that it is having an extraordinary effect on all aspects of culture—including what might still be called THE FOLK SCENE, THE CITY FOLK MUSIC SCENE, only the scene is very small as regards its original purpose." He sensed ongoing complexities in presenting roots musicians to an urban audience. "More time and effort have to be devoted to some traditional performers to make them feel at home," he wrote. "Some traditional performers are idolized and not let alone, most, though, are ignored until their appearance on stage. I wonder what they think of it all. . . . What happens when the traditional person's gift is used up, analyzed and taken over by the city person, and then is discarded as has been happening the past several years." Izzy had long developed a convoluted relationship to the commercial marketplace. "Can we help it if in OUR culture we sing for money, we make money out of the things we love. . . . What good does all our erstwhile labors do the present, living traditional person who can't compete with us on our turf and on his own turf is unemployable as the newer technology replaces them [sic] in the economic sphere, too." But he had no answers. Feeling uncomfortable with Sing Out! editor Happy Traum, Izzy progressively confined his writing to his own newsletter. Only two "Frets and Frails" columns appeared in 1969, the last in September, his tenth anniversary.[56]

While some shunned the commercial limelight, popular folk and rock continued to garner attention and analysis. Burt Korall focused on "The Music of Protest" in the Saturday Review. "Those who register complaint and desperation today are not far removed in spirit from Guthrie and other bards of yesterday, like black artists Big Bill Broonzy and Leadbelly, who spoke out of their experience and tried to bring mass focus to inequality and the number of sicknesses in the land." His discussed Dylan, Otis Redding, Richie Havens, the Doors, and Frank Zappa's Mothers of Invention. Herbert Rosscol followed in High Fidelity with a roundup of popular folk: "The gallant sweet-singer has stepped down from the tapestry, the unshaven folkie has put on his shoes, and both have climbed up into the pop charts. . . . What hasn't been grasped by untrustworthy over-thirties is the fact that folk music has been kidnapped (or raped) by the Now generation." Rosscol seemingly longed for the traditional songs, or at least something fresh.[57]

In the spring of 1968 the venerable Club 47 in Cambridge folded. Manager Jim Rooney had left in late 1967 to become a fieldworker and talent coordinator for the Newport jazz and folk festivals, soon followed by longtime club stalwarts Betsy and Bob Siggins. They moved to Washington, where Betsy worked with Rinzler on the Festival of American Folklife. The core Cambridge folk community, closely linked with Newport and Berkeley, had disintegrated. But newcomers continued to filter into the scene. Bonnie Raitt had entered Radcliffe College in 1967, partly because of its proximity to Club 47, and quickly met Son House, Buddy Guy, and other bluesmen through her relationship with photographer and promoter Dick Waterman. "I went to Europe for the summer, and when I got back things had changed," she recalled. "The 47 was gone. About the best you could do for music was the Ultimate Spinach at the Tea Party or Canned Heat at the Psychedelic Supermarket." Deftly steeped in the blues, she would soon make her mark on the music world.[58]

Folk music found itself caught in the backdraft of external forces as the decade waned. Sing Out! shied away from taking editorial stands on the passing political scene, but Pete Seeger continued his drumbeat for rebellion and change. "Part of what we must do is act—the most definitive communication," he proclaimed in his column. "Not only peace and freedom workers have become actionists. Conservationists have also. . . . Take it from an old blacklisted banjopicker, this land does belong to the hardworking people who love freedom, to you and me." A few months later he launched the sloop "Clearwater," the symbol and means of his commitment to cleaning up the Hudson River. The floating folk festival included in the crew, at various times, Len Chandler, Jimmy Collier, Reverend Frederick Douglass Kirkpatrick, Jack Elliott, Don McLean, Lou Killen, and Gordon Bok, all skilled musicians. Initially seeming a quixotic venture, the "Clearwater" eventually proved a vital component of the environmental movement and helped establish Seeger's wide public acceptance[59]

In a *Rolling Stone* article ironically entitled "The Swan Song of Folk Music," *Sing Out!* editor Happy Traum made a strong case that folk was thriving. He argued that "folk music is not only alive, but is more influential than at any other time in our post-ethnic civilization. It is no longer a thing to be set aside and regarded as a museum piece by anthropologists, left-wing politicians, and old record collectors." He found folk's influences, broadly construed, all around, in the music of the Grateful Dead, Canned Heat, and the Byrds, as well as the British groups Pentangle and the Young Tradition. Moreover, crowds "still flock to see bluegrass bands, old-time fiddle contests, country blues pickers, gospel shouters, and mountain balladeers, as well as the newer folk-pop singer-songwriter stars." He lamented, however, the dearth of commercial venues for mainstream folkies. All was not roses, yet "what we are left with is an exciting new music based on many past experiences and influences, and a healthy respect for the traditional music from whence it all came." He repeated these sentiments in his *Sing Out!* column, writing that "folk and other acoustic sounds are coming back again after the last few years of hard rock."[60]

Rock dominated the music charts through 1969 and rock festivals dotted the landscape, highlighted by the mostly mellow Woodstock gathering of 400,000 in mid-August. Jimi Hendrix, Janis Joplin, Joan Baez, Blood, Sweat and Tears, the Jefferson Airplane, and Sly and the Family Stone topped the bill at Woodstock. "Joan Baez, the square, six months pregnant, the wife of a draft resister, endlessly proselytizing about the war," as she later reminisced, felt both awkward and awed, certainly out of place among drugs and rock. "I just stood up there in front of the residents of the golden city who were sleeping in the mud and each other's arms, and I gave them what I could at the time. And they accepted my songs."[61]

Newport and California

Newport once again became the focus of folk attention in midsummer, though it had long faded from the national headlines. "Everyone is curious to see if the big, expensive Newport Folk Festival can survive in 1969 USA," Seeger mused. He hoped this year's festival would return to first principles, down-playing commercialism and focusing on roots performers and audience partic-ipation.[62]

Riots at the recent Newport Jazz Festival (shades of a decade before) were a strong warning that trouble might be brewing for the folk festival. A week before the scheduled mid-July opening, the Newport City Council passed a list of festival do's and dont's: no rock music, a heavy wire fence around the center field for crowd control, additional security guards, seating limited to eighteen thousand for the evening concerts, and all concerts to end by 12:15 A.M. Local and state police would be quite visible, strictly enforcing the midnight-to-7:00 A.M. curfew on city beaches. Tensions in Newport mirrored national trends. The festival was hardly a raucous affair, however, featuring mostly traditional musi-cians such as Brownie McGhee, Sleepy John Estes, and Willie Mae "Big Mama" Thornton, along with Arlo Guthrie, James Taylor, Joni Mitchell, the Everly Brothers, Muddy Waters, Jesse Fuller, and the country quartet of Johnny Cash, June Carter, Doug Kershaw, and Carl Perkins. Even a reconstituted Weavers made their appearance, with Eric Darling, Lee Hays, Fred Hellerman, and Ronnie Gil-bert. The general lack of big names produced a rather small crowd, though 16,000 attended Saturday night's concert. "In an attempt to stay away from the star system, the festival lacked excitement and direction," Jan Hodenfield carped in Rolling Stone. He preferred the informal workshops to the nighttime concerts.[63]

The press reports, such as they were, remained generally positive. Not so the folk establishment. Sing Out! editor Traum lamented that the "over-all feeling of Newport 1969 was that of an armed camp." The hot, dusty grounds proved quite uncomfortable, and the food vendors had little to offer, but the depth and variety of performers showed that the board of directors had style and imagination. The crowd was drawn to the big names, again ignoring the work-shops and unknowns. Barbara Dane had refused to lead a "Songs of Liberation" workshop, rejecting the festival's commercial slant. "If it intends to be one more music festival, then say so and pay the performers accordingly," instead of the standard token payment for all. "If it means to be serious about its dedication to the music of the people, then it must relate to and respond to the conditions under which those people live."[64]

Izzy concurred with Happy Traum in questioning the security measures and commercial overtones. "My main impression with the new 25,000 dollar fence, and the policemen all around, is that the people have no contact with the people on the stage, and the photographers in the pit have no connection with either. . . . Doug Kershaw, cajun, tells the audience to buy his record for he needs the money. What kind of shit is that to hand out to the audience," he wrote. "If Newport is Mecca then why are there no folksingers here for pleasure?" At the party on Saturday night, Jim Rooney, Bill Keith, and one of the Everly Brothers were picking and singing "so nicely and quietly—why can't they do it on the stage at Newport," Izzy wondered. He preferred to continue his own music series in the back room of the Folklore Center, one or more a week, drawing small crowds and making a few dollars.[65]

Though an artistic success—at least for some—the Newport festival once again lost money. Splitting the cost of the $28,000-dollar mile-long fence with the jazz festival was a blow for the festival board, along with the added costs for security guards. The foundation found itself increasingly strapped, and so canceled the 1970 festival. Festival organizer George Wein promised a festival in 1971 to show that "folk music can communicate to youth in the same way that rock music has," but riots at the 1971 jazz festival forced cancelation of the folk festival just a week before its opening. The Newport Foundation was forced to borrow $8,000 to help pay its debts; two benefit concerts in July 1972 raised another $30,000, after which the foundation was dissolved. (Rock promoter Frank Russo's 1979 attempt to resurrect the festival proved stillborn, following dismal ticket pre-sales. After another decade, in 1988 Ben and Jerry's Newport Folk Festival renewed the tradition through the end of the century.)[66]

Other festivals struggled to continue, with mixed results. Izzy made his second trip to the West Coast to visit the modest Sweet's Mill festival near Fresno. Izzy loved the music (Dr. Humbead's New Tranquility String Band, Mark Spoelstra, Sandy and Jean Darlington), the rustic setting, the manageable audience, and the mellow atmosphere. "What was particularly attractive about Sweet's Mill this year was the attempt to relate folkmusic to cultural change and revolution in American life," he reported to *Sing Out!*'s readers.[67]

Izzy appreciated that West Coast rock groups seemed more political than mercenary, donating their time in late spring to support People's Park in Berkeley, for example—the aborted attempt to convert a parcel of university-owned land designated for construction into a green space. "The most ambitious undertaking so far of trying to bring art to the people free, or almost free, was planned by Ralph Gleason and Barry Olivier to take over Golden Gate Park with folk music, jazz, opera, ballet, poetry, and so on," Izzy reported. But the event was canceled when the Black Panthers and Third World Conference "wanted the event to be more revolutionary in a political way rather than accept a group of people fighting through alternate life styles. Probably at this time there is no way to accommodate both views and that is a shame for bringing music and art to the people free is a good starting point for everybody."[68]

As the Golden Gate festival, to be called "Wild West," was scheduled for August, the Berkeley Folk Festival had to be postponed until fall. Always one to avoid politics, if possible, Olivier was caught off guard by "a number of gross misunderstandings between some of the radicals and the controlling group of rock people. In the end the Chairman had his life threatened and violence was promised if we tried to do it, so we called it off," as he later explained. He substituted a few rock concerts at the Fillmore and Family Dog ballrooms in San Francisco. Exhausted from the "Wild West" fiasco, Olivier had little enthusiasm or stamina for the Berkeley festival, yet still managed to pull off a minor success with Brownie McGhee and Sonny Terry, Arthur "Big Boy" Crudup, the Youngbloods, Doug Kershaw, Commander Cody and His Lost Planet Airmen, Country Joe and the Fish, and Charles Seeger. Olivier concluded that having the festival during the semester worked well to attract students. Phil Elwood wrote in the *San Francisco Examiner*, "The . . . Berkeley Folk Festival indicated that there are still thousands of folk who appreciate informal, low-pressure, distinctive performances by self-taught artists who are not generally of the ultra-hype, expansive-electronic, $100,000 star-fee types."[69]

"Late in 1969 (even before Altamont) we decided that we were about through with festivals," Olivier reminisced, "but decided that it would be nice to do one more if we could get Pete Seeger to come." Surprisingly, not only did Seeger agree to appear in October 1970, but Olivier also managed to snag for his finale a stellar lineup: Peggy Seeger and Ewan MacColl, Ramblin' Jack Elliott, Joy of Cooking, Mimi Fariña, Sam Chatmon, Big Mama Thornton, Big Brother and the Holding Company, and the last-minute addition of Joan Baez. "This proved a perfect ending note for the Festivals at Berkeley," Olivier wrote some years later, "with a total success, combining beautiful music, sharing of ideas, feelings of unity, and good attendance (which brought financial success, also)." He had done his work for thirteen years, through good times and bad, and now felt it time to move on. "I busted my ass and so did the other people working on it with me, some of whom were volunteers, some of whom were paid something, to manage it well. But it just got harder and harder to have to deal with all the provisions for things that could go wrong." Oddly, considering all the struggles to obtain funding and pay the bills, a savior now appeared in the form of Manny Greenhill, the successful manager of Baez and many others. Attending his first festival in 1970—though his son Mitch had long been involved—Greenhill volunteered to secure backing for future festivals. But Olivier stuck to his decision to bow out.[70]

Olivier now preferred the low-key, all-volunteer approach of the one-day Berkeley Fiddlers' Convention and contests, first held in 1968. First prize was 5 pounds of rutabaga, and second prize 10 pounds. Ralph Gleason touted the strictly acoustic policy and jocular atmosphere, a far cry from the raucous psychedelic rock concerts he usually covered. "There was an absence of politicos and no speeches," he thankfully commented, referring to the "17th Annual Fiddlers' Convention" in June 1969 (it was only the second). "In contrast to the competitive stance of most festivals, this one was totally relaxed." While Berkeley continued to boil, with the National Guard occasionally occupying the city and demonstrations almost daily, folk music still had something to offer. Olivier organized local Baez concerts for a few more years, then settled into teaching guitar classes, averaging four hundred students a week in the mid-1970s.[71]

Farther to the south folk tried to compete with rock. "The LA scene is closest to NYC, naturally, because of the recording studios, singers getting discovered and people generally on the make," Izzy wrote during his western trip, "all conspiring to overshadow the quieter scene in most of the rest of California where evidently more and more people want to pick and play with other people, get into country music, or write songs in a country vein."[72]

Ed Pearl's Ash Grove remained part of the traditional music landscape, though the owner was becoming increasingly radical and disillusioned. He recalled, "Things were getting drugged-out, and the path wasn't as clear as what it had been in the earlier periods. I mean, it was very simple at the beginning to welcome all folk music, whether it was sophisticated or real or not, just the idea of putting different sounds before the American people." While proud of the stars he had nurtured—Linda Ronstadt, Jackson Browne, Taj Mahal, Ry Cooder, and the Chambers Brothers—Pearl preferred the traditional sounds. But he also turned the club into a political forum, with an initial show in early 1969 supporting the black student strike at San Francisco State University, featuring Country Joe McDonald. Soon after, while Pearl was preparing for a discussion on Cuba, the Ash Grove burned down. Pearl was convinced an anti-Castro group was responsible. It took him six months to reopen. The club struggled into the next decade, only to experience two more fires, but changing musical tastes and a fracturing radical movement proved most discouraging. In particular, Pearl concluded that "traditional country music was dead—totally dead—bluegrass, unaccompanied ballad singing, string band music. Nobody would come to see it, period."[73]

An Era Passes

Folk music coexisted somewhat uneasily alongside rock and pop as it tried to maintain a separate identity, fill a musical and political niche, and recruit fresh voices and styles. Sing Out! editor Happy Traum expressed the upbeat side of the story:

> Folk music is playing an increasingly important part in the everyday lives of the American people, whether it is a participant in a small-town old-time fiddler's society, a song-swap club member, the avid folk/rock festival fan, or the anti-war G.I. listening to folk performers in a local coffee house. Because it is so diversified, it can't be called a 'movement,' but the signs of a new and hopefully different kind of 'folk-boom' (for lack of a better term) are definitely in the air.

The same issue recognized the passing of the torch, with the singer-songwriter Don McLean penning a singular, pained portrait of Josh White, who died on September 6, 1969. Sing Out! limped through the next decade until fully resurrected in the 1980s.[74]

Broadside, now appearing every month or two while the editors somehow survived endless financial, health, and family problems, also weathered the decade and continued to encourage political songwriting. Gordon Friesen celebrated publication of the hundredth issue in mid-1969, with songs by Mike Millius, Jimmy Collier, and Pete Seeger, and Nina Simone's "Revolution." "Music took strange turns in the 60's," the editors ruminated. "Some singers who began with straight folk and direct political statement gradually changed to inane flowers, clouds, gardens poetry of the [Leonard] Cohen-[Rod] McKuen sort. The biggest development, of course, was rock." They were not discouraged, for rock "reinforced protesting youth, emotionally if not intellectually." There was hope, despite the rapacious conduct of the music industry, that the revolution would yet arrive. As for the second Woody Guthrie tribute, held at the Hollywood Bowl in September 1969, the editors wrote: "What would 'really be a tribute' to Woody would be to restore the image of the man he really was—a Revolutionary, a loyal Communist Party member, an unwavering fighter for a Socialist world in which not only would uncharted diseases [for example, Huntington's] be remedied, but already existing cures applied to millions of suffering human victims." They particularly resented the inclusion of Joan Baez, "with her simpering pacifism and repeated blasts at student and black militants."[75]

"We're living in a more violent time," Izzy said in an interview in RAT, an underground paper, in early 1969. "In America, if you have a bad heart, they'll cure the bad heart but never change the conditions so you won't get a bad heart to begin with. It's hard to talk about violence and nonviolence 'cause the violence is all around us." At year's end he took his first, tentative expatriate step, a trip to Stockholm. "Tonight I am presenting my last concert in America at Eagleton Institute on the Douglas Campus of Rutgers University," he wrote in his notebook in mid-November. Featuring Paul Siebel, Gary White, Rosalie Sorrels, and Dominic Behan, it "is the best NYC has to offer and I am the only one able to get it together." Izzy would take another three years, in 1973, to pull up stakes and relocate to the peaceful, socialist haven of Stockholm, but his mental move had already begun with the passing of the 1960s.[76]

Irwin Silber's political and musical disillusionment also mounted. "Since severing my connections with Sing Out . . . I have been less and less involved with the folk song scene," he informed Eric Winter, editor of the British *Sing*. "Actually, I am quite alienated (both politically and emotionally) from the whole song movement in the country. Ever since it was co-opted out of its role as an alternate culture through the merchandising process, it began to hold less and less interest for me. As a result, I find myself very much at odds with many old friends and co-workers of long standing." He was quite proud of his work with Barbara Dane on *The Vietnam Songbook* and increasingly threw his efforts behind revolutionary songs from around the world; the two launched Paredon Records in 1969, devoted to circulating such music. Dane also devoted much energy to singing for antiwar soldiers. About the same time Silber remarked that ten years earlier he and others believed that "if 40 million American would begin to sing the songs of Woody Guthrie we would be living in a better society. That the rediscovery and reclamation of our folk music heritage would inspire a new democratic vigor in the life of our morally moribund society." With Vietnam and so many other horrors, however, "the America of Walt Whitman and Mark Twain, of Carl Sandburg and Woody Guthrie, the America of the democratic frontier and libertarian populism is dead."[77]

Folksingers were coming and going, grabbing for the commercial brass ring as best they could, with some falling by the wayside. Phil Ochs struggled into the 1970s, until spinning out of control in early 1976; his suicide was shocking, yet not entirely unexpected. Dylan, Baez, Collins, and many others continued to record and perform. A *Life* cover featured Collins in May 1969, a "gentle voice amid the strife." Others such as Harry Chapin, who was steeped in Seeger, the Weavers, and others of the founding generation, began the slow climb to fame and fortune. And if Newport and the Berkeley Folk Festival had vanished, other festivals—Philadelphia, University of Chicago, Fox Hollow—filled the gaps, presenting a compound of styles to the mixed crowds of students and their parents.[78]

"I have been sitting here thinking about myself and where I've been over the past couple of years," Janis Ian, not yet twenty but a seasoned performer, wrote to Sis Cunningham and Gordon Friesen in early 1970. "I thought back to the first Broadside hoot I was at—remember that? Phil, Tom, Len, the SNCC singers, Peter Seeger, god it seems like everyone in the whole world was there for *Broadside*."[79]

The folk revival had run its course, or had it? Folk music—acoustic, traditional, with or without a message, hard to pin down but seemingly identifiable; blues, Cajun, klezmer, old-time, country, Celtic, bluegrass—would continue to flow along in both commercial and private channels, as it had long done, continuing to capture and charm. If folk reached its commercial peak sometime in the mid-1960s, this was only a fleeting recognition of its potential ability to reach out beyond the small, scattered groups of performers and political activists who had long been its champions. The story neither begins in 1940 nor ends in 1970; but this was a period when a remarkable number of performers, collectors, organizers, managers, academics, journalists, record company owners, writers, store owners, and many others coalesced to promote the music. They were driven by an odd mixture of commercial, political, and aesthetic motives.

"A slow but dramatic metamorphosis in contemporary musical expression is transforming most 'popular' music into 'folk music,'" Gene Youngblood forcefully contended in the hip *Los Angeles Free Press*, while reviewing the film *Festival*, filmed at Newport from 1963 to 1966. "The young generation is a generation of plug-in troubadors. Slung over their back is an electric fuzz bass instead of a homemade lute. . . . And because of them it is increasingly true: 'pop' music is 'folk' music, from Beatles to Baez to Dylan and Donovan." Bubbling up from the grassroots, rock and roll was surely as much folk as was the deepest southern blues or hillbilly string-band music. "This new music may have its roots more in technology than in turf," Youngblood continued, "but because of our affluent and technological society, the Moog Synthesizer, the wah-wah peddle [sic] and the Vox amp are as accessible and intrinsic to the new troubador as the jug and Jew's Harp were to the mountain moaner. And if the message has changed from dirt to dope it still is a message, still personal, still reflective of the attitudes of the 'folk.' "[80]

Notes

Preface

1. Jim Bessman, "Rising Singer/Songwriters Redefine Folk in the '90s," *Billboard*, July 16, 1994, 1, 36.

2. Lynn Van Matre, "The Unbroken Circle: A Folk Resurgence Is Blowing in the Wind as a New Generation Discovers Old-time Sounds," *Chicago Tribune*, May 16, 1993, section 5, 7.

3. Nat Hentoff, "The Odyssey of Woody Guthrie: The Rebel Who Started the Folk-song Craze," *Pageant*, Mar. 1964, 103.

4. Pete Seeger, *Where Have All the Flowers Gone: A Singer's Stories, Songs, Seeds, Robberies* (Bethlehem, Pa.: A Sing Out Publication, 1993), 67; Harold Meyerson and Ernie Harburg, *Who Put the Rainbow in The Wizard of Oz?: Yip Harburg, Lyricist* (Ann Arbor: University of Michigan Press, 1993), 135, 224.

5. Theodore Bikel, *Theo: The Autobiography of Theodore Bikel* (New York: HarperCollins, 1994), 167–68.

Prologue

1. Cohen interview with Guy Carawan, Gary, Ind., Jan. 24, 1991. Cohen interview with Frank Hamilton, Atlanta, Ga., Nov. 2, 1990 (revised Mar. 2, 1993).

2. Cohen interview with Guy Carawan, Jan. 24, 1991; Cohen interview with Frank Hamilton, Nov. 2, 1990.

3. "Guy's Journal, Summer 1953," 1, 6 (copy of MS courtesy of Guy Carawan). On Lunsford, see Loyal Jones, *Minstrel of the Appalachians: The Story of Bascom Lamar Lunsford* (Boone, N.C.: Appalachian Consortium Press, 1984).

4. "Guy's Journal, Summer 1953," 7; Cohen interview with Frank Hamilton, Nov. 2, 1990.

5. "Guy's Journal, Summer 1953," 10.
6. "Guy's Journal, Summer 1953," 19–20, 23. On Highlander, see John Glen, *Highlander: No Ordinary School, 1932–1962* (Lexington: University of Kentucky Press, 1988).
7. "Guy's Journal, Summer 1953," 30–32. On Black Mountain College, Martin Duberman, *Black Mountain: An Exploration in Community* (New York: Anchor Books, 1973).
8. Cohen interview with Billy Faier, Woodstock, N.Y., Aug. 8, 1992.
9. Cohen interview with Frank Hamilton, Nov. 2, 1990. Hamilton to Cohen, Oct. 5, 1994.

Chapter 1

1. Blanche Lemmon, "American Folk Songs," *Etude* 58 (Apr. 1940), 220.
2. Lemmon, "American Folk Songs," 220, 274; Alan Lomax to Ronald Cohen, Dec. 6, 1993.
3. D. K. Wilgus, *Anglo-American Folksong Scholarship since 1898* (New Brunswick: Rutgers University Press, 1959), xix. See also Norm Cohen, "The History of the Folksong Revival," in the booklet accompanying the CD boxed set *Folk Song America: A 20th Century Revival* (Washington, D.C.: Smithsonian Collections of Recordings, 1990), 5–9.
4. Georgina Boyes, *The Imagined Village: Culture, Ideology and the English Folk Revival* (Manchester, U.K.: Manchester University Press, 1993). Boyes does not mention Sharp's collecting in the United States. For a more critical view of Sharp and others, David Harker, *Fakesong: The Manufacture of British "Folksong" 1700 to the Present Day* (Philadelphia: Open University Press, 1985).
5. David Whisnant, *All That Is Native and Fine: The Politics of Culture in an American Region* (Chapel Hill: University of North Carolina Press, 1983); Henry D. Shapiro, *Appalachia on Our Mind: The Southern Mountains and Mountaineers in the American Consciousness, 1870–1920* (Chapel Hill: University of North Carolina Press, 1978), chap. 10; Eileen Boris, *Art and Labor: Ruskin, Morris, and the Craftsman Ideal in America* (Philadelphia: Temple University Press, 1986); Benjamin Filene, *Romancing the Folk: Public Memory and American Roots Music* (Chapel Hill: University of North Carolina Press, 2000), chaps. 1–2; Richard A. Peterson, *Creating Country Music: Fabricating Authenticity* (Chicago: University of Chicago Press, 1997).
6. Charles Seeger, notes in booklet for *Peggy Seeger, The Folkways Years, 1955–1992: Songs of Love and Politics* (Smithsonian Folkways CD, SF 40048).
7. Penelope Niven, *Carl Sandburg: A Biography* (New York: Scribner's, 1991), 444, 448–63.
8. Carl Sandburg, *The American Songbag* (New York: Harcourt, Brace, 1927); Judith Tick, *Ruth Crawford Seeger: A Composer's Search for American Music* (New York.: Oxford University Press, 1997).
9. For a helpful discussion of the state of folk song scholarship and collecting at the time, see Debora Kodish, *Good Friends and Bad Enemies: Robert Winslow Gordon and the Study of American Folksong* (Urbana: University of Illinois Press, 1986), chap. 1.
10. Engel quoted in Peter T. Bartis, "A History of the Archive of Folk Song at the Library of Congress: The First Fifty Years," unpub. Ph.D. diss., University of Pennsylvania, 1982, 1. On Gordon's life, see Kodish, *Good Friends and Bad Enemies*.
11. For various views of Lomax, see Nolan Porterfield, *Last Cavalier: The Life and Times of John A. Lomax, 1867–1948* (Urbana: University of Illinois Press, 1996); Charles Wolfe and Kip Lornell, *The Life and Legend of Leadbelly* (New York: HarperCollins, 1992); Jerrold Hirsch, "Modernity, Nostalgia, and Southern Folklore Studies: The Case of John Lomax," *Journal of American Folklore* 105 (Spring 1992), 183–207; Gene Bluestein, *The Voice of the Folk: Folklore and American Literary Theory* (Amherst: University of Massachusetts Press, 1972); Wilgus, *Anglo-American Folksong Scholarship*; and John A. Lomax, *Adventures of a Ballad Hunter* (New York: Macmillan, 1947).
12. On the Lomaxes and their role in collecting and shaping vernacular music, see Filene, *Romancing the Folk*, chap. 2.

13. Alan Lomax, *The Land Where the Blues Began* (New York: Pantheon, 1993), 286. On John Lomax's conservative views, see Hirsch, "Modernity, Nostalgia, and Southern Folklore Studies." And see, in general, Wolfe and Lornell, *The Life and Legend of Leadbelly* and Porterfield, *Last Cavalier.*

14. Whisnant, *All That Is Native and Fine,* Seeger quote on 207, and see chap. 3 in general. Timothy Lloyd, "Whole Work, Whole Play, Whole People: Folklore and Social Therapeutics in the 1920s and 1930s America," *Journal of American Folklore* 110:437 (Summer 1997), 239–59.

15. See the fascinating discussion in Norm Cohen, "Minstrels & Tunesmiths: The Commercial Roots of Early Country Music Illustrated with Early Recordings from 1902–1923," booklet to accompany the album of the same name (John Edwards Memorial Foundation LP-109). Archie Green, *Only a Miner: Studies in Recorded Coal-Mining Songs* (Urbana: University of Illinois Press, 1972), chaps. 1 and 2.

16. Charles Wolfe, *The Devil's Box: Masters of Southern Fiddling* (Nashville: Country Music Foundation Press and Vanderbilt University Press, 1997). Andre Millard, *America on Record: A History of Recorded Sound* (New York: Cambridge University Press, 1995). William H. Kenney, *Recorded Music in American Life: The Phonograph and Popular Memory, 1890–1945* (New York: Oxford University Press, 1999).

17. Paul Oliver, Max Harrison, and William Bolcom, *The New Grove Gospel, Blues, and Jazz, with Spirituals and Ragtime* (New York.: W.W. Norton, 1986). Lawrence Cohn, ed., *Nothing but the Blues: The Music and the Musicians* (New York: Abbeville Press, 1993). Paul Oliver, *The Blackwell Guide to Recorded Blues* (Cambridge, Mass.: Blackwell, 1991).

18. For a discussion of other styles of black music, see Paul Oliver, *Songsters and Saints: Vocal Traditions on Race Records* (New York: Cambridge University Press, 1984).

19. Jean A. Boyd, *The Jazz of the Southwest: An Oral History of Western Swing* (Austin: University of Texas Press, 1998).

20. Lawrence Gellert, *Negro Songs of Protest* (New York: American Music League, 1936), 7. Bruce Harrah-Conforth, "Laughing Just to Keep from Crying: Afro-American Folksong and the Field Recordings of Lawrence Gellert," unpub. M.A. thesis, Indiana University, 1984, 64–73. Some of Gellert's recordings were finally released: *Negro Songs of Protest* (Rounder Records 4004) and *Cap'n, You're So Mean* (Rounder Records 4013).

21. Herbert Halpert, "Federal Theater and Folksong," *Southern Folklore Quarterly* 2, 83; Halpert, "American Folk Songs," *The American Music Lover* (Mar. 1938), 414, 416.

22. Clark D. Halker, *For Democracy, Workers, and God: Labor Song-Poems and Labor Protest, 1865–95* (Urbana: University of Illinois Press, 1991). Philip S. Foner, *American Labor Songs of the Nineteenth Century* (Urbana: University of Illinois Press, 1975). Archie Green, "Homestead's Strike Songs," in *Wobblies, Pile Butts, and Other Heroes: Laborlore Explorations* (Urbana: University of Illinois Press, 1993), 229–72; David King Dunaway, "Music and Politics in the United States," *Folk Music Journal* 5:3 (1987), 268–94.

23. Green, "Singing Joe Hill," in *Wobblies, Pile Butts, and Other Heroes,* 77–94. Lori Elaine Taylor, "Joe Hill Incorporated: We Own Our Past," in *Songs about Work: Essays in Occupational Culture for Richard A. Reuss,* ed. Archie Green (Bloomington, Ind.: Special Publications of the Folklore Institute No. 3, 1993), 23–36. Joyce L. Kornbluh, ed., *Rebel Voices: An I.W.W. Anthology* (Ann Arbor: University of Michigan Press, 1964). A good selection of recordings of Joe Hill songs is *Don't Mourn—Organize: Songs of Labor Songwriter Joe Hill* (Smithsonian Folkways SF 40026). The first complete publication of his songs is Barrie Stavis and Frank Harmon (aka Fred Hellerman), *The Songs of Joe Hill* (New York: People's Artists, 1955). For McClintock's recordings, see Harry McClintock, *Hallelujah! I'm a Bum* (Rounder Records 1009).

24. Shelly Romalis, *Pistol Packin' Mama: Aunt Molly Jackson and the Politics of Folksong* (Urbana: University of Illinois Press, 1998).

25. Bill Malone, *Country Music U.S.A,* rev. ed. (Austin: University of Texas Press, 1985), 129–35. R. Serge Denisoff, *Great Day Coming: Folk Music and the American Left* (Urbana: University

of Illinois Press, 1971), chap. 2. Richard A. Reuss with JoAnne C. Reuss, *American Folk Music and Left-wing Politics, 1927–1957* (Lanham, Md.: Scarecrow Press, 2000). Archie Green's notes for *Sarah Ogan Gunning, "Girl of Constant Sorrow"* (Folk-Legacy Records FSA-26). John Greenway, *American Folksongs of Protest* (Philadelphia: University of Pennsylvania Press, 1953). Edith Fowke and Joe Glazer, *Songs of Work and Freedom* (Chicago: Roosevelt University, 1960). Alan Lomax, comp., *Hard Hitting Songs for Hard-Hit People* (New York: Oak Publications, 1967). See, in general, Green, *Only a Miner*, particularly chap. 3; Guido Van Rijn, *Roosevelt's Blues: African-American Blues and Gospel Songs on FDR* (Jackson: University Press of Mississippi, 1997). Two excellent compilations of recorded rural protest songs are *Hard Times* (Rounder Records 4007) and *Poor Man, Rich Man: American Country Songs of Protest* (Rounder Records 1026).

26. On the Communist party, see Fraser M. Ottanelli, *The Communist Party of the United States: From the Depression to World War II* (New Brunswick, N.J.: Rutgers University Press, 1991), and Harvey Klehr, *The Heyday of Communism: The Depression Decade* (New York: Basic Books, 1984).

27. See Chris Waters, *British Socialists and the Politics of Popular Culture, 1884–1914* (Stanford: Stanford University Press, 1990), chap. 4, and Kenneth Teitelbaum, *Schooling for "Good Rebels": Socialist Education for Children in the United States, 1900–1920* (Philadelphia: Temple University Press, 1993), 163–67.

28. Charles Seeger, "Music in America," *Magazine of Art*, July 1938, 411, 436.

29. *Workers Song Book* (New York: Workers Music League, 1934), 3. Workers Music League, *Red Song Book* (New York: Workers Library Publishers, 1932). Denisoff, *Great Day Coming*, chap. 3. Reuss, *American Folk Music and Left-wing Politics*, chap. 3.

30. Seeger quoted in Ann M. Pescatello, *Charles Seeger: A Life in American Music* (Pittsburgh: University of Pittsburgh Press, 1992), 135. William F. McDonald, *Federal Relief Administration and the Arts* (Columbus: Ohio State University Press, 1969), 636–41.

31. John Hammond, *John Hammond on Record: An Autobiography* (New York: Penguin Books, 1981), 200. Mark Naison, *Communists in Harlem. During the Depression* (Urbana: University of Illinois Press, 1983), 211–13. Malcolm Goldstein, *The Political Stage: American Drama and Theater of the Great Depression* (New York: Oxford University Press, 1974), 197–205. Eric A. Gordon, *Mark the Music: The Life and Work of Marc Blitzstein* (New York: St. Martin's Press, 1989), 176–77. Barbara Stratyner, " 'Significant Historical Events . . . Thrilling Dance Sequences': Communist Party Pageants in New York, 1937," *Studies in Dance History* 5 (Spring 1994), 31–49. On the Communist party and popular culture, see Paul R. Gorman, *Left Intellectuals and Popular Culture in Twentieth-Century America* (Chapel Hill: University of North Carolina Press, 1996), esp. chap. 5, and Michael Denning, *The Cultural Front: The Laboring of American Culture in the Twentieth Century* (New York: Verso, 1997).

32. Helen Lawrenson, "Black and White and Red All Over," *New York*, Aug. 21, 1978, 36–42. Denning, *Cultural Front*, chap. 9. David W. Stowe, "The Politics of Cafe Society," *Journal of American History* 84:4 (March 1998), 1384–1406. Max Gordon, *Live at the Village Vanguard* (New York: St. Martin's Press, 1980). Elijah Wald, *Josh White: Society Blues* (Amherst: University of Massachusetts Press, 2000).

33. Julia S. Ardery, ed., *Welcome the Traveler Home: Jim Garland's Story of the Kentucky Mountains* (Lexington: University Press of Kentucky, 1983).

34. John Lomax to Alan Lomax, April 25, 1940, Lomax Family Papers, American Folklife Center, Library of Congress, Washington, D.C. Alan Lomax, "Saga of a Folksong Hunter," *HiFi/Stereo Review*, May 1960, 40.

35. Alan Lomax, "Songs of the American Folk," *Modern Music* 18 (Jan.-Feb. 1941), 138. Ray had started with the Department of Agriculture's Resettlement Administration in 1937, along with Charles Seeger. Ostensibly in charge of local theater activities, Ray also traveled around recording traditional musicians, and had become familiar with Aunt Molly Jackson and other performers while sharing a house with the Lomaxes.

36. Alan Lomax to Woody Guthrie, February 4, 1941, Woody Guthrie Publications,

Inc./Woody Guthrie Archives, New York City. Lomax and Guthrie quoted in Bernard Eisenschitz, *Nicholas Ray: An American Journey* (London: Faber and Faber, 1993), 60, and see 39–72, and 499 for lists of the radio shows.

37. Henrietta Yurchenco, "The Beginning of an Urban Folk-song Movement in New York: A Memoir," *Sonneck Society Bulletin* 13 (Summer 1987), 39–40. Yurchenco, *A Mighty Hard Road: The Woody Guthrie Story* (New York: McGraw-Hill, 1970), 104–6; Joe Klein, *Woody Guthrie: A Life* (New York: Knopf, 1980), 165–70.

38. Stephen West, "Americans Want American Music! A Conference with Elie Siegmeister," *Etude*, Jan. 1944, 54. Naomi Feld, "Singing Is a Form of Battle," *Daily Worker*, Dec. 28, 1942. Elie Siegmeister, ed., *The Music Lover's Handbook* (New York: Morrow, 1943), 19, 679–82. Horace Grenell also carried on the choral tradition during World War II with the American People's Chorus, mixing Left politics, European classical music, folk music, and grassroots democratic convictions. Grenell taught music at Brooklyn College and was fired during the Red Scare; in the 1940s he founded Young People's Records, a mail-order company, with stories and folk music, that included Pete Seeger, Oscar Brand, and Tom Glazer. Becoming Children's Record Guild in 1950, the company was shipping 200,000 records a month at its height.

39. Irene Tannenbaum, "Mass Folk Music Aim of Workers Order Chorus," *Daily Worker*, May 27, 1939. *Reader's Digest* quoted in "Paul Robeson Broadcast Brings Cheers from Vast Radio Public," *Daily Worker*, Nov. 20, 1939. Roger Kerran, "National Groups and the Popular Front: The Case of the International Workers Order," *Journal of American Ethnic History* 14 (Spring 1995), 23–51. See, in particular, Earl Robinson with Eric A. Gordon, *Ballad of an American: The Autobiography of Earl Robinson* (Lanham, Md.: Scarecrow Press, 1998).

40. Sally Osborne Norton, "A Historical Study of Actor Will Geer, His Life and Work in the Context of Twentieth-Century American Social, Political, and Theatrical History," Ph.D. diss., University of Southern California, 1980, 328.

41. Roy Harris, "Folksong—American Big Business" *Modern Music* 18 (Nov.-Dec. 1940), 10–11. Barbara A. Zuck, *A History of Musical Americanism* (Ann Arbor, Mich.: UMI Research Press, 1980), 139–53.

42. Chester Kallman, "I Hear America Singing," *Harper's Bazaar*, June 1941, 86.

43. "September Records," *Time*, Sept. 15, 1941, 51; George Lewis, "America Is in Their Songs," *Daily Worker*, Mar. 24, 1941.

44. "DISCussion," *Promenade* 2 (Nov. 1941). Letter from John Hammond et al., n.d., about "Songs for John Doe," MS copy in Seeger scrapbooks. Pete Seeger to Millard Lampell, Oct. 1, 1987 (courtesy of Pete Seeger).

45. FBI report, "Almanac Singers," Oct. 29, 1941. J. Edgar Hoover to SAC (Special Agent in Charge), New York, Apr. 28, 1943, FBI office files, U.S. Department of Justice, released under a Freedom of Information Act request.

46. Pete Seeger, *Where Have All the Flowers Gone: A Singer's Stories, Songs, Seeds, Robberies* (Bethlehem, Pa.: Sing Out, 1993), 22.

47. "September Records," *Time*, Sept. 15, 1941, 51. See Goldstein, *The Political Stage*, 215.

48. Pete Seeger to Millard Lampell, Oct. 1, 1987.

49. Gordon, *Live at the Village Vanguard*, 44–53.

50. Flyer for "Victory Campaign Rally," in Seeger scrapbooks.

51. Pete Seeger to Millard Lampell, Oct. 1, 1987.

52. Seeger to Lampell. Bruce Bastin, *Red River Blues: The Blues Tradition in the Southeast* (Urbana: University of Illinois Press, 1986), chap. 15. See also Agnes "Sis" Cunningham and Gordon Friesen, *Red Dust and Broadsides: A Joint Autobiography* (Amherst: University of Massachusetts Press, 1999).

53. Gordon Friesen, "Open Door at Almanac House," *Broadside* 7 (June 1962), 6. Anne Chester to the Almanac Singers, Dec. 13, 1941, in Richard A. Reuss Papers, Indiana University Archives, Bloomington, Ind. (hereafter cited as Reuss Papers).

54. Friesen, "Winter and War Came to Almanac House," *Broadside* 8 (June 30, 1962), 7. Robert Stephens, " 'Peace Choir Changes Tune," *New York Post*, Feb. 17, 1942.

55. Eugene Burr, "From Out Front," *Billboard*, June 27, 1942. Army staff sergeant Lampell wrote numerous air force radio series, including *First in the Air* for CBS, *I Sustain the Wings* for NBC, and *Return to Duty* for the Mutual network, in which he occasionally named fictional characters after his friends Pete Seeger, Cisco Houston, and Lee Hays. See Sgt. Millard Lampell, *The Long Way Home* (New York: Julian Messner, 1946).

56. Arthur Stern to Pete Seeger, late 1942, in Reuss Papers.

57. Stern to Seeger.

58. Pete Seeger to Millard Lampell, Oct. 1, 1987. On the party during the war, see Maurice Isserman, *Which Side Were You On? The American Communist Party during the Second World War* (Middletown, Conn.: Wesleyan University Press, 1982).

59. Ellen Graff, *Stepping Left: Dance and Politics in New York City, 1928–1942* (Durham: Duke University Press, 1997), chap. 6.

60. Pete Seeger to Gordon Friesen, n.d., quoted in Reuss, *American Folk Music and Left-wing Politics*, 174.

61. John Hasted, *Alternative Memoirs* (Itchenor, West Sussex: Greengate Press, 1992), 121, 124.

62. "That's Gold in Them Thar Hillbilly and Other American Folk Tunes," *Billboard*, Band Year Book, Sept. 26, 1942, 86. "Hillbilly Disks Hit New Midwest High, Say Dealers," *Billboard*, July 31, 1943, 16. "Folk Music Takes Hold in the Jukes," *The Billboard 1944 Music Year Book*, 343, and see also 353.

63. Peter Goldsmith, *Making People's Music: Moe Asch and Folkways Records* (Washington, D.C.: Smithsonian Institution Press, 1998), 109–10. When the Soviet Union pulled out of the New York World's Fair in mid-1939 it left behind tens of thousands of Russian records, including the "Red Army Chorus," which Harris sold briskly to American-Soviet friendship groups. With the materials shortage during the war Asch supplied the recordings and Harris the shellac. Harris, a Communist party member, committed suicide in 1956, perhaps a casualty of Khruschev's revelations of Stalin's crimes.

64. Seymour Peck, "America Sings for Asch," *PM*, Sept. 19, 1944. The American Federation of Musicians, led by James C. Petrillo, struck the major record companies in August 1942 (until November 1944), attempting to lessen the competition with live performances. Many black performers, relegated to Jim Crow locals, continued to record for smaller labels, however, which greatly benefited Asch.

65. "Offbeat," *Time*, Feb. 25, 1946, 65; Goldsmith, *Making People's Music*, 169–70.

Chapter 2

1. Ted Zittel, "Ballads Are Booming," *Everybody's Digest*, undated clipping [1945], 71.

2. Oscar Brand, *The Ballad Mongers: Rise of the Modern Folk Song* (New York: Funk & Wagnalls, 1962), 82–83. "New Series of Folk Song Dramatizations," *Daily Worker*, Oct. 7, 1946.

3. Elie Siegmeister, "Probing the Treasury of Native Minstrelsy," *New York Times*, undated clipping [ca. early 1945].

4. Goldsmith, *Making People's Music*, chap. 4.

5. Pete Seeger, "Report from the Marianas—Number 8," June 9, 1945, mimeographed (copy in author's possession).

6. Pete Seeger to Moses Asch, Apr. 18, 1944, quoted in Goldsmith, *Making People's Music*, 140. Pete Seeger, "Report from the Marianas—Number 9," Aug. 12, 1945, mimeographed.

7. Cohen interview with Mario "Boots" Casetta, Los Angeles, Dec. 5, 1991.

8. Len DeCaux, "A CIO Staffer Works and Dreams," in *The Cold War against Labor*, ed. Ann Fagan Ginger and David Christiano, vol. 1 (Berkeley, Calif.: Meiklejohn Civil Liberties Institute, 1987), 132.

9. See David Leviatin, *Followers of the Trail: Jewish Working-class Radicals in America* (New Haven: Yale University Press, 1989), 15–16, 32–37. Robbie Lieberman, *"My Song Is My Weapon": People's Songs, American Communism, and the Politics of Culture, 1930–1950* (Urbana: University of Illinois Press, 1989), 18, 60–62. Arthur Liebman, *Jews and the Left* (New York: John Wiley and Sons, 1979), 321–24, 557. Paul Mishler, *Raising Reds* (New York: Columbia University Press, 1999), chap. 5.

10. Program for "All-day Conference on Folklore in a Democracy," Elisabeth Irwin High School, Mar. 10, 1945. Program for "Folklore in the Metropolis: An All Day Conference on the Collection and Utilization of Folklore in a Democracy," Elisabeth Irwin High School, May 4, 1946.

11. Lee Hays to Earl Robinson, ca. Dec. 1945, Earl Robinson Papers, University of Washington–Seattle Archives.

12. Woody Guthrie, *Pastures of Plenty: A Self-Portrait*, ed. Dave Marsh and Harold Leventhal (New York: HarperCollins, 1990), 158–59. Cohen interview with Bernie Asbell, State College, Pa., Aug. 14, 1992. Pete Seeger, "People's Songs and Singers," *New Masses*, July 16, 1946, 8. David Dunaway, *How Can I Keep from Singing: Pete Seeger* (New York: McGraw-Hill, 1981), 118.

13. Mike Gold, "Change the World," *Daily Worker*, Jan. 2, 1946. *People's Songs* 1:1 (Feb. 1946), 1.

14. Guthrie, *Pastures of Plenty*, 161–63.

15. *Pittsburgh Press*, Mar. 23, 1946; Louise Levitas, "The Blues up to Date," *PM*, Apr. 2, 1946.

16. Waldemar Hille to "Dear Songwriter," Aug. 17, 1946 (copy in author's possession).

17. "People's Songs Designed to Fight Discrimination," *The Afro-American*, May 4, 1946. "Hootenanny," *Time*, Apr. 15, 1946, 71–72. N.C., " 'Free World' Hoot: Music in Action," *Daily Worker*, Oct. 22, 1946.

18. Edwin Gordon, "Cultivating Songs of the People," *New York Times*, Aug. 25, 1946. Hille edited *The People's Song Book* (1948), successor to *A People's Songs Wordbook* (1947).

19. Ann Seymour, "At Your Service," undated clipping [ca. 1946].

20. Beth McHenry, "Lee Hays and His Buddies Hit the Picket Line Again," *Daily Worker*, May 15, 1946. Margot Mayor, "Wanted: Criticism," *Promenade* 5:3 (June-July 1946), 1.

21. Minutes of the National Board Meeting, People's Songs, Inc., Oct. 27, 1946, in Reuss Papers.

22. George Margolin, "Sidewalk Hootenanny," *People's Songs* 2:1, 2 (Feb.-Mar. 1947), 6.

23. "PAC Urges Councils to Seek Free Time," *Broadcasting*, Sept. 9, 1946, 30. George Sokolsky, "These Days," *New York Sun*, Sept. 13, 1946. Frederick Woltman, "Communist Minstrels Set Tunes for PAC," *World-Telegram*, undated clipping. See Ellen Schrecker, *Many Are the Crimes: McCarthyism in America* (Boston: Little, Brown, 1998).

24. "Report of Publicity Director and Production Manager," minutes of the National Board Meeting, People's Songs, Inc., Oct. 27, 1946, in Reuss Papers. Woody Guthrie to DISC Company of America, July 14, 1946, Smithsonian Folkways Collection, Center for Folklife and Cultural Heritage, Smithsonian Institution, Washington, D.C. (hereafter Smithsonian Folkways Collection).

25. Asch Records, "For Immediate Release, New Folk Series Is Announced by Asch Records," mimeo, n.d. [ca. late 1946]. For more on Brownie McGhee's career at this point, see *Guitar Styles of Brownie McGhee* (New York: Oak Publications, 1971), 12–16.

26. Robinson with Gordon, *Ballad of an American*, 207–12.

27. "Report of the National Director," minutes of the National Board Meeting, People's Songs, Inc., Oct. 27, 1946, in Reuss Papers.

28. Some of Wolff's papers are in the Southern Folklife Collection, Wilson Library, University of North Carolina at Chapel Hill. Sonny Vale formed the Los Angeles People's Songs chorus in June 1947. Left choruses, never abandoned, still existed in New York,

including the Jefferson Chorus, part of the Communist-affiliated Jefferson School, and the American Ballad Singers, directed by Elie Siegmeister, which preferred traditional folk songs. The American People's Chorus, organized in 1938, changed its name to the Jefferson School Chorus after affiliating with the school in 1943. First conducted by Earl Robinson, then Horace Grenell and Herbert Haufrecht, and finally in 1948 by Elmer Bernstein, the group issued Picket Line Songs on Moe Asch's short-lived Union label in 1946. The Jewish Peoples Fraternal Order formed the Jewish Folk Singers in October 1946.

29. Stuart Timmons, The Trouble with Harry Hay: Founder of the Modern Gay Movement (Boston: Alyson Publications, 1990), 127–29.

30. Cohen interview with Mario Casetta, Los Angeles, Dec. 5, 1991. With much difficulty, Casetta continued the company while in New York; its last gasp, the "Peekskill Story," documenting the militant side of the conservative backlash, appeared in late 1949.

31. "Boots" Casetta, "One Big State," People's Songs 2:1, 2 (Feb.-Mar. 1947), 4.

32. Carl Williams, "Working and Singing in Unison," Daily People's World, Apr. 24, 1947. Mike Vance, "Songster Jerry Walter: A Culture from the People," Daily People's World, July 12, 1948.

33. Raeburn Flerlage, "The People's Music," Chicago Star, clipping dated Dec. 1946. Flerlage, "The Ballad of Burl Ives; A Saga of Rags to Riches," Chicago Star, Jan. 25, 1947. See also Raeburn Flerlage to Felix Landau, Jan. 23, 1947, in Pete Seeger scrapbooks.

34. Mike Scott, "Singing People," People's Songs 1:9 (Oct. 1946), 2. Eric Von Schmidt and Jim Rooney, Baby, Let Me Follow You Down: The Illustrated Story of the Cambridge Folk Years, 2d ed. (Amherst: University of Massachusetts Press, 1995), 76.

35. "Miserable but Exciting Songs," Time, Nov. 26, 1945, 52.

36. "Americana on Records," Newsweek, Sept. 22, 1947, 83. Alan Lomax, "Introduction to American Folk Music Series," Sing-Along-Book of Cowboy Songs and Negro Spirituals Sung by Carl Sandburg (Decca Records A-356).

37. John S. Wilson, "Lomax Brings in the Roots," PM, Nov. 4, 1946. Virgil Thompson, "Music," New York Herald Tribune, Nov. 11, 1946.

38. Alan Lomax, "The Best of the Ballads," Vogue, Dec. 1, 1946, 208. Lomax, "America Sings the Saga of America," New York Times Magazine, Jan. 26, 1947, 16.

39. "Editorials," Christian Science Monitor, Mar. 4, 1947. New Yorker, Dec. 21, 1946, 81–82. Billboard, Mar. 15, 1947.

40. "New Folk Singer," Life, Oct. 29, 1945, 137.

41. David Platt, "Josef Marais and Miranda, Ballad Singers of the African Bushveld," Daily Worker, Nov. 16, 1946.

42. Gordon, Live at the Village Vanguard, 57. Elaine Lambert Lewis, "City Billet," New York Folklore Quarterly 2 (Nov. 1946), 284–85.

43. Horace Reynolds, "Collecting Our Living Folksong," New York Times Book Review, Mar. 2, 1947, 7. Reynolds, "Heard It Ring-nnng: Library of Congress Provides Songs and Tunes of Early Americans," Christian Science Monitor, May 17, 1947, 6. See Bill C. Malone, Southern Music/American Music (Lexington: University Press of Kentucky, 1979) and Malone, Singing Cowboys and Musical Mountaineers: Southern Culture and the Roots of Country Music (Athens: University of Georgia Press, 1993).

44. Courtlandt Canby, "Voice, Heart, Memory," Saturday Review of Literature, Nov. 15, 1947. Elaine Lambert Lewis, "City Billet," New York Folklore Quarterly 4 (Autumn 1948), 235. Trying to establish her folk credentials, Stafford established an annual folklore prize of $250 in 1948, judged by a committee of the American Folklore Society, for the best collection of American folklore by a university student.

45. Frederick Woltman, "Reds' Class Struggle Singers Hold Forth on WNYC," New York World-Telegram, undated clipping [ca. mid-1947]. See also Cederic Belfrage, The American Inquisition, 1945–1960 (Indianapolis: Bobbs-Merrill, 1973), chaps. 6–7.

46. Irwin Silber, "United Songsters Make a Chain," People's Songs 2:10 (Nov. 1947), 3.

47. *Hootenanny* pamphlet [ca. late 1946], 7.

48. "The Un-American Menace," *People's Songs* 2:11 (Dec. 1947), 2. Pete Seeger to "Dear Friend," Jan. 26, 1948, in Pete Seeger scrapbooks.

49. Robert Friedman, "People's Song Book," *Daily Worker*, Feb. 20, 1948. Pete Seeger to members, n.d. (copy in author's possession).

50. For a partial list of the signers of the statement, see "500 Leaders in Arts and Sciences Back Wallace," *Daily Worker*, Oct. 19, 1948.

51. Mario Casseta to Bill Oliver, Sept. 4, 1958, in Mario Casseta Papers (in author's possession). Cohen interview with Mario Casetta, Los Angeles, December 5, 1991. See also Curtis MacDougall, *Gideon's Army* (New York: Marzani and Munsell, 1965), 651. For Robeson's role in the campaign, see Martin Bauml Duberman, *Paul Robeson* (New York: Knopf, 1988), chap. 16.

52. *People's Songs* 3:10 (Nov. 1948), 1, and see MacDougall, *Gideon's Army*, 651.

53. *People's Songs* 3:11 (Dec. 1948), 2.

54. Minutes of the Meeting of National Board of Directors of People's Songs, December 18, 1948, in Reuss Papers.

55. *People's Songs* 4:1 (Feb. 1949), 2. Sidney Finkelstein, "The Folk Song's Back to Stay," *Worker Magazine*, Mar. 6, 1949, 2.

56. Barnard Rubin, "Broadway Beat," *Daily Worker*, Apr. 8, 1949.

57. Roger Butterfield, "Turkeys in the Straw," *Saturday Review of Literature*, Jan. 31, 1948, 56.

58. Gilbert Chase, "Folk Music on Records," *The Music Journal*, Jan.-Feb. 1948, 15. Howard Taubman, "Records: From U.S. Folksong Archive," *New York Times*, Apr. 10, 1949.

59. Charles Seeger, "Reviews," *Journal of American Folklore* 61 (Apr. 1948), 216–18. Horace Reynolds, "Kingdom of American Balladry," *Saturday Review of Literature*, June 26, 1948, 15.

60. Harold H. Martin, "Minstrel Man of the Appalachians," *Saturday Evening Post*, May 22, 1948, 31.

61. Bascom Lamar Lunsford to Zilphia Horton, Mar. 23, 1946 and Jessie O'Connor to Zilphia Horton, Oct. 6, 1947, Highlander Folk School Collection, Tennessee State Library and Archives, Nashville, Tennessee. On folk music at Highlander, see John M. Glen, *Highlander: No Ordinary School, 1932–1962* (Lexington: University Press of Kentucky, 1988), 37, 54.

62. Dan Singer, "Susan Reed Replaces Leadbelly, Performing in Folk Festival," *The Phoenix* (Swarthmore College), Apr. 28, 1948, 1. Ralph Lee Smith, "If I Had a Song," *Swarthmore College Bulletin*, Mar. 1997, 17–20, 62.

63. Ben Gray Lumpkin, *Folksongs on Records* (Boulder, Colo.: Ben Gray Lumpkin, 1948), 2. Ben Gray Lumpkin with Norman L. McNeil, *Folksongs on Records*, (Boulder, Colo.: Folksongs on Records, 1950).

64. People's Songs press release, Sept. 10, 1948, in Reuss Papers.

65. Program for "Elsa Maxwell's Americana Party," May 11, 1949. For this period, see Belfrage, *American Inquisition*, chaps. 9–10.

66. "Launch New People's Music Group July 8," *Daily Worker*, July 4, 1949. "Paul Robeson to Star in Outdoor Concert for Harlem Civil Rights," *Daily Worker*, Aug. 15, 1949.

67. Irwin Silber, in *"Wasn't That a Time!" Firsthand Accounts of the Folk Music Revival*, ed. Ronald D. Cohen (Metuchen, N.J.: Scarecrow Press, 1995), 99. Duberman, *Paul Robeson*.

68. Lee Hays, "Simon McKeever at Peekskill," *Daily Worker*, Sept. 18, 1949. See Dunaway, *How Can I Keep from Singing*, chap. 1, and Duberman, *Paul Robeson*, chap. 18.

69. Pete Seeger, "Interim Newsletter," no. 1 (Oct. 7, 1949), 1.

70. "From Kentucky Mountain Ballads to Chinese People's Songs," *Daily Worker*, June 14, 1949. Seeger proudly announced in the "Interim Newsletter" that the Weavers had "added a new member, Hope Foye. It is the first professionally rehearsed such group," in contrast to the Almanacs, a loosely knit organization with a floating membership and little sustained

discipline. Starting at Barney Josephson's Cafe Society Downtown in 1944, Foye had moved to the Uptown location, performed with Josh White, and later appeared with Robeson. She appeared frequently as a member of People's Songs. Only briefly one of the now integrated Weavers, Foye joined on their American Labor Party recordings, but not on the Charter releases "Wasn't That a Time" and "Dig My Grave." "Interim Newsletter," no. 1 (Oct. 7, 1949), 3.

71. "Corn of Plenty," *Newsweek*, June 13, 1949, 76–77. Malone, *Country Music U.S.A.*, chap. 7.

72. Quoted in Peter T. Bartis, "A History of the Archive of Folk Song at the Library of Congress: The First Fifty Years," Ph.D. diss., University of Pennsylvania, 1982, 175.

73. "Leadbelly Dies; Twice Sang Way Out of Prisons," *New York Tribune*, Dec. 7, 1949. Earl Robinson, "America's Greatest Folk Singer," *The Worker Magazine*, Apr. 2, 1950.

74. Cohen interview with Joe Jaffe, Berkeley, California, June 29, 1992.

75. Cohen interview with Mike Fleischer, Chicago, Illinois, Dec. 1, 1989, 1.

76. Barney Josephson's Cafe Society, forced to close in early 1949, proved another economic as well as political casualty. David W. Stowe, "The Politics of Cafe Society," *Journal of American History* 84:4 (Mar. 1998): 1384–406.

Chapter 3

1. Brand, *The Ballad Mongers*, 142–43.

2. Frederic Ramsey, "Leadbelly's Legacy," *Saturday Review*, Jan. 28, 1950, 61.

3. "Harold Leventhal," in Joe Smith, *Off the Record: An Oral History of Popular Music* (New York: Warner Books, 1988), 152. "Folksongs at 8 at Panel Room," *Daily Worker*, May 5, 1950. Harold Leventhal with Robert Santelli, "Remembering Woody," in *Hard Travelin': The Life and Legacy of Woody Guthrie*, ed. Santelli and Emily Davidson (Hanover N.H.: Wesleyan University Press, 1999), 14–21. For the Weavers early recordings, see *Songs for Political Action: Folkmusic, Topical Songs and the American Left, 1926–1953* (Bear Family Records, BCD 15720), and *Goodnight, Irene: The Weavers, 1949–1953* (Bear Family Records, BCD 15930 EK).

4. Jenkins quote in Doris Willens, *Lonesome Traveler: The Life of Lee Hays* (New York: W.W. Norton, 1988), 125.

5. Pete Seeger with Robert Santelli, "Hobo's Lullaby," in Santelli and Davidson, *Hard Travelin'*, 32.

6. "Good Night, Irene," *Time*, Aug. 14, 1950, 38. Galen Gart, comp., *First Pressings: The History of Rhythm & Blues Special 1950 Volume* (Milford, N.H.: Big Nickel Publications, 1993), 99, 111.

7. Jim Capaldi, "Wasn't That a Time! A Conversation With Lee Hays," *Sing Out!* 28 (Sept.-Oct. 1980), 5.

8. "Out of the Corner," *Time*, Sept. 25, 1950, 69.

9. James Dugan, "Birth of a Song Hit," *Maclean's Magazine*, Sept. 15, 1950, 50. Gilbert Millstein, "Very Good Night: An Old Lament in Waltz-Time for a Girl Named Irene Is a National Musical Wonder," *New York Times Magazine*, Oct. 15, 1950, 41. Pete Seeger, *The Incompleat Folksinger* (New York: Simon and Schuster, 1972), 22.

10. Woody Guthrie to Moe Asch and Marian Distler [sic], Oct. 23, 1950, and Asch to Guthrie, Oct. 29, 1950, Smithsonian Folkways Collection. Goldsmith, *Making People's Music*, 231–32.

11. Hazel Meyer, *The Gold in Tin Pan Alley* (Philadelphia: Lippincott, 1958), 195–97. Meyer is not quite accurate, and I thank Fred Hellerman for giving me the full story. There were also popular recordings by conductors Mitch Miller and Ralph Flanagan, as well as singer Vic Damone, in 1950. "Wimoweh" also has had copyright problems; see Rian Malan, "Money, Greed and Mystery: Who Wrote 'The Lion Sleeps Tonight,' " *Rolling Stone*, May 25, 2000, 54–66, 84–85.

12. See Hugh Mooney, "Just before Rock: Pop Music 1950–1953 Reconsidered," *Popular Music and Society* 3 (1974), 65–108. Steve Chapple and Reebee Garofalo, *Rock 'n' Roll Is Here to Pay: The History and Politics of the Music Industry* (Chicago: Nelson-Hall, 1977), chap. 1. By 1950, the year "Your Hit Parade" switched from radio to television, there were four million television sets, with a concentration in New York City. A large youth market, soon to dominate the record industry, had not yet made itself felt, however.

13. "Fred Hellerman," in Griffin Fariello, *Red Scare: Memories of the American Inquisition: An Oral History* (New York: W.W. Norton, 1995), 367. *Counterattack*, Letter No. 159 (June 9, 1950).

14. *Counterattack*, Letter No. 174 (Sept. 22, 1950). Frederick Woltman, the Red-baiting reporter for the *New York World Telegram*, reminded readers in August 1951, "Pete has a long record of singing for the revolution—the Communist revolution, that is." Woltman stretched back to the Almanac Singers and beginnings of People's Songs in recapping Seeger's career. Woltman, "Melody Weaves On, along Party Line," *New York World Telegram*, Aug. 25, 1951.

15. See, in general, David Caute, *The Great Fear: The Anti-Communist Purge under Truman and Eisenhower* (New York: Simon and Schuster, 1978). John E. Haynes, *Red Scare or Red Menace? American Communism and Anticommunism in the Cold War Era* (Chicago: Ivan R. Dee, 1996). And particularly Schrecker, *Many Are the Crimes*.

16. "The Inside on 'Counterattack,'" *Billboard*, Sept. 9, 1950, 4.

17. Jerry Wexler and David Ritz, *Rhythm and the Blues: A Life in American Music* (New York: St. Martin's Press, 1993), 66. Peterson, *Creating Country Music*, 198–99.

18. Irwin Silber, "Some Hootenanny Opinions (regarding January 13, 1950 Hoot)," in Reuss Papers.

19. *Sing Out!* 1:1 (May 1950), 2.

20. "Songmakers Salute 10th Anniversary," *Songmakers Almanac* 2:6 (June 1963). Bart and Edna van der Schelling, who had been active in People's Songs in Los Angeles and held hootenannies at their home in the Hollywood Hills, fled to Mexico about 1950; Bart, a Spanish Civil War veteran and not a citizen, feared being deported.

21. Cohen interview with Noel (Oliver) Osheroff, Venice, California, July 31, 1993.

22. Cohen interview with Frank Hamilton, Decatur, Georgia, Nov. 2, 1990 (revised by Hamilton Mar. 2, 1993).

23. Cohen interview with Hamilton.

24. Frank Hamilton to Ronald Cohen, Mar. 1993.

25. Seeger, *Incompleat Folksinger*, 22. Irwin Silber, "The Weavers—New 'Find' of the Hit Parade," *Sing Out!* 1:9 (Feb. 1951), 6, 12.

26. Wally Hille to Bob Black, Mar. 6, 1951, in Reuss Papers.

27. Quoted in Willens, *Lonesome Traveler*, 134.

28. Walter Lowenfels, "New Hootenanny Records by People's Artists," *Daily Worker*, Dec. 28, 1949. Cohen interview with Irwin Silber, Oakland, California, Dec. 13, 1991. Most of the Hootenanny records featured one or more of the People's Artists integrated quartet: Laura Duncan, Ernie Lieberman, Betty Sanders, and Osborne Smith. The Weavers single sold the most copies, almost fifteen hundred over three years; the popular Martha Schlamme's ethnic "Johnny I Hardly Knew You" (Irish) / "Rabbi Elimelech" (Yiddish) ran a close second—an indication of the tastes of the New York market, where she had a twice-weekly radio show.

29. "Sing Out—One Year Old," *Sing Out!* 2:1 (July 1951), 2.

30. Fred Moore, "Decca Issues Folk Song Album with the Weavers," *Sing Out!* 2:4 (Oct. 1951), 6. "Weavers' Yarn," *Newsweek*, Aug. 6, 1951, 80.

31. "Testimony of Harvey M. Matusow, of Dayton, Ohio, February 25, 1952," *Report of the Un-American Activities Commission, State of Ohio, 1951–1952* [Columbus, Ohio, 1953], 106, 109. Harvey Matusow, *False Witness* (New York: Cameron & Kahn, 1955), 51. "Ronnie

Gilbert," in Fariello, Red Scare, 372. Bert Spector, "The Weavers: A Case History in Show Business Blacklisting," Journal of American Culture 5 (Fall 1982), 113–20. Robert Lichtman and Ronald D. Cohen, Deadly Farce: Harvey Matusow and the Workings of the Informer System in the McCarthy Era (Urbana: University of Illinois Press, forthcoming).

32. Allen Churchill, "Tin Pan Alley's Git-tar Blues," New York Times Magazine, July 15, 1951.

33. Lloyd W. Schram to Burl Ives, Sept. 19, 1950. Ives to "Whom It May Concern," Sept. 28, 1950, in Burl Ives Papers, University Library, Western Illinois University, Macomb, Illinois. In a private letter to the university Ives cautioned, "the book Red Channels, where the organizations with which my name has been linked are listed, has had an unfortunate affect [sic] in that many innocent people like myself are victimised [sic] by it." Ives to Lloyd Schram, Sept. 28, 1950.

34. "Testimony of Burl Icle Ives," May 20, 1952, Subcommittee to Investigate the Administration of the Internal Security Act and Other Internal Security Laws of the Committee on the Judiciary, United States Senate, 82d Congress, 2d Session on Subversive Infiltration of Radio, Television, and the Entertainment Industry, Mar. 20, 26, Apr. 23, and May 20, 1952, part 2 (Washington, D.C.: Government Printing Office, 1952), 208, 220, 228. For the larger context, see Victor Navasky, Naming Names (New York: Viking, 1980).

35. "Burl Ives Sings a Different Song," Sing Out! 3:2 (Oct. 1952), 2. Pete Seeger, "Sea Song Paperback," Sing Out! 6:4 (Winter 1952), 21. In his obituary of Dyer-Bennet, who died on December 14, 1991, Oscar Brand reminded Sing Out!'s readers that after Ives's testimony, "in a short time, right-wing protests began to cause cancellation of Dyer-Bennet concerts. Richard told me he wasn't angry with anyone but the Committee and with remarkable aplomb proceeded to rechart his life." Brand, "Richard Dyer-Bennett (1913–1991), 20th-Century Minstrel," Sing Out! 37:1 (May-June 1992), 45. In early 1993 Ives and Seeger finally appeared together in a concert in New York City. See also A. V. Shirk, "Richard Dyer-Bennett: The Classical Folksinger," Sing Out! 43:2 (Fall 1998), 56–62.

36. "The Un-American Subpoenas," Sing Out! 2:9 (Mar. 1952), 2. "The 'Un-Americans' Retreat," Sing Out! 2:10 (Apr. 1952), 11.

37. "Josh White: Mr. Folksinger," Our World 4:3 (Mar. 1949), 13. White had long been dogged by the bureau, which did not cease its snooping with his committee testimony.

38. Robert Shelton, ed., The Josh White Song Book (Chicago: Quadrangle, 1963), 33, 35. Wald, Josh White. Duberman, Paul Robeson, 388–91. On Allan and "Strange Fruit," see David Margolick, Strange Fruit: Billie Holiday, Café Society, and an Early Cry for Civil Rights (Philadelphia: Running Press, 2000).

39. Counterattack, Letter No. 172 (Sept. 13, 1950). Josh White, "I Was a Sucker for the Communists," Negro Digest, Dec. 1950, 31. White quoted in Dorothy S. Siegel, The Glory Road: The Story of Josh White (New York: Harcourt Brace Jovanovich, 1982), 124.

40. Irwin Silber, "Editorial," Sing Out! 2:4 (Oct. 1951), 10.

41. Counterattack, Letter No. 202 (Apr. 6, 1951). Merle Miller, The Judges and the Judged (Garden City, N.Y.: Doubleday, 1952), 110.

42. Irwin Silber, "Folk-singer Oscar Brand Joins Witch-hunt Hysteria," Sing Out! 2:5 (Nov. 1951), 2. Cohen interview with Oscar Brand, Great Neck, N.Y., Sept. 29, 1991. Brand, Ballad Mongers, 135, 139.

43. Counterattack, Letter No. 236 (Nov. 30, 1951). In February 1954, Counterattack, losing its clout, again detailed Belafonte's alleged Communist connections, and also the singer's denials and assurance that "as a Roman Catholic, a Negro and an American he hates Communism and everything it stands for." Counterattack 8:7 (Feb. 12, 1954).

44. Counterattack 7:8 (Feb. 20, 1953). "Testimony of Lee Hays," Aug. 16, 1955, Investigation of Communist Activities, New York Area, Part VI, U.S. Congress, House, Committee on Un-American Activities, Hearings (1955), 2359. "Folk Singer Is Heard," New York Times,

Aug. 17, 1955. On Robinson's music and ongoing political struggles, see Robinson with Gordon, *Ballad of an American*, esp. 201–69.

45. "Testimony of Tony Kraber," Aug. 18, 1955, Investigation of Communist Activities, New York Area, Part VII, U.S. Congress, House, Committee on Un-American Activities, *Hearings* (1955), 2436–37. "Un-Americans," *Sing Out!* 5:4 (Autumn 1955), 2. For Seeger's testimony, see Eric Bentley, *Thirty Years of Treason: Excerpts from Hearings before the House Committee on Un-American Activities, 1938–1968* (New York: Viking, 1971), 686–700. Millard Lampell had testified before the Senate Internal Security Subcommittee of the Judiciary Committee on April 1, 1952, when he repeatedly took the Fifth.

46. Ad for "New Year's Atom and Eve Ball," *Daily Worker*, Dec. 10, 1947. Paul Boyer, *By the Bomb's Early Light: American Thought and Culture at the Dawn of the Atomic Age* (New York: Pantheon, 1985). Margot A. Henriksen, *Dr. Strangelove's America: Society and Culture in the Atomic Age* (Berkeley: University of California Press, 1997).

47. *Counterattack*, Letter No. 173 (Sept. 15, 1950). Victor Riesel, "Inside Labor," undated clipping. See also Harold Bernz, "Atom Discs for Peace," *Sing Out!* 1:5 (Sept. 1950), 11.

48. Vern Partlow, "Just a Song at Twilight: *Old Man Atom* vs. the Cold War," in *Give Peace a Chance: Music and the Struggle for Peace*, ed. Mariane Philbin (Chicago: Chicago Review Press, 1983), 96. "Sleeper of the Week," *Cash Box*, July 15, 1950.

49. "No Private Censors," *Life*, July 11, 1950. "The 1950 Silly Season Looks Unusually Silly," *Saturday Evening Post*, Nov. 18, 1950. *New York Times* editorial cited in "Muir-'Atom' Issues Wide Coverage," *Variety*, Sept. 13, 1950.

50. Carl Bernstein, *Loyalties: A Son's Memoir* (New York: Simon & Schuster, 1989), 210–11.

51. "Sing Out for Hallinan and Bass," *Sing Out!* 3:1 (Sept. 1952), 2. R. Serge Denisoff and Richard A. Reuss, "Songs of Persuasion and Skits of American Trotskyists," in *Sing a Song of Social Significance*, 2d ed., ed. Denisoff (Bowling Green, Ohio: Bowling Green State University Popular Press, 1983), 80–96. For more information on Glazer and Friedlander, see Cohen and Samuelson, *Songs for Political Action* and the songs in *Ballads for Sectarians*, included in *Songs for Political Action*. See also Joe Glazer, *Labor's Troubadour* (Urbana: University of Illinois Press, 2001), 125–27.

52. "Golden Age of Hootenany," *Saturday Review of Literature*, Nov. 24, 1951, 75.

53. "Freedom Festival," Sept. 20, 1951, MS program in the People's Songs Library Collection, box 21, folder 12, 2, 13, Archives of Labor and Urban Affairs, Walter P. Reuther Library, Wayne State University, Detroit, Michigan.

54. *Sing Out!* 3:11 (Oct. 1953), 2. *Sing Out!* 3:10 (June 1953), 10–11. The first and only issue of an enthusiastic rival magazine, *American Folk Music*, with Gordon Burdge as publisher and the folklorist Kenneth Goldstein listed as managing editor, had recently appeared, filled with articles on various performers and concerts, reviews, a few songs, and a listing of future articles. Certainly premature, this apolitical, commercial effort died with hardly a trace. (Goldstein had little connection with the magazine and was shocked to see himself named as managing editor; he briefly thought of suing.)

55. John Gould Fletcher, "A Songbag from the Ozarks' Hollows and Ridgy Mountains," *New York Times Book Review*, May 28, 1950. On folk music scholarship, see Wilgus, *Anglo-American Folksong Scholarship*.

56. Charles Edward Smith, "Folk Music, the Roots of Jazz," *Saturday Review of Literature*, July 1950, 48.

57. Horace Reynolds, "America Singing for Sure," *Christian Science Monitor*, Oct. 7, 1950, 18. Reynolds, "Songs Made to Work With," *New York Times Book Review*, Feb. 18, 1951.

58. *New York Times*, clipping dated 1952. Robert Cantwell, *When We Were Good: The Folk Revival* (Cambridge: Harvard University Press, 1996), chap. 6. Greil Marcus, *Invisible Republic: Bob Dylan's Basement Tapes* (New York: Henry Holt, 1997), chap. 4. And the booklet accompanying the *Anthology*'s reissue by Smithsonian Folkways Recordings in 1997.

59. "South African 'Country,' " Time, Feb. 2, 1953, 36. Sigmund Spaeth, "Folk Music to the Fore," Theatre Arts 37 (July 1953), 10–11.

60. Oscar Brand, "The Authentic Version," Saturday Review of Literature, Aug. 29, 1953, 54.

61. Duncan Emrich, "The Authentic Version," Saturday Review of Literature, Nov. 28, 1953, 96.

62. Pete Seeger to Dr. Ray Lawless, Feb. 18, 1953, and Gil "Cisco" Houston to Lawless, May 30, 1955, Ray M. Lawless Collection, Archive of Folk Culture, American Folklife Center, Library of Congress, Washington, D.C.

63. Sing Out! 4:2 (Jan. 1954), 2. Sing Out! 4:7 (Fall 1954), 30.

64. Jac Holzman and Gavan Daws, Follow the Music: The Life and High Times of Elketra Records in the Great Years of American Popular Culture (Santa Monica, Calif.: FirstMedia Books, 1998), 1–15. "There are, at the present writing, some 300 LP records devoted to folk music," Donald Ritchie calculated in late 1953. Donald Ritchie, "A Survey of Folk Music on Long Play," American Record Guide, Oct. 1953, 35. See also Oscar Brand, "Old Folk Songs at Home," Saturday Review of Literature, Dec. 12, 1953, 43.

65. Cohen interview with Jac Holzman, Los Angeles, June 27, 1990.

66. R.P., "Folk Music on Disks," New York Times, Feb. 7, 1954. Fredcrick Ramsey Jr., "Leadbelly's Last Sessions," High Fidelity Magazine, Nov.-Dec. 1953, 133–34. On Folkways' economic history, see Anthony Allan Olmsted, " 'We Shall Overcome': Economic Stress, Articulation and the Life of Folkways Records and Service Corp., 1948–1969," unpub. Ph.D. diss., University of Alberta, 1999.

67. Russell Ames, The Story of American Folk Song (New York: Grosset and Dunlap, 1955), 276.

Chapter 4

1. Roy Harris, "Folk Songs," House and Garden, Dec. 1954, 165, 170.

2. Ralph J. Gleason, "The Gateways Are 'Puttin' on the Style' in a Big Way," San Francisco Chronicle, Feb. 10, 1957.

3. Jim Walls, "The Gateway Singers: Their Slam-Bang Impact," San Francisco Chronicle, Mar. 16, 1958.

4. Jeff Greenfield, No Peace, No Place: Excavations along the Generational Fault (New York: Doubleday, 1973), 40–41, 43. Richard A. Peterson, "Why 1955? Explaining the Advent of Rock Music," Popular Music 1 (1990), 97–114.

5. Thomas Doherty, Teenagers and Teenpics: The Juvenilization of American Movies in the 1950s (Boston: Unwin Hyman, 1988). On rock and roll, see Ed Ward, Geoffrey Stokes, and Ken Tucker, Rock of Ages: The Rolling Stone History of Rock and Roll (New York: Rolling Stone Press, 1986). Charlie Gillett, The Sound of the City: The Rise of Rock and Roll, rev. and expanded ed. (New York: Pantheon, 1983). Philip K. Eberly, Music in the Air: America's Changing Tastes in Popular Music, 1920–1980 (New York: Hasting House, 1982), chap. 14. Philip H. Ennis, The Seventh Stream: The Emergence of Rocknroll in American Popular Music (Hanover, N.H.: Wesleyan University Press, 1992), part two. Reebee Garofalo, Rockin' Out: Popular Music in the USA (Boston: Allyn and Bacon, 1997), chaps. 4 and 5. Malone, Country Music U.S.A., chap. 8.

6. Greenfield, No Peace, No Place, 60. Linda Martin and Kerry Segrave, Anti-Rock: The Opposition to Rock 'n' Roll (Hamden, Conn.: Archon, 1988). James Gilbert, A Cycle of Outrage: America's Reaction to the Juvenile Delinquent in the 1950s (New York: Oxford University Press, 1986). Ronald D. Cohen, "The Delinquents: Censorship and Youth Culture in Recent U.S. History," History of Education Quarterly 37:3 (Fall 1997), 251–70. Elaine Tyler May, Homeward Bound: American Families in the Cold War Era (New York: Basic, 1988).

7. Dan Wakefield, Going All the Way (New York: Dell, 1970), 199, 201 (ellipsis in the original).

8. Marge Piercy, Braided Lives (New York: Fawcett, 1982), 114.

9. Burl Ives, "What Is a Folk Song?" *Variety*, Jan. 5, 1955.

10. Max Gordon, *Live at the Village Vanguard*, 87–88. Henry Louis Gates Jr., *Thirteen Ways of Looking at a Black Man* (New York: Random House, 1997), 155–79.

11. Quoted in Arnold Shaw, *Belafonte: An Unauthorized Biography* (Philadelphia: Chilton, 1960), 125, 197. Howard Taubman, "A Folk Singer's Style," *New York Times*, Feb. 7, 1954. "Belafonte's Best Year," *Ebony*, Mar. 1956, 58, 60.

12. Donald R. Hill, *Calypso Calaloo: Early Carnival Music in Trinidad* (Gainesville: University Press of Florida, 1993).

13. Joel Whitburn, *The Billboard Book of Top 40 Albums* (New York: Billboard, 1991), 37.

14. Harry Belafonte letter to the *New York Mirror*, May 5, 1957. " 'I Wonder Why Nobody Don't Like Me,' " *Life*, May 27, 1957, 85. "The Storm over Belafonte," *Look*, June 25, 1957, 141. Jeanne Van Holmes, "Belafonte Gives It All He's Got," *Saturday Evening Post*, Apr. 20, 1957, 76.

15. For the lure of exotic music in the 1950s, see, for example, the essays in *Incredibly Strange Music*, vol. 2 (San Francisco: Re/Search Publications #15, 1994).

16. John Hasted, "A Singer's Notebook," *Sing* 3:4 (Dec. 1956-Jan. 1957), 70. Hasted, "A Singer's Notebook," *Sing*, 3:6 (Feb.-Mar. 1957), 81. Chas McDevitt, *Skiffle* (London: Robson, 1997).

17. John Hasted, "A Singer's Notebook," *Sing* 4:1 (Apr.-May 1957), 13. Hasted, "A Singer's Notebook," *Sing* 4:2 (June-July 1957), 22.

18. John Hasted, "Don't Scoff at Skiffle," *Sing Out!* 7:1 (Spring 1957), 29. John Hasted, *Alternative Memoirs* (Itchenor, West Sussex: Greengates Press, 1992), 144.

19. Irwin Silber to Ronald Cohen, Jan. 15, 1998. Irwin Silber, "Five Years Old," *Sing Out!* 6:1 (Winter 1956), 2. Pete Seeger, "Johnny Appleseed, Jr.," *Sing Out!* 6:1 (Winter 1956), 44.

20. "Un-Americans," *Sing Out!* 5:4 (Autumn 1955), 2.

21. "Tin Pan Alley, Folk Songs, and the Weavers," *Sing Out!* 6:2 (Spring 1956), 2.

22. Leventhal notes in booklet accompanying *The Weavers: Wasn't That a Time* (Vanguard CD box VCD4-147/50), 22.

23. Robert Shelton, "The Weavers," *High Fidelity Magazine*, Dec. 1960, 122. *New York Times* quote on back of album jacket, *The Weavers at Carnegie Hall* (Vanguard Records VRS-9010).

24. Bruce Sylvester, "Vanguard Records: Cutting Edge before There Was Cutting Edge," *Goldmine* 464 (May 8, 1998), 74–80.

25. Irwin Silber, "Carnegie Hall Rocks as the Weavers Return," *Sing Out!* 6:1 (Winter 1956), 31–32.

26. Seymour Raven, "Folk Singers Are Cheered by Audience," *Chicago Tribune*, May 19, 1956.

27. Letter from Pete Seeger to People's Artists, Nov. 2, 1956, quoted in Reuss, *American Folk Music and Left-Wing Politics*, 265–66.

28. *Counterattack* 10:48 (Nov. 30, 1956), 192.

29. Irwin Silber to Archie Green, Jan. 7, 1957, and Silber to Green, Nov. 26, 1957, Archie Green Papers, Southern Folklife Collection, University of North Carolina at Chapel Hill (hereafter cited as Green Papers).

30. Cynthia Gooding Ozbekkan to Lou Gordon, Apr. 26, 1954 (copy in possession of author from privately held Gooding Papers).

31. Woody Guthrie, *California to the New York Island*, ed. Millard Lampell (New York: Guthrie Children's Trust Fund, 1958).

32. Dan Wakefield, *New York in the Fifties* (Boston: Houghton Mifflin, 1992), 81, 192.

33. Jo Mapes, "Passing Through" (manuscript in author's possession), chap. 10; *Theo*, 155–56.

34. Noel Clad, "Greenwich Village—1955," *Cosmopolitan*, Apr. 1955, 87. Craig Harris, "A Mosaic of Stories: Ramblin' Jack Elliott," *Dirty Linen* 63 (Apr.-May 1996), 15–17, 119.

35. Bikel, Theo, 159–60.

36. Van Ronk quoted in Robbie Woliver, Bringing It All Back Home: 25 Years of American Music at Folk City (New York: Pantheon, 1986), 11–12. See also Ronald Sukenick, Down and In: Life in the Underground (New York: Morrow, 1987), which says little about the folk scene, and Ronald D. Cohen, "Singing Subversion: Folk Music and the Counterculture in the 1950s," in Beat Culture: The 1950s and Beyond, ed. Cornelis A. van Minnen, Japp van der Bent and Mel van Elteren (Amsterdam: VU University Press, 1999), 117–27.

37. Wakefield, New York in the Fifties, 313. Mike Porco had purchased William Gerdes's restaurant on West 3d Street with his brother and cousin in 1952, then moved to West 4th four years later, with an occasional piano player or trio, but as yet no folk music and little business.

38. Cohen interview with Orrin Keepnews, Berkeley, California, Oct. 19, 1990.

39. Neil Rosenberg interview with Kenneth S. Goldstein, Jan. 2, 1979, 33, copy of the manuscript in author's possession and used with permission of .Neil Rosenberg and partially printed as "A Future Folklorist in the Record Business," in Transforming Tradition: Folk Music Revivals Examined, ed. Neil V. Rosenberg (Urbana: University of Illinois Press, 1993), 107–21.

40. Wm. Hugh Jansen, "Balladry and Ballad Singers," Saturday Review, Mar. 30, 1957, 50. Goldstein, "A Future Folklorist," in Transforming Tradition, 114–15.

41. Cohen interview with Jac Holzman, Los Angeles, June 27, 1990. Holzman and Daws, Follow the Music, 34.

42. Cohen interview with Oscar Brand, Great Neck, Long Island, Sept. 29, 1991. In the early 1970s Brand finally issued, through Roulette Records, an album of unexpurgated songs, wrapped in brown paper with an X on the cover, which barely circulated, so Brand reissued the songs in an album with a plain white cover. See also Ed Cray, The Erotic Muse: American Bawdy Songs, 2d ed. (Urbana: University of Illinois Press, 1992).

43. Cohen interview with Oscar Brand, Great Neck, Long Island, Sept. 29, 1991; Cohen interview with Jac Holzman, Los Angeles, June 27, 1990.

44. Roz Baxandall, "Another Madison Bohemian," in History and the New Left: Madison, Wisconsin, 1950–1970, ed. Paul Buhle (Philadelphia: Temple University Press, 1990), 135.

45. Ron Radosh, "Problems of a College Folk Music Group," Caravan, Oct.-Nov. 1958, 27.

46. Cohen interview with Les Brown, New York City, Mar. 8, 1994.

47. Cohen interview with Odetta, New York City, Aug. 6, 1992. Theo, 161. Bob Gibson and Carole Bender, Bob Gibson: I Come for to Sing (Naperville, Ill.: Kingston Korner, 1999), 33–37.

48. Cohen interview with Les Brown, New York City, Mar. 8, 1994.

49. Gerry Armstrong, "Studs Terkel's 'Almanac' Keeps Chicago Folksong-Conscious," Sing Out! 7:3 (Fall 1957), 31.

50. The original Folksong Society, initiated in 1945, perished after one year, then re-merged around 1951 as the Folk Union, which soon became the Folklore Society, since "union" had radical overtones, while "folklore" appeared academic.

51. Studs Terkel to Moe Asch, n.d., Smithsonian Folkways Collection.

52. Hoke Norris, "A Singing Man Sits Silent at His Rousing Benefit," Chicago Sun-Times, Nov. 29, 1957. See Mark A. Humphrey, "Bright Lights, Big City: Urban Blues," in Nothing but the Blues, ed. Lawrence Cohn (New York: Abbeville, 1993), chap. 5.

53. Cohen interview with Odetta, New York City, Aug. 6, 1992. Lisa Grayson, ed., Biography of a Hunch: The History of Chicago's Legendary Old Town School of Folk Music (Chicago: Old Town School of Folk Music, 1992), 1–2.

54. Cohen interview with Frank Hamilton, Decatur, Georgia, Nov. 2, 1990.

55. Sam Hinton, "The Singer of Folk Songs and His Conscience," Western Folklore 14 (1955), 171.

56. Bikel, *Theo*, 161–62.

57. Bikel, *Theo*, 163.

58. Israel G. Young, *Autobiography. The Bronx, 1928–1938* (New York: Folklore Center Press, 1969), 11.

59. B. A. Botkin and William G. Tyrrell, "Upstate, Downstate," *New York Folklore Quarterly* (Spring 1957), 66. Richard A. Reuss interview with Israel G. Young, New York City, July 8, 1965 (copy of the transcription in author's possession).

60. "Folklore Center," *Sing Out!* 7:1 (Spring 1957), 33. Israel G. Young, "A New Secret History of Folklore U.S.A.," Feb. 26, 1957 (unpublished manuscript).

61. Lee Shaw, "Skiffle Stateside," *Caravan* 6 (Jan. 1958), 5.

62. Israel Young to Archie Green, Apr. 20, 1958, Green Papers.

63. LH, "Folkmusic: What Is It?," *Choog Two-Four*, May 1957, 2. Editor, "No Matter How You Sing It," *Choog Two-Five*, Summer 1957, 2.

64. "Jon Pankake," in Cohen, *"Wasn't That a Time!,"* 106. Cohen interview with Lee Hoffman and Aaron Rennert, Port Charlotte, Florida, Jan. 2, 1990.

65. Blind Rafferty, "The Elektra Catalog—A Sarcophagus," *Caravan* 1 (Aug. 1957), 4. Lee, "The New York City Scene," *Caravan* 1 (Aug. 1957), 15.

66. Arlene E. Kaplan, "A Study of Folksinging in a Mass Society," *Sociologus* 5:1 (Spring 1955), 15.

Chapter 5

1. "Folk Concerts Jazz Up B.O.," *Variety*, Feb. 26, 1958, 43.

2. Sven Eric Molin, "Lead Belly, Burl Ives, and Sam Hinton," *Journal of American Folklore* 71 (Jan.-Mar. 1958), 63.

3. Sam Hinton, "Last Words," *Journal of American Folklore* 71 (Jan.-Mar., 1958), 75–78.

4. Cohen interview with Barry Olivier, Berkeley, California, July 2, 1990. An attorney and dulcimer expert from Virginia, Summers had begun recording for Columbia Records in 1941, and later turned out a string of traditional albums for Moe Asch; see Douglas Summers Brown, "Sweet Singer of the Virginia Highlands: Andrew Rowan Summers," *Virginia Cavalcade* 45 (Winter 1996), 101–8.

5. Al Fischer, "Northgate Restaurant Featuring 'Popular' Folk-singing Concerts," *Daily Californian*, clipping, n.d. Morton Cathro, "Return of the Troubadour," Parade section, *Oakland Tribune*, Oct. 20, 1957.

6. Von Schmidt and Rooney, *Baby, Let Me Follow You Down*, 78.

7. Billy Faier, "Message from the West," *Caravan*, Apr. 1958, 18. Barry Olivier to Mrs. B. Connors, Committee on Drama, Lectures, and Music, May 14, 1958, Berkeley Folk Festival Artist Archive, Special Collections Department, Northwestern University, Evanston, Illinois. Olivier had discovered that Charles Seeger had organized a folk concert on campus in 1913, soon after his faculty appointment, probably the first such university activity.

8. *Folk Song Arts* 7:1 (June 6, 1958).

9. Billy Faier, "Message from the West," *Caravan*, Aug.-Sept. 1958, 17.

10. Barry Olivier, "The University of California Folk Music Festival: This Year and Last," [1959], Olivier, "A Personal Beginning," Berkeley Folk Festival Artist Archive.

11. Alfred Frankenstein, "UC's Folk Festival Is Skillfully Shaped," *San Francisco Chronicle*, July 4, 1960.

12. Page Stegner and Zonweise Hubbard, "Message from the West," *Caravan*, Feb.-Mar. 1959, 27.

13. Billy Faier to Ray Lawless, Nov. 29, 1957, Ray Lawless Collection, Archive of Folk Culture, American Folklife Center, Library of Congress.

14. Michael Rossman, "The Berkeley Folk Music Scene in the Sixties: Reflections on a Poster Exhibition," undated MS in author's possession.

15. "Lou Gottlieb," in Cohen, *Wasn't That a Time!*," 149. See also the discussion in "Dave Samuelson," 79–85. The trio's recording career and much else can be traced in Benjamin Blake, Jack Rubeck, and Allan Shaw, *The Kingston Trio on Record* (Naperville, Ill.: Kingston Korner, Inc., 1986).

16. Paul Coburn to Dave Guard, Bob Shane, and Nick Reynolds, Aug. 8, 1958, Dave Guard and Richard Johnson Kingston Trio Papers, University Manuscript Collections, University of Wisconsin-Milwaukee.

17. James T. Fisher, *Dr. America: The Lives of Thomas A. Dooley, 1927–1961* (Amherst: University of Massachusetts Press, 1997), 1–11.

18. "Hanged Man in Hit Tune," *Life*, Dec. 15, 1958, 81.

19. Robert Cantwell, *When We Were Good: The Folk Revival* (Cambridge: Harvard University Press, 1996), 1–10. John Cohen avers that according to Guard the Kingston Trio learned the song from the Folksay Trio's recording, with its "calypso rhythm jump" at the start; see "John Cohen II" in Cohen, *Wasn't That a Time!*," 177.

20. "Dave Guard: The Kingston Trio," in Bruce Pollock, *When Rock Was Young: A Nostalgic Review of the Top 40 Era* (New York: Holt, Rinehart and Winston, 1981), 136–37.

21. "Three Daring Young Men," *Redbook Magazine*, May 1959, 12. "A Trio in Tune Makes the Top," *Life*, Aug. 3, 1959, 61, 64.

22. "Tin Pan Alley: Like from Halls of Ivy," *Time*, July 11, 1960, 56–57.

23. Ann Grisby and Susan Wichman to Dave Guard, Bob Shane, and Nick Reynolds, Jan. 5, 1960, Dave Guard and Richard Johnson Kingston Trio Papers. Stephanie P. Ledgin, "Doc Watson: An Unbroken Circle," *Sing Out!* 44:2 (Winter 2000), 65.

24. *Life* quoted in Doherty, *Teenagers and Teenpics*, 52. Gilbert, *A Cycle of Outrage*. Grace Palladino, *Teenagers: An American History* (New York: Basic Books, 1996).

25. Paul Goodman, *Growing Up Absurd: Problems of Youth in the Organized Society* (New York: Vintage, 1960), 11.

26. Pete Seeger, "Johnny Appleseed, Jr.," *Sing Out!* 7:4 (Winter 1958), 33.

27. Robert Shelton, "Popular American Folk Songs on LP," *New York Times*, Jan. 26, 1958.

28. Robert Shelton to Archie Green, Jan. 17, 1959, Archie Green Papers, Southern Folklife Collection, University of North Carolina at Chapel Hill (hereafter cited as Green Papers).

29. A. L. Lloyd, "American Folk Song: The Present Situation," in Lloyd, *Recorded Folk Music*, vol. 1 (Mar.-Apr. 1958), 14. In her scholarly article, "Some Currents of British Folk Song in America, 1916–1958," *Journal of the English Folk Dance and Song Society* 8:3 (Dec. 1958), 137, Evelyn K. Wells argued: "This [current] popularizing of folk song, real and pseudo, in some respects deplorable, is not to be discounted, since to-day's devotees of popular song sometimes become tomorrow's students of folk song, and since comparison of the two is wholesome for the traditionalist."

30. Ron Radosh, "Commercialism and the Folk Song Revival," *Sing Out!* 8:4 (Spring 1959), 27–29.

31. Malvina Reynolds, "Walla Walla Bing Bang," *Sing Out!* 9:1 (Summer 1959), 28. Alan Lomax, "The 'Folkniks'—and the Songs They Sing," *Sing Out!* 9:1, 30–31. John Cohen, "A Reply to Alan Lomax: In Defense of City Folksingers," *Sing Out!* 9:1, 33–34. For discussions of the complexities of defining authenticity, see "Ed Kahn" and "Dave Samuelson" in Cohen *"Wasn't That a Time!,"* 57–69, 79–84.

32. Alan Lomax liner notes to *Guy Carawan—Vol. II* (Folkways Records FG3548, 1959).

33. B. A. Botkin, "Reading and Writing," *New York Folklore Quarterly* 14 (Summer 1958), 153.

34. Michael James, "Balladers Lure Crowd to Washington Square," *New York Times*, May 25, 1959.

35. Barry Kornfeld, "Folksinging in Washington Square," *Caravan*, Aug.-Sept. 1959, 11.

36. "Roy Berkeley" in Cohen, *Wasn't That a Time!*," 190.

37. Cohen interview with Lee Shaw and Aaron Rennert, Port Charlotte, Florida, Jan. 2,

1990. Van Ronk quoted in Robbie Woliver, *Bringing It All Back Home: 25 Years of American Music at Folk City* (New York: Pantheon, 1986), 39.

38. "New York Scene," *Caravan*, May 1958, 29, 30.

39. Wakefield, *New York in the Fifties*, 313.

40. Barry Kornfeld, "The Folklore Center," *Caravan*, Aug.-Sept. 1958, 29–30. Bruce Nyland to Folklore Center, Nov. 28, 1958, in Reuss Papers.

41. "Folk Song as It Is," *Newsweek*, Apr. 14, 1958, 80. Pete Seeger, "Welcome Back, Alan," *Sing Out!* 8:3 (Winter 1959), 7. For a less enthusiastic review of Lomax's work, see Roger D. Abrahams, "The Flesh, the Devil, Alan Lomax, and the Folk," *Caravan*, Aug.-Sept. 1959, 31.

42. John S. Wilson, "Program Given by Alan Lomax," *New York Times*, Apr. 4, 1959. Aaron Rennert, "Folksong '59: A Review," *Gardyloo* 2 (May 1959), 7. Richard Reuss interview with Israel G. Young, New York City, July 8, 1965 (in author's possession).

43. Alan Lomax, "Bluegrass Background: Folk Music with Overdrive," *Esquire*, Oct. 1959, 108. Neil Rosenberg, *Bluegrass: A History* (Urbana: University of Illinois Press, 1985), 143–55.

44. Israel G. Young, "Frets and Frails," *Sing Out!* 9:3 (Winter 1959–60), 34.

45. "Folk Music Guide," *Sing Out!* 9:2 (Fall 1959), 44.

46. Israel G. Young, "Predictions of the Folklore Center," *Record Research*, June-July 1959, 2.

47. Irwin Silber to Archie Green, Sept. 21, 1959, Green Papers.

48. Jac Holzman to Israel Young, Oct. 19, 1959, in Reuss Papers.

49. Billy Faier to Archie Green, May 4, 1959, Green Papers. The acerbic John Greenway carped to Archie Green: "I still get *Caravan*, but as yet I don't share your enthusiasm for it. I have had for some time the feeling it will become a voice for the Beat Generation, and, having passed the age of adolescence, I don't have a great deal of toleration for such goings-on." John Greenway to Archie Green, Dec. 21, 1958, Green Papers.

50. Cohen interview with Billy Faier, Woodstock, N.Y., Aug. 8, 1992. "Editor's Page," *Caravan*, Aug.-Sept. 1959, 4.

51. Dick Ellington to Archie Green, Sept. 17, 1958, Green Papers. Fred G. Hoeptner, "Folk and Hillbilly Music: The Background of Their Relation, Part II," *Caravan*, June-July 1959, 28. John Greenway had published an article on Jimmie Rodgers two years earlier; the highly influential "Hillbilly Issue" of the *Journal of American Folklore*, edited by Greenway and D. K. Wilgus, would not appear until 1965. Scholars such as Hoeptner, Archie Green, Ed Kahn, Greenway, and Wilgus would carry the torch for early commercially recorded country music for many years.

52. Cohen interview with Aaron Rennert and Lee Shaw, Port Charlotte, Florida, Jan. 2, 1990.

53. Lee Shaw to Archie Green, Feb. 5, 1959, Green Papers. "Editor's Note," *Gardyloo* 1 (Apr. 1959), 4.

54. "John Cohen I," in Cohen, "*Wasn't That a Time,!*" 35. Philip F. Gura, "Roots and Branches: Forty Years of the New Lost City Ramblers, Part 1," *Old-Time Herald* 7:2 (Nov. 1999-Jan. 2000), 26–33.

55. Grace Jan Waldman, "Life among the Guitars," *Mademoiselle*, May 1959, 88, 32.

56. Ren Grevat, "Folkniks on March; Hill Sound Upsurge," *Billboard*, June 8, 1959, 1. T. E. Rafferty, "Hootennanies Hit Tin Pan Alley," *Knave* 1:4 (July 1959), 30, 64.

57. Ren Grevatt and Paul Ackerman, "Folk Music Becomes Big Business in Pop Field," *Billboard*, July 13, 1959, 8.

58. Robert Shelton, "Folk Joins Jazz at Newport," *New York Times*, July 19, 1959. Robert Shelton, "Folk Music Festival," *The Nation*, Aug. 1, 1959, 59. Robert Shelton to Archie Green, Aug. 22, 1959, Green Papers.

59. Robert Gustafson, "First Newport Folk Festival," *Christian Science Monitor*, July 14,

1959. Frederick Ramsey Jr., "An Arena for Folk Music," *Saturday Review*, Oct. 31, 1959, 51, 53. And see, in general, Cheryl Anne Brauner, "A Study of the Newport Folk Festival and the Newport Folk Foundation," unpub. M.A. thesis, Memorial University of Newfoundland, 1983.

60. Mark Morris, "Newport Report," *Gardyloo* 5 (Sept. 1959), 10, 12. Irwin Silber and David Gahr, "Top Performers Highlight 1st Newport Folk Fest," *Sing Out!* 9:2 (Fall 1959), 21, 24.

61. Israel G. Young, "Newport Folk Festival," *Caravan*, Aug.-Sept. 1959, 25, 27. Israel G. Young to Billy Faier, *Caravan*, Jan. 1960, 7.

62. Joan Baez, *And a Voice to Sing With: A Memoir* (New York: Summit Books, 1987), 60. See also Bill Carpenter, "The Voice and Vision of Folk Music: Joan Baez," *Goldmine*, Jan. 17, 1997, 18–22.

63. Cohen interview with Manny Greenhill, Santa Monica, California, June 21, 1990. Manny Greenhill to Israel Young, Sept. 10, 1959, Reuss Papers.

64. Bernie Krause, *Into a Wild Sanctuary: A Life in Music and Natural Sound* (Berkeley, Calif.: Heyday Books, 1998), 16.

65. Krause, *Into a Wild Sanctuary*, 22–24.

66. Cohen interview with Frank Fried, San Diego, California, June 19, 1990.

67. Cohen interview with Frank Hamilton, Decatur, Georgia, Nov. 2, 1990.

68. Paul Endicott to Marian Distler, Oct. 29, 1958, Smithsonian Folkways Collection.

69. Guy Carawan to Israel Young, Aug. 24, 1959, Reuss Papers. John M. Glen, *Highlander: No Ordinary School, 1932–1962* (Lexington: University Press of Kentucky, 1988), 193–95.

70. Paul Endicott to Moe Asch, Aug. 29, 1959, and Ernie Marrs to Moe Asch, ca. Fall 1959, Smithsonian Folkways Collection.

71. Billy Faier, "Folk Music, Los Angeles," *Caravan*, Apr.-May 1959, 4, 5, 20. Gerald McCabe to Billy Faier, *Caravan*, Apr.-May 1959, 11.

72. Edwin Pearl to Israel Young, Oct. 10, 1959, Reuss Papers.

73. Ed Kahn to Moe Asch, June 8, 1959, Smithsonian Folkways Collection.

74. Cohen interview with Herb Cohen, Los Angeles, Aug. 2, 1993.

75. Miriam Makeba, *Makeba: My Story* (New York: New American Library, 1987), 83.

76. Howard Koerpel to Moses Asch, Sept. 28, 1959, Smithsonian Folkways Collection.

77. Erik Darling, "About Folk Songs and Their Singers," *Music Journal*, Sept. 1959, 97–98.

78. Robert Gustafson, "Folk Music Draws a Crowd," *Christian Science Monitor*, Sept. 9, 1959.

79. Wilgus, *Anglo-American Folksong Scholarship since 1898.*

80. Ellen Sander, *Trips: Rock Life in the Sixties* (New York: Scribner's, 1973), 11.

Chapter 6

1. Donald Katz, *Home Fires: An Intimate Portrait of One Middle-Class Family in Postwar America* (New York HarperCollins, 1992), 146–49.

2. Jay Milner, "The Folk Music Craze," *New York Herald Tribune*, Feb. 11, 1960. "Turkeys in the Craw Dept.," *Mad*, Jan. 1960, 24–25.

3. Carroll Calkins with Alan Lomax, "Getting to Know Folk Music," *House Beautiful*, Apr. 1960, 141, 205. Alan Lomax, "Saga of a Folksong Hunter," *HiFi/Stereo Review*, May 1960, 46.

4. Michael Rossman, *The Wedding within the War* (Garden City, N.Y.: Doubleday, 1971), 65–68.

5. Jack Newfield, *A Prophetic Minority* (New York: New American Library, 1966), 33–34.

6. Todd Gitlin, *The Sixties: Years of Hope, Days of Rage* (New York: Bantam, 1987), 75.

7. Harriet Van Horne, "Square Toes Blues," *World-Telegram and Sun*, June 17, 1960. "Folk Sound USA," *Variety*, June 22, 1960, 29.

8. "It's Folksy. . . ." *Newsweek*, June 6, 1960, 112. "Folk Frenzy," *Time*, July 11, 1960, 81.

9. "Folk Frenzy," *Time*, July 11, 1960, 81.

10. Robert Shelton, "40 Amateurs Join Hootenanny as Newport Folk Festival Ends," *New York Times*, June 27, 1960.

11. Izzy Young, "Frets and Frails," *Sing Out!* 10:3 (Oct.-Nov. 1960), 48.

12. Israel Young to Pete Seeger, July 6, 1960, and Seeger to Israel Young, July 9, 1960, Reuss Papers.

13. Robert Shelton, "Folk Music Makes Mark on City's Night Life," *New York Times*, Nov. 17, 1960.

14. Ned Polsky, "The Village Beat Scene: Summer 1960," *Dissent* 8 (1961): 354. As an example, Polsky notes in a footnote: "When the Fire Department raided beat coffee shops, the proprietor of The Folklore Center [Izzy Young] on Macdougal Street went so far as to issue a mimeographed broadside [dated June 12, 1960,] praising this action and condemning the beats. Shortly thereafter he had his window broken." According to Young, his window was broken after he posted a sign naming local clubs that did not pay their folk singers. Izzy later remembered: "I also learned from the Mafia captain that Izzy, in a democracy or an other form of life you can go against Commies, Mafia, Wife-slayers, Capitalist-pigs but *never* name names. That was a great lesson in life, well worth a smashed window." Israel Young to Ronald Cohen, June 4, 1996.

15. "Joan Baez," in Joe Smith, *Off the Record: An Oral History of Popular Music* (New York: Warner, 1988), 156. Sander, *Trips*, 13. Richie Havens with Steve Davidowitz, *They Can't Hide Us Anymore* (New York: Avon, 1999), 30.

16. "Izzy Young," in Woliver, *Bringing It All Back Home*, 18. Israel G. Young, "Frets and Frails," *Sing Out!* 10 (Apr.-May 1960), 38.

17. Israel G. Young, "How the Fifth Peg Came into Existence," July 1984, copy in author's possession. "Izzy Young Notebook," May 14, 1960, copy in author's possession (the quote about English, Shelton, and Scott was left out of the printed version in *Sing Out!* 18 [June-July 1968]).

18. "Israel Young's Notebook (May 14, 1960)," *Sing Out!* 18 (June-July 1968), 48–49. "Israel Young's Notebook (May 15, 1960)," *Sing Out!* 18 (Aug.-Sept. 1968), 11.

19. Archie Green to Israel Young, Jan. 5, 1960, and Ellen Stekert to Young, Feb. 15, 1960, Reuss Papers.

20. Barbara Dane to Israel Young, Jan. 6, 1960, and Dick Weissman to Young, June 5, 1960, Reuss Papers.

21. Irwin Silber, "They're All Talking about the *Little Sandy Review*," *Sing Out!* 10 (Oct.-Nov. 1960), 26.

22. "Editor's Column," *Little Sandy Review*, no. 1 (none of the issues were dated), 2. "Jon Pankake," in Cohen, *"Wasn't That a Time!,"* 107.

23. "Jon Pankake," in Cohen, *"Wasn't That a Time!,"* 109. Paul Nelson to Moses Asch, Mar. 26, 1960, and Asch to Nelson, Apr. 26, 1960, Smithsonian Folkways Collection.

24. "Jon Pankake," in Cohen, *"Wasn't That a Time!,"* 109–10.

25. "Manny Solomon Speaks Out!" and "An Open Letter to Manny Solomon," *Little Sandy Review* 6, pp. 16–21. "Folkum" was their term for slick, commercial recordings.

26. "The Year's Best," *Little Sandy Review*, no. 11, 3. Billy Faier, "Little Sandy Review," *Caravan*, June-July 1960, 34–35.

27. Cynthia Gooding, "Everybody's 'Midnight Special . . . ,' " and Bruce Cook, "The Kingston Trio," *Rogue*, Oct. 1960, 77, 78.

28. Susan Montgomery, "The Folk Furor," *Mademoiselle*, Dec. 1960, 99, 118.

29. Gene Bluestein, "Songs of the Silent Generation," *New Republic*, Mar. 13, 1961,

22. Nancy Lynch, "Silent Generation—Loud Protest," *New Republic*, Apr. 17, 1961, 22–23.

30. Israel G. Young, "Frets and Frails," *Sing Out!* 11 (Apr.-May 1961), 47. Sandy Paton, "Horton Barker—An Appreciation," *Sing Out!* 13 (Apr.-May 1963), 5–6.

31. "John Cohen I," in Cohen, *"Wasn't That a Time!,"* 36.

32. "The First Annual University of Chicago Folk Festival," *Little Sandy Review*, no. 12, 3, 10.

33. Pete Seeger to Israel Young, Feb. 9, 1961, Reuss Papers. Robert Shelton, "Students Import Folk Art to Chicago," *New York Times*, Feb. 12, 1961.

34. Norma Lee Browning, "Are You a Folknik in a Hootenanny?" *Chicago Daily Tribune*, June 24, 1960.

35. Archie Green to Israel Young, Mar. 17, 1961, Reuss Papers. Archie Green, "The Campus Folksong Club: A Glimpse at the Past," in Rosenberg, *Transforming Tradition*, 63–64.

36. Archie Green, "Folksong on Campus," *Autoharp* 1:1 (Apr. 7, 1961), 3. FKP Jr., "Tom Ashley at Madison," *Autoharp* 2:6 (May 4, 1962).

37. "The Second Annual University of Chicago Folk Festival," *Little Sandy Review*, no. 21, 35. In March 1962 John Cohen's "Report from Chicago" launched the first issue of the L.A. Broadside, a small-format folk magazine with local news and articles that would run for a few years: "Fireball Archie Green and Studs Terkel had a job on their hands trying to successfully introduce the traditional performers to a city audience," Cohen wrote. "Studs was more successful this year, although Archie had a bit of a chip on his shoulder trying to whoop everyone up to the realization of their own lack of understanding." John Cohen, "Report from Chicago: Part I," *Broadside* (L.A.) 1 (Mar. 1962), 7.

38. Rinzler's memories are available in the notes to *The Original Folkways Records of Doc Watson and Clarence Ashley: 1960–1962* (Smithsonian/Folkways CD SF40029/30).

39. Israel G. Young, "Frets and Frails," *Sing Out!* 10 (Dec.-Jan. 1960–61), 48. John Cohen, "Field Trip—Kentucky," *Sing Out!* 10 (Summer 1960), 13. "The Friends of Old Time Music," *Sing Out!* 11 (Feb.-Mar. 1961), 63–64.

40. Cohen interview with Ed Pearl, Los Angeles, Jan. 30, 1993. Cohen interview with Ralph Rinzler, Washington, D.C., May 15, 1990.

41. John Cohen to Israel Young, ca. Sept. 1961, Reuss Papers. And see Phillip Drammond, "Folk Music in Southern California," *Sing Out!* 10 (Oct.-Nov. 1960), 44.

42. Barry Olivier to Alfred Frankenstein, May 29, 1961, Berkeley Folk Festival Artist Archive.

43. "Three from Arhoolie," *Little Sandy Review*, no. 16, 4. On his second trip Strachwitz also heard Cajun music in Louisiana, though its revival would have to wait a few years.

44. Pete Welding, "The Rise of Folk-Blues," *Down Beat*, Sept. 14, 1961, 15–16.

45. Glen Alyn, comp., *I Say Me for a Parable: The Oral Autobiography of Mance Lipscomb, Texas Bluesman* (New York: W. W. Norton, 1993), 406, 419. I have generally recast the quotes into standard English.

46. "Jon Pankake," in Cohen, *"Wasn't That a Time!,"* 113–14.

47. John Fitz to Barry Olivier, July 1, 1962, Berkeley Folk Festival Artist Archive.

48. "The Kingston Trio: Pied Pipers to the New Generation," *Look*, Jan. 3, 1961, 54, 60. "Night Clubs: The Faculty," *Time*, June 16, 1961, 56. Herbert Kamm, "Oldtime Folk Singers Hum a Bigtime Tune," *New York Herald-Telegram and Sun*, Aug. 28, 1961.

49. Pete Seeger to "Dear Friends," Aug. 10, 1960, Smithsonian Folkways Collection. "Pete Seeger Concert, December 17, 1960" in "Dick Reuss Manuscript Concert Notes, 1958–63," bound manuscript in author's possession.

50. "The Pete Seeger Benefit Concert," June 18, 1961, flyer. Article on the Weavers, *New York Times*, Jan. 3, 1962. Following intermission during a Theo Bikel concert at the University of California at Berkeley, Bikel announced the news of Seeger's victory and the crowd erupted in cheers.

51. Israel G. Young, "Washington Square—Without a Song!," *Sing Out!* 11 (Summer 1961), 19. Paul Hoffman, "Folk Singers Riot in Washington Square," *New York Times*, Apr. 10, 1961.

52. "Folkways: The Foggy, Foggy Don't," *Time*, Apr. 21, 1961, 69–70.

53. "Weaver's Concert, Carnegie Hall, May 6, 1961," report by Jeff Stull in "Dick Reuss Manuscript Concert Notes, 1958–63," bound manuscript in author's possession. Israel G. Young, "Frets and Frails," *Sing Out!* 11 (Oct.-Nov. 1961), 51. Brand, *Ballad Mongers*, 171.

54. "The Brothers Four, Ohio Wesleyan, May 3, 1961" in "Dick Reuss Manuscript Concert Notes, 1958–63," bound manuscript in author's possession.

55. Nat Hentoff, "The Rise of Folkum Music," *Commonweal*, Oct. 20, 1961, 99. For another survey, see "Hoots and Hollers on the Campus," *Newsweek*, Nov. 27, 1961, 84.

56. Malvina Reynolds, letter, *Sing Out!* 10 (Dec.-Jan. 1960–61), 2. Pete Seeger, "Johnny Appleseed, Jr.," *Sing Out!* 12 (Feb.-Mar. 1962), 58.

57. Cunningham and Friesen, *Red Dust and Broadsides*, 278.

58. Editorial, *Broadside* 1 (Feb. 1962).

59. Josh Dunson, *Freedom in the Air: Song Movements of the Sixties* (New York: International Publishers, 1965), 57. And see, in general, Cunningham and Friesen, *Red Dust and Broadsides*, chap. 9. *The Best of Broadside, 1962–1988: Anthems of the American Underground from the Pages of Broadside Magazine* (Smithsonian Folkways Recordings, SFW 40130), which includes five CDs and extensive notes.

60. Israel Young Manuscript Diary, Oct. 13 and October 23, 1961, copy in author's possession. Robert Shelton, "Bob Dylan: A Distinctive Folk-song Stylist," *New York Times*, Sept. 29, 1961, reprinted in Craig McGregor, ed., *Bob Dylan: The Early Years, A Retrospective* (New York: Da Capo, 1972), 17. See also Robert Shelton, *No Direction Home: The Life and Music of Bob Dylan* (New York: Beech Tree Books, 1986). Bob Spitz, *Dylan: A Biography* (New York: McGraw-Hill, 1989). Clinton Heylin, *Bob Dylan: Behind the Shades* (New York: Summit Books, 1991). David Hajdu, *Positively 4th Street: The Lives and Times of Joan Baez, Bob Dylan, Mimi Baez Fariña, and Richard Fariña* (New York: Farrar, Straus and Giroux, 2001). Howard Sounes, *Down the Highway: The Life of Bob Dylan* New York: Grove Press, 2001).

61. Israel G. Young, "Frets and Frails," *Sing Out!* 12 (Feb.-Mar. 1962), 51. Israel G. Young, "Frets and Frails," *Sing Out!* 12 (Apr.-May 1962), 45. "David Blue" in Woliver, *Bringing It All Back Home*, 84. Gil Turner, "Bob Dylan—A New Voice Singing New Songs," *Sing Out!* 12 (Oct.-Nov. 1962), 5–10.

62. "Bob Dylan" and "Editors' Column," *Little Sandy Review*, no. 22, 12, 18, 46. "THE FREEWHEELIN' BOB DYLAN," *Little Sandy Review*, no. 27, 24. Editors, *Little Sandy Review*, no. 25, 7.

63. Josh Dunson, "Birth of a Broadside," *Broadside* 20 (Feb. 1963). Michael Schumacher, *There but for Fortune: The Life of Phil Ochs* (New York: Hyperion, 1996).

64. Peter Goldsmith, *Making People's Music: Moe Asch and Folkways Records* (Washington, D.C.: Smithsonian Institution Press, 1998), 308–10. Broadside Records appeared sporadically through the 1970s, giving voice to the famous and the obscure; a posthumous Phil Ochs album appeared as late as 1980. For the songs and detailed information, see *The Best of Broadside, 1962–1988*.

65. Makeba, *Makeba*, 103.

66. Joe Hickerson to Marion Distler, 8, 1960, Smithsonian Folkways Collection.

67. Irwin Silber, "He Sings for Integration," *Sing Out!* 10 (Summer 1960), 4.

68. Guy Carawan to Irwin Silber, ca. Feb. 1965, People's Songs Collection, box 23, folder 2, Archives of Labor History and Urban Affairs, Wayne State University, Detroit.

69. Tom Paxton, "Courting the Muse," *Sing Out!* 41 (Aug.-Sept.-Oct. 1996), 96.

70. Brian Ward, *Just My Soul Responding: Rhythm and Blues, Black Consciousness and Race Relations* (Berkeley: University of California Press, 1998), 269–71. For an overview of civil rights recordings, see *Voices of the Civil Rights Movement: Black American Freedom Songs, 1960–1966* (Smithsonian Folkways Collection, 1980), and Goldsmith, *Making People's Music*, chap. 7.

71. Bernice Johnson Reagon, "Songs of the Civil Rights Movement 1955–1965: A Study in Cultural History," unpub. Ph.D. diss., Howard University, 1975, 127–28. See also Guy and Candie Carawan, comp. and ed., *Sing for Freedom: The Story of the Civil Rights Movement through Its Songs* (Bethlehem, Pa.: A Sing Out Publication, 1990), a republication of their two earlier collections. And Pete Seeger and Bob Reiser, *Everybody Says Freedom* (New York: W. W. Norton, 1989).

72. Robert Shelton, "Songs a Weapon in Rights Battle," *New York Times*, Aug. 20, 1962. For an insightful discussion analyzing why mostly white folksingers were more involved in the early freedom struggle than black rhythm-and-blues performers, see Ward, *Just My Soul Responding*, 293–310. But Ward comments: "While civil rights workers were deeply appreciative of the public and artistic stands people like Seeger, Baez and Dylan were taking, it was usually their politics and the money and public sympathy they generated for the Movement, rather than their music, which appealed to black activists. These preferences were even more evident beyond Movement circles, where few blacks gave a hootenanny about folk" (309).

73. Robert Shelton, "Singing for Freedom: Music in the Integration Movement," *Sing Out!* 12 (Dec.-Jan. 1962-63), 17.

74. Robert Shelton, "Carnegie Is Still Going Strong: Capacity Crowd at Hootenanny," *New York Times*, Sept. 24, 1962.

75. Charles Portis, "Marching Down the Avenue," *New York Herald Tribune*, Jan. 30, 1962.

76. "Leisure: String 'Em Up," *Time*, Jan. 5, 1962, 46. "The Folk-Girls," *Time*, June 1, 1962, 39. "Real Long Hair," *Newsweek*, July 9, 1962, 53.

77. "Folk Singing: Sibyl with Guitar," *Time*, Nov. 23, 1962, 54, 56, 59, 60. "Corn on the Campus," *Song Hits Magazine*, Nov. 1962, 8. Many folkies bridled at *Time's* "snide sensationalism" and focus on money, but Ellen Stekert cautioned that this was to be expected as part of the music's growing pains. The "problem is with *Time* and what *Time* stands for and does to things it touches," she explained. "As long as folksinging keeps growing there will be more *Time* articles." She particularly complained about the captions under the photos of Frank Proffitt ("Out of the sour mash") and Jean Ritchie ("Over the dinner dishes"). Ellen Stekert, "Views & Reviews," *Tune Up* 1:4 (Jan. 1963), 4–5.

78. Judy Collins, *Trust Your Heart: An Autobiography* (Boston: Houghton Mifflin, 1987), 77. Holzman and Daws, *Follow the Music*, 53. See also Judy Collins, *Singing Lessons: A Memory of Love, Loss, Hope, and Healing* New York: Pocket Books, 1998), chap. 5.

79. "Carolyn Hester" in Wolliver, *Bringing It All Back Home*, 100. Hammond, *John Hammond on Record*, 349–51.

80. "Mary Travers" in Wolliver, *Bringing It All Back Home*, 58. "Mary Travers and Peter Yarrow" in Smith, *Off the Record*, 162. Fred Goodman, *The Mansion on the Hill: Dylan, Young, Geffen, Springsteen, and the Head-on Collision of Rock and Commerce* (New York: Times Books, 1997), 82–90.

81. "Eric Weissberg" in Wolliver, *Bringing It All Back Home*, 55.

82. "Mary Travers and Peter Yarrow" in Smith, *Off the Record*, 160. Jerry Wexler and David Ritz, *Rhythm and the Blues: A Life in American Music* (New York: St. Martin's, 1993), 199. William Ruhlmann, "Peter, Paul and Mary: A Song to Sing All Over This Land," *Goldmine*, Apr. 12, 1996, 20–151. On Warner Bros. Records and Grossman, see Goodman, *Mansion on the Hill*, chaps. 3, 5.

83. Von Schmidt and Rooney, *Baby, Let Me Follow You Down*, 147.

84. "Commissioner of Police Opens Probe in Jackie's Assault Case," *Broadside* 1 (Dec. 19, 1962), 8.

85. Von Schmidt and Rooney, *Baby, Let Me Follow You Down*, 149–50.

86. Cohen interview with Manny Greenhill, Santa Monica, California, June 21, 1990. Baez, *And a Voice to Sing With*, 106.

87. Von Schmidt and Rooney, *Baby, Let Me Follow You Down*, 129.

Chapter 7

1. "Hootenanny on TV Soon," Billboard, Mar. 2, 1963, 18.

2. Joan Barthel, "From the Bitter End," New York Times, May 20, 1962.

3. "Industry Eyes Campus and Civic Entertainment," The Scene 1 (Mar. 1963), 1.

4. Dave Wilson, "Rambin' Round," Broadside (Boston) 1 (Jan. 25, 1963), 4. Broadside 21 (Feb. 1963).

5. Nat Hentoff, "That Ole McCarthy Hoot," Village Voice, Mar. 14, 1963, 5. "The Folknik Show," Newsweek, Mar. 18, 1963, 64. "Talent Boycott Threatened in Ban of Seeger, Weavers on 'Hootenanny,' " Variety, Mar. 20, 1963, 86.

6. Israel Young's Notebooks, Mar. 17, 1963, and Mar. 20, 1963, copy in author's possession.

7. Israel Young's Notebooks, Mar. 25, 1963, and Mar. 26, 1963, copy in author's possession. Ren Grevatt, "Greenbriars Balk at 'Hootenanny' Booking," Billboard, Apr. 13, 1963.

8. Jack Gould, "TV: 'Hootenanny' Debut," New York Times, Apr. 8, 1963. Barry Kittleson, "Hootenanny on TV Needs Life," Billboard, Apr. 27, 1963, 16.

9. "John Cohen I" in Cohen, "Wasn't That a Time!," 28–29.

10. Israel Young Notebook, Nov. 11, 13, 1963, copy in author's possession.

11. Gordon Friesen, "There's No Blacklist in Heaven," Broadside 24 (Apr. 1963). Pete Seeger, "Johnny Appleseed, Jr.," Sing Out! 13 (Apr.-May 1963), 63. Collins, Trust Your Heart, 100.

12. Pete Seeger to ABC, quoted in Dunaway, How Can I Keep from Singing, 217.

13. Paul Gardner, " 'Hootenanny' Sends Sound of Folk Music through Halls of Ivy," New York Times, Nov. 17, 1963.

14. Jo Mapes, "Passing Through," unpub. manuscript autobiography in author's possession, 116.

15. Terry Turner, "ABC Bounces Hootenanny for Fall," Chicago Daily News, June 11, 1964. "News and Notes," Sing Out! 14 (Apr.-May 1964), 4.

16. "Beach Hoot a Splashing Success," Billboard, Apr. 27, 1963, 16.

17. Maggie Puner, "Folk Music as I See It," Seventeen, Jan. 1963, 29. Joyce Maynard, Looking Back: A Chronicle of Growing Up Old in the Sixties (New York: Doubleday, 1973), 31–33.

18. "Fourth Man Makes the Trio Tick," Business Week, Feb. 23, 1963, 58.

19. Art D'Lugoff, "Greenwich Village at Night," Cavalier, Mar. 1963, 31. Folk music shared the stage in Greenwich Village with a variety of musical styles, dance, theater, and other avant-garde arts; see Sally Banes, Greenwich Village 1963: Avant-Garde Performance and the Effervescent Body (Durham, N.C.: Duke University Press, 1993).

20. Dion DiMucci with Davin Seay, The Wanderer: Dion's Story (New York: Morrow, 1988), 147–49.

21. David Crosby and Carl Gottlieb, Long Time Gone: The Autobiography of David Crosby (New York: Dell, 1988), 72.

22. Meryle Secrest, "College Folk Music: They Explore in Song . . . Love, Money, and Disaster," Washington Post, May 5, 1963. James O'Neill, "Folk Music? The 'Hooenanny' May Be a Step Forward, but Noisy," Washington Daily News, July 24, 1963.

23. Barry Shank, Dissonant Identities: The Rock 'n' Roll Scene in Austin, Texas (Hanover, N.H.: Wesleyan University Press, 1994), 39–48. Doug Rossinow, "The New Left in the Counterculture: Hypotheses and Evidence," Radical History Review 67 (Winter 1997), 90–91. Laura Joplin, Love, Janis (New York: Villard Books, 1992), 91–103.

24. Notes by Israel Young in his scrapbook, Feb. 1963, copy in author's possession. In 1965, middle-aged Sam and Eve Gordon frequented their favorite Long Island club, El Patio, where they heard Trini Lopez, "a great favorite at the clubs, singing 'If I Had a Hammer' and 'Sinner Man' over and over by special request. If he tried to take a break,

the crowd went crazy—truly crazy, Sam and Eve both thought." But by then the revival had already peaked. Katz, Home Fires, 202.

25. Nat Hentoff, "Folk, Folkum and the New City Billy," Playboy, June 1963, 95, 170.

26. Israel Young Notebook, Mar. 5, 1963, copy in author's possession. Ben A. Botkin, "The Folksong Revival: A Symposium," New York Folklore Quarterly 19 (June 1963), 109.

27. Israel Young Notebook, Mar. 5, 1963, copy in author's possession. "Dick Weissman" in Cohen, "Wasn't That a Time!," 170.

28. Mike Gross, "Mass Market Yens New Songs," Variety, July 3, 1963, 1.

29. Robert Shelton, " 'Freedom Songs' Sweep North," New York Times, July 6, 1963. Reagon, "Songs of the Civil Rights Movement 1955–1965, 146–70.

30. Pete Seeger, "The Integration Battle: A 'Singing' Movement," Broadside 30 (Aug. 1963). "Folk Music: They Hear America Singing," Time, July 19, 1963, 53.

31. Baez, And a Voice to Sing With, 103. On Josh White's career in the 1960s, see Wald, Josh White, 258–95.

32. Reagon, "Songs of the Civil Rights Movement, 1955 1965," 165–66. Robert Sherman, "Sing a Song of Freedom," Saturday Review, Sept. 28, 1963, 65.

33. John Phillips, Papa John: An Autobiography (New York: Dell, 1986), 158–60. Phillips was not considering white country performers, who were often conservative, if political at all.

34. Josh Dunson, "Slave Songs at the 'Sing for Freedom,' " Broadside 46 (May 30, 1964). Josh Dunson, "Freedom Singing Gathering in the Heart of Dixie," Sing Out! 14 (Sept. 1964),

35. "Len Chandler" in Cohen, "Wasn't That a Time!," 136. See also Guy and Candie Carawan, "Carry It On: Roots of the Singing Civil Rights Movement," in Freedom Is a Constant Struggle: An Anthology of the Mississippi Civil Rights Movement, ed. Susie Erenrich (Montgomery, Ala.: Black Belt Press, 1999), 143–51.

35. Julius Lester, "Freedom Songs in the South," Broadside 39 (Feb. 7, 1964). Julius Lester, "Freedom Songs in the North," Broadside 42 (Mar. 30, 1964).

36. Julius Lester, Search for the New Land: History as Subjective Experience (New York: Dell, 1969), 56–57.

37. "News and Notes," Sing Out! 14 (July 1964), 3.

38. Bob Cohen, "The Mississippi Caravan of Music," Broadside 51 (Oct. 20, 1964). "News and Notes," Sing Out! 14 (Nov. 1964), 3. Bob Cohen, "Sorrow Songs, Faith Songs, Freedom Songs: The Mississippi Caravan of Music in the Summer of '64" in Erenrich, Freedom Is a Constant Struggle, 177–89.

39. Lester, Search for the New Land, 68–69. Cohen interview with Carolyn Hester, Los Angeles, August 3, 1993. "Without These Songs . . . ," Newsweek, Aug. 31, 1964, 74. Schumacher, There but for Fortune, 85–88. Collins, Singing Lessons, 130. Collins, "Mississippi," in Erenrich, Freedom Is a Constant Struggle, 201–7.

40. Taylor Branch, Pillar of Fire: America in the King Years, 1963–65 (New York: Simon and Schuster, 1998), 436.

41. Bikel, Theo, 180.

42. "Folk Festival at Newport Revived," Sing Out! 13 (Apr.-May 1963), 76. Cheryl Anne Brauner, "A Study of the Newport Folk Festival and the Newport Folk Foundation," M.A. thesis, Memorial University of Newfoundland, 1983; see especially 254–58 for the "Proposal for the Newport Folk Festival to be held in Newport July 1963 on the 26th, 27th and 28."

43. Robert Shelton, "Folk Music Fete Called a Success," New York Times, July 29, 1963. Leroy Aarons, "Folk Music Digs In to Stay," Washington Post, Aug. 4, 1963. "The Milk Drinkers," Newsweek, Aug. 12, 1963, 80. On Bill Monroe's revived career and role in the folk revival, see Richard D. Smith, Can't You Hear Me Callin': The Life of Bill Monroe. Father of Bluegrass (Boston: Little, Brown, 2000), chap. 6.

44. Josh Dunson, "Workshops Key to Newport '63," *Broadside* 31 (Sept. 1963). Israel G. Young, "Frets and Frails," *Sing Out!* 13 (Oct.-Nov. 1963), 63. "Newport 1963—A Good Year," *Song Hits Magazine*, Jan. 1964, 8.

45. "Folk Festivals Are 'In,' " *Sing Out!* 13 (Oct.-Nov., 1963), 24.

46. John Cohen and Ralph Rinzler, "The University of Chicago Folk Festival," *Sing Out!* 13 (Apr.-May 1963), 8. Rita Weill, "Concerts, Hoots, Workshops Highlight UCLA Folk Festival," *Sing Out!* 13 (Summer 1963), 43.

47. Cohen interview with Ed Pearl, Los Angeles, June 25, 1990 (corrected copy Jan. 30, 1993). Bess Hawes, "Impression of Newport," *Broadside* (Aug. 1963), 4.

48. Ralph J. Gleason, "The Boredom of Folk Music," *San Francisco Chronicle*, May 21, 1963. Ralph J. Gleason, "Monterey's Test of Fire," *San Francisco Chronicle*, May 22, 1963.

49. Barry Olivier, "A Personnel Beginning," Berkeley Folk Festival Artist Archive.

50. Josh Dunson, "Folk Music from Horse Pastures to Concert Halls," *Broadside* 32 (Sept. 20, 1963).

51. "Hoots the Name of the Game This Year," *Billboard*, Aug. 17, 1963, 1. Barry Kittleson, "New Folk Breed Spells 'Meat,' " *Billboard*, Aug. 17, 1963, 16. "Folk Trend Shows No Sign of Let-up," *Billboard*, Oct. 19, 1963, 18. Pete Seeger, "Dear Fellow Humans," *Seventeen*, Nov. 1963, 199. Robert Shelton, "New Trend: City Musicians Writing Folk Songs," *New York Times*, Dec. 15, 1963.

52. Aaron Sternfield, "Collegians Shape Nation's Musical Tastes," *Billboard Music on Campus*, Mar. 28, 1964, 11. Mike Gross, "New Talent Influx Assures Steady Folk Field Growth," *Billboard*, Apr. 4, 1964, 1.

53. Mary Kelly, "Guitar Twangs Folk Song in the Wind," *Christian Science Monitor*, Apr. 4, 1964. "Just Playin' Folks Sonic Boom in U.S.A.," *Saturday Evening Post*, May 30, 1964, 25. Chris Welles, "The Angry Young Folk Singer," *Life*, Apr. 10, 1964, 109. Whitney Balliett, "Jazz Concerts," *New Yorker*, May 30, 1964, 133–34.

54. Irwin Silber, "News and Notes," *Sing Out!* 13 (Feb.-Mar. 1963), 47. Silber, "Folk Music—1963," *Sing Out!* 13 (Oct.-Nov. 1963), 3–4.

55. Bob Shelton to Archie Green, July 28, 1962, Green Papers.

56. "Where We're at and Where We're Going," *Hootenanny* 1:1 (Dec. 1963), 5. "News and Notes," *Sing Out!* 13 (Dec.-Jan. 1963–64), 4. Bob Shelton to Archie Green, Jan. 23, 1964, Green Papers. Bob Shelton, "Judy Collins—Why I Quit the A.B.C. Show," *Hootenanny* 1:2 (Mar. 1964), 29.

57. John Greenway, "The Anatomy of a Genius: Woody Guthrie," *Hootenanny* 1:3 (May 1964), 17. Bob Shelton, "The Kingston Trio vs. Beatlemania," *Hootenanny* 1:4 (Nov. 1964), 66.

58. Bob Shelton to Archie Green, Oct. 31, 1964, Green Papers.

59. Theodore Bikel, "Random Thoughts on the Folk Scene," *ABC-TV Hootenanny Show Magazine* 1:1 (Jan. 1964), 19.

60. *Good News* 1:1 (Apr. 1961), 4. For the larger musical context, see Barney Hoskyns, *Waiting for the Sun: Strange Days, Weird Scenes and the Sound of Los Angeles* (New York: St. Martin's, 1996), chaps. 2–3. Timothy White, *The Nearest Faraway Place: Brian Wilson, the Beach Boys, and the Southern California Experience* (New York: Henry Holt, 1994).

61. Joe McDonald, "Thoughts on 'Et Tu,' " *Et Tu* 1 (Aug. 1964).

62. Israel G. Young, "Frets and Frails," *Sing Out!* 14 (Apr.-May 1964), 77. Irwin Silber, "Folk Yearbook," *Sing Out!* 14 (July 1964), 83. Jim Clark, ed., *Folk Music Yearbook of Artists 1964* (Fairfax, Va.: Jandel Productions International, 1964).

63. "Editorial," *Sing Out!* 14 (Feb.-Mar. 1964), 3.

64. Ren Grevatt, "Bloom off the Folk Rose?," *Music Business*, July 18, 1964, 18.

65. Gordon Friesen, "Something New Has Been Added," *Sing Out!* 13 (Oct.-Nov. 1963), 13. Betty Rollin, "A New Beat: Topical Folk Singers, Their Songs," *Vogue*, Sept. 1, 1964, 130.

66. Josh Dunson to Seeger, Aug. 5, 1965, in author's possession.

67. Dunson, Freedom in the Air, 71, 111.

68. Mark Spoelstra to Moe Asch, Dec. 3, 1963, Smithsonian Folkways Collection.

69. Robert Shelton, "Cream of Newport Folk Festival," New York Times, July 19, 1964.

70. Robert Shelton, " '64 Folk Festival Ends in Newport," New York Times, July 27, 1964. Bikel, Theo, 182.

71. Shelton, No Direction Home, 261. Johnny Cash, Cash: The Autobiography (New York: Harper San Francisco, 1997), 197–98.

72. Shelton, No Direction Home, 258.

73. Irwin Silber, "Editorial," Sing Out! 14 (Sept. 1964), 3. Paul Nelson, "Newport: The Folk Spectacle Comes of Age," Sing Out! 14 (Nov. 1964), 7.

74. Paul Nelson, "Newport: Down There on a Visit," Little Sandy Review, no. 30 [Apr. 1965], 48–49, 53, 58, 66, 67.

75. Josh Dunson, "Newport: Two Workshops of Our Times—Part One," Broadside 49 (Aug. 20, 1964). Josh Dunson to Theodore Bikel, Sept. 8, 1964, in author's possession. Josh Dunson, Bill Martin, and Agnes Friesen, "Report on the 1964 Philadelphia Folk Festival," Broadside 50 (Sept. 22, 1964).

76. Richard Fariña, "Baez and Dylan: A Generation Singing Out," Mademoiselle, Aug. 1964, 342. Robert Shelton, "Joan Baez Sings at Forest Hills," New York Times, Aug. 10, 1964.

77. Irwin Silber, "An Open Letter to Bob Dylan,"Sing Out! 14 (Nov. 1964), 22–23. Paul Wolfe, Broadside 53 (Dec. 20, 1964).

78. Phil Ochs, "An Open Letter from Phil Ochs to Irwin Silber, Paul Wolfe, and Joseph E. Levine," Broadside 54 (Jan. 20, 1965). Ralph J. Gleason, "The Voice of the New Generation," San Francisco Chronicle, Oct. 11, 1964. Nat Hentoff, "Profiles: The Crackin', Shakin', Breakin' Sounds," New Yorker, Oct. 24, 1964, 66, 90.

79. Robert Shelton, "Bob Dylan Shows New Maturity in Program of His Folk Songs," New York Times, Nov. 2, 1964. Israel Young manuscript notebooks, Nov. 8, 1964.

80. "A Minstrel with a Mission," Life, Oct. 9, 1964, 61.

81. Pete Seeger's notes, "Bon Voyage Concert: Pete Seeger," pamphlet.

82. Baez, And a Voice to Sing With, 118.

83. Baez, And a Voice to Sing With, 119. David Lance Goines, The Free Speech Movement: Coming of Age in the 1960s (Berkeley, Calif: Ten Speed Press, 1993). Terry H. Anderson, The Movement and the Sixties (New York: Oxford University Press, 1995), chap. 2.

84. Michael Rossman, "The Berkeley Folk Music Scene in the Sixties: Reflections on a Poster Exhibition," in author's possession. Ralph J. Gleason, "Songs Born of the UC Rebellion," San Francisco Chronicle, Nov. 16, 1964. Irwin Silber, "Songs from Berkeley," Sing Out! 15 (May 1965), 18. Goines, Free Speech Movement, 712–28 (includes the complete song book).

85. Lawrence Linderman, "Big Folk at Berkeley," Cavalier, Nov. 1964, 60.

86. Gene Lees, "The Folk-music Bomb," HiFi/Stereo Review, Nov. 1964, 57–58, 60. Arnold Shaw, "Gitars, Folk Songs, and Halls of Ivy," Harper's Magazine, Nov. 1964, 43. Robert Shelton, "Folk Music: Pompous and Ersatz?," New York Times, Nov. 29, 1964.

87. "Rally Right," WIRE (publication of the California Young Republicans), Aug. 1964, 12. Jere Real, "Folk Music and Red Tubthumpers," American Opinion, Dec. 1964, 19–20. The Goldwaters Sing Folk Songs to Bug the Liberals was issued on Greenleaf Records.

88. "Togetherness," Newsweek, May 13, 1963, 95.

89. "News and Notes," Sing Out! 14 (Feb.-Mar. 1964), 5, 62.

90. Sander, Trips, 39.

Chapter 8

1. Ralph J. Gleason, "The Times They Are A Changin'," Ramparts, Apr. 1965, 37, 48. Lenore Hershey, "Sight & Sound," McCall's, June 1965, 8.

2. Anderson, *The Movement and the Sixties*, chaps. 2–3. Tom Wells, *The War Within: America's Battle over Vietnam* (Berkeley: University of California Press, 1994), chap. 1. Not all students were left-wing, however; the conservative Young Americans for Freedom claimed a membership of twenty thousand in 1965, a portent of things to come.

3. "Neil V. Rosenberg" in Cohen, *"Wasn't That a Time!,"* 75.

4. Jack Newfield, "Blowin' in the Wind: A Folk-music Revolt," *Village Voice*, Jan. 14, 1965, 4. John Denver with Arthur Tobier, *Take Me Home: An Autobiography* (New York: Harmony, 1994), 46.

5. Pete Seeger to *Broadside*, Mar. 24, 1965, *Broadside* 57 (Apr. 10, 1965). Reagon, "Songs of the Civil Rights Movement 1955–1965, 173, 175. See also Len H. Chandler, "Selma: A Folksinger's Report," and Pete Seeger, "You Can't Write Down Freedom Songs," *Sing Out!* 15 (July 1965), 7–10, 16–18; 11.

6. Margaret Long, "Let Freedom Sing," *Progressive*, Nov. 1965, 29. And see Ward, *Just My Soul Responding*, chap. 8.

7. Guy and Candie Carawan, "Carry It On," in Erenrich, *Freedom Is a Constant Struggle*, 148–50.

8. Alan Lomax et al., "Report on the Conference for Southern Community Cultural Revival," Oct. 1–2, 1965, 2, 3, copy in author's possession.

9. Alan Lomax, "First Conference on the Southern Grass Roots Culture," copy in author's possession.

10. For the larger racial, cultural, political, and musical context, see Ward, *Just My Soul Responding*.

11. "Inter-racial Folksong Group on Tour through the South," *Sing Out!* 16 (July 1966), 9.

12. Irwin Silber, "Fan the Flames," *Sing Out!* 15 (Mar. 1965), 47, and *Sing Out!* 15 (May 1965), 63.

13. Israel G. Young, "Frets and Frails," *Sing Out!* 15 (May 1965), 75.

14. Notice, *Sing Out!* 15 (Mar. 1965), 90.

15. Richard A. Reuss, "Folk Scene Diary Summer 1965," Reuss Papers.

16. Pete Seeger to Irwin Silber, Jan. 5, 1965, copy in author's possession. KAY guitar ad, *Sing Out!* 15 (Mar. 1965), 94. Silber to Seeger, Jan. 27, 1965, copy in author's possession.

17. Irwin Silber, "What's Happening," *Sing Out!* 15 (Sept. 1965), 5, 97.

18. Reuss, "Folk Scene Diary Summer 1965," 16.

19. Robert Shelton, "Folklorists Give Talks at Newport," *New York Times*, July 24, 1965.

20. Von Schmidt and Rooney, *Baby, Let Me Follow You Down*, 253, 258. Cohen interview with Paul Rothchild, Los Angeles, June 26, 1990. Ed Ward, *Michael Bloomfield: The Rise and Fall of an American Guitar Hero* (New York: Cherry Lane, 1983), 39–48.

21. Cohen interview with Paul Rothchild, Los Angeles, June 26, 1990. No two studies seem to agree on the sequence of events at Newport. Perhaps the best is Spitz, *Dylan: A Biography*, 301–8; see also Heylin, *Bob Dylan*, 137–45.

22. Shelton, *No Direction Home*, 302–3. Cohen interview with Paul Rothchild, Los Angeles, June 26, 1990.

23. Von Schmidt and Rooney, *Baby, Let Me Follow You Down*, 265.

24. Bikel, *Theo*, 271–72.

25. On the connections among folk, rock, the Byrds, and the L.A. scene, see Hoskyns, *Waiting for the Sun*, 69–76, and Johnny Rogan, *Timeless Flight: The Definitive Biography of The Byrds* (Essex, Eng.: Square One, 1990).

26. Reuss, "Folk Scene Diary Summer 1965," 24–25.

27. Robert Shelton, "Folk Music Fills Newport Coffers," *New York Times*, July 26, 1965. In his biography of Dylan, Shelton devotes three pages to Newport '65, with a defense of Dylan. Shelton, *No Direction Home*, 301–04.

28. Irwin Silber, "What's Happening," *Sing Out!* 15 (Nov. 1965), 3–4.

29. Paul Nelson, "What's Happening," *Sing Out!* 15 (Nov. 1965), 6, 8. Paul Nelson to Jon Pankake, Aug. 10, 1965, Reuss Papers.

30. Ed Freeman, "Notes from a Variant Stanza Collector," *The Broadside* 4:13 (Aug. 18, 1965). Robert Shelton, "Beneath the Festival's Razzle-Dazzle," *New York Times*, Aug. 1, 1965. Arthur Kretchmer, "Newport: It's All Right, Ma, I'm Only Playin' R&R," *Village Voice*, Aug. 5, 1965, 6. Mississippi Phil Ochs, "The Newport Fuzz Festival," *Realist* 61 (Aug. 1965), 11–12.

31. Robert Shelton, "Folk Music Marathons," *Cavalier*, Nov. 1965, 42, 61, 62.

32. Mary Travers to Archie Green, Aug. 6, 1965, Green Papers.

33. Israel Young manuscript notebook Aug. 25, 1965, copy in author's possession.

34. Robert Shelton, "Dylan Conquers Unruly Audience," *New York Times*, Aug. 30, 1965. Dick Reuss notes, "Bob Dylan Concert, August 28, 1965," Reuss Papers. For a creative account of Dylan's trip through England, and much more, see Greil Marcus, *Invisible Republic: Bob Dylan's Basement Tapes* (New York: Henry Holt, 1997), esp. 34–41.

35. Quote in Brauner, "A Study of the Newport Folk Festival," 122–23.

36. Jim Rooney, "Reflections on Newport '65," attached to Rooney to Irwin Silber, Aug. 6, 1965, copy in author's possession.

37. Israel Young manuscript notebook, Aug. 10, 1965, copy in author's possession.

38. Israel Young to Pete Seeger, Aug. 25, 1965, copy in author's possession.

39. Reuss, "Folk Scene Diary Summer 1965," 104–5. Robert Lurtsema, "On the Scene," *The Broadside* 4: 16 (Sept. 29, 1965). Michael Cooney and Irwin Silber, "What's Happening," *Sing Out!* 15 (Jan. 1966), 4.

40. "Rock 'n' Roll," *Time*, Sept. 17, 1965, 102. "The Folk and the Rock," *Newsweek*, Sept. 20, 1965, 88. Nora Ephron, " 'Folk Rock'—What the Shouting's All About," *New York Post*, Sept. 26, 1965. The quarterly *Rock Folk Song Folio* appeared in early 1966 and lasted for over a year; it featured an odd assortment of songs and stories, trying to cash in on folk rock, broadly conceived.

41. Ian Whitcomb, *Rock Odyssey: A Musician's Chronicle of the Sixties* (New York: Doubleday, 1983), 200–1.

42. Sander, *Trips*, 55.

43. Whitcomb, *Rock Odyssey*, 203–4. "Bits and Pieces," *The Broadside* 4:21 (Dec. 8, 1965), 23.

44. Ed Freeman, "Notes from a Variant Stanza Collector," *The Broadside* 4:15 (Sept. 15, 1965). "An Interview with Phil Ochs," *Broadside* 63 (Oct. 15, 1965). Dave Wilson, "Boston Roundup," *Sing Out!* 16 (Feb.-Mar. 1966), 81.

45. "Folkin' Around," *Sounds* 1: 9 (Nov. 8, 1965).

46. Josh Dunson, "Folk Rock: Thunder without Rain," *Sing Out!* 15 (Jan. 1966), 17.

47. "Len Chandler at Odyssey," *The Broadside* 4:20 (Nov. 24, 1965), 13.

48. Israel Young manuscript notebook, "Sing In Committee for Peace," August 25, 1965, 21, 29.

49. Jim Dillin, " 'Sing-in' Assails Vietnam war," *Christian Science Monitor*, Sept. 27, 1965. Irwin Silber, "Fan the Flames," *Sing Out!* 15 (Jan. 1966), 71–72.

50. Israel Young, "Bob Dylantaunt," *East Village Other* 1:1 (October 1965).

51. Moe Asch, "An Explanation and a Plea for Consideration: To Whom It May Concern," Nov. 14, 1965, copy in author's possession. Goldsmith, *Making People's Music*, chap. 6.

52. "An Open Letter to Open Minds," *Washington Post*, Nov. 11, 1965. Ralph Gleason, "Surrounded by 'Subversive' Music," *San Francisco Examiner and Chronicle*, Nov. 14, 1965.

53. Jay L. Kraus to Irwin Silber, Nov. 17, 1965, W. W. Nelson to *Sing Out!*, Nov. 23, 1965, in Reuss Papers. Irwin Silber to Michael Asch, Nov. 16 1965, in Reuss Papers.

54. Donald Myrus, *Ballads, Blues, and the Big Beat* (New York: Macmillan, 1966), 118–19.

55. Israel Young to Pete Seeger, Dec. 7, 1965, copy in author's possession.

56. Israel Young to Irwin Silber, Dec. 21, 1965, copy in author's possession. Israel G. Young to Jesse, Dec. 10, 1965, in Reuss Papers.

57. "The Children of Bobby Dylan," *Life*, Nov. 5, 1965, 43. "A Night with Bob Dylan," *New York: The Sunday Herald Tribune Magazine*, Dec. 12, 1965, 18.

58. Russell Baker, "Observer: Down with Musical Uplift," *New York Times*, Dec. 17, 1965.

59. "Growing Up," *Sing Out!* 15 (Jan. 1966), 2. John Cohen to Archie Green, Jan. 2, 1966, Green Papers.

60. Pete Seeger, "A Challenge to Our Readers from Pete Seeger," *Sing Out!* 16 (Feb.-Mar. 1966), inside front cover, and 88 for the Hagstrom ad.

61. "Man of the Year: The Inheritor," *Time*, Jan. 6, 1967, 18, 23.

62. Robert Shelton, "On Records: The Folk-Rock Rage," *New York Times*, Jan. 30, 1966. Irwin Silber to the Editor, *New York Times*, Feb. 20, 1966.

63. Robert Shelton to the Editor, *New York Times*, Feb. 20, 1966. Paul Nelson to the Editor, *New York Times*, Feb. 20, 1966.

64. Israel G. Young to Howard Klein, February 23, 1966. Israel Young manuscript notes, February 24, 1966, both in Reuss Papers.

65. Israel Young manuscript notes, February 26, 1966. Robert Shelton to "Whom It May Concern," Feb. 28, 1966, both in Reuss Papers.

66. Robert Shelton to "Whom It May Concern," Feb. 28, 1966, in Reuss Papers. Shelton, *No Direction Home*, 313.

67. Israel G. Young, "Dear BROADSIDE," *The Broadside* 5:8 (June 8, 1966), 25.

68. "Cavalier's Second Speak Out at the Village Vanguard," *Cavalier*, Mar. 1966, 60, 61.

69. Ralph Earle, "Folk at Winterfest," *The Broadside* 5:2 (Mar. 16, 1966), 6.

70. See Joel Selvin, *Summer of Love: The Inside Story of LSD, Rock & Roll, Free Love, and High Times in the Wild West* (New York: Dutton, 1994).

71. Cohen interview with Barry Olivier, Berkeley, California, July 2, 1990.

72. Faith, "Hurrah! Plaudits! Acclaim! More!," the *folknik* 2:3 (May 1966), 3.

73. Ralph J. Gleason, "Airplane, a Rabbi, and Gypsy Fiddlers," *San Francisco Chronicle*, July 6, 1966. Bill Haigwood, "'Jefferson Airplane'; Big Hit at Annual Folk Festival Here," *Berkeley Daily Gazette*, July 4, 1966. Ralph J. Gleason, "The Performer-Composer Era," *San Francisco Examiner and Chronicle*, July 17, 1966.

74. Cohen interview with Joe McDonald, Berkeley, California, Apr. 24, 1992.

75. Rock Scully with David Dalton, *Living with the Dead: Twenty Years on the Bus with Garcia and the Grateful Dead* (Boston: Little, Brown, 1996), 43.

76. Cohen interview with Ed Pearl, Los Angeles, June 25, 1990. Hoskyns, *Waiting for the Sun*, chap. 4.

77. Phillips, *Papa John*, 195.

78. "Los Angeles," *Sing Out!* 15 (Nov. 1965), 11. On Taj Mahal and Ry Cooder, see Fred Metting, *The Unbroken Circle: Tradition and Innovation in the Music of Ry Cooder and Taj Mahal* (Lanham, Md.: Scarecrow, 2001).

79. D. K. Wilgus, "Who Says Interest in Folk Music Is Waning," *Los Angeles Times*, May 16, 1965. D. K. Wilgus to Miss Frances Inglis, Fine Arts and Public Lectures Department, October 22, 1965, D. K. Wilgus Papers, Southern Folklife Collection, University of North Carolina at Chapel Hill (hereafter Wilgus Papers).

80. D. K. Wilgus to Miss Frances Inglis, Nov. 8, 1965, Wilgus Papers.

81. Robert Shelton, "6th Folk Festival Ends in Newport," *New York Times*, July 25, 1966.

82. Bruce Jackson, "Newport," *Sing Out!* 16 (Sept. 1966), 13. Bruce Jackson, "Newport '66—Good Music, Diabolical Programming," and Irwin Silber, "Fan the Flames," *Sing Out!* 16 (Oct.-Nov. 1966), 16–17, 33.

83. "Notes," *Broadside* 73 (Aug. 1966), 16.

84. "Editorial Extending Our Borders," *Sing Out!* 16 (Oct.-Nov. 1966), inside front cover.

85. Lester, *Search for the New Land*, 118. Julius Lester, "The Angry Children of Malcolm X," *Sing Out!* 16 (Oct.-Nov. 1966), 25.

86. Robert Shelton, "Folk, Blues, and Country Music: The Year in Review," *Cavalier*, Dec. 1966, 90–91.

87. Shelton, "Folk, Blues, and Country Music," 91.

88. Israel Young manuscript notebook, Nov. 1966, 5. Israel Young, "A Quick Report from the Folklore Center," Dec. 2, 1966, copy in author's possession. Israel Young manuscript notebook, Sept. 5, 1966. On *Crawdaddy* and Landau, see Goodman, *Mansion on the Hill*, 18.

89. Israel Young manuscript notebook, Nov. 1966, 6–8.

90. Cohen interview with Jac Holzman, Pacific Palisades, California, June 27, 1990. Aaron Sternfield, "Elektra Makes Move as Full-line Diskery," *Billboard*, Aug. 7, 1965, 1. Holzman and Daws, *Follow the Music*.

91. Bruce Pollack, *When the Music Mattered: Rock in the 1960s* (New York: Holt, Rinehart and Winston, 1983), 20–21, 24.

92. Von Schmidt and Rooney, *Baby, Let Me Follow You Down*, 301; Israel G. Young, "Frets and Frails," *Sing Out!* 16 (Aug.-Sept. 1966), 41.

93. Ellen Stekert, "Cents and Nonsense in the Urban Folksong Movement: 1930–66," originally published in *Folklore and Society: Essays in Honor of Benjamin A. Botkin*, ed. Bruce Jackson (Hatboro, Pa.: Folklore Associates, 1966), and republished in Rosenberg, *Transforming Tradition*, 104; see 84–92 for her more recent thoughts on the original essay.

94. Ian Tyson with Colin Escott, *I Never Sold My Saddle* (Vancouver, B.C.: Greystone, 1995), 27.

Chapter 9

1. Israel Young manuscript notebook, Jan. 8, 1967, 18, copy in author's possession.

2. Israel Young manuscript notebook, Jan. 6, 1967.

3. Kristin White, "Where Have All the Folkies Gone?," *Billboard Music on Campus*, Apr. 8, 1967, 24–25.

4. Editorial, "A New Chapter Begins," *Sing Out!* 17 (Aug.-Sept. 1967), inside front cover.

5. Irwin Silber to "Dear Owner et al.," July 22, 1967, copy in author's possession.

6. Mike Asch et al. to Pete Seeger, Aug. 2, 1967, Silber Papers. Ed Badeaux to Seeger, Aug. 31, 1967, copy in author's possession. Israel Young manuscript notebook, Aug. 16, 1967.

7. Israel G. Young, "Meeting of Sing Out! Stockholders and Editorial Board," Sept. 6, 1967, in Reuss Papers.

8. Ibid. Irwin Silber, "A Personal Statement," *Sing Out!* 17 (Dec.-Jan. 1967–68), 35.

9. Irwin Silber to Francine Brown et al., Apr. 8, 1968, copy in author's possession.

10. Israel Young manuscript notebook, May 11, 1968, copy in author's possession. Irwin Silber argues that *Sing Out!* had been supported by Oak Publications, which helped pay the bills, and the move to the larger format was not a financial disaster: "We thought it worth trying to get wider circulation through more traditional magazine distributors and networks principally as a means of increasing subscriptions. The additional expense was really minimal since it only involved printing additional copies of each issue, making the extra copies fairly inexpensive. The larger $8\frac{1}{2} \times 11$ format also meant a slight increase in cost. On the other hand, because we could offer a wider circulation, we got a boost in advertising revenue." Silber to Ronald Cohen, Apr. 24, 1998. Conditions changed when Oak was sold and *Sing Out!*'s collective ownership struggled to stay afloat.

11. Irwin Silber to Pete Seeger, Sept. 6, 1968, Silber Papers. Irwin Silber and Barbara Dane, *The Vietnam Songbook* (New York: A Guardian Book, 1969), 7.

12. "Notes, Comments, Changes & Things," *Broadside* 78 (Jan. 1967), 9. Paul Nelson, "Popoeuvres," *Sing Out!* 17 (Apr.-May 1967), 59.

13. Irwin Silber, "Fan the Flames," *Sing Out!* 17 (Apr.-May 1967), 33. Paul Nelson, "Popoeuvres," *Sing Out!* 17 (June-July 1967), 49. Ed Badeaux, "The Spectacle Moves On," *Sing Out!* 17 (Aug.-Sept. 1967), 12.

14. Lester, *Search for the New Land*, 127. Lester, "Mirror of evoL," *Sing Out!* 17 (Oct.-Nov. 1967), 7, 9.

15. "A Letter from Julius Lester," *Broadside* 84 (Sept. 1967), 7–8. Letter from Dick Reuss, *Broadside* 85 (Oct. 1967).

16. Julius Lester to Irwin Silber, Oct. 13, 1967, copy in author's possession.

17. Julius Lester, *Falling Pieces of the Broken Sky* (New York: Little, Brown, 1990), 133.

18. Young, "Meeting of Sing Out! Stockholders and Editorial Board, September 6, 1967."

19. Irwin Silber, "Fan the Flames," *Sing Out!* 17 (Feb.-Mar. 1967), 31. David A. Noebel, *Rhythm, Riots, and Revolution* (Tulsa: Christian Crusade Publications, 1966), 15. William S. McBirnie, *Songs of Subversion* (Glendale: A Voice of Americanism Publication, n.d.).

20. Irwin Silber, "Fan the Flames," *Sing Out!* 17 (Feb.-Mar. 1967), 31.

21. Baez quoted in Irwin Silber, "Fan the Flames," *Sing Out!* 17 (Apr.-May 1967), 33. Baez, *And a Voice to Sing With*, 127.

22. "Folksinger Quits SNCC to Protest Attack on Israel," *Louisville Courier-Journal*, Aug. 17, 1967. Bikel, *Theo*, 259.

23. Bikel, *Theo*, 259–62.

24. Olivier, "A Personal Beginning," Berkeley Folk Festival Artist Archive.

25. Julia Bidou, "Berkeley Folk Music Festival—1967," *the folknik* 3:3 (July-Aug. 1967), 3.

26. Phillips, *Papa John*, 227, 244. Joel Selvin, *Monterey Pop: June 16–18, 1967* (San Francisco: Chronicle Books, 1992). Selvin, *Summer of Love*.

27. Ellen Sander, "Monterey," *Sing Out!* 17 (Oct.-Nov. 1967), 2, 28.

28. Ralph Earle, "Newport 1967," *The Broadside* 6:12 (Aug. 2, 1967), 21.

29. Irwin Silber, "Festivals: Newport," *Sing Out!* 17 (Oct.-Nov. 1967), 1.

30. Pete Seeger to Irwin Silber, Nov. 13, 1967, Silber Papers.

31. Kathy Kaplan, "New York News & Notes," *The Broadside* 6:16 (Sept. 27, 1967), 11.

32. *The Folklore Center–Fretted Instruments Newsletter* 2, Feb. 17, 1967. "Keep in Touch with the Folklore Center," *Sing Out!* 17 (Feb.-Mar. 1967), 59. *The Folklore Center–Fretted Instruments Newsletter*, Mar. 17, 1967. Ray G. Alden, in "The Continuing Folklore Center Folk Festival," *Sing Out!* 21 (Jan.-Feb. 1972), 10–11, notes that the larger concerts moved to the Washington Square Methodist Church in early 1968.

33. Israel Young, "Open Letter to Greenwich Village," *Village Voice*, Mar. 16, 1967. Israel Young manuscript notebook, Apr. 19, 1967.

34. *The Folklore Center–Fretted Instruments Newsletter*, Aug. 14, 1967. "Ellen Faust's Sweets Mill Thoughts," *the folknik*, 3:4 (Oct. 1967), 2. Patty Hall, comp. and ed., *At the Mill: The Story of Sweet's Mill of California* (n.p., 1975).

35. "Transcription of Interview Michael Asch and Israel Young, December 21, 1967," by Gail Porter for Methods and Problems in Anthropology, Fall 1967, in Reuss Papers.

36. Israel G. Young Notebooks, Jan. 16, 1968, copy in author's possession. Billy Faier, "Music," *Woodstock (N.Y.) Week*, Jan. 25, 1968.

37. Ralph J. Gleason, "The Strong Songs of Woody Guthrie," *San Francisco Examiner and Chronicle*, Oct. 22, 1967.

38. Ellen Willis, "In-Person: A Tribute to Woody Guthrie," *Cheetah*, Mar. 1968, 19. Clive Davis, *Clive: Inside the Record Business* (New York: Ballantine, 1976), 68–69.

39. Bob Shelton to Archie Green, June 10, 1967, Green Papers. "Notes," *Broadside* 89 (Feb.-Mar. 1968), 14. Schumacher, *There but for Fortune*, 180–82.

40. David A. DeTurk and A. Poulin Jr., eds., *The American Folk Scene: Dimensions of the Folksong Revival* (New York: Dell, 1967), 13–14. Joe Hickerson, "The Meaning of Folksong Revival," *The Sunday (Washington, D.C.) Star*, Oct. 29, 1967.

41. Tom Phillips, "Vietnam Blues," New York Times Magazine, Oct. 8, 1967, 26, 32. David E. James, "The Vietnam War and American Music," in The Vietnam War and American Culture, ed. John Carlos Rowe and Rick Berg (New York: Columbia University Press, 1991), 226–54. James Perone, Songs of the Vietnam Conflict (Westport, Conn.: Greenwood Press, 2001).

42. "Folk Music: Sing Love, Not Protest," Time, Feb. 23, 1968, 90.

43. Robert Shelton, "Dylan Sings of Lovers, Losers," New York Times, Jan. 14, 1968.

44. Ralph J. Gleason, "Bob Dylan: Poet to a Generation," San Francisco Sunday Examiner and Chronicle, Aug. 18, 1968.

45. Israel G. Young, "Frets and Frails," Sing Out! 18 (Mar.-Apr. 1968), 37. Baez, And a Voice to Sing With, 146–53.

46. Richard Madden, "New York Leads Songs of Protest," New York Times, Aug. 29, 1968. Anderson, The Movement and the Sixties, chap. 4.

47. Robert Shelton, "Folk Music Trends Emerge at Newport Festival," New York Times, July 30, 1968.

48. Richard Goldstein, "Newport (Cont'd)," Village Voice, Aug. 8, 1968. Ellen Willis, "Newport: You Can't Go Down Home Again," New Yorker, Aug. 17, 1968, 87, 88. Jon Landau, "The Newport Folk Festival," Rolling Stone, Aug. 24, 1968.

49. Israel Young manuscript notebook, July 26, 1968, copy in author's possession. See also Irwin Silber, "Newport: Playing the System's Game," Guardian, Aug. 17, 1968.

50. Anthony R. Dolan, "Letter from Newport: Heroes in the Seaweed," National Review, Oct. 8, 1968, 1011–12.

51. Irwin Silber, "The Topical Song 'Revolution' and How It Fizzled Out," Guardian, Sept. 28, 1968.

52. Olivier, "A Personal Beginning," Berkeley Folk Festival Artist Archive.

53. The Folklore Center–Fretted Instruments Newsletter, Feb. 9, 1968.

54. John Cohen, "Chicago Festival," Sing Out! 18 (June-July 1968), 65.

55. Jonathan Eberhart, "The Smithsonian Institution Festival of American Folklife," Sing Out! 18 (Oct.-Nov. 1968), 67. Josh Dunson, "1968 Festival of American Folk Life," Sing Out! 18 (Dec. 1968-Jan. 1969), 3. Robert Cantwell, Ethnomimesis: Folklife and the Representation of Culture (Chapel Hill: University of North Carolina Press, 1993), 215–17.

56. Israel Young manuscript notebook, Nov. 13, Nov. 16, 1968, copy in author's possession.

57. Burt Korall, "The Music of Protest," Saturday Review, Nov. 16, 1968, 37. Herbert Russcol, "I Gave My Love a Cherry, So, Tell It Like It Is, Baby!," High Fidelity 18 (Dec. 1968), 55–56.

58. Bonnie Raitt quoted in Von Schmidt and Rooney, Baby, Let Me Follow You Down, 308.

59. Pete Seeger, "Johnny Appleseed, Jr.," Sing Out! 19 (Apr.-May 1969), 23. Richard W. Wilkie, "The Hudson River Sloop Restoration," Sing Out! 19 (July-Aug. 1969), 2–3.

60. Happy Traum, "The Swan Song of Folk Music," Rolling Stone, May 17, 1969, 7–8. Happy Traum, "What's Happening," Sing Out! 19 (July-Aug. 1969), 45.

61. Baez, And a Voice to Sing With, 164, 165.

62. Pete Seeger, "Johnny Appleseed, Jr.," Sing Out! 19 (July-Aug. 1969), 37.

63. Jan Hodenfield, "Newport 1969," Rolling Stone, Aug. 23, 1969, 20.

64. Happy Traum, "What's Happening," Sing Out! 19 (Sept.-Oct. 1969), 35. Barbara Dane, "Newport Folk Fest: Business as Usual," Village Voice, July 10, 1969.

65. Israel Young notebook, July 1969, copy in author's possession.

66. George Wein quoted in New York Times, May 27, 1970.

67. Young, "Frets and Frails," 26.

68. Young, "Frets and Frails," 27.

69. Olivier, "A Personal Beginning," Berkeley Folk Festival Artist Archive. Phillip Elwood, "UC Festival Brings out the Folks," San Francisco Examiner, Oct. 27, 1969.

70. Olivier, "A Personal Beginning," Berkeley Folk Festival Artist Archive. Cohen interview with Barry Olivier, Berkeley, California, July 2, 1990.

71. Ralph J. Gleason, "Strings Sing in a Berkeley Happening," *San Francisco Chronicle*, June 23, 1969.

72. Young, "Frets and Frails," 27.

73. Cohen interview with Ed Pearl, Los Angeles, June 25, 1990. Hoskyns, *Waiting for the Sun*, chaps. 5–6.

74. Happy Traum, "What's Happening," *Sing Out!* 19 (Winter 1969–70), 34.

75. "Editorial," *Broadside* 100 (July 1969). "Editorial," *Broadside* 108 (July-Aug. 1970). For the larger political context for the later sixties and into the seventies, see Anderson, *The Movement and the Sixties*, part 2, and Wells, *The War Within*, chaps. 6–10.

76. P. Dingle, "Israel Young . . . The Music Belongs to the People," *RAT*, Mar. 7–13, 1969, 14. Izzy Young manuscript notebook, Nov. 12, 1969, copy in author's possession.

77. Irwin Silber to Eric Winter, June 10, 1969. Silber to Sharyn Harris, Sept. 25, 1969, Silber Papers.

78. *Life*, May 2, 1969. See Peter M. Coan, *Taxi: The Harry Chapin Story* (New York: Lyle Stuart, 1990). Kristin Baggelaar and Donald Milton, *Folk Music: More Than a Song* (New York: Crowell, 1976). Craig Harris, *The New Folk Music* (Crown Point, Ind.: White Cliffs Media, 1991). Dave Laing, Robin Denselow, Karl Dallas, and Robert Shelton, *The Electric Muse: The Story of Folk into Rock* (London: Eyre Methuen, 1975), 66–78. For the British story, see Dave Laing and Richard Newman, comps. and eds., *Thirty Years of the Cambridge Folk Festival* (Cambridge, Eng.: Music Maker Books Ltd., 1994).

79. Janis Ian to Sis Cunningham and Gordon Friesen, Apr. 4, 1970, copy in author's possession.

80. Gene Youngblood, "Change in Contemporary Folk Music Chronicled on Film," *Los Angeles Free Press*, Nov. 17, 1967, 13.

Index

Young, Israel Goodman "Izzy," 108, 120–
22, 136–37, 138–39, 140; advice for
Maynard Solomon, 260; arrested, 278–
79; on Bikel, 196–97; on bluesmen,
247–48; on Butterfield Blues Band, 240;
on Paul Clayton, 274–75; on commercialism, 252, 263; on death of folk music, 275; on Bob Dylan, 181, 182, 245–
46; on folk festivals, 161; on *Folk Music
Yearbook of Artists 1964*, 217; "Frets and
Frails" column, 139–42, 274, 282; on
future of traditional performers, 281–82;
launches newsletter, 274; on Alan Lomax, 163; moves to Sweden, 288; on
Newport Folk Festival, 147, 161, 210,
279–80, 284–85; on New York Folklore
Society, 203; opens Fifth Peg, 162–64;
organizes concerts, 144, 260, 288;
press regarding, 275; on recording
black music, 233; reflects on his career,
274, 275; regarding *Hootenanny* television
show, 196, 197–98; relationship with
Little Sandy Review, 165; on Robert Shelton, 163, 250–51; and "Sing-In for
Peace," 245; on *Sing Out!*'s future, 241;
on *Sing Out!*'s reorganization, 265; Sing

Out! stake, 264; starts Friends of Old
Time Music, 173; studied by Margaret
Mead, 275; on Sweet's Mill festival, 285;
on University of Chicago Folk Festival,
168; on the Washington Square riot,
178, 179; and West Coast scene, 275,
285, 287; on Paul Williams, 259
Young, Neil, 255
Youngblood, Gene, 289
Youngbloods, 264; at Berkeley Folk Festi-
val, 286
Young Communist League, 26, 43
Young Tradition, 279, 283
Young Workers League of America: *The
March of the Workers and Other Songs*, 19
Your Ballad Man (radio show), 57
Youth market, 133–34, 157–58, 167–68,
248; press regarding, 213
Youth rebellion, 182, 229, 253, 267
Yurchenco, Henrietta, 25–26; aids Alma-
nacs' recording, 30

Zappa, Frank, 282
Zimmerman, Robert. *See* Dylan, Bob
Zittel, Ted, 39

RONALD D. COHEN was born in Los Angeles in 1940. He received his B.A. in history from the University of California, Berkeley, and his M.A. and Ph.D. in history from the University of Minnesota, Minneapolis. He has taught since 1970 at Indiana University Northwest, Gary, Indiana, where he is a professor of history. Among Professor Cohen's publications are *Children of the Mill: Schooling and Society in Gary, Indiana, 1906–1960* (Indiana University Press, 1990). He has edited several works, including *Red Dust and Broadsides: A Joint Autobiography,* by Agnes "Sis" Cunningham and Gordon Friesen (University of Massachusetts Press, 1999), and *Golden Threads: An Illustrated History of Folk Music in the United States* (Folk Music Museum in Greenwich Village, forthcoming). Professor Cohen has coproduced a number of retrospective CD collections, including *Songs for Political Action: Folk Music, Topical Songs, and the American Left, 1926–1953* (Bear Family Records, 1996) and *The Best of Broadside, 1962–1988: Anthems of the American Underground from the Pages of Broadside Magazine* (Smithsonian Folkways Recordings, 2000), which was nominated for a Grammy Award. He has been president of the History of Education Society (1996–1998), president of the Historians of American Communism (2000–2002), and vice president and cofounder of the developing Folk Music Museum in Greenwich Village, which will house his extensive collection of artifacts and memorabilia on the folk revival. He is the father of two children, Alysha and Joshua, and lives in Gary, Indiana, with his longtime companion, Nancy DelCastillo.